Books by Allan W. Eckert

THE WINNING OF AMERICA SERIES

OTHER BOOKS

Twilight of Empire

Twilight of Empire

A NARRATIVE

By

ALLAN W. ECKERT

LITTLE, BROWN AND COMPANY
BOSTON · TORONTO · LONDON

FIRST EDITION

Library of Congress Cataloging-in-Publication Data

Eckert, Allan W.
    Twilight of empire / Allan W. Eckert. — 1st ed.
        p.   cm. — (The Winning of America series)
    Bibliography: p.
    Includes index.
        1. Frontier and pioneer life — Illinois.   2. Frontier and pioneer
    life — Northwest, Old.   3. Illinois — History — 1778–1865.
    4. Northwest, Old — History — 1775–1865.   5. Indians of North America —
    Wars — 1815–1875.   6. United States — Territorial expansion.
    I. Title.   II. Series: Eckert, Allan W.   Winning of America series.
    F545.E24 1988
    977 — dc19   88-7305
                                                                                CIP

10   9   8   7   6   5   4   3   2   1

MV

Published simultaneously in Canada
by Little, Brown & Company (Canada) Limited

PRINTED IN THE UNITED STATES OF AMERICA

To my dear friend —

RANDY WHITE

— with deep regard and affection

*"I liked my town, my cornfields, and the home of my people.
I fought for them."*

— BLACK HAWK (Makataimeshekiakiak)
Wisconsin Historical Collections, II: 265.

*"There was a total absence of discipline — orders were obeyed
or disobeyed as suited the pleasure or convenience of the men;
and in this way men grow grey in service without becoming
soldiers."*

— WILLIAM ORR, written anonymously as
"a Citizen of St. Clair County" to
criticize Illinois Governor John Reynolds
and the Illinois State Militia officers.

"I tell you what, Sam, there is no fun in fighting Indians. . . ."

— CAPTAIN JOHN THROCKMORTON,
skipper of the Mississippi River
steamboat *Warrior*.

*"I fought hard. I was no coward. Much blood was shed.
But the white men were mighty. They were as many as
the leaves of the forest. The Indians are but few.
They are brave, but they are few."*

— BLACK HAWK (Makataimeshekiakiak) in a
speech made in Philadelphia, June 14, 1833.

AUTHOR'S NOTE

TWILIGHT OF EMPIRE is fact, not fiction. The incidents described here actually occurred; the dates are historically accurate; the characters, regardless of how major or how minor, actually lived the roles in which they are portrayed.

This book is meant to provide the reader with an accurate and comprehensive — yet swiftly paced and dramatic — picture of the events and people of the period it covers. It is the result of extended and intensive research through a great multitude of original documents of the time period covered, including many hundreds of personal letters and notes, memoranda, general orders, special orders, diaries, legal papers, journals, deeds, military records, depositions, tribal records where they exist, governmental reports, logbooks, and many other sources, including historical accounts produced subsequent to the events herein portrayed.

Of all The Winning of America series of historical narratives, this present volume has been by far the most difficult to write. The reason for this has been, largely, the uncommon plethora of accounts describing particular events that are, all too often, at variance with one another in regard to the same incidents. The main reason for such variance of accounts is that the principal event of this volume is the Black Hawk War, which, on the side of the whites, was fought — or participated in — in large measure by militia units raised from counties in Illinois, Indiana, Michigan (which at the time included present Wisconsin), and Missouri. This was also a time when an almost incredible number of these militiamen — from generals to privates — were actively seeking public office, either through election or reelection. Offices ranging from sheriffs to commissioners and judges, from congressmen to governors and even to presidents, were filled by men who participated in one way or another in this war; all of whom were extremely conscious of establishing advantageous war records. As a result, there was a phenomenal amount of posturing and politicking going on, during and after the war. It was especially *after* the conflict that an amazingly large number of accounts were published in newspapers, periodicals, and books, with each writer tending to glorify his own role in the events — or demean the roles of others — often to the great exaggeration or distortion of the truth. Thus, it has been most difficult to ferret out and piece together what actually occurred and when. Every effort has been made to study and present these events in the manner in which they truly transpired, in as unbiased and thorough a manner as possible. If errors have occurred, and it is hoped there are few, they are honest errors and not meant to fit a preconceived notion or plan.

Within the text there are occasional consecutively numbered passages keyed to an Amplification Notes section at the back of the book. These notes include tangential material meant to provide the reader with increased understanding of the events portrayed, as well as the pinpointing of historic geography to present-day locales.

Since English translations of the names of Indians tend, in many cases, to become derogatory or repetitive, I have endeavored to refer to these Indians, wherever practicable, by their actual Indian names. The tribes most concerned in this work are the Sac, Fox, Winnebago, Potawatomi, Sioux, Menominee, and Kickapoo. Occasionally, in cases where the Indian name involves difficulty of pronunciation, the English form is used. Two cases in point in this book where the English is much simpler and more practical for use are the names of the Sac leader, Black Hawk, and the Winnebago chief, White Crow — whose lengthy Indian names, respectively, are Makataimeshekiakiak and Kauraykaw-sawkaw.

As in the other five volumes of The Winning of America Series, certain techniques normally associated with the novel form have been utilized to help provide continuity and narrative flow, but not at the expense of historical accuracy. Where dialogue is used, it is actual quoted conversation from historical sources (and, in some cases, stilted due to the expressive forms used in those days), or is reconstructed from historically recorded interchanges between individuals but written then as straight exposition rather than as dialogue — in essence, what I call "hidden dialogue." In occasional other instances, historical fact has been utilized in the form of conversation to maintain dramatic narrative pace, but always meticulously in keeping with the character and the fundamental leanings of the individual to whom the words are attributed.

As a further aid, there is, at the back of the book, a chapter-by-chapter listing of the principal sources for the facts, dialogue, and possibly controversial information in the text. There is also a bibliography and complete index.

Twilight of Empire is the sixth volume in the author's in-progress series entitled The Winning of America. Other volumes in the series, in the order in which they were written, are: *The Frontiersmen, Wilderness Empire, The Conquerors, The Wilderness War,* and *Gateway to Empire.* The individual books do not depend on one another, yet they strongly complement each other, and characters who appear in one volume sometimes appear in others. All six of these books contribute to the principal theme of the series: how the white man took North America from the Indians. Step by step, this series moves across the continent, showing clearly and in the most fundamental terms how the land was won — through encroachment, trickery, warfare, deceit, treachery, purchase, alliance, gift, theft, and treaty. In point of time, *Twilight of Empire* essentially picks up the narrative thread where it left off in *Gateway to Empire*.

As in past volumes of The Winning of America Series, it is neither the intention nor the desire of the author to champion either the cause of the Indians or that of the whites; there were heroes and rascals on both sides; humanity and atrocity on both sides; rights and wrongs on both sides. The facts are presented chronologically and without projection, just as they occurred, and with the greatest possible degree of accuracy. There has been a minimum of author intrusion, editorializing, or moralizing. It has not been necessary. The facts speak amply for themselves, and whatever conclusions are drawn must be drawn solely by the reader.

— ALLAN W. ECKERT

Bellefontaine, Ohio
January 1988

MAPS

Twilight of Empire

PROLOGUE

[*July 4, 1767 — Saturday*]

HER NAME was Kneebingkemewoin — Summer Rain — and she was a very short woman.[1] Even when standing as tall as she could, the top of her head barely reached the level of Pyesa's shoulder, and Pyesa was not a large man.[2] She had awakened at dawn on this fine summer day, as she usually did, and stepped outside to begin her chores, but took no more than a few steps when the first contraction seized her and her water broke. She had stopped at once, straddle-legged, and remained rooted in place until it ceased, then retraced her steps into the broadly domed structure.

Now, late in the afternoon, sitting on the platform of layered reed matting in the dimness of the lodge, Summer Rain reached out and squeezed the hand of the man squatted beside her in the dimness, who was staring unseeingly toward the skin-covered doorway. Pyesa turned and, when their eyes met, knew at once that it was time. Though he remained expressionless, the spark of a smile kindled in his eyes. He squeezed her hand in return, and for just an instant placed his hand on the great mound of her abdomen. Wordlessly, he rose and dipped his head to his mother and her sister, who had been waiting patiently across from them. As they moved toward his wife, he strode from the wigwam, head high, the knowledge strong within him that no longer would the tongues of the old men waggle after he passed; no longer would the pregnant squaws, fearful of causing embarrassment, scurry from sight when his woman came toward them.

For nine summers they had been husband and wife; each of their years together, after the first, made more difficult than the preceding because no children had been borne of their union. They had lived with ever-increasing whispers that the *sholee* — black vulture — that had circled incessantly high above the village on the day they had been wed was but a vessel for an evil spirit who had cursed her womb so that it could produce no offspring. That was no longer true if, indeed, the *sholee* had brought such a spirit on that otherwise auspicious day. The medicine he had so frequently made — guttural incantations over bones and stones strewn from his pouch — had at last dispelled the evil.

Though of less than medium build, Pyesa cringed before no man, for his was the proud heritage of the Thunder Clan, a patrilineal descent bestowing upon him considerable stature in the tribe. Pyesa was the foremost medicine man of the Sac tribe, as had been his father, Kiakukiak, before him.[3] Before that, his grandfather, Nanamakee, had been a war chief of legendary prowess, and the father of his grandfather, Mukataquet, had been the most outstanding and powerful principal chief the Sac had ever had.[4]

Now, as he was striding away from the lodge, Pyesa's gaze missed nothing among the similar structures in this village named Saukenuk. One of the largest Indian villages presently existing in America, it boasted well over four hundred single-family wigwams — those dome-shaped dwellings of skins or bark stretched over a framework of bent boughs — as well as about one hundred of the larger and more permanent bark-covered quonset lodges, each about twenty feet wide and fifty feet long and in each of which resided from three to a dozen families or more. All these structures were clustered on the north side of the Rock River, three miles upstream from the Mississippi.[5] It was not the dwellings that Pyesa was looking at just now. What he sought to see was a sign from the Great Spirit that would signify what his firstborn should be named. He walked to the bank of the Rock River, where it slid past the doorstep of the tribe's most substantial village, but though he stopped and stood quietly there for long moments, the only movement he perceived was that of the water itself. At length he shook his head and began following the course of the stream toward its junction with the great grandmother of all rivers, the Mississippi. The place where these two rivers met was, he knew, a magical area held sacred by his tribe; a place where he was certain he would encounter *something* that could only be interpreted as the sign. Nor was he wrong.

In the last rays of the sunlight, as he stopped close to the point where the clearer waters of the Rock swirled into the mud-stained Mississippi, it was his ears rather than his eyes that first detected the sign — a high-pitched and sustained *killy-killy-killy* from above. He looked up and saw a small falcon hovering in place on rapidly fluttering wings. Abruptly the shrill cry ceased and the bird plummeted earthward, braking only an instant before alighting spread-taloned on a huge grasshopper.

It was a sparrow hawk, which would have been significant of itself, but this was not an ordinary hawk of the species. It was a rare melanistic variety — its normal coloration of barred cinnamon-red on back and crown, blue-gray on wing coverts, and daintily masked eye replaced with black. The bird clutched the grasshopper in one taloned foot for a moment, maintaining its balance with partially spread wings. Then it took off, still clutching its prey, its triumphant *killy-killy-killy* one more time piercing the air as the bird sped away southward across the mouth of the Rock River and then over the east bank of the Mississippi.

Pyesa watched until the bird disappeared and then he walked back to the village. A number of chattering, smiling villagers had gathered and they spoke to him as he threaded his way through them to his lodge, congratulating him, but refraining from asking what the child's name would be. They did not even know what sex the baby was, only that it had been born.

As Pyesa entered the dwelling, his mother and aunt rose from where they were squatted beside the recumbent form of Summer Rain and moved past Pyesa, speaking soft words of pleasure and praise on their way out. When they were gone, Pyesa kneeled beside Summer Rain and touched her cheek gently with his hand. She smiled and reached up, pressing his hand against her mouth so that her lips met his palm.

"We have a son, Pyesa," she murmured and took great pleasure in the joy that sprang into his eyes as she pulled back the light coverlet of rabbit skins and exposed the tiny form couched in the warm curve between her arm and breast.

He nodded. "It is good. And the Great Spirit has given a good sign."

Close at hand on the floor were two little wooden bowls, one in which there was some milk-white paint, while the other contained black. These were the paints favored by the Sac and which separated individuals in the tribe's social stratification. By tradition, the face of each male in the tribe was, at birth, daubed with either black or white, thereby forever establishing the particular band of the tribe with which that individual would be associated. The particular face color used would distinguish the individual as he grew up, determining what side he would be on in the tribal games as the youths teamed with or against others, in tribal ceremonies, in the more serious feats of individual skill or daring, where the warriors vied for honors, and, most important, in competition for the greatest of all honors, in warfare.

Pyesa reached out and took up the farthest of the bowls and dipped his fingertips into the viscous fluid. He daubed this in spots and small smears on the forehead, cheeks, and chin of his new son. The baby squirmed a little but made no sound as he applied it.

There was no surprise in the voice of Summer Rain when she spoke softly. "Muckataiwah" — Black.

Pyesa glanced up at her and smiled. "My son's name," he said gravely, "is Makataimeshekiakiak" — Black Sparrow Hawk.[6]

[July 4, 1777 — Friday]

During the week when he reached his tenth summer, Black Hawk began to feel that the world had passed him by; that all the wonderful things that could be accomplished had already happened and that all the great honors of war had already been won.

What inspired all this and sent him spiraling into the depths of the first real depression he had ever experienced were the hours his father, Pyesa, had spent with him, instructing him in the history of his tribe and the world that surrounded it and sometimes infringed upon it.

"We have had many enemies in the past," Pyesa said, speaking softly to his son as they sat together beneath a great oak tree high on a bank overlooking the Rock River several miles above their village of Saukenuk, "but we have defeated them. The worst of these have been the tribes west of the great river — especially the Osage but also, at times, the Kansa, the Sioux, and the Otoe. Now we are at peace, or at least in a state of truce, with these tribes."

Black Hawk stood up and faced his father. Already recognized as a leader among the youths his own age or even somewhat older, he yearned with unbearable intensity to prove his worth among the Sacs. He was of average height for his age, leanly muscled and alert. At the moment his dark eyes were wide and searching, his visage troubled. "Father," he said earnestly, "if all the wars have already been fought, where will I be able to gain my honors? How will I ever be able to wear the feathers of a warrior?"

Pyesa reached out and placed a hand on his son's shoulder and let it rest there a moment before speaking. "Makataimeshekiakiak, so long as there are men, so long as there are different tribes, so long as the whites continue to push into Indian lands, there will be wars."

"But all the great wars have already been fought," Black Hawk objected. "I have been born too late." He was close to tears and horrified at the thought that his emotion would spill into view and add shame to his already unbearable deprivation.

"Not true, my son," Pyesa said, doing his best to mask the smile that tugged at his mouth corners. He knew what Black Hawk was feeling and turned his gaze upward into the branches of the oak, so that if his boy's emotion should surface, he would not see it and his son would not be embarrassed. "Long, long summers ago, when I was like you — young and filled with the fire of needing to prove myself — I sat with your grandfather, Kiakukiak, and spoke to him as you are now speaking to me. I thought there could be no more great wars then, but I was wrong. He told me what I am telling you, but I found it very hard to believe. Then, the very next summer — we were then living far north of here, near the south end of the Bay of Bad Smells — the Chippewas brought a war upon us that we had no reason to expect.[7] My father and his two brothers, Namah and Paukahummawa" — Sturgeon and Sun Fish — "went off to fight them.[8] They were gone long and long and when they returned it was with great honor and the war had ended. But the honors won by Kiakukiak were never known by him, because he was killed. That was why I became close to my uncles,

Sturgeon and Sun Fish, for they took upon themselves the duties toward me that would have been my father's, had he lived."

Pyesa dropped his hand and stood up, still not looking at Black Hawk, his gaze directed upriver but focused only on the past. He shook his head faintly. "I was, and remain, something of a disappointment to them. Great warrior chiefs that they are, they had wished for me to follow their path but I did not, because the death of Kiakukiak had changed me. I turned from the path of the warrior and became instead a learner of the arts of tribal medicine at the side of old Koweeth, who told me that had I known the medicine he knew and been able to be beside my father with this knowledge, I might have saved his life. When Koweeth died and his place was taken by Nothamukano, I then worked beside him and learned from him what there had not been time to learn from Koweeth."[9]

"But you *are* a warrior as well as a medicine man," Black Hawk said quickly. "I have heard from you and others of the war parties you raised and led and the honors you won."

"I have earned such honors," Pyesa admitted, "and I may win others in time to come, but they are secondary for me. More important to me is continuing in the work of Koweeth and Nothamukano as they correctly said I would do when they were gone. So here I am, with a few honors of war, but not ashamed that I do not have more. For some — not necessarily for you, but for some — there are honors of other kinds that are equally important."

"Come along," he said, slipping his arm over his son's shoulder. He began walking with him past the tribe's extensive cornfields and gardens toward the village, resuming his narration of the tribe's history as it had been told to him and as he had himself lived part of it. And much later that night, as the steadied breathing of his father and mother bore testimony to their sleep, Black Hawk pondered over what he had learned in these past days. The depression he had suffered had been short-lived, largely due to the final remarks his father had made this day.

Two hundred summers ago, Pyesa had told him, their tribe had lived close to where Montreal was now located. Then, less than a century ago, the tribe had moved far west, to a location above the Bay of the Saginaw in a distant land called Michigan, where they were allies with other Michigan tribes, including the Fox, against a common and terrible foe to the east — the Iroquois, which was a powerful confederacy of five tribes. Their strength was great, and they did not live in wigwams but rather in long houses, each of which contained many families. They likened their confederacy to a long house as well, naming it Iroquois. Its front door, where the Mohawks lived, faced onto a river that ran southward to the sea at a place now inhabited by whites and called New York. Their back door, guarded by the Senecas, faced onto the powerful waterfall over which eventually tumbled all the waters that sprang up in the Great Lakes as they flowed on their eastern journey to the sea. The tribes inhabiting the interior of the long house were the Oneidas and Onondagas and Cayugas, fierce fighters all.

Together these five tribes, by uniting their strengths, had conquered tribes far and away beyond their own lands, and wherever the cry was raised, "The Iroquois are coming!," even the bravest of other tribes fled before them. Those who defied them were destroyed.

"Inhabiting the area between us and them," Pyesa had said, "was the Erie tribe, who made the mistake of giving shelter to the Hurons, who were enemies of the Iroquois League. The Iroquois thereupon descended upon the Eries and destroyed every man, woman, and child, so that now all that remains of a once proud and strong tribe is a memory that warns others. The Hurons fled their land and came to live in the Michigan land to the south of us, still very fearful of the Iroquois."

"Didn't the Iroquois ever come after them, too?" Black Hawk had asked.

"They would have, in their own time," Pyesa replied. "They were planning to. But partly because of the whites — and one among them in particular, an adopted brother of the Mohawks, called Warraghiyagey by the Iroquois and William Johnson by the whites — a peace was arranged between them. And after a while the whites, as they always seem to do, made even the Iroquois no longer able to venture far from their long house.[10]

"Then, nearly eighty summers ago, when the Huron tribe split and half of them became known as Wyandots, we found that the hunting grounds had now become too crowded with hunters, for in addition to the Hurons and Wyandots and Foxes and Sacs, there were Ottawas and Chippewas and Potawatomies. So we spoke among ourselves on this matter over many council fires with our Fox brothers and finally agreed to move far and far away. Our two tribes crossed over the land on top of the great blue water sea also called Michigan, and we established our villages near the south end of the Bay of Bad Smells near our friends the Menominees. To the southwest of us, the Fox people — those the Frenchmen called Reynards — settled among their old friends the Winnebagoes along the river they call Wisconsin.[11] But farther to the north, the Chippewas suddenly brought war upon us for injuries they imagined we had done them in passing through their lands. And that was when the body of Kiakukiak was borne home by his brothers, my uncles."

Pyesa had gone on to tell Black Hawk that just as the Sacs had their troubles with the Chippewas, so the Fox tribe, who were as interested in the fur trade as the Sacs, soon became involved in a series of wars with the whites called French. Because, Pyesa went on, both our tribes, but especially the Foxes, were on the trading route, their existence was constantly upset by these Frenchmen, so the tribes moved again and settled on lands along the Wisconsin near the Mississippi and down the grandmother of rivers from there.[12] The Sac and Fox warriors drove away the hunters of other tribes who had long been coming here — the Missouri and Kansa and Osage — so they became our bitter enemies. And now the Sac and Fox villages were here in this Illinois land and across the river among our friends the Iowas, from across from the mouth of the Wisconsin to as far south as the river that borders the territory of the Missouri, the river the Frenchmen call Des Moines. "And here we are still," Pyesa had concluded, "and we are very strong."

"What about Pontiac?" Black Hawk had prompted eagerly. He had heard the story before, but never tired of hearing it again.

"Yes, Pontiac," Pyesa had replied. "I knew him. He was a strong chief of the Ottawas in Michigan when I was a young man there. He was very partial to the French, and when the British came and drove the Frenchmen out, he hated them and vowed vengeance. He remembered the strength the Iroquois had when they united into a league and he decided to do the same himself. He sent war belts to all the tribes, inviting them to join him in making a surprise attack upon the British, and many tribes, including the Sacs and Foxes, joined him. I was there. Almost overnight, to the east as far as the former land of the Eries and to the west as far as where we had lived, at the Bay of Bad Smells, all the British forts were captured."

"All but one," Black Hawk had corrected.

Pyesa's lips quirked. "Yes, all but one. Only Detroit did not fall at once, and Pontiac kept the soldiers boxed up in there for many moons and almost had them ready to give way when the tribes who were supporting him began to abandon him. It was their way to fight as men, in open warfare, not as little children with sticks waiting for the rabbit to come out of his hole. At last Pontiac had no other choice than to sue for peace, but even after that he still planned to raise another army of tribes and finish what he had begun. By then, many of the tribes had gone to the great waterfall for a grand council.[13] Some of our chiefs were there and signed the peace treaty, but there were others of us who were willing to take up the hatchet again with Pontiac to drive the British out. Pontiac, in an effort to get more tribes to support him, visited the Illinois country and tried to convince the thirteen tribes of the Illinois Confederacy, led by the Peorias, Cahokias, and Kaskaskias, to pledge him their support. But they were a cowardly group and, fearful that he would bring the wrath of the British down upon them, they invited him to a council and then murdered him. That happened when you were approaching your second summer, Black Hawk.[14]

"So angered were all the other tribes," Pyesa continued, "that they joined together and swept down on the Illinois Confederacy and wiped them out. This, then, left their lands open for the taking. We, along with the Potawatomies and Kickapoos and Winnebagoes and others, claimed the land by right of conquest and it has been ours since then. And now there are new dangers to face. The whites have begun moving into the Illinois country. They are still few in number and weak, and we should drive them out now, but we will not. We wait instead for others to do it for us."

"Who?" Black Hawk had asked, just as they finished walking past the cornfield and started to pass the principal cemetery of the Sac nation.

"The Shawnees," Pyesa said promptly. "They and the Delawares and the

Hurons and the Miamis, all of whom are between the whites and us." He paused and then added, "They must stop the whites or be destroyed. They know this and it makes them very uneasy. As some of their chiefs are already saying, If the great Iroquois could not stand before the whites, what chance, then, can individual tribes have who are of lesser strength?"

They were just now entering the great village of Saukenuk with its half a thousand wigwams and quonsets spread out in picturesque manner before them. Black Hawk was silent for a long while as they walked, and then he looked at his father. "You do not think they will be able to stop the whites?"

They had stopped before the entry to their lodge and Pyesa had regarded his son steadily for some time before replying. "You worry that you will have no war to fight to bring honor to yourself in battle. I tell you now, Black Hawk, the whites will come — probably with their hands outstretched in friendship first — and you will eventually go to war against them, and it will be a war more terrible for us than our people have ever known before. You will be very brave and you will win many honors. But, hear me, Black Hawk, this may be the war that we cannot win."

Now, listening to the breathing of Pyesa and Summer Rain across the interior darkness of the wigwam from him, the ten-year-old Black Hawk felt a surge of excitement rise in him as he thought of the glory of war and the honors he would gain. And though he would never have admitted it to anyone, deep in his heart an uncomfortable kernel of shame for his father had taken root because Pyesa had suggested the possibility that if war with the whites was to come, the Sacs might not win.

[*July 22, 1783 — Tuesday*]

Flames from the large fire in the central clearing of Saukenuk caused the surrounding forms of the wigwams and larger quonset huts to loom and fade eerily in the darkness as the shadows of the dancers, barefoot and clad only in loincloths, leaped and spun and whirled across them. More than seven hundred Sacs sat in a wide circle about the fire, watching intently and approvingly the thirty-one warriors who were involved in the scalp dance. Each dancer was, in his own way, reenacting the role he had played in the recent foray against the Osage tribe. Screeches and howls rent the heavy night air and were echoed by the spectators in a wild cacophony, accompanied by the drums, rattles, and reed flutes of the musicians, the cadenced clapping by virtually all in attendance, and a persistent underlying clinking of strands of clamshells about the ankles and wrists and necks of the dancers.

Spaced at intervals around the fire were nine slender poles impaling the earth at a near-sixty-degree angle, and from the top of each, strung in place with thin rawhide tugs, a scalp depended, swaying and turning in the breezes generated by the fire and the passage of the dancers. For more than an hour the dance continued as squaws moved silently about the inner perimeter of the spectators, placing mats at intervals and heaping them with arrays of fruits and vegetables, newly baked breads, dried strips of meat and fish, whole roasted haunches and sides of venison, along with large communal bowls of thick stew. So long as the dancing continued, the food remained untouched.

Gradually the general dancing of the returned war party subsided as, one by one, the individual warriors who had actually taken the scalps from their enemies separated themselves from among the thirty-one. Each, in turn, became the center of attention for two or three wildly gyrating turns about the fire, relating in chanting sing-song the details of how he had taken the ultimate trophy from his foe, the individual dance culminating in the warrior snatching from among the slanting poles the enemy scalp he had taken. And each, as he finished, won more than just the applause and cheers of the assemblage. Each was approached by Kataka, leader of the victorious war party, and gravely presented with an eagle feather to be worn as a headdress with the one or two or several similar feathers the warrior had already won, as a token of prowess as a warrior; a token that brought to each a new permanent honor in the tribe.[15]

At last only one scalp remained attached to its pole. Kataka walked to it and, facing the fire, raised both arms high and uttered a shrill cry. In one hand was a single eagle feather. Instantly all sounds from participants and spectators ceased, and the crackling of the fire heightened in the expectant hush. Kataka, clad only in a loincloth just as the dancers had been, was an imposing figure, tall and sinewy and bald, the hair of his head having been plucked away to leave only a shining pate except for an inch-diameter scalp lock above and behind his right ear, to which were attached in descending fashion a string of eleven eagle feathers similar to the one in his hand. The left half of his body had been painted jet black and the right side stark white. All eyes were locked on him as he removed the final scalp from its pole, held it high in his free hand, and silently paced two complete circuits around the fire.

"A boy accompanied our war party when we left Saukenuk one moon ago," he said loudly as he came to a stop, "but when we returned, only men were with us. One summer ago he accompanied us, and at that time he wounded an enemy and won his first honor as a young warrior; but he was still a boy. This time the boy leaped to the front as we attacked and grappled with the Osage who led their party. The Osage was larger and stronger than the boy, yet it was the boy who plunged his knife into the enemy's heart. It was the boy who cut this scalp from that warrior chief's head. It was the boy who gave the victory cry as he held the scalp aloft for all to see." He paused and then dramatically pointed the feather toward the crowd before him. "That boy," he said loudly, "now no longer a boy, was the son of Pyesa. Come forward, Black Hawk."

Bursting with pride, the sixteen-year-old, clad as the other dancers had been and his face bedaubed with streaks of black paint, stepped forward and stopped before Kataka.

"Black Hawk," Kataka said solemnly, "you have shown great courage and, in facing and slaying a powerful enemy, have brought honor to yourself, to your family, and to your tribe. You are, as of this night, no longer a boy. You are a brave henceforth with the right, if you should so choose and if there is the proper justification for doing so, to organize your own war party of any who will choose to follow you."

The youth said nothing as Kataka stepped to his side and began attaching the coveted single eagle feather to his hair at the right temple, but his eyes glinted and a faint smile tilted his lips. Only rarely had such an honor come to one so young among the Sacs. There was far more behind Kataka's simple utterance than was apparent. Black Hawk was well aware of the ramifications, since they had been explained to him over a year ago by his father.

"Any male of our tribe who accompanies a war party," Pyesa had told him then, "is considered a warrior, but not all warriors have the right to lead war parties. This honor is reserved only for the braves — those who have already proven themselves in battle by overcoming an enemy and killing him under circumstances involving considerable personal danger."

"Such as hand-to-hand fighting?" Black Hawk had asked then, intensely interested.

"Yes," his father said, "usually hand to hand. But just because one has been honored with the status of brave, he does not have the right to organize a war party on a whim. There is a traditional process that must be followed. Most important, there has to be justification for it."

"What kind of justification, father?"

Pyesa grunted, detecting a trace of disappointment in his son's voice, but he answered the question as if he did not notice. "One that derives from some member of the tribe, especially a member of one's immediate family, having been killed or insulted or in some manner injured. But there's a certain amount of leeway in this. For example, if you have the status of brave and you even have a powerful dream that such an insult or injury or death has occurred — or sometimes even *might* occur — then that is at times considered proper justification for you to try to organize a retaliatory war party.

"To do this," Pyesa went on, "you, as a brave, must openly declare in full tribal council that you wish to avenge the actual or dreamed slaying or insult. You thereupon call for volunteers to form a war party under your leadership. At this point, any warriors in attendance who are interested in the project — or simply interested in following the man who will be the leader — may offer themselves for it. This could result in no one at all volunteering, which would be a mark of shame against you and could even result in your status as a brave being revoked or suspended. The usual result, however," he added hastily, "is that a war party does form."

"Of how many warriors?" the boy asked. "And how long would they be gone?"

Pyesa shrugged. "It depends on many things, Black Hawk. There may be as few as six or seven warriors in addition to the organizer, or, in especially popular causes involving tribal honor or accepting a war belt circulating from other tribes that are allies, as many as six or seven hundred. Often, too, more than one such party of volunteers are formed if more than one brave at the council calls for volunteers. Depending on circumstance, others in the tribe — sometimes the chief, but more often women and old men — will either encourage the volunteer warriors to go or advise them against it. If the party actually does head out, it is with the understanding that the organizer is the leader, even though others of higher tribal rank may be in his party, and their travel and fighting are under the tight discipline established by the leader. If, however, the leader exhibits cowardice or makes errors, those following him have the right to discuss this with him and, if they choose, to abandon the project and go home without dishonor.

"As for how long they will stay out, it could be only a week or two. Or, in a major war, they might stay away for two or three years."

Black Hawk was clearly fascinated. "Is there a particular method of fighting they have to do, father?"

Pyesa shook his head. "Again, much depends on circumstance. If at all possible, an attack is made from ambush or by surprise. Often what it amounts to is cutting off stragglers of larger groups of the enemy. Sometimes it involves boldly attacking small groups like hunting parties or, especially among the whites, isolated cabins or farms. Then again, as happened with those who followed Pontiac's leadership, it may involve laying siege to fortified camps or villages.

"Finally, when the war party returns with scalps or captives, the ceremonies are held. If there are captives, some might be adopted into the tribe, but more often they will be tortured to death. If there are only scalps, then a celebration is prepared and the scalp dance is held, followed by feasting, which may last for two or three days."

Pyesa had stopped then, and after a moment Black Hawk, with a start, had realized his father was finished talking, but the boy himself wanted to know more.

"Father, you said the chiefs or others might sometimes try to discourage warriors for volunteering for a war party. Why would they do this?"

Pyesa looked at his son steadily for a long while and then said slowly, "I think I have not a son who will become a medicine man like his father and grandfather. He will, I think, become a fighter and perhaps a war chief like his father's uncles." He sighed, but then, after a moment, went on more briskly. "The chiefs — or others — might feel the party's preparations are not good enough, or the justification sufficient enough, to warrant the act. Then, too, they might weigh the possible consequences of such a war party's attack and decide that it could provoke retaliation that would be too destructive to the tribe as a whole. Or the war party may wish to attack a valuable ally, and that would have to be discouraged except in the most extreme cases. Chiefs tend to consider such things very carefully, whereas young warriors are more hot-blooded and inclined to react more from the heart than from the head. The chiefs might then attempt to dissuade the party through reasonable argument, but if the warriors will not listen, the chiefs may take stronger steps, such as confiscating their amulets and potions or other medicine. They might also appeal to the women of the tribe to speak to their warriors and dissuade them as only women can dissuade men at times."

The memories of this conversation that had crowded back on Black Hawk were abruptly thrust aside as Kataka finished attaching the eagle feather and stepped back. He placed a hand on the boy's shoulder.

"If," he intoned, "you participate in any more war parties or eventually lead one yourself, may the Great Spirit remain at your side and continue to bring you honor."

Only one thing had ever brought Black Hawk more pleasure than this moment of triumph before his tribe. It was the incredible exhilaration he had felt at the moment his blade had found the heart of his adversary and he had felt the body of the Osage relax in death beneath him. This had whetted an appetite in him that would not easily be sated and, though Black Hawk dipped his head in humble acknowledgment, humility was not in him. He knew it was not a question of *if* he participated, but *when*. And it would be often. And he, Black Hawk, would lead.

CHAPTER I

[*January 10, 1801 — Saturday*]

A VERITABLE LEXICON of adjectives would have been required to describe the tall and slender young man who was so intensely engrossed in his writing under the glow of a shiny brass chimney lamp as midnight approached. *Industrious* would have been an obvious choice. *Successful*, certainly, as attested to by his fashionable garb and the elegant furnishings of his quarters. But other terms, far less immediately obvious, were decidedly applicable: intelligent, ambitious, aggressive, persuasive, opportunistic, deceitful, indefatigable, tenacious, and a host of others. Of them all, perhaps none was so thoroughly appropriate as *ambitious*.

The gaunt featured young man with permanently brooding expression beneath a shock of reddish hair was only twenty-seven years old, and yet earlier this very day he had become one of the most powerful men in the United States; certainly *the* most powerful in the young nation's raw northwestern frontier. Almost beyond doubt, any other individual achieving the status that had been bestowed upon him this morning would have been celebrating or at least, considering the rigors of this day, relaxing. Not he. His pen sped across the page before him, creating calligraphic line after line. He paused briefly at short intervals to thrust his pen nib swiftly and unerringly into the inkpot and, at somewhat longer intervals, to blot his finished page and begin another. Occasionally he referred briefly to one or another of the multitude of books, pamphlets, reports, and correspondence spread out close at hand.

He glanced up at a slight sound and smiled at his wife standing in the doorway, the ivory lace of her nightgown's collar exposed at the neck of her voluminous, floor-length, deep-blue robe. She held a lamp similar to his but smaller, her delicate finger curled through the decorative coiled brass handle.

The light of its flame softened the lines of worry on her brow, but the anxiety in her voice was clearly evident.

"William?" She was hesitant. "Will you be coming to bed soon?"

"Yes. Yes, of course. Soon." He began leaning toward his work again. "You go on, Anna. I'll be there shortly."

He was gone, immersed in his work again, oblivious to time, oblivious to her, even though she remained a while longer. She knew it would be hours before he broke off, perhaps not at all, and at length she turned and walked away. Her footfalls on the steps were briefly audible, but he took no notice.

For William Henry Harrison, a new job — an immensely important new position — demanded immense attention, and he was willing, eager in fact, to give it. Earlier today, by appointment of President John Adams, he had been sworn in as the governor of Indiana Territory, a vast expanse extending all the way from the Ohio Territory to the Mississippi River and northward to Canada. In all this land he would be the final authority, responsible to no one but the President of the United States and holding unto himself the power of life or death over any inhabitant.

Harrison had no fear that this appointment by a lame-duck president would be short-lived. As favored as he continued to be by President Adams, he was held in even greater esteem by Vice President Thomas Jefferson, who had won the recent election and would be taking over the reins of the nation in less than two months. Already Jefferson had made his desires concerning the West abundantly clear to Harrison, and the latter found that, if anything, he would have an even freer hand with Jefferson than with his predecessor.

In the year and a half that he had served as secretary of the Northwest Territory he had learned a great deal about this rough frontier and its Indian inhabitants. He had acquired a comprehensive grasp of its turbulent past and uneasy present. Now, in his new exalted position, he could envision its future as well; a future that he, with the sanction of incoming President Jefferson, had the power to carve. A lesser individual might have seen himself as instrumental in the months and years to come in creating counties and maintaining a quietly benevolent godhead attitude. But already William Henry Harrison's gaze went far beyond such shallow aspirations. This vast territory would become states of the Union under his guidance — states that he already thought of as Indiana and Michigan and Illinois, possibly a couple more in the expansive region to the west and northwest of Lake Michigan. His immediate ambitions were to prove his worth to his president and countrymen through acquisition of lands far beyond what was projected by even the most liberal. At present the Indiana Territory was heavily populated by Indians of a dozen or more different tribes, but only about fifty-five hundred whites. It would take treaty, treachery, outright thievery, and perhaps even warfare to uproot and remove the tribes, but he was certain that no man alive knew better than he how this could be accomplished. And in the very doing of it, the watered seed of his even grander ambition would be able to swell, burst, and take root in the fertile soil of his amazing accomplishments. Though he would not have had the foolish temerity to make a public utterance of it at this stage of his career, he was fully confident that one day *he* would be president of these United States.

First things first, however, so even though his knowledge of this land and its people was prodigious for one so young, he continued to study — even on this day of his installation as governor.

His own career had been meteoric. His father, Benjamin Harrison, signer of the Declaration of Independence, had been a close friend of George Washington. The elder Harrison had wanted his son to become a doctor, but such a profession was not even remotely a stepping-stone to William's goal, so when his father had died a decade ago, William had immediately taken advantage of his father's friendship for the president and begged the chief executive to appoint him an officer in the United States Army. Washington granted the boon, and Harrison was commissioned an ensign. A second favor was also granted: assignment with the U.S. Tenth Regiment at Fort Washington — Cincinnati — under General Arthur St. Clair, another friend of Washington's. He had arrived there mere days too late to join St. Clair's campaign against the amalgamated tribes — Shawnees, Delawares, Miamis, Weas, Piankeshaws, and others — under the formidable joint leadership of Chief Blue Jacket of the Shawnees and Chief Little Turtle of the Miamis. His initial dismay at missing the expedition quickly turned into relief, for St. Clair's army was devastatingly attacked and suffered the most shattering defeat at the hands of the Indians by any military force in North American history, with two-thirds of his force of over nine hundred men killed and only two dozen men who returned uninjured. The Indians lost only sixty-six men.[16]

Congress investigated the affair and, though St. Clair was exonerated of any blame for the disaster and continued as governor of the Northwest Territory, command of the Army of the West had been put into the hands of General Anthony Wayne. Harrison, keenly aware of the value of proximity and never one to let an opportunity pass him by, quickly got himself appointed as Wayne's aide-de-camp. He remained with Wayne through the general's decisive victory against the Indians at the Battle of Fallen Timbers on the Maumee River, and also learned valuable lessons from him in respect to treaty making with the Indians. Wayne indisputably secured for the United States more than half of the Ohio Territory by means of the Treaty of Greenville in 1795, a treaty the defeated Indians had no choice but to sign. Dispossessed of their southern Ohio lands, the Shawnees had moved north of the treaty line or westward into the Indian territory. Pleased with the performance of his aide-de-camp through all this, Wayne not only had Harrison promoted to captain, but secured for him command of Fort Washington.[17]

Then came one of the major turning points in Harrison's life. He was offered the opportunity to resign his military commission in favor of becoming secretary of the Northwest Territory under St. Clair. He hesitated not one moment in turning his back on the military career for the more political and influential berth. For a man of only twenty-five, he had certainly made great strides, but he knew he was far from finished. He was very correct. Three months before the end of the century, when Governor St. Clair called a meeting in Cincinnati to establish the newly authorized territorial legislature, the man elected as delegate to the United States Congress was, to no one's surprise, William Henry Harrison.

The young delegate had wasted no time getting into the thick of the action. As the new century blossomed, Harrison took the floor in Congress Hall and introduced a bill proposing that Congress divide the Northwest Territory into two distinct areas politically independent of one another. Knowing that his own fortunes would be predicated upon a swift and voluminous increase in the white population of the frontier, he further introduced a bill that permitted whites to purchase tracts of 320 acres each at a cost of only $160 down and three successive annual payments of the same amount. Not only was the latter bill passed handily, the Congress also passed his proposed Division Act, and last May 7 the Northwest Territory as such had ceased to exist, replaced by the creation of the Ohio Territory and the Indiana Territory. The Ohio Territory was already on the verge of statehood and, as Harrison was only too well aware, the new Indiana Territory required a governor. Harrison had adroitly maneuvered himself into the perfect situation, because that governorship was an appointive post, and where lame-duck President Adams and President-elect Jefferson were concerned, no one else was so qualified for the job as he. And so had come the most prestigious single advancement of his career thus far.

Harrison had discovered, during his years with St. Clair and Wayne, that one of the surest ways to keep his fingers on the pulse of the frontier was to keep a force of spies constantly on the move throughout the territory and to pay close attention to every little detail they reported. Very often, he knew, these little details, seemingly insignificant at the time, turned out to be pivotal factors in what course of action would ultimately ensue.

[*March 9, 1804 — Friday*]

Black Hawk stood at the window of the governor's mansion in St. Louis and watched with a sour expression what was occurring on the open ground below them. A large number of chiefs from various tribes were assembled there, each with a small contingent of blanket-wrapped followers. A United States Army officer, Captain Amos Stoddard of Connecticut, was stepping from group to group and, through an interpreter, greeting and speaking to each for a few minutes before moving on.

"They do not seem to mind, Black Hawk," Charles Delassus said at his side. "Perhaps they realize they have no choice and are making the best of the situation." The inflection in his voice made it clear he hoped the Sac would come to the same conclusion as the other tribes.

"I mind," Black Hawk responded sharply. "I do not believe there is no choice and will have no part of this." He turned to face the governor. "I am sorry you are leaving and will miss you. My people will miss you. I will take my men and leave now."

Governor Charles Dehault Delassus realized the futility of trying to dissuade him from his stand, and so they simply shook hands in silence. As Black Hawk turned and walked away, Delassus felt the frustration rise in him again at the implacability of these events. An era that had involved him deeply was ending, and there was nothing he could do to alter matters.

The group of warriors standing or squatting in the elegant entry hall of the mansion straightened as Black Hawk came into view descending the broad stairs. They read his expression and none spoke as he passed through them toward the massive, carved, walnut double doors. A butler opened the door as he approached and stepped back as he passed through to the outside, followed by his warriors. At the foot of the stairs they stopped as Black Hawk paused to watch Captain Stoddard shake hands with the final chief — a Kansa named Chiryskata.[18]

The officer finished with Chief Chiryskata, turned, and walked toward the mansion, closely followed by his interpreter and two noncommissioned officers, as the bulk of his company remained in formation well behind. When Stoddard's eye fell upon Black Hawk and the Sac men behind him, he smiled the same smile he had donned for the other chiefs and approached with hand outstretched. Black Hawk neither smiled nor waited for the captain to speak.

"We do not know you," he said, ignoring the attempt at friendliness. "We do not *wish* to know you. We are not like the others who have come here" — his gaze flicked to the assembled tribal contingents well away from them, then back to the officer — "and we do not welcome you. We do not, as they do, offer respects to a new father, for we still love our old father, whom you are today dispossessing."

Even as Black Hawk was speaking, the interpreter was repeating *sotto voce* in English for Captain Stoddard's ears, but Black Hawk ignored him, making no attempt either to pause or to slow his oration. "Those tribes," he continued, "may fear the strength of your father Jefferson's arm, but the Sacs and Foxes do not. We cannot keep you from being here in St. Louis, but do not make the mistake of thinking you can ascend the Grandmother of Rivers and enter our land with your empty promises. Your chief named Harrison has sent us many messages asking for councils with us, but what he wishes to discuss is taking our land, and we do not want that. We have asked that an agent be provided to be our eyes and ears and voice between us and the whites, but the white Chief Harrison ignores this, so we choose now to ignore him and you. Our friends the British, who have posts at Prairie du Chien and elsewhere in our country — *with our permission* — supply us with what we need. We have learned that you do not become friendly unless you want something. We do not wish your friendship. We do not *need* your friendship. We wish only that you avert your greedy eyes from the land of our fathers, which we will never let you take from us."

Admirably, considering Black Hawk's rapid delivery, the interpreter finished only a few beats after the Sac speaker. Stoddard, who had dropped his out-stretched hand self-consciously as Black Hawk spoke, now faced him with a smile still on his face, though decidedly strained. He listened without change of expression as, apart from his duty, the interpreter murmured a string of words close to his ear. He nodded as the interpreter finished and stepped back.

"You are Black Hawk," he said. "I am told that you are not a chief and do not have authority to speak for your tribe. Nevertheless, I will tell you this: we do not wish your land. That is not the purpose of our visit here. The Sacs have heretofore ignored the hand of friendship extended to them from our great father, the president, and his representative, William Henry Harrison, in Vin-cennes, but our great father is as patient as he is powerful, and when the time is right he will prove to you that he means you no harm, and he will make it possible for your people and ours to meet in amity and discuss matters to our mutual benefit."

Black Hawk understood much of what Captain Stoddard said, but he waited until the interpreter had finished and then repeated himself in a tone even colder than before. "I am not a civil chief among my people, no, but I have long been a leader of war parties among the Sacs. I say to you, as one who carries great strength in my hand, that we do not wish to speak to you or to your father or any of his emissaries. I say only that you will *not* have the lands of the Sac and Fox."

Without waiting for the interpreter to finish, he stepped past the officer and, followed by his own contingent, made his way toward the Mississippi River. As he walked, he thought of what had brought this confrontation about. A mes-senger had arrived at Saukenuk several weeks ago with word from Governor Delassus that he wished to have Black Hawk come to see him for a talk at this time. That same messenger had also carried a message for the Sac council — a loose body of civil chiefs who made up the governing faction, such as it was, of the Sac tribe.

The message that had been brought was an invitation for whatever chiefs were inclined to do so, to present themselves for an important discussion about what was in store for Sac lands. This was nothing new. Emissaries from Governor William Henry Harrison, western chief of the great father called Jefferson, had brought them messages many times, asking meetings to discuss possible purchase of lands, but they had always turned a deaf ear to them. The latest message had similar effect; the chiefs discussed it among themselves, and since, so far as they were concerned, nothing was in store for Sac lands except at the discretion of the Sacs themselves and they had no desire to dispose of any of their lands on either side of the Mississippi, what purpose would be served should they travel so far a distance? The consensus was, as always before, that they would stay at home.

Black Hawk, however, because of his personal friendship with Delassus, had decided to go. It had been many moons since they had met. The warriors he brought along were those who had accompanied him on numerous successful forays into enemy territory and who would volunteer to do so again when the time came. Thus, even though this was not a mission of warfare, which they would have preferred, they had elected to join him.

Three days ago the large dugout canoe, laboriously carved from the trunk of a single, huge elm tree and containing two dozen Sacs, had reached its destination. Twenty-two of the men, eleven to a side, were paddlers, whose well-coordinated strokes, aided by the strong current of the Mississippi, had moved the long craft swiftly along less than an arrow's flight from the steep bluffs of the west shore. The only two who had not done any paddling were the individuals in bow and stern. The former was Nepeek — Dark Water — a well-built man of about thirty who was second in command of the party and its lookout. His gaze was restless as he studied the shoreline and the river ahead. As they moved around a projecting point of the west shore, a large settlement loomed in the distance ahead, and Nepeek broke into a broad grin, exposing the gap where one of his upper incisors was missing. He swiveled about and shouted to the man in the rear.

"Black Hawk! There it is!"

Black Hawk nodded as he saw the extensive Louisiana Territory settlement of St. Louis. At once he issued a guttural order that caused the paddlers to send their canoe skimming toward the main landing area, where a variety of boats were anchored, tied to wharves or drawn up on the sharply sloped shoreline. This was by no means his first visit to the largest and most important city of the whites within hundreds of miles.

In 1763, four years before Black Hawk was born, the French, who had long claimed all this vast area west of the Mississippi, ceded it to Spain through the Treaty of Paris. Quick to take advantage of their acquisition, the Spaniards had immediately sent an expedition under Pierre LaClede upriver from New Orleans to establish a principal fur trading station near the mouth of the Missouri River. For thirty-seven years under Spanish dominion, St. Louis grew. Then, only three and a half years ago — on October 1, 1800 — France struck a secret agreement with the Spaniards in the Treaty of San Ildefonso, and the Louisiana Territory was returned to the French, with the proviso that they guaranteed never to transfer it to any power but Spain. And, though the Louisiana Territory was again under French ownership, full transfer of authority was slow in occurring and had not yet been carried out everywhere. Upper Louisiana was still under the Spanish governorship of Charles Dehault Delassus, who had been appointed to that post five years ago.

Now St. Louis was forty years old and had become a major metropolis of the frontier. The initial cluster of rough cabins built by LaClede and his stepsons —

the young Chouteau brothers, Auguste and Pierre — had evolved into a rowdy and wildly robust frontier town, but a well-organized one. Today there were carefully laid-out streets, hundreds of houses and governmental buildings — some of very substantial and impressive architecture — as well as churches and schools and an all but unbelievable multitude of stores. Many of the shops satisfied the needs of the town's residents, but as many or more were outfitters catering to the needs of those heading upriver or down on the Mississippi and, even more pertinently, to those hardy traders and trappers who were penetrating the vast unknown lands to the west by moving upstream on the strong and unpredictable Missouri River. St. Louis was also a powerful draw for the Indians, who could come here and trade their furs for the staples they needed, such as gunpowder, weapons, blankets, and tools, to say nothing of whiskey.

While Black Hawk's warriors were looking forward most especially to the whiskey that they could get here, Black Hawk himself wished only to see the man who had become his friend over these years, Governor Delassus. Their approach caused little interest among the people moving about. Indians in the streets and business places of St. Louis were very nearly as commonplace as whites. When the canoe scraped ashore, the men dropped their paddles and leaped out, dragging it a full boat length from the water before looking to Black Hawk. He merely waved them off with a gesture and, as they walked laughing and joking toward the waterfront saloons, he strode toward the governor's mansion. Not until he had covered half the distance did he realize that many of the people he was seeing on the streets looked very morose. Recognizing a taciturn French trader who often dealt with the Sacs, he stopped him.

"What is happening here?" he demanded. He flung out an arm in an encompassing gesture. "Why do so many wear long faces?"

The trader smiled thinly in recognition. "Ah, *mon ami* Black Hawk. You are a long way from home. You have heard, eh?"

"What? What is it I am supposed to have heard about?"

The trader squinted at him. "You don't know, do you? I feel regret for you, *mon ami*. Go see Monsieur Delassus. He will tell you the bad news." He appeared on the point of saying more, then shook his head, stepped around Black Hawk, and walked off.

Black Hawk watched him go, then continued toward the mansion, but no longer with the sense of anticipation that had filled him earlier. Several minutes later, when he presented himself to Delassus, the governor welcomed him warmly, bade him sit, and poured them each a glass of wine from a decanter. Though Black Hawk had never learned to appreciate the taste of alcohol, he accepted the glass and took a small sip. Despite the governor's cordiality, it was clear that Delassus was infected with the same aura of gloom that was cloaking the town.

"Black Hawk," he said, wheezing as he settled himself in a brocaded chair an arm's length from his guest, "I am glad you have come as I requested. I am only sorry that it is at such a bad time. The news is not good. This is very probably the last time we will meet."

The Sac sat quietly a moment and then nodded as he remembered a conversation they had had many months ago. "It is as you told me would happen? The French are coming to claim this place?"

Delassus shook his head. "Not the French. The Americans."

Black Hawk frowned, not understanding. "You said it was the French who regained the Louisianas from you."

The governor sighed and sipped at his wine. "That was true. But strange things have happened. You remember I told you of the French foreign minister across the sea — Monsieur Charles de Tallyrand?" At Black Hawk's nod, he continued. "When the bargain was struck between the French and my people for us to return this land to them, Tallyrand promised he would never give possession of it to anyone but us, the Spanish. Now he has turned his back on that promise. Not until it was done did we learn he had sold Louisiana to the American president, Jefferson.[19] A messenger has brought word that a company of American soldiers will arrive here tomorrow. At that time, under an authority that has been granted to him, a Captain Amos Stoddard will formally accept the Territory from Spain in the name of France. On the day after that, in a similar ceremony, he will accept the Territory from France on behalf of the United States and become its acting governor. When that is accomplished, I am done here and will leave for New Orleans, and from there for Spain."

It had occurred as Delassus had said it would, and now Black Hawk's mood was bleak as his men launched the canoe and they began moving upstream away from St. Louis. The Americans! These were the ones who had come under the chief named George Rogers Clark — after he had taken the British at Kaskaskia and Cahokia — and burned Saukenuk when Black Hawk was only in his thirteenth year.[20] The Sac could still remember peering from the bushes where he and Pyesa were hidden, watching as their wigwams were burned, as their whole town was destroyed, just as every Indian town in Clark's path had been destroyed if its inhabitants had given aid or shelter to the British. In one of those Saukenuk wigwams had been Kneebingkemewoin — Summer Rain — who was very ill, on the point of death, and could not be moved. But they had not let her have the death the Great Spirit had meant for her to have, quietly and at peace, with her husband and son beside. The whites had not even known she was there, nor would they have cared if they had. The Sacs had returned when the Americans were gone and the fire was out. Eventually Saukenuk was rebuilt even better than before, but the fire of hatred for the Americans that had been ignited in the hearts of Black Hawk and Pyesa had never diminished.

"Portage des Sioux, Black Hawk," Nepeek called out, interrupting the Sac leader's reverie.

Black Hawk motioned his men to continue paddling upstream, but he looked toward the west bank and saw the trading post and scattered shed and wigwams surrounding it. They were all familiar with the place. Located six miles above the mouth of the Missouri, this stopping place had been established five years ago. For those coming downstream on the Mississippi and intent upon ascending the Missouri, the short portage here to the Missouri cut off many miles of paddling down to the big tributary's mouth and then upstream again. It was a route often taken by the Sac war parties when they moved out against the hated Osages.

Again Black Hawk became lost in memories. Good memories. Memories of the war parties in which he had participated as a warrior and later, when considerable fame had come to him among his people as a leader of war parties. But what he hoped for so desperately — to be named war chief of his nation — was an honor not yet acquired. It was a lifetime post awarded only when the present war chief died or was incapacitated or stepped down, and was given only when a noted warrior announced his intention of raising an expedition to go against enemies and called for volunteers. If that warrior had been successful in earlier expeditions, he usually had no trouble in getting volunteers to join him, at which time he became nominally a war chief. But if he made errors in judgment or showed cowardice in any way, he might never again find volunteers to accompany him, and the title of war chief could conceivably be taken away from him.

It had been only a few months after Black Hawk had officially become a warrior at the scalp dance when he announced his intention of going against the Osages and asked for volunteers. There were not many who were willing to be led by a youth of sixteen summers who had taken only one scalp, but two of the warriors who had been on the previous expedition and had seen him fight joined him, along with four of the younger men still yearning to take their own first scalps and become entitled to the elite warrior status.

The seven-man war party left Saukenuk in light canoes, heading downstream. They had passed across Portage des Sioux and penetrated deeply into the territory of the Osages, almost to the land of the Omahas and Poncas. Eventually they had come across the trail of a large Osage party — far larger than their own and surely upwards of one hundred strong. The other members of the party urged him to turn back, since it would be no disgrace for them to avoid engagement with so large a force of the enemy. The choice was Black Hawk's, and he had ordered they go on until they engaged the enemy. With that utterance, any who turned back would be guilty of cowardice and possibly have to live with that stigma the rest of their lives. They had overtaken the enemy at night, having painted their faces black in the almost sure knowledge that they would be killed once their presence was discovered. But Black Hawk had ordered that they shriek as loudly as they could when the attack was made, strike hard, and then retreat immediately with whatever trophies they had taken. Five guards were near the fire, and they fell upon them by surprise. Three of the guards were wounded immediately, and another who rushed to meet the enemy was slain by Black

Hawk's slashing tomahawk. The single guard still unharmed was terrified and raised the cry to flee, that a great force of Sacs was attacking them. So, as the Osages fled in one direction through the darkness, Black Hawk and his six men fled in the other, and gripped in Black Hawk's hand was the scalp of the guard he had killed. The honor that was his after this — a tiny band of seven attacking a hundred of the enemy, taking coup, even taking a scalp, and then getting away without the loss or even injury of a single man — was enormous. No longer would there be any reluctance among warriors and untried young men to volunteer to serve under his leadership.

It was well that he won such high honors, for on the expedition he led the following year, with 180 warriors in the party behind him, matters had not initially gone so well. They traveled far up the Missouri to the Osage River, and then up that stream to where Black Hawk had been told by a trader that there was an Osage village. But when they arrived there they found the village deserted, and this was construed as an error on the part of Black Hawk. Most of his followers became dissatisfied and mistrustful of his leadership and abandoned him. But Black Hawk and five loyal followers had gone on and finally found an Osage family. They attacked, scattered the family, killed a man and a boy and took their scalps, and returned with them to Saukenuk, where more honor was heaped upon Black Hawk for persevering even under great disadvantage. Despite the honor, he had lost a certain amount of his coveted prestige, not only because of his miscalculation about the village but because he had been unable to control the warriors who followed him and had allowed them to desert him.

The Osages retaliated, of course, mounting several war parties in succession to come against the Sacs. They caused considerable damage and a few deaths before retreating across the Mississippi and back into their own country. Black Hawk wanted to lead a party after them immediately, but the loss of face he had suffered still plagued him, and it was not until the following summer that he recruited enough men to follow him. At the head of two hundred warriors he again penetrated the Osage country, and they came up against a band of enemies similar in number to themselves. A hard battle was fought, and the Sacs, inspired by the fierceness of Black Hawk in their van, who was striking left and right with deadly precision, managed to overcome the Osages. One hundred of the enemy were killed, as opposed to only nineteen Sac deaths, and Black Hawk alone had killed and scalped six men and a squaw. A great scalp dance was held, and not only had he again won extremely high honors in his tribe, the Osages were demoralized by the defeat and sued for peace. A truce was established between the two tribes that lasted for many years afterward.

The Osages were not, however, the only enemy of the Sac and Fox. A powerful ally of the Osages was the Cherokees, far downriver on the Mississippi. In the summer of 1788, after years of uneasy peace between the Sacs and the Cherokees, active warfare had broken out again when a boatload of Sac travelers — a few men, but mostly women and children — had stopped to camp overnight on the west shore of the Mississippi just below St. Louis. A party of Cherokees fell upon them and killed all but one youth, who managed to escape and eventually get back to Saukenuk to report what had happened. Oddly, though, despite the outrage of the incident, the majority of the Sacs were hesitant to declare war on the Cherokees, whose great power and organization and alliances with other southern tribes were distinctly to be feared.

Pyesa, however, had been furious and announced his intention, even if not sanctioned by the council of civil chiefs, to lead a retaliatory war party. His nineteen-year-old son, Black Hawk, was first to volunteer to go with him. About forty others, mostly young men without warrior status, also volunteered, and downriver they went in a small flotilla of canoes. It was they, however, who were ambushed just below St. Louis near the mouth of the Meremec River by that same party of Cherokees, much greater in number than they, and a hot battle broke out. Early in the action an arrow hummed in and buried itself in Pyesa's thigh, very nearly coming out the other side. Black Hawk, seeing his father fall, rallied the other Sac fighters, who were on the point of fleeing, and led them in a spirited charge.

In the intense hand-to-hand fighting that followed, Black Hawk killed three men and wounded several others. In all, twenty-seven Cherokees were killed and the southern band was put to flight. When they were gone, Black Hawk hastened back to his father, who was sitting with his back against a large tree, mesmerized by the continuing flow of scarlet blood from his wound soaking into the ground. Black Hawk tried to staunch the bleeding but could not, and in a short while his father slumped over in death. As was his right, the grieving Black Hawk removed the medicine bag that his father had always carried and slung it over his own shoulder. Within that skin bag were the magical accoutrements of the tribal medicine man — a variety of charms and amulets, some natural and some carved, the dried skin of a sparrow hawk, a bag of cedar needles, a length of tightly braided sweetgrass, a coarsely haired section of bison tail, a deformed antler from a deer. These would now be his for so long as he lived, and would give him the right to hold the title of medicine man, even though he might never choose to follow that profession. Singing the melancholy death song, Black Hawk and his men returned with their seven dead and buried them with great ceremony in the Saukenuk graveyard adjacent to the village. The entire tribe went into mourning, since Pyesa had been their most esteemed medicine man. Black Hawk began a special mourning period of his own, blackening his face and, at regular intervals over the next five years, as was the custom among his people, fasting, neglecting his appearance, and praying to the Great Spirit. During this period he was required to give up warfare and serve as a civil chief, and he could engage in no intertribal activities beyond hunting and fishing.

But though the Sacs were a tribe of fierce and greatly feared warriors, war was always considered by them as more a luxury than a way of life. During the years that followed Pyesa's death, a period of more normal activities settled over the

Sac and Fox tribes. The strong binding factor between these two tribes, whose internal political organization was weak, was their strongly similar social organization. Their combined territory stretched outward from both sides of the Mississippi from just above the mouth of the Wisconsin River on the north to the Missouri River on the south. Eastward it extended to the middle of the Illinois country and westward to the high ground that separated the tributaries of the Des Moines River and the Missouri. This latter area was shared by a longtime ally, the Iowa tribe. Numerous villages dotted this entire area, but the major Sac and Fox settlements were along the Mississippi. One was in the area of the lead mines adjacent to the settlement of the Frenchman named Julien Dubuque, who was so beloved of the tribes that in 1788 they had given him and his companions a grant of land all their own in the midst of their territory, learning from him the most modern methods of mining and smelting the rich deposits of lead here — lead that the Sac and Fox could sell or trade much to their advantage in St. Louis.

Two villages — Saukenuk and Musquakenuk — were at the mouth of the Rock River. The Sac had also established other lead mines in the area of Galena, on the Illinois side of the river some fifteen miles southeast of the Dubuque Mines. Other major Sac and Fox villages were located at the mouths of the Iowa River and Des Moines River on the west side of the Mississippi, and at Henderson Creek on the east side. In addition to permanent villages, there were also numerous summer villages throughout their whole territory, but especially in the great prairie lands of the Illinois country, where the deep black soil was incredibly fertile. The land was used not only for the hunting of small game but for growing plots of corn, beans, squash, and other vegetables.

The years fell into a distinct pattern of cyclic activities for the Sac and Fox peoples. The hardest part of winter was spent near the permanent trading posts, but in the spring Black Hawk's band returned to Saukenuk. On arriving at the village they would greet the small number who always remained behind to keep up the village and guard it from intruders. But the past winter would always have taken its natural ravages, and so the men set up wigwams and repaired and rebuilt their more permanent lodges while the women would open the caches containing the bark-covered packages that had been hidden the preceding autumn. These caches were usually holes in the ground into which parcels were carefully placed, separated from one another by partitions of soil and layers of dried grasses. When filled in this manner with parcels, the caches were carefully covered with a foot of soil and topped with sod that blended perfectly with the surrounding ground. No one who did not know their exact location would have any chance of finding them. Once the caches were opened by the returned villagers, the parcels were recovered, taken into the village, and opened. For several days the people would literally gorge themselves on the contents, which were the sorts of foods that had largely been unavailable to them all winter — dried squash, crab apples, beans, and corn.

After that the women, including Black Hawk's wife, Asshawequa — Singing Bird — would all go to the north of Saukenuk where they always planted the specially preserved seeds in a great tract of some three thousand acres well above the Mississippi floodplain — a field that each year yielded an enormous crop of squash, pumpkins, beans, and corn. While they did this, Black Hawk and the other men would sit together to smoke and tell stories as well as to deal with the many traders who came through. Unlike most of his fellows, Black Hawk always avoided hard liquor, despising both its taste and physical effect. Therefore, when trading was finished he usually had come off better than those of his companions who gave away much of their lead or furs for spirits. Once the crops were planted, flimsy pole fences were erected around the plots to help keep the deer away. The women would then join their men for the customary ceremonial dances and feasting.

Soon most of the villagers would disperse. Many of the women and children and old people of both tribes would fish and set about gathering up bark and reeds for the weaving of mats and long, slender, pliable poles for the construction of the dome-shaped wigwams or the larger quonsets. The Fox men would go principally to the lead deposits for extensive mining and smelting. By summer's end they would have smelted upwards of two tons of lead for use in trade with the whites. The majority of Sac men, on the other hand, moved westward for the summer hunt. Black Hawk and his companions greatly enjoyed these hunting expeditions, and they would often travel all the way to the prairies well beyond the Council Bluffs to hunt buffalo, elk, and antelope. At such times they might encounter similar hunting parties of Osages, Cheyennes, Arapahos, Sioux, Poncas, Omahas, Dakotahs, and Mandans, but because all were garbed and equipped for hunting rather than warfare, their unspoken tribal agreement would prevail and they would deliberately avoid one another. Almost nothing of the game they downed was wasted. The meat they acquired was dried in strips as jerky or salted down in wide flat slabs for winter consumption. The hides were salted and rolled into snugly tied bundles to be taken back for tanning; the leather was used in coverings for the wigwam or quonset framework or for making clothes or for trading.

Before the end of two moons they would all reassemble at their villages, and there would be more ceremonies and dances and feasting as they shared the fruits of their combined labors. There were tribal and intertribal sports competitions — lacrosse games and medicine ball and horse racing, with the heavy gambling that always accompanied these pursuits. All this would end as soon as the crops came to maturity. Then they would have the harvest, in which all would participate. Following this, again they would gorge themselves on whatever was not to be wrapped in bark parcels and hidden in the caches for winter. The autumn hunt, often in the Two Rivers area, would last until the winter turned very severe, at which time they would move to areas close to established traders with whom they dealt.[21] Here they would set up wigwams and remain snug inside, close to the cheery central fires. On comfortable mats and cloaked with beautifully tanned fur skins to keep them warm, they would while away the long nights with tales of their hunts or battles or listen carefully to the tribal histories being passed along from father to son.

As winter was ending, the tribes would again be on the move; the women and children heading out to set up sugar camps and tap the maple trees of their sweet sap, the men setting up their individual trap lines to catch the mink, fox, raccoon, beaver, muskrat, weasel, and otter when their pelts were in their prime condition. The trapping was an extremely important aspect of the Sac and Fox economy. In the last year alone, $60,000 worth of furs had been brought in by them and sold at the trading posts in St. Louis. They rarely took cash, of course, preferring to trade for the supplies that were the necessities of life for them — guns and gunpowder, steel knives and tomahawks, shovels, picks and other mining equipment, hoes, wire, salt, cloth, beads, awls, steel traps, tobacco, and, of course, whiskey. And each year, when the annual fur trapping was finished, the disparate parties would all converge again at a previously agreed-upon rendezvous point and then journey together to their villages to begin the cycle anew.

It was during these years that Black Hawk had become a frequent visitor to St. Louis and, as a result, found a friend in Governor Delassus, to whom he referred as "my Spanish father." Now that particular friend and ally would no longer be in St. Louis, his place usurped by the hated Americans. The Sac tribe had, with the exception of a few parties who went out on their own, avoided the war being waged in the Ohio and Indiana country between the Americans and the tribes of that area, principally the Miamis and Shawnees. When the Americans won in 1794, due to the skill of General Anthony Wayne at the Battle of Fallen Timbers, a great council of all the tribes and the Americans had been held at Greenville, Ohio, the following year and the Treaty of Greenville was agreed to and signed. The Sacs were among the limited number of tribes who refused to sign the treaty, along with the breakaway group of Shawnees under the leadership of Tecumseh, the son of a former Shawnee war chief.

Since that time, more and more whites were pouring into this land, and little settlements and isolated cabins were springing up everywhere, though mainly in the area of the southern Illinois country where no tribes except for some scattered bands of Kickapoos were resident. The encroachment moved farther north in the Illinois country each season, and still the Sac council refused to recognize the signs of approaching conflict, preferring to remain aloof and convincing themselves that the whites were really only settling in the southern Illinois country because it was on the route to St. Louis, being followed by those who were settling there and farther west.

The only real war action for the Sacs recently occurred last year when Black Hawk had led a minor expedition downriver into Cherokee country to exact vengeance for his father's death, but the expedition had turned out to be largely a fiasco. Though they had searched over a wide area, they found only a party of six Cherokee men, whom they captured easily. Deciding it would be cowardly to kill them, Black Hawk took them prisoner to St. Louis and turned them over to Governor Delassus. He then returned to Saukenuk and, still determined to wage war, raised a party of half a thousand seasoned Sac and Fox warriors and an additional hundred warriors from among the Iowa. The object was to hit the Osage tribe and teach it a lesson for the long series of hit and run attacks they had been perpetrating against the Iowa tribe. After a long journey up the Missouri and into Osage country, they fell upon a village of forty lodges and killed everyone with the exception of two squaws taken prisoner by Black Hawk. Many of the finest warriors of the Osage were killed in this action, and once again the aggressive Osages pulled in their horns and ceased their incursions eastward. And once again the fame of Black Hawk as a great fighter spread throughout the Mississippi Valley.

Black Hawk abruptly shook away the memories that had been flooding his mind and came back to the present. He pulled his blanket more closely around him and watched as the paddlers skillfully avoided blocks of ice still floating downstream on the river's surface.

"This is *our* land," he muttered to no one in particular. "Ours alone. The only way the Americans will have it is to take it from us by force."

At this same moment, Captain Amos Stoddard was in his rather sumptuous quarters in the governor's mansion — having some time ago finished his official ceremony with Governor Charles Dehault Delassus in which he took possession of the Louisiana Territory in the name of the United States — and was now in the process of penning his report of the past three days to United States secretary of war Henry Dearborn. He wrote with controlled agitation about his encounter with Black Hawk in front of the mansion earlier this day:

The Saucks . . . . certainly do not pay that respect to the United States which is entertained by the other Indians — and in some instances they have assumed a pretty elevated tone.

[*September 8, 1804 — Saturday*]

The party of nine Sacs moving along the bank of the Cuivre River cautiously approached the first of several new settlements of whites they had been instructed to visit here in the Missouri country.[22] There were only three small buildings here and they were hardly more than poorly thrown-together log cabins. The Indians exhibited signs of peace as they neared, even though the very fact that they wore no paint and their number included two women and three children should have sufficed to show they had no malicious intent. As they had been forewarned to do, they also called out cheerfully and waved friendly greetings. The four men in the Sac party carried no firearms but, as was customary, they wore tomahawks and knives in their belts.

Because of his ability to speak English, Nepeek was in charge of this small party, and just to his right and a pace behind was his wife, Stonkah — Small Feathers. She was an uncommonly attractive woman of about thirty and, like her husband, was smiling as they advanced toward the cabins. Their group had been sent here specifically by the Sac council at Saukenuk to have a peaceful discussion with the six men who lived in the settlement. Now, as they approached the crude log structures, the door of one opened and five men emerged, three of them carrying rifles. Nepeek could not tell whether the sixth man was still in one of the cabins or was away somewhere.

"What d'ya want?" growled the man in the lead, coming to a stop a few paces before the Sac party, who had also stopped. He was a short, hard-looking man with heavy black beard and cold eyes that slid away from Nepeek and rested brazenly on Stonkah before returning to her husband. The bearded settler had not raised his gun, but the two armed men with him had stopped with their rifles held hip high, generally pointed toward the Sacs.

Nepeek took a step forward, extending his hand. "I am Nepeek," he said, speaking slowly and distinctly. "We come in peace, sent by our chiefs in Saukenuk to discuss things of importance."

"You gonna believe that, Charley?" snorted one of the armed men to their bearded leader.

"What things?" the man named Charley replied, ignoring both his companion and Nepeek's outstretched hand.

"Our chiefs," Nepeek went on, dropping his hand and his manner stiffening, "have heard disturbing things about you. We wish to resolve this problem before it becomes more troublesome."

"What things?" Charley repeated, his voice flat.

"First, I am told to tell you that where you are is Sac land. This is where many of our people spend the fall and winter hunting. You have made your place here without asking us, but our chiefs are willing that you may stay, so long as you remain in peace."

"We ain't hurt nobody," said one of the unarmed whites, a buck-toothed, obviously nervous youth of about nineteen.

"Yet," added one of the other men, moving the muzzle of his rifle slightly but significantly toward Nepeek's middle.

Nepeek did not even glance at them, his gaze locked on the bearded spokesman. "What you are doing here causes troubles," he continued. "Our chiefs have heard that you have given food and refuge to some Osage war parties who have been making raids against Sac and Iowa villages. That must stop. You must not give aid to our enemies."

The attack came wholly without warning, taking Nepeek and the Sacs by surprise. The bearded man barked an order as he lunged forward. The butt of his rifle rammed into Nepeek's stomach. As the Indian doubled over and fell, the other two armed whites aimed their guns at the remaining Sacs. The man called Charley, rifle still gripped in his left hand, reached out and grabbed the loose neckline of Stonkah's soft doeskin dress and yanked savagely downward. It tore slightly at the shoulder, but not as much as the man had intended. She fell, and instantly he dropped his gun and was astraddle her supine form on his knees, pinning her arms and still ripping at her garb.

The blow that had felled Nepeek was painful, but it had not struck the solar plexus and incapacitated him. He rolled to his knees, coming up with his tomahawk in hand, and struck, burying the blade in the bearded man's head. A shot rang out, and Nepeek felt the lead ball tear harmlessly through his hair just above the ear. The man who shot dropped his gun and was clawing for his knife, while the other man was swiveling away from the rest to point his gun at Nepeek. The Sac was too fast for him. He leaped and grappled with the man before he could bring his gun to bear. The impact knocked the man backward and sent his rifle spinning away. Nepeek had his knife out as they fell together and the blade found his adversary's heart before they stopped rolling. He sprang up to face the man who had been drawing his knife, but saw that he had already been felled by a tomahawk blow from another of the Sacs. The remaining two whites, weaponless, were plunging away. In an instant they had disappeared into the heavy brush surrounding the small clearing.

Nepeek, breathing heavily, the blood-stained knife still in hand, helped Stonkah to her feet. She was upset but unhurt. He turned from her and grimly took the scalps from the two men he had killed, while the warrior who had downed the third white man scalped him. At Nepeek's order the Sacs all ran to their canoe and in a moment were paddling rapidly downstream toward the Mississippi.

"Such a thing as this should never have happened," Nepeek said aloud to no one in particular. "There was no reason for it. We came in peace. The council will not be pleased that this has happened."

"That is true, Nepeek," responded one of the other warriors. "Still, they will praise you for the way you acted so swiftly and well in such a situation, where everything was against you. It is nothing to mourn that three white men died. Those were bad men, and they deserved what happened to them. Nothing will come of this."

But he was very wrong. Unwittingly, Nepeek had this day altered the course of history.

[*September 13, 1804 — Thursday*]

The great mansion called Grouseland stood in anachronistic splendor amidst the rough frontier cabins of the Indiana Territory town called Vincennes. Surrounded by beautifully landscaped gardens and arbors, Grouseland Manor had taken the better part of two years to construct. It was a massive edifice of red brick and native stone, with four great chimneys thrusting proudly a full nine feet above the highest point of the mansard roof. This was the governor's mansion — the home of William Henry Harrison.

Within the structure were thirteen huge rooms, those of the main floor with great beamed ceilings and fine draperies flanking real glass windows. Flocked wallpaper of exquisite patterns covered the walls, and the woodwork was solid walnut, much of it skillfully carved under the hands of artisans in New England. Each of the high-ceilinged rooms was appointed with the finest in furnishings; each had walls adorned with mirrors framed in painstakingly scrolled woodwork. Everywhere there were polished hardwood floors and Persian rugs of incomparable beauty. Large pedestal vases stood here and there, and an exquisitely hand-carved balustrade guarded the elegantly curved staircase that swept gracefully from entry hall to second floor. In the drawing room, for the continuing pleasure it brought Anna, there loomed a magnificent piano of hand-polished mahogany upon which she unstintingly practiced each afternoon; her current study, at which she was already accomplished, was a piece entitled *Sonata Quasi una Fantasia*, written two and a half years ago by Ludwig van Beethoven and first introduced in Vienna.[23] Fine crystal chandeliers hung from the ceilings and were kept sparkling by the large staff of Negro servants, as were the various items of brass and silver. The servants were, in essence, slaves, but since the Ordinance of 1787 had prohibited possession of slaves in the Northwest Territory, the term "servants" was applied. The separate kitchen even boasted a Moore box — the device patented a year ago by its Maryland farmer inventor, Thomas Moore, and now nicknamed "ice box" — which, when properly stocked with block ice, kept perishable foods in edible condition for considerable periods.

Although surrounded by such splendor, Harrison saw little of it, deluged as he was by duties. The Indiana Territory had been phenomenally expanded by virtue of the Louisiana Purchase. The territory lying westward of the Mississippi River, from its mouth northward, had quickly been divided into two sections by an act of Congress. By far the smaller of these, to be known as the Territory of Orleans, was a substantial tract encompassing both sides of the Mississippi River from the Pearl River in the east and to the Sabine in the west, upstream as high as the mouth of the Red River, and then only the west side of the Mississippi from that point to thirty-three degrees north latitude.[24] The remaining portion, all the way up the Mississippi and westward to the Rocky Mountains — to be known as the District of Louisiana — was now under the jurisdiction of the Indiana Territory. Thus, William Henry Harrison was governing an area virtually two-thirds larger than the remainder of the United States.

In addition to being named interim governor of the now gigantic Indiana Territory until an actual appointment of a Louisiana Territory governor could be made by the president and approved by Congress, the thirty-one-year-old Harrison had also received a special appointment from President Jefferson as special Indian affairs commissioner, with power to treat with the Indians over land matters. He was accountable only to the president and the secretary of war. As a result, the luxury of the Grouseland mansion was little used by Harrison, since he spent most of his time in his private study, poring over the multitude of

reports that regularly found their way here, conferring with delegates and emissaries and spies, writing voluminous reports of his own to the president or
secretary of war at the country's new capital, in Washington, D.C., correspond-
ing with — and issuing orders to — the Indian agents in the Indiana Territory,
and learning the pulse and tempo, the treasures and perils, of this vast wild
land.[25] It was in this room that he sat now, reading the message received by
express a short while ago from Pierre Chouteau, the United States Indian agent
in St. Louis.

His initial reaction to Chouteau's report was controlled anger. The blasted
Sacs creating problems again! Of all the tribes in the territory, he had more
difficulty communicating with them than with any other. It was not so much
that they caused trouble for the whites settling in this area; the Kickapoos and
Potawatomies and Osages were far worse in that respect. Nor was it so much that
they were tough in negotiations. That, in fact, was the crux of the problem with
them; they not only were not tough in negotiations, they were apathetic about
them, and it was extremely difficult even to get them to attend a treaty council.
They had the loosest form of government among all these tribes and had almost
no interest in hearing proposals for sale of the land that Harrison coveted so
much. Where other tribes had distinct principal chiefs with the power to negotiate for their people, the Sacs had numerous village or band chiefs, usually
without power on a tribal basis, and only an ill-defined tribal council that might
or might not have such power, but usually wasn't interested enough to discuss
anything.

It was two and a half years ago when Harrison suggested to the then relatively
new secretary of war Henry Dearborn that he be given leave to call a grand
council of the tribes of the Indiana and Illinois country — the Kickapoos,
Potawatomies, Miamis, Weas, Eel Rivers, Kaskaskias, and Sacs — in order to
establish permanent boundaries between them and the United States. To help
pave the way with the Sacs, who were notoriously disinclined to sign treaties, he
also noted that even though the Sacs had refused to sign the Greenville Treaty
of 1795, they were now complaining that they were receiving no annuities such
as the other tribes were getting, so might it not be a good idea now to append
their tribe to the Greenville Treaty? Dearborn had replied immediately, giving
Harrison the permission he sought to negotiate with the tribes and also to give the
Sacs the benefit of the Greenville Treaty annuity ". . . *if their conduct and
disposition shall appear to deserve it . . . ,*" and if so, that it be made up from
portions of the annuity presently going to the Kickapoos, Kaskaskias, and
Piankeshaws. This would hardly have sat well with the latter three tribes, but it
never came to the test — once again the Sacs refused even to appear at the grand
council, which was held at Grouseland the following September 17, leaving
Harrison still just a bit bewildered about how to deal with such a disinterested
tribe. That very disinterest had served a purpose for the tribe in protecting the
Sacs and Foxes from a land grab of which they were wholly ignorant. Having

dealt frequently with the British at the posts in Prairie du Chien, Green Bay, and Mackinac, they were accustomed to the British practice of giving annuities to the tribes they dealt with merely to establish good will.

The continued and growing influx of whites into the territory was the genesis of many problems. Incidents of varying degrees of severity were becoming more and more frequent between settlers and Indians. Thefts and murders were attributed to both sides, and it seemed to Harrison his time was largely being taken up with conciliatory acts for both factions. Yet, no matter how strongly he stressed the need to bury the hatchet, the outrages continued, and sooner or later they could evolve into outright war. Where Dearborn might lean toward the idea of war to get possession of the territory the United States wanted, Harrison, while not opposed to war if it came to that, tended to lean in the other direction. More than once he had reminded hawks in the administration of George Washington's wise words a quarter of a century ago: "There is nothing to be obtained by an Indian war but the soil they live on, and this can be had by purchase at less expense."

The present president, Thomas Jefferson, publicly ascribed to this philosophy, but privately he felt that perhaps the most important single task for the United States during his administration was to acquire as indisputable U.S. territory as much of North America as possible. Thus, while he openly exhibited concern for the native tribes and advocated fair and just treatment for them, his real aim was to learn as much as possible about the West and then snatch, by any means possible, those areas that would be best for mining, farming, industry, transportation, lumbering, and other exploitation by the whites. In a directive to Harrison last February 21, meant to become public knowledge, Jefferson had written:

Our system is to live in perpetual peace with the Indians, to cultivate an affectionate attachment from them, by everything just and liberal we can do for them within the bounds of reason, and by giving them effectual protection against wrongs from our own people.

What followed, however, was not meant to become public at all. It was extremely urgent, Jefferson contended, that steps be taken at once and by any means possible, to bring the tribal leaders into council so that concessions could be obtained from them. Part of the reason why this had not heretofore been the success Jefferson had hoped was the continued presence of the British traders throughout the area, especially in the Michigan, Wisconsin, and Minnesota regions and, most particularly, along the upper Mississippi. So long as the Indians could depend on the British, working out of Canada, to provide them with the goods they needed, usually without strings attached, they would not be inclined to come to council meetings meant to discuss land cessions to the United States. Three things had to be done: get them under control on smaller pieces of land by making them more dependent on crops and livestock than on hunting, and thus more apt to fall into debt, through which pressure could be applied; secondly, where such tribes might refuse to relinquish their hunting and trapping pursuits and nomadic life styles, which demanded vast tracts of land that were essentially uninhabited, there was another way to approach the problem. Some of the tribes, Jefferson reminded Harrison, had been clamoring for more and better government trading posts to be established in their country, and as the president saw it, therein lay the key. He wrote to Harrison:

When they [the Indians] *withdraw themselves to the culture of a small piece of land, they will perceive how useless to them are the extensive forests and will be willing to pare them off in exchange for necessaries for their farms and families. To promote this, we shall push our trading house, and be glad to see the good and influential individuals among them in debt, because we observe that when these debts go beyond what the individual can pay, they become willing to lop them off by a cession of lands. But should any tribe refuse the proffered hand and take up the hatchet, it will be driven across the Mississippi and the whole of its lands confiscated.*

The third thing needing to be done was the establishment *within the territory of the tribes* strong United States forts, which would be built allegedly to protect the Indians from white incursions and provide them with government "factories" for fur trading purposes, but, in the long run, to give the United States firm toeholds in the regions that might ultimately become enemy territory in a contest for possession. In this respect, plans were already under way to establish a new fort at the southern tip of Lake Michigan at the settlement of Chicago, presently a regular stopping place for the fur traders on the route between the great fur center at Mackinac and the Illinois River, which led to the Mississippi Valley.[26] Further plans of the president called for a string of forts up the Mississippi River from St. Louis — especially one to usurp the power and influence of the British at their important trading post at Prairie du Chien in the Wisconsin country.

Henry Dearborn, a pragmatic, no-nonsense military man who was far more comfortable as a general planning campaign strategy than officiating in Washington, was also a man who had little but scorn for the Indians and was not as convinced of the necessity of this course as was Jefferson. He reluctantly acquiesced to the plan but, convinced it was a waste of time, money, and manpower, was determined that since construction of such forts fell under his department's jurisdiction, he would spend as little on them as possible. He wrote to the president:

War Dept., 28th June, 1804

SIR — *Being of opinion that, for general defence* [sic] *of our country, we ought not to rely on fortifications, but on men and steel; and that works calculated for resisting batteries of cannon are necessary only for our principal seaports, I cannot conceive it to be useful or expedient to construct expensive works for our interior military posts, especially such as are intended merely to hold the Indian in check. I have, therefore, directed stockade-works, aided by block-houses, to be erected at Vincennes, at Chikago [sic], near the mouth of the Miami of the Lakes [the Maumee River], and at Kaskaskias, in conformity to the sketch herewith enclosed, each calculated for a full company; the block-houses to be constructed of timber, slightly hewed, and of the most durable kind to be obtained at the respective places; the magazine for powder to be of brick of a conic figure, each capable of receiving from fifty to one hundred barrels of powder. Establishments of the kind here proposed will, I presume, be necessary for each of the military posts in Upper and Lower Louisiana, New Orleans and its immediate dependencies excepted. I will thank you to examine the enclosed sketch, and to give me your opinion on the dimensions and other proposed arrangements. You will observe the block-houses are intended to be so placed as to scour from the upper and lower stories the whole of the lines. The back part of the barracks are to have port-holes which can be opened when necessary for the purpose of musketry for annoying an enemy. It will, I presume, be proper, ultimately, to extend the palisades around the block-houses.*

In his private communication with Harrison, President Jefferson stressed the need for action to be taken, particularly in respect to the Sac and Fox tribes, who for all intents and purposes controlled the Mississippi River north of the mouth of the Missouri. Also, the superb farming land of the Illinois country prairies was needed for national expansion, so he was directing Secretary of War Dearborn to authorize Harrison, *by whatever means it took*, to effect the desired goal. Dearborn, in turn, had written to Harrison:

. . . It may not be proper to procure from the Sacs, such sessions [sic] on either side of the Illinois, as may entitle them to an annual compensation of five or six hundred dollars; they ought to relinquish all pretensions to any land on the southern side of the Illinois, and a considerable tract on the other side.

President Jefferson had also confided in Harrison, shortly after his bold Louisiana Purchase had been consummated, that he intended, as soon as possible, to mount a number of major expeditions into the vast unknown country that had doubled the size of the nation. One of these he meant to go up the Missouri to its headwaters and, even though the legal possession of the United States ended at the Rocky Mountains, to penetrate beyond and discover not only a passage to the Pacific Ocean, but what kind of lands, resources, and people were there, all with an eye toward even greater expansion for the United States at some time yet to come. Another expedition he had in mind, Jefferson said, was one to explore upstream on the Mississippi all the way to its headwaters, not only to find the source of this great river but also to note the resources of the land and its probable value for exploitation. A third expedition was planned to ascend the Arkansas River from its mouth at the Mississippi to its headwaters, then perhaps even beyond into the Spanish territory of the southwest — territory that also might well, at some future time, become part of the United States expansion. There were other exploratory expeditions being contemplated as well.

That Jefferson had gone ahead at full speed with his plan became obvious when he presented modified versions of the plans to Congress and asked for funding. Congress, not wholly aware of the extent of the plans, approved and voted

. . . *the sum of $2,500 for the purpose of extending the external commerce of the United States.*

Jefferson had selected his personal secretary, thirty-year-old Captain Meriwether Lewis, to command the most important and extensive of the expeditions — up the Missouri River and to the Pacific — and Captain Lewis had, in turn, suggested that Captain William Clark be his co-leader on the mission. The expedition had begun just four months ago, on May 14, when Lewis and Clark had embarked from St. Louis, a party of forty-five men in a fifty-five-foot keelboat and two smaller advance boats for the guides.[27] For the Mississippi River headwaters expedition — another reason, Jefferson pointed out, why it was necessary to come to some kind of accord with the Sac and Fox tribes — the president was considering Captain Zebulon Montgomery Pike. Leadership of the other proposed expeditions was still undetermined.

Harrison's overwhelming burden of responsibility would soon be somewhat eased, since the United States Congress had just been asked to confirm President Jefferson's choice of a man to become governor of the District of Louisiana at St. Louis — General James Wilkinson. Nevertheless, it would be some while before the confirmation could take place and, even then, a substantial period before Wilkinson would arrive to take over the reins of his new office. In the interim, Harrison would continue as governor of Louisiana, and he had been directed to organize the administration of that gigantic district. In addition, since he was still functioning as the special Indian affairs commissioner, Harrison continued to be deeply occupied in matters involving the tribes.

With the Potawatomies and other tribes claiming ownership of lands in the Wabash flowage of the Indiana Territory, Harrison had made significant strides. A year ago last June he had finalized the Vincennes Tract boundaries, over the objections of Chief Michikiniqua — Little Turtle — of the Miamis, in a treaty signed at Fort Wayne.[28] Right after that he had made another treaty of consequence, this time with the Kaskaskia and Miami tribes, by which he obtained for the United States a clear title to a large extent of the great Illinois prairie country south of the Illinois River. These were significant accomplishments that brought the Indiana Territory governor accolades from the government, but he personally considered them as only a starting point.

Harrison's intensive study of the problem relating to the Sac and Fox tribes was resulting in his gaining a fairly clear picture of a complex situation. For many years the Sac and Fox had dealt with white traders — first with the French, then with the Spanish, and finally with the British, with some trading with United States citizens thrown in, such as with John Kinzie, who operated the important trading post at Chicago. The majority of their dealings with the traders involved the purchase of goods on credit. The Indians would buy their traps, gunpowder, and provisions for the forthcoming fall and winter hunting and trapping season on credit. When the season ended in spring, they would appear at the trading posts with their peltry and other goods, trade off their furs and maple sugar to pay their debts, and use what was left over to trade for whatever they needed for the summer and fall. When autumn came, again they were without funds and again they went into debt in the continuing cycle. The white traders liked this sort of arrangement because the Indians were almost universally honest in their dealings, and having accepted credit from a trader for goods received, the Indian was sure to return to the same post in the spring rather than go to the post of a competitor. If the Indian had an especially bad year and could not pay off his entire debt, the trader was willing to extend and even increase the credit for the next year, putting the Indian even deeper into his debt. If the debt wasn't paid in two years, the trader began to consider its ultimate payment as uncertain. If not paid in three years, the trader could be reasonably sure it would never be paid — at least not in the normal manner, with furs. But there was another way of collecting on such debts; they could be written into treaties. What this meant was that when the tribe made a treaty with the United States and received, as payment for land, an annuity, part of this annuity would then automatically be deducted from what the Indians received, as payment of the outstanding debt. Or, even more to the point, the government could — and often eagerly would — buy the debts from the trader who held them and then trade them to the Indians for land cessions.

For a long while this whole system of trade had worked very well, but with more and more traders coming into the frontier, along with a continuous flow of settlers, the problems began to magnify. Settlers complained that Indians returning from unsuccessful hunts — unsuccessful because the game had been killed or frightened away by settlers or white hunters — were not opposed to shooting "deer with bells on their necks" or knocking down fences or stealing a horse or two to replace those that had died during their hunts; they complained as well of occasional beatings and murders suffered at the hands of the Indians. On the other hand, the Indians complained of land frauds, trade frauds, theft of horses, theft of crops while they were away, and white hunters infringing on the traditional Indian hunting grounds, as well as occasional beatings and murders suffered at the hands of the whites.

That was further emphasized by the letter just received from Pierre Chouteau, recounting a disturbing incident that had occurred between white settlers and Sacs on the Cuivre River less than forty miles northwest of St. Louis. A party of Sacs from their principal village at the mouth of Rock River had approached a white settlement on the Cuivre River and killed three of five men on hand at the time, then fled back to their village with the scalps they had taken. Chouteau continued:

In furthering my investigation into the afair [sic] *I must, on behalf of the Saukes involved, admit that there is a strong likelyhood* [sic] *that the Indians approached peacefully and were profoundly insulted by an attack by a white man on a Sac woman in the party, whereupon one of the braves kilt* [sic] *the attacker with his hatchet, whereupon a general fighting broke out in which two more whites, including a boy of 19 years, were killed and two others fled. While not conclusive, the evidence so far indicates the attack by the Sacs was justified by means of defending an unarmed female from attack and by further means of self-defence* [sic]. *However, it behooves me to add, Your Excellency, that the white people in this place are both frightened and very angry. Rumors are common that the Sacs are circulating a war belt. Some of the Sac bands living closest to St. Louis have, as a result of the troubles, moved farther up the Mississippi. The people here are demanding retribution for the killings and they insist that the Sac murderers be brought to an early justice. What are your directions in this respect?*

The initial anger that suffused Harrison on first reading the letter was short-lived. Dusk was filling the room, and as he leaned forward and turned up the flame on the crystal chimney lamp, the warm glow showed that a small smile had appeared on his lips. Knowing by now the basic propensity of the Sacs for loose organization and lack of coordination in matters affecting the tribe as a whole, he was beginning to sense that this incident might just provide the key he sought to bring the Sacs at last to the bargaining table. He now dashed off a quick letter to Pierre Chouteau, in which he wrote:

. . . and it is my intention to arrive in St. Louis one month from now. In addition to the steps I will be taking, as aforementioned, to organize the civil department there, I would wish to meet with various tribal chiefs in order to bestow upon them gifts in the name of President Jefferson. It is of particular importance to me that special envoys be sent to the Osages in the territory westward of you and to the Sacs at Rock River, requesting that they be on hand to receive gifts from their father. The Sacs should further be admonished to bring with them the perpetrators of the murders of the white men at the river Cuivre, so that the anger of the residents of St. Louis will be cooled and so that the men in question may receive fair and just treatment. Be sure to impress upon them that if this is not done, it is likely that the whites in the vicinity of St. Louis, though

not authorized to do so, are prepared to rise in their anger and bring down the fire of destruction upon the Sacs.

[*September 24, 1804 — Monday*]

The Sac ceremonial pipe was a fine, large-bowled calumet fashioned of the hard, bright-red clay being found in only two locations in the Wisconsin country.[29] Occurring in a bed sixteen inches thick lying beneath a heavy deposit of quartzite, the red clay had long been quarried by the Indians in those two locations. They would pry away the quartzite and split out slabs of the hard clay in pieces from one to four inches thick. From these slabs, pieces of convenient size were separated and then cut and fashioned with steel blades, becoming very smooth in the process. The sections were hollowed out into fancy pipe bowls and the outer surface carved into unusual symbolic shapes, usually geometrical or animal. It was a laborious process, and when finished, the handsome brick-colored bowl was fitted to a yard-long pipe stem cut from a very straight hickory sapling previously hollowed out and polished. The pipe stem, sometimes itself carved, was then decorated with small strands of wampum, colored ribbons, and half a dozen eagle feathers. The raw clay itself was a very valuable item in the Indian trade with other tribes and white traders. A tribe's or village's official calumet was a very treasured item and always carefully protected.

A very fine yard-long Sac ceremonial calumet was presently being passed from chief to chief in the large council lodge. There were some forty chiefs and a number of influential warriors, most with blankets wrapped about them, seated on mats in a circle about a central council fire, their backs to the wall of the large council quonset. The calumet — in this case an official council pipe — was just completing its third complete circuit, each of the chiefs in turn puffing from it before passing it on. The calumet bowl required repacking with a fresh mixture of kinnikinnick and tobacco several times on each circuit, and the air inside the building was filled with an aromatic blue-white haze.

Now, as the pipe finished its third circuit, a loud call was given. In response, a young man of medium height, heavy build, and broad, pleasant features entered the doorway and strode through the seated throng to stand before them at the council fire. He stood quietly until the faint murmur of voices faded away and all eyes were directed toward him.

The chiefs knew this young man well and looked forward to what he would say, for he was gifted with uncommon intelligence and enviable eloquence, and he consistently exhibited a mature judgment that had won the approval of even the oldest and wisest of the chiefs. As a young boy he had traveled to many distant places with his father, who was himself a civil chief in the tribe. Together they had gone to St. Louis and to New Orleans, as well as to Mackinac and Montreal and even to Boston, New York, and Philadelphia, when his father had been invited to meet with President Washington. He had been exposed to fine art and culture and had developed an uncanny knack for learning different languages. Aided while away by skilled teachers and at home by the Indians of other tribes and the traders who often came here, he honed his innate abilities, and with remarkable swiftness had become fluent in English, Spanish, and French, plus at least half a dozen Indian dialects.

Thoughtful, gentle, and reasonable, the young man had become a favorite among the traders and, because of his broad knowledge and decided impartiality, was often summoned to settle disputes. He had never killed a foe in battle and thus was not qualified for a seat in the Saukenuk council meetings. Nevertheless, two years ago when the young man's father had died, the chiefs had bestowed a unique honor on the son as a token of respect for the older man, allowing the youth to stand just outside the doorway and listen to the speakers. On rare occasions, because of his eloquence and clear thinking, he was even invited to address the council.

The young man's name was Keokuk — He Who Has Been Everywhere. [30]

There were very few Keokuk met, Indian or white, who did not immediately like him and quickly develop an enormous respect for him. But foremost among that small number who did not admire him was Black Hawk, who, seated in the council circle, scowled as Keokuk nodded pleasantly to the assembled chiefs. It irked Black Hawk that for so many years he had fought and risked his life and taken the lives of others in order to win acclaim and prestige in his tribe and a seat in the council, yet he came nowhere near receiving the honors in council that were afforded to this young man who was fourteen years his junior and who had never even slain a man. The jealousy was a constant gorge in Black Hawk's throat, and he let no opportunity pass to oppose Keokuk's views. In doing so, he besmirched only his own image, for no one in the tribe was unaware of the jealousy he harbored. His intense and barely controlled dislike of the young man was further exacerbated by the fact that Keokuk never rose to his frequent baiting, refused to take offense at the unjustified enmity, and always treated Black Hawk in a respectful manner. Now, with the attention of the circle of chiefs upon him, Keokuk began speaking, and the richness of his voice filled the oversized quonset.

"Our good friend in St. Louis, Pierre Chouteau, has sent us word by his agent, Nicholas Boilvin, that the powerful white chief of the country, Harrison, has asked some of us to come to St. Louis to meet him. As before, he says this has to do with our land and that Governor Harrison wishes to help us protect it from our enemies."

"There are no enemies," Black Hawk spoke up rudely, coming to his feet, "that we cannot protect ourselves from." That he had insulted the speaker with his interruption was of no concern to him, and he continued in a voice that, after Keokuk's, sounded gravelly and irritating. "At no time before this have we needed anyone's help to protect what is ours. Why should we need it now?" He sat down again, glowering.

"A good question from Black Hawk," Keokuk said, addressing the chiefs rather than the warrior, "and a point well taken. We are a proud and strong people. Why now, more than in times previous when we have been asked to attend councils, should we even consider it?"

"You see," Black Hawk called out, not even coming to his feet this time, "I am right!"

"Very possibly Black Hawk *is* correct," Keokuk acknowledged. He paused, and the momentary silence gave his next words, spoken no more strongly than before, increased emphasis. "Yet, the world about us is changing, and we leave ourselves open to grave danger if we ignore those changes. In years past, the whites have been busy fighting the Shawnees and Miamis and other tribes who lay between us and them. And when the fighting was finished, the white chief Harrison continued to be busy with council after council among the tribes. So, even though he often sent us invitations to these councils, he was not greatly concerned that we did not attend. But now there is no more war, and the treaties with the other tribes have been signed. Now the whites are driving their posts into the ground close enough that we can almost hear them, and soon, no matter how much we try to keep them away, they will be here. They will try to take our lands."

"If they do," Black Hawk spoke up again, "we will kill them."

"Yes, we will kill them. And then there will be war. Against any other tribe who might make war on us, we would almost surely win. At least we would be able to hold what we have, and eventually the war would end and we would be where we have always been. But this time we have an enemy who has fighters more numerous than the leaves in the forest. Even should we kill twenty of them for each of us who is killed, yet they have enough to keep coming and coming. Eventually there would no longer be any way to oppose them, and all we have would be lost. Perhaps now, for the first time *and for our future*, it might be wise for us to talk with these people."

One of the Sac chiefs, Hashequarhiqua — Bear — rose now and spoke gravely.[31] "You put to words what many of us have thought, Keokuk," he said. "The whites are moving around us. We find them in the woods, in the prairies, on the river. They build log houses on our land and take offense when we tell them to go away. They are going far beyond us. In the past Planting Moon a small army of them went up the big river of the Missouris, and already they have gone farther toward the setting sun than we ourselves have gone. Others will follow. Soon they will be all around us. Perhaps it is as you say. Perhaps it is time to protect with paper and writing what we will not very long be able to protect with gun and bow."

One by one, those chiefs who wished to be heard arose and spoke their peace. They were almost evenly divided on whether it would be better to negotiate now for the tribe's probable safety later or to sit where they were, as always before, and reject such proposals, as always before, and finally fight for what was theirs when it came to that.

"What," said one of the minor chiefs at last, "is *your* thought, Keokuk? On which wind do we ride?"

"I think we should not accept this invitation just now," Keokuk said deliberately, "lest the chief Harrison begin to think we are negotiating through fear. Would it not be better, instead, to send Chouteau's man back with word that we are considering his request and might come if the chief Harrison truly does come to St. Louis, at which time he could invite us once more and we could once more consider this matter."

There was a general nodding at this and a soft rumble of voices, which stilled as Keokuk raised his hand. "Chouteau's man, Nicholas Boilvin," he said, "who even now waits in my wigwam for our answer to Chouteau, says there is one other thing we must consider. He was told to tell us what we already know — that Chouteau wishes us to bring to St. Louis the persons who killed the three white men on Cuivre River. He guarantees their safety if they come, but says he cannot guarantee *our* safety if they do not, since the whites have become very angry over this matter and are calling for war."

"I will speak to that." The words came from Nepeek who, cloaked in a green blanket, had come to his feet. "I, and no one else, am responsible for the three men who were killed. I brought the scalps here and put them before you, proud of what I had done in protecting the honor of my wife, myself, and my tribe. I, and no one else, should go to St. Louis to speak of that matter. I do not fear that I will come to harm. The Great Spirit will be with me, and when the whites learn the truth, they will be appeased. What I did was justified and in defense of my wife and myself. We came to them in peace. They tried to bring us dishonor and death, but brought it upon themselves only. If the council feels I should go, I will do so and gladly."

There was a general discussion of this, and the consensus was that *if* another invitation came from St. Louis and *if* they decided to accept it, then Nepeek could go along and surrender himself *if* he wanted to. That would be his choice alone.

[*October 29, 1804 — Monday*]

That William Henry Harrison was in solid control of the meeting that had convened in the palatial home of Auguste Chouteau was clearly evident in the deference being paid him by the other six men present. For most, though they had corresponded with him many times, his visit to St. Louis marked the first time they had come face to face with the aggressive young governor of the Indiana Territory. The power of his personality was little short of overwhelming. It had quickly become obvious to those who had assembled that Harrison depended on solid facts and his superior quality of logic to dictate his course of action; that he assumed little and evidently never jumped to conclusions.

They had just finished a sumptuous meal in the spacious Chouteau dining room. Auguste Chouteau had been forced to excuse himself early in order to take care of an unexpected business matter that had arisen. His wife was here, however. When she gaily led the other wives to the parlor for *demitasse*, the men adjourned to the library, settled back in comfortable chairs, and lighted cigars while a servant poured brandy from a beautiful cut-glass decanter. As soon as he had finished and left the room, quietly closing the double doors behind him, the seven men prepared to discuss the matter of the moment — the situation shaping up in regard to the Sacs. During the phenomenally busy seventeen days since his arrival here, Harrison had concentrated on a variety of matters not directly related to the Sacs. Both circumstance and choice had combined to have him put off that knotty situation until other matters had been cleared up. General James Wilkinson had still not arrived to assume his duties as governor of the District of Louisiana, so Harrison was continuing to act in that capacity.[32]

On their arrival in St. Louis, Governor and Mrs. Harrison had been enthusiastically received by the townspeople, who had turned out in force to welcome them. The Harrisons had been duly impressed with the obviously rapidly growing city, which already had over a hundred thriving businesses and some two hundred houses, including a number of exceptional mansions. They had graciously accepted the invitation of the town's most prominent and wealthy landowner and fur trader, the influential Auguste Chouteau, to be guests in his home.

In his customary manner, as soon as he had Anna ensconced in their temporary quarters, Harrison had turned his energies to the business of civil affairs that had initially dictated his coming here. Since Congress had, for administrative purposes, attached the District of Louisiana to the Indiana Territory, it was necessary for a formal civil organization to be established. Thus far, during the first half of his stay here, Harrison had, with the able assistance of Judge John Griffin, who was one of the guests this evening, drawn up the district's civil code, reorganized its courts, and reestablished its militia.

The next matter had been, with Pierre Chouteau at his side, meetings with the chiefs of the various tribes who had converged here. To the Otoes, Poncas, Omahas, Kaskaskias, and Kickapoos who had assembled, he presented token gifts of food, blankets, tobacco, and trinkets. To the Osages, however, with whom the United States had been on much better terms of late, he gave a much greater supply of gifts, along with strong assurances of continued friendship from President Jefferson. There was sufficient reason for this blooming amity on the part of the Osages. In early August a war party of some three hundred Sacs under Black Hawk, en route to attack the Osages, had been stopped by a force of United States troops under Captain Stoddard and asked to turn back. Undesirous of engaging in open hostilities with the United States, the Sacs had turned back, though smoldering with anger at what appeared to them to be partiality on the part of the Americans for the Osages. Just three days ago, after having received their lavish gifts from Harrison, the Osages had left St. Louis to go home, greatly pleased with the council just concluded and having promised to avoid committing any outrages against the whites. The other tribes were so clearly envious of this apparent favoritism toward the Osages that some of the U.S. officers stationed in St. Louis feared the consequences.[33] Now, with the Osages finally gone and the other matters out of the way, that left only the present thorny problem with the Sacs.

Harrison, seated in Auguste Chouteau's favorite deep leather chair, began the discussion. "Before we become involved too deeply in regard to the party of Sacs who arrived the day before yesterday and set up their camp here," he said, letting his gaze move across the others, "I'd like to backtrack a bit and hear a more complete account of the incidents that have brought us to this point. Perhaps Pierre Chouteau can start us off."

"Yes sir," said Chouteau, setting down the crystal brandy snifter from which he had been sipping. "You are aware, of course, as all of us here are, of the Cuivre River affair in which the three settlers were killed. As soon as I received your letter in answer to mine, I dispatched my assistant, Nicholas Boilvin," he tilted his head toward the lanky, dark-haired interpreter sitting beside him to his right, "to Saukenuk with an invitation to the chiefs to come here for talks with you. Mr. Boilvin waited while they councilled and returned with their decision, which was to consider the request but to remain in place until they received another invitation assuring them of your arrival in St. Louis, at which time they would again discuss whether or not they would come."

"Mr. Boilvin," Harrison put in, "did they, at that first meeting, discuss the matter of surrendering the murderers of the Cuivre River settlers?"

"They did, sir," replied Boilvin. "The killings were done by at least two of the Sacs who were in that party, although the blame for all the deaths is being shouldered by only one — a respected warrior named Nepeek, who is a close friend of one of the tribe's most noted warriors, Black Hawk. In regard to the Cuivre River incident, as I was led to believe, Nepeek and his party returned to Saukenuk after the affair and tossed down the three scalps before the chiefs, telling them he was proud of what he had done because it was justified for the preservation of his and his wife's honor and that there had been an element of self-defense involved as well. Nepeek volunteered to surrender if that was the will of the council. The council considered this and countered that it would be Nepeek's own decision whether or not he would surrender himself."

"The other settlers of the Cuivre River area and the citizens of St. Louis were by this time concerned?" Harrison asked.

"I believe I can reply more directly to that, sir," spoke up one of the two neatly uniformed officers across the table. He was Major James Bruff of the artillery, who was second in command of the United States Army detachment stationed here. "Immediately following the incident, a deputation of settlers from the Cuivre River and areas between here and there came to me demanding immediate retaliation on the Sac villages closest to us, and saying that if the Army would do nothing, they would attack the villages themselves. With some difficulty I managed to convince them that such a course could well lead to war and that they should let the government handle the matter. I promised that ample justice would be forthcoming."

"I understand," Harrison said, tapping the ash of his cigar into a small silver ashtray on the table beside his chair, "that there were some Sacs here in St. Louis at this time?"

"Not exactly, Governor," put in the short, swarthy Noel Mongrain, who was sitting to Pierre Chouteau's left. He, like Boilvin, was one of the interpreters at the St. Louis Indian agency. "I brought them here. I was at one of their lower towns — the closest to the Cuivre River settlement — when word of the incident arrived. They went into pretty much of a panic about the whole thing and were afraid there would be reprisal. They immediately began to abandon the town, intent on crossing over the Des Moines River to get into the greater safety of the midst of their people. However, before they could all leave, I convinced two of the chiefs — assuring them of their safety as long as they were with me — to accompany me to St. Louis and to talk with Major Bruff here and convince him that the Sacs, as a tribe, were not on the warpath."

Bruff, faintly annoyed at having been interrupted, resumed his narration. "Before they arrived, I'd already been visited by that deputation from the settlements who were demanding arms, ammunition, and reinforcement. They were full of rumors of war belts circulating, of the Sacs holding war talks with the Potawatomies and Kickapoos, and of Sacs insolently riding around with American flags tied to the horses' tails. As I already mentioned, Governor Harrison, I dissuaded them from taking the matter into their own hands. Then, when Mongrain here arrived with the chiefs, I discussed the matter with them and they confirmed the news of the killings. I demanded that they surrender the warriors involved, but they were very evasive about that and said that they were only village chiefs and had no control over hot-blooded young men from other villages. They asked me how the Sacs could cover the dead men to bring satisfaction to the whites."

"Cover them?" Harrison said, raising his eyebrows. He knew full well the meaning of the term as applied to certain tribes in the Ohio and Indiana country, but wanted clarification that it was the same with the Sacs.

"Sir," Pierre Chouteau spoke up again, "it is customary among the Sacs to atone for killings that might have widespread ramifications by doing what they call covering the dead, which is usually an intertribal measure to prevent war. Evidently they are under the impression that we engage in it, too. What it means is that the offending tribe pays for the people killed, covering their blood with the payment and thus satisfying the relatives of the man or men who have been killed. This is their only way of saving one of their people who has killed another."

Harrison nodded, his head momentarily wreathed in cigar smoke. It was essentially the same with the other tribes. Satisfied, he motioned to Bruff to continue.

"I told them," the major resumed, "that this was not our way and that the offenders would have to be turned in to face justice in a white court of law. I then sent them back to their own country with a stongly worded demand for the surrender of the guilty men. Following that, I immediately wrote to my superior officer, General Wilkinson, warning him."

"In what way, Major?" Harrison interjected. "How did you word this warning to the general?"

"I recounted the events as I knew them, sir, and concluded with the warning, which was, as nearly as I can recall the exact wording, quote, Sir, There is but one opinion here: that unless those murderers are demanded, given up, and examples made of them, our frontier will be continually harassed by murders and robberies, unquote. I heard nothing further from them, and it was shortly afterwards that we learned of your impending arrival here in St. Louis." Bruff leaned back in his chair and picked up his glass.

"Thank you, Major," Harrison said, then directed his next remark to the portly officer seated beside Bruff. "Captain Stoddard, you've been relatively close to matters here in regard to the British traders. Have you uncovered anything that would indicate they have abetted or fomented this situation?"

Amos Stoddard, who was neither smoking nor drinking, shook his head. "No, sir, not in this matter. I don't think they even knew about it until some while after we did. Of course, when they did learn of it, they weren't entirely displeased. They haven't been guiltless when it comes to stirring up difficulties for us here."

"Clarify that, please."

"Well, sir, a prime example occurred last March, just before Captains Clark and Lewis started out on their expedition. Captain Lewis had heard that early on in the expedition they'd be traveling the Sac country, and in an effort to avert possible hostilities, he sent a message to the Sac chiefs in Saukenuk explaining his mission and stressing the point that he'd only be passing through their territory, not stopping there for long and certainly not establishing forts or settlements. Unfortunately, the message arrived while a British trader was there, and unable to read it themselves, they asked him to translate it for them. He did so, but in a vein that was very unfavorable to the United States. Fortunately word of this was brought to me, and I immediately went to see them, along with Mr. Boilvin here, whom they admire and trust. He then read the message to them as it was meant to be, and they were mollified. It is, however, indicative of the way British traders continue to try to undermine us in the eyes of all the tribes with whom they have any contact."

"We'll certainly have to do something about that, won't we?" Harrison murmured. "Thank you, Captain." He turned his head to face the Indian agent again. "Now then, Mr. Chouteau, on my arrival here I requested that you send another message to the Sacs stressing the urgency of their being here as requested and to bring along the men of their tribe who were guilty of the murders. The Sacs are presently camped nearby, so they obviously received that message. Nevertheless, I'd like to hear about it, please."

Chouteau nodded. "I wrote a message to them, sir, as you asked. Mr. Boilvin was not here at that time, so I had another assistant, Louis Honore, carry it to them. He's an excellent interpreter whom they trust, and he read them its contents. I had advised him, as you suggested, to make every effort to bring back with him some of the chiefs and other important men of the tribe. Even some of the Fox chiefs, if he could."

"You advised him not to mention that this was in regard to a treaty of land acquisition?"

"I did, sir. Mr. Honore assured me he did not even touch upon that subject."

"Excellent. Go on."

"I also asked Mr. Honore to try to find out how affairs stood at this time between them and the British, and he did so. It does not essentially differ from what Captain Stoddard just reported. I should point out, sir, that, as you stressed should be done, I advised him to treat the Indians with great courtesy and, in the matter of getting them to agree to come here and bring the guilty warriors with them, to exercise gentle persuasion in convincing them how important this was if they were to maintain peace with the United States. They . . ."

"Excuse me, Mr. Chouteau," Harrison interrupted, "do you have a copy of the written message you sent them by way of Mr. Honore?"

"Yes, sir, I do." He patted his coat. "Right here."

"I think it might serve us well if you were to read it to us, please."

Chouteau nodded and removed a folded paper from his inner breast pocket and opened it. "It says, Governor, 'My Brothers — The great chief of the seventeen great cities of America having chosen me to maintain peace and union between all the red skins and the government of the United States, I have in consequence just received the order from the great chief of our country, who has just arrived from the post of Vincennes, to send for the chiefs of your villages with some important men, and to bring with them those of you who recently killed his children. I enjoin you to come at once, and if some great reasons prevent you from bringing the murderers with you, this is not to prevent you from obeying the orders which I transmit to you. When you carry them out, you will be treated as chiefs and you will go home after having listened to the word of your Father, and then you can make it understood by your elders and your young people; so open your ears and come at once. You will be treated as friends and allies of the United States.' " He refolded the paper and returned it to his breast pocket. "That's it, sir, so far as the message is concerned. I questioned Mr. Honore closely when he returned, and he said that one of the foremost reasons why the Sacs did decide at that time to send along a deputation of their tribe with him on his return was because their long-term hostilities with the Osages made them particularly anxious to come to terms with us, believing our troops could then become a barrier for Osage war parties coming against them. That was why they were so upset when they arrived here and learned of our government's generosity to the Osages. A runner went back to the tribe with this news immediately, and it is feared this might cause some of the Sac hot-bloods to go on the warpath after the Osages again."

The faintest expression of discomfiture flickered momentarily in Harrison's eyes. "But the Sacs did indeed decide upon sending a deputation here, as well as one of the murderers. How was this decided upon?"

"Louis — Mr. Honore, that is — told me that immediately after he read them my message they held a major council. They agreed that it was time they came to a meeting with the whites, and a deputation was named to go. This deputation included the chiefs named Quashquame and Pashepaho, along with two honored warriors, Outchequaha and Hashequarhiqua, who were authorized to do all they could to pay for the persons who were killed, thus covering the blood and satisfying the relatives of the settlers who were killed.[34] Immediately upon their being selected, Mr. Honore told me, the leader of the party of Sacs who killed the settlers — a warrior named Nepeek — volunteered to accompany them here and surrender himself to the American father; that is, Governor, to you. Mr. Honore further said that when he was on the point of leaving Saukenuk with the deputation and Nepeek, much of the population of the village turned out to see them off with good wishes. He said the relatives of Nepeek had blackened their faces and declared that they were now fasting, in the hope that the Great Spirit would take pity on them and quickly return Nepeek to his wife and children.

"When Mr. Honore and the deputation with Nepeek arrived here in St. Louis, he brought Nepeek to me, and I, in turn, since this was a matter for the civil courts rather than the military, turned him over to Judge Griffin. He was immediately arrested, shackled, and placed in a jail cell, where he is at this time, under heavy guard."

"I take it" — Harrison's gaze shifted to the judge, who had not yet spoken — "that this Nepeek has been questioned?"

"He has," Judge Griffin replied, "with both Mr. Chouteau and Mr. Boilvin serving as interpreters. Immediately after questioning him, we then questioned again — separately — the two settlers who escaped with their lives in that affair." He paused.

"And?" Harrison prompted.

"Nepeek told them a very straightforward account of what had occurred at the Cuivre River settlement. However, the two settlers told stories somewhat at variance to one another, and when they were more closely examined in view of what Nepeek had told us, finally broke down and more or less corroborated Nepeek's version. There are still some discrepancies, but I would be inclined to accept what the Sac said as the truth of the matter."

"Which is what?"

"That the Sacs had come in peace, with women and children in their party, and approached to tell the settlers that they were on Sac land. They did this and told them they were welcome to stay so long as they remained at peace. It was at this time, as we reconstruct the matter, that Nepeek was attacked — knocked to the ground with a rifle butt — and the . . ."

"Were the Indians armed?" Harrison interjected.

"Not with guns, Governor. However, as is customary, they did have knives and tomahawks in their waistbands."

Harrison nodded. "Go on."

"After knocking Nepeek down, the leader of the settlers then knocked down Nepeek's wife and attempted to rip her garment from her while his companions held leveled guns on the other Sac men in the party. Nepeek recovered more swiftly than expected and struck his and his wife's assailant with his tomahawk, killing him. One of the other whites fired at him at that point but missed, and that was when one or both of the others were killed. We're not sure whether or not another of the Indian men helped in this. The two surviving whites fled. The Indians took the scalps of the men they had killed and immediately left and returned to Saukenuk and reported what had happened. The Sac council was greatly alarmed, some fearing reprisals. Others, however, including the noted warrior, Black Hawk, were evidently hoping for exactly that."

"I don't know that I believe that story," Harrison said. The men around the table shot unbelieving glances at one another but had no chance to say anything. "Suppose," mused the governor, ignoring their astonishment, "we assume the killings to have been unjustified and consider this Sac Indian to be guilty of murder. It seems apparent that he did not kill all three men himself. What if we were to offer a pardon to the others involved if they were to testify against him?"

Boilvin was aghast. "Sir, excuse me, but that would never wash. Never. The Sacs know what happened. He is innocent in their eyes. They would never agree to such a thing."

"Then," Harrison continued, unruffled, "to gain the good will of the tribe, if that would be of benefit, what if we release Nepeek on a technicality — say we declare that the crime was committed while Spanish law was still in effect and we specify a defunct court to deal with it?"

"Damn it, sir, you can't do that!" Major Bruff had leaped to his feet. Immediately he realized what he had said and backed off a bit. "Excuse me, Governor, I forgot myself. But sir, do you realize what you're saying? The local population would be up in arms in a minute."

"Besides which," put in Judge Griffin with a dry chuckle, "it wouldn't be legal, would it?"

The governor did not reply, and the judge fell silent. For a long moment no one said anything, all eyes on Harrison as he pulled on his cigar, put his head back, and let a great blue-white tendril of smoke curl upward from his mouth. In a moment he straightened.

"And so here we are," he murmured, more to himself than to them. Abruptly he nodded and went on more briskly. "I will write to the president tomorrow and request an executive pardon for Nepeek. That, gentlemen, is confidential. In the meanwhile, Mr. Chouteau, you will continue your efforts with . . ." He hesitated.

"Quashquame?" Chouteau supplied.

"Yes, of course, Quashquame. Nothing new to report in that direction?"

"Nothing of any real significance, sir. They've been joined by another Sac chief who arrived in town just before noon today. His name is Layowvois.[35] I know him well. I spoke to him for some time before he joined the others. He will go along with us and could possibly be of some aid in convincing Quashquame and Pashepaho."

"Fine," Harrison approved. "Continue with your best efforts along the lines we discussed. I don't think I need to reemphasize the extreme importance of your succeeding. When you consider the time appropriate for it, you may present the proposition you and I agreed upon concerning Nepeek. The treaty papers are all drawn up and ready, awaiting only their signatures. Keep Mr. Honore or Mr. Boilvin with you, and the moment you get them to agree, send one of them to me immediately. That messenger is to be instructed to interrupt me irrespective of whatever else I am doing, so the matter can be seen to without delay. Understood?"

"Yes, sir."

"Excellent, excellent." He ground out the stub of his cigar in the ashtray and stood up. "I suggest, gentlemen, that we rejoin the ladies now."

[*November 2, 1804 — Friday*]

In their camp on the outskirts of Shallow Water — which is what they called the St. Louis area — the five Sac Indians sat hunched by the fire, blankets pulled firmly around them to ward off the chill of the evening. In all their lives, these five had never had such an abundance of liquor supplied to them. It would be a week tomorrow since four of them had arrived here and been met almost at once by their white brother, Pierre Chouteau. He had always been kind and generous to them on those occasions when they visited Shallow Water or when he stopped by their villages, but never had he lavished such attention on them as he was doing this time, nor had he ever been quite so generous as this.

Quashquame, Pashepaho, Outchequaha, and Hashequarhiqua had never had it so good. The first evening of their stay, Chouteau and his man, Honore, had come with several bottles of rum for each of them, and the Indians had sat at this very spot until the small hours, renewing their friendship and becoming progressively more mellow as the night deepened. It was unlikely that any of the four Sacs was aware that Chouteau and his assistant, when a bottle would be passed to them, tilted it to their lips but actually did little swallowing. That first night had set the pattern for the nights that followed, except for Monday night, when

Chouteau had arrived quite late and apologized profusely to them, explaining that he had had other business to attend to.

They were simple men, these four Sacs, with essentially guileless minds, innocently willing to accept events as they occurred without extensive analysis. Their attention was far more directed to their conversation with Chouteau, their egos well swollen with his attentions to them, their minds hazily projecting toward the honor that would be theirs when they returned to their nation and boasted of how this great man — agent to all the tribes here — had singled them out for such attentions.

How sympathetic Chouteau was to those matters that bothered them! What other white man would have understood so well the love they felt for their brother, Nepeek, now in irons in a small jail cell merely for doing what any Sac who was a man would have done under similar provocation? As they drank into the night, Chouteau and his helper felt so deeply for them that they even wept with them at the plight of their friend. And how reassuring the agent was that things would go well for Nepeek in the end; that he would be happily reunited with his people, with his wife and children. Provided, of course, this contingent of Sacs was sincere in their desire to help him.

After a full night and a day and another night of drinking, with only sporadic periods of eating and sleeping, the two chiefs and two warriors had been joined by another chief, Layowvois, who was only too eager to share the largess they were receiving from Chouteau. What a selfless man the Indian agent was! He could easily have taken all the credit himself for supplying them with such an abundance of spirits, yet he was clear in pointing out that all this was a gift from the white chief of all this country, Governor William Henry Harrison, who was so very concerned for them and for the plight of their friend. They must know that he wanted with all his heart to be friends with the Sacs; that he wanted to help them and their tribe in any way he could.

There had been some anger in the four at first. They had learned almost immediately on their arrival that the Osages had already been here and left, loaded down with a fantastic array of gifts — far more than any of the other tribes had received — and the Sacs initially took this to be confirmation of the partiality the Americans were showing of late for the Osage tribe, beginning with that humiliating time three months ago when American soldiers had turned back the war party led by Black Hawk that was on its way against the Osages. Quashquame and his party were outraged, and easing this resentment alone took many bottles of rum, but Chouteau had finally convinced them that their great father in Washington loved *all* the tribes equally and only wished to keep them from hurting one another. What the Osages got from the great father, Chouteau explained, was actually much less than what was in store for the Sacs if only they would let bygones remain bygones and exhibit, in a tangible way, their own respect and love for him.

How could they do this? What sort of tangible evidence of their sincerity could they provide? Well, now, how fine it was of such brave and renowned men of such a brave and renowned tribe to inquire in such a direction, since it was obviously an indication that they were truly sincere. Cool night, isn't it? Have a few more swallows of that good rum to warm the insides and we'll talk about it some more. There, that's better. Surely they were aware that the great father needed more land, weren't they? Hadn't they noticed that more and more whites were coming into this country? The reason was that the great father had so many children that there was little room left for them anymore in the east. But where were they to come to in the west? Everyone knew that when they stopped and tried to sink their roots in lands owned by the Indians, it caused only trouble, but where were these poor souls to go? Now the Sacs might just have an answer for that. They had so *much* land, and what better way to show their love and respect for their great white father than to help his children become settled on land where their presence would not cause friction because they were trespassing? Oh no, the great white father would never consider just reaching in and taking such land, even though he was certainly powerful enough to do so if he chose. No, he only wanted a little more land, and he was willing to pay a very handsome price for it.

The gist of the conversation began getting through to Quashquame and the others, and they countered in the way Chouteau had anticipated they would. No, he responded to them, the great father was not asking for a very large cession of lands that belonged to the Sacs. How peculiar an idea! Surely they were aware that where large land cessions were involved, there was always a definite protocol that was observed. Had the Sac tribe received a formal invitation to come and make a major land cession treaty? Certainly not. Had such a proposed land cession been formally discussed in tribal council? Of course not. Had the Sacs dispatched a huge delegation of their most prominent chiefs and orators to this place for such treaty making? Obviously not. Had wampum belts been made for the occasion? Definitely not.

But then, Quashquame and the others wondered, if this was not a major land cession treaty, what was it? Well, now, didn't Quashquame have land that was essentially his own — that is, land owned by the Sac band over which he was chief? Yes, he did. Didn't Pashepaho and the others have similar lands? Yes, they did — all of these were areas of Illinois country south of the Rock River. But any cession of land would have to be these lands that were intrinsically theirs, not the tribe's. None of these five had any authority to speak or act for the tribe as a whole, except in the matter of "wiping away the tears" of the relatives of the dead settlers by making some sort of payment to them, as authorized by the tribal council. But as for selling Sac lands, oh, no! Ah! Then surely if they wished to sell pieces of this land that they spoke of as their own, it was not a tribal matter, was it? And think of what great benefit they would derive from it; what a fine price the great father would pay them for this boon. Not only a huge quantity of goods and money to begin with, but annuities that would last them all a lifetime.

Well, in that sort of light, it was an appealing proposition, wasn't it? Especially in the rosy glow of an alcoholic haze. But no, Quashquame and the others reluctantly shook their heads and mumbled that they didn't think they could do that. It was far beyond their authority.

How sad, Chouteau murmured. How deeply he sympathized with his red brothers for being on the brink of losing an opportunity such as would never again come along in their lifetime. Well, let's forget about that for now and consider the plight of our beloved friend, Nepeek. Poor man! During those first days since his arrival here, it had seemed there would be no problem in effecting his release. But this had changed a little. Wasn't this obvious to them? Hadn't they noticed the anger of the whites over what had happened at Cuivre River? Three of their beloved white brothers had been slain, and if some sort of reparation was not made, well, maybe Nepeek was in more trouble than any of us initially realized. For instance, did you know that in the white man's courts — where Nepeek would be tried, of course — the penalty for murder was death? Or at least a lifetime in chains and behind bars? How sad for Nepeek. How sad for Nepeek's wife and children. How sad for the Sacs, for such a thing would bring a great shame to the entire Sac nation, wouldn't it? And how sad for Quashquame and his four comrades here, for weren't they sent to St. Louis with specific instructions from their tribe to wash away the tears of the relatives of the dead men? What would be the reaction of their tribe when they failed in a duty they had been trusted to perform?

Quashquame and Pashepaho and the others objected, thickened tongues blurring their words. No, there should be no death penalty or life imprisonment for Nepeek in this matter, and certainly there should be no shame for the Sac nation. That should not be necessary at all. Their people had sent them here to prevent such a possibility. We *have* come here prepared to cover the dead and salve the hurt of the relatives and friends of those men who died. What *is* it that the whites would like us to pay to accomplish this? That is why we are here, friend Chouteau.

Well, there, you see, you *may* have the answer in the palms of your hands without even realizing it. Is not the life of your friend, Nepeek, dear enough that you would consider covering the dead by offering the land that the great father so desperately needs? And it's not as if you would be *giving* the land. Oh, no. Our great father would not expect that of you. Here is what he would pay you for such a cession . . . and a long discussion of gifts and annuities bedazzled their blunted minds. And think! If they did this, not only would they receive such generous payment, but they could continue living in peace on that very land for as long as the United States owned it. And, beyond that, all charges against your brother, Nepeek, would be dropped and he would be released from jail. What great men they would be to return to Saukenuk not only with money and gifts and lifetime annuities and with the land essentially not lost to them at all, but bringing along with them their dearly beloved brother!

For six days and nights the arguments had been hammered home, subtly, skillfully, convincingly, until now, as midnight was approaching, Quashquame and the others caved in.

"We will give our lands," he mumbled. "When the sun comes up tomorrow, we will put our marks to the great father's paper."

Instantly Chouteau dispatched Louis Honore to alert Governor Harrison to have the land cession treaty ready for signing at sunrise. He, Chouteau, would personally bring the five Sacs. And as Honore thundered off, Chouteau went to his horse, opened his saddlebag, and extracted five more bottles of rum.

"We must celebrate this wonderful occasion, my friends," he said, and he returned to the fire and distributed the bottles to the Sacs.

[November 3, 1804 — Saturday]

Under the brilliant morning sun of this crisp day, William Henry Harrison stood patiently, masking the exultation that surged within him as the five Sac Indians awkwardly made their marks on the final page of the treaty, just below his own flourished signature. The pen marks made by the Indians were very shaky — quite as much from their inexperience in the use of such an implement as from the fact that all five were still in the midst of a mind-deadening, rum-induced alcoholic blur. Not one of the five could read, write, or speak the English language, so the wording on the treaty was just so much scribbling so far as they were concerned. But their good friend, Pierre Chouteau, had carefully explained to them the salient points of the document to which they were appending their marks.[36]

All five of the Indians were wearing the new coats that had been presented to them this morning — United States Army wear with insignia and rank removed, but still resplendent with brilliant brass buttons. Around the neck of each Indian on a broad scarlet ribbon was a large bronze medal with a depiction of the President of the United States in relief on one side and two hands, Indian and white, clasped in friendship on the other. They also had several smaller medals attached to the breast of their coats. Each Sac wore a fine new felt hat, and in the band of each was anchored the quill of a huge, frilly ostrich plume. Off to one side were the boxes and bales and bags containing goods to the value of $2,234.50. And, as the Indian agent so carefully explained to them, their signing also guaranteed that every year hereafter the combined Sac and Fox tribes would receive, in goods, an annuity to the value of one thousand dollars — six hundred of this for the Sacs, four hundred for the Foxes.[37] In addition, Chouteau said, so long as the lands being ceded to the United States this day remained public lands and were not sold by the United States, the Sacs and Foxes were free to live on them and hunt on them.

Article Two of the treaty, describing the boundaries of the land cession being consummated here, was read quickly and in such a dead monotone that all on hand lost interest long before it was finished. Chouteau was careful to reiterate to the five Sacs that only when a piece of land was sold to a settler would the Indians have to vacate that piece of land; but, he assured them, that possibility was so far in the future — perhaps twenty or thirty years — they certainly needn't be much concerned about it.

Immediately after the chiefs had appended their marks where indicated, eleven St. Louis men — including the two sworn interpreters on hand — signed the treaty as witnesses.[38] Then William Henry Harrison soberly shook hands with each chief. Major James Bruff detailed a squad of soldiers to carry the stack of goods to the riverfront and carefully load all the items into the canoes of the Sac signers. With that, it was over.

The borders of this cession of land began at the mouth of the Illinois River on the Mississippi just above St. Louis, followed the Illinois River upstream to the mouth of the Fox River, then upstream on the Fox River to Fox Lake, then on a due northwest line to a point on the Wisconsin River thirty-six straight-line miles above its mouth, then down that river to its mouth at the Mississippi at Prairie du Chien, then down the Mississippi to the starting point, plus a parcel on the west side of the Mississippi running upstream along the north shore of the Missouri River for about one hundred miles to a point directly opposite the mouth of the Gasconade River, then on a straight line north by northwest for another eighty miles, then directly eastward down the south shore of the North River to its mouth at the Mississippi River, and finally, down the Mississippi River to the starting point at the mouth of the Missouri River.[39]

On this bright November morning, William Henry Harrison, for an incredibly paltry sum, had just purchased for the United States of America a parcel of land encompassing 51 *million* acres!

There was one other unwritten part of the deal remaining to be completed. The Sac party was told that Governor Harrison had written to the great white father, Jefferson, asking for a presidential pardon for Nepeek, still in jail and accused of murder. There was no doubt, Harrison assured them through Chouteau, that the pardon would be issued. As soon as it was received, Nepeek would be released. In the meanwhile, his leg irons had been removed and he would be receiving very good treatment.

As night fell on this significant day, however, a shadowy figure slunk unseen into the jail. A voice, speaking somewhat less than fluently in the Sac tongue, whispered through the darkness to Nepeek in his cell. It told him that the anger of the whites of St. Louis had overflowed and a large party of them were at this moment en route to the jail to kill him, and that he must flee at once. There was the clicking of metal against metal as the door was unlocked — then silence. Nervously, Nepeek swung the door open and paused, looking and listening intently. He neither heard nor saw anything. He felt his way to the outer door and found it ajar. He poised, muscles tensed, then leaped outside, running as fast as he had ever run in his life.

He was no more than twenty feet from the door when three or four voices

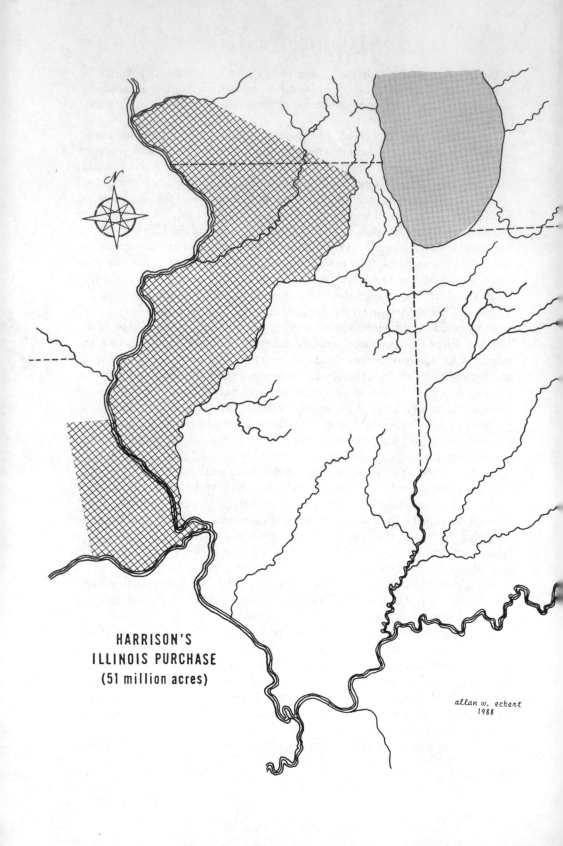

HARRISON'S
ILLINOIS PURCHASE
(51 million acres)

allan w. eckert
1988

boomed out simultaneously in the darkness: "He's escaping! He's escaping!" On the heels of the exclamations came a dozen or more shots. At least half of the bullets slammed into the Sac, shattering his skull, bursting his heart, severing his spine.

Nepeek was dead before his body struck the ground.

[*December 31, 1804 — Monday*]

The year came to a quiet close with virtually no Indians — certainly none among the population of nearly eight thousand Sacs and Foxes — fully grasping the significance of what had occurred at the St. Louis Treaty in November. All they knew was that the deputation they had sent to secure the release of Nepeek from captivity ultimately returned wearing fine new coats and shiny medals and with a great many gifts from the Americans.

Quashquame and his four companions said the American officials in St. Louis had treated them regally, although they shamefacedly admitted that they didn't remember a great deal of what had transpired, since they were drunk almost all the time they were there. They reported that their mission to aid Nepeek had been successful, in that they had received assurance from Governor Harrison himself that Nepeek would subsequently be pardoned and released. Unfortunately, before this information could be relayed to Nepeek, he had mysteriously made an attempt to escape from jail and was shot and killed in the process. It was very sad, they said, but no one was to blame, and it seemed obvious that they must take the forfeiture of Nepeek's life as being the will of the Great Spirit.

As an aside, Quashquame also admitted that his little deputation had ceded a small piece of land to the Americans in exchange for the gifts they had brought back with them, plus an annuity for both the Sacs and Foxes. Their remembrance of the matter was very foggy due to their overindulgence in liquor, but certainly it did not amount to much of anything, and it not only established better relations with the whites, it provided an annuity that could be of considerable benefit, especially during lean years when crops or trapping were not at their best.

The concept of this five-man deputation under Quashquame having engaged in land dealings at all, however insignificant, caused a certain degree of unpleasant murmuring among the tribesmen since, by tribal law, no individual or small deputation had any authority whatsoever to sell lands to the whites. Quashquame and the others were mildly censured for overstepping their authority, but no one thought much of it beyond that. Everyone in the tribe was quite well aware that there were a number of distinct steps that had to be taken before any tribal lands could be disposed of in any way.

In a legitimate land treaty, first of all, the tribal council would have to receive an official invitation from the white authorities to discuss a possible cession of land. This, by tradition, had to be followed by an announcement to all members of the tribe that such an issue was pending, after which the principal people of the tribe, men and women alike, would meet to discuss the advisability of the matter. Irrespective of what decision would then be reached, whether for or against the proposed cession, a formal reply would be returned to the prospective purchaser, along with wampum belts to signify the official nature of the response.

If the preliminary decision had been to go further into the matter of a proposed land cession treaty, then a great tribal meeting would be scheduled and held in which the actual full tribal council and a representative sampling of the whole population, including warriors and women and even children of both tribes, would be on hand, and a decision would be made as to what land would be sold and for what sort of concessions. If the women, who were essentially the cultivators of the land, were opposed to the sale, there would be no such sale. And if the women were not consulted at all, then no sale of land could be valid.

Assuming, in such a land matter, that the women by and large agreed to the proposed sale, then this great tribal meeting would be followed by the formation of a large formal treaty deputation, which would be given explicit instructions on what to say in the meetings with the whites, and there would be considerable movement of runners back and forth as negotiations were made. As a result, at most treaty councils involving Sac and Fox tribes, invariably a large portion of the tribe's population — including numerous women — would be on hand at the time the treaty was consummated. Finally, when all points were agreed upon and the issue had been put to a vote and won the approval of the tribe as a whole, then belts of wampum would be made to fully establish both the formality and legality of the transaction. So this was why, when Quashquame's little five-man deputation returned from St. Louis and spoke of having given the Americans a land cession, no one believed it could possibly mean anything more than perhaps granting the Americans a certain right of safe traverse across the Sac and Fox lands.

At this time, far to the east, the strength of Thomas Jefferson as president of the United States had just increased enormously through his having won reelection by an overwhelming plurality of 162 electoral votes to only fourteen for his opponent, Charles C. Pinckney. And the crest of popularity Jefferson was riding was in no way diminished by the incredible coup that had been pulled off by his able appointee, William Henry Harrison, in having acquired ownership for the United States of 51 million acres of land, largely in the Illinois country. Congress was jubilant at what the young politician had accomplished, and already the Senate, at the urging of Jefferson, was rushing to ratify the St. Louis Treaty as quickly as possible.[40]

There were few voices raised, questioning whether or not the Indians understood what they had agreed to and, if so, why they had sold themselves out for so ridiculously paltry a sum? These voices were generally ignored, even when they went on to gloomily forecast that sooner or later great troubles were bound to erupt as a result of it. Where most senators and representatives were concerned, the important thing was that the treaty *had* been made, that there was no doubt it *would* be ratified very soon, and that the United States had once again — as it had with the Louisiana Purchase — very cheaply come into legal ownership of a vast section of land to which it had previously held no title.

The adroitness of Harrison in lulling Indian anxiety and forestalling the ultimate confrontation was apparent in Article 7 of the treaty, which allowed the Indians to live and hunt on the land and use it as they always had, so long as the United States owned it. It might be twenty or thirty years before the United States was ready to sell the land to individuals. Who would then be around to remember whether or not the land cession was properly made? And what tribe, by then, could dare to make any attempt to thwart the United States in whatever disposition it cared to make of the lands it had purchased?

CHAPTER II

[*December 31, 1829 — Friday*]

IN THE QUARTER-CENTURY that had passed since the unauthorized representatives of the Sac and Fox tribes had signed the treaty that William Henry Harrison had placed before them in St. Louis, vast changes had taken place throughout the Mississippi Valley frontier. Yet, oddly enough, though these great changes had roiled and seethed around them, the Sacs and Foxes had remained essentially untouched until only recently. It was a situation that could not last, and in a rare moment of eloquence at a recent large Sac and Fox council of chiefs, Makataimeshekiakiak — Black Hawk — had gravely spoken of it.

"When I was ten — fifty-three summers ago — my father, Pyesa, led me to the river and told me to sit on the edge, in a place where the clear water flowed only a finger deep over a bed of stones. From the bank nearby he dislodged a large chunk of earth and held it before my eyes. 'Consider this,' he told me, 'as being the land of your people.' He placed it gently on the gravel, and the water parted and flowed around the earth. He touched the water with his finger and said, 'Consider this our worst enemies — not those who come and try to destroy us in one great wave, but those who have the patience to nibble at us and gradually wear us away.' Together Pyesa and I watched, and at first there was little change. Then a tiny piece of the soil fell off to one side and was swept away, then another on the other side. Bit by bit and piece by piece the land crumbled away, and though there was never a great wave to sweep over it, yet by little bites it disappeared until at last it was all gone, and there was no way to bring it back. Pyesa told me this was what would happen to the Sacs and Foxes if we were not watchful, if we did not discourage those who came to nibble away little bites of us. My brothers, bit by little bit we are being nibbled away."

The words he spoke were true. In those twenty-five years a war had intervened — a war that had begun in 1812 and that some called the second war of the revolution. It was preceded by a bold march of William Henry Harrison's army toward Tecumseh's village on Indiana's Tippecanoe River during that Shawnee leader's absence. That approach did exactly what Harrison had planned for it to do — it provoked an attack by Tecumseh's brother, Tengskwatawa, and gave Harrison's army the justification it needed to respond.[41] The Indian confederation it had taken Tecumseh many years to establish was wiped away and most of the tribes abandoned him, and so he had been left with no recourse at last but to throw the weight of what remaining strength he had to the British, as the War of 1812 broke out.

Black Hawk had led a large contingent of Sac and Fox warriors all the way to Detroit to help Tecumseh in the battles occurring on that front, but the action was mostly finished when he arrived; supplies for the Indians were meager at best, and the anticipated spoils of victory were absent. For a long while they stayed and fought as part of Tecumseh's confederacy of tribes, but without significant reward for their efforts. The resentment Black Hawk's warriors exhibited was palpable. Their accusing glances that blamed him for being at the wrong place at the wrong time were more humbling than verbal abuse, and so the disgusted Sac chief turned his back on Tecumseh and the British, leaving them to fight the Americans in the Detroit area while he led his warriors back to Saukenuk. Black Hawk vowed that hereafter he would fight in his own way, in his own time, and at a place of his own choosing.

Black Hawk's disenchantment had turned to bitter discouragement when he reached the principal Sac village and learned that, while he was absent, Keokuk had been elevated to the rank of war chief of Saukenuk, which in essence made him war chief of the entire tribe. Black Hawk was stunned. This was the post he coveted most, the prize he had attempted to win for years by leading so many dangerous expeditions against fierce enemies. And then the post had been awarded to a smooth talker who had never even been in battle.

"How?" Black Hawk had directed the question in a brittle, strained voice to his elder son.

Nasheweskaka had grimaced.[42] "While you were away, father," he replied, "runners came to Saukenuk with the news that a large force of American soldiers was coming to destroy us. A council was called, and it was decided that our best course would be to leave Saukenuk and cross the Mississippi to the side of the setting sun, to get out of the way. That was when Keokuk spoke and —"

"How could Keokuk be in tribal council," Black Hawk had interrupted, "when he has never killed an enemy?"

"He was not *in* the council," Nasheweskaka explained. "As usual, he was standing outside the doorway listening, and when he heard what the council was deciding, he beckoned old Chief Wacome to him."[43]

"Wacome is an old woman!" Black Hawk growled. "All his life he has been an old woman. He has white doves fluttering in his heart."

Nasheweskaka had only shrugged and gone on with his relation. "Keokuk asked Wacome to tell the council that he was very anxious to address them on the matter under discussion. Wacome returned to the council and told them, recommending that Keokuk be allowed to speak, and the chiefs thereupon bade Keokuk to enter and say his thoughts. What he said was strong, and all of us remember the words well." He paused.

"Tell me!" Black Hawk had gritted, knowing his son would, without deletion or embellishment, repeat to the best of his ability exactly what Keokuk had said.

Nasheweskaka had nodded, sat still for a moment, and then nodded again and spoke the words as Keokuk had uttered them: 'My fathers, my brothers, I have heard with sorrow that you have determined to leave our village and cross the Mississippi, merely because you have been told that the Americans were seen coming in our direction. Would you leave our village, desert our homes and fly before an enemy approaches? Would you leave all — even the graves of our fathers — to the mercy of an enemy, without even attempting defense? Give *me* charge of your warriors. *I* will defend the village and you may sleep in safety.' "

Nasheweskaka, who had spoken as if in a trance, had paused then and swiveled his head to look at his father. "The council agreed to what Keokuk said and named him temporary war chief, since all our bravest warriors were away with you and others. Keokuk then called up his braves and sent out spies to reconnoiter in all directions, while he led a large party of warriors toward where the enemy was supposed to be. They saw no one, and no danger threatened. But because of the courage he had shown to willingly lead a small party of inexperienced warriors against what was reported as a large army of whites, when he returned to Saukenuk his place as war chief was made permanent. That is where he is now. He sits in all councils and speaks much, although since that time he has spoken only of peace, not war."

Black Hawk had been filled with bitterness toward the younger man who had so easily seized what Black Hawk himself had so long coveted. And when word came that the great Tecumseh had been killed by General William Henry Harrison's army in the Battle of the Thames, the Sac council concluded that this would not have occurred had not Black Hawk abandoned Tecumseh in his need. Black Hawk's reputation was badly tarnished.[44]

Keokuk was well aware of and took pleasure in his verbal powers, reveling in letting his well-modulated, convincing words roll over each assemblage like a gentle touch. An imposing figure who thoroughly enjoyed the pomp of ceremony, he had taken to wearing the same colorful garb each time he addressed tribal councils — immaculate, beautifully tanned doeskin shirt and leggins, knee-high soft leather moccasins, necklace of black bear claws separated by polished wooden ovals, and an ermine cape slung over his shoulders. In stately elegance he wore a massive buffalo headdress, its shiny black horns upcurved and glinting in the firelight. As impressive as he was to behold, even more magnetic was his manner of speech. His audience clung to his words, stirred by the passion of his oratory and swayed by the inexorable logic interwoven in his words. Black Hawk, poor speaker that he was, greatly envied Keokuk's talent and, in envying him, despised him as well.

"Consider, my brothers," Keokuk had said in the first council after Black Hawk's return, "the dangerous position in which we have now been placed by what has been occurring around us. We are plucked at from all sides. For many summers we have lived at peace with the Winnebagoes, our neighbors, and so it has been as well with the Potawatomies, and yet now many of the Winnebagoes have become strongly supportive of the British and as strongly against the Americans, while with our neighbors, the Potawatomies, the opposite is true.[45] And each plucks at us in his own way to support them. The Winnebagoes suffered terribly at the hands of the American chief Harrison at Tippecanoe, and now suddenly these same Winnebagoes war with our brothers, the Foxes, who have appealed to us to help them, just as the Winnebagoes have appealed to us to help *them*. So where does that leave us?

"Some of our lodges," he continued after a moment, "have gone to help our Fox brothers. Others" — his glance shifted momentarily to where Black Hawk sat — "are inclined to aid *anyone* against the Americans. Ten of our lodges have moved farther up the Rock River to remain neutral, and they tell the emissaries of the Foxes that though they are our comrades and brothers, the Sacs cannot help the Foxes this time lest it bring down on their own heads the wrath of the British and Winnebagoes. But they are in danger trying to hold that country. We, here, are in a hard place, and soon we must decide which way we must go or the decision will be taken from us, almost surely by the Americans."

In the pregnant pause that followed Keokuk's sober words, Black Hawk threw off the blanket that cloaked him, came smoothly to his feet, and spoke loudly. "What then does Keokuk, who seems to have the answers for all the ills of the Sac and Fox, suggest we do? For my part, and those who follow me, we will not become the frightened dog with tail between legs before the Americans. We will oppose them always. *Always!*"

"That, then, is your choice, Black Hawk," Keokuk replied reasonably, "and there are many here who will adopt your choice. But there are as many and more who will think and act from a cool mind that weighs consequences rather than from a hot heart that veils the eyes to what is and what must be." He abruptly clapped a hand to his bare chest with a resounding smack and spoke again, now with greater force. "*My* heart and mind are as one in what I say now. If we support the British, we are told we will be provided with guns and powder and food and necessaries, but such promises have failed to materialize in the past. If we support our Indian friends who support the British, we are told that a great nation of Indians will come into being that will drive out the enemy whites. Yet, this I say to you: However much those choices appeal to us, in doing so we would ultimately lose all. In the same way, if we support the Americans and stand by them, we stand to lose as much. Yet there is a way we may avoid both. The

Americans have offered to let us be as we are, unencumbered by alliances that require we raise our tomahawks in war. They have offered a great tract of land for us to reside upon under their protection, far up the Missouri River, away from the bad influences we face here. They have guaranteed that our long-time enemies near there, the Osages, have agreed not to bother us if we do not bother them. In my heart I feel we must give such an opportunity a chance, and should it not work to our liking, then certainly we may return here and be in a position no worse than we now occupy. My fathers, my brothers, my heart and mind say we should accept."

Obviously, Keokuk's words at that time had touched his audience profoundly, for there had risen a great din of clapping hands and stamping feet along with loud cries of approval. Black Hawk had not joined in the demonstration, and he was somewhat cheered to see that there were others who hadn't, either. The tribe was being pulled in opposing directions, wooed by the British on the one hand and by the Americans on the other, and as a result, it began to split into three different factions — one, essentially led by Keokuk, that wished peace and favored cooperation with the Americans; another, essentially led by Black Hawk, that wished war and favored aiding the British and was quickly dubbed "the British Band" of Sacs; and finally another, led essentially by Pashepaho, that wished only total noninvolvement.

That last faction was a plum ripe for the plucking by the governor of the Missouri Territory, William Clark — the same Clark who had shared leadership of the great westward expedition to the Pacific with Meriwether Lewis.[46] Through his emissaries, Clark had offered the Sac and Fox a new tract of land of their own — the one Keokuk had referred to — well up the Missouri River, and he had been well pleased when the Sac tribe split and about a quarter of the population, some fifteen hundred men, women, and children, had accepted the offer with high praise for the generosity of the Americans.

That supposed generosity did not keep the Americans from doing all they could to gain a territorial toehold in the Sac and Fox country. The whites had boldly come up the Mississippi River from St. Louis and established Fort Madison on the west shore of the river some fifteen miles above the mouth of the Des Moines River, allegedly as an American fur trade factory.[47] The Sacs, however, especially the so-called British Band, viewed it as an unwarranted encroachment into their territory and responded by making a series of harassing attacks against it, until eventually, in April 1814, it was abandoned and burned by its escaping garrison.

General Howard had then led an expedition up the Illinois River to the Peoria area and razed the Potawatomi villages, after which he built a new fort that was called Fort Clark. Not to be outdone, Governor Clark sent a force up the Mississippi, which briefly engaged and cowed the Sac and Fox at the mouth of the Rock River, then continued up the Mississippi to the mouth of the Wisconsin River, where, adjacent to the long-established British fur trading post of

Prairie du Chien, they built an installation named Fort Shelby, after Governor Isaac Shelby of Kentucky. The fort, staffed with a weak garrison, immediately became a target for attack by a British force led out of Fort Mackinac by Lieutenant Colonel William McKay. Although a reinforcement for Fort Shelby had been sent upriver by Clark, the boats were attacked by the Sacs at Rock River simultaneously with the attack by the British and Indians on Fort Shelby. The Americans were defeated and thrust back to St. Louis, and the British took over the Prairie du Chien fort and renamed it Fort McKay.

Despite some moderate successes by the Americans, the fortunes of war seemed to be favoring the British. The American attack on Fort Mackinac was repulsed, the United States capitol was burned, and when an American force led by Zachary Taylor moved up the Mississippi and built Fort Johnson on the Illinois side opposite the mouth of the Des Moines, Black Hawk's force attacked and defeated them; just before the war finally ended, Fort Johnson was evacuated and burned. Yet, no amount of resistance seemed to deter the Americans for long. Fort Howard, named after General Howard, who died on September 18, was built in the Missouri Territory at the mouth of the Cuivre River. The British Fort McKay at Prairie du Chien, because it was too far into the wilderness for support, was evacuated and burned by its own troops. With the War of 1812 over, a number of Indian treaties were made by the United States — one at Portage des Sioux, one at Prairie du Chien, one at Spring Wells near Detroit, and then another at Portage des Sioux.

Gradually the nibbling at the land was occurring. Surveyors came, and there were skirmishes and troubles with objecting Sacs and Foxes, but nothing of a truly serious nature, and the surveyors did not stay for long, as they had things to do in other areas surrounding the Sac and Fox territory. It became the habit of the Sacs to follow the type of policy Keokuk advocated — to ignore the encroachments of the whites so long as these encroachments were not on what the Sacs still considered to be their own property. Thus, on April 13, 1816, when Indiana had finally become one of the states in the Union, there was little Sac concern because the Indiana country was largely the territory of such tribes as the Miami, Piankeshaw, Delaware, Kickapoo, and some Potawatomi and Ottawa.

With the end of the war, a flurry of American frontier development began, including construction of a federal highway from east to west — an amazing fifteen-foot-wide, hard-packed gravel artery of transportation that was spearing into the wilderness, beginning at Fort Cumberland in Maryland and planned to end at St. Louis.[48] In addition, a number of new fortification projects were undertaken throughout the northwestern frontier, but the Sacs generally chose to disregard their deadly potential. Fort Dearborn, at Chicago, which had been destroyed early in the war at the time of the Fort Dearborn massacre, was rebuilt, but this was not a concern, the Sacs told one another, because it was located in Potawatomi territory.[49] In Prairie du Chien another fort was built, this one called Fort Crawford, but it was not considered a direct Sac concern because it was in

Winnebago territory.[50] And the Americans had finally taken over Fort Mackinac, but that was in the territory of the Chippewas, as was the new fort built at Sault Sainte Marie — Fort Brady. A new Fort Howard was built at Green Bay, but that was in Menominee territory, and a new Fort Shelby built at Detroit was in Ottawa country, as was Fort Saginaw at Saginaw Bay.

So far it was all the other tribes who were most directly concerned with where the Americans were sinking new roots on the frontier, but before very long the white expansion struck closer to home for the Sacs. Almost on the ruins of where Fort Johnson had been, on the east side of the Mississippi across from the mouth of the Des Moines River, the Americans built a new fort that they named Fort Edwards.[51] And worse things were to come. In May of 1816, Black Hawk, Keokuk, and numerous other Sac and Fox chiefs and influential warriors had journeyed to St. Louis at a summons from Governor Clark, to speak of peace. This time, however, the Americans were not so conciliatory as they had been in previous meetings. Clark and the military officers in attendance accused the Sacs of a multitude of hostile acts, from small misdeeds to major crimes, not the least of which was still leaning in their sympathies toward the British. The chiefs tried to explain that it was the American attitude toward the tribes that had *forced* a portion of the Sac tribe to join the British, and when the chiefs accused the Americans of lying, the Americans became offended at the insult and, in their anger, threatened to break off the talks and just go to war against the Sacs. The rift was eventually smoothed over, and a pipe of peace was smoked. A new treaty was drawn up between them, which the chiefs were told merely confirmed previous treaties of peace between them — but which also reaffirmed the 1804 St. Louis Treaty — and for the first time Black Hawk put his name to it.[52] But then, when the Sac delegation returned home, they found that in their absence a detachment of Americans under Major Morrell Marston had come in and, on Rock Island in the Mississippi, less than six miles from Saukenuk, were building a large military installation called Fort Armstrong.[53]

Apprehensive as a result of the treaty meeting just completed in St. Louis, where the Americans had seriously threatened them with war, the Sacs were afraid to complain about the presence of the new fort, but it bothered them greatly. This was the best and most beautiful island on the entire Mississippi. It had long been used by the Sacs as a place for rest and relaxation during the summer. Here they swam and fished and helped themselves to the abundant fruits that grew on the island's surface — apples, plums, strawberries, gooseberries, and nuts of different kinds. But there was even stronger reason for the Sacs to be upset about this intrusion on Rock Island. In the limestone rock of which it was formed were a series of caves, and the Sacs all knew that the winged spirit who lived in the caves was a good spirit, protective of the island and benevolent to those who came and used it in quiet peace. This spirit, claimed to have been seen at various times by many of the Indians, was known to wear a long white robe and had powerful wings ten times as large as those of a swan. The Sacs made it a point, when moving about on that part of the island the spirit supposedly inhabited, to be very quiet so as not to disturb him. Now Fort Armstrong was being built directly over the caves, and the Sacs sat back and waited for the wrath of the spirit to descend upon these defilers. Finally, when the fort was completed and that hadn't happened, they ruefully reckoned that early on during the construction, the noise had driven the good spirit away and a bad spirit had come to take its place, so now the Sacs rarely came to Rock Island anymore.

The Americans professed to having the best interests of the tribes in mind with every expansionist movement made, and they established Indian factors and factories as well as Indian agencies and agents, subagents, and interpreters at various posts in the Indian territory. Sometimes, as in the case of Nicholas Boilvin and Maurice Blondeau, who continued to serve Governor Clark, they were roving subagents, but it was agents such as Alexander Wolcott for the Potawatomi in Chicago and Thomas Forsyth for the Sac and Fox at Rock Island who played the most important role as intermediaries between Indians and whites and who, without exception, professed to champion the rights of the Indians among the whites. And very often, though not always, this was true.

Among the more visible signs of increasing white encroachment were those that were water-borne. In 1817, during the administration of President James Monroe, paddle-wheeler steamboats had appeared on the Mississippi. Equally, on the Great Lakes, fine schooners like the *Baltimore* and *Hercules* had begun making reasonably regular runs between Mackinac and Chicago.

The entire frontier area was being infiltrated by whites in a number of ways, and aware of the Indian-white land disputes that must soon arise, President Monroe laid a groundwork of justification by commenting, "The hunter or savage state requires a greater extent of territory to sustain it than is compatible with progress and just claims of civilized life . . . and must yield to it." The Ohio Indians had recently done just this, signing a treaty ceding to the United States their remaining four million acres of land in that state in exchange for guaranteed annuities and reservations all their own far west of the Mississippi. Vaguely established and highly flexible boundaries were gradually solidifying, and there was the continuing clamor of districts vying to be established into territories and territories to be made into states. The Territory of Arkansas had been created, and in relatively rapid succession, statehood had been granted to Mississippi, Illinois, Alabama, and Maine. And Missouri became, in August 1821, the first state entirely on the *west* side of the Mississippi.

Whether welcomed or not, civilization was definitely pushing its way into the frontier. The University of Cincinnati was founded in Ohio, and the University of Michigan was established at Ann Arbor. Employees of John Jacob Astor's monopolistic American Fur Company spread all throughout the area from the company's new northwestern headquarters on Mackinac Island, founding posts in areas where, now that the United States-Canada border was established, new United States licensing regulations had effectively prohibited British fur traders.

To help enforce these regulations, secretary of war John C. Calhoun ordered the erection of a substantial fort at the confluence of the St. Peters River and the Mississippi, and Lawrence Taliaferro established his headquarters there as Indian agent to the Sioux tribe.[54]

As white settlement in Illinois moved in more and more from the south and the white population of the state increased to more than fifty thousand, it caused the Sac and Fox to abandon areas where they used to hunt and go farther west and northwest, across the Mississippi River and into the traditional hunting areas of the Iowas and the Dakotah Sioux. Not unexpectedly, clashes broke out among the Indians, and the threat of new tribal wars became very real. The Sioux were very strong, but they were also spread out over a territory to the west that was far more vast than that of the Sacs and Foxes. The very concentration of the latter tribes tended to balance the inequality of tribal numbers, and in 1818 the strength of the Sacs had been increased rather unexpectedly. On July 30 that year, for three thousand dollars worth of goods and a guaranteed annuity of two thousand dollars in silver for fifteen years, the Kickapoo tribe had ceded the last of their Illinois lands to the United States and agreed to remove to a reservation on the Osage River in Missouri. But one faction of the Kickapoos was very much opposed to the cession. Instead of agreeing to be resettled west of the Mississippi with the remainder of the tribe, they appealed to the Sacs for asylum and received it. The fifty families of Kickapoos pledged their strength and loyalty to the Sacs and, late in the year, took up residency in a new village they built close to Saukenuk.

Thomas Forsyth had long operated the trading post at Peoria and had been appointed Indian agent by President James Madison. In April 1819, he had been assigned permanently to Fort Armstrong by Governor Clark. It did not sit well with Forsyth that his charges, the Sacs and Foxes, remained so obtuse in respect to the lands they were occupying. Trying to explain to them that they were presently on land the United States government had bought in 1804 was like talking into a windstorm; he could shout himself hoarse, but his words still would not get through. The Sacs, especially those of Black Hawk's British Band, would simply close their ears to the idea that they no longer owned this land, that they were only here at the sufferance of the government, who had guaranteed them in that 1804 treaty the right to live and hunt on the land and cultivate it so long as the government should own it. Now white settlers were beginning to move in and squat on it, and a strong belief prevailed among them that very soon the government was going to open these lands for sale to U.S. citizens.

Well known and respected by the Indians, Forsyth was particularly well suited for his job, and almost immediately after his appointment the Indians began to lay troubles at his doorstep. Shortly after his arrival at the Rock Island agency, while talking with two friends — the enormously fat Fort Armstrong interpreter, twenty-two-year-old Antoine LeClaire, and one of the local traders, George Davenport — Forsyth was confronted by a confused and concerned delegation of

Sacs, including Keokuk and Black Hawk. Both the dapper, thirty-seven-year-old Davenport and the nearly four-hundred-pound LeClaire — who was the half-breed son of a Potawatomi woman and a French trader-blacksmith — were well liked by the Indians, who had no reticence about speaking of their problems in front of them.[55]

"What is happening in our lands?" Black Hawk had asked. "Why do we find white people on them wherever we go, whether it be our summer places or our winter hunting camps? This past winter I hunted as usual on the Two Rivers.[56] I was out one day hunting in a bottom and met three white men. They accused me of killing their hogs. I denied it, but they would not listen to me. One of them took my gun out of my hand and fired it off, then took out the flint and gave back my gun. Then they began beating me with sticks and ordered me off. I was so badly bruised that I couldn't sleep for several nights."

"Did you retaliate?" Forsyth had asked, his eyes locked on Black Hawk's.

"No." The Sac shook his head. "Perhaps we should have. Others of our party had experiences even worse. One of my braves, not long afterward, went out and cut a bee-tree when it was too cold for the bees to fly. He carried the honey to his lodge, but very soon a party of whites who had followed his tracks in the snow came to his lodge and told him that the bee-tree was theirs and that he had had no right to cut it. My brave told them he was sorry, that he did not know that. He pointed to the combs that were in a container to one side and told them to take the honey. They did, but they were not satisfied with this. They also took all the packs of skins that he had collected during the winter and carried them off. Those were the skins with which he was to clothe his family and pay his trader in the spring. Now he was destitute."

After a momentary silence, Forsyth had spoken quietly. "And you still did not retaliate?"

"No. We had always been prepared to offer friendship to the whites wherever we encountered them, but how could we like such people who treated us so unjustly? We determined to break our camp early and return home lest the whites do even worse to us, and it was probably wise that we did. When we joined our people here at Saukenuk, we found that a great many were complaining of having been treated similarly to the way we were treated."

Thomas Forsyth had nodded sadly. "Thank you for telling me this," he said, then turned slightly to address his remarks to all the Sacs who were present. "My brothers, it causes my heart to become heavy to learn of these things, and I wish I could tell you that it will change and become better. Instead," he lowered his head slightly, "I must tell you that it will probably only become worse, especially since you persist in flying the flags and wearing the medals given to you by the British. This makes your great father in Washington unhappy with his red children. Don't you see? Only when you leave your village for good and cross over the Mississippi to stay in the Iowa country, as you agreed to do, will things become better for you."

George Davenport, whom the Sacs continued to like and trust, agreed with Forsyth and began urging Black Hawk to leave Illinois permanently, but Black Hawk was staring at Forsyth and not hearing the trader's words. He interrupted Davenport by addressing the Indian agent intently.

"What do you mean, as we agreed to do?" he demanded. "When have we *ever* agreed that we would give up our lands or our village of Saukenuk?"

"It was in the original 1804 Treaty of St. Louis, signed by your chiefs, and in the treaties since then which reaffirmed those terms, signed by other chiefs and even by you, four summers ago, Black Hawk. It is why the Sacs have for many years been receiving an annuity of goods from the government. The payment is, and always has been, for your Illinois lands, including the site of Saukenuk. I can't believe —"

Forsyth broke off as Black Hawk reached out and strongly gripped the Indian agent's wrist and stared into his eyes. "I tell you now," the Sac chief gritted, "that this is the first I have ever heard of such a thing. It is and has been our belief that the annuities paid us each year by your great father were to give you safe passage in our lands and as a token of the great white father's esteem for his red children. But as a payment for *purchase* of our land, *no!* No chief of Saukenuk has ever — or *would* ever — sign away our right to this land, where the bones of our fathers lie in peace."

Forsyth sighed, gently pulled free of Black Hawk's grip, and repeated, "The treaties were first signed, Black Hawk, by your chiefs in St. Louis in 1804, and reaffirmed several times since then — including by you in 1816 — and —"

"No!" Black Hawk shouted, then repeated less excitedly. "No, *you* must listen to *me*. If any of us signed any paper saying such a thing, it would only be because we could not read the words and they were not truly translated to us and we would therefore have been lied to and cheated and the agreement would be false and we could not be held to its false promises. I will now tell all of our people that they are no more, ever, to accept annuities from you, for by such you are trying to buy our land from us, and one day you will try to claim those lands."

There was genuine sorrow in Forsyth's voice when he replied. "You must try to understand, we are not *trying* to buy your lands. The lands *have already been bought* by the United States government long ago. The treaty of November 4, 1804, said that the Sac and Fox nations would be allowed to live and hunt on the lands they ceded for as long as those lands belonged to the United States. But soon, you see, your great father in Washington will wish to sell these lands, and once this is done, the lands no longer belong to the United States, and the Sac and Fox can no longer legally stay on them. So you see," Forsyth finished apologetically but firmly, "you really must leave here, because the lands *are* going to be sold before long, and it can only become very much harder for you if you do not."

For the first time Keokuk spoke, cutting off Black Hawk, who was just about to reply. "We will give consideration to what you have told us," he said. "If those you name who supposedly sold the lands to you so long ago actually *did* sign such papers as you say, then that is the word of the Sacs, and we must live up to our word. I will talk with those who look to me as their war chief and I will tell them what you have said, and where our honor lies, and we will then act as honorable men must act."

"You will be speaking for yourself, Keokuk," Black Hawk said tightly, "and for the few others who may also wish a cowardly way out of difficulty. No one person or small handful of men of this tribe had any right to sell our lands, and even if Quashquame should say that is what occurred, it is not a legal sale according to our laws. As for me, whichever way this goes, I have no intention of permanently leaving Saukenuk and our lands here on Rock River."

Hardly had the Sac delegation returned to Saukenuk when word of the meeting they had had at the Indian agency flashed through the entire village, and soon no one was speaking of anything else but the astounding possibility of abandoning Saukenuk and their territory east of the Mississippi River. That Keokuk was prepared to do just this became clear when, a short while later, he sent a crier through the village with the loudly uttered message that it was the will of the great father that the Sac people should remove to the west side of the Mississippi, and Keokuk recommended a place on the Iowa River as a good site for the new village. The crier concluded the message by saying that Keokuk, as war chief of the Sacs, wished his party to make whatever arrangements were necessary before they started out in the fall for their hunt, so as to preclude the necessity of returning to Saukenuk the following spring — or ever again.

A stunned sense had settled over the village, and then a delegation of those opposed to leaving Saukenuk had come to Black Hawk and asked his opinion and whether or not he would lead them in opposition to Keokuk's proposal. Black Hawk had just finished speaking privately with Quashquame and Pashepaho and found to his dismay that both chiefs were very hazy about what they put their names to on the 1804 treaty, but that they had indeed signed it, as had the other three, who had died since then. Black Hawk could not even begin to comprehend that such a fraudulent treaty could be taken seriously, and he had no need to deliberate much before responding to the villagers who had come to him.

"I have spoken to Chief Pashepaho and Chief Quashquame in this matter," he said, "and they have assured me that they never consented to the sale of our village, but even if they had, how could such a treaty be binding on our entire nation? No, I cannot follow what Keokuk proposes. As you ask me to, I promise now to be your leader and raise the voice of opposition to Keokuk, with a full determination not to leave my village."

Black Hawk had then gone to Keokuk to see if this difficulty with their great father, the president, could not be settled. "I propose," he told Keokuk, "that we give some other land, any that our great father might choose — even our valuable lead mines — if we may be peaceably permitted to keep the small point of land on which our village and cornfields are now. [57] I must tell you, Keokuk, that I am of the opinion that the white people have plenty of land and would never take our village from us."

Keokuk had nodded, but his demeanor lacked conviction. "I will make such an exchange if possible," he had said, "and will apply to our agent, Forsyth, and his chief, Clark, at St. Louis, who has charge of all the agents, for permission to go to Washington to see our great father for that purpose."

It had been an acceptable response that satisfied Black Hawk and those who sided with him. That fall they had gone to their hunting grounds filled with the hope that during their absence something would have been done for them. Black Hawk and his followers established their winter camp ten days' journey from Saukenuk, this time near the headwaters of the North Fork Salt River. [58] And it was there, with that winter not half gone and the new year only ready to begin, that a runner had come with an urgent piece of news for Black Hawk. They had gone into Black Hawk's lodge, where the runner was given heavy fur robes to warm his outside and hot food to warm his inside and a hot pipe to warm his mind. When the pipe was done and set aside, the runner spoke.

"Black Hawk, in your absence three families of whites have come to Saukenuk. They have destroyed some of the lodges in our village. One of their families is living in your lodge. They are building fences to divide our cornfields for their own use, and they are even quarreling among themselves about their lines in the division. That is what I have come to say."

Black Hawk had sat for a long moment staring into the fire, and finally the runner had asked, "What will you do now?"

Black Hawk stood up and pulled a thick buffalo robe around him. "I will go immediately to talk to these whites," he said grimly, "and tell them to leave our village and our fields."

[*January 31, 1830 — Friday*]

Because Black Hawk suffered from what might generously have been described as an abrasive disposition, few people had ever become very close to him. Not that he was unable to find followers when he wished to undertake a raid against enemies, but followers and friends are not quite the same. Even his wife, Asshawequa — Singing Bird — could not truly have been considered a friend; she served him as he wished her to, bore his children, cooked his meals, and cared for him, in return for which he showed her a certain deference, protected her against enemies, and provided her a home in his lodge when in Saukenuk and in his wigwam when elsewhere.

But there was one who was a friend, a follower, virtually a disciple, and that individual was Neapope. [59] A tall, lanky, morose-looking individual of about forty-five, Neapope had been with Black Hawk on scores of raids and extended expeditions over the years, and had become closer to Black Hawk and more trusted than any other person had ever been. Black Hawk, though influential, was still not a civil chief, though many considered him the leader of the British Band.

Actually, Bad Thunder was the principal chief of the British Band, seconded equally by Chief Ioway and Chief Namoett; but behind the scenes it was always Black Hawk whose word and wishes carried the most weight.[60] At times Black Hawk leaned on these three very heavily, but none was so close or devoted to him as Neapope. There was virtually nothing Neapope wouldn't do for Black Hawk, and he was fierce in his protectiveness of the Sac. Actually, Neapope, no more a civil chief than Black Hawk, was a very good leader in his own right, yet almost always he chose to look to Black Hawk for leadership and guidance. It was only because Neapope was away from the hunting camp at the time Black Hawk had gone back to Saukenuk that he did not accompany his chief. But it was probably just as well, since Neapope often had a great deal more difficulty controlling his temper than Black Hawk and was inclined to act very rashly with minimal provocation.

Thus, it was not unusual that when Black Hawk returned from his midwinter journey to Saukenuk, he closeted himself with Neapope and spoke for a long time, telling his lieutenant all that had occurred during the month-long absence.

"Was it true, Black Hawk?" Neapope asked. "Were the whites really in your lodge in Saukenuk as it was reported to you?"

Black Hawk nodded. "It was true. I went to my lodge and found a white family occupying it, and I asked them why and by what right they had moved in, but they did not understand my tongue and I did not understand theirs; but they made threatening gestures toward me, and so I left and went to Fort Armstrong to complain about what was occurring."

"Did you talk with Forsyth there?" Neapope asked.

"No. He was gone from Rock Island, and it was said he was in St. Louis. But I talked with LeClaire. He could not come back to the village with me, but I told him what I wanted to say to those people, and he wrote down the words so I could take it to them."

"What did you have LeClaire write to them?"

"I said that they were not to settle on our lands, nor trouble our lodges or fences." Black Hawk's expression tightened. "I said there was plenty of land in the country for them to settle on if that was what they wanted, and they did not need to come into Saukenuk to settle. I said that we had not abandoned our village, but that it was our way to leave it in the fall to go to our hunting camps, but that we always returned in the spring, which was what we would be doing again before long. That is what I told LeClaire, and that was what he wrote on the paper that he gave to me to give to them."

"And you gave it to them?"

"Yes, and they read it and were not happy with the words that were there. They talked to me in an excited way, but I could not understand what they were saying, and after a while they stopped talking and I left. I fully expected they would remove themselves as I requested they do and so I left, telling them I would come back. It was getting much colder, and I returned to Rock Island and spent the night there in the Agency with LeClaire. Davenport was visiting him, and we three talked far into the night, but they were not encouraging about our returning to Saukenuk. Our friend Davenport, especially, urged us not to return there. Both Davenport and LeClaire said the white men were no doubt planning to stay, and it would be much better for everyone if we just gave up and made our village with Keokuk on the Ioway River. I told him I would not, and that I spoke as well for those who followed me."

Neapope made an approving grunt. "And did you then return to Saukenuk to make sure the Americans had gone away?"

"No. Not then. In the morning I went toward the sunrise and crossed the Mississippi again on bad ice, but the Great Spirit made it strong that I might pass over safely. I walked for three days more and then visited the agent for the Winnebagoes and told him of our difficulties with the whites at Saukenuk, but he told me the same as Davenport and LeClaire had done — that we should give up and go live on the Ioway River where the chiefs of our tribe have considered setting up our new village and where Keokuk and his followers are talking of joining them. I left him and continued up the Rock River to the Winnebago Prophet's Town.[61] I did so because it had struck me that it would be appropriate to get the reaction of a very wise man, and I know of none other so wise as the Prophet."

"Wabokieshiek? You visited Wabokieshiek?"[62]

Black Hawk had nodded. "I explained everything to him as it is. He agreed with me at once that I was right and advised me never to give up Saukenuk to the whites, for them to plow up the bones of our people. He told me that if we remained at Saukenuk, the whites would not trouble us. Where Keokuk was concerned and those followers of his who consider going with him to the Ioway River, he advised me to convince them to return and stay at Saukenuk. I think if we do that, showing that we are strong in our resolve, we will have no more trouble with the Americans."

Black Hawk could not have been more incorrect. The whites — some of them, at any rate — were still in Saukenuk when the late-winter trapping and sugar making ended and the Sacs returned to their principal village. Ill feelings prevailed, and at times it was only with the greatest of difficulty that Thomas Forsyth, reluctantly acting as mediator between the Americans and the Sacs, was able to forestall open hostilities. It was a situation that could only become worse as, inexorably, the whole frontier seemed to be blossoming.

There were good reasons why the American squatters were attracted to the area of the mouth of the Rock River and to the whole region north of there to Prairie du Chien. Where Saukenuk was concerned, its site was not only extremely beautiful, it was in close proximity to government protection in the form of Fort Armstrong on Rock Island; it was a natural stopping place for any river travelers; moreover, the soil of the area was wonderfully fertile and had been worked into perfect loam through years of cultivation by the Sacs, so that new ground bound tightly by the roots of buffalo grasses did not have to be broken. Where the area to the north was concerned, the great attraction was the abundance of mineral wealth, particularly lead. For many years the Indians had mined lead in a rather primitive manner in holes dug into the ground in the northwestern Illinois country, southwestern Wisconsin area, and adjacent Iowa across the Mississippi, especially in the area called Dubuque's Mines. They had learned to smelt the lead in small amounts with log fires. What had more or less opened the door to the whites and caused the boom in mining in this lead-rich country occurred nearly a decade ago, with the July 20, 1820, Treaty of Prairie du Chien. At that time certain factions of the Chippewas, Ottawas, and Potawatomies, who had no real claims to the territory in question, had ceded all rights to northwestern Illinois lands to the United States government. Word spread of lead being in great abundance, and this quickly attracted miners. Almost overnight, it seemed, small white settlements had begun to appear in the Fever River District — settlements like Galena, which was even named after the mineral the miners sought.[63] Now Galena, which only seven years ago had just one house, was a rapidly growing mining town where this year alone over 12 million pounds of lead had been mined.

Among the many whites that had been flocking into the lead mine region was a six-foot-tall, strong-visaged individual named Henry Dodge, who had arrived early in 1828. Born forty-seven years ago in southwestern Indiana, Dodge had spent his childhood in Kentucky before moving with his parents to the Sainte Genevieve district of Missouri when it was still Spanish territory. An aggressive young man, at the age of twenty-three he had become sheriff of that district, and eight years later, in 1813, had become marshal of the Missouri Territory and rose to the rank of major general in the Missouri Militia. Now he was certain that the future for an enterprising person on this frontier lay in the lead mining area just opening to exploitation, and he meant to be a part of it. The possibility of difficulty with the Indians bothered him not at all. When Joseph Street at Prairie du Chien threatened to use troops to evict Dodge and others from the Indian land, Dodge replied scornfully, "Let them march, sir; with my miners I can whip all the old sore-shinned regulars that are stationed at Prairie du Chien."

Matters between the Sacs and whites had continued to degenerate over these passing years. During the customary winter absence of the Sacs at their hunting camps, the whites had begun moving in and illegally taking possession of Saukenuk. They destroyed some of the more permanent quonset lodges and smashed or burned many of the larger boats owned by the Sacs. Such acts unfailingly stirred the wrath of the Indians when they returned in the spring. Then when many of their number would depart for the summer hunt, the few who remained to guard the Sac holdings had almost daily squabbles with the white settlers. The whites were not at all averse to becoming squatters on the Indian lands, but they deeply resented it when the returned Indians hunted among their settlements. They claimed that with the wild game all but gone —

a fact no one disputed — some of the Indians had taken to killing the settlers' cattle for meat. Most of the Sac annuities were never seen by the Indians and instead were distributed by their agent to settlers who had lodged damage claims against them. It availed Black Hawk nothing to point out that the tribe was being severely pinched — they couldn't hunt any longer to the south because now this country was all settled by whites, so the Sac hunters were having to travel upwards of three hundred miles to the north and west to reach good hunting. In doing so, they were being forced to enter the territory of the Dakotah Sioux, who objected to the Sac incursions and darkly threatened war.

When the Sacs complained to Thomas Forsyth about outrages being committed against them by squatters, the Indian agent could do little more than shrug and advise the Indians to abandon Saukenuk and go settle across the Mississippi in the Iowa country. It was particularly futile for Forsyth to explain the treaty to the settlers and the right of the Indians to remain on the land until the United States government sold it. The squatters merely pointed out they were staying, and it was only a matter of time until the land was brought into the public market sale and settlement, so state and government officials should remove the Indians from Saukenuk now, by force if necessary, and get it all over with.

Frictions increased, but nothing concrete was being done to resolve the situation. Dissatisfied with getting no results, the squatters began to try almost anything to so annoy the Indians that they would leave here just to end the aggravation; they shot the Indians' dogs, claimed the Indians' horses as their own, accused the Indians of stealing vegetables from settler gardens and of killing their hogs and cattle, and bitterly complained that the Indian horses were breaking into their fenced cornfields — fields they themselves had usurped from the Indians — and causing damage to their crops, for which the settlers demanded, and received, recompense in cash from the Sac annuities. Worst of all, perhaps, was the traffic in liquor. Many of the more unscrupulous settlers were taking advantage of the Indian weakness for whiskey, plying them with it and collecting in return many times its value in fur skins — valuable pelts that the Indians owed their traders for credit advanced. Some of the chiefs — Black Hawk prominently among them — beseeched the agent and even the settlers themselves not to sell whiskey to the young men, but these requests and wishes and even threats had little effect. Occasionally government agents tried to break up the liquor traffic, but to little avail. Exasperated, Forsyth wrote to his superior, William Clark, in St. Louis:

It is truly shameful that such quantities of whiskey are sold and traded with the Indians on this river. Almost every settler's home is a whiskey shop, and will buy from the Indians the most trifling articles for whiskey.

At one point the disgusted Forsyth encouraged his charges to forcibly take back from the whites the property that the whites had purchased with liquor. This backfired badly, because sometimes the drunk Indians threatened the owners of property that they had no claim upon and committed some acts that injured innocent white men. Clashes began breaking out between Indians and whites, more often than not with the Indians on the receiving end. In numerous cases the whites badly beat the Sacs with the Indians' own swords and ramrods. Black Hawk long ago had vowed he would never forget, or forgive, the American settlers for so severely beating him as they had, and those who knew him well knew he would hold that grudge for the rest of his life. One white settler threatened to shoot a young Sac who objected to the fact that the settler had struck the Indian youth's mother. In another case, a clash occurred between some Potawatomies and whiskey peddlers Samuel Mallory and Tom McNeale near the mouth of the Spoon River in central Illinois, and one of the Indians was killed. The government investigated and placed the blame on the settlers, but little was done about it, and anti-Indian fervor increased among the whites. A comment all too frequently heard among the whites was that killing an Indian served a better purpose than killing a deer. Yet, treaties with the Indians continued to be negotiated.

Another major treaty that benefited the Americans was concluded at Chicago on August 29, 1821, after two weeks of negotiations with some three thousand Potawatomies, Ottawas, and Chippewas. As the days of negotiation wore on, the Indians became more and more desirous of the whiskey they had been promised but which was being withheld. Finally one of the leading Potawatomies, Chief Topenebe, rose and said in all seriousness, "We don't care about the land or the money or the goods — it's *whiskey* that we want. Give us whiskey!"[64] That was exactly what the chief commissioner for the United States, Michigan Territory governor Lewis Cass, had been waiting for. "I'll tell you what," he said. "If you'll just get on with this treaty, I promise you enough whiskey to make every Potawatomi man, woman, and child drunk." The negotiations went swiftly after that, and the Indians ceded to the United States their claim to five million acres of land in southwestern Michigan, northern Indiana, and northern Illinois in exchange for a six-thousand-dollar annuity, plus a promise of lands of their own west of the Mississippi and a government blacksmith shop to be established in Chicago for their use and supported by a one-thousand-dollar annuity for twenty years.[65] As soon as the treaty was signed, the governor of the Michigan Territory gave the Indians a very large supply of whiskey. Not unexpectedly, the Indians very soon were roaring drunk. Old tribal animosities flared, and in the resultant brawl eleven Indians were killed.

Periodically, as time passed, the Sac and Fox denied the validity of the 1804 treaty, and just as often Thomas Forsyth confirmed it, and warned darkly on each occasion that the time was coming when the government would sell the lands, and then they would *have* to leave for good.

Perhaps no single event brought home more emphatically to the Indians along the Mississippi how their world was gradually changing into a white man's land than when, on April 21, 1823, the first steamboat ever to ascend the river — the *Virginia* — left St. Louis and arrived nineteen days and 729 miles later at Fort St. Anthony. Steamboats, along with the new steam locomotives that ran across the face of the earth on shiny steel rails, were ushering in a whole new means for white expansion into the American wilderness. Not only that, a short time later the Erie Canal opened, and the Great Lakes became directly linked with the Hudson River, New York City, and the Atlantic Ocean. Suddenly places like Rochester, Syracuse, Cleveland, Detroit, and Chicago began to boom as port cities, since the time required to move freight from Illinois, Michigan, and Ohio to the Atlantic dropped from thirty days to ten days or less, and freighting rates dropped from one hundred dollars per ton to five dollars.

At almost the same time as the passage of the *Virginia* up the Mississippi, the Sacs entered into a brief and very fierce war with the Iowa tribe. A huge Sac and Fox force led by Chief Pashepaho and seconded by Black Hawk crossed the great river and fell upon the Iowas, virtually annihilating them and confiscating their lands. What few Iowas survived were assimilated into the Sac tribe. And in June of 1827, the very real threat of an all-out war between the Dakotah Sioux and the Sac and Fox ended, to everyone's relief, when the Dakotah Sioux chief Wabeshaw sent a peace pipe and conciliatory message to the Fox chief Pamoske at the village near Dubuque's Mines and to the Sac chief Pashepaho at Saukenuk.[66]

A great blow was felt by the tribes with the death at St. Louis of one of the Indians' greatest white champions, Nicholas Boilvin, who had been one of the pioneer settlers of Prairie du Chien. His place as Indian agent at Fort Crawford was filled by the appointment of Joseph Street, a general in the Illinois Militia. Another and more overwhelming shock wave was soon felt by the Sacs. Increasingly in these years, the Illinois settlers were finding the presence of the Indians to be thwarting them in their desire to settle on lands to the north and west of the Rock River. Though aware that the Sacs still had every right to be there, they were growing impatient with waiting for the government to do something. In Springfield, Ninian Edwards, who had recently been elected governor of the State of Illinois, reacted to the will of his constituency and sent a formal appeal to the United States secretary of war for the removal without delay of all Sac and Fox Indians from ceded lands in Illinois.

Whatever might have happened then was abruptly overshadowed by the outbreak of hostilities from an unexpected quarter. The Winnebagoes had long been overrun and mistreated by the white miners who had been coming into the lead-rich country of southwestern Wisconsin and northwestern Illinois. Finally, pushed beyond the limit by the frequent galling clashes from which the Winnebagoes always seemed to emerge a little worse off than before, a young chief named Red Bird decided, in the summer of 1827, to declare war on the whites. Black Hawk, with a select following, agreed to support him. Early in June a large council was held at the Lake Geneva village of Potawatomi chief Mawgehset, whom the whites knew as Big Foot.[67] Red Bird attended with his small band of fanatic followers and displayed a war belt, asking the Potawatomies to join with him and Black Hawk's band and some of the Sioux, who were also on hand, in a general uprising against the Americans. Big Foot agreed at once, for he despised the Americans, but the rest of the Potawatomies in attendance refused the war belt and immediately dispersed to their villages.

The Winnebago War, as it was dubbed — though wholly undeserving of the name — was by no stretch of the imagination an uprising of the entire Winnebago tribe. It began when Chief Red Bird, with Wekau — The Sun — and Chichonsic — Little Bull — came to Prairie du Chien on June 26, 1827, and got some ammunition and whiskey from a trader.[68] The trio then walked two miles to the cabin of a miner who had been particularly offensive to the Indians, Registre Gagnier, who was living in the cabin with his wife, a young son, an infant daughter named Louisa, and an old discharged American soldier named Solomon Lipcap.[69] The three Winnebagoes entered, catching the whites off guard, and instantly shot and killed Gagnier and Lipcap. Snatching up her husband's gun, Mrs. Gagnier got her small son safely behind her and finally, after the Indians had entered the bedroom and seemed to have killed her baby girl, drove them outside, where they scattered. She then ran to Prairie du Chien with the boy and got armed men to return with her. The party found the baby Louisa still alive on the bed, though her neck had been cut and she had been scalped.[70] Meanwhile, Red Bird and his cohorts had moved off to another cabin where they killed a settler named Méthode, his wife, and five children.

Black Hawk and his party of Sacs and Winnebagoes did their part by intercepting the keelboat *Oliver H. Perry* as it was coming down from Fort Snelling. In a well-planned assault of murderous concerted gunfire, they attacked it at the mouth of Bad Axe Creek, a full day's journey above Prairie du Chien. Two crew members were killed outright, two others were mortally wounded and died later, and two others were slightly wounded. Only one Indian was killed. The boat managed to get away from the strong attacking force and reached Prairie du Chien with 693 bullet holes in it.

Word of the attacks spread swiftly, and a great nervousness arose among the whites, especially in Chicago. Big Foot and his Potawatomies showed up in Chicago to collect their annuities and stayed around to watch a dance being held in the soldiers' barracks. The festivities were interrupted by a storm, during which lightning struck the barracks and set the building afire, along with an adjacent storehouse and a guard house. Everyone had to help stop the blaze before it destroyed the entire fort, but the Potawatomies simply stood and watched and would not help. A great apprehension was aroused by this strange behavior, and as a result the Chicago Militia was quickly organized.

The United States Army was swift to take action. General Atkinson, who was commander of the United States Army's western district and had earned the sobriquet White Beaver from the Indians, was no stranger to the western frontier.

He had accompanied two expeditions up the Missouri River to the Yellowstone and had been involved in many major Indian councils. A tall, whipcord North Carolinian currently stationed at Jefferson Barracks adjacent to St. Louis, he quickly received orders to inflict exemplary chastisement and immediately came upstream with a strong force of both federal and militia troops.[71] Local militia forces were being raised elsewhere, and in the lead district, Colonel Henry Dodge was quickly chosen by the miners as their leader. On the arrival of the U.S. Army, he placed his little force under General Atkinson's command.

Strong enough and wise enough to listen to and heed the advice of those in a position to know, Atkinson did not launch an all-out attack against the Indians. Instead, he followed William Clark's advice and stopped off at Rock Island to appeal to Sac war chief Keokuk at Saukenuk to help. He gave Keokuk a fine saddle and bridle and won his support and that of the majority of the Sacs. With such an addition to his already strong force, the Army was very powerful, and Red Bird realized that resistance was pointless, so he and his two lieutenants, Chichonsic and Wekau, surrendered. They were transported in chains to Jefferson Barracks and incarcerated there to await trial. Black Hawk was arrested and accused of leading the attack on the keelboat at Bad Axe, but due to lack of evidence no indictment was brought against him, and he was released. The Winnebago War, such as it was, had ended. Red Bird was never brought to trial because he died of an intestinal ailment in his cell at Jefferson Barracks on February 16, 1828.

Nevertheless, Illinois governor Ninian Edwards had had his fill of Indian problems, especially in respect to the Sacs. He strongly disliked their continued occupation of the ceded lands and didn't even want them hunting in it or traversing it. He had no sympathy whatever for the justice of their complaints about the squatters on their land and condemned them for their protests. *"Such conduct,"* he wrote to the secretary of war, *"has been borne by the people for a few years past with great impatience and cannot be submitted to much longer."* He cared nothing for the fact that the Sac and Fox were caught in the jaws of a constantly tightening pincers — an inexorably advancing line of settlers to the south and east and, to north and west, the scalping knives of the Dakotah Sioux.

Last May Thomas Forsyth had one more of his many meetings with the Sac who remained in the Saukenuk area and implored them to leave, to cross the river into Iowa before great trouble should descend on them, but Black Hawk and others of those who remained would not hear of it. Quashquame and Pashepaho, signers of the 1804 treaty, responded angrily, reiterating as always that they, even by the terms of that disputed treaty, had never sold *any* land above the mouth of Rock River — which included Saukenuk — or any land northward and westward of that river. They adamantly refused to move from the land where the bones of their ancestors lay, and vowed they would defend that land against any intruder.

The weariness of waiting for the federal government to do something about the situation was wearing very thin indeed the patience of Governor Edwards. Following one more of the interminable disputes between miners and Indians in the Fever River district, he wrote with barely controlled anger to William Clark in St. Louis:

May 25, 1828

Sir —

I have only time to ask you whether any and what definitive arrangements have been made for removing the Indians from the ceded lands of this State, in pursuance with the directions of the Secretary of War, and what is the prospect of immediate success? The Secretary's letter gave me reason to believe that this measure would have been accomplished before this time. The General Government has been applied to long enough for its own action to have freed us from so serious a grievance. If it declines acting with effect, those Indians will be removed, and that very promptly. . . . You have done all that can be accomplished without coercion. Repeated exertions have been made for the past several years to induce those Indians to remove from the seat of the lands of Illinois. I trust you must see the necessity of substituting force for persuasion. Their continued presence is an invasion of the rights of a sovereign and independent state, and if these Indians do not remove at once, either the President must use force or I will, on my own responsibility.

Four separate events during the remainder of 1828 had created great jubilation among the settlers. The first was the promise made by the new secretary of war, Peter B. Porter, that except for some Kickapoos, all Indians in Illinois would be removed *"beyond the Mississippi to lands unsuitable for white settlement by May 25, 1829."* The second event was the late-summer proclamation issued by President John Quincy Adams opening western Illinois lands — including the area of Saukenuk — to settlement and development. Then there was the long-awaited trial, held August 25, in the United States Circuit Court, Crawford County, Prairie du Chien, of Wekau and Chichonsic. The two Winnebagoes were found guilty of murder in the witnessed killings of Registre Gagnier and Solomon Lipcap and the scalping of Louisa Gagnier with intent to kill, and were sentenced to be executed on December 26. The final event was the execution itself, which took place as scheduled the day after Christmas. Once that had been accomplished, a great sense of relief filled the settlements. Now the Indians would have to know the United States meant business and they better get out.

Early this past spring the various bands of Sacs, returning from their winter's absence, rendezvoused across the Mississippi from Saukenuk and crossed over to the Illinois side to plant this year's corn before returning across the river and going to the new village site that had been established by their chiefs on the Iowa River. Black Hawk and his band crossed to the Illinois side with them and, as the year before, found some of their lodges destroyed and the best cornfields taken over by squatters and fenced. The Indians promptly knocked the fences down and planted their corn where they had always planted it. The whites were extremely upset and were highly vociferous about *their* rights being infringed upon. At once they went to Rock Island and presented themselves to Forsyth and the commanding officer of Fort Armstrong as peaceful settlers who had come to Rock River expecting that the Indians, who had been ordered to remove, would not return. However, they *had* returned and were knocking down their fences, stealing their horses, and threatening to kill them if they did not leave Saukenuk. The commanding officer only shrugged sympathetically and said he lacked the authority to remove the Indians, while Forsyth said he could only request to the Sacs that they depart. The settlers were disgruntled and threatened to appeal directly to Governor Edwards. Forsyth had sighed and told them that was their right if they chose to, and was very pleased that for the moment, at least, outright violence had been averted.

As for the Indians, with the season's corn planted, the majority of the Sacs crossed back to the Iowa side, but Black Hawk refused to go with them, saying he did not fear the Long Knives and would remain in Saukenuk. He had added ominously that if the Americans tried to keep him from the land of his fathers, their scalps would be hung in his lodge. The Sac chiefs, with Pashepaho as their spokesman, deputized Keokuk to remain east of the Mississippi with Black Hawk in the hope of preventing trouble. Not pleased with the assignment, Keokuk obeyed, but he was aghast when Black Hawk, Neapope, and Quashquame planned to go to Fort Armstrong and complain about the whites still squatting in Saukenuk. He refused to accompany them.

Forsyth listened to the Sacs attentively at first but then with growing impatience when, after he explained he was powerless to help them, their harangue went on and on. As soon as they left, the frustrated Indian agent had written to Clark:

> Rocky Island
> 22 May 1829
>
> Sir —
>
> *I have to acquaint you that I was visited yesterday by all the principal Sauk Indians now at their village on Rocky River (Keocuck [sic] and principal braves excepted) on the subject of their land where their Village is on Rocky River.*
>
> *Three Sauk Indians — Black Hawk, Neapope and Quashquame — spoke very fiercely on the subject and said the land was theirs, that they never sold the Land, that their Land contained the bones of their ancestors, and [they] would not give it up; that they had defended it against all your power during the late war [the War of 1812], and would again defend it as long as they existed; that they had*

formed an alliance with the Chippeways, Ottoways, Pottowatomies, Kickapoos & Menomonies, who were ready to assist them at any time in defending their country against any force whatever. A number of Chippeways, Ottoways and Pottowatomies with some Kickapoos were present and assented to what the Sauk Indians had said. Keocuck with some of his Braves were on the Island at the time of the Council, & told my interpreter [Antoine LeClaire] after all was over that the Sauks who spoke did not know what they were saying, which was the reason he would have nothing to do with their talk.

It appears that yesterday some of the Settlers commenced ploughing up a patch of ground belonging to a Sauk Indian (who stands next to Keocuck among the Braves) when on seeing the whites ploughing up his ground, he wished to prevent them, telling them he was going to plant corn there himself. One of the white men struck him with a bean pole, & drove him away: This is only the beginning of more serious consequences which must happen when the Indians get any whiskey during the summer months from below [meaning from the white settlements southward from Saukenuk in Illinois and Missouri].

The Indians and myself had a great deal of talk at this meeting, the most of which was quite unnecessary, & at the winding up of which I told the Indians I would not listen to any complaints that might come in [the] future from any Indians who would remain at Rock River.

I have done everything in my power to get the Indians to remove [to] their own lands [Iowa], but the Black Hawk with a few others are the Indians who are making all this fuss. The Stabbing Chief, Pishkenawer [Pashepaho] and all the influential Indians have gone to their own Country during the last month to a new village, and there are some going daily from Rocky River.[72]

Those who have planted corn will remain & they will be few in number to the whole population of the Socks [sic].

The Chief Keocuck enquired of me, in private, if he & some of his friends could remain at Rock River to raise the corn they had planted? Saying at [the] same time that more than half of those now at Rock River would go shortly [to the Iowa River village]. I told Keocuck that he had heard what I said to the Indians in council, and that it was out of my power to give any Indian such permission as he asked for.

It is my opinion that but few Indians will remain at Rock River this summer, but yet I am fearful that some difficulty will take place between them and the settlers during the ensuing summer.

All the Fox Indians, formerly residing in the vicinity have gone and made a new village at the Grand Mascouteen.[73]

23rd. Keocuck called on me this afternoon alone and told me that the Indians now at Rocky River [Saukenuk] did not like him, and his intention was to go down to the Iowa River to reside, but that the head chiefs, who were now at Ioway River directed him to remain at Rocky River to keep things in order if possible, and *that he must obey the Chiefs, otherwise him and those of his family now here would have been at their new village at Ioway River long since. That he had succeeded in preventing two partisans (who have been fasting for the last winter) from going to war.*

Keocuck appears to be much dejected, from his Chiefs compelling him to stay at Rocky River, as part of his large family is already at Ioway River, indeed he sees the necessity that the Indians should abandon their old village at Rocky River and live on their own Lands.

> *Respectfully I remain, Your Obdt. Servt.*
> *Thomas Forsyth*
> *Genrl. William Clark, Supt. Ind. Affairs St. Louis.*

Oddly enough, though Forsyth had little evident sympathy for the Sacs in late May, on June 17 he wrote Clark:

It appears hard to me that the Indian property should be stolen, their huts torn and burned down, and their persons insulted by Strangers . . . who are now quarreling and fighting with each other about the cornfields. I hope our government will render some justice to those Indians, and not encourage those intruders.

All these matters in the Rock River area, however, were overshadowed by the major Indian council held at Prairie du Chien on July 29 for the express purpose of resolving the Indian versus white question of territorial possession in southwestern Wisconsin and northwestern Illinois. Various tribes were invited by Thomas L. McKenney, head of the Indian Bureau of the War Department, but he declined to include the Sacs and Foxes in the invitation, because to include them in the discussion of Indian claims to land east of the Mississippi might imply that they had such claims. The eighty Potawatomies from Wisconsin and Illinois who attended were led by Mawgehset—Big Foot—and the brothers Black Partridge, principal chief of the Potawatomies, and the younger Waubansee, war chief of the tribe. They were accompanied by their two extremely influential, adopted half-breed chiefs. The first of these was Sauganash — Billy Caldwell — who was actually the son of an Ottawa chief's daughter and a British officer, Captain William Caldwell; the second was Chechepinqua — Alexander Robinson — who also was the son of an Ottawa woman but whose father was a Scots trader.[74] Of the eighty, thirty-five signed a treaty and gave up land that the Winnebagoes, Sacs, and Foxes had as much claim to as they, if not more — two large tracts west of the Rock River and south of Prairie du Chien, including the lead-rich Fever River district. They also ceded a large triangular tract north of the Fox River and due west of Chicago. For this cession the Potawatomies received twenty thousand dollars in goods, an additional perpetual annuity of sixteen thousand dollars to be paid at Chicago, the promise of another gift of goods valued at twelve thousand dollars to be paid at the next annuity payment, and several smaller items that included fifty barrels of salt annually and a permanent blacksmith shop in Chicago. The government also agreed to pay to various traders in Illinois and Wisconsin the outstanding debt of $11,600 owed them by the tribe.[75]

Despite Thomas McKenney's efforts to keep the Sacs and Foxes in the dark about the major council, they got wind of it, and a small delegation under Keokuk made a late but dramatic entrance. The Sac war chief brought along two Fort Crawford deserters he caught as they were fleeing downriver. After turning them over to the Americans, he led a ferocious war dance meant to intimidate the Sioux and Winnebagoes. When queried on whether the Sac and Fox might be interested in selling their mineral lands west of the Mississippi, Keokuk vocalized his tribe's reluctance to get involved in any more land deals with the United States. In a rare moment of not toadying to the Americans, he declared that General Harrison had obviously cheated them in 1804 and that Chief Quashquame and Chief Pashepaho and the other three, now dead, had deceived the tribe also, but that he, Keokuk, did not propose to be cheated. Other Indian delegates on hand sided with the Sac war chief in refusing to sell mineral sites and railed against the trespassers in their lands. The United States treaty commissioners warned wearily about the consequences to the Sac and Fox should there be any renewal of intertribal hostilities with the Sioux, as seemed to be happening. Keokuk attributed that trouble to the Fox chief Allotah — whom the Americans called Morgan — but added that there was good reason; the more the Americans forced the Sacs and Foxes out of their own territory, the more they were forced to go into Sioux territory to survive. The council ended, as it always seemed to, with the United States getting a great deal more than it gave.

There had been little good news for the Indians all this year, and Andrew Jackson's taking over the reins of the presidency was in keeping with the ill fortune. He made no secret of his dislike for the Indians generally, and he very quickly issued an order meant to end the problem of Indians and whites contending over the ceded land still owned by the government. Jackson directed the United States General Land Office to advertise immediately the sale of government lands in northwestern Illinois — including the site of Saukenuk. The United States Land Office in Springfield, Illinois, announced that the land sale would begin on the third Monday of October.

As if things were not bad enough with all of that, when the Sacs showed up for the annuity of two thousand dollars they were supposed to receive from Forsyth, he had the money for them all right, but they had to turn over nineteen hundred of it to the traders Russell Farnham and George Davenport, to apply to the debt they had run up. The remaining one hundred dollars was retained by Forsyth to satisfy claims made by settlers for Indian depredations.

Throughout the remainder of the summer and into early fall, matters between Indians and whites continued to degenerate in the lead-mining areas. Traders had begun seriously making dire predictions about a general Indian war shaping up, yet somehow gunfire was avoided. In late September, Thomas Forsyth came to Saukenuk as the Sacs were preparing to leave for their autumn hunting camps. He was not pleased to see that Black Hawk's band had been augmented by the hundred Kickapoo warriors and their families under their young war chief Panoahah, who had led them out of the Sangamon Valley of central Illinois.[76] Forsyth called an assembly of the chiefs and principal warriors — specifically Keokuk, Black Hawk, Quashquame, and Panoahah — and made it as clear as he could to them that this land where they stood now was going to be sold by the United States in a matter of weeks and they must not — *could not!* — return here next spring. As usual, the Indians paid little heed to his words. When the meeting was over, Keokuk came up to the Indian agent, shaking his head sadly. Having been reproached by Pashepaho on the Iowa River for not having kept Black Hawk under better control during the summer, and being openly reviled by Black Hawk and the entire British Band of the Sacs, Keokuk was disgusted and depressed. "If," he said glumly, "any Indians do attempt to return and reside at Rocky River next spring, they must take their chances. I will not be with them to ward off tragedy."

The Indians went off to their hunting camps within the next few days, and as Forsyth had told them would occur, the ceded lands held by the government went on sale at the U.S. Land Office at Springfield on October 19. At the time there were about twenty families of white squatters in Saukenuk and its vicinity, but only one man among them who had enough money to buy a quarter-section. But a buyer was on hand who had plenty to spend and was eager to do so. This was the wealthy trader George Davenport — made wealthy from many years of dealing with the Indians, fairly in most respects, but unfailingly to his own advantage. Now, at the land sale, he bought over two thousand acres — land that included all of Saukenuk, including its graveyard and a large portion of its cornfield acreage. Nevertheless, a great deal of the available land went unsold, and so, according to the terms of the 1804 treaty, the Indians still had the right to reside and hunt on these lands. President Andrew Jackson was determined to change that. In his annual message to Congress earlier this month he angrily denounced the presence of *any* Indians within state boundaries as a flagrant violation of that state's rights — a situation, he warned, that would not be tolerated.

To strengthen the United States position in that portion of the Michigan Territory known as southwestern Wisconsin, a new fort was built on the Wisconsin River at the portage that led to the Fox River and ultimately down that waterway to Lake Winnebago and Green Bay and the upper Great Lakes. The new installation was called Fort Winnebago, and the new Indian agent appointed for the bands of Winnebagoes in that area was John H. Kinzie, the son of the trader who had been so instrumental in the foundation and growth of Chicago from a trading post to a young city, who had died there only last year. And accompanying the twenty-six-year-old appointee to his new post was his nineteen-year-old brother, Robert Allen Kinzie, who would be employed as sutler to the fort.

So now it was the end of the Ice Moon, and a deeply pervasive gloom had settled over the Sac Indians under Black Hawk at their traditional Two Rivers hunting camp in Missouri. Not only had hunting been much worse than usual here this season, but scattered throughout this area they had always hunted were now the new cabins of settlers who had moved in — settlers who were sharply suspicious of Indians coming anywhere near their property and who often ordered them away at gunpoint. That alone could have been responsible for the gloom, but it was more than that. Only today a runner had brought word to Black Hawk that, as their agent had warned them would occur, the entire site of Saukenuk, including even the graves of their ancestors, had been sold by the United States government, and that the buyer had been none other than the trader they had so trusted, George Davenport, and that undoubtedly he had made the purchase at least in part with the very money they had paid him last August from their annuities.

In the dimness of his wigwam this bitterly cold night, Black Hawk sat quietly before the central fire, a deep-red blanket draped over him. He stared at the flames for a long while and then lifted his eyes to look at the two Indians who shared the warmth on the other side of the fire — the young Kickapoo war chief, Panoahah, and Black Hawk's own closest friend, Neapope.

"Now, at last," Neapope said, "our eyes are opened to why our trader was so eager for us to leave." He paused and then added bitterly, "Who would have believed that he, of all the whites who have come among us, would be the one who coveted our lands the most?"

"What do we do now, Black Hawk?" asked Panoahah.

"To go back now would almost surely mean war," Neapope pointed out quickly, before Black Hawk could respond, "but I, for one, think we should go back and claim what is rightfully ours."

"We will go back," Black Hawk said slowly, "but not now. In the spring, as we usually do. Then we will go back and see for ourselves what has happened there. We will return to our lodges, if they still stand, and if force is used to remove us from them or remove us from Saukenuk, as it probably will be, then *we* will be forced to retaliate. Many will be killed."

They were silent for a long while, and then Neapope spoke again. "I make this promise to you, Black Hawk. If what you say takes place, then I promise you that with my own hand I will kill all those who are directly to blame for our misfortune — the trader Davenport and the interpreter LeClaire and the one among our own people who has betrayed us with his love for the whites, Keokuk."

Black Hawk looked at Neapope speculatively across the fire and finally shook his head. "You are a good friend, Neapope, and I have no doubt you would do as you say. Perhaps the time may come for that, but not yet. Not yet. The trader Davenport has been my friend for many years, and I have never known him to wrong the Indians in his dealings with them. Before we decide he has become an enemy, we must at least hear what he has to say in his own defense. I'll see him immediately on our return to Saukenuk."

CHAPTER III

[*March 22, 1830 — Monday*]

THERE WAS A HEAVINESS in the steps of Black Hawk as he entered the quarters of George Davenport at Fort Armstrong and took the seat offered him before the trader's fireplace. A biting chill was in the air outside and the warmth of the hearth felt good, yet his expression remained frozen in a scowl as he watched the tall trader take a seat opposite him and cross his legs comfortably, waiting for the Sac to speak.

"These years have come to be bad times," Black Hawk said.

"Aye," Davenport replied, "for many they have. For the Sac and Fox this is especially true. I didn't know whether you would come back this spring or not. I should have known you would."

"It is my home. I was born here. My father is buried here. I cannot turn my back on it."

"No, of course not." The trader raised an eyebrow. "The winter was not good for you, I know. How was it for those of your people who have made the new village on the Iowa River?"

"No better for them. And our women have received bad accounts from the women that have been raising corn at the new village. They complain of the difficulty of breaking new ground with their hoes and the small amount of corn they raised. They fared no better than we."

"Sad," Davenport said with genuine sympathy. "Keokuk did not come back here this spring?"

Black Hawk shook his head. "I asked some of his band to return this spring to our village here, but they would not return with us. I hoped that if he had come with us we might get permission to go to Washington to settle our affairs with our great father. I have just come from visiting Forsyth, and he is displeased because we have returned to Saukenuk. Again he told me what he said that his chief in St. Louis instructed him to tell me — that we *must* remove to the west of the Mississippi. I told him plainly that we would *not!* I told him that we found one of the white settlers continuing, despite our warnings that he stop, to sell liquor to our people, and so I led a party of our young men to his place and broke all his barrels and poured his liquor on the ground, so that no young Sac warrior might get drunk and kill a white in his anger. At this Forsyth was even more angry. He accused my people of being responsible for a settler who was stabbed in several places recently, and would not listen when I told him truthfully that we had heard of this and had determined that it had been done by a Winnebago warrior from the Prophet's village up Rock River. But the anger of Forsyth remained, and he said that on the recommendation of Keokuk he would henceforth be withholding from us the services of the blacksmith appointed for the Sacs here on Rock Island, and further, that he had requested of Clark that three or four hundred militia soldiers be sent up from St. Louis to Rock Island to persuade us to leave Saukenuk. When I heard that, I had nothing more to say to him. From there I went and visited our interpreter, LeClaire, at his house, and he advised me to do as Forsyth directed. Now I have come here."

The trader nodded and tapped the tip of his pipe's mouthpiece against his front teeth. "A long time ago it was the Osage you warred against, and the Otoe. Then, and sometimes now, your tomahawks were raised against the Chippewas and Sioux and sometimes the Winnebago. But as much as you fought against them in the past, and may still fight them in the future, they did not take from you what the Americans have taken from you without the use of bullets and swords."

Black Hawk's gaze scowled. "You are one of those Americans," he pointed out.

Davenport knew that now the Sac was finally getting down to the issue that had brought him here. "Aye, but I would never take from you what was yours to keep, Black Hawk."

"You bought our lands!" There was a sudden sharpness in Black Hawk's voice. "You *knew* they were our lands and yet you bought them. Why have you betrayed us?"

The trader took no offense and merely shook his head. "I didn't betray you. Black Hawk, you and I have been friends for many years, and you must know that I would never do that. Yes, I bought your lands, but if I had not done so, some other person would have — someone you wouldn't even know — and any chance of getting those lands back would be gone. But I have them now, and if our great father will make an exchange with us, I will willingly give up the land I have purchased to the government, which will again give you the right to live there."

Black Hawk considered this and finally grunted in a more satisfied manner.

"That, I think," he said, "is fair of you, and I do not think you have acted badly, as we first thought."

"Is your lodge at Saukenuk still standing?"

"Yes, but it has been damaged by fire. Most of our lodges were burned down this past winter or were severely damaged by fire. We are rebuilding them now and erecting some new ones to take the place of those that were destroyed. And our women are planting corn in some small patches where the whites have not yet taken the ground within their fences. We are working hard to raise something for our children to live on, but it is very difficult."

Davenport sighed, recognizing Black Hawk's ploy for sympathy, but he couldn't blame him. He nodded. "Yes, I know. It is very hard for you and your people, Black Hawk. Consider this, though: according to the treaty, you have no right to remain upon the lands that have been sold, and believe me, the government will force you to leave them. But — and this is important — only a small portion of the ceded lands has been sold, and the balance remains in the hands of the government. There is a belt of land fifty miles wide just to the east of here that is practically unoccupied, which is part of the ceded lands. This is the land you should inhabit — the land you have the best right to occupy."

"We have been talking with our Winnebago friends far up the Rock River, and they have invited us to sink roots among them, but whether or not we do this depends first on other things we must see to." Black Hawk stopped speaking abruptly, as if he had said too much. He came to his feet and looked down at the trader. After a moment he extended his hand, and Davenport accepted it. "Despite what has happened," the Sac said, "you are still our friend. I will not doubt you again."

Davenport rose and walked to the door with the Indian, curious about what he was up to. "What will you do now, Black Hawk? Where will you go?"

"For now my people will remain here, in Saukenuk, while I go on an important mission. I will see you when I return."

Black Hawk left and returned to his lodge in Saukenuk and made preparations. Within twenty-five hours he was on his way to the nearest major British post, Fort Malden, near the mouth of the Detroit River. It was time, he felt, that his British father helped the Sac people, as Sac warriors had so often in the past helped the British.

[*April 4, 1830 — Sunday*]

The huge blacksmith was an extraordinarily powerful man with a dense shock of black hair and a thick black beard. He strode along the shoreline of Big Indian Creek with strong, tireless pace, scarcely slowed by the occasional jumbles of stream-deposited brush heaps or fallen trees. His piercing black eyes constantly swept the landscape ahead, looking for the right place. He didn't know exactly what it would be, but he knew he would recognize it when he saw it.

Several miles behind, he had left his party camped on the riverbank at the place where this small, clear stream called Big Indian Creek flowed into the Fox River.[77] Some of the others had volunteered to accompany him on the journey afoot up the creek, but he had waved them off. He meant to move rapidly and be back as quickly as possible, and anyone who came with him would only slow him down. No one had argued with him, but then William Davis was not a man people argued with very often, even when they disagreed. He had been known to break a man's nose — or arm — for laughing at the wrong time, or questioning a decision the huge man had made.

Now, following the creek past the place where a smaller creek entered and then around a low rise, he paused abruptly, and his eyes glittered.[78] This was the place. Ahead, the creek came through a sort of gap between low hills on both sides. Above this was a meadow that formed a natural basin, its edges against a great grove of fine hardwoods — oaks, hickories, ash, maples — the type of wood that burned best and hottest for smithing. This was where he would settle. This was where he would build the dam he would need for the mill he planned to build. This was the perfect spot.

The creek, he'd been told, was named after the Potawatomies. They had a village right on this creek, about six miles upstream from here. It was not a large village, nor was its chief, Meau-eus, renowned in the tribe except for having a distinct antipathy toward Americans.[79] And, though Davis had been told that there was little possibility the chief might object to the Davis party settling here, it would not be wise to offend him.

Davis was not at all concerned about whether he offended any Indians. Who cared what the Indians thought? Or wanted? They'd all soon be living west of the Mississippi anyway, wouldn't they? If they didn't like the presence of his party here, that was just too bad — they could head west right now.

For another few minutes the big blacksmith stood surveying this land he had chosen, then turned and headed back downstream to get the others, including his wife and seven children, and lead them back here. He was unaware that he had been watched from a screen of brush this whole time by two young Potawatomi braves named Toquamee and Comee.[80] As Davis disappeared from sight downstream to get his party, the pair raced off upstream to warn Chief Meau-eus of this intrusion into their territory.

[April 11, 1830 — Sunday]

No one knew for certain exactly when Ogee's Ferry was established by the Potawatomi-white half-breed named Joseph Ogee, only that some years ago he had built a crude log hut alongside the Rock River and began operating a rope ferry there — a wide, flat-bottomed skiff that could carry people, goods, and even horse carriages across the broad swift surface.[81] Since there were no bridges anywhere along the Rock River's entire course, Indians and whites for scores of miles in all directions had gladly availed themselves of the ferry service. Soon there was a little community there, and even a post office had been established last year. But Ogee, decidedly unambitious, quickly became disenchanted with the amount of work and responsibility entailed in being a ferryman and let it be known that he was willing to sell out. Before long a buyer showed up who was quite pleased to relieve him of the burden. The man who purchased the business was a prematurely gray, forty-six-year-old former New Yorker named John Dixon.

Ten years ago, Dixon had operated a clothing business in New York City, where he had been suffering from a respiratory ailment that just would not clear up. On the advice of his doctor and some friends, he packed up his wife and children, plus his sister and her husband and family, and moved west in the hope that a different climate might help.[82] The large party traveled all the way to the valley of the Sangamon River in the Illinois country before putting down roots — a move that seemed to help, for Dixon's hacking cough cleared up and his chronic chest pains disappeared. Dixon's brother-in-law, Oliver W. Kellogg, became a county constable and was also awarded the mail contract to Lewistown. Dixon, however, was not so fortunate in finding work, and after five years in the Sangamon Valley without finding any job that really held his interest for long, he had moved on with his family to Peoria.

It was that same year, 1825, that Kellogg began opening a carriage road from Peoria to Galena, a project that took him two years. The road went northward from Peoria up the Illinois River to where the river turned eastward, then directly north to Ogee's Ferry and from there northward and then westward to Galena. This coach road, almost 150 miles long and built to facilitate mail delivery and the rapidly increasing traffic to the lead mining district, had become known as Kellogg's Trail even before its completion. In the laying out of it, Oliver Kellogg had also found a home site. So taken was he by a grove of burr oaks some thirty-seven miles north-northwest of Ogee's Ferry that he built his home and outbuildings there and encouraged others to settle in the area. The little community soon came to be known as Kellogg's Grove.[83]

Meanwhile, in Peoria, John Dixon had earned the sobriquet of Father Dixon, not only because his long white hair gave him the appearance of age, but also because of his kindly features, gentle personality, and helpful ways.[84] Everyone loved him, but though he was trying his hand at various county jobs, which included deed recorder, clerk for the county commissioners' court, circuit clerk, and finally justice of the peace, he just wasn't satisfied. At the end of three years he moved again, this time northward up Kellogg's Trail to where the Illinois River turned eastward and where there was a little frontier community called Boyd's Grove.[85] Two rather unrewarding years were spent there until the day when his brother-in-law stopped by and told him that Joe Ogee was offering his Rock River ferry for sale. Dixon somehow knew at once that this was exactly the

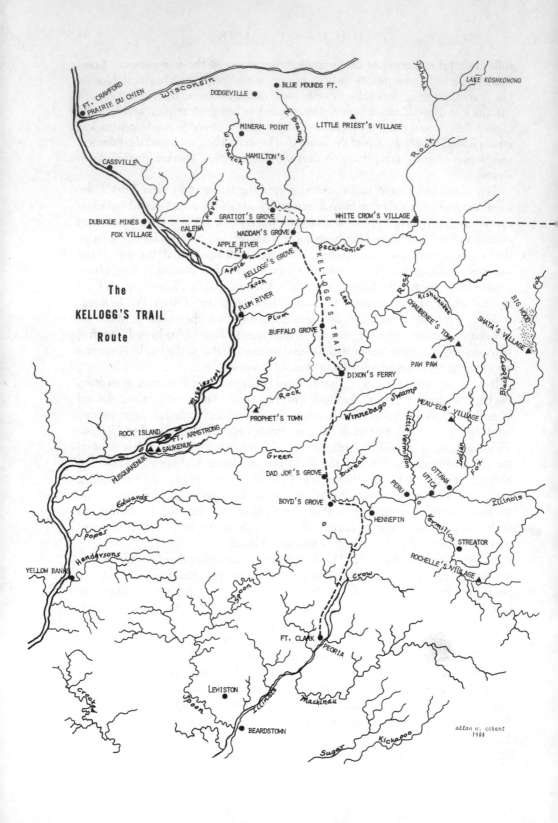

sort of thing he'd been looking for. He promptly bought out Ogee and took over the business. He had moved his family to the community just a few weeks ago, on April 11, and the settlement was immediately renamed Dixon's Ferry.[86]

Having used all his funds for the purchase, Dixon applied for and was appointed to the position of postmaster and received a contract to carry the mail from Peoria to the lead miners in Galena and Gratiot's Grove.[87] As in the other areas where he had lived, Dixon quickly became very popular, not only with his neighbors — about twenty families — but with the Potawatomi, Sac, and Winnebago Indians of the area. The Winnebagoes liked him so much they adopted him into their tribe and named him Nachusa — Long-Hair White. And now, less than a month since the purchase, he was already erecting a building ninety feet long and divided into three sections — a store in which to do business with the whites and trade with the Indians, a hotel for weary travelers, and his family's own living quarters.

John Dixon had at last found his niche on the frontier.

[*May 5, 1830 — Wednesday*]

The three sleek canoes, each with six occupants, had come up the Mississippi from the Fox village just below Dubuque's Mines. Now, with the sun already set and darkness gathering, they coasted in to shore less than half a mile from Prairie du Chien and close to the mouth of the Wisconsin River.

This was the usual camping place for the parties of Sac and Fox that came to attend the peace councils held periodically at Prairie du Chien — a place where they could prepare their evening meal and get a good night's rest before the council began the next day. They were pleased that this particular council had been called, and since the summons had been delivered to them by a runner sent by Forsyth's Fever River subagent, Captain Wynkoop Warner, it was undoubtedly important.

Warner's title of captain was strictly unearned — one that he had bestowed upon himself because he was once in charge of some boats of the American Fur Company's fur brigade. He was not a particularly bright individual, though he had a rather exalted notion of his own capabilities and how far he was going to go. Actually, apart from his very limited duties as subagent in the mining district, he was merely an employee of the company's factor here at Prairie du Chien, Joseph Rolette. But Wynkoop Warner was always on the watch for that big opportunity he knew would come someday, the opportunity to show what he could do and lift him above the less than mediocre level of his existence.

Wynkoop Warner felt he knew the Indians very well; knew them and considered them as something quite less than human and wholly incapable of logical thought. Which was why, when the two Sioux warriors had approached him and mumbled something about wanting peace with their traditional enemies, the Foxes, he suddenly realized that the opportunity he had always hoped for had just fallen into his lap. The Sioux did not know that Warner was wholly without authority to arrange any sort of peace councils on his own, but they read his ambitious nature very well indeed. Immediately upon the subject being broached to him, all Warner could think of was that the Sioux and the Sac and Fox had been at war for a great many years without any real coming to terms between them, and if, on his own, he could arrange a peace council that would forever end that war, it would bring him great renown and perhaps even appointment as Indian agent in his own right. For that matter, he might even win the supervisory position William Clark was still holding. After all, Clark was sixty years old, and sooner or later — hopefully sooner — he would be leaving office.

Thus, with the Dakotah Sioux obviously so sincere in their desire for peace, Warner, suspecting no deviousness in what they proposed and without notifying any other whites, lest they take the credit that would be rightfully his, proceeded exactly as the Sioux wished him to, by sending a runner to the chiefs of the principal Fox village near Dubuque's Mines, where old Chief Pamoske and young Chief Allotah were foremost in authority.[88] The message was a request for them to attend an important peace council at Prairie du Chien. And since only a week before, the Sacs and Foxes had received a letter from Clark suggesting a peace council be held at Prairie du Chien, they thought that this was a part of the same thing. In choosing the Fox village just below Dubuque's Mines, the Sioux had acted very shrewdly. As one of the Fox towns closest to Sioux territory, the village was always in danger of attack from the Sioux, and to negate such a possibility would be to lift a great burden from the shoulders of these Fox Indians.[89] With the invitation to the peace council having come directly from the Sac and Fox agent, the Foxes considered it — as the Sioux had known they would — an official invitation on behalf of the agent at Prairie du Chien, Joseph Street, as a bona fide representative of the United States government. Warner did nothing to clarify that misinterpretation. And when the runner had returned to Warner with word that the invitation had been accepted, and that the Fox peace party would arrive to meet "General" Street at Prairie du Chien early in the morning of the appointed day, the Fever River subagent had been nearly beside himself with exultation. What a coup this would be for him!

Wynkoop Warner sent the runner off immediately to the Sioux to let them know, as they had requested he do, that the Fox had accepted the invitation and exactly when they would arrive at Prairie du Chien. He had no way of knowing that the Indians he considered less than human and essentially stupid had just very neatly duped him. The Sioux quickly sent out runners of their own to the Menominees and Winnebagoes, neither of which had any love for the Foxes. The Sioux were quite well aware of the fact that the party of Foxes coming to the council would not only be traveling with virtually no weapons, as peace council protocol dictated, but that they would, as customary, be stopping at the Sac and Fox traditional camping site just below Prairie du Chien the evening before the council so as to arrive fresh for the meeting on the scheduled morning.

The morning of the day before Warner's scheduled council, a party of some fifty Sioux, having descended the Mississippi in canoes from their village on the west shore of the great river, arrived at a rendezvous point on an island directly across the Mississippi from Prairie du Chien.[90] Shortly after their arrival they were joined by two dozen Menominee warriors and a similar number of Winnebagoes. They were led by a short, powerfully built, fifty-seven-year-old Sioux chief whose sinister aspect was enhanced by the black patch he wore over an eye that had been blinded and severely mutilated in a fight with the Foxes many years ago — for which he had never forgiven them. His name was Wabasha.[91] All the Indians were heavily armed with rifles, tomahawks, war clubs, and scalping knives. They held a brief council to discuss their plans and then spent another hour or so applying war paint to their exposed skin. Then, close to the west shore, they went downstream until out of sight of Prairie du Chien before crossing over to the east side and coming ashore at the traditional Sac-Fox camping site.

The large war party was very careful. None of the canoes was allowed to scrape ashore on the mud and thus leave evidence of its presence. The light craft were picked up in the shallows and carried well into the brush, where they were carefully hidden. All footprints in the shallows or on shore were meticulously obliterated, and the entire party of warriors went into hiding in the undercover within easy gunshot range of the landing place. By mid-afternoon there was no suggestion that anyone was at the camping site.

The afternoon dwindled away, and the sun set behind the limestone bluffs of the west side of the river. When, from far downstream, the three canoe-loads of Fox Indians hove into view, a faint whistle remarkably similar to that of the evening call of the cock robin broke the stillness on shore. It was answered by similar calls in several locations nearby.

In the lead canoe, Chief Pamoske scanned the shoreline carefully, watching for any telltale sign to indicate possible danger. He did not expect any, of course, since this was a peace mission, but one could never be too careful. There was nothing in view to indicate that anyone had been there for some time. Pamoske, who had ordered that Allotah remain at the Dubuque Mines town with the majority of the villagers, had brought, along with his fifteen warriors, his wife, Minnctana, and fourteen-year-old Masheptah, the son of his own son and the captured Winnebago squaw he had taken to wife.[92] Though the knives of the men were in sheaths at their belts or around their necks, the few other weapons they had with them — several rifles, some tomahawks and war clubs — were discreetly stowed away out of sight in the bows of the three canoes, where they would remain.

The canoes scraped ashore, but no one disembarked at first except Pamoske. He walked along the water's edge and studied the mud, then walked farther up on the shore and looked around carefully, but saw nothing suspicious. He moved to the campfire site and placed his hand on the residue of ash and charcoal bits, but it was cold. He nodded and called out a command, and immediately the remainder of the party alighted and drew the canoes well up on shore. Food parcels were brought out of the canoes, and some of the men began spreading out in search of firewood in the gathering darkness.

At that moment a great barrage of shots erupted, accompanied by fearful cries as a horde of nearly one hundred painted warriors burst from cover and attacked. By prearrangement, a handful of the attackers closest to the water raced forward to shove the Fox canoes out into the current so the enemy would have neither access to any weapons nor to escape by boat. One Fox warrior managed to snatch a rifle from a canoe he was near and get off a single shot, which killed one of the charging Sioux. But the goal was accomplished, and the canoes were set adrift while more than half of the Fox warriors fell dead in the first moments of the attack. Those who managed to survive that initial onslaught leaped away as quickly as possible into the brush. The firing of guns fell off rapidly and became sporadic, though the shrieking continued unabated as the attackers tried to intercept the enemy Foxes before they could reach the brush or began following those who were successful in penetrating their line. In the gloom of the now deeply shadowed underbrush hiding became easier, but the attackers knew exactly how many Foxes had arrived, and not until all but one of them had been killed did the search end. The single exception was the fourteen-year-old, Masheptah.

In less than an hour all gunfire had ended, and the bodies of the Foxes were carried into the clearing and dumped there, where a fire had been built. The knives and ornaments of the fallen Foxes were taken and all the dead were scalped, the hair sections then mounted on poles. Pamoske's chest was opened and his heart was removed to be later ceremonially roasted and eaten so that the victors could take unto themselves the strength and courage of their fallen foe. The fingers, toes, ears, noses, genitalia, and occasional whole hands or feet of all the dead were cut off and strung on cord or tied to the scalp poles, to be exhibited during a victory dance tomorrow to the accompaniment of drums and rattles and belled ankles and wrists.

Young Masheptah, certain that he was to be slain at any moment, stood trembling to one side, under guard and cradling an arm broken by the blow of a war club, his quavering voice raised in the Fox death song. One of the Fox canoes that had wedged in shoreline brush a short way downstream was retrieved and the goods taken from it. Masheptah was placed in it with a single paddle and told to go home and tell his people that what he saw here was in store for all Foxes and Sacs. The canoe was pushed away from the shore and rapidly swallowed up in the darkness.

The excitement of the attackers was abruptly contained, and they moved about in a much more subdued manner as they put out guards and began setting up their own camp for the night. There would be a great celebration for this victory, but not until tomorrow morning, when, with all their grisly trophies on display, they would enter Prairie du Chien and dance in wild triumph before the town's six hundred or so residents.

[*July 26, 1830 — Monday*]

The superintendent of Indian affairs at St. Louis, William Clark, sighed as he dipped his goose quill into the inkpot preparatory to writing more, then left the quill standing upright in the pot as he leaned back and rubbed the heels of his hands into both eyes. The letter to his superior in the War Department, Thomas McKenney, head of the Bureau of Indian Affairs, could wait.[93] He wished he could take a little nap, but there just wasn't time. The thought flitted across his mind that he was really beginning to feel his age these days, because no matter how many hours of sleep he was able to get, it never seemed to be enough. And truth be known, at times of crisis such as these past few weeks had been — ever since the Dakotah Sioux attack on the Foxes at Prairie du Chien — he was rarely able to sleep more than four or five hours at a time.

That damned nincompoop, Wynkoop Warner! What a hornet's nest he had stirred up. How grand that he would no longer have to deal with such a stupid, shortsighted man. And now that he had explained the whole idiotic affair to McKenney, he was sure his superior would hold no brief about the peremptory discharging of Warner from further duties in the Indian Department.

Immediately following that terrible incident almost in the shadow of Prairie du Chien, the Dakotahs continued to hover close to the Fox village in the vicinity of Dubuque's Mines, and Allotah's people were extremely fearful for their lives, expecting an overwhelming invasion by those Sioux at any moment. For the first time in many years, the Foxes appealed to the Sacs to help them in this emergency. Had Black Hawk been on hand, there could be no doubt he would have led an immediate retaliatory expedition against the Dakotah Sioux, but he was on his way to visit the British at Malden, and the Sacs remaining were hesitant, despite the provocation, to mount a force to attack them. Neapope did go at once to the Dubuque's Mines village with two hundred warriors and evacuated the remaining Fox populace, establishing them in a temporary site on the Iowa side of the river directly opposite Fort Armstrong. Sac and Fox met in council, and when War Chief Keokuk refused to take a command position in this affair, the Fox chief named Katice was given that rank on a temporary basis.[94]

Katice had immediately raised a force of five hundred warriors — as did the Sioux — and the two Indian forces were suddenly teetering on the brink of attacking one another. That might well have occurred, except for the frenzied intervention of the Indian agents at Fort Armstrong and Fort Snelling —Thomas Forsyth and Lawrence Taliaferro — who did everything in their power to keep an all-out Indian war from bursting forth. They knew only too well that if such a thing occurred, it would spill over to involve all whites on the frontier and the possible loss of the very country the United States had been gradually acquiring. There was only one way this could be avoided — by the United States' shouldering the responsibility of "covering the dead" — and Clark had authorized their proceeding in this vein while he had urgently communicated with McKenney to get the government to underwrite what he was proposing. The two agents were able to persuade Katice on the one side and Wabasha on the other to hold off marching to war while the Americans made every effort to cover the dead.

Throughout all the tribes of the northwest, "covering the dead" was the only means of preventing immediate and deadly retaliation for the killing of any members of an individual tribe. What it meant was that the relatives of the person or persons who had been killed had to be appeased by a payment in the form of horses, gunpowder, traps, staple goods, weapons, blankets, or actual cash money in such amount so as to mollify their injured feelings and thus "cover" the dead. Even the chiefs of a tribe did not have the power to prevent offended relatives from taking to the warpath if their dead remained uncovered. The attack by the Dakotah Sioux and the death of seventeen members of the tribe, including a chief as important as Pamoske, demanded a substantial covering to mitigate the deed and ward off retaliation. And though at first this current problem seemed insurmountable, Clark soon came to the conclusion that the United States government could turn the affair to its own advantage by taking an immediate initiative.

Clark's proposal was that the United States hold a treaty council with the tribes involved, in which the government would cover the dead on all sides. This would, he believed, eliminate the primary motivation for warfare. It would be expensive, Clark had pointed out to McKenney, but far less expensive than would be the military intervention necessary to quell a general Indian war. Besides, Clark pointed out, what had occurred could be traced to the failure of the United States to clearly fix boundaries in past treaties — not only boundaries between the tribes and the United States, but boundaries between the tribes themselves, which it had obligated itself to establish in the Treaty of 1825. If the tribes were reluctant to come to such terms, Clark advocated that the United States threaten them with military invasion as the result of refusal.

It had been a bold step and it had worked, but just barely. Clark had received the authorization he requested, and Forsyth and Taliaferro had managed to persuade Katice to hold off attacking the Dakotah Sioux while a delegation of 213 Indians of both tribes, after meeting at Fort Armstrong, visited Clark in St. Louis. In view of what had occurred, the Sac absolutely refused to meet for the other peace council that Clark had proposed at Prairie du Chien. Keokuk, who was acting spokesman for the two tribes, stated the Sac and Fox position eloquently to Clark.

"We cannot do that on land where the blood of our people has not even dried." He paused for a long, uncomfortable while and then went on gravely. "When our people are killed in war, our hearts are not grieved, but when they are killed while trying to do a good act — while trying to make peace and when obeying the words of the agent — it makes us feel bad. It was the death of Pamoske, first chief of the Fox tribe, that made both our nations [Sac and Fox] very angry. He always advised peace. Yet, he was killed. They took out his heart to add to their strength, and they put a hook in his mouth and a rope around his neck.[95] He was sent for by General Street to meet the Menominees, the Sioux, and the Winnebagoes, and was killed on his way up. My father, we always take notice of your words and our great father's [Clark's] words. Twelve days after we received a letter from you advising peace and a meeting at Prairie du Chien, our people were killed. Now we do not wish to go to Prairie du Chien. We wish to meet you at Rock Island. Our reason is that we do not want to see Chief Pamoske's grave. . . . I cannot shake hands with the Sioux and Menominees until we are paid for covering our dead." Keokuk had shaken his head and paused again, trying to find the words to make Clark understand how the Sac and Fox felt about this whole affair. He went on, "If *your* great father were to send for you and you obeyed his words by going where he directed, and you were killed on the way when not expecting mischief, he would feel sorry for you and take revenge for your death. So we now feel. Our chief was sent for and killed when thus obeying the instructions of the agent."

In answer to the Indian superintendent's urgent request that the government move swiftly to cover the dead, McKenney had authorized Clark to pay the Sacs up to five thousand dollars. Always the negotiator, however, Clark had the feeling they might settle for much less than that, and he was correct. He had been greatly relieved when he was able to mollify them with one thousand dollars for their loss. As a matter of fact, after the Indians were paid, their visit had become so amicable that Clark even suggested once again, as he had on numerous past occasions, that they sell to the United States that part of their country west of the Mississippi in the area of Dubuque's Mines, for which they would receive in payment an annuity sufficiently large to allow them to move westward well away from the Mississippi, and which would provide the whole tribe with all the financial support it needed. He suggested they discuss this further at a peace treaty council in Prairie du Chien in July, but that was pushing it too far, and Keokuk reiterated what he had said earlier: "To do so, we would feel that we were walking over the graves of our dead relatives to shake hands with our enemies. We cannot do that."

But Clark knew the tribe very well, and he was heartened by the absence of Black Hawk and his British Band. With the volatile Sac and his followers temporarily gone, the Indian outbreak everyone had forecast to occur this summer might be delayed yet another year. And though he said nothing more about it at that moment, Clark felt quite sure he could persuade the Sac and Fox to attend his proposed Prairie du Chien peace meeting in July. Nor had he told them that on May 28, just over three weeks after the Sioux attack on the Foxes, President Andrew Jackson had signed the long-awaited Indian Removal Act — an act of Congress that permitted appropriation of half a million dollars for the purpose of removing the Sacs and Foxes from any land they were residing on in any state or territory — in essence, allowing for the forcible exchange of Indian lands east of the Mississippi for lands that were west of the Mississippi, that were unsuitable for white habitation, and that were not presently part of any state or territory.[96]

The fact of the Indian Removal Act had not stopped Clark from going ahead with his plans for the Prairie du Chien council. Now he smiled wearily as he picked up his pen again, shook ink from the nib, and continued writing his report to Thomas McKenney. He explained how, early this month, he had ascended the river and stopped at all the Sac and Fox villages en route, haranguing them as forcefully as he could to accompany him to Prairie du Chien for the peace council. What changed their minds more than anything else was the strong stand he took against a determined group of whites. These were miners who had been on the east side of the Mississippi until they heard about the evacuation of the Dubuque's Mines village by Allotah's people. Almost immediately the whites had crossed the river and occupied the lead mines first developed by Julien Dubuque and then carried on after his death by the Foxes themselves. At the request of the Sacs and Foxes, Clark ordered the whites back to the east side of the Mississippi and warned them that if they tried one more time to squat on the Indian property west of the river, he would have them locked up permanently in the detention building at Jefferson Barracks. They believed him and left. With that, Allotah and Keokuk and their followers had been among the first to fall in line, and then the others had quickly done the same. The upshot was that by the time he reached Prairie du Chien he had some seventy Sac and Fox Indians in tow, and they found as many more Menominees, Dakotah Sioux, Chippewas, Winnebagoes, and Potawatomies awaiting them there.

Had it not all been so deadly serious a business, Clark informed McKenney, one might have enjoyed the color and pageantry, the drama, and even the humor of the situation of the enemy tribes confronting one another on that bright warm morning of July 8. The Potawatomies, Menominees, and Chippewas were clad in their finest raiment and accoutred with spears and bows, tomahawks and clubs and guns — all of which they displayed with great show at first, then ceremoniously laid aside as the time for the talks approached.

The Sioux and Winnebagoes displayed no weapons at all, but the Sioux wore flamboyant fur headdresses made of skunk pelts, symbolizing that they neither feared nor ever ran away from any enemy. And the Sacs and Foxes, in the boats behind, were a rather frightening parade as they broke into war chants and stood upright in the boats, paddling back and forth cautiously a few yards from the shoreline several times before coming in for a landing. Their scalp locks were dyed red, cut and groomed to stand erect like the fearsome crest made famous many years ago by the Mohawks. Except for the crests, the warriors had shaved and painted their heads, and long tufts of red-dyed horsehair depended from their elbows and armpits. Necklaces of downward-curved bear claws encircled their throats, and the only garb of most was a buckskin breechclout, leggins, and moccasins. A fair number of the warriors carried small drums, which they beat in cadence upon stepping ashore from their boats, blending into a rhythm with one another, to which the feet of the nondrummers immediately began moving in concert. In their hands they carried spears and knives, clubs and tomahawks and guns, and for a few minutes after landing they brandished them as if ready to do battle. But then, as their opponents had done, they put the weapons aside.

The treaty negotiations took nine full days and were exhausting, but, when completed, had brought peace between tribes that had not had true peace existing between them for scores of years. What it amounted to was the United States buying a strip of land twenty miles wide on the nebulous border of the Sioux territory from the Sac and Fox, and buying a similar strip from the Sioux on the border of the Sac and Fox territory. This then created a forty-mile-wide strip of land that belonged to the United States, not to any tribe. This strip, Clark informed them, was hereafter neutral ground, upon which members of the opposing tribes could enter to hunt or fish unmolested. The finally negotiated purchase price gave the Sac and Fox an annuity of $6,500 for the next ten years.

Clark chuckled to himself as he recalled what had happened next. It seemed an appropriate time to try once again to buy the Iowa mineral lands rights from them, but now all at once the Sac and Fox became very cagey, as if for the first time beginning to realize just how valuable that land was. The tribes owed the American Fur Company — represented here by traders Russell Farnham and George Davenport — a total of $40,000 in back debts, and the Indians suggested that if the government paid this debt, plus giving them an annual payment of $32,000 for half a century, plus keeping them well provided with salt and tobacco, they *might* consider the transaction. There was no possibility of Clark guaranteeing this, so that portion of the negotiations came quickly to a dead end.[97]

Thus, Clark wrote in concluding his report to McKenney, the situation in the Indian territory was better now than it had been for some time, but that was partly because Black Hawk was still away from the tribe with his rebellious faction, and the Sacs and Foxes had no idea yet of the significance of the passage of the Indian Removal Act.

[*October 7, 1830 — Thursday*]

Felix St. Vrain, at age thirty-one, was tall and slender, with a shock of curly black hair and an easy smile. An affable, sympathetic man who had been born in St. Louis to a French family that was once very powerful in the government of France, he hardly considered himself any sort of candidate for an appointment in the United States Indian Department.[98] Yet here he was, a man with almost no knowledge of the Indians, appointed to the position of Indian agent to the Sac and Fox tribes, replacing a highly experienced man he had never even met, Thomas Forsyth, who, rumor had it, was fired by William Clark for dereliction of duties. His own appointment, St. Vrain knew, was what came of knowing someone who knew someone.

The St. Vrain family, despite having been ostracized from France during the Reign of Terror, still had powerful connections, and when the Louisiana Territory became part of the United States, certain members of the family had been appointed to governmental positions. Felix's brother, Ceran, had no desire to be connected with the government and instead became a well-known and highly respected trader to the Indians well up the Missouri River. Felix, whose ambitions, political or otherwise, were relatively undefined, had moved into the Illinois country and settled there with his wife, Marie.[99] For a while, in Kaskaskia, he had served as quartermaster of the Second Regiment, Illinois Militia, and later, a Randolph County commissioner and public administrator. He was still aimlessly drifting when he became a county-employed steam sawmill operator in Peoria. But among his circle of family friends was United States senator Elias Kent Kane, who was also a close friend of the Indian superintendent at St. Louis, William Clark.

For the past couple of years, Clark had grown increasingly exasperated with the incipient unreliability of Thomas Forsyth. The man had an excellent background of Indian knowledge, but to Clark it seemed that whenever he wanted Forsyth, the agent was off somewhere else, and all too often on his own business. Long ago, despite Clark's orders that he refrain from doing so, Forsyth had taken to leaving his post at the agency on Rock Island and spending most of the winter in comfortable quarters in St. Louis, which put him no closer to the pulse of Indian affairs up the Mississippi than was Clark himself. After the near-disastrous events between the Sioux and the Sac and Fox, which the Indian superintendent had felt would not have occurred had Forsyth been more available to his Indian charges, Clark had become convinced that Forsyth was more a liability to the Indian Department than an asset.[100]

The discharging of Forsyth had left open the position of Indian agent, and when Clark's friend Senator Kane suggested his own friend for the job, Clark passed along the recommendation of Felix St. Vrain to his superior, Thomas McKenney, in the Indian Bureau of the War Department. That recommendation was accepted and the appointment made, so now St. Vrain, wholly inexperienced in the matter of Indian affairs, was the new agent to the Sacs and Foxes.

Having assumed his duties at Fort Armstrong on Rock Island, St. Vrain was almost immediately besieged by complaints from whites and Indians alike, each accusing the other of various outrages. But while inexperienced at dealing with Indians, St. Vrain was not a stupid man, nor an unsympathetic one. He immediately resolved to himself that he would not, as his predecessor had, try to threaten the Indians into compliance, because, obviously, when the Indians didn't comply, the threats proved to be empty and the strength and integrity of the Indian agency was proportionately diminished. So far as Felix St. Vrain was concerned, that was not going to happen again. But the new Indian agent was also aware that he had been placed in a position that would become increasingly untenable.

St. Vrain knew, for example, that there were only two reasons why no serious eruption of trouble had occurred between the Americans and the Sac and Fox this year. First, because for most of the summer Black Hawk and his bellicose band had been away visiting their British friends at Malden and looking for support from them. Second, there had been the outbreak of trouble between the tribes, and that had overshadowed everything else. But what about next year? St. Vrain could only envision severe problems coming, and he was already getting a foretaste of it.

There was no problem with Keokuk and his band, since for the most part they were staying west of the Mississippi, as recommended by the agency. But now Black Hawk and his people had returned to the Rock River area, surly at having been refused support of any kind from his former British allies and irate at finding Saukenuk almost entirely occupied by whites. Aware that by the terms of the 1804 treaty, he and his people had every right to live and hunt on the ceded land still owned by the government, Black Hawk was shrewd enough not to attempt to openly occupy Saukenuk again, but stayed farther upstream on the Rock River, on unoccupied government lands. Under cover of darkness the Indians came in and methodically destroyed virtually the entire crop of corn planted by the whites in the former Sac cornfields, and though everyone knew it was Black Hawk's band that was guilty of the depredation, there was no proof and nothing St. Vrain could do.

The new Indian agent felt very helpless, and had he been more experienced in dealing as an intermediary between the Indians and the Americans, he might have thrown up his hands in despair. Instead, his very lack of knowledge and experience made him all the more determined to exert himself to the utmost to aid both the Indians and the whites to the best of his ability and in as impartial a manner as possible. In this respect it was quite likely that the appointment of Felix St. Vrain as agent to the Sac and Fox was the best thing that could have happened for both sides.

[December 31, 1830 — Friday]

As surely as if no tensions of any sort existed on the Mississippi River Valley frontiers of America, growth and development continued unabated. A slow but steady influx of settlers trickled into the land and settled as new landowners or squatters wherever it most suited their fancy, despite whatever frictions this might inspire among the native inhabitants.

The Sac and Fox, along with other tribes still to some extent occupying the Illinois country, had yearned for the time when the great father of Illinois — Ninian Edwards — would leave his office, as they were assured would someday occur. They may or may not have been aware of the old saw about being careful what you wish for, since your wish might come true. In this case it did. The Illinois elections were held, and the openly Indian-disliking Governor Edwards was, after a four-year term of office, bested in the gubernatorial race by the St. Clair County representative John Reynolds. It was, the Indians quickly learned, no cause for rejoicing.

Ninian Edwards may have disliked the Indians, but he was a man of a raised degree of breeding and culture who was keenly attuned to the problems of his state's frontiers. Reynolds, on the other hand, who had spent his entire life on the frontier and was a previous resident of Tennessee, was a generally tricky man always on the alert to take advantage of any situation that presented itself. Of Irish heritage, he was a hot-tempered individual who had served as a ranger in the War of 1812, who was strongly in favor of slavery, and who was also very openly an avowed hater of Indians, considering all red men incapable of being civilized, and those living in the State of Illinois a particular pain in the neck. He was always open to the complaints of any whites against the Indians — complaints of destruction of property, theft, trespassing, and even rape and murder, no matter how outlandish or unjustified — but nearly always had a totally deaf ear for any complaints by the Indians against the whites. Almost immediately after his election, he appealed to the General Assembly for the authority to call out the militia and use force to oust from the state all Indians still remaining within its boundaries. Obviously, in view of the federal treaties still in effect, this could not be done and his appeal was rejected, but it left no question in anyone's mind, red or white, in which direction Reynolds's sympathies lay.

Chicago, which had been growing very rapidly since Lake Michigan was being connected to the Illinois River and Mississippi River system by the long-dreamed-of Illinois and Michigan Canal, now had its first bridge over the Chicago River, a permanent population of over one hundred, and had only recently been platted into lots and received its first legal geographic location as a town. [101]

As part of the insidious encroachment of civilization into the frontier from a burgeoning United States population of 13 million, a military road was quietly laid out along the Wisconsin River all the way upstream from Prairie du Chien to the portage that connected to the upper Fox River. [102] Another road of even greater significance was simultaneously being carved by a wagon train into the western wilderness from the Missouri River to the Rocky Mountains — a wagon train that closely involved a trio of men whose names were essentially unknown to anyone beyond the frontier — William "Bill" Sublette, Jedediah Strong Smith, and James "Jim" Bridger — men who were rapidly coming to epitomize a new breed of rugged western frontiersmen, the mountain man.

The frontier, which had for so long been almost stationary in the Illinois country, was now spreading westward with an increasing momentum that was no longer even slowed by what was once felt to be a barrier it could never overcome — the Mississippi River. Fearful of such growth and envisioning what appeared to be in store for the future, Mexican legislators passed a law forbidding any further colonization of its Texas territory by United States citizens. But, like so many acts meant to thwart the young country's growth, it was too little and much too late.

The United States was clearly unstoppable in its major move west.

[*May 26, 1831 — Saturday*]

The frustrating Indian situation in the Rock River Valley of Illinois finally began coming to a head as soon as the Sacs under Black Hawk returned from their fall and winter hunting and trapping activities. Everyone had predicted it. Now it was time for armed retaliation on the infernal red man. Certainly, the residents of Illinois agreed, provocation enough had been there. How many more outrages must United States citizens endure before their government would act? Black Hawk's band had to be stopped. Soon. All the settlers had been waiting, almost holding their breaths for word that the government had finally made its move against the Indians. Then Black Hawk had returned, the depredations had begun again, and still no relief was in sight.

It was in early spring that Black Hawk, though not officially a chief except by self-proclamation, contested Keokuk's power in the tribe, and though there had been no clear winner, there could be no doubt that he had enhanced his own position and reduced that of Keokuk. And from what Governor John Reynolds could deduce from his spies, it all stemmed from Black Hawk's principal lieutenant, Neapope, visiting Wabokieshiek at the Prophet's Town.

Wabokieshiek had just had his own first confrontation with some whites. Two Illinois settlers, Hiram Sanders and Ammyson Chapman, had become aware of John Dixon's success with his ferry far up the Rock River and were convinced they could cash in on that success by establishing a ferry of their own between Dixon's and the mouth of Rock River. They had set about doing so, but were not very circumspect about the location they chose or the way they did it. Just outside the Prophet's Town, the two whites had taken over the lodge of a Winnebago who was absent, moved in some goods of their own, and begun setting up their ferry virtually on the doorstep. Naturally, this news was carried to Wabokieshiek at once, and within hours he sent them word by the same messengers to leave while they could do so peaceably, because if they didn't, he would forcibly eject them. When the whites refused, Wabokieshiek had soon arrived in person with a group of warriors. He then again told the pair to leave peacefully while they could, this time backing up his words by having his braves throw out the furniture that the whites had brought into the lodge. This time Sanders and Chapman took the hint and left, but were furious at the treatment they had received at the hands of the Prophet and vowed darkly that they'd make him rue the day.

Neapope, after having politely listened to Wabokieshiek's story, spoke on

Black Hawk's behest, asking the Prophet what he could see in the future should Black Hawk take up the hatchet actively against the whites occupying his former village site at Saukenuk. Wabokieshiek bade Neapope to sit before him and then, after smoking a pipe and murmuring a string of unintelligible incantations, scattered the contents of his medicine bag on the soft buckskin he had spread out before himself. For long moments he had studied the jumble of feathers, bits of bone and antler, quartz crystals, waterworn pebbles, and other items that had spilled from his pouch, and then he had smiled and addressed Neapope.

"Tell Black Hawk," he said in a pleased voice, "that I see nothing but good fortune in store for him and his followers. The whites greatly fear him, and if he will take up the hatchet against them, he will have the Great Spirit on his side, and not only will those who are faithful to him fall into place behind him, many others who have said they would not help, now will. He will easily vanquish his foes in this country and restore to his people the lands they have lost."

Neapope had immediately rushed back to Black Hawk with this good news, and that was when Black Hawk had defiantly marched into Keokuk's village on the Iowa River and disputed Keokuk's peaceful stance. He spoke to his tribesmen with great force, stirring them to a considerable pitch of excitement and reimbuing them with a sense of nationality that had long been eroding away. Many of Keokuk's people had deserted him at that juncture and threw their weight behind Black Hawk, increasing his strength and prestige in the tribe.

In an effort to thwart his rival, Keokuk also addressed the assemblage, seemingly backing up Black Hawk at first but actually trying to undercut him with rhetoric. "If this is what you wish," Keokuk had cried, "then I, as your war chief, will lead you into battle against the Americans." There were great cheers at that, and he waited until they died away before going on. "But before we move against them," he added, "I implore you to do one thing that will ease the pain you will surely face later if you do not. I direct you now, kill your children, your wives, your parents, your grandparents. Destroy all those who cannot fight beside you, so they might die quickly and mercifully at your hands, and so that later you need not watch their suffering as the whites kill them little by little, reveling as they will in their screams for mercy. Kill them! Do that, and I promise you I will personally lead you into battle against the whites — and I assure you, it will be our final battle!"

The speech gave them pause, and many who had raised their voices only moments before in favor of Black Hawk, now swung back again to the pacifism Keokuk always advocated. Nevertheless, Black Hawk left the Iowa River Valley with more strength by far than when he had arrived, and he returned at once to the site of Saukenuk, where forty white families were now living. It was shortly after that when the white residents in the area begged Governor Reynolds for help. Their petition minced no words.[103]

April 30, 1831

His Excellency, the Governor of
the State of Illinois —

We, the undersigned, being citizens of Rock River and its vicinity, beg leave to
state to Your Honor the grievances we labor under, and pray your protection
against the Sac and Fox tribe of Indians, who have again taken possession of our
lands near the mouth of Rock River and its vicinity. They have, and now are
burning our fences, destroying our crops of wheat now growing by turning in [to
the cornfields] *all their horses. They also threaten our lives if we attempt to plant*
corn and say they will cut it up and that we have stolen their lands from them and
they are determined to exterminate us provided we don't leave the country without
[delay]. *Your honor no doubt is aware of the outrageous* [acts] *that were commit-*
ted by said Indians here before, particularly last fall. They almost destroyed all
our crops and made several attempts on the owners' lives when they attempted to
prevent their depredations, and actually wounded one man by stabbing him in
several places. [104] *This spring they act in a much more outrageous and menacing*
manner, so that now we consider ourselves compelled to beg of you protection
which the agent and garrison on Rock Island refuse to give, inasmuch as they say
they have no orders from [the] *government. Therefore, should we not receive*
immediate aid from Your Honor, we shall be compelled to abandon our settlement
and the lands we have purchased of the government. [105] *Therefore, we have no*
doubt but [that] *Your Honor better anticipate our condition than it is represented*
and grant us immediate relief in that manner that to you seems most likely to
produce the desired effect. The number of Indians now among us are about six or
seven hundred. They say there are more coming and that the Potawatomies and
some of the Winnebagoes will help them in case of an eruption with the whites.
The warriors now here are the Black Hawk's party with other chiefs, the names of
which we are not acquainted with. Therefore, looking to you for protection, we beg
leave ever to remain yours, &c.

The petition was signed by thirty-eight white residents of the Saukenuk area. [106]
As soon as he received it, Governor Reynolds himself had requested intervention
by regular army forces of the United States on behalf of the residents, but this was
refused because there were no orders from the secretary of war to this end. When
Reynolds threatened to call up the Illinois Militia and send it in, he was gravely
warned by Captain John Bliss, the commander of Fort Armstrong, not to attempt
to do such a thing without the consent and cooperation of William Clark as well
as the commanding general of the Western Department of the United States
Army, General Edmund P. Gaines. Reynolds immediately wrote to Clark and
Gaines and waited for a response from them.

In the meanwhile, the Rock River settlers Hiram Sanders and Ammyson
Chapman, making good on their threat to cause problems for Wabokieshiek, had

given a deposition to a justice of the peace that was now delivered to John Reynolds. The governor's expression turned sour as he read it quickly:

State of Illinois, Fulton County

Personally appeared before me, Stephen Dewey, an acting Justice of the Peace in and for said County of Fulton, and State of Illinois, Hiram Sanders and Ammyson Chapman of the aforesaid county and state, and made oath that some time in the month of April last, they went to the old Indian Sac town, about thirty miles up Rock River, for the purpose of farming and establishing a ferry across said river, and the Indians ordered us to move away, and not to come there again, and we remained there a few hours.

They then sent for their chief, and he informed us that we might depart peaceably, and that if we did not, he would make us go.

He therefore ordered the Indians to throw our furniture out of the house; they accordingly did so; and threatened to kill us if we did not depart. We therefore discovered that our lives were in danger, and consequently moved back again to the above county.

We supposed them to be principally Winnebagoes.

H. Sanders
A. Chapman

Sworn and subscribed this 11th day of May, 1831

Stephen Dewey, J.P.

Angry as he was over the way his constituents were being treated, Reynolds nevertheless continued to hold off any action against the Indians while he awaited a reply from William Clark. It had been during that interval that the governor received another petition from the settlers at Saukenuk. It had been carried to him by a special courier, Benjamin F. Pike, who was himself a three-year resident of the Saukenuk area and well respected by his neighbors. This one was more desperate than the first, wondering, in addition, if they had been abandoned to their fate by the governor. Furious at the position in which he was being placed, Reynolds was now goaded beyond restraint and decided to wait no longer. He issued an immediate mobilization call for seven hundred Illinois militiamen, mounted, to rendezvous at Beardstown, Illinois, on June 10. Then he wrote strong letters to General Edmund P. Gaines at Jefferson Barracks and William Clark at St. Louis. The letter to Clark was very blunt:

Belleville, 26th May, 1831

Sir — In order to protect the citizens of this State, who reside near Rock River, from Indian invasion and depredations, I have considered it necessary to call out a force of militia on this State of about seven hundred strong, to remove a band of Indians who are now about Rock Island. The object of the government of the State is to protect those citizens, by removing said Indians, peaceably, if they can, but forcibly if they must. Those Indians are now, and so I have considered them, in a state of actual invasion of the State.

As you act as the public agent of the United States in relation to those Indians, I considered it my duty to inform you of the above call on the militia, and that in about fifteen days a sufficient force will appear before said Indians to remove them, dead or alive, over to the west side of the Mississippi; but to save all this disagreeable business, perhaps a request from you to them, for them to remove to the west side of the river, would effect the object of procuring peace to the citizens of the State. There is no disposition on the part of the people of this State to injure those unfortunate and deluded savages if they will let us alone; but a government that does not protect its citizens deserves not the name of a government. Please correspond with me to this place on this subject.

Your obedient servant,
John Reynolds

Gen. Clark, Supt., etc.

[*May 30, 1831 — Tuesday*]

At fifty-four, Edmund Pendleton Gaines could very advantageously have posed for a portrait of what a general of the United States Army should look like. He was slightly taller than medium height, with strong, chiseled features beneath a slightly receding hairline. His eyes were a steady, warm gray that could, under provocation, become the cold color of pewter. His demeanor was one of quiet strength, and after thirty years of military service, he was quite capable of taking virtually any crisis in stride.[107] That included the present situation as it had been laid out to him in letters from William Clark in St. Louis and Governor Reynolds in Belleville, Illinois.

Reynolds's letter, written two days before, had reached him early yesterday, as had a letter from Clark, who enclosed the letter he also had received from Reynolds. The governor's letter to Gaines was brief and very direct:

Belleville 28th. May 1831

General Gaines

Sir, I have received undoubted information that the section of this State near Rock Island is actually invaded by a hostile band of the Sack [sic] Indians, headed by the Black Hawk. And in order to repel said invasion, and to protect the citizens of the State, I have, under the provisions of the constitution of the United States, and the laws of this State, called on the militia to the number of seven hundred men, who will be mounted and ready for service in a very short time.

I consider it my duty to lay before you the above information so you, com-

manding the military forces of the United States in this part of the Union, may adopt such measures in regard to said Indians, as you deem right.

The above mounted volunteers (because such they will be) will be in readiness immediately to move against said Indians. And I, as the Executive of the State of Illinois, respectfully solicit your co-operation in this business.

Pleas [sic] honor me with an answer to this letter.

With Sincere respect for your Character, I am your obt. Servt.

John Reynolds

Gaines had long been opposed to the Indian removal program as it was presently being handled, but his duty lay in maintaining the peace and protecting the lives and property of United States citizens. While he had no doubt that Governor Reynolds believed in the rightness of his actions in response to the petitions of the citizens, Gaines was not convinced that those documents had presented a true picture of what was occurring in the Rock River Valley. The last thing he wanted to see right now was the outbreak of a general Indian war due to the rash acts of an essentially undisciplined and largely irresponsible mob acting under the mantle of militia. Immediately Gaines had replied:

Hd. Qrs. Western Department
29 May 1831

His Excellency Governor Reynolds

Sir — I do myself the honor to acknowledge the receipt of your letter of yesterday's date, advising me of your having received undoubted information that the section of the frontier of your state near Rock Island is invaded by a hostile band of Sauk Indians, headed by the chief called the Black Hawk; that in order to repel said invasion and protect the citizens of the state, you have called on the militia to the number of seven hundred mounted men, to be in readiness immediately to move against the Indians, and that you solicit my cooperation.

In reply, it is my duty to state to you that I have ordered six companies of the regular troops stationed at Jefferson Barracks to embark tomorrow morning and repair forthwith to the spot occupied by the hostile Sauks. To this detachment I shall, if necessary, add four companies from Prairie du Chien, making a total of ten companies.[108] With this force I am satisfied that I shall be able to repel the invasion and give security to the frontier inhabitants of the state. But should the hostile bands be sustained by the residue of the Sauk, Fox or other Indians, to an extent requiring an augmentation of my force, I will in that event communicate with your Excellency by Express and avail myself of the cooperation which you have proposed. But under existing circumstances and the present aspect of our Indian relation on the Rock Island section of the frontier, I do not deem it necessary or proper to require militia — or any description of force — other than that of the Regular Army at this place and Prairie du Chien.

> *I have the honor to be, very respectfully,*
> *Your obd Servt*
> *Edmund P. Gaines*
> *Major Gen by Brevet, Commanding*

Later in the day Gaines became concerned that, despite the letter he had written to the Illinois governor, Reynolds might act rashly. It was a reasonable concern, considering the fact that Reynolds had a reputation for acting rather precipitately at times. The general therefore prepared to make the short journey to Belleville personally and speak with Reynolds at length; but Reynolds surprisingly showed up himself at Jefferson Barracks headquarters, and the two men conferred together well into the night. Gaines assured the governor that he would, within a week, inform Reynolds by express of what was occurring at Rock River. Grudgingly acquiescing to be led by what General Gaines proposed, Reynolds had then gone on to St. Louis to discuss the same matter with Clark.

Now, with the hubbub of preparations clearly audible from outside, Gaines signed with a flourish the letter he had just completed to Adjutant General Roger Jones in Washington:

> *Hd. Qrs. Western Department*
> *30 May 1831*

Sir:

I have the honor to report, for the information of the proper authorities, that the Sauk Indians, settled near Rock Island on the Illinois side of the Mississippi River, called the "British Band of Sauks" headed by the Black Hawk and for some years past extremely restless and insolent, have recently become disorderly and, as I learn from the Governor of the State of Illinois, have assumed the attitude of open hostility and, as he conceives, have actually invaded the border of the state — whereupon he has ordered seven hundred mounted militia to be in readiness immediately to march against those Indians. See the enclosed copy of Governor Reynolds' letter, marked A.

I yesterday had a conference with the Governor, which resulted in an understanding that I should make an effort to repel the supposed invasion, and to remove the offenders to their nation on the right bank of the Mississippi, and that in the meantime the mounted militia are not to be called out. But should I find the hostile band sustained by any considerable number of the neighboring Indians in that quarter, I am in this event to communicate with the Governor by express and to avail myself of the assistance and cooperation which he has offered. I enclose herewith a copy of my letter to the Governor, marked B.

My present purpose is to embark this day on board a steamboat with six companies of the 3d and 6t Regiments [of] Infantry, with two light 6 pounders, a supply of muskets and 100 Halls patent rifles, with 100 rounds fixed ammu-

nition (*buck shot and ball, and grape and canister*) *for each arm — with one month's supply of hard bread and fifteen days' supply of salted pork — together with a moderate supply of camp equipage suited to the present mild season and to an active temporary movement. Should I find the Indians in a state of actual hostility, as reported, I shall use force and, if necessary, strengthen myself by calling down from Prairie du Chien four or five companies of the first Regiment Infantry. I trust, however, that they may not have commenced actual hostilities. In this case I shall urge them to cross the Mississippi to their proper position belonging to their nation. In any event, I shall endeavor to do the best that can be done with the Regular troops until I am honored with the views of the President of the United States upon the subject. I expect to obtain from Governor Reynolds and General Clark some documents in relation to this matter, when I will write and communicate to you whatever may seem worthy of notice.*

Very Respectfully, I have the honor to be
Edmund P. Gaines, Major Genl. by Bt. Cmg.

CHAPTER IV

[*June 5, 1831 — Sunday*]

IN HIS TEMPORARY QUARTERS at Fort Armstrong, General Edmund Gaines had dismissed his aide, Lieutenant George McCall, for the night. Now he was finally alone, and he exhaled deeply and rubbed his nape with one hand. He crossed the room and, in the light of the chimney lamp, held up his hand with his fingers widespread and stared at it, fully expecting to see a trembling. He was mildly surprised and pleased when he saw that it was very steady. He grunted softly to himself; considering what had transpired since his arrival here, anyone would have been justified in exhibiting nervousness. He sat down heavily in the chair and prepared to write the letter to Governor Reynolds that he had been putting off. But first he reviewed in his mind the events of these past two days.

He had finally met the infamous Black Hawk and some of the principal chiefs, if such any chiefs could be called, of the Sac and Fox tribes — Pashepaho, who was probably the most influential and whom the Americans called the Stabbing Chief; Keokuk, of whom he had heard so much praise from Clark, LeClaire, and St. Vrain; Kinnekonesaut — who was so volatile and evil-tempered; Wapello, the gentle peace lover; Allotah — Morgan — of the Foxes, who constantly gave the impression of being a very dangerous man; Quashquame — the Jumping Fish — who still carried himself with dignity but who, with his advanced years, was becoming unsteady in his movements; Neapope, young and hot-tempered and far more inclined to action than words.[109] And then there was Black Hawk — Makataimeshekiakiak — who, though not a chief in the strictest sense of the word, was perhaps the most noteworthy adversary among all the Indians who had gathered, and who was the direct cause of Gaines preparing to write now to the governor of Illinois.

The steamboat had deposited Gaines and his small force of regulars at Rock Island in the middle of the afternoon on June 3, four days after their departure from Jefferson Barracks. Without delay he had sent his aide, Lieutenant McCall, to fetch the Indian agent and the interpreter, Felix St. Vrain and Antoine LeClaire. McCall was soon back with the two men in tow, and the displeasure of Gaines became evident as they told him that evidently Black Hawk had learned of the whites' mounting a force to come here even before they had, and that he had gone away for a few days on a trip, the purpose of which remained a mystery. General Gaines had asked the agent and the huge interpreter if they would please send runners at once to wherever the Indians were encamped and ask the warrior Black Hawk and the chiefs Bad Thunder and Quashquame and others of the British Band, along with Keokuk and whatever other more peaceably inclined Sac and Fox chiefs were on hand, to attend an urgent council at Rock Island beginning the next morning. The rest of the evening and much of the night he had spent in lengthy private conference with Felix St. Vrain.

Black Hawk, clad in his finest and most flamboyant garments, had been at the head of a large number of warriors and women of the British Band yesterday morning as they approached the council house. He was heavily armed, as were all of the Indians in his party, men and women alike — a bristling array of lances, war clubs, strung bows with arrows, spears, even a few rifles. The majority of the regulars were drawn up in formation with their weapons, but they were fully a quarter-mile distant and would have been unable to respond quickly enough in the event of an outbreak of violence, which now seemed altogether possible. It was wholly against the protocol of council meetings to arrive armed in such a manner, and to make matters worse, the whole of Black Hawk's party was singing a war song as they arrived at the door and waited for their leader to enter. For a short while no one seemed quite sure whether there would be talking or fighting, and since the Indians at the council chambers outnumbered the whites nearly ten to one, it was a tense moment.

This demonstration of strength was so alarming that the entire command of regulars under General Gaines was kept under arms and tightly alert, but against such odds the soldiers would have had little chance, had the Indians elected to attack. A tight little smile played briefly on Black Hawk's lips, but it faded as he let his eyes sweep across the assemblage already inside the council house, and he remained rooted at the entry instead of walking inside. With the Americans was another substantial contingent of Indians, the more peaceable members of the Sacs and Foxes from across the Mississippi, led by Pashepaho, Wapello, and Keokuk. Black Hawk's glance continued moving across the group until it fell on the fat interpreter, paused there a moment, then moved again to stop on the individual beside him, General Gaines.

"Why is it," the Sac spoke loudly, pleased to note that immediately LeClaire had begun interpreting *sotto voce* for the American general, "that at a council convened for us," he made a gesture that took in those crowded behind him, "we find so many others in the room that are opposed to our views? Is this part of how the Americans divide their opponent in order to conquer him? I do not object to the presence of the principal men, but I will not enter and speak unless those who do not have a rightful place here leave at once. Those people know who they are."

There was an uncomfortable stirring among the Indians inside, but General Gaines only waited for LeClaire to finish his interpretation and then raised his hand for silence. "The Black Hawk is, I think," he said, "within his right to so question. The Sac and Fox presently within this chamber are not those about whom the settlers on this side of the Mississippi have made complaint. Therefore, except for their chiefs and principal speakers, I will ask that they leave this chamber so that the British Band may enter and council with me."

It took some minutes for all this to be accomplished, but at last those whose presence Black Hawk had objected to were outside, while most of Black Hawk's people were inside. Keokuk, staring angrily at Black Hawk, had remained, as had Wapello and Pashepaho. Black Hawk ignored them, his gaze still on Gaines, waiting. The American general stood and picked up a sheet of paper from the small table before him. He glanced at it and opened his mouth to speak, but it was the voice of Kinnekonesaut that filled the chamber.

"When white men talk," he said accusingly, "they talk from papers, but when red men have anything to say, they speak from the heart."

Edmund Gaines frowned, and the faintest touch of color came to his cheeks as he replied. "When I speak for *myself* and about my own affairs, I usually speak without paper, but when I am in the performance of a public duty and speak not for myself alone but for others, then I deem it proper to speak that which is written." He stared at Kinnekonesaut, waiting to see if he had a reply, but the Sac sat down, and Gaines dismissed him by shifting his attention back to Black Hawk.

"I have heard," he began, "many reports of the improper conduct of the Sac Indians near this place, and I have called the chiefs and principal braves together to talk with them face to face and inquire into the truth of those reports."

He waited until LeClaire caught up to him with his interpretation, then continued. "Twenty-seven years ago, a treaty was made between the United States and the Sacs and Foxes for the land on which you now reside. Sixteen years ago that same treaty was renewed. It is now six years since yet another treaty was made between the United States and the Sac and Fox Indians together with several other tribes, the second article of which expressly says" — he glanced at the paper and read aloud — " 'The Sacs and Foxes relinquish all their claim to lands east of the Mississippi River.' "[110]

The American general made a brief gesture that took in the Indians in attendance. "Although," he went on, "you are known as the British Band of the Sacs — often our enemies in war and never believed to be our friends — yet the humane disposition of the United States and their kind feelings" — he glanced at Pashepaho, Keokuk, and Wapello — "towards the great and good chiefs of your nation, who long ago left the land they sold us and settled beyond the Mississippi River, have induced them to attribute your conduct to ignorance rather than to any desire or intention to quibble and lie. Wishing to treat you as friends and brothers, your great father in Washington has allowed you to remain on the lands you sold until the present time. But, having heard of the difficulties constantly arising between you and the white inhabitants, he is now convinced of the impossibility of your living peaceably together. He very much wants — and is bound in this respect by the law of the land and the oath he has taken — to do equal and exact justice to all people subject to his control, both red and white, and to see that the laws are faithfully executed. A part of the land in question has been sold to our white brothers of Illinois and other people, and it is now evident that you cannot in justice be permitted to remain on that part of it any longer. You must, therefore, *without delay*, move to the west side of the Mississippi, where you own a rich and beautiful country abounding in game and where you may live comfortably without labor, and live in peace with your neighbors.[111] Your great father in Washington is so much displeased with your conduct that he will no longer allow you to remain on the Rock River lands, and I can only add that you *must* move off those lands as soon as practicable." Gaines looked around at his audience, and his voice went higher as he concluded with a ringing segue into the golden rule: "Go to your own fine country and be obedient to your chiefs and do unto other men as you would they should do unto you."

The officer sat down as LeClaire finished his interpretation, and then it was the Jumping Fish — Quashquame — who was first to respond. "My braves have heard what you have said," he replied, "but they do not know what sales or bargains you speak of. I do not have any idea what was put down upon paper at the talk. We have always believed that the Great Spirit is with the people who make talks on paper, and if so, I don't believe your people would write down lies while the Indians speak from their hearts. Some time ago," he continued, regret becoming heavy in his voice, "I sold a part of the land of the Sacs in order to purchase the release of one of our braves, Nepeek, who was in the white man's jail. But Nepeek was killed when, as we were told, he tried to escape, and neither I nor any of my braves know of any sale of *all* our lands east of the Mississippi River. I am a redskin, and I do not use paper at a talk, but my words are in my heart, and I do not forget what has been said."

"I have never," General Gaines replied quickly and rather defensively, "made or attended a treaty with your nation, but" — he picked up a volume that St. Vrain had loaned him the previous evening, in which the text of various treaties was printed — "the names of the chiefs who sold the land in question are in this book. Here are their names." He then read aloud the names of all those Indians who had made their marks to the treaties involved, which took a considerable while. When he was finished it was Black Hawk who spoke up.

"What," he asked, "was given to *us* at the second treaty?"[112]

"The treaty will show what was given," Gaines replied at once. "The annuities were to have been divided equally among the different bands of the Sacs and Foxes. The friendly and the good men of the nation," he added pointedly, "received their part and moved off the lands. Why didn't you follow their example? Your great father in Washington appointed an agent to attend to the affairs of the red men. Every year he sends the agent a great sum of money, for them" — he glanced at Keokuk — "and for you. Just recently he sent eight thousand dollars to be divided among his red friends.[113] You," he continued, looking back at Black Hawk, "are in the habit of going often to visit your old friends at Malden and of running after the British for what little money and goods they can allot you." He paused, and when no one spoke he made an effort to wrap things up. "We do not wish to injure you," he said reasonably, "but you must not again interfere with the whites. Now I want you to let me know how many days it will take you to be ready to move. If you wish it, we will help you cross the Mississippi in our boats. You *must* go soon."

A strained silence followed the words, and then, as if drawn by a powerful magnet, the eyes of the Indians in attendance swung to Black Hawk and locked on him. He stood looking at the floor at his feet for a long while, and when he finally raised his head, his jaw was set in a determined line.

"We," he said, " — those who follow me and I — are of a single mind in our desire to remain in our old fields. We wish to raise our corn and will do it peaceably, as we have no evil in our hearts against the whites. It is there, in those fields, that the Great Spirit placed them so long ago, and now they have no desire to leave their homes. Perhaps," he added with a speculative lifting of his brow, "the whites have something very valuable in the land, and that is why they wish the Indians removed." He didn't mention the rich lead deposits that were largely responsible for bringing whites to this region to begin with, and Gaines was wise enough not to bring them up himself.

"We know of nothing uncommonly valuable in the land," said Gaines, "but it *is* ours — purchased and paid for. As you know, a part of it is under cultivation. The good chiefs of your nation have sold it to us, and you no longer have any right to remain on it. I repeat, *you must leave it!*"

The general let his eyes move across the assembled Indians and shook his head faintly, with just the right suggestion of sadness. "The Black Hawk has received bad counsel," he said softly, "and he has given bad counsel to his braves." He pointed to the object of his comments and raised his voice a few decibels. "Who is *he* that he should assume the right of dictating to his tribe and lead his people into difficulties?" Gaines hardly took note of it when Black Hawk, with flared nostrils, sat down among his followers. The general placed a hand flat against his breast and continued. "I, as a friend to all *good* red men, advise them to move at once. I did not come here to talk," he added, his words abruptly laced with faint menace, "and I have said enough. The world is wide enough for all of us. This" — he pointed to the ground where he stood — "is *our* part of it, and *that*" — he pointed westward — "is yours."

If the general thought that would do the trick, he was seriously mistaken. Kinnekonesaut — He-Who-Strikes-First — leaped to his feet, his expression pinched with the anger that had risen in him. "The braves have heard what you have said," he shouted, "but they do not agree to it. You have no *right* to the land. Last summer some of our people went to General Clark and sold part of our country, yes, but who sold this little strip we are on? We never sold it!"

Black Hawk now came to his feet again and moved closer to the table behind which General Gaines was still standing. There was a dangerous look in his eyes, and a sudden hush fell as everyone waited for what would come next. One of the American soldiers brought his gun up to hip height, and though the noise his movement caused was slight, it was inordinately loud in the stillness. Black Hawk paid no attention to him, his dark eyes unwaveringly on the general's.

"You asked who am I. *I am a Sac!* My fathers were great men, and I wish to remain where the bones of my fathers are laid. I want to be buried with my fathers. Why, then, should I leave their fields?"

Edmund Gaines was taken slightly aback, but his voice was firm when he replied. "The whites are often obliged to leave the lands of their ancestors, and when they sell their lands, they leave them immediately. I wish you to think of what I have been saying to you until tomorrow morning. After you have slept on it, let me hear from you." He turned and, without another word, even before LeClaire had finished interpreting, walked out of the chamber.

Had he slapped the Sac in the face, the insult could hardly have been worse. And later, when this was explained to him in his quarters, he was considerably chagrined, and sent LeClaire to Black Hawk with his apology and a sincere hope they could talk more in the morning. LeClaire shook his head as he left on the mission, not in the least optimistic about that.

The morning had dawned beautifully bright and clear, and when an orderly tapped on the general's door and announced that some Indians were seeking an audience, Gaines was pleased, sure it was Black Hawk. It was not. Instead, it was Pashepaho, foremost civil chief of the Sacs, and Keokuk, still considered by the majority of the Sacs as their war chief. A sizable cortege of their chiefs, braves, and women were in attendance. Rather than try to invite them in, Gaines came out and stood waiting expectantly.

"My Father," Keokuk began, in passable English, a vaguely ingratiating tone in his voice, "yesterday in the council I stood near the lesser chiefs of the British Band and listened to your words. I was close to them because some have been my friends in the past, and I have been trying for many summers to draw them off from Black Hawk. I have already drawn off ten or twelve large lodges — near fifty families — and I expect to draw off more as I continue to pull at them until I have taken as many as I can to the west side of the Mississippi. That is why I have come here. I wish to ask that you not apply force to Black Hawk's band until I can get all my friends and relatives across the river."

Gaines considered this and nodded. "That sounds reasonable. How long will it take?"

Keokuk made a face. "Long. They have planted corn at the Rock River, and it is now too late in the season to prepare new ground for new cornfields, and if they cannot reap what they have sown here this spring, they will suffer badly from want of food next winter."

"It is not the purpose of my army here to punish those who are not at fault," Gaines told him. When Keokuk remained standing before him, Gaines realized the Sac war chief was not finished. "What else?"

"My Father," Keokuk went on, the sense of obsequiousness still cloaking him, "the Dakotah are making a habit of coming into Sac and Fox country, hunting our game, trapping our furs, sometimes killing our people. We have often wanted to fight back, but we have been as often warned by our white friends to avoid war with the Sioux or other tribes, that this is a bad thing. We wish to do what our agent and his chief say we should, but we need your help to do this. We wish that you would write to your chief soldier at Fort Crawford in Prairie du Chien and instruct him, as well as others of your soldier chiefs on the Mississippi, that the Sioux and other tribes be told that they must no longer hunt on or even enter Sac and Fox lands."

General Gaines considered this and then nodded. He reached out and took Keokuk's hand and shook it, then did the same with the hand of Pashepaho. "You have made our hearts glad in the way you have urged your friends who are part of the British Band to cross over the river with you to your own lands. Yet, I must assure you that if that band does not move in a few days, they will be visited by my troops and they will be *driven* off these lands. In the meantime I need to learn from you, Keokuk, and from Pashepaho as well, who are those who are of that band, and who are those who are not. Only by knowing this will it be possible for me and my officers and men to be able to tell our friends from our enemies. That is very important, because it is not the wish of our great father in Washington to punish the innocent for the crimes of the guilty."

"I will see that those who are friends are pointed out to you before this day is done," Keokuk promised, "and those who are of the British Band and follow Black Hawk."

"Good. Very good." Gaines was pleased. "And I promise you that I will write to the officers commanding Fort Crawford and Fort Snelling and direct them to forbid the Dakotah Sioux or any other tribes from passing into Sac and Fox country anymore. And in a few days more from now, the British Band will no longer be here."

"What of those of our friends here who have planted their corn in the field by Saukenuk? Will they be able to come back and harvest their corn in the fall?"

The general shook his head. "No. The Indians must not come back here. It will no longer be permitted. But this I promise you also, Keokuk. Those of your friends here who have voluntarily left Black Hawk's British Band by the end of this day will, four moons from now, in October, be given — at any landing place they designate on the Mississippi River — as much corn as they would have harvested in the fields they had planted."

Obviously impressed by the offer, Keokuk interpreted this for Pashepaho, who then asked him a question in return. Keokuk faced the officer again. "Pashepaho asks" — he relayed the question somewhat apologetically — "who is to say how much corn they would have harvested?"

Gaines laughed, appreciating the irony. "Tell him," he said at last, still chuckling, "that the amount given will be what, in the judgment of any two good men — one appointed by the agent, one by the Sacs — the Indians would have raised in their fields."

They talked some more, and Gaines learned that Black Hawk had no intention of coming to see Gaines personally, as Gaines had suggested, and that if he wished to talk with the British Band again, he would have to call for the council to resume tomorrow morning. "But," Keokuk warned, "even if you do that, you will be making a mistake to think you will convince Black Hawk to leave Saukenuk." He looked around suspiciously and lowered his voice. "I must tell you that when Black Hawk learned of your planning to come here, he went away on a mission."

"I had heard of that," Gaines admitted, "but the one who told me did not know what his mission was or where he went."

"But *we* know," Keokuk said, indicating Pashepaho and himself. "Black Hawk went and visited the Prophet, Wabokieshiek, and other chiefs of the Winnebago, Kickapoo, and Potawatomi, and asked them to join with him in opposing the Americans. What response Black Hawk had from them I cannot positively say, but I do not think he was successful. Regardless of whether or not he was successful, you will not," Keokuk reiterated, "be able to convince him to leave Saukenuk."

"Whether I will be able to convince him or not is more his problem than mine," Gaines rejoined grimly. "Just tell him to come with his British Band to the council house tomorrow morning when the sun has been up for one hour. Tell him he has no choice."

Now it was early evening, and he was alone in his quarters preparing to write the letter to Governor Reynolds that he had hoped would be unnecessary. He sighed, experiencing the aversion the regular army officers always seemed to feel when put into the position of having to accept the services of a militia force. He dipped his pen, and the words flowed swiftly onto the page before him.

> *Head Quarters Rock Island*
> *5th June, 1831*

To His Excellency John Reynolds Governor of Illinois
 Sir — I do myself the honor to report to your Excellency the result of my conference with the Chiefs & Braves of the Band of Sauk Indians, settled within the limits of your State, near this place. I called their attention to the facts

reported to me of their disorderly conduct toward the white inhabitants near them, but at the same time [they] adhered with stubborn pertinacity to their purpose of remaining on the Rock River land in question.

I notified them of my determination to move them (peaceably, if possible) but at all events to move them to their own side of the Mississippi River, pointing out to them the apparent impossibility of their living on lands purchased by the whites, without constant disturbance.

I have this morning learned that they have invited the Prophet's band of Winnebagoes on Rock River, with some Potawatomies & Kickapoos to join them. If I find this to be true, I shall gladly avail myself of my present visit to see them well punished. And, therefore, I deem it to be the only safe measure now to be taken, to request of Your Excellency, the battalion of mounted which you did me the honor to say would cooperate with me. They will find at this post a supply of rations for the men, with some corn for their horses, together with a supply of powder & lead. I have deemed it expedient, under all the circumstances of the case, to invite the frontier inhabitants to bring their families to this post until the difficulty is over.

> *I have the honor to be, with great respect,*
> *Yr. Obdt. Servt.*
> *Edmund P. Gaines*
> *Major Gen. by Brevet Commanding*

[June 7, 1831 — Tuesday]

Although General Gaines had told Keokuk to notify Black Hawk that the council was to convene in the morning an hour after sunrise, Black Hawk had shown his scornful independence by not showing up until early in the afternoon, and this time with a retinue comprising as many women as men. The general was not at all pleased at having been kept waiting.

Black Hawk spoke first, gesticulating fiercely with virtually every point he made. "The Great Spirit," he said loudly, "made this land for all men, the red as well as the white. And the Great Spirit has placed these people where they are now. He did not put the red men here so the white men could come in and say the red men must move. Our women," he indicated the squaws with a wave of his hand, "have worked this ground, until now, after many summers, it is easy of cultivation. This was diffcult to do, for we do not have the tools of the white man for breaking and turning the earth. But we did it, and we did it with the care and love that we always have for our land. And now that the land is good and easily planted and grows crops well, now is when you say we must leave it and go somewhere else where the ground is hard and filled with roots, and we must start all over to break it and try to make it good? No. Our women are unwilling to leave these fields they have worked so hard to make right. They are unwilling and they refuse."

"They cannot refuse," Gaines told him shortly. "They must leave."

"No," Black Hawk repeated. "The Great Spirit has never directed that we sell our land, and if you say some chiefs sold it to you, then that was not a legal sale that was sanctioned by all our people. We do not believe that our great father in Washington has directed that we should be driven off our land. We believe the Sioux have whispered into the ears of the whites and told them to make us go away so that they can have access to our lands, too — lands which the Dakotah Sioux have coveted for more years than you and I are old."

When Black Hawk fell silent, one of the squaws in his contingent came to her feet. She was an old woman who appeared to be unwell. "I am Cheeto-chena," she said in a gravelly voice, "daughter of Chief Quiltohame, who was killed in battle many years ago against our enemies, the Osages.[114] Because he was a great chief, it is my right to speak, and I will speak for all the Sac women who are here." Her gaze was leveled at the general. "We do not know of politics and agreements and stories of things that took place or did not take place. We know only that this is our land, that it is where we grow the food for our people, that it was not sold to the whites and never would have been sold to them."

Quashquame stood when Cheetochena was finished and briefly agreed with what she had said and her right to say it, speaking for the Sac women generally. But now Edmund Gaines was weary of all the haranguing, and he was shaking his head even before Quashquame had finished. His expression was stern, and he began speaking as soon as LeClaire had finished interpreting what Quash-quame had said.

"Such a dialogue as this accomplishes nothing and gets us nowhere. We are not here to debate any further the issue of whether or not the Sacs sold the land to the Americans. The treaties that have been signed in the past show that they did, and that they reaffirmed these treaties with other treaties over the years, so I will not discuss that point any longer. I have only to say that the Sac have often been reminded of the sale they made of their land to the United States government. Now you are obliged to move, and very soon at that. The time has come, and there will be no more leeway for you. You *must* move in three days, or you will be forcibly moved across the river! I want you to think about what I have told you, and when you have decided among yourselves when you will leave, then we will assist you across the river. There is nothing more to say at this time. The council is over."

The Indians filed out sullenly, but even before Gaines could gather up his papers and leave the chambers, Black Hawk returned with Antoine LeClaire and they approached him. The general straightened and waited for him to speak.

"Our annuity is due at this time," the Sac said, LeClaire interpreting as rapidly as he spoke, "and it has been withheld from us."

"It has only been delayed until this business is settled," Gaines replied.

"I ask," Black Hawk said, "for the sake of our women who are hungry, that you give them some food."

"It will be done," Gaines agreed. "We are not here to be needlessly cruel. I will order that food be given to them. At the same time I remind you that you have but three days to leave the east side of the Mississippi with your people — *all of them.*"

Black Hawk looked at him steadily, then bobbed his head once. "If Bad Thunder and the other chiefs of the Sacs who follow me agree to that, then I will no longer oppose the movement. But if they do not agree, we will stay, and our bones — as well as yours — will whiten the prairies before we will remove. We who are of what you call the British Band want peace, and we will not strike the first blow."

[*June 15, 1831 — Wednesday*]

It was primarily because his own force was not mounted that General Edmund Gaines had not followed through with his three-day ultimatum to Black Hawk. He preferred to await the arrival of Governor Reynolds's mounted volunteers, who were already en route to Rock River. They would be far more able than his own force to pursue and dislodge the well-mounted Indians should the Sacs be heading for the white settlements to create havoc.

Although Gaines had never before met Colonel Henry Gratiot, the newly appointed subagent to the Winnebago Indians in the Rock River Valley, his brief association over these past three days with the man had made him quite certain that here was an extremely capable individual upon whom he could depend fully for almost any task involving gathering intelligence about what the Indians were up to. [115] The subagent was fearful that the Prophet, whom he characterized as a very unpredictable and dangerous individual with a disturbing amount of influence over the young men of his own and neighboring tribes, would support Black Hawk to the fullest. Which was why Gaines had commissioned Gratiot to do a job of spying. The subagent's first report was on the desk before him, and he picked it up and read swiftly through it again to refresh his mind about the details before beginning his own writing.

Rock Island June 11th. 1831

Majr Genl Gaines U.S. Army Comdg W. Dept.

Sir — I have the honor to report to you that agreeably to my intimation to you, I visited the village of the Sac & Fox Indians near this place last evening, for the purpose of persuading off the Winnebago Prophet and some young men of his band, who I knew had previously been there (and I believe with an intention to support those Indians).

I learned on my arrival that the Prophet had just left there to return to his village, which is on Rock River, and although he had previously promised me that he would return home and remain there, I have reasons to believe that his object is to engage as many warriors of his (and of the other bands of Winnebago Indians who reside on Rock River within my Agency) as he can for the purpose of joining the Sac and Fox Indians and supporting them in thier [sic] present pretensions.

I have recently been at some of the principal villages within my agency and I understand from unquestionable authority that although the Indians have been solicited to join the Sac and Fox band under Black Hawk, they have refused to do so. I am, however, of the opinion that it will be advisable for me to follow the Prophet and prevent him from exercising his influence amongst them, I will (if you think it important) return immediately to this place and bring with me some of the influential Chiefs who can be relied on and who will, with my assistance, be able to controul [sic] them. It is my opinion that there are at least four hundred warriors at the Black Hawk's Village, which I visited yesterday, apparently determined to defend themselves in their present position.

On receipt of your letter of the 4th Inst. (in which you instructed me to investigate Sauk recruiting among the Rock River Winnebago and to forward any information obtained to Captain Legate at Galena) we came to the conclusion that a personal interview would perhaps be the most satisfactory to you.[116] *I therefore hastened to this place, to give any information upon the subject of your letter, within my knowledge, and also to tender my services in any way which you may think them useful.*

> *I am with Great Respect Sir Yr Obt. Svt*
> *Henry Gratiot U.S. Sub-Indian Agent*

It appeared to Gaines, at least on the surface of matters, that the Sac and Fox threat was slackening to some degree. Nevertheless, the day before yesterday he had ordered the civilian steamboat *Winnebago* to be armed and to go up the Rock River and reconnoiter the Sac position. For many of the officers on the boat, this view of Saukenuk was the first Indian village they had ever seen, and they gawked at it with unabashed interest, quite surprised at the size of the place, the number of lodges, and the sturdiness of their construction. Some of the lodges in the village had been taken over by the whites, and so far as could be ascertained from aboard the steamboat, the only Indians to be seen anywhere were women, children, and old people, all of whom were greatly alarmed at the boat's smoke-belching appearance. In accordance with the commander's orders, the steamboat withdrew and returned to Fort Armstrong without firing its guns. Although General Gaines had no idea of the whereabouts of the missing Sac warriors, the continued presence of the women, children, and old people at Saukenuk made him certain they would soon return and had not crossed to the west side of the Mississippi. It was at Saukenuk that he meant to attack them as soon as the Illinois Militia arrived.

General Gaines had long ago concluded that the most exasperating chore in any campaign was the necessity of writing letters and reports to keep his military superiors in Washington and the War Department informed of what he had done and was planning to do. Nevertheless, irksome though the chore was, he performed it with satisfactory regularity and completeness, and as he had not reported to Adjutant General Roger Jones since June 8, the day after giving Black Hawk his three-day ultimatum, it was time to bring him up to date. He wrote swiftly, and for a long while the scratching of his pen nib was the only sound in his chambers.

Head Quarters, Western Department
Rock Island, 15th June, 1831

Sir, — In my letter of the 8th instant (written in great haste to be sent by the commander of a steamboat reluctantly detained for the purpose), I stated that the British Band of Sauk Indians on Rock River, having failed to obtain the assistance of the Winnebagoes and Potawatomies, and having been abandoned by the friends and relatives of Keokuk, one of the principal chiefs of the friendly party settled on the Ioway River west of the Mississippi, appeared disposed to listen to my counsel; that I had notified them to move off in three days, & had assured them that if they did not move themselves in that time I would move them. The facts and circumstances which follow suggested to me the propriety of affording these Indians a little more time for reflexion [sic].

I. I have ascertained (through the able services of the excellent subagent of the Winnebagoes of Rock River, Colonel Henry Gratiot, who visited them in their village) that they were visited by upwards of a hundred Potawatomies, with some Winnebagoes and Kickapoos, & have determined not to move without being forced off. They say they will not fight, but there is reason to believe that as soon as they are forced off, they will attack the frontier settlements of the State of Illinois. These settlements are even more sparse & feebler than I had anticipated. Few of the inhabitants are supplied, as our border men used to be, with good rifles or with other means of defence [sic] such as Block-houses &c., &c. A section of near 300 miles of this description of frontier, embracing the old hunting & fishing grounds of these Sauks & their allies, the Foxes, Potawatomies, Kikapoos [sic], & Winnebagoes (the three former speaking the same language), lies open to the incursions of these Indians who, if disposed to engage in a war against us, would have it in their power to do much havoc upon this exposed border before it would be possible to arrest the evil by the employment of other than mounted men — most of the Indians being well mounted and well armed.

II. Notwithstanding it was the opinion of Colonel Gratiot that neither these [Winnebagoes] nor the Potawatomies would join the hostile Sauks, yet I have learned from him soon after the date of my last [letter], that he had seen recent cause to doubt the correctness of his previous impression upon this point. He therefore determined to visit the Sauk Village of Rock River and, if possible, separate the Indians of his agency from the hostile party. His report is enclosed herewith, marked "A".

III. The companies which I sent for to Prairie du Chien could not join me as soon as I desired because I did not deem it proper to call troops from that post without making the time of their departure to depend on the arrival there of the companies ordered from Fort Winnebago, and they had not arrived. Besides, even if I had the four companies expected from Prairie du Chien (though this force, added to the six companies here, would have enabled me to punish and disperse these Indians, unaided by any of their allies) yet, as they are all mounted and my force on foot, they might have made a heavy stroke upon the frontier settlements without the possibility of being overtaken before the arrival of the mounted Militia.

IV. I have recently learned from the public interpreter at this post (and I have the promise of a written communication from the agent, Mr. St. Vrain, stating the particulars, which I will forward with this if it be received in time,), that three of the Sauk chiefs sent by this band in the last year to visit & enter into alliances with all the Indian tribes along our southwestern frontier to Texas, inclusively; that they did visit and treat with 12 different nations. Two of the chiefs died on the way, after visiting Texas.[117] The other one returned to his band but a few weeks past. He reports that they were all well pleased with the friendly reception they met with from the natives and with the country in and near Texas, whither the band is believed to have some intention of moving. They seem, therefore, willing to abandon their country here, west of the Mississippi, if compelled to leave their present position at Rock River, and they have intimated an expectation that a war upon this frontier and as far as Texas (in which many different nations will be engaged) is likely to occur within a year or two. These anticipations are, however, doubtless more the result of their sanguine hopes and wishes than of their reasonable expectations. Their English friends, they say, have spoken to them of an intended war with us & call the attention of the Indians to the trading establishments of the English at the mouth of the Columbia River as evidence of their continued efforts to secure, in such a war, the cooperation of all American Indians.[118] These speculations will serve to show their continued, deep-rooted infatuation toward England and relentless enmity towards the United States.

The foregoing views appear to suggest the propriety of my abstaining from any measures calculated to excite a spirit of active hostility among these Indians until they actually strike, or attempt to strike, a blow in that spirit, until I am favored with the President's view upon the subject. My present authority only embraces the simple duty of PROTECTION to the citizens, soldiers & public functionaries of the United States. Whenever this duty calls for the application of powder & ball, they shall be freely applied. But whilst our neighboring Savages, blinded as they are by the unconquerable force of habitual prejudice & hatred, forbear [sic] to strike, I must not dare to strike a deadly blow. I shall therefore, if possible, *remove them without bloodshed. But I shall not, during the continuance of their present conduct & caution, attempt to move them by force until I possess the means of protecting the frontier settlements.*

I cannot but conclude that the present is an auspicious occasion to treat with these people for the whole of the country west of this place, than which no measure could tend more to the immediate security & permanent prosperity of the northern & western parts of the states of Missouri & Illinois.

I am now satisfied that the friendly professions of Keokuk & Morgan & their followers west of the Mississippi are not much to be relied on. The latter spoke to me of his intention to comply with the late treaty, but was manifestly much dissatisfied with some parts of it.[119] He inquired whether we did not wish to obtain more than their land. I afterwards learned that his band, the Foxes, were disposed to sell.

Accompanying this I send you a copy of the memorandum of my aide de camp, Lt. McCall, of the substance of my talks held with these Indians. I have notified them that I can hear nothing more upon the subject of the removal of the Sauks until they shall have removed, or come to notify me that they will move forthwith.

All which is respectfully submitted for the information of proper authorities.

> *Edmund P. Gaines*
> *Major Genl. by Brevet, Commdg.*

General Gaines was blotting his final words when his aide, Lieutenant George A. McCall, tapped respectfully at the door and entered, spoke briefly to the commander, and then left. Gaines considered what McCall had just told him and then dipped his pen and added a postscript to his letter to Adjutant General Jones:

P.S. Since writing the foregoing letter, I have obtained more satisfactory information than that on which my remarks respecting Keokok [sic] were founded. A confidential agent was employed to visit Keokuk's village, about 45 miles west of this place and reports that all but two of the friendly warriors of that chief are with him at the village, preparing to go still farther up the Iowa River on a hunting party, and that the two others referred to are endeavoring to separate their friends from the British Band.

I enclose herewith the letter of F. St. Vrain Esq., Indian Agent, referred to in the 4th paragraph of the foregoing letter, Marked "C".   E.P.G.

[June 23, 1831 — Thursday]

To Lieutenant George Archibald McCall, this present assignment on the northwestern frontier was undoubtedly the best thing that had happened to him since his graduation at age twenty from the United States Military Academy at West Point nine years ago. Throughout his Pennsylvania boyhood, the glamour of a military career had appealed to him. But then, when his West Point graduation was followed by a series of lackluster assignments at posts in Georgia and the Carolinas, he had begun to feel he had made a serious error in becoming an officer in the United States Army. At one point he had even contemplated resigning from the service — and then had come this present duty, which he quickly found so fascinating that any thought of leaving the Army was thrust aside for once and all.

The stories that had reached his ears of the irascibility of General Edmund Pendleton Gaines had not caused him even a moment's hesitation in accepting the post as the general's aide de camp. He knew of scarcely any way better for an ambitious young officer to get ahead than to be working closely with a commanding general and having contact with the wide variety of people an aide had to deal with, both civilian and military. And while Gaines *was* at times a bit hard to get along with, Lieutenant McCall didn't know anyone who wasn't testy at times, himself included. The secret to getting along, he found, lay in merely learning to read the general's moods and anticipating his needs. By doing so in these first three months of this assignment, he had made himself invaluable to the general.

Though he would not have told anyone, the one thing about his own life that bothered George McCall more than anything else was that he was lonely. As a youth he had harbored a great affection for a young lady in Philadelphia and had escorted her to a number of affairs before his appointment to West Point. He had assumed she was as interested in him as he was in her, but such was evidently not the case. She wrote to him at first, but then her letters became fewer and farther apart, until finally they ceased. And though he had continued writing to her, there was no response. When, after earning his commission, he returned to Philadelphia on furlough, he was stunned to find that she had married a prominent Boston surgeon, and he never saw her again. Only twice in his military career since then had he encountered fellow officers whom he truly considered friends and whose company he enjoyed. In each case reassignment had eventually separated them, and the loneliness returned. As a refuge from it, he had become an outstanding correspondent who wrote long, interesting letters describing the people, places, and events of his existence. And while he wrote to a number of people, to none did he write more fully or faithfully throughout the years than to his beloved father, Archibald McCall.

Tonight, by the light of the brass lamp affixed to the wall over the small writing desk, he continued the letter that had occupied his free time off and on for the past week. A bell dinged on deck, and the sound filtered pleasantly into his cabin aboard the *Winnebago*. He was very tired and looking forward to stretching out in the somewhat cramped quarters of his bunk, but he would gladly have foregone his rest for an opportunity to talk some more with the young woman he had met on board, the so wonderfully attractive and intelligent Susan Shelton. That, of course, was impossible here in the quarters where total privacy was unachievable; yet, as an alternative, the compulsion to write — to *talk*, as it were — to his father was too great to allow him to merely turn in for the night. Over the past week he had written in this same letter at four different sittings, and he was fairly certain that it still wouldn't be finished when this night's stint was over.

The long letter was addressed to the elder McCall, who, almost as much as George himself, had been delighted at the duty assignment that had finally taken his son out of the South and placed him in the western frontier, and which was made even more exciting now by the growing likelihood of a major Indian war in the offing. And, as he often did when continuing a letter begun at an earlier time, Lieutenant McCall read quickly through what he had already written, beginning with the more or less narrative account he had penned a week ago today.

> *Headquarters, Western Department*
> *Rock Island, Ill. — June 16, 1831*

My dear Father: —
Your letter of the 5th inst. reached me this morning, having been forwarded from St. Louis by the steamboat Winnebago, *bound to Galena. . . .*

Lieutenant McCall had gone on to say that the *Winnebago* had moored at Rock Island, and half the freight for Fort Armstrong — the arms, ammunition, and food supplies consigned to the fort's commander, Major John Bliss — had already been unloaded when something unusual occurred. A "sucker" arrived at Fort Armstrong — "sucker" being the term Missourians used to designate an inhabitant of Illinois. The sucker, McCall told his father, had come upriver by himself in a canoe all the way from the Red Banks, which was sixty-five miles downstream from Rock Island.[120] He was bearing an express addressed to General Gaines. It was a special request for help from two merchant keelboat crews. They had written:

> *We beg that General Gaines will understand the gravity of our situation (which the bearer will explain) and send downstream to us an escort to guard our valuable cargo of merchandise and protect our vessels as well as our lives, on our journey upstream as far as Rock Island.*

The express, after thankfully devouring some food provided for him at the general's request, carefully explained his mission. It seemed that while the two keelboats put to shore to lay up for the night at the Indian-French settlement near the rapids just above the mouth of the Des Moines River, a party of four Sac Indians came in. They acted very friendly and claimed they were part of Keokuk's band. They loitered around the fire where the keelboat crews were preparing their supper and engaged the boatmen in conversation. They seemed genuinely interested in everything the boatmen said and asked a wide variety of questions. Then they had begged some whiskey from their "very good white friends" and departed for their own camp to drink it. Not until after they had been gone for a while did the boatmen realize that among the questions they had innocently answered was the nature of the cargo of the keelboats — a quantity of red cloth, gunpowder, ball, whiskey, and other goods intended for the traders far up the Mississippi who lived among and were doing business with the old enemies of the Sac and Fox, the Dakotah Sioux.

The express, who had many years of experience dealing with the Indians and knew their language well, then told General Gaines that he had suddenly been struck by a strong hunch that something was very wrong. "I told the others in our party that although those Indians were undoubtedly Sacs, I was beginning to doubt that they were part of Keokuk's band, as they had claimed. In fact," he said, "I was convinced they were actually part of the British Band under Bad Thunder, Quashquame, and Black Hawk."

After a grateful sip at the cup of hot tea that had been handed to him, the express had gone on. "Since I understood their language better'n any of the others, I told them that I figgered it might not be too bad an idea to slip into their camp and do some judicious spying. By this time, I said, they had prob'ly finished eating and were well into the whiskey we'd given 'em, which maybe would loosen their tongues. The others agreed with me, so I slipped through the woods to the camp of the Indians. I got in almost right up to their fire, and the very first words I overheard convinced me my impression was correct, that these Sac were of the British Band, not Keokuk's, and the one doing most of the talking was Neapope, Black Hawk's right-hand man. I'll try to repeat what he said, exactly the way he said it.

" 'My brothers,' said he, 'the braves of the pale-faces are at this moment surrounding our homes; their watch fires light up the forests of our ancestors, their great guns are pointed, their long knives are bared, and they only wait for the arrival of their horse soldiers to drive us from our lodges, our fields, and the graves of our forefathers.' When he stopped talking for a moment, the other three gave out with a long, shrill, sad-sounding war whoop. Neapope then continued talking and said, 'These boats of the pale-faces,' and by that he meant *our* party's keelboats, 'are going to our old enemies, the Sioux, the very ones who fourteen moons ago killed our unarmed chief and his whole party while they were on their way to talk peace.[121] Answer me, my brothers! Shall the treasures of the pale-faces reach their destination?' A fierce negative shouting from the others was the only answer to this question, but it told me exactly how eager they were to get their hands on our cargo. They developed their whole plan while I listened. One of the Indians of this party was going to set out in the morning to get a reinforcement, while the other three were going to stay out of sight on shore, keeping an eye on our boats as we worked our way upstream on the Mississippi.

They figured to have Black Hawk's warriors intercept us by surprise in the middle of the night about halfway between the Red Banks and here — I guess about thirty miles downstream from here."

The boatman paused and finished his tea, then went on. "They figgered on killing us and taking the whole cargo. Once that was settled, Neapope had raised the bottle from the ground and held it up against the firelight to see how much was left inside. I didn't wait around to watch 'em finish it. When I got back to my old friends and told 'em what I'd overheard, some were in favor of lifting anchor at once and making the best of a good head start. Others were for returning to St. Louis. I didn't agree. I told 'em I didn't think there was any real danger at present, and that we didn't have anything to fear until we reached the point where they planned to ambush us. I figgered as long as we didn't try to make a run for it, they wouldn't realize we knew what was planned, and we could make it to the settlement at Red Banks, where we'd be able to stay in safety until an escort could be procured from you folks here at Rock Island, which I volunteered to come here to try to get."

Lieutenant McCall had paused as he remembered the scene, but in a moment he lowered his eyes and continued reading what he had written to his father:

His advice was followed and here he is, having just put me in possession of the facts nearly as I have given them to you.

As these boats have on board some ammunition essential to the perfect efficiency of the troops, the General has engaged the captain of the Winnebago *to return for them.*[122] *A company will be put on board, and the General will avail himself of the opportunity to examine more closely the country about the mouth of Rock River, by the* "Great cut-off."

We shall go on board as soon as the steamboat has discharged its freight, which I think will be about midnight; and if I can find the time tomorrow, I will give you a sketch of our history since we left St. Louis.

It was not until the next day, after they had been to the Red Banks and were on their way back to Rock Island that George McCall was able to get back to the letter he was writing to his father, and he started with an entirely new page, which he again dated as originating from Headquarters, but this was not an error. As he had explained to Archibald McCall long ago, as commander of the Western Department of the Army, General Gaines *was* headquarters, and wherever he happened to be was so described. Therefore, at this particular time, headquarters turned out to be a boat afloat on the Mississippi. Captain Hunt, the civilian skipper of the steamer, had not been at all pleased to be pressed into escort duty that not only put him far off his schedule and discommoded his passengers, but also could be distinctly hazardous. He had protested at first, but General Gaines had insisted, and told Hunt that he could volunteer to help and remain the boat's captain, or the *Winnebago* could simply be commandeered in the name of the United States government and a captain and crew appointed from among the general's troops. Captain Hunt, with somewhat poor grace, elected to "volunteer," not wishing any unfamiliar hands operating *his* boat.

> *Hd. Qrs Western Department*
> *On board Steamer Winnebago.*
> *Near the Red Banks, June 17 1831*

My dear Father: — About midnight we got on board and soon after were under a press of steam, moving down the bright current of the father of waters. The moon was full and the night beautiful. The mild prairies on our right, smiling in the soft moonlight, were finely contrasted with the dark and frowning woodland that overhung and shaded the water on our left. The air was redolent with the rich offering of a thousand prairie flowers, and love and poetry, as they accepted the offering, pronounced the hour to be their own.

McCall shook his head as he looked up from his own writing. He knew he tended to be flowery in his prose, but in reading it over like this, he was finding it a bit too much and wondered if he should scratch it out. No, his father would be amused, and after all, it did express the rather romantic sense he was experiencing as he wrote that particular passage, and with good reason, considering the ladies that were on board the *Winnebago* — and the one in particular who was so painfully touching his emotions at the moment, Susan Shelton. He shook his head again and continued reading, eager now to review what he had said to his father in his first mention of her.

The boat was filled with passengers for Galena, among whom were (and are, for they are still with us) four ladies. Their berths were all filled, so that I had full time to contemplate the scene along the hurricane-deck.

Having been at work all day, I at length lay down in my cloak and slept for an hour, but was up again at four o'clock, preparing a dispatch for the Governor of Illinois — which we sent off about breakfast-time. I also sent a letter addressed to yourself, which I trust will reach its destination.

Now for Indian affairs. The day after our arrival at Fort Armstrong, Black-hawk, with his principal braves, met the general in council. They approached the council-house, bounding from the earth and whooping, in all the extravagance of the war dance. We observed, too, that they were much more completely armed than is usual on such occasions and many of them, indeed, had their bows bent — so unequivocal an indication of their hostile feeling that it was thought proper privately to increase the guard and keep the whole command under arms, for which purpose the usual drill afforded a sufficient pretext. And I observed during the session of the council, some of the old traders were evidently uneasy and constantly on the qui vive, and they afterwards told me that never before at a similar scene did they see so strong a demonstration of hostility as on this occasion.

The next half-dozen pages of McCall's letter detailed the meetings General Gaines had had with the Indians — how he rebutted their claims to the land by outlining the details of the several treaties by which the United States had purchased the land, and how, despite such evidence, the Indians persisted in claiming they had never sold their lands north and west of the Rock River, which included their town of Saukenuk, to the United States. He told of the haranguing that had gone on and of the adamant stand of the British Band of the Sac to follow the lead of Black Hawk and remain on the east side of the Mississippi. As McCall put it to his father:

The general told him his great chief had sold the land and they no longer had the right to occupy it and that go they must. *"Who is the Black Hawk that he should assume the right of dictating to his tribe?" said the General. "I know him not — he is no chief. Who is he that he should take it upon himself to speak for his tribe?" The old* Hawk, *who is upwards of seventy, was very much cut down by this and took his seat quite mortified, but after a little he rose and, with infinite dignity and energy of manner addressing the General, said, —*
"You have asked who is the Black-Hawk? Know that I am a Sac. My fathers were great men. They have left their bones in our fields, and there I will remain and leave my bones with theirs."

Lieutenant McCall continued to chronicle the details of the confrontations with the Indians after that and was obviously much impressed by the Sac war chief, describing Keokuk as *"a perfect Apollo in figure, and one of the most graceful and eloquent speakers I have seen among the Indians of any tribe."* The army lieutenant went on to explain to his father how, despite the sternness of General Gaines, the British Band of the Sacs refused to acquiesce to him, and finally the general had been forced to lay down an ultimatum. As the lieutenant had written in his letter:

The General is, of course, desirous to remove them, if possible, without bloodshed, and on that account gave them three days to effect the movement, on hopes that in the interim they would see the folly of their decision.
They say that they wish to be at peace, that they will not fight if attacked, but that they are as firmly resolved to remain and lay their bones beside those of their ancestors.
This is, of course, Indian talk. The Sacs are perhaps the most warlike and the fiercest, as well as most determined, Indians in our country, as their conduct during the last war exemplified. Some of them were killed at the very cannon's mouth, and if they could now raise sufficient force to make a successful stand and

take a number of scalps before they cross the river (which they well enough know they must *do,) they would delight in seizing any opportunity that would afford them revenge; — but they are fortunately so well acquainted with what would be the consequence to themselves to think of such a thing for one moment, and their only object, I am of the opinion, is to extort further annuities or presents from the Government.*

The General has called for me on the hurricane-deck to take notes of the country and make a topographical sketch of this "slough".[123] *Adieu.*

The following day — June 18 — Lieutenant McCall did not add to the continuing letter to his father, not only due to the press of his own duties, but because of the time he was spending in the company of the lovely and lonely Susan Shelton. But on the day after that he was again relating his views on paper.

Hd. Qrs Western Department
On board the Winnebago June 19, 1831

My dear Father: — For two days I have been on the hurricane-deck of the boat, many hours at a time, taking notes and sketches of the country east of the "slough," which we have been navigating ever since our return from the "Red Bank" with the two keel-boats before mentioned, which were placed in safety under the guns of the fort.

As we put the crew of the boat — the Winnebago *— and the passengers under the semblance of martial law, three of the ladies soon tired of the noise of the new-made soldiers and took refuge in the fort with the more orderly regulars, but the fourth, Mrs. S———, a fine-looking young woman, the daughter of Judge D——— of Arkansas, was too much of the heroine to desert her post and remained, as she told me, to see that her better half did his duty toward his country. The better half, however, is far from being a moiety of "the one flesh"; he is near double her age, a sot, and never leaves the card table till he is carried by the waiter to bed. She is pretty, as I told you, and being full of life, I discourse with her by the hour when I am not on deck. And, as the General and I have now half of the ladies' cabin, I of course see her frequently.*

We shall continue to cruise these waters, observing the motions of the red-skins, till the arrival of the Governor with some hundreds of mounted militia. He is expected on the 21st instant.

As the Black-Hawk declined to move, and we have learned from good authority they would be joined by the Prophet's band of Winnebagoes and Kickapoos, to the amount of some hundreds — I know not how many for they, of course, lie perdu *and no man can calculate the strength of an Indian war-party till he sees them in the field — at least under the present circumstances. This, as I observed, being the case, the General determined not to strike a blow until he could array such a*

force as would make resistance hopeless; for though it would be easy enough to
drive them from their present position across the river, yet without a large body of
mounted men it would be impossible to protect this extensive frontier settlement
from their ravages in case they should recross either above or below for purposes of
revenge. I counted, the other day, a hundred and twenty canoes in front of the
friendly town, in one mass, besides numbers in every direction — at least half of
which probably belong to the British Band and their allies — numbers of whom,
I have no doubt, have sought the sanctuary of the white flag, under which they
will lie at their ease until they see how the scale turns, for the "friendly" party (so
called) is, I believe, at most but neutral.

But I have no doubt that when a sufficient force is brought to bear upon them,
they will still without hesitation sign the articles of agreement, and quietly
relinquish their lands.

Again the brass bell on the deck of the *Winnebago* dinged and jarred Lieutenant McCall from his reverie. He dipped his pen and bent to the task of
bringing Archibald McCall in Philadelphia up to date on what had been occurring here these past four days, during which he had not written.

June 23

Here we have been threading this slough twice a day for a week, and no
Governor arrived yet. The high state of the waters which cross his line of march
have doubtless been a greater obstacle to the celerity of his Excellency's movements
than any he had anticipated would be opposed to him. I am wearied of the
sameness of the scene, for as he has been expected daily and almost hourly for some
days past, we have visited the point of concentration regularly with a supply of
ammunition and provision, both of which he stands in need of.[124] *We have*
examined Rock River as high up as the town and found the channel good. The
town is prettily situated and has some fine land adjacent to it, all of which is
finely commanded by some heights upon its left.[125]

As we passed the town we observed a number of horses — picketed and at
large — but no inhabitants but a few old women and children. The ravines in the
rear of the town, which are both long and numerous and moreover thickly clad
with underbrush, would afford a covering for an immense number of Indian
warriors, but still could be swept in a few minutes by some pieces of artillery on
the heights above mentioned.
Our lady . . .

McCall paused in his writing, smiling as he thought of Susan Shelton and
wishing, as he often did lately, that he and she were free to spend more time
together. Obviously her husband, one of the newer recruits, cared little about

her and much preferred the companionship of his drinking, card-playing fellow soldiers than hers — a condition McCall found difficult to understand or accept. He had even considered interceding on her behalf with Private Shelton, but was wise enough to realize this would have been a very foolish gesture on his part. He sighed deeply and bent to his writing again.

Our lady still remains with us, nothing daunted by the warlike preparations she sees around her, but she has too much sense and has seen too much of the Indian character in her own country to be alarmed at outward appearances. I collect her bouquets of prairie-flowers daily and we discuss their beauties with great apparent interest; indeed, the colors and delicacy of some of these are truly exquisite, though they have little fragrance.

The weather some days has been charming, and nothing can be more brilliant than the nights. We sleep under the guns of the Fort, and the other night, returning later than usual, we discovered at some distance a canoe apparently floating with the stream. Suspecting that it contained some red-skins, the General ordered the pilot to steer for it. The steamboat accordingly changed her course and began to plough the waves in the direction of the object which, gliding along in the shade of the woody bank, would, to an inexperienced eye, have passed for one of the numerous pieces of floating timber which are at this season borne seaward on the bosom of the mighty Mississippi.

It was as we had anticipated, but the courage of the midnight wanderers was constant and true to their purpose. They lay perfectly concealed in their shell of a boat until another revolution or two of the wheels of the Winnebago *would have brought her upon them and buried them and their canoe in the turmoil of waters that burst and parted beneath her angry prow. But then, as it were by magic, five forms simultaneously appeared above the low sides of the hollow trunk, and one simultaneous sweep of five light paddles darted the canoe like an arrow to the shore where, leaving it to the guidance of the current, they sprung on land and instantly disappeared in the thicket. As we were running close to shore and parallel to it, we passed within a few yards of them as they vanished from our sight, but, as the object was not to injure them (which, from their boldness, they were probably aware of), they were permitted to escape unhurt.*

The whisper of a gentle touch on his shoulder caused George McCall to jerk so unexpectedly that a blot of ink arced from his pen and spattered to the edge of the paper. He started upward and to his right, where a shadowy form loomed close. It was higher than the warm dome of yellow light that spread beneath the sconce, but a faint aroma touched his nostrils, and, instantly recognizing it, he came hastily to his feet. The touch on his shoulder slid down his arm and remained there, incredibly light and almost unbearably *present*. The softness of the voice seemed more imagined than heard.

"Would the lieutenant care to share a breath of the fragrant night air?"
Indeed the lieutenant would.

[*June 25, 1831 — Saturday*]

It was just after the sun had cleared the eastern horizon that the horsemen, four abreast, broke out of the forest and onto the high prairie overlooking the Mississippi Valley. Row after row emerged behind the leaders until it seemed they would never stop appearing, and the four-abreast formation became a sinuous dark line with its head more than a mile into the open prairie while its tail was still lost along the trees. There were some sixteen hundred men in this formation and, with pack and wagon animals included, nearly two thousand horses. Near the center of the long column rode their commander, Brigadier General Joseph Duncan, close to a wagon in which rode the man who had inspired this army's creation, Illinois governor John Reynolds.

The sixteen hundred were the men who, with their animals ranging from fine thoroughbreds to heavy-footed plow-horses, had risen to the published proclamation of the governor, which called for volunteers to march against the Sac and Fox Indians and any other tribes foolish enough to espouse a cause that opposed white settlement. The governor had issued his call hoping to raise a force of seven hundred men, asking them to rendezvous at the little village of Beardstown on the Illinois River on June 10, bringing their own weapons and provisions.[126] By the end of the first week of June they had begun arriving, and by the tenth over one thousand had come, and more were still arriving. Not until all who were coming had been given a chance to arrive could the militia begin to organize itself, and so they set up camp and waited . . . and waited. New arrivals finally tapered off sharply on June 14, and concrete steps were taken for the formation, the following morning, of this mass of humans into an organized, well-functioning army.

There was a great feeling of *esprit de corps* among the men, but it was not altruism alone that had brought them here. Some realized that if the Indians were, in fact, finally driven out, a whole new safe region of wonderful farmland or land abundant in mineral wealth would open to settlement. Others were even more crass. Illinois was growing, as was the nation, and there was no doubt in anyone's mind that if another great Indian war was shaping up, there were wonderful political careers to be forged in the crushing of the red menace. Cases in point included such nationally prominent figures as Henry Knox, Lewis Cass, William Henry Harrison, Henry Dearborn, John Calhoun, and none other than Andrew Jackson, all whose powerful political careers had stemmed from meteoric military leadership experiences. Thus, while many ordinary settlers were on hand simply to help their state when it needed help, a great many were there essentially to stand up and say, "Here I am! Look at me and remember my name when it comes time to vote. I was here and did my part!" And not in the least exempt from political posturing of this sort was the Illinois governor himself. Reynolds fancied himself still to be a rising star in the political galaxy, and the particular constellation he had his gaze locked on at the moment was the United States Presidency. If Jackson could do it, then, by grab, so could he! That, of course, was what had influenced him in his decision to accompany the militia army to the Rock River — not in a command position, but simply as a patriot. Of course, it wouldn't hurt a thing to have the people, some time in the not-too-distant future, remember that it was good ol' stalwart Johnny Reynolds who'd ridden into the very den of the bloodthirsty savages with no motive at all other than to inspire the militia with his presence and his sharing of the privations and toils of the campaign.

Though volunteers had been asked to bring their own horses, weapons, and provisions — and many did — a great number showed up with nothing more than the tired old steed that had transported them bareback to the rendezvous. The early appointment of Colonel Enoch C. March and Colonel Samuel C. Christy as quartermasters was little short of a stroke of genius, for these two had the capability of performing miracles of outfitting and provisioning. One small example of their ability was how they had quickly located a merchant in Beardstown, Francis Arenz, who had a quantity of brass guns on consignment for the South American trade. At the persuasion of Colonels Christy and March, Arenz was quickly made to see that the course of duty lay in donating weapons to the state's militia.

Organizing the great congregation of men into a brigade was a task Governor Reynolds delegated to his two principal aides, Milton K. Alexander and James D. Henry. A strong commanding general was needed, and to this post, with the rank of brigadier, Reynolds appointed Joseph Duncan of the Illinois State Militia. Named as brigade quartermaster was William Thomas. William G. Brown became paymaster general. E. D. Taylor became General Duncan's adjutant, while J. J. Hardin was appointed his inspector general. He was given three well-qualified men as personal aides — Aaron Atkins, Isom M. Gillham, and Enoch B. Wethers.

The brigade itself was divided into two regiments, plus a spy battalion and an odd battalion. The two regiments were split into seven companies each, the spy battalion into four companies, and the odd battalion into three companies.[127] The only fly in the ointment of this whole State Militia establishment was the weather. A series of heavy thunderstorms had filled every stream bank full, and crossings became major problems that caused long delays — and the puzzlement of General Gaines over why the militia army was so late.

But now, at last, the whole force, weary from its protracted march but undaunted in spirit, had at last arrived at its rendezvous point along the Mississippi only a few miles below the mouth of the Rock River. The worst part was over; all that remained now was to engage and defeat the enemy.

[*June 26, 1831 — Sunday*]

It was Neapope who, two hours before dawn, brought word to the large lodge that final preparations were being made by the Americans for their attack on Saukenuk.

"The great white chief who has been on the noise-boat all these days will be coming at us from the north with all his soldiers who dress the same and march as one. The great white chief we do not know — he who has arrived from below with more horses and warriors than we have ever seen here — will be coming at us from the other side of Rock River, crossing to the island and then to our shore. The noise-boat, with many thunder guns pointing toward us, will be coming up Rock River. There is not much time."

Black Hawk suddenly looked older than his sixty-four years and very tired. As he had known it would, the time had come at last. For all his bravado, and his claims that he would never leave Saukenuk and that his bones would whiten on the land where the bones of his fathers lay, now he was indeed being forced to leave. A great sadness rode him and he nodded, but made no reply.

"What do I tell our people now, Black Hawk?" Neapope asked after a moment.

"Tell them to leave. Now. Without delay. Tell them to meet where I have said we would meet. The hidden place on the west side of the Mississippi.[128] Tell them that once across, they must stay out of sight. I will join them soon. Tell them . . ." His voice trailed off.

"Tell them what, Black Hawk?"

"Tell them that no matter what happens or what this move across the river looks like, we are not done. We leave Saukenuk for this moment only, merely because we have no other choice and we have not the strength to oppose. But we *will* be back. Saukenuk is ours, and we cannot give it up for all time." He paused, as if gathering himself to say more, but at last he simply shook his head and turned away. "Go, Neapope," he said, his back to the younger man. "There is no time for them to waste. They must leave now. All of them. Go."

[*June 29, 1831 — Wednesday*]

Lieutenant George McCall bade General Gaines good night and then left the large, partitioned stateroom of the *Winnebago* for the pleasant night air on deck. He was, of course, hoping that Susan would be there, but she was not. Though he waited for nearly an hour, she did not show up. That probably meant she was nursing her pitiful excuse for a husband through another of his besotted states, and he wished there was some way he could help *her* through it.

The whisper came from close behind him. "Excuse me?"

He gasped and spun around, momentarily disconcerted, since he had heard no one approach. It was a woman, barely visible in the darkness, but he knew that it wasn't Susan.

"Ma'am?" he replied, his own voice low. "May I help you?"

"Your name," she said. "Tell me your name, please."

"McCall, ma'am. George McCall. Lieutenant."

He felt a folded paper being nudged into his hand. "You're the one, then," the woman murmured. "A friend sends this." She stepped back into the deeper shadows.

McCall waited for her to say more, and when she didn't, he stepped forward into the heavy darkness where she had been and discovered she was gone, having departed as silently as she had come. He turned and made his way back to his own partitioned quarters. His lamp was glowing at low wick and he left it that way, glancing about to make sure he was unobserved, then opening the folded paper. There was neither salutation nor farewell — only a block of neatly written words — but he knew full well the author.

He suspects but does not know for certain when or how or who — and never will. You and I cannot meet again, ever. We had nothing, yet we had so much. So fleetingly. Do not endeavor to change the situation; you cannot, nor can I. Thank you for showing me the flowers.

McCall returned to the deck and walked to the leeward rail. Slowly, methodically, he tore the note into halves five times and then extended his arm to its full length, opened his hand, and let the bits of paper flutter away toward the wet darkness below. He knew he would never see Susan again, and he was paradoxically saddened and relieved.

Ten minutes later, back at his cramped little desk, he turned up the wick a little and found his solace as so often in the past, through writing to Archibald McCall in Philadelphia.

> *Hd. Qrs. Western Department*
> *On board steamer* Winnebago
> *June 29, 1831*

My dear Father: — On the 25th instant the Governor arrived with fifteen hundred mounted men, under command of General Duncan, and took up his quarters with us on board the Winnebago.[129] *Having accompanied the militia of his State, merely with a view of inspiring them by his presence and participation in the toils and privations of the campaign with a portion of his own patriotic feelings, the Governor took no active command; but rumor, ever busy with the actions of the great, imputed his high military ardor to no other incitive than the promised advancement of his own politic views. On the evening of the 25th, an advanced company of the* Spies (*a battalion, under that title, commanded by Major Samuel Whiteside*) *reached the bluff where the militia were ordered to unite with us and notified General Gaines of the approach of the command. They had* encamped about ten miles to the southeast of our position and the next morning, soon after sunrise, we discovered the heads of their columns upon the summit of a distant hill which rose gradually and regularly from the river-bank.[130]

Of this part of the country, which is beautiful rolling prairie, the upper or, as it is called, hurricane deck of the Winnebago commanded a perfect view; and as they advanced in four columns directly in front of us and marched slowly down the sloping plain, I thought I looked upon one of the prettiest pictures of the kind ever presented to my view. General Gaines directed me to meet them and invite the Governor, with Gen. Duncan and his staff, to breakfast with us on board.

On reaching the head of the left centre [sic] column, which had now halted on a spacious level, I inquired for the Commander-in-Chief and was informed that I should find him about the centre of that column. Having proceeded thither, I soon discovered a small knot of better than ordinarily mounted men, whom I rightly conjectured to be the persons I sought.

Having welcomed the General in the name of General Gaines, I inquired for the Governor and was conducted by General Duncan towards a vehicle which, had I met it elsewhere, I should have taken for a Jersey fishcart, but which, from its situation and position in the file, I now set down in my mind for an ammunition caisson. Approaching it, however, the General raised a leather curtain — for it was with these able barriers that the stronghold was defended on all sides from the weather — and there, Jupiter tonans! [sic], there lay his linsey-woolsey Excellency, coiled upon a truss of tarnished straw. By preventing an apoplexy of admiration (with which I was at the moment attacked) from gaining vent in an uncourtly cachinnation, I had like to have died. But I bowed me to the earth in token of respect and, in so doing, recovered sufficiently to deliver my message.

The invitation was declined because, as his Excellency said, he had had for three days "the chills and fever." I persuaded him, however, on that account, to take a state-room on board the boat, as he would then be able to contend with his malady on a fairer footing, and finally prevailed upon him to do so.

As we had a pretty substantial breakfast, I had the satisfaction of seeing our guests, who had been on plain allowance for some time, do ample justice to our steamboat fare; but this is a subject I will not descant upon as I am myself, especially after being on horseback an hour or two before day, apt enough to be seduced by the alluring savor of beefsteaks and collops far beyond the pale of classic epicurism.

The whole day was absolutely necessary for the issuing of ammunition, the cleaning of arms and, finally, putting the men in effective fighting order after the fatigues of the march. But the next morning's sun [June 26], which rose lurid and threatening, saw our columns on the march towards the Sac village. The United States Infantry of the 1st and 6th Regiments debouched from Fort Armstrong and, crossing the narrow channel to the mainland, moved down upon the village (which is about four miles from the fort) in two good columns, supported by one *company of artillery; while the mounted men under General Duncan advanced in the opposite direction.*[131] *As these latter were obliged to ford Rock River immediately above the village, the* Winnebago, *with one company of artillery on board, proceeded up the river to cover their passage.*

The companies arrived simultaneously at the designated points and the artillery, having taken possession of the heights on the right of the village, a few shots were fired through the ravines and the brushwood on the island, over which the trace to the ford passed, and the head of the column of militia entered the river.[132]

Some troops of the Spies battalion having effected their passage, the General landed and, having thrown out some light infantry, mounted and began to reconnoiter, more minutely than he had hitherto done, the ground about the village. I knew that the position of the Indians was a strong one, but I now saw that it was much more tenable than I had even imagined. Had they been disposed to maintain it, it would have given us some trouble to dislodge them. But they had (as soon as they saw their fate was inevitable and that they were, poor fellows, doomed to quit forever their much loved homes) wisely decided to abandon their village. This, however, was not concluded until they saw from our preparations that they could trifle no longer with impunity. They had remained in their village until just before day on the morning of our entrance, when, collecting their canoes, a greater portion of them crossed to the western shore of the Mississippi; and some, indeed, had clung to their miserable dwellings until within a short time of our arrival, as we discovered by the fresh tracks of the trace leading to the Winnebago Prophet's town some distance up the river.

Of course, they were not pursued, as the object — now that they were driven from their old haunts and saw that we had a sufficient mounted force to protect the frontier — was to let them quietly settle on the lands appropriated to them and then call the chiefs to a council for the purpose of renewing the treaty and securing their pledges to preserve order and quiet among their followers.

Keokuk, who has talent with great shrewdness and is, withal, an eloquent speaker, has been unremitting in his efforts to move the hearts of the people of the British or Black-Hawk Band to yield gracefully, or at least appear to acquiesce in what must at last prove to be inevitable. In truth, the difficulty has been in bringing about not a conviction that their country was inevitably wrested from them (for that was apparent to the most obtuse), but to overcome a determination to die rather than relinquish the land of their birth and the graves of their ancestors. Keokuk accomplished the latter point — the former required no prompting.

Just a short while ago that artful negotiator called on the General in all the finery of official dress, conspicuous in which was a necklace of the formidable claws of the Grizzly Bear (which, by the by, it is whispered he procured with "the silver bullet"; but Keokuk is nevertheless acknowledged to be a brave and able leader on the war-path as well as a wise man in council); and in a grandiloquent speech reported the success of his mission and that Black Hawk

*would come in tomorrow and renew the treaty, relinquishing the territory lat-
terly in dispute.*[133]

I am called off and must close my letter. Adieu.

[*June 30, 1831 — Thursday*]

The large council chamber at Fort Armstrong on Rock Island droned with the murmur of scores of individual low conversations as the delegates settled themselves and waited for the most significant Indian group to make its appearance.

Behind the semicircle of tables were seated the principal whites of this scenario — General Edmund P. Gaines, resplendent in his fine uniform, seated to the right of a smiling though still rather peaked Governor John Reynolds, who claimed to have lost at least a dozen pounds on this expedition. The general's aide de camp, Lieutenant George A. McCall, sat to his immediate right with a sheaf of papers in a folder on the table before him — the treaty that he had been ordered by General Gaines to draw up. A handful of freshly trimmed goose-quill pens lay to one side, next to an inkpot. Colonel Willoughby Morgan of the U.S. 1st Infantry, commander of Fort Armstrong and as neatly clad as Gaines, sat to the right of the general's aide, with Brevet Major John Bliss, commander of Fort Crawford at Prairie du Chien, beside him. Extending outward on Governor Reynolds's left sat the United States Indian agents from Prairie du Chien and Rock Island, Joseph M. Street and Felix St. Vrain, as well as the grossly corpulent half-blood interpreter, Antoine LeClaire. The remaining seven white men at the table were officers of the Illinois militia — Samuel Whiteside, John S. Greathouse, M. K. Alexander, A. S. West, Joseph Danforth, Dan S. Witter, and Benjamin F. Pike.

Governor Reynolds fidgeted a bit as they waited, but General Gaines sat calmly and quietly at attention, only breaking into a half-smile when a growing sound of voices and movement outside heralded the arrival of the Indian contingent that was being awaited. Bad Thunder and Quashquame, the titular chiefs of this so-called British Band of Sacs, approached the building at the head of nearly five hundred warriors. All eyes, however, were on the hairless, eagle-featured Indian directly behind the two chiefs, Black Hawk, resplendent in immaculate doeskin and wearing a forty-piece grizzly claw necklace. The latter strode with firm step, his gaze straying neither left nor right as they approached the council house. It was his voice that barked out a guttural command, and at once all but fifty of the principal chiefs, subchiefs, and important braves of this contingent stepped apart to wait outside while the fifty entered. They wore their finest garb and ornamentation, though many were bare-chested. Heavy breechclouts and leggins of finely tanned buckskin covered their lower bodies and they were shod with moccasins colorfully decorated with beads and dyed porcupine quills. Most had light blankets, folded to a third of their length, draped over a bare shoulder, and no man among them had a visible weapon of any kind on his person, although those who had remained outside were heavily armed.

The fifty Sacs took their place where space had been left vacant for them, and at a hand gesture from Bad Thunder, all sat down. As General Gaines came to his feet, a hush settled over the assemblage of close to two hundred Indians and whites now inside the council chambers. Immediately interpreter LeClaire also rose and took position within a few feet of the general, prepared to interpret for the Indians every utterance of the white chief and vice versa.

"In the name of the President of the United States," Gaines said, his voice clear and measured, "I welcome our red brothers to this treaty council and extend the bough of permanent peace between us. In preparation for this long-awaited day, I have directed that a treaty be drawn up in which all points of agreement between our peoples are carefully and clearly stated. So that there will be no misunderstandings here and in later times as to what was stated in this treaty, I now direct my aide, Lieutenant McCall, to read this treaty sentence by sentence, with interpretation by Antoine LeClaire to be similarly given sentence by sentence. If at any time during this reading or afterwards, until the signing of the treaty is completed, there is any question by any principal involved, it is his responsibility to bring it up in discussion. If no question is asked and the treaty is signed by the principals, then it must be understood now and forever afterwards that all who are here involved knew exactly what the treaty contained and approved of its contents entirely and without reservation." He paused until LeClaire had caught up with him in the interpretation, then turned to his aide. "Lieutenant McCall, please begin your reading of the treaty at this time."

George McCall murmured, "Yes sir," and opened the folder before him. He began to read in a loud, clear voice, pausing at the end of each phrase until that phrase had been interpreted aloud by Antoine LeClaire.

"Articles of agreement and capitulation made and concluded this thirtieth day of June, one thousand eight hundred and thirty-one, between E. P. Gaines, major-general of the United States Army, on the part of the United States; John Reynolds, governor of Illinois, on behalf of the State of Illinois; and the chiefs and braves of the band of Sac Indians usually called the British Band of Rock River, with their old allies of the Potawatomi, Winnebago, and Kickapoo nations:

"Witnesseth: That, whereas the said British Band of Sac Indians have, in violation of the several treaties entered into between the United States and the Sac and Fox nations in the years 1804, 1816, and 1825, continued to remain upon and to cultivate the lands on Rock River, ceded to the United States by the said treaties, after the said lands had been sold by the United States to individual citizens of Illinois and other states; and, whereas the said British Band of Sac Indians, in order to sustain their pretensions to continue upon the said Rock River lands, have assumed the attitude of actual hostility towards the United States, and have had the audacity to drive citizens of the State of Illinois from their homes, to destroy their corn, and to invite many of their old friends of the Potawatomies, Winnebagoes, and Kickapoos to unite with them (the said British Band of Sacs) in war, to prevent their removal from said lands; and, whereas many of the most disorderly of these several tribes of Indians did actually join the said British Band of Sac Indians, prepared for war against the United States, from which purpose they confess that nothing could have restrained them but the appearance of force far exceeding the combined strength of the said British Band of Sac Indians, with such of their aforesaid allies as had actually joined them; but being now convinced that such a war would tend speedily to annihilate them, they have voluntarily abandoned their hostile attitude and sued for peace.

"First — Peace is therefore given to them upon the following conditions, of which the said British Band of Sac Indians, with their aforesaid allies, do agree; and for the faithful execution of which the undersigned chiefs and braves of the said band, and their allies, mutually bind themselves, their heirs and assigns forever.

"Second — the British Band of Sac Indians are required peaceably to submit to the authority of the friendly chiefs and braves of the united Sac and Fox nations, and at all times hereafter to reside and hunt with them upon their own lands west of the Mississippi River, and to be obedient to their laws and treaties; and no one or more of the said band shall ever be permitted to recross this river to the place of their usual residence, nor to any part of their old hunting grounds east of the Mississippi, without the express permission of the president of the United States or the governor of the State of Illinois.

"Third — the United States will guarantee to the united Sac and Fox nations, including the said British Band of Sac Indians, the integrity of all lands claimed by them westward of the Mississippi River pursuant to the treaties of the years 1825 and 1830.

"Fourth — the United States require the united Sac and Fox nations, including the aforesaid British Band, to abandon all communication, and cease to hold any intercourse, with any British post, garrison, or town, and never again to admit among them any agent or trader who shall not have derived his authority to hold commercial or other intercourse with them by license from the president of the United States or his authorized agent.

"Fifth — the United States demand an acknowledgment of their right to establish military posts and roads within the limits of the said country guaranteed by the third article of this agreement and capitulation, for the protection of the frontier inhabitants.

"Sixth — it is further agreed by the United States, that the principal friendly chiefs and headmen of the Sacs and Foxes bind themselves to enforce, as far as may be in their power, the strict observance of each and every article of this agreement and capitulation, and at any time that they may find themselves unable to restrain their allies, the Potawatomies, Kickapoos, or Winnebagoes, to give immediate information thereof to the nearest military post.

"Seventh — and it is finally agreed by the contracting parties that henceforth

permanent peace and friendship be established between the United States and
the aforesaid band of Indians.

"In witness whereof we have set our hands, the date above mentioned."

Lieutenant McCall glanced up from his papers and added, "This instrument
of treaty, agreement, and capitulation, will now be signed by Edmund P.
Gaines, major-general by brevet, commanding, and John Reynolds, governor of
the State of Illinois, after which all twenty-eight Indian principals named —
chiefs, subchiefs, and braves — shall come forward and sign their names or
make their official marks at the place indicated, after which the thirteen designated witnesses will duly affix their signatures to the document in attestation of
its validity."

In order, then, following General Edmund Gaines and Governor John Reynolds signing the treaty, the principal Indians were called, each by his Indian
name and its English counterpart, and each thereupon made his official mark
where appropriate on the document. All this took some time, and it was followed
by the thirteen officially designated witnesses adding their signatures to the
treaty. With that, the threat of possible war with the Sac and Fox Indians seemed
to have been negated, and the 1831 Treaty of Rock Island now became history.[134]

As something of a postscript to the day, General Gaines and Governor Reynolds briefly visited Black Hawk's hidden camp on the west side of the Mississippi
and were sobered by the impoverished state in which they found the women and
children, many of whom hardly even had clothing to cover themselves and were
making do with bits of rags. And though Governor Reynolds — still gravely
considering his public image — refused to have any part of it, General Gaines
authorized that the Indians of Black Hawk's band be helped, and that they be
given enough food and other goods from the store of provisions at Fort Armstrong to last them until the fall crops could be gathered, and that Black Hawk
distribute this largess among his people. With genuine gratitude, Black Hawk
accepted the gift.

Well after midnight, beneath the yellow glow of his lamp, George McCall
again closed his long day by writing to his father.

> *Hd. Qrs. on* Winnebago
> *Before dawn July 1, 1831*

My dear Father: —

*The treaty is done. At the appointed time, Black-Hawk appeared, accompanied
by "The Jumping Fish," the legitimate chief, who was by heredity right, so far as
that was acknowledged, and for the rest of the election, the head and front of the
Band, but whose negative character gave way before the bold and active prompt-
ings of his prime-minister, Black-Hawk.[135] There were in attendance about fifty
sub-chiefs and distinguished warriors, but all on this occasion were unarmed.*

All being seated in due form, the treaty, which in the interval I had been

*ordered to draw up, I, by direction of the General, now read sentence by sentence,
as it was translated by the interpreter, Saint Clare, a half-blood French-
Indian.*[136] *This being accomplished, and the purport of the treaty being acknowledged as understood and agreed to by* The Jumping Fish, *I called up Black-Hawk
to affix, in his official character as prime minister, his sign-manual to the paper.
He arose slowly and with great dignity, while in the expression of his fine face there
was a deep-seated grief and humiliation that no one could witness unmoved. The
sound of his heel upon the floor as he strode majestically forward was measured
and distinct. When he reached the table where I sat, I handed him a pen and
pointed to the place where he was to affix the mark that would sunder the tie he
held most dear on earth. He took the pen — made a large bold cross with a force
which rendered that pen forever unfit for further use. Then, returning it politely,
he turned short upon his heel and resumed his seat in the manner he had left it.*

*It was an imposing ceremony and scarcely a breath was drawn by anyone
present during its passage. Thus ended the scene — one of the most impressive of
the kind I ever looked upon. And with it terminated the duty which had led our
General to visit Fort Armstrong.*

*I must not omit to mention that during our stay here, the General had our
horses put on board a boat in which we crossed the river. We ascended a steep bluff
and, on attaining its summit, there was laid open to our view a boundless, rolling
prairie — the first I had ever laid eyes upon. We rode out upon it some distance.
I was greatly exhilarated and proposed to the general to breathe our horses. To this
he responded by putting spurs to his charger, and bounded off like a boy. I at once
discovered that the old gentleman was a fine horseman and bold rider. After a
pleasant ride, we returned — both, I believe, much refreshed and benefitted after
being shut up on the steamer.*

It is late at night and I must close my letter. Adieu.

CHAPTER V

[*December 31, 1831 — Saturday*]

THOSE WHO HAD THOUGHT the ousting of the British Band of the Sacs from Saukenuk six months ago would relieve the tension existing on the Illinois frontier were greatly in error. There was the prevailing feeling — without concrete justification but, nevertheless, definitely there — that the military action had been nothing more than the first confrontation in a general Indian war. There was also the strong feeling that General Gaines had been much too easy on Black Hawk and other leaders of the Indians who had been occupying the Rock River area, and that they should have been taken into custody and incarcerated at Jefferson Barracks, not only as an example to those who might have similar anti-white inclinations, but also as hostages against such a possibility. When word spread that Gaines had actually given the Sacs food and other supplies to tide them over for the loss of the crops they had planted on the east side of the Mississippi, many were scornful, saying the Indians should have been on the receiving end of bullets, not food, and they referred to the entire military action against them, such as it was, as the "corn war."

Even the most highly placed government officials — the president and the secretary of war — had begun to question whether the United States' response to the threat had been punitive enough. Sharply worded letters were sent to all the principals involved — Gaines, Reynolds, Duncan, and Clark, as well as all the Indian agents and interpreters — ordering each to explain in his own way the factors that had caused the whole situation to occur and whether calling up the militia in such numbers had been justified. And though, in the end, the government agreed with the steps Gaines had taken, there was still a strong sense of unease on the frontier and a presentiment that more trouble from the Sacs was to come.

The response of Governor Reynolds to the secretary of war left no doubt as to his feelings in the matter, and his determination to be much tougher the next time, if there were a next time:

Belleville 7th July 1831

To the Hon. *the Secretary of the Department of War*

Sir: — *I consider it my duty to inform you of the late Indian hostilities and of the measures which were adopted to repress them.*

The Indians, with some exceptions, from Canada to Mexico, along the northern frontier of the United States, are more hostile to the whites than at any other period since the last war. Particularly, the band of Sac Indians usually, and truly, called the "British Band" became extremely unfriendly to the citizens of Illinois and others. This band had determined for some years past to remain, at all hazards, on certain lands which had been purchased by the United States, and afterwards some of them [the lands] sold to private individuals by the General Government. They also determined to drive off the citizens from this disputed territory. In order to effect this object they committed various outrages on the persons and property of the citizens of this State.

That this band might more effectually resist all force that would be employed against them, they treated with many other tribes to combine together for the purpose of aiding this British Band to continue in possession of the country in question.

These facts and circumstances being known to the frontier inhabitants, they became much alarmed and many of them abandoned their homes and habitations.

In this situation of affairs, I considered the State to be actually invaded and the country in "imminent danger," so much that I immediately called on part of the militia nearest the disputed territory to be ready to march to repel said invasion and to restore peace to the frontier. I informed Genl. Gaines of the situation of the State and of my preparatory movements. After the General became acquainted with the numbers and disposition of the Indians and the exposed situation of the frontier, he very rightly determined on making a requisition on me for a number of mounted militia. These mounted volunteers, whom I had organized for the same purpose, cheerfully marched at the call of the United States. The great extent of the frontier from Lake Michigan to the Mississippi in the State, including part of the mining country, made it necessary to have the service of mounted men to protect the citizens. There are great numbers of Indians who reside near the northern border of this State and it was probable that all might be joined in a war. I have no hesitation in stating that it was necessary to make the call and that a considerable number of mounted men ought to be used in this service. It has been the case in many military operations that a sufficient force has not been in the first instance employed and the consequence has been disaster and defeat. This was not the case in this military movement. A sufficient force of mounted men — and none too many for the purpose — was immediately called into the field. This efficient and bold movement intimidated the Indians and compelled them to abandon their hos-

tile attitude without bloodshed, whereas a small number of mounted men would probably have led on to a general war.

Thus I have presented to you the general outlines of this military movement — which has terminated so fortunately for all concerned.

In the council, or treaty, with the Indians, General Gaines requested me to be associated with him as a commissioner. You will see by the agreement that these Indians are to remain in [the] future on the west side of the Mississippi. The policy to separate them from the whites is the only sure course to preserve peace with them.

There is a village of bad Indians on Rock River, about thirty miles from its mouth, whom I would recommend you to have moved to the west side of the Mississippi.[137] This may save a great deal of trouble, as I do assure you that if I am again compelled to call on the militia of this State, I will place in the field such a force as will exterminate all Indians who will not let us alone.

I have the honor to be your obt. Servt.

John Reynolds

By July 6 the majority of the regulars were back at St. Louis, and the militia was well on its way home and ready for disbanding. But there was a definite change. Before the militia left, Saukenuk was destroyed, and many of the Indian graves were opened so that the ornaments and implements that had been buried with the dead could be stolen. In some cases the exhumed dead were maliciously chopped apart, and in one case a body believed to be that of a recently deceased chief was placed atop a bonfire and burned. The fury of the Indians, when these outrages became known, was intense. Also, for the first time many would-be settlers realized what wonderfully fertile country the Rock River Valley was, and now, with the hazard of the British Band of the Sacs having been removed, they began to flock into the territory to buy the land or simply claim it as a squatter. When the Indians tried to return to rebury their disinterred dead, the new settlers drove them off. When the supply of corn General Gaines had given them turned out to be insufficient to tide them over and a party of warriors slipped back across the river in an attempt to harvest the fields they had planted, they were fired on by the whites and driven off.

The agent at Rock Island, St. Vrain, was sympathetic to his charges and tried to help them, but he was almost universally thwarted by the settlers, and he was sure new Indian problems on this frontier were virtually inevitable under the existing circumstances — a state of affairs he tried to put across in St. Louis to the commanding officer of Jefferson Barracks, who also happened to be the newly appointed commander of the right wing of the Army's Western Department, Brigadier General Henry Atkinson. This general, who privately harbored his own sympathies for the Indians, was still too new in his position to be of any great assistance. Felix St. Vrain then appealed to his own immediate supervisor, William Clark:

Rock Island Indn. Agency
July 23, 1831

Sir:

At the time I made application to the Indians for the payment of the claims which were handed to me against them, they said that it was no more than justice for the Government to pay them for the mineral that was taken from their land at Dubuque's Mines, and likewise for other property which the white people took from them. Wapello — the Prince — a Fox chief, says that a rifle worth thirty dollars was taken from him by a white man and broken; this was done within the State of Missouri, near Des Moines Rapids, at a time when Wapello was returning to his village from a visit he had been paying on you at St. Louis.

I am sorry to say that after the departure of the troops, complaint was made to me by the Indians that the white people living at or near the old Sac village on Rock River would not permit them to go over to that place for the purpose of covering their dead which had been disturbed by the militia; that some of the Indian graves had been uncovered, of which I immediately informed the Govr. of Illinois. He assured me that it should be stopped. When the Indians came to let me know that they could not have the privilege of covering the graves which had been so shamefully disturbed, I told them to meet me the next day at the village and I would see that they should not be injured. I accordingly went with my interpreter and found to my astonishment that about fifteen or twenty graves had been uncovered, and one entire corpse taken out from the grave and put into the fire and burned; some of the bones were found in the ashes. Some of those [white] inhabitants make it their business to shoot at the Indians as they peaceably pass in the river; and if they happen to land, their canoes are either destroyed or taken from them.

I had occasion to give a pass to an Indian (whose horse had been taken by a white man) to go over in the State of Illinois to get his horse. The pass was examined and returned to the Indian, after which they took his gun and broke it and gave him a severe whipping.

I am perfectly satisfied from the information I have been able to get, that those who are guilty of the above charges are none but the squatters on the public lands.

I have the honor to be, Your Obt. Servt.,
Felix St. Vrain, Ind. Agt.

Though undoubtedly St. Vrain was correct in his assessment that serious problems were looming, the volatile frontier situation was abruptly exacerbated by a horrifying act of revenge. Though a military invasion against them had intervened, the Sacs and Foxes had not forgotten the ambush and annihilation of the peace party of Foxes at Prairie du Chien by a party of Sioux, Menominees, and Winnebagoes. To the majority of the Sacs and Foxes, their dead had never been sufficiently covered. In their hearts the insult and indignity of the murder of Chief Pamoske and sixteen of his unarmed followers and the desecration of their bodies was still a fire of hatred that could only be quenched by revenge. Now, at last, they got that revenge. Only a few hundred yards from old Fort Crawford in Prairie du Chien, a party of thirty to forty Menominee warriors had camped and were given a large supply of liquor by the traders. It began turning into a debauch, and the squaws of the party, fearful that their men would harm one another in their drunken reveling, gathered up all the weapons and hid them. Two hours before dawn, a force of about one hundred Sacs and Foxes, led by two prominent warriors named Pankeene and Natauetaheka, burst upon the scene and silently, using only their knives, tomahawks, and spears, killed twenty-six of them and wounded several others before slipping away in the darkness.[138]

The Indian agent at Prairie du Chien, Joseph Street, wholly overlooking the fact that the attack was strictly an Indian matter, a matter of honor among the Sac and Fox for an injury earlier inflicted upon them in part by the Menominee and in direct retaliation for that previously unpunished act, castigated the Sacs and Foxes severely, accused them of insulting the United States, and loudly demanded that the government step in and "signally chastise and deeply humble" them or else whites would be next to be attacked.

Even President Andrew Jackson got in on it, concurring with Street's opinion and ordering that the Indian agents demand of the Sac chiefs that the perpetrators of the "massacre" be turned over to them for trial as murderers. Immediately General Atkinson ordered the Fort Armstrong commander, Major John Bliss, to call a council of the Sac chiefs at Rock Island, interrogate them on the matter, and insist that the murderers plus some hostages be turned over to the government.

The council was held on September 5 by Major Bliss and Felix St. Vrain. Various chiefs and influential braves spoke at length, including Quashquame, Black Hawk, Bad Thunder, Tiomay — the Strawberry, Allotah, and Kattekennekak — Bald Eagle — all more or less in the same vein, but none with more force or concern or controlled anger than Keokuk, who was at last bitterly incensed at what was occurring. He referred back to the massacre that had been perpetrated by the Sioux, Menominees, and Winnebagoes on the Foxes, when Pamoske and his party had been attacked, and then continued with quiet vehemence.

"If what *they* and what now *we* have done were put on a scale, it would balance. So why do you criticize *us* so much? I suspect it is because our names are Sacs and Foxes that you make a noise about it. Why do you only think things are bad when it is *we* who have done them? Look now. After we did this thing to the Menominees at Prairie du Chien, the Sioux and Menominees then turned and took a vengeance on us. A band of our Fox people under Chief Kettle, living at Dubuque Mines, made an appointment to meet the agent at Prairie du Chien. But the agent told the trader John Marsh, and John Marsh told the Sioux of the time and place. The Sioux and Menominees then went fifteen miles below Prairie du Chien, where the river channel the canoes follow passes close between the islands where there are thick bushes, and here they waited in ambush. Our Chief Kettle came to this place in his boat with his people, and as he passed through they rose from hiding and killed him and several others, and those who got away fled back to Dubuque's Mines. Yet the whites do not ask the Sioux or the Menominees to account for this or to turn over to them those who did the shooting, so they can be tried in white man's court for murder. Why, then, are *we* singled out for such treatment from you?"

Keokuk glared at the whites in attendance, but they knew he was not finished and made no response. "Last winter," he continued, "I went to the Missouri, and there, at the treaty, an Ioway killed an Omahaw. So why did you not ask that the Ioway be surrendered up to the whites for trial for murder? Why was *he* not hanged? *Our* chiefs were killed with the pipe of peace and wampum in their hands."

He looked around and fastened his gaze on St. Vrain. "This is all I have to say. As for my chiefs and braves, they will do as they please. I have said all I have to say on that subject, but why do you not let us fight? You whites are constantly fighting — why do you not interfere with them? Why do you not let us be as the Great Spirit made us, and let us settle our own difficulties?"

All the Indians in attendance broke into applause and hoots of approbation at this. When quiet was finally restored, Major Bliss again demanded an answer about whether or not the guilty Indians would be turned over to him. Keokuk shook his head, and there was an unbreachable finality in his voice when he replied.

"The answer you wanted you have heard from the chiefs. Many are absent now, and before they could be collected it would be so late as to cause us to lose our fall hunt. But during our hunt we shall be able to talk over this matter and early next spring give an answer."

"I expect," John Bliss said reproachfully, "that much mischief may occur before next spring, and an answer before then would be desirable."

Again Keokuk shook his head. "We cannot do as you say. We cannot go and get them and bring them to you. *They* must offer to give *themselves* up. Before we can take them, we must persuade them to give themselves up. That is our way. It is not in our power to take them. We cannot take them without their consent and the consent of their relations, some of whom have gone over on the Missouri to hunt."

With that the council had broken up. The whites had been thwarted for the moment, but they let it be known they were not yet finished. Black Hawk was, at this point, extremely discouraged over the treatment the Sacs and Foxes were receiving at the hands of the whites. He based the discrimination solely on the fact that even though the whites had gotten Saukenuk and the Sac lands east of the Mississippi, now they had their greedy hands poised to grasp the lead mines of the Dubuque area *west* of the Mississippi and would not be satisfied until they had them.

The massacre of the Menominee party had rekindled a fire in Black Hawk's heart that had been banked for a long time. When the Sacs and Foxes who had been involved in it came to him and asked his advice about whether or not they should turn themselves in to the whites, Black Hawk was flattered that they should have sought out his opinion, while at the same time angered that they should even *consider* surrendering themselves in a matter that was no business of the whites to begin with. As a result of his views in regard to the situation, many of the Sacs and Foxes that had earlier turned their backs on him now began throwing their support behind him again.

It was at this opportune time that Neapope returned. He had been gone since the time when General Gaines had first put his army in the noise-boat to come upstream to attack Saukenuk. As the rest of the Sacs had fled across the Mississippi to the hidden camping place, Neapope — following the directions of Chiefs Bad Thunder and Quashquame, at Black Hawk's instigation — headed for a visit to the British at Malden, seeking their advice and quite possibly even their support in the great problem facing them with the Americans.

Now, in the dubious warmth of the wigwam, with the bitter wind howling without, Neapope gave Black Hawk a glowing report. The British had offered their aid! A particular British agent, he said, had told him to tell his chiefs that if the Sacs had not sold their village to the Americans, then those whites had no right to it. Neapope took a stance before Black Hawk and, eyes glittering with excitement, spoke earnestly.

"The British father told me to tell my Sac and Fox chiefs that the right to Saukenuk and the lands east of the Mississippi belongs to the *entire* tribe, and since the tribe has what he calls a vested right, the land and village can be transferred only by the voice and will of the whole nation in agreement. He said that since the Sac and Fox had never given their consent for the sale of their country, it remains our exclusive property, from which we cannot legally be forced. He said that in the event of our going to *war* with the Americans, we should have nothing to fear, as our British friends will stand by us and assist us!"

Neapope grinned, pleased with being the bearer of such news. "When I left Malden," he continued, "I was given messages from the British to carry to Wabokieshiek. The messages promised Wabokieshiek and his combined force of Winnebagoes, Chippewas, Ottawas, Potawatomies, and Kickapoos that if they agreed to help the Sacs and Foxes, the British would, in the spring, send guns, ammunition, clothing, provisions, and other supplies to help support them in their struggle against the Americans; that the vessel to bring these goods would come by way of Milwaukee. And the British message also said that even if the worst occurred and the Indians were defeated, they could retreat to the Red River area of Canada, west of Lake Superior, where the British would gladly give them refuge.

"When I stopped to see the Prophet he was very receptive to the British offer, and has already asked for and received commitments from the five tribes, and he has them all under his command. Now he has told me to tell you, Black Hawk, that he wishes you to recruit as many Sacs and Foxes as possible for the forthcoming contest, and he says we are all going to be happy once more."

Black Hawk's eyes were alight. "I am pleased," he said, "to hear that our British father at last intends to see our wrongs righted. We have been driven from our lands without receiving anything for them, and I now begin to hope that my people will once more become happy. If I can accomplish that, I will be satisfied. I am growing old, and I can spend the rest of my days anywhere, but first I want to see my people happy. I begin to hope that our sky will soon be clear."

Neapope grunted an assent. "We must go and see the Prophet. I will go first. You had better remain and get as many of our people to join us as you can, now that you know and can tell them everything that has been done. The Prophet leaves with you the matter of making arrangements among our people as you please. I will return to the Prophet's village tomorrow, and you can, in the meantime, make up your mind as to the course you will take and send word to the Prophet by me, as he is anxious to assist us."

"I do not need to wait until the morrow to give you the message to return to him," Black Hawk said, reaching out and squeezing the shoulder of the younger man. "Tell the Prophet that even though Black Hawk six moons ago put his name to a treaty that would keep him out of his own country, now he promises that in spring he will cross the Mississippi one more time and retake Saukenuk and the Indian lands that the Americans have illegally taken as their own."

[*January 4, 1832 — Wednesday*]

The giant blacksmith, William Davis, could hardly believe his eyes when he looked from the window shortly after dawn on this bright, unseasonably warm day and saw the three Indians trying to destroy his mill dam. One of them was using a heavy iron rod to poke savagely at the raceway in an effort to damage it, and the other two were pulling away the chunks being dislodged. Without even pausing to snatch up his coat, Davis burst from the house and ran to the dam. His son Bill, pausing only to snatch a rifle from its pegs on the wall, followed closely behind.

More than anything else in his life, the elder Davis was proud of this little community he had created in the Illinois wilderness. Word of the beauty of the place he had chosen in the valley of Big Indian Creek, a dozen miles north of Ottawa, had spread widely, and many visitors had come to see his property, which included not only the substantial house he had built for himself and the other eight members of his family, but also a large blacksmith shop and adjoining gristmill. Throughout the entire summer newly arriving settlers had come and, as Davis had anticipated they would, decided this was a wonderful place to put down their roots and built their houses close to his. Now there were a dozen families living here who looked to one another for companionship and even assistance if it should come to that.[139] The blacksmith and his wife, Martha, rather liked the idea of establishing a town and even considered the immodesty, when the time came to think of such a project, of naming it Davis. As a matter of fact, it was already being called the Davis Settlement, and that pleased him inordinately.

The single construction of which he was most proud at this new location was the dam and mill he had built on Big Indian Creek. Construction had been completed a few months before, and now the impounded waters slid powerfully into the millrace and onto the blades of the great waterwheel at the side of the mill. The heavy rumbling sound of the wheel as it turned and caused the huge millstone inside to revolve and ponderously crush the grain was a comforting drone, and it had been busy all this past fall grinding the wheat and corn that had been brought in by settlers not only of the Davis Settlement, but for many miles in all directions.

There had been only one minor black cloud in the midst of this sanguinity, and that was when, about six weeks ago, a delegation of five Potawatomi Indians from the village of Chief Meau-eus, some six miles upstream from here, had come to ask that the dam Davis had built be torn down.[140] The reason for their request, the spokesman named Toquamee said in passable English, was that the economy of their village depended on the free flowage of Big Indian Creek. Each spring there was a significant run of spawning fish up this stream to the area of their village, which was why their village had been located there to begin with. During the spawning season, they caught and dry-cured a great many of the fish and then used them as trading items within their own tribe, with other tribes, and with white traders. Now the dam Davis had built was preventing the fish from coming upstream to their natural spawning area and thus ruining the economy of Meau-eus Town. Would Davis please tear down the water obstruction?

Davis would not. Not only had he coldly and flatly refused even to consider the request, he had ordered Toquamee and the other two Potawatomies away with thinly veiled threats of what he would do to them if they stayed or if they showed up here again to make trouble. Almost certainly there would have been serious repercussions to this but for the intervention of the powerful and influential Chief Chaubenee, whose village was on the same creek some eighteen miles above Meau-eus Town.[141]

Chaubenee had gotten wind of the developing crisis and had hastened to Meau-eus Town while a council was still in session discussing whether or not an immediate attack should be made on the whites at the Davis Settlement. Skilled negotiator and speaker that he was, Chaubenee had managed to convince his fellow Potawatomies that not only were the whites in this country to stay, but that any conflict between themselves and the whites would serve no purpose but to cause immediate and deadly retaliation by the Americans and a resultant loss of the Potawatomi claims in the area. While it was extremely inconvenient for them, he made them see the wisdom of simply going to a different location, downstream from the Davis dam, to engage in their annual harvest of the spawning fish next spring.

Even though Chief Meau-eus and his Potawatomies had agreed not to fall upon the whites at the Davis Settlement, Toquamee continued to carry a bitter resentment within him for the insult that had been handed him by the big blacksmith. For weeks the rancor had grown within him, until finally, unable to contain it any longer, he had decided on his own to destroy the dam. Shortly after darkness had fallen last night, he had come to the Davis property, slipped into the blacksmith shop and found an iron rod, and begun poking and prying at the dam with it. He was sure that if he could just start a rift in the dam, the pressure of the water in the impoundment would be sufficient to rip the dam apart as it poured through the gap he made.

That might have been exactly what occurred, except for the discovery by Davis early this morning of the damage being done by Toquamee and his two friends, Comee and Pukemus.[142] Arriving on the scene, the elder Davis stiff-armed Comee and Pukemus out of the way, ripped the iron rod out of Toquamee's grasp and threw it some distance away, then knocked the Potawatomi down with a tremendous blow to his face that broke Toquamee's nose and caused a gout of bright red blood.

While young Bill Davis covered the other two Potawatomies with the rifle, his father dragged the stunned Toquamee away from the dam by his hair and then proceeded to beat and kick him unmercifully until Bill began to fear his father was going to kill the Indian. He yelled at him to stop.

The shouted words penetrated at last and the elder Davis stepped back, breathing heavily, his great fists still clenched and nostrils flaring. He bent over and took the injured Indian's knife and tomahawk, then strode to the other two Potawatomies being held at gunpoint by his son and similarly took their weapons. He then indicated to these two that they were to pick up the man on the ground, who had now struggled dazedly to a sitting position, and take him away.

Comee and Pukemus edged nervously past Davis and his son and got Toquamee to his feet, draped his arms over their shoulders, and half-carried, half-dragged him away. By the time they had reached the edge of the woods several hundred yards distant, Toquamee had regained his senses enough to be walking by himself with their assistance. The three Potawatomies paused before entering the grove of hardwoods and looked back at the two whites, who were still standing where they had been, watching the departure.

Toquamee, smudging away the blood from his lower face, glared malevolently through eyes swollen almost shut, spat out a broken tooth, and spoke a muffled, implacable threat.

"These whites are dead men."

[*March 30, 1832 — Tuesday*]

"Come in," William Clark said loudly, in answer to the respectful tapping on his office door. It was sunny but quite crisp in St. Louis today, and yet, though it was cool in the room and there were only dimly glowing embers in the fireplace, the Indian supervisor was working in shirtsleeves. His desk was littered with letter pages scrawled with messy handwriting and smudged with occasional ink blots. He sighed and looked up as a clerk opened the door and leaned his head inside.

"Excuse me, Governor Clark," he said, but there's an officer here to see you with a message from General Atkinson."

Clark nodded. "Send him in," he said.

The officer who stepped inside smartly was Lieutenant George Shaver, a junior headquarters aide from Jefferson Barracks. In his left hand was an envelope. "Sir," he said, snapping a smart salute, "General Atkinson is planning to come by to see you within the next few days, but he asked me to let you see this letter he has received from Major Bliss, commander of Fort Armstrong. The general said that since it involved Black Hawk, you'd probably want to look it over."

Clark returned the salute in a lackadaisical manner and extended his hand. "Let's see it," he said.

Lieutenant Shaver stepped forward, handed the envelope to him, and then stepped back a pace and stood waiting at attention. The governor continued looking at him, smiling faintly as he extracted the folded sheets from the envelope and began to open them. "Relax, Lieutenant, while I read it. Have a seat."

The officer murmured a "Thank you, sir," and sat at attention on a nearby chair, his eyes straight ahead as Clark read through the three pages of small, neat handwriting. The governor's shoulders seemed to slump a little, and when finished he set the letter in a small clear spot on the right-hand side of his desk. Deep inside he had a feeling such as he had experienced on numerous occasions before — a feeling of impending trouble. He chewed at his lower lip as he considered what he had just reviewed in the other letters that evidently tied in so well with what Major Bliss had written to General Atkinson. One of those letters had been from Joseph Street, the Indian agent at Prairie du Chien, who had written:

The Sioux of the lower bands and those near St. Peter are collecting on the Cannon & Root Rivers, and tho' engaged in hunting, are passing wampum with the Menominees, and evidently preparing for a Spring campaign against the Sacs & Foxes; and have, in their encampments, declared as much. . . . The Chippewas are also near them, with whom a peace has been lately concluded.[143] *Their avowed intention is to go against the Sacs & Foxes in the Spring if the murderers of* [the Menominee party at] *Prairie du Chien are not before that time given up. . . . The Winnebagoes continue to assure me they will not join in the war so long as I advise them not. They say they made peace with the S & F. . . . The Sacs & Foxes, I learn, expect retaliation and will be in preparation to meet them.*

I think, therefore, a bloody contest may be expected. I can only remark in much haste, that the information now given . . . will show the necessity of an early interference, if any is intended.

An almost identical report in substance had been received from Elias T. Langham, the Indian subagent at the Sioux Agency at St. Peters in the Minnesota country. No less disturbing was the terse little letter Clark had received from Illinois governor Reynolds in regard to the Kickapoos still lingering in the state and evidently just waiting to see if Black Hawk was going to come back, so they could take up the war club alongside him. Reynolds had written:

I have received a letter . . . that there are about one hundred Indians in the Illinois River bottom near the mouth of Spoon River . . . & the citizens & they are not on friendly terms. . . . I fear some mischief may be done. The same letter informs me that the Whites had whipped several of them "in a most inhuman manner."

More evidence of the probability of trouble brewing was the note Clark had received from John Dougherty, the Indian agent at Cantonment Leavenworth, who stated that Jaton, the principal chief of the Otoes, had reported that the Sacs and Foxes on the Mississippi had invited them, as well as the Iowas and the Missouri Sacs, to join them in a war against the Americans, but that all had refused.[144]

These reports had concerned Clark enough that he had written a letter to his superior in the War Department, Indian commissioner Elbert Herring:

. . . By the report of Genl. Street, the Indians of the upper Mississippi seem determined on War against the Sacs & Foxes, if the murderers of the Menominees at Prairie du Chien are not given up. And from the report of Mr. Dougherty, it would appear that the Sacs & Foxes of the Mississippi had solicited aid of some of the Missouri tribes and intended opposition. No information has been received from Mr. St. Vrain in relation to the hostile intentions of the Sacs: that agent set out about the middle of last month to the Sac & Fox hunting camps high up the Demoine [sic] and Ioway [sic] Rivers for the purpose of obtaining the surrender of the murderers of the Menominees; or to learn the views & intentions of those Tribes in regard to the demand which has already been made of them for those murderers; and also to learn the particulars in relation to the Sac killed by the Sioux in the early part of the winter.

Shortly after that, St. Vrain had finally emerged from the wilderness again, and from his agency office at Rock Island immediately penned a gloomy report to Clark:

Sir, I was very much delayed in coming to my agency by bad weather and ice. . . . On my way from the lower rapids I had occasion to see a number of the Sac & Fox Indians, which had come in from the Des Moines River. They said to me that there was no news, except the fact of the report of the murder of the son of Kemanssa, a Fox Indian. The Indians report it was done by the Sioux and Menominees. . . . It is reported that the young men of the Sac & Fox nations of Indians will go to war against the Sioux; this I endeavored to prevent by sending a message to the principal chiefs, to interpose and stop them. . . . As to the surrender of the murderers of the Menominees, they say little about the matter, but it is my opinion that they will not give them up. . . .

Another brief message from St. Vrain came to Clark with word that a deputation of the peaceful Sacs in Iowa had come to him with a message from Keokuk, stating that Black Hawk was planning to lead his band of followers back into Illinois very soon; that the party, which might have from 250 to five hundred warriors and nearly three times that many women, children, and elderly, was planning to assemble at the site of old Fort Madison on the west side of the Mississippi, cross the big river, and move up to the Rock and follow it to its headwaters, where they planned to stay. After Black Hawk's ouster from Illinois last year by General Gaines, Clark found it hard to believe that the belligerent Black Hawk would be so foolish as to actually try to return once more. Yet, knowing very well the anger and frustration that was in the Sac, he conceded to himself that what Keokuk warned was altogether possible. Clark couldn't help feeling a surge of sympathy for the Sacs, since everything seemed against them. That feeling was underlined by news just received of two recent United States Supreme Court decisions that were bound to have strong ramifications here: on March 3 the court had ruled that the federal government had exclusive authority over tribal Indians and their lands within any state, and a fortnight after that another Supreme Court ruling held that an Indian tribe may not sue in federal courts, since the tribes are not foreign nations. Everything possible, it seemed, was being done to hamstring the Indians.

The final straw seemed to have come with official orders just received from Commissioner Herring in the War Department:

I am instructed to say to you that you will cause measures to be taken for the immediate surrender or apprehension of the Sacs and Foxes who murdered the Menominees last summer, or so many of them as may be sufficient for the purpose of example and justice — and that if it be impracticable to apprehend them, you will cause four or five of each tribe to be taken and detained as hostages, to constrain the surrender or delivery of those murderers. Troops have been ordered from Jefferson Barracks to proceed up the Mississippi to prevent the threatened hostilities of the Indian tribes and to aid you in effecting the apprehension of the before-mentioned murderers or the seizure of four or five of each tribe (Sacs and Foxes) as hostages for the purpose aforesaid.

William Clark again picked up the letter just brought to him by Lieutenant Shaver and reread it. Certain phrases Major Bliss had used seemed to leap out of the page at him. Keokuk and Chakeepashipaho had visited Fort Armstrong and told him that the deputation of Sac chiefs that was supposed to come down to St. Louis to talk with Clark had now decided not to do so after all. They also said that they had tried to keep Black Hawk and his people from returning to Illinois but were failing, and that if they should not succeed, they would be glad to see Black Hawk evicted by the whites. The chiefs had said that Black Hawk's prestige in the tribe had taken a sharp rise, and that they could make no satisfactory arrangements with him for the union of his band into the Iowa faction. And they had also said that as the Menominee murderers had not surrendered to them, they could not and should not interfere between them and the whites. Bliss went on to say that St. Vrain reported Neapope was with the Black Hawk band, that the band was expected to invade Illinois in the Rock Island area within the next ten or twelve days, and that Black Hawk had sworn to grow corn again at Saukenuk and to kill St. Vrain, George Davenport, and others. Bliss then added:

. . . These reports . . . have occasioned considerable agitation in this settlement. Interpreter LeClaire, however, attaches but little weight to these boasts and threats of Black Hawk, as [such are] *common to all Indians, and attributes his conduct to the rivalry existing between him and the chiefs above named.*

The governor wore a thoughtful expression as he quietly folded the letter and returned it to its envelope. He looked at the lieutenant, who immediately came to his feet and approached the desk.

"Sir?"

"I presume you are aware of the orders General Atkinson has received from Washington?"

"Concerning the move upriver on the Mississippi? Yes, sir."

"When does he plan to leave?"

"The posted orders call for departure on April eighth, sir. But as I mentioned, General Atkinson plans to visit you before our departure."

Clark handed him the envelope and leaned back in his chair. "There will be no written response," he said. "Just tell the general that I look forward to seeing him. You may also tell him that although I will not be accompanying this expedition, I will order whatever agents of this department that he meets to cooperate with him fully." It was a dismissal.

"Yes, sir!" Shaver saluted, spun on his heel, and left the room, closing the door behind him.

"And God help you all," Clark murmured.

[*April 5, 1832 — Thursday morning*]

The fifth day of April dawned on the Mississippi River with a brilliantly clear sky for a change, and with the voices of newly returned robins and red-winged blackbirds raised in declaration of territorial rights. It was going to be a beautiful day, and a fan of tiny crows-feet appeared at the outer corners of Black Hawk's eyes as he raised his arm. The birds he considered a good omen, for as they were declaring their territorial rights, so, too, at last, was he.

Beside him on a chestnut mare was Neapope, now rightfully Chief Neapope, civil head of the British Band since the recent death through illness of Chief Bad Thunder. Beyond these two leaders stretched out a multitude of Indians, well over a thousand individuals, along the Mississippi shoreline. The 350 Sac and Fox warriors, as well as the thirty-six Kickapoo warriors, were, like Black Hawk and Neapope, mounted on horses whose manes and tails were decorated with dyed feathers and numerous strands and bows of colored yarns. On the shoreline beyond them were over six hundred women, children, and elderly, malnourished, weak, and destitute due to a particularly bad winter's hunt far up on the headwaters of the Iowa. Despite their obvious poor condition, each had his own burden to carry — the entire material wealth of the band: household items, clothing, traps, blankets, cookpots, lodgepoles, weapons, skins, and a variety of other items, including a very limited amount of ammunition and foodstuffs. In addition to everything else they carried, they had nearly a hundred portage canoes.[145]

The fine white stallion upon which Black Hawk was mounted snorted and pawed the ground impatiently, and Black Hawk, arm still raised, called out loudly. "This is where we cross! This is where we return to our own land, to our own Rock River."

His moccasined heels thumped into the sides of his horse, and the animal instantly plunged out into the turbulent, spring-swollen waters of the broad river and began swimming across. The entire assemblage began to follow, and it was a grand spectacle as the many scores of horses and canoes and people began the crossing. The force of the current carried them almost half a mile downstream before they emerged on the opposite side. It took a long time for the entire party to reach the east shore, and while the crossing was still in progress, Black Hawk dispatched runners — not to the Winnebago Prophet at his village thirty-five miles up the Rock River, who Black Hawk knew was already en route to meet him, but to the Potawatomies in their various villages far up near the headwaters of the Rock and along the Fox River and in the country of the Four Lakes.[146] The runners carried his invitation to meet for a war council on the Rock River at the mouth of the Kishwaukee River.[147]

It took nearly until the sun was at its zenith to complete the crossing of the Mississippi, since each of the canoes had to make two or three trips in order to bring across all the people and their goods, but remarkably, considering the flooded state of the river, it was accomplished without a single accident to claim life or goods.[148] When it was finished and they were rested, once again Black Hawk came before them on the big white stallion and stilled them with his raised arm.

"We have come home," he said loudly. "We will not, for now, bother the whites who are here, but neither will we allow them to bother us. Now we go to Rock River, and I promise you, we will leave our *bones* on its shores if necessary before giving it up to the whites."

[*April 5, 1832 — Thursday afternoon*]

Felix St. Vrain's brows pinched together in a frown, and an angry undertone entered his voice. "Are you *sure* that's an accurate interpretation of what he said, Antoine?"

Not accustomed to having his interpretive abilities questioned, Antoine Le-Claire held his own anger in check with difficulty and spoke in a strained tone. "It is what he said, Monsieur St. Vrain, but if it will make you feel better, I will ask him to repeat what he said."

The Rock Island interpreter rattled off a few words to the Indian standing before him and then listened as Wabokieshiek — the Winnebago Prophet — responded. LeClaire turned back to St. Vrain. "It is exactly as he said it before, monsieur. He says, 'I think you should know, so that we may avoid trouble, that I have invited Black Hawk and Neapope to bring their band of followers to my village this spring, so they may raise their corn there, since they can no longer do so in Saukenuk.' "

"God damn it," St. Vrain thundered, "where does he get off pulling a stunt like that?" It was a rhetorical question and LeClaire made no comment, although Major John Bliss, standing to one side, muttered heavily, "There'll be hell to pay if that happens!"

St. Vrain was glaring at Wabokieshiek, who was looking innocently unconcerned with a half-smile on his lips. Without taking his eyes off the Winnebago, St. Vrain addressed the fat interpreter. "Ask him, Is he not aware that the confederated tribes agreed last June not to recross the Mississippi?"

LeClaire posed the question and Wabokieshiek spread his hands in a little helpless gesture, though his dark eyes glittered, as if he were finding this whole conversation very amusing. Through the interpreter he replied, "I had heard something of that, but I thought the restriction only applied to Rock Island and the mouth of the Rock River up to Saukenuk."

"If you are *that* careless about understanding agreements," St. Vrain responded through the interpreter, "then it just may be that you, too, will be ordered from your village by the whites."

Wabokieshiek's smile faded as he heard the words, and he rolled his eyes from the agent to the Fort Armstrong commander. Though he replied to St. Vrain, his cold gaze was locked on Bliss. "Perhaps you might expect to do so, but if that is tried, either your bones or mine may finally lay there."

"We just may put that to the test," St. Vrain said. "What do you think of that?"

Wabokieshiek let his gaze slide back to the Sac agent and stared at him a long, hard moment. Then he walked to the door, opened it, and turned, his hand still gripping the latch. "I have nothing more to say beyond this," he said. "If *you* think so, we can make war, but those Sacs are my young men, and I can call on them and the Winnebagoes for their strength at any time. I am half-Sac and half-Winnebago!"

He turned and was gone even before LeClaire had finished interpreting, and John Bliss released a harsh oath. "Do you believe that insolence?" he stormed. "Mr. St. Vrain, if you wish, I'll have him placed in irons and sent down to St. Louis."

St. Vrain shook his head. "No, I think not, Major. But like you, I think if Black Hawk *is* coming back with his people, whether at the Prophet's invitation or not, there's going to be hell to pay!"

[*April 10, 1832 — Tuesday*]

On the anchored Mississippi River steamboat *Chieftain*, General Henry Atkinson stood at the bow and stared morosely upstream in the gathering dusk. Apart from a single, huge, snaggly-rooted tree trunk floating downstream in the muddy expanse of swiftly flowing water, nothing caught his eye. Sentries patrolled the deck of the big ship ceaselessly; they would be on watch all throughout the night until the ship weighed anchor again in the morning. Atkinson paid little attention to them, thinking instead of his comfortable quarters at Jefferson Barracks and wishing he were back there now, wondering when or even *if* he would return.

The presentiment of great danger ahead had manifested itself in the general's mind since the meeting he'd had with Clark in St. Louis. It had only intensified since then, and with good reason, he thought, considering the dispatches and intelligence he'd been receiving. He and Clark had discussed his orders and what he was expected to accomplish, and at one point Atkinson had murmured to the Indian superintendent, "I am apprehensive that I shall have more trouble in settling the difficulties there than I at first expected."

A native North Carolinian, the tall, fifty-year-old General Henry Atkinson was really not well chosen for this assignment; he was much too easy-going, too little of the hard disciplinarian and too much of the benevolent commander. He had been in the United States Army for twenty-four years — establishing a career that was unblemished but also one not marked by signal achievement. He had led the two relatively uneventful Yellowstone expeditions of 1819 and 1825, and had commanded the United States troops in the lackluster little conflict now called the Winnebago War five years ago, in which the Indians had given him the name of White Beaver, but his only truly notable accomplishment thus far had been his construction of Jefferson Barracks in 1826. He had been in command of the installation ever since.

General Gaines, now headquartered in Memphis, was his immediate superior and still commanded the Western Department of the Army, but he had earned the War Department's displeasure last summer by his uninspired handling of the Black Hawk affair. It was clearly an official snub when orders from the commander of the entire United States Army, Major General Alexander Macomb, had bypassed Gaines and gone directly to Atkinson. Actually, after having read them, Atkinson would have greatly preferred they had been sent to Gaines. Received by Atkinson on April 1, the orders minced no words:

> *Headquarters of the Army*
> *Washington — 17 March 1832*

Sir: Information has been received at the War Dept. that the Menominees, with such other tribes as they may be able to enlist in their behalf, contemplate, as early as the season will admit of their moving, to make an attack on the Sacs and Foxes, in consequence of their having murdered a number of the Menominees at Prairie du Chien, in August last. . . .

In order that the murderers may be apprehended and delivered to the civil authority, and with a view also to put a stop to the threatened hostilities among the Indians, the Government has determined, for these purposes, to employ the troops stationed on the Mississippi and at Fort Winnebago. You will therefore proceed forthwith to Fort Armstrong, with the efficient force now at Jefferson Barracks, and if the Sacs and Foxes do not deliver up as many of the persons concerned in these murders as may be sufficient for the purposes of example and justice, say not less than eight or ten, including some of the principal men, you will then use force to apprehend them or to take hostages, not exceeding the number above stated. Which of these measures shall be adopted is left to your discretion on a full view of the circumstances. The hostages, if apprehended, will be humanely treated, and secured til [sic] the determination of the government is made known to you or some of the murderers are surrendered.

In the execution of this duty, I rely on your well-known judgement that force will not be used, til it becomes absolutely necessary; and that then so used, that the Indians will see that the object of the United States is to punish the guilty, not to injure the innocent.

It is important that the attack contemplated by the Menominees and their allies, should be prevented, and you will therefore take such steps, as in your judgement will best effect the object, taking care to apprise the Menominees of the intentions of the Government in regard to the murderers. . . .

General Clark and the Agent and sub-agents must be possessed of every information connected with the subject of the Indians. . . . . You are distinctly to understand that in the present instance no temporizing is to be allowed. The force placed at your disposal to carry into execution the views of the Government, is to be exerted to the utmost, should you find it necessary.

In withdrawing the effective force from the posts of Jefferson [Barracks], Rock Island, and Forts Crawford and Winnebago, it is to be expected that there will remain a sufficient number of men unfit to march, who will be capable of guarding the respective posts, at each of which a suitable portion of officers should be left on duty. . . .

You will keep me informed as early and as often as practicable of your movements and operations, that I may communicate the same to the Secretary of War.

> *I have the honor to be very respectfully Sir,*
> *Yr. Obt. St.*
> *Alex Macomb Major General Com:g the Army*

General Atkinson had responded to Macomb's letter on April 3, explaining the steps he was taking to put the operation into effect and stating that he expected to load his troops — six companies — aboard the steamships *Chieftain* and *Enterprise* within three or four days to embark for Rock Island.[149] He was optimistic about the prospects, expressing to Macomb that:

. . . From a personal acquaintance with many of the principal Indians among the Sacs and Foxes & a knowledge of the country, and of their character, I am persuaded that I shall be able to carry your views into effect without much difficulty. . . .

At that point in the letter a little warning bell had sounded in Atkinson's mind, and he paused, considered what he'd written, and then, with his characteristic of conservatism, added the waiver:

. . . In this however I may be mistaken.

Atkinson had begun his operational Order Book at once upon being assigned his task, and among the initial orders given was one to the company commanders to make sure that each soldier in the command was supplied with a greatcoat, a blanket, two shirts, a gray jacket, two pairs of pantaloons, a shako, a pair of boots, and a pair of shoes.[150] Preparations for departure were going along quite smoothly until a report from Felix St. Vrain jolted Atkinson into the realization that what lay before him was rapidly becoming a business far worse than anticipated and possibly even a war.

Another letter had come from the War Department, this one not bearing orders but merely advising the general that in view of the increase in tensions on the northwestern frontier, the long-abandoned post of Fort Dearborn at Chicago would soon be regarrisoned. The responsibility for procuring the necessary supplies and transportation would be under direction of Major Henry Whiting at Detroit. Atkinson considered that good news, but soon after the good came some bad.

Rumors had come to St. Louis and Jefferson Barracks that the British Band of Sacs under Neapope and Black Hawk were planning to return to Illinois again to reoccupy their old village site and grow more corn . . . and resist any attempts to oust them. At first Atkinson did not give the reports credence, but then came the report from St. Vrain, and it was chilling in its portent.

The Sac agent had learned that the British Band, numbering possibly as many as two thousand individuals, were definitely on the march to return to Illinois and would be crossing the Mississippi in the vicinity of the Upper Yellowbanks only a few days before the steamboats carrying the army would pass there; that once they got across they would detach the women, children, and elderly to a secret location to set up a permanent camp, while the men would be free to reoccupy their village and commit any mischief, then return to their secret family encampment for safety. St. Vrain had also reported that a story was circulating which, at first widely believed, held that the British were going to help the Sacs regain and retain possession of their lands, since the British were preparing to go to war with the United States again anyway. Closer investigation of the story, however, showed that the story had originated with Black Hawk and Neapope, and evidently had no basis in fact. Nevertheless, St. Vrain had gravely warned, the Sacs and Foxes had worked themselves into a state where many were now willing to follow Black Hawk and Neapope to the point of throwing their lives away. Further, there were inklings of some sort of intertribal coalition being formed as soon as Black Hawk reached the village of the Winnebago Prophet, Wabokieshiek. St. Vrain added that there was virtually no likelihood of the Sacs turning over to the Americans the murderers of the Menominees. It was believed that those murderers, numbering about fifty warriors, had attached themselves to Black Hawk, not so much because they believed in his leadership or his cause but because if they stayed with the peaceful Sacs — Keokuk, Chakeepashipaho, and others — they ran the risk of being turned in by their own people. The air was atingle with war talk everywhere on the frontier, St. Vrain had concluded, and if war *did* come, he doubted that the peaceful Sac and Fox chiefs would be able to prevent at least half of their young men from joining under Black Hawk's banner.

General Atkinson notified Macomb of all this in a letter just before embarking, still saying that he could hardly think that Black Hawk and his band had any serious intention of reoccupying their old village, but if they attempted to do so, he would prevent it if he could, although his own force, numbering a total of 280 officers and men, was much smaller than the numbers that had been quoted of Indians he would be opposing. There was a faintly querulous sense to the letter that the commanding general was certain to recognize. In another letter to General Gaines, Atkinson wrote:

. . . Our transports will be down this evening and I shall embark the command in the morning and proceed without delay to Rock Island.[151] *Then in person to Prairie du Chien for the purpose of adopting such measures as may be necessary to prevent the Sioux and Menominees from moving against the Sacs & Foxes.*

It still had not been indisputably confirmed that Black Hawk and the British Band had actually crossed the Mississippi until just a short time ago, as the troops reached the section called the Lower Rapids near the mouth of the Des Moines River. Here they were joined by an express sent to them by Captain Gustavus Loomis, commanding officer of Fort Armstrong at Rock Island. His report solidified all the worst fears the general had harbored. It told, with irrefutable detail, that the Sac crossing had been confirmed, and that there was good evidence the Winnebagoes would side with the British Band because of the recent activities and remarks of the Prophet, Wabokieshiek.

Now, standing at the bow rail of the *Chieftain,* General Atkinson turned his gaze to the deeply silhouetted eastern shoreline of the river. Black Hawk had crossed the river five days ago and was somewhere over there. But where? And even if he located them soon and confronted them, could two hundred soldiers force a couple of thousand Indians to go back? A little shiver touched the general's back, and turning away from the rail, he returned to his cabin in a dejected manner. At the small desk he swiftly wrote a terse little letter to the commanding general, to be expressed back to St. Louis tonight and eastward from there.

Head Qrs Right Wing West. Dept.
Lower Rapids 10th. April 1832

Sir On my arrival at this place an hour ago, I received information from Rock Island and the country occupied by the Sacs and Foxes in the intermediate distances. The Prophets band of Winnebagoes residing some thirty miles up Rock River have assumed a hostile attitude . . . at least one of defiance. And Black Hawk's band of Sacs have crossed the Mississippi near the mouth of the Ioway River, and are on the move for their own villages, or with a view to join the Prophet. Whether they intend commencing hostilities, or put themselves in an attitude of defiance against their being removed again to the west side of the river is a matter of doubt. Probably they will join The Prophet and refuse to recross the river. On this event, what is to be done? The regular force put at my disposal is not sufficient to contend successfully against eight hundred or a thousand well armed Indians.

I shall proceed on without delay to Rock Island, whence I will communicate to you the state of things.

Gen: Atkinson to Major Gen: Macomb:

[*April 11, 1832 — Wednesday*]

In a dense grove of trees about a mile south of their old village site of Saukenuk, Black Hawk stood and listened to what the Winnebago Prophet was saying to the many warriors and their families of the British Band. Clad as he was, in pale, almost white, doeskin shirt and leggins, the firelight highlighted Wabokieshiek well in the gathering darkness, glinting off the silver and brass ornaments he wore around his neck. Black Hawk marveled at how fresh and clean he looked, and wondered by what magic he had managed it.

When the Prophet and Black Hawk had finally joined early this morning, Wabokieshiek was riding a badly mud-splattered horse and was himself nearly as muddy. The rains of the past week had turned the earth into slick mud and the streams into torrents, so that each crossing of a creek or branch became a major undertaking. Yet, even though Wabokieshiek had no more baggage than his blanket roll, somehow he had managed to transform himself into this spotlessly clad, imposing figure whose strong words could be heard by every member of the large assemblage.

Thoughts of the mud caused Black Hawk to recall briefly the difficult time his own people had been having. It had taken them six days of hard marching just to reach this point near Saukenuk, a bit less than halfway to the Prophet's Town, and there were even more difficult stream crossings to be made between here and there, so it could take another eight or ten days before they arrived. This was especially so because of being slowed as they were by those on foot, many of whom among the elderly could not travel far without pausing to rest. With all the baggage they had to carry, five miles in a day's time was the best they had been able to manage. This would improve when the torrentially swollen river could be safely navigated, for then most of the goods and all those who were ill or lame or elderly could be transported by canoe. As it was, only about twenty of the one hundred canoes started up the Mississippi from the Lower Rapids, each paddled against the turbulent current by two powerful young men who had volunteered to do that rather than to portage their canoes so long a distance. They had come to regret their choice, and though they finally entered the equally swollen mouth of the Rock River and got close to Saukenuk, they had finally given up and, with blistered and bleeding hands and aching bodies, carried the canoes inland and intercepted the main party.

The progress of both parties of Sacs had been noted by a number of different traders and settlers. Black Hawk was aware of it, but he ignored them and ordered his followers to do the same. In each case the observer watched from hiding as the walkers or paddlers passed him, then raced away as soon as possible to carry the news to Fort Armstrong or to other settlements.

"No!"

The exclamation by Wabokieshiek jerked Black Hawk back to what was occurring here at the camp. The Prophet stood with a clenched fist held high and repeated himself. "No! My children, you need have no fear! Our spies have brought word that the American war chief, White Beaver, has brought a little army up against us and is now sitting on Rock Island, and you think he is ready to spring out upon us and do us harm. No! I will not listen to such talk, because no war chief dares molest us as long as we are at peace. We do not wear war paint. We do not threaten the few whites we encounter. We only mind our own business and continue toward my village, where perhaps you will grow corn and remain at peace."

He had been punctuating each sentence with upward thrusts of his extended fist, but now he dropped his arm. "You need only follow us and act like braves, and then there will be nothing to fear but much to gain. The American war chief might come to us, but he would not — he *dares* not! — interfere with us as long as we act peaceably."

The Winnebago Prophet paused and then slowly let a small smile spread his lips and gradually evolve into a broad grin. "We are not yet *ready* to act otherwise. Not yet! We must wait until we ascend Rock River and receive our reinforcements. The Winnebagoes have decided to support their brothers, the Sacs and Foxes, and will fight beside them, if necessary, against any who would do us harm. *Then* we shall see who it is who controls this land. *Then* we will be able to withstand *any* army, be it Sioux or Menominee or American — or all of them at once!"

There was a chorus of hoots and excited cries from the Sacs and Foxes. Wabokieshiek waved to them and then stepped down and rejoined Black Hawk. "That should keep their spirits high until they reach the village," he said, placing a hand on Black Hawk's shoulder. "I will be getting back now. By the time you get there, the other chiefs will have arrived, and then we will be able to decide who leads."

The Prophet squeezed Black Hawk's shoulder and then went to his horse, mounted with a lithe bound, and without looking back, rode off into the darkness.

"I have already decided," Black Hawk murmured, "who leads."

[*April 13, 1832 — Friday*]

Because he wished to confer with his officers aboard the other steamboat, General Atkinson had transferred from the *Chieftain* to the *Enterprise* for the remainder of the trip upriver from the Lower Rapids to Rock Island. As they approached the mouth of the Iowa River, a lookout spied a party of Indians on the point of land where the Iowa emptied into the Mississippi. In their midst was a bearded white man waving both arms to attract the crew's attention. A look through the ship's brass telescope disclosed that the bearded man was the well-known Josiah Smart, an employee of trader George Davenport, and beside him were Pashepaho, the number-one civil chief of the friendly Sacs, and Keokuk.

Instructions were called to the other steamboat to continue without pause to Rock Island, that the *Enterprise* would be along soon. The latter ship stopped and anchored so that the Indian delegation and Josiah Smart could be ferried aboard in the little lifeboat. A double squad of soldiers had been given instructions and stood ready with their weapons in case of trouble, but there was none. The Indians, with Smart acting as interpreter, had merely wished to convey to the great white war chief that they did not support the British Band in anything they were doing and that if a conflict was to come, they wanted no part of it and did not wish to be held responsible for the actions of Black Hawk and others of his errant crowd.

Atkinson was cool in his response to them and indicated how very seriously the United States government viewed this whole situation. He said there were many questions he wished to ask the chiefs of the friendly Sacs and Foxes, but aboard a steamship was hardly the place. Would they be agreeable to formal council at Rock Island as soon as the general could arrange it up there, probably the day after his arrival? Yes, they would. And they would even send a runner from their party to go to Wapello's village and get him to attend with his delegation as well.

Pashepaho and Keokuk requested permission, along with their party, to continue with the general to Rock Island aboard the *Enterprise*. Atkinson had no objection to that, but first asked permission from the ship's captain. Permission was granted, and by the time that was done and a runner had been given instructions and taken back to the west shore to move quickly up the Iowa to Wapello's village, several hours had passed. The *Chieftain* had long since passed from view, and as the *Enterprise* weighed anchor and resumed her passage up the turbulent river, General Atkinson closeted himself with Josiah Smart and questioned him closely about the Indian situation developing here.

When they had arrived at Rock Island near midnight last night, they found the *Chieftain* riding at anchor. [152] Henry Atkinson had wasted no time starting things moving, despite the late hour. He went ashore at once and was cordially greeted by the commanding officer of Fort Armstrong, Major John Bliss. Then, with Keokuk beside him, he met with Felix St. Vrain, who was more than a bit nonplussed to see the commanding general and one of the principal Sacs disembark together. St. Vrain quickly brought Atkinson up to date on events so far as he knew them, and agreed to take care of all the arrangements for the council the general wanted scheduled for the next afternoon with the friendly Indians. Atkinson then spoke for a short while with Major Bliss and learned from him what precious little he knew about this present invasion of the British Band. By that time it was nearly two o'clock, and the general turned in, knowing he'd have to be rested for the busy day coming.

First thing this morning after rising and getting dressed, even before having any breakfast, Atkinson had gone to the Indian agency house, where he found St. Vrain and five traders seated close together deep in conversation — George Davenport and his employee, Josiah Smart, plus three other traders to the Sacs and Foxes, Andy Hughes, Nate Smith, and Tom Taylor.

"You gentlemen," he had said, after the initial introductions were completed, "obviously know these Indians very well. You see a lot and hear a lot and undoubtedly have a good grasp of what goes on. With the exception of Mr. Smart, with whom I've already spent several hours in discussion, I urgently request that each of you hand to me, before noon today, a written account of what you personally know in regard to this movement of the British Band back into Illinois."

Not in the least overjoyed with the assignment, the traders nonetheless acquiesced, and by noon all four of the reports had been delivered to the general. They were not models of neatness and style, and the grammar and spelling left much to be desired, but the intelligence they passed along Atkinson found to be most useful. Davenport wrote that he'd been informed by the assistants he had wintering with the Indians that the British Band of Sacs was determined to make war upon the frontier settlements. He said over the winter he'd heard of the British Band planning to rendezvous at old Fort Madison and recruit any other Indians that came in, which they had, including about fifty of the party that had killed the Menominees. Then they planned to cross the Mississippi at Upper Yellowbanks, go up the Rock River to some swampy country where they could hide their womenfolk and goods, and then, after being joined by Winnebagoes, Potawatomies, and other Indians, to come back down in war parties and kill all the settlers on the frontier. And, Davenport had gone on:

. . . agreeable to the above plan the British Band of Sack Indians did Randevouse at Old Fort Maddison and Indused a great maney of the yong men to Join them. at their arrival at the yallow Banks they Crossed about five hundred horses into the State of Illinois . . . and will no doubt endeavour to reach their stronghold in the Rock River Swamps if thay are not entersepted.

from evrey Information that I have recd I am of oppinion that the Intentions of the B Band of Sack Indians is to commit depredations on the Inabitents of this frontier. I am Satisfied that, KeOkuck Pasheppaho Wapellow and thier bands of Sack & Foxes have nothing to do with the Br. Band.

Thomas W. Taylor — a slightly better speller, though definitely not perfect — was not quite so informative in his report as Davenport had been. He wrote:

In reply to the request, you made this morning, respecting the present hostile intentions of the Socks, Foxes & Kickapoo, Indians against the Americans — I now beg leave to refer you more particularly to Mr. Smith's Letter. Mr. Smith was my Interpreter (on the river Desmoines) for the purpose of Trading with the Socks & Foxes, during the winter season.

I visited my hands once this winter at the trading house on the Desmoines river. While there the Kickapoos asked permission of me to go over on the Illinois side to hunt. this I forbid, telling them at the same time I had no authority to give them permition.

I have not had any communication with any of them since then, but . . . I was informed that Black Hawk & his party intended to raise corn at the old village or & Prophets Town this summer.

The letter from Nathan Smith was a bit more definitive. He wrote, in his cramped style of handwriting, that while on the Des Moines River during the winter:

. . . I have been able to judge from their actions and conversation that they intended to commence hostilities on the Americans in the Spring and I know from the conversations of a small band of Kickapoos they have been urging the Sacks & Foxes to be hostile

One Sack indian (a Brave) told me last winter that he would rather kill Genl. Gaines than any other being on earth. Whenever talking with them on the subject, they have always appeared to have a wish to fight the Americans, they have always said to me that the Americans were certainly afraid of the Winnebagoes.

A few days ago . . . I arrived opposite to the mouth of the Ioway river, where I was informed that Black Hawk's party had crossed over to the Illinois side . . . they were determined to live on Rock River or up at the Prophets village also they have stated to me that they are going to the British. I told them that it was contrary to their Treaty last Summer. The Sacks & Foxes told me last Summer that they were not affraid of the regular Troops that it was not them that sent them across the river, that they never would have crossed but for the fear they had of the mounted Troops. My opinion is that the Black Hawk's old men, women & children have been sent up to wards the Prophets village, this is formed from the signs and trails I seen & examined.

Finally, Andrew S. Hughes had written his report in a somewhat more impassioned manner, saying:

. . . during the last fall & winter, I heard of many threats that had been made by Black Hawk's party in relation to their determination to reoccupy their old village on Rock river . . . against the americans. . . . I was informed that he and his party had crossed the Mississippi at Yellow Banks . . . I determined to examine for myself and to follow the trail of the Indians so far as I might be enabled, [to] judge the direction the old men and squaws had taken, as well as to

ascertain the position of the warriors. My opinion is that the squaws & old men have gone to the Prophets town on Rock river and the warriors are now only a few miles below the mouth of Rock river within the limits of the state of Illinois. That those indians are hostile to the whites there is no doubt, that they have invaded the state of Illinois to the great injury of our citizens is equally true — hence it is that the public good requires that strong as well as speedy measures should be taken against Black Hawk and his followers.

Other traders and settlers had been coming to Fort Armstrong all morning, greatly upset over the "invasion" and demanding that something be done about it immediately. General Atkinson questioned as many of them as he could before the time appointed for the council, but got little more than reaffirmation of the things the traders had written. Estimates of Black Hawk's strength from those who had seen the Indians and tried to make a count varied from as few as five hundred warriors to as many as eighteen hundred. All the citizens were very fearful, and not in the least assuaged by the fact that the intruding Sacs had thus far not harmed anyone in the least.

A few minutes ago, escorted by Felix St. Vrain, Major Bliss, Lieutenant Johnston and a squad of guards, interpreter Antoine LeClaire, and the four traders the general had interviewed, Atkinson entered the council chamber and found about seventy Indians awaiting him. It was a small delegation for three chiefs so important as Pashepaho, Keokuk, and Wapello, but there had been little time for the usual protocols of Indian councilling. However, this was simply a formal council, not a major treaty-making council, so a slight bending of protocol was acceptable.

Now, with the murmur of voices died away and everyone waiting expectantly, Brigadier General Henry Atkinson addressed the assembled Indians in a clear, firm voice, pausing occasionally to let LeClaire keep pace with his interpretation.

"I am directed by your great father to come here and place myself between the Menominees and Sioux, and you — the Sacs and Foxes. Your great father has been informed that the Menominees and Sioux have been collecting together to come down and strike you." He paused, and the brief delay added emphasis to his next words. "I will send to the Menominees and Sioux and tell them to stay at home. Your great father will settle the difficulties between the Sioux and Menominees, and Sacs and Foxes."

Atkinson's gaze shifted only far enough to move from Keokuk to Pashepaho to Wapello and back to Keokuk, but there was great impact in that look, as if he were measuring each man's worth in turn and not disclosing, by any trace of expression, his conclusions. The silence stretched out to a nearly unbearable point and then split with the impact of a gunshot with the next measured sentence the general spoke: "My great father has directed me to tell the Menominees and Sioux that they *shall* listen to his voice!"

Whatever other qualities Henry Atkinson may have had, there was no doubt that he was a superbly skilled speaker who could wring emotion out of his listeners, lift them high in expectancy, hold them tense in anticipation, then impale them on the point of his words with the rapier sharpness of a skilled swordsman. A universal gasp erupted from the Indians, and no individual among them doubted the truth of what White Beaver had just said. A murmur arose from them and almost immediately died away in embarrassed silence at this breach of council protocol.

"I will now tell you," Atkinson went on, as if he had not even noticed their reaction, "what your great father has directed me to say to *you*. The summer before last you made a treaty at Prairie du Chien. Many of you were present and signed that treaty." Atkinson abruptly raised his right hand, holding up his index finger ramrod straight. "In violation of which, some of your angry young men went up to Prairie du Chien and killed many Menominees. This has greatly displeased your great father, who says that at the same time that I compel the Sioux and Menominees to do right, I must also exact justice from the Sacs and Foxes. You *must* surrender eight or ten of the murderers."

Atkinson paused again, and when he resumed there was less of the tenseness in his voice, yet more of a thread of anger. "When I left home," he said, "I had no information of the bad conduct of these people *over here* — the band of the Black Hawk. I heard of it at the Lower Rapids." He made a sudden slashing gesture with his hand. "I care nothing for it — they can be as easily crushed as a piece of dirt!" There was another muted gasp, since this was a terrible insult to Black Hawk and his band. But if that remark stunned them, what followed had even greater impact. "If they do not recross the river," the general continued grimly, "measures will soon be taken to compel them. I will not ask them to go back. I will not speak to them until they recross to the west side of the Mississippi. I will treat them like dogs. I am not going to call them into council, to tell me lies." His gaze, which had slid over to Pashepaho, snapped back to Keokuk as he raised his hand in a sudden point at the Sac. "Keokuk knows that his great father can *cover* these plains with men!"

Keokuk nodded and spoke a single word. "Yes."

The barest ghost of a smile flickered for an instant in Atkinson's mien, more expressed in his eyes than on his lips, but there was no sense of softening in his words when he spoke again. "If Black Hawk's band strikes *one white man*, in a short time they will cease to exist."

While they mulled over that open threat, Atkinson turned his stern face away from them and back to the tables behind him where the rest of the whites sat. He reached down and moved a few papers, as if he were studying them, but he never even looked at them. Instead, he gave Felix St. Vrain a long, deliberate wink. Then he turned back to the assemblage and his voice became brisk. "I want to know how many Indians have joined Black Hawk."

The three chiefs looked at one another, and it was Pashepaho who responded. "Five hundred."

Atkinson nodded. "I am going myself to Prairie du Chien to attend to the business with the Menominees. The Sacs and Foxes who have not joined the band of Black Hawk must keep themselves away. They must not go where *they* are. Now, because I have given you much to think about and discuss, I am quite willing, if you like, to temporarily adjourn this council and let you withdraw to privacy for discussion and decisions."

"The White Beaver is very kind," Pashepaho said. "Yes, we will accept this offer and return to these quarters before long."

The Indians filed out and reassembled a few hundred yards away in an open glade where the dry grasses had just begun to show a hint of summer's coming verdancy. Here they sat in a circle while one after another rose to speak. In just over an hour, they returned to the council house, and it was Keokuk who stepped forward first to speak.

"We, the chiefs and warriors of the Sac and Fox nations, do not know what to answer, since we have been put *out*." He gestured, open palm upward, toward Atkinson. "You tell the truth with regard to the treaty two years ago. When Colonel Morgan took us up to the prairie, he made us make peace with the Sioux.[153] He told us to go up with them, and he wanted to arrange all matters."

Keokuk slapped his hands to his sides in a small gesture of futility. "We did not wish to make peace, but we *did* make peace for fear of the Americans." His voice took on an accusing tone. "We acted from fear, like whipped children. And when he spoke at Prairie du Chien, he told me he would hold each village accountable for its own conduct. When Governor Clark went up, he invited those Indians over here, Black Hawk's band, to go up, and they would not." He looked at Pashepaho. "*My* chief would not go. *I* went up. I got a copy of the treaty and explained it to my band, and also to the Rock River Indians."

Keokuk paused and shook his head sadly. "My village and the British Band do not like each other. They will not listen to us, and that is the reason we do not know what to do. You say *they* must give themselves up, or the *chief* must do it." He held up both hands in a supplicating gesture. "We *can't* give them up. It is out of our power. All of the Sacs engaged in the murder of the Menominees are off, or with Black Hawk's party. We are unfriendly to that band."

The Sac paused, spent of words, wearied of pleading the case. His shoulders slumped and he shook his head, realizing it was no use. When he spoke again, the words seemed to come from far away rather than from him. "We will tell them what you say. Last fall we had a meeting on invitation of Major Bliss and our agent. As soon as the council was over, those who are with Black Hawk's party went away, and we never could get them to speak to us since. If the war party had started from our village we would feel ourselves bound to give them up, but as it is, we are unable. You wish us to keep at peace and have nothing to do with the Rock River Indians. We will do so in token of our intentions." He pointed to the doorway, where a large number of flint-headed spears were propped against the wall. "You see, we have lain our spears there, all together. While you are gone to Prairie du Chien we will endeavor to speak to them and try to persuade them to go back. If we do not succeed, we can do no more — then we will go home and try to keep our village at peace. The one," he concluded bitterly, "who has raised all this trouble is a Winnebago called the Prophet."

He turned and took his place with the others and at once Wapello — the Prince — foremost civil chief of the Fox tribe, rose and spoke loudly. "You have heard what my friend has said concerning the treaty at Prairie du Chien, and I will tell what I have heard from you to those chiefs that belong to the Fox village of Allotah — he that you call Morgan. It is a pity that those who command this village are only boys. While you are gone to Prairie du Chien, I will tell them what you have said today. I do not doubt that they will say they do not know what to do. This is all I can say, perhaps. If I were to promise more, I could not do it. One of our young men was killed out here last fall by the Sioux, Menominees, and Winnebagoes — we judged so by some articles of dress and other signs."

That was an area of discussion it would be pointless at this juncture to argue in view of his orders, so Atkinson changed the subject, asking sharply, "Where is Pankeene?"[154] Pankeene, all present knew, had been one of the leaders of the massacre of the Menominees at Prairie du Chien.

Wapello did not hesitate in his response. "At Morgan's village. Nataueta-heka," he volunteered, "another principal man engaged in the murder, is also there."[155]

"Why didn't Morgan's band come in to council?"

Wapello shook his head and glanced at St. Vrain. "I don't know. The agent sent for them. They said they would come here."

General Atkinson considered this, made a notation on the paper before him on the table, and spoke again without looking up. "Were there more Sacs than Foxes engaged in the murder?"

Wapello shrugged, looked at Pashepaho, then back at Atkinson, who had raised his head and now was regarding the Fox chief levelly. "About equal numbers of each," the chief replied. He stepped backward a pace, indicating he was finished speaking.

The silence drew out, and at last Henry Atkinson came slowly to his feet and spoke without addressing any one of the three chiefs in particular. "When I told you that I would stand between the Menominees and Sioux and you, it was under the supposition that you would be able to settle this difficulty. I can do nothing more than tell the Menominees to wait till I hear from their father again." Atkinson sighed, genuinely distressed that it had come to this. "I am instructed by your great father to tell you that if you cannot give up the murderers, you must give up hostages. I was told to take the hostages and treat them kindly until the difficulty could be settled. If you think proper to leave some of your people here, I will stand between you and the Menominees. As you have been invited by me to come here, I will not insist on it, but leave it to your own good sense. They are not to be tried — they are to be kept till the murderers are given up. Hostages are required in order to show that you are disposed to do right. The Winnebagoes gave us hostages," he added, in reference to the Winnebago War of 1827. "When our difficulties were settled, I gave them up."

"I would speak if given permission to do so," spoke up a young warrior abruptly.

"Identify yourself," Atkinson said, inwardly amused at the effrontery.

"I am Apenose," he said proudly, offering no further explanation.

Keokuk stepped forward. "This," he said, somewhat apologetically, "is the son of the great Fox chief, Taimah, whose village is at the Flint Hill."[156]

Unable to hide it any longer, Atkinson smiled openly and dipped his head at the young Fox warrior. "Speak," he said.

"My Father, I came up in one of those boats with the troops. I thought after seeing what would happen, I would go and tell the Indians of Black Hawk's band of it. I went into the lodge of one of the leading chiefs, Neapope, where he is camped on Rock River. I began to talk to him gently, but before I finished he stopped me and began to scold me violently. He did not strike me. That is all. He said *you* will be very pitiful after a while. After I was so badly treated, I went away to the braves' lodge. I tried to get one of my married sisters to come away. As soon as they found I was trying to get my sister away, they sent a crier through the camp, telling the women and children not to go away, that they would be happy and the rest of us miserable. I got there a little too late. The Prophet's message had been received before I got there."

Atkinson had become suddenly alert at the mention of the camp on Rock River. "Where," he asked, "is Black Hawk's band?"

"Near the head of the rapids of Rock River."

The general leaned over and asked St. Vrain in a whisper where that was located, and the agent told him it was about six or eight miles away. Atkinson nodded thoughtfully and returned his attention to young Apenose. "Where are they going?"

"They would not tell me."

"Where are their women and children?"

"With them."

"How many men have they?"

"I could form no estimate, and they wouldn't tell me." He stepped back, indicating there was nothing more for him to say, and once again Keokuk spoke up.

"You have just now heard the way our friends behave. That is the reason we never could fix the business. When you observed that the only way would be to give some up, I thought I told you if they did not belong to our band, we could do nothing with them. After hearing how our message was received, we consulted and thought we could not give ourselves up, as we had nothing to do with the murders. We leave it to you to do with those chiefs what you can. We are now speaking to you here: if you will take notice you will hear that *we* will be the first who are killed. We heard a good while ago that they were going to kill us. The man who was the crier in the camp also said so."

General Atkinson's expression had become grim on hearing the refusal to offer hostages. "Your great father will not be satisfied. You ought to do your part to give up the Foxes."

Exasperated and barely able to keep his temper at the obstinacy of the officer, Keokuk slapped his hand to his side and replied in a harsh manner: "I have nothing to do with the Foxes, but I will attend to it."

The commander, realizing he had pushed matters about as far as possible in this meeting, came to his feet and spoke matter-of-factly. "This present council is ended. I direct now that Morgan's band be sent for. There will be another council between us and the chiefs of the Sacs and Foxes on the sixth day from today — April nineteenth." He gestured to Major Bliss. "I wish all these chiefs that are present here now to remain here until Morgan's band comes."

So, though not quite in the manner he had anticipated, Atkinson had three hostages, anyway — Wapello, Pashepaho, and Keokuk. Though angry looks were sent his way, there were no objections. As Atkinson turned and began to leave, he heard the voice of Wapello behind him, and St. Vrain, who caught up to him, said the Fox chief had given one of his braves an order to fetch Morgan here as quickly as possible. Atkinson smiled, thanked the agent, and continued to his quarters. In moments he was hurriedly writing a letter to Alexander Macomb:

> *Head Qrs Right Wing Western Depart:*
> *Fort Armstrong 13th April 1832.*

General — I arrived at this place last night at 12 O'clk. I find a state of things existing in this quarter that I did not apprehend.

The Band of Sacs, under Black Hawk, joined by about one hundred Kickapoos, and a few Pottawattomies, amounting in the whole to five hundred warriors, have assumed a hostile attitude. They crossed the Mississippi on the 5th. at Yellow Banks, sixty miles below this, and are now moving up toward The Prophet's village on Rock river. [157] *I have thought it most advisable not to pursue them, as my force is too small to oppose them with a prospect of success without great risk, and to make an unsuccessful attempt would only give them confidence and add to their numbers the wavering and disaffected. Besides, it would subject our frontier to attack. As yet they have committed no act of hostility, and probably will not, till measures can be taken to protect the frontier.*

I enclose herewith copies of several communications which contain information relative to the views and movements of the hostile Indians.

A day or two will more fully develope [sic] *the intention of the Indians, of which I will inform you as soon as ascertained. I write by this conveyance to the Governor of Illinois giving him all the information I possess touching the subject. If things assume a more threatening aspect it will be necessary for the Governor to call out the Militia to protect the frontier. I will give him all the assistance in my power.*

I held a council to day [sic] *with the Chiefs and head men of the friendly Sacs, and some of the Chiefs of the Foxes, they profess not to be able to surrender the Menomine* [sic] *murderers, alleging that the principal persons engaged in that affair have joined the hostile Indians.*

They refuse at this time to give up hostages on the ground that none of the men of their band were concerned. As they were brought together by my invitation, I do not feel justified in detaining any of them, but shall wait for a proper occasion to effect the object, if indeed the present aspect of affairs will justify the course.[158]

I have but a moment to write. In a day or two I will communicate fully my views relative to the posture of affairs and the measures necessary to be taken.

Brig: Gen: Atkinson to Major Gen: Macomb.

Having completed the letter, Atkinson blotted the ink with rocking movements of a crescent blotter, folded the letter, and placed it, along with copies of the missives he had received from the four Fort Armstrong traders, into an envelope, to be wax-sealed along with the second letter he was now ready to write. This one was to Governor John Reynolds.

Fort Armstrong 13th. April 1832

Dear Sir — The Band of Sacs, under Black Hawk, joined by about One hundred Kickapoos, and a few Pottawattimies [sic] *amounting in all to about five hundred men have assumed a hostile attitude. They crossed the Mississippi at the Yellow Banks on the 5th Inst: and are now moving up on the east side by Rock river, towards the Prophet's village. They have not yet committed any act of hostility, and they profess, I understand, not to intend to strike the first blow, but to resist any attempt to remove them once again from the Rock river Country. I enclose to you by Mr. Taylor, a gentleman of intelligence, copies of several communications relative to the views and movements of the hostile Indians. These with the information that Mr. Taylor can give will put you in possession of all the facts and circumstances that have come to my knowledge.*

The regular force under my command is too small to justify me in pursuing the hostile party. To make an unsuccessful attempt to coerce them would only irritate them to acts of hostility on the frontier, sooner than they probably contemplate. Your own knowledge of the character of these Indians, with information herewith submitted, will enable you to judge of the proper course to be pursued.

I think the frontier is in great danger, and I will use all the means at my disposal to co-operate with you in its protection and defence [sic]. *Two or three days will more fully develope the intentions of the Indians, when I will again write to you, and should I think it necessary I will return immediately to St. Louis to confer with you upon the course to be pursued.*

Genl. Atkinson to Gov: Reynolds.

[*April 13, 1832 — Friday*]

On the southwestern shore of Lake Michigan, in the little village of Chicago, the white inhabitants had no inkling of the Indian problem shaping up to the west of them. Among these whites it was simply another day of business as usual, with a special term of the Court of County Commissioners being held for the purpose of establishing certain price control regulations and also fixing taxes on certain items so the County Commission could sustain itself and properly administer the duties of civil government. No steps were being considered at this time to revamp or regarrison Fort Dearborn, which the United States War Department had abandoned many years before. Instead, as befitted a rapidly growing town, a tax levy of one-half of one percent was instituted for such property as town lots, pleasure carriages, distilleries, horses, mules and cattle older than three years, and on watches and clocks.

There were already a couple of thriving taverns in the town, but now, with the new regulations being inaugurated, these and other businesses would have to be licensed. Today, two in-town tavern licenses were granted, one to Elijah Wentworth for a fee of seven dollars and another for five dollars to Samuel Miller for his somewhat smaller establishment.[159] With the licenses issued, a price control scale was instituted governing not only what was sold at the taverns but also by merchants.[160] Three licenses were issued for merchants to sell goods — one to Miller and another to Robert A. Kinzie, whose establishments were in town, and a third to Barney H. Laughton, who had a store a few miles up the South Branch of the Chicago River.[161]

Finally, action was taken by the commissioners for the establishment of a regular ferry operation across the Chicago River, to be located across the main body of the stream just below where it was formed by the mergence of the North Branch and South Branch. Use of the ferry was to be free for all residents of Cook County and whatever vehicle the individual might be using. All others would have to pay ferrying fees for themselves plus their baggage and transportation. A scow was purchased by the commissioners from Sam Miller for sixty-five dollars for this purpose, and whoever was to be appointed ferryman — at the next meeting — would be required to pay the county fifty dollars and file a bond in the sum of two hundred dollars for the faithful performance of the duty.[162]

But while the white residents of Chicago and Cook County were busy with their civic matters and not at all apprehensive about any sort of Indian problem, three of the well-known and highly respected resident Indian chiefs, Chaubenee,

Sauganash, and Chechepinqua — Coalburner, Billy Caldwell, and Alexander Robinson — were extremely nervous about what was currently in the wind. A runner had just arrived with an invitation for Chaubenee to attend, on behalf of the Potawatomies, a council called by Black Hawk of the Sacs, to be held at the mouth of Sycamore Creek. The runner had also told them that en route to Chicago he had stopped off at the village of Chief Mawgehset — Big Foot — at the eastern extremity of Lake Geneva. [163] Mawgehset, whose volatile nature and intense antipathy toward the whites were widely known, had immediately signified his eagerness not only to attend Black Hawk's planned council, but to support the Sacs in their avowed intention of using that council to get support from other tribes and then to openly declare war on the Americans.

Chaubenee agreed to attend also and, with the help of Sauganash and Chechepinqua, had every intention of seeing what would develop at that council.

[April 15, 1832 — Sunday]

It seemed to General Henry Atkinson that he had been in constant motion ever since first learning three days ago of Black Hawk's crossing of the Mississippi in violation of the treaty. Now, in the interval having councilled with the Indians at Fort Armstrong on Rock Island, and having gone farther upriver on the steamboat and visited with officials in the bustling lead-mining town of Galena, he had come to Fort Crawford at Prairie du Chien and would almost immediately be heading back downstream again to Galena and Rock Island.

The trip upriver had been for two primary reasons — first, to inspect the defenses at Galena in case of an outbreak of actual hostilities — which, though determined to discourage, he considered entirely possible — and secondly, to secure reinforcements to his own force from the regular troops garrisoned at both Fort Crawford and Fort Winnebago. In the first instance he had found Galena to have woefully inadequate defenses and encouraged the immediate erection of some sort of fortification wherein the settlers and miners of the surrounding area could take refuge if necessary. In Prairie du Chien he had reviewed the Fort Crawford garrison and ordered its commander, Captain Gustavus Loomis, to position five or six boats in a line across the Mississippi just below the mouth of the Wisconsin in order to intercept any parties of Menominees or Sioux that might be on the move to attack the Sacs and Foxes. He similarly sent a message to the acting commander of Fort Winnebago, Captain Joseph Plympton, to block the Wisconsin near the portage and turn back any advancing Menominees there. [164] Atkinson was able to get two companies of the First Infantry, stationed at Fort Crawford, detached to his service under command of Lieutenant Colonel Zachary Taylor. [165] They would be returning with him to Fort Armstrong. Others at Fort Winnebago were to hold themselves in readiness to join General Atkinson when summoned. In written orders to the Indian agents at Rock Island, Prairie du Chien, Fort Winnebago, and Green Bay — respectively, Felix St. Vrain, Joseph Street, John H. Kinzie, and Samuel C. Stambaugh — he directed that their Indian charges should be informed of the invasion of Black Hawk's band into Illinois and its present movement up the Rock River, and that they should give their Indian charges very stern warnings against considering joining with the pugnacious Sacs and Foxes in any move against the whites, or of aiding them in any way by providing them food, ammunition, shelter, or other necessaries.

It was during his overnight stop at Galena that Atkinson had written letters to two of the most able whites on this frontier. The first, written the evening of April 14, was to Henry Dodge, the strong-willed elected leader of the miners in the southwestern Wisconsin mining communities of Wiota, Mineral Point, Dodgeville, and Blue Mounds. The second, written the following morning before embarking for Prairie du Chien, was to Henry Gratiot, the highly competent subagent to the Winnebagoes. Though under direct command of the Winnebago agent, John H. Kinzie at Fort Winnebago, Gratiot operated most often from his home in Gratiot's Grove, and that was where the general addressed the letter. In like manner Atkinson informed both men of the invasion of the British Band under Black Hawk, its size and apparent hostile nature, and its advance up the Rock River, adding that "*. . . They say they will not strike first, but it is believed by some well-informed men they will strike as soon as they secure their women and children in the fastnesses of the Rock River swamps.*" To Dodge the general had added that he wished him to warn the settlers and miners in his area and toward the Rock River to guard against any hostile moves by the Indians. Then Dodge was to meet him in Galena when Atkinson returned there on the 17th of the present month after visiting Prairie du Chien.

The following morning, before leaving Galena, Atkinson had written to the capable Gratiot, giving him an even more demanding and dangerous assignment. The Winnebago subagent was not only to similarly warn the settlers in his area and farther southeast toward the Rock River of the Sac and Fox invasion, but he was also to visit with some of the leading Winnebagoes in an effort to glean whatever information he could about the movements and final destination of Black Hawk's band. Equally important, Gratiot was to endeavor to determine the views and intentions of the Winnebagoes in these matters. Atkinson had concluded, "*. . . inform me of the results of your enquiries* [sic] *and observations as early as possible. I shall be found after four days at Rock Island.*"

Now, confident that he had done all that could reasonably be accomplished on this brief swing up the Mississippi, General Atkinson reboarded the steamboat for the journey back to Galena and Rock Island with Zachary Taylor's two companies.

[*April 17, 1832 — Tuesday*]

Hardly had General Atkinson's letter of April 13 reached him the day before yesterday than Governor John Reynolds had plunged into action, dictating a whole series of letters to militia commanders throughout the state, though primarily north and west of the Illinois River, instructing them to call immediately for sixteen hundred volunteers to meet and drive off the invading enemy. As if that were not enough, he dictated an impassioned plea to be posted in prominent view in a score or more locations:

FELLOW CITIZENS:

Your country requires your services. The Indians have assumed a hostile attitude and have invaded the State in violation of the treaty of last summer.

The British band of Sacs and other hostile Indians, headed by Black Hawk, are in possession of the Rock River country, to the great terror of the frontier inhabitants. I consider the settlers on the frontiers to be in imminent danger.

I am in possession of the above information from gentlemen of respectable standing, and also from General Atkinson, whose character stands high with all classes.

In possession of the above facts and information, I have hesitated not as to the course I should pursue. No citizen ought to remain inactive when his country is invaded and the helpless part of the community are in danger. I have called out a strong detachment of militia to rendezvous at Beardstown on the 22d instant.

Provisions for the men and food for the horses will be provided in abundance.

I hope my countrymen will realize my expectations and offer their services as heretofore, with promptitude and cheerfulness in defense of their country.

The call affected a great many citizens of the state, since members of the militia included, by law, all males aged eighteen to forty-five. "And if they don't volunteer," Reynolds muttered darkly, on finishing dictation of the appeal, "they'll be drafted."

This year, however, was not to see a repeat of the great throng of volunteers flocking in answer to the call. Not only was last year's debacle still uncomfortably fresh in their minds, this year there was a significant difference. The spring thus far had been not only very chilly, there had been an abnormal amount of rainfall, which had effectively delayed the plowing of fields that were subsequently to be planted. This meant that work which should already have been done was not yet even begun, and if the men who were supposed to do that work were off chasing and fighting Indians, there might not be a satisfactory corn crop. In addition, while Reynolds was attempting to raise an army of mounted volunteers, an existing grain shortage had left the majority of the horses in the state in generally poor condition, with fewer than one in five really fit for a campaign such as was now being organized. Then, too, last year's campaign, which had so unsatisfactorily fizzled out, made prospective volunteers or draftees only too aware of the poor payment a member of the state militia received. A private would receive only twenty-one cents per day, a corporal only two cents more than that, and a sergeant just twenty-five cents. That hardly encouraged enlistment. As an editorial in the *Sangamo Journal* in Springfield put it, following a schedule outlining the pay volunteers would receive:

> *Twenty-one cents a day and found! Call our farmers from their ploughs, our mechanics from their benches, our merchants from their stores, in the most busy and important season of the year, and give them twenty-one cents a day as compensation! . . . Members of Congress, no better than they are . . . contentedly receiving eight dollars a day, give to the volunteer soldier twenty-one cents a day!*

Yet, despite the disadvantages involved in volunteering, word of the call flashed across the state with breathtaking and almost unbelievable speed, and a surprising number of the young men began flocking to their respective county seats or the general rendezvous point at Beardstown, ready to lay down their lives, if necessary, to protect the state from the red terror that loomed so horrifyingly in the imagination. Of course, once again a very telling factor was involved in this apparent altruism: it was an election year, and maybe — just *maybe* — this would be the campaign that could launch spectacular political careers.

Among the many hundreds of eager young men who read the notice was a long, lanky youth of twenty-three years who was a grocery clerk at Denton Offut's store in New Salem. This young man had a hunch that if he didn't hesitate to volunteer in the defense of his state, it might go far in his being able to win a seat in the Illinois House of Representatives, so he took off his apron and headed for the mustering-in area as soon as he heard the call.

"What's your name, son?" asked the portly company clerk who was signing up the volunteers.

The lean young man grinned, swallowed, and replied, "Lincoln, sir. Abraham Lincoln."

Throughout all of Illinois the news of the invasion spread with greater speed than a prairie fire in a windstorm. Not all who heard it were impelled to rush heroically to the state's defense. A reasonably large number of them rushed, all right, but eastward or southward out of the supposed path of the red invaders and into the sanctuaries of larger towns and cities with stronger forts and means of defense. Some left the state entirely, never to return. Others, especially those in the frontier areas, congregated at the closest community to where they lived and helped in the frenzied construction of local forts in which they and their families could find refuge if real danger threatened. In this way a whole collection of cabins, houses, barns, and outbuildings throughout the northern third of Illinois and all of southern Wisconsin became crudely fortified installations that were dubbed with the term "fort," just in case some dullard could not recognize their new status as such.

In Galena, on the heels of General Atkinson's comments about its defenselessness, citizens worked together to fortify a structure grandiosely called Fort Galena even before it was finished. Apple River Fort appeared almost overnight in the tiny Apple River community. Fort Clark was refurbished at Peoria, and the still abandoned Fort Dearborn became suddenly important again to the citizens of Chicago and Cook County. Then there was Fort Deposit at Wilbourn, Fort South Ottawa, and Dixon's Fort, along with Fort Hennepin and West Bureau Fort, Fort Kellogg's Grove and Buffalo Grove Fort. In the Wisconsin country, near Henry Dodge's community of Dodgeville, miners turned a local house into Fort Union, and another tiny installation, grandly called Fort Defiance, sprang into being on Parkinson farm some five miles southeast of Mineral Point. At Wiota, a building at William Hamilton's smelting works became Fort Hamilton, and Blue Mounds Fort came into being about a mile and a half south of East Blue Mound. Little Wingville became the site for Parish's Fort, built at the smelter of Tom Parish, and a host of other buttressed buildings became forts named after their communities at Cassville, Diamond Grove, Gratiot's Grove, Elk Grove, Old Shullsburg, Platteville, and White Oak Springs. Not all that construction occurred overnight, but under the present scare sweeping the countryside, it didn't take long.

Yesterday John Reynolds had paused long enough in the flurry of his activity to quickly dictate a response to General Atkinson in which he proudly let it be known that no grass was growing beneath his feet. He wrote:

> State of Illinois — Belleville
> 16th April 1832

Dear Sir — I had the honor yesterday of receiving your letter dated Fort Armstrong 13th inst. and the accompanying documents, all shewing [sic] the necessity of energetic movements to protect the frontier settlements. I am happy to have the honor of your cooperation in the defence of our border.

And in order to effect this object I have ordered Genl. [Isaiah] Stillman of the militia to organise four companies of mounted men of fifty each. And for him to command them as Major. This battalion is ordered to range on the frontier under Major Stillman's command from the Mississippi eastward. The major will report as soon as his command is organised.

In order to be ready for war or peace, I have judged it proper to call out . . . the militia, who will be mounted and will rendezvous at Beardstown on the Illinois River on the 22nd inst. I consider it necessary for me to be there on that day to cause the detachment to be organised. I am satisfied that the good of the country requires this movement of the militia in order, if necessary, to be ready to deal out distruction [sic] to the hostile Indians in defending our border.

Beardstown is a central point, and Should the Indians commence hostilities on our frontiers, from this place the militia can be marched in a few days to the scene of the action. Should the militia not be wanted, it will not be difficult to return home from this point.

Thus you see my preparatory movements, and you see likewise the necessity for me to be informed of your views on the subject. . . .

The more John Reynolds considered the developing situation, the more eager he became to have that situation develop into a hot war, in the pursuit of which the mettle of his state's militia could be tested and proved to the greater glory of the governor, who might just possibly find this whole business a first rung on the ladder to the presidency. That was why, having now gotten all the balls rolling that he could set into motion, Reynolds sat down this morning at his desk and, in a somewhat less frenetic frame of mind, wrote to Lewis Cass, the United States secretary of war:

Sir — The State is again invaded by the hostile Indians and the country is in imminent danger. This is made manifest to me by Official Communications, a part of which I herewith transmit to you, and by other information.; The regular troops under the command of an excellent officer of the U. States Army, Gen. Atkinson, is too small to pursue the Indians, as you see in his letter to me, and the frontier [is] in great danger.

In this situation I have hesitated not a moment. I have called out a strong detachment of the militia to rendezvous near the frontier on the 22nd. instant. Beardstown on the Illinois River is the place of Rendezvous. This is within three or four days march of the enemy, and is a place where supplies can be furnished by water. While the militia is organizing, I will hope to see Gen. Atkinson and know the precise situation and intentions of the Indians.

I am satisfied the country requires this movement and I hope the Militia will not be ordered home before these Indians are chastised.

I will march with the militia and go all lengths within my constitutional authority and the laws of the land to protect the frontier by chastising these insolent and restless Indians.

With sincere Respect I am Your obt Servant
John Reynolds.

[*April 18, 1832 — Wednesday*]

The conference General Atkinson had with Henry Dodge and town officials at Galena was inconclusive. Dodge tended to believe this whole business was an act of bravado on the part of Black Hawk's band and that they would quickly sue for peace if truly threatened by a white force of any consequence. Dodge felt that the whole thing could blow over very easily, or, if improperly handled, could evolve into a significant war. It was up to those in power to keep a tight control over the developing situation and not be stampeded into rash acts.

Galena officials asked for help with their defense measures, and Atkinson tentatively authorized the town's newly formed militia to draw arms and ammunition from Fort Crawford if the British Band became more threatening. Dodge promised to keep on top of things as best he could and keep the general informed, and with that Atkinson returned to Rock Island for the second council with the friendly Sacs and Foxes.

On his arrival at Fort Armstrong, Atkinson was met by a delegation of Sacs and Foxes, who now promised in a rather contrite manner to surrender at the council on the morrow all of the warriors among them who were involved in the deadly attack on the Menominees last year. That, however, amounted to only three warriors. The rest of the attackers were either scattered into the wilderness or else had joined with the British Band. Keokuk and Felix St. Vrain had both sent messengers to Black Hawk in an effort to get him and other leaders of his band to attend the next day's council, but none of those Indians had appeared and it was unlikely that they would. St. Vrain was entirely convinced that nothing short of powder and ball would stop the British Band in its gathering momentum, and by the time his second council with the Indians was concluded an hour ago, General Atkinson had begun to feel that the Sac agent might be correct.

Three minor chiefs had been surrendered during the council. One was Kakekukanuck — Chief-of-the-Soldiers — who was a war chief and son of the great Chief Kettle. The second was Wameykay — the Wandering Wolf — whose father had been killed by the Menominees and who was himself a nephew of Chief Katice. The third, Poyekakanumeta — The-One-We-Don't-Know — had lost a nephew to the Menominees. [166] All three were resigned to receiving a death penalty from the United States and had surrendered themselves in an effort to prevent the Americans from further harassing the friendly Sacs and Foxes.

Atkinson was sure at this point that if they pushed the friendly Indians any harder, those very Indians that had been trying so hard to comply with his directives would simply turn against the Americans and add their strength to Black Hawk's band. He could not help but feel that the government really had no business interfering in the conflicts that arose between tribes, yet it was not his place to suggest this, though he found it difficult not to let his controlled anger show through in the letter report he wrote now to General Alexander Macomb:

> *Head Quarters Right Wing West Dept.*
> *Fort Armstrong 19th. April 1832.*
>
> *General — I have the honor to inform you that the Chiefs of the friendly Sacs and Foxes, with whom I have been in council for several days, have this morning, after* [my] *urgently pressing upon them the necessity of a compliance, surrendered up three of the principal men under their influence who were concerned in the attack and massacre of the Menominees last summer at Prairie du Chien. They allege an inability of giving up a greater number of any note implicated in the affair, as the other principal persons who were concerned have gone off with the hostile Indians*

to Rock river. I am disposed to be content with what has been done, as the men delivered up are of rank and connexions [sic] & descendants of the Fox Chiefs murdered by the Menominees in 1829. I might, probably, have obtained the surrender of one or two more of less note, by a further course of perseverance, but I consider men of this character of but little consequence and that the number and weight of character of those given up is, under the existing state of things, sufficient for all purposes of maintaining principle in the case, and of example, particularly as those equally implicated in the commission of the offence who have joined the hostile band of Sacs and their associates, should be held equally accountable, and a persevering course pursued until they are brought to justice. Moreover, the conduct of the friendly chiefs, Wapella, Stabbing Chief & Keokuck, has been so decidedly earnest and persevering to obey the orders of the Government in bringing the matter to a satisfactory conclusion. I have felt it but just not to press them beyond their ability to comply, as a contrary course might tend to drive to the enemy a still greater number of their young men. Under the present arrangement it is probable the Bands now on the west side of the river may remain quiet and friendly, even whilst measures are in operation to coerce the combination of Outlaws and invaders.

It is not understood that the unfriendly Indians have as yet made any direct hostile movement upon the white settlements. I shall keep a strict eye upon them until orders are received as to the course to be taken in relation to the attitude they have assumed, or until they make a stroke. I shall be enabled in a day or two, I presume, to give you information of a more decided character.

General Atkinson to Major Gen. Macomb.

[*April 20, 1832 — Friday*]

Except for a single factor, the powerful forty-five-year-old Winnebago chief named Kauraykawsawkaw — White Crow — could well have epitomized the ideal appearance of an American Indian.[167] He was powerfully, muscularly built without any semblance of being overdeveloped or misshapen. Only slightly taller than the median height of his fellows, he was a strikingly handsome man with well-chiseled features — wide brow, high cheekbones, strong chin, and the domineering aspect of an eagle due to both a direct, penetrating eye and a well-formed, slightly hooked nose. His hair — shoulder-length and very dark except for a slight, distinguished graying at the temples — was normally allowed to fall freely, though sometimes, as now, held in place out of his face by a red headband. The single factor that marred his perfection of appearance was what had, many years ago when he was a young man, caused the French traders to dub him Le Borgne — the One-Eye. As a youth, while walking through the woods in the dark, he had walked into a stub of broken branch that had punctured his left eye as neatly as if it had been purposely aimed at him. After that, when the wound had healed and left an empty socket, a French trader had given him a fine black silk cloth, which, ever since, he had worn over the old injury. Oddly, instead of detracting from his appearance, it imparted a sort of rakish insouciance and had become his trademark.

Now, in the British Band's temporary camp along Rock River just outside Prophet's Town, White Crow smiled grimly as he watched a war fever that had started very slowly take on a momentum of its own and sweep through the assemblage of Indians. Not only were Black Hawk's own 350 Sac warriors and six hundred women, children, and old people on hand, there were also the over three dozen displaced Kickapoo braves that had joined him, plus several hundred other warriors, mostly young hotheaded Winnebagoes, who were committed to the leadership of the Prophet, Wabokieshiek, and openly dedicated to destruction of the Americans. In addition, there were numerous other chiefs and warriors of the Winnebago tribe who, like himself, were vocally uncommitted to any cause but who secretly hoped for the destruction of the whites, while at the same time realizing that such a consummation was extremely unlikely. A sizable number of these uncommitted Winnebago warriors on hand had come here from White Crow's own Turtle Village on the Rock River.[168] Even more Winnebago warriors, as yet also largely uncommitted, had come here from the Four Lakes region of Wisconsin under the powerful chiefs known to the whites as Whirling Thunder, Spotted Arm, and the Liar.[169] But of all those Winnebagoes committed to Black Hawk or those opposed to him or those yet uncommitted in either direction, there were no more than a few on hand who, like White Crow, were walking that delicate and difficult balance between two increasingly festering protagonists, maintaining a protective self-interest while at the same time giving an outward appearance of neutrality, yet at the same time convincing each side of his tacit support. In such a balanced position he could quite neatly play both sides against the middle, with himself personally being exposed to the least risk and simultaneously gaining the greatest benefit.

It amused White Crow to see the change in Black Hawk. When he had first started leading the British Band up the Rock River, Black Hawk had been very unsure of himself and ready at a moment's notice to run or sue for peace if threatened by the whites. He had even been fearful, at first, of the messengers sent to him by the White Beaver — General Atkinson — and the Sac agent, St. Vrain, demanding that he turn back and lead his followers out of the Illinois country and back across the Mississippi. Now, having reached Prophet's Town, and in view of the support he was receiving from so many of the Winnebagoes, he had become far more self-assured in his manner and more boastful in his speech. When the young Fox, Apenose, and the French-Sac half-breed François Labussier had returned with yet another message from Keokuk and St. Vrain to stop and turn back before matters got out of hand, he treated them insultingly and sent them away with warnings that if they came to him again bearing white messages, their scalps would decorate his lance. For the first time, Black Hawk had begun eagerly looking forward to the meeting he would soon be having with the Potawatomies at the mouth of Sycamore Creek, since now he was taking it for granted that they, like the Winnebagoes and the scattered few Potawatomies here, would unite under his banner to drive the Americans out of this land.

There was good reason for Black Hawk's newfound confidence. He had received all manner of promises of backing from many of the Winnebago chiefs, and solid support from the Winnebago Prophet and his followers here at Prophet's Town. Now his British Band was no longer merely a splinter faction broken away from the majority of the Sacs and Foxes. With the Kickapoos and Winnebagoes joining him and the Potawatomies almost certain to do the same, the band was becoming a true confederation, like those brought together in the past by the great Shawnee leader Tecumseh and by the powerful Ottawa chief Pontiac. In fact, during the major council just concluded here, leadership positions had been named for those who would no doubt soon be opposing the American soldiers. Chiefs were chosen from among the Sacs, Foxes, and Winnebagoes in a descending order of nine leaders who were already chiefs in their own right. In addition, five head braves were chosen from among those who were distinguished warriors but not presently chiefs.

The head chiefs chosen as leaders of the new group, in order of their new rank, were the Winnebago Prophet, Wabokieshiek, as the number-one head chief, followed by Neapope — Broth — as second head chief, and Pamisseu — He-That-Flies — as third head chief. In succession, then, came Weesheet — Sturgeon Head — as fourth chief, Chokepashepaho — Little Stabbing Chief — as fifth, Chekokalauko — Turtle Shell — as sixth, Ioway as seventh, Pamaho — He-That-Goes-on-the-Water — as eighth, and finally, Towaunonne — the Trader — as ninth head chief.[170] The five chosen as head braves were Black Hawk as the number-one head brave and beyond any doubt the number-one leader of the entire anti-American faction, despite his lack of chieftainship, Menakau — the Seed — as second head brave, Makatauauquat — Black Cloud — as third, Pachetowart — the Liar — as fourth, and Kinnekonesaut — He-That-Strikes-First — as fifth head brave.[171]

Now White Crow approached Black Hawk and gripped his broad shoulders with both hands. "They know," he said, his head briefly tilting toward the others, "that for all the chiefs that have been chosen, none but the Black Hawk can really be the leader. You are the one that all will follow."

Black Hawk smiled, reveling in the role that he had so long coveted. "Does that include White Crow?" he asked.

White Crow grinned and his uncovered eye glittered. "You know it does," he said. "Even when I am sitting in the palm of the White Beaver and he thinks I am his good Indian chief and his soldiers are all around us, what I am gaining from him I am *getting* for you. My ear to his lips will be the means for you to know his plans as well as his own lesser chiefs know them."

Black Hawk smiled, pleased with having such an able spy. And the one-eyed Winnebago chief smiled back, wondering what the old Sac leader would think if he knew that with but a few minor transpositions of names, White Crow had already made similar comments to Henry Dodge, Felix St. Vrain, and Henry Gratiot.

[*April 20, 1832 — Friday*]

In the governor's mansion in St. Louis, William Clark quickly opened and began reading the letter just handed to him that had come from up the Mississippi aboard the newly arrived steamboat. The handwriting was distinctive enough that he didn't have to look at the signature to know it was from the Sac agent.

Rock Island Ind. Agency
Apl. 18 1832

Genl. Wm. Clark Supt. Ind. affairs St. Louis
   Sir — I was somewhat in a hurry when I wrote you my last of the 14th inst., but knowing it would be some satisfaction to you to have an imperfect idea of the movements of the Indians, that I sent it in that state; since that time I have got news, almost dayly [sic], that the unfriendly band of Sac Indians were constantly recruting [sic] their forces, and that they were determined to make a stand. I state this more positively because Apenose, a Fox brave, and Francis Labusier went to Rock River on the 16th inst. by request of Keokuck, Wapala, &c. to persuad [sic] some of their relations to return and be at peace, but the Messengers were received with suspision [sic] and even threatened to be punished for their audacity. A Potawatomi knocked Labusier's hat off and said that he (Labusier) came there to tell lies that he (the Potawatomi) had seen and heard from several nations who were ready to aid the Sacs in their undertaking. One of the Menominee murderers brandished a lance, saying that it had only served to kill some of the Menominees at Prairie du Chien, but he hoped to brake [sic] or wear it out on the Americans. The Black Hawk said he would be prepared to die in twenty days. Every thing goes to show that they are determined for war against the United States. Those who have seen them say there are at least six hundred warriors, among which are Kikapoos [sic], Potawatomies, Winnebagoes &c. Those, joined to the Proffet's [sic] band (who has no doubt been recruting his forces) will make a formadable [sic] resistance.
   The arrival of the Troops seems to have considerable affect [sic] on the friendly Indians, but it appears that nothing short of Arms will deter the British Band from their purpose. It is not for the want of an invitation that they did not come to the Council with the friendly bands, for I repeatedly sent them word to come up, but they said that I, nor not [sic] any person else on the Island, was their friend. . . .

I have the honor to be, Your Obt Servt.
Felix St. Vrain Ind. Agt.

[*April 30, 1832 — Friday*]

It was the chunky, thirty-four-year-old attorney, James McGowan Strode who, during his brief visit to Dixon's Ferry, convinced Dick Young and Ben Mills of the utmost urgency of writing to Governor Reynolds for help. A round-faced individual with perpetually turned-down mouth and heavily lidded eyes, Strode had been a resident of Galena for the past five years and colonel of the Jo Daviess County Regiment of Illinois Militia for the past two. Though he had never undergone real military action, he unabashedly considered himself the equal of any soldier on earth. He was also convinced that he would make a wonderful congressman and was presently a candidate for Illinois state senator. One way of getting votes next fall, he reasoned, was to make himself well known to the populace right now as a man concerned for the people. Thus, a request to the governor for assistance would no doubt make the citizens here at Dixon's Ferry remember him for coming to their aid and would simultaneously let the governor know that he was a strongly civic-minded individual and therefore an asset to the state in general. Though it was he who actually wrote the letter, he gave Young and Mills the honor of signing it first, after which he signed his own name, slightly larger and more boldly, on a separate line.

Letter to Governor Reynolds —
Dated at Mr. Dixon's upon Rock River

To his Excellency John Reynolds — We are instigated by the pressing necessity of the settlers of this neighbourhood, to address your Excelly [sic] in their behalf, but not at their direct solicitation. The hostile Sacs & Foxes from Missouri have come in considerable force to the prophets Village upon this River. Mr. Smith from Rock Island is here by the direction of Gen Atkinson and Gratiot is at the Turtle Village for the purpose of procuring intelligence of the disposition of the Potawatomies and Winnebagoes. Mr. Smith has had much conversation with the Indians this evening. We regard it as entirely certain that the Potawatomies will join the Sacs & have little doubt that, if their first effort should not prove disastrous, the Winnebagoes will unite their forces with the others. We are upon the spot and therefore have an opportunity of perceiving & feeling much more than can come to your knowledge at the distance at which you are placed or than we can well communicate upon paper without occasioning suspicions which would be without foundations. But of one thing we are certain — that the condition of the exposed settlements is much more critical & alarming than is generally believed and we are therefore induced in their name & in the name of the justice & protection which the government owes to them, to request of you to direct to this place a force of at least two hundred men for their protection. As far as the Sacs are concerned, who are only a few miles below here, We look upon War as inevitable & without immediate aid the settlers in this section will be cut off. We do not hesitate to state to you our conviction that an efficient force ought to be sent to this point without delay. *We speak particularly of this point because it is a central point of communication, not only to the white inhabitants, but it is also nearly central between the Sac Village and the Potawatomi Villages above. There is also a considerable Winnebago force near this place at this time & will be supplied with munitions.*

> *We are Your obt Servts —*
> *Richard M. Young   Benjamin Mills*
> *J.M. Strode*

[*April 21, 1832 — Saturday*]

> U.S. Sub-Indian Agency
> Fort Winnebago, Apl. 21st, 1832

To Brigdr. Genl. Atkinson, U.S.A. Fort Armstrong

Sir — . . . I yesterday held a Talk with a party of the Menominees and signified to them your desire of promoting tranquility, and purpose of enforcing, should it be necessary, the stipulations of the Treaty of Peace of 1830, between them and other tribes. They expressed to me the intention of their nation to remain quiet and not to avenge the murder of their people at Prairie du Chien until they learn whether their Great Father has succeeded in bringing the offenders to justice.

Captn. Plympton (the commanding officer at this place) has united with me in assembling to-day some of the principal Winnebago chiefs of this neighbourhood, and we have communicated to them the substance of what I made known to the Menominees, and the evils which would result to them should any of their nation co-operate with the disaffected band of Sacs. They expressed to us in Council their disapprobation of the procedure of those Indians and their determination not to participate in any hostile movement. They have promised to despatch [sic] runners to their brethren on Rock River to dissuade them from uniting with the malcontents.

Any information I may receive in [the] future of the movement of the Sacs &c. I shall immediately transmit to you.

> *Very Respectfully, Sir Yo. Obt. Sevt.*
> *Jno. H. Kinzie Sub-Agt. Ind. Affs:*

[*April 24, 1832 — Tuesday*]

Governor John Reynolds viewed with undisguised pleasure the assemblage of some one thousand men who had thus far gathered at the Beardstown rendezvous site during the past week since he issued his call-up of the Illinois Militia. Many more were still en route, but the various county militias had responded well to the governor's call in view of the fact that many were farmers and this was the season for preparing the earth and planting, and if not as yet at the Beardstown rendezvous, they were certainly well on their way. Of course, that in no manner meant that the army of the State of Illinois was ready to move. Far from it. Supplies had yet to be ordered up, requisitions made to the government for funds for the purchase of arms and ammunition, and orders issued for the transportation of supplies to meet the troops somewhere along the Mississippi River well below Rock River, probably at either Yellow Banks or the mouth of Henderson Creek. More horses and arms had to be requisitioned for those several hundred volunteers who had shown up or were still en route without either. There were also endless details of formation to be taken care of, not the least of which was the often lengthy and frequently contentious business of the election of officers among the companies, battalions, and regiments. Clearly, it would still be a number of days before the force would be able to move out.

The establishment of the major commands had moved along well enough, and over the past couple of days the assembled force had been organized into four regiments under command of four colonels — John Thomas, Jacob Fry, Abraham Dewitt, and Samuel M. Thompson, plus a spy or scout battalion under Major James D. Henry and two "odd" battalions under two other majors, Thomas James and Thomas Long. The 5th Regiment, under command of Colonel James Johnson, had been formed earlier with Isaiah Stillman, militia general, as battalion major in charge of specially recruited companies.[172]

It was while the militia volunteers were beginning to get themselves organized for the campaign lying ahead that Governor Reynolds had become very angry on receipt of the alarming letter expressed to him from the three men at Dixon's Ferry. Fearful that it betokened a forthcoming slaughter of settlers on that part of the frontier, he yesterday sent a special order to the senior officer of the Illinois 38th Regiment, in Tazewell County:

To Col. David Bailey: You are hereby commanded to raise two hundred mounted men — volunteers, if possible, to be raised in the counties of Macon, Tazewell, McLean and Peoria, in equal proportions in relation to the militia in each county — to be formed into four company [sic] and to elect their company officers. If volunteers cannot be had, then in that event you will draft that number. And you are hereby appointed to command said Corps as major. You will receive your provisions for the volunteers and corn for their horses at Peoria . . . and you will proceed to Dixons on Rock River or its vicinity for the protection of the frontier — Tour of duty not to exceed thirty days.

Now, with the main militia army assembled here at Beardstown having been placed under command of Brigadier General Samuel Whiteside and presently being readied to march north to join the regulars under General Atkinson, Governor Reynolds penned a hasty letter to Isaiah Stillman, who as battalion major had been ranging his companies throughout the country eastward from the Mississippi for the past week. Reynolds wrote:

Dear Sir: I will try to march from this place on the 28th inst. with 1,500 mounted men to the Mississippi at or near the mouth of Hendersons [Creek]. This Route is taken, as the road direct to Rock River is impassible [sic] with wagons. Supplies will meet us on the river.

I have advised Gen. Atkinson of my movement and am informed by him that arms are furnished to the Citizens at Hendersons.

The damage on the Frontier seems to be great.[173] *I have ordered out 200 mounted men to range about Dixons on Rock River.*

You will be vigilant in your exertions.

With respect your obt sevt John Reynolds.
To Gen Stillman.

CHAPTER VI

[*April 26, 1832 — Thursday*]

THE WINNEBAGO subagent Henry Gratiot, through all his years of dealing with the Indians, had never truly felt threatened by them until now. But today there was no doubt in his mind that he was very close to being executed, and it was only with the greatest of difficulty that he was able to maintain a calm front. Still, his eyes kept drifting nervously to the door of the large wigwam, because it would be from the next individual who arrived that he would learn his fate. While he waited, he thought again of the events that had brought him to this point.

It had been eleven days ago, on April 15, that he had received the letter written by General Atkinson, informing him about the British Band of Sacs having crossed the Mississippi and ordering him to range southeastward from Gratiot's Grove to warn white settlers of the possibility of danger from hostile Indians ascending the Rock River and also telling him to visit the Winnebago villages to determine, if he could, their views and intentions in the matter.

The following morning, accompanied by Gratiot Grove's only schoolteacher, George Cubbage, who was also a clerk employed by Gratiot, and his very competent nineteen-year-old Winnebago interpreter, Catherine Myott, the subagent had set out on his mission.[174] He stopped at every settlement and isolated cabin and warned all whites encountered of the dangerous developing situation, and finally, on April 19, reached Turtle Village on the Rock River at the Illinois border. This was White Crow's village, but because of the chief's absence — they did not tell him that White Crow was then at Prophet's Town — the other chiefs on hand did not grant him a council until April 22, by which time White Crow had returned.

A council was convened, and Gratiot, speaking through Catherine, asked the Winnebagoes if they were aware of Black Hawk's invasion of Illinois and his advance up the Rock River. They were, but — White Crow spoke gravely —

they thought it was a very bad thing, and they abhorred the idea of warfare possibly breaking out between Indians and whites. "War belts were sent to us by the Sacs," White Crow said, adjusting the black silk band over his blind eye, "but we returned them at once. The Americans are our friends, and we do not wish to see them hurt. Nor do we wish to be drawn into a war by either whites or Sacs. You tell us it is your intention to continue down this river to Prophet's Town to warn the white people along the way and to discover from the Winnebagoes there what they plan to do. This could be very dangerous for you, so a party of us will accompany you there in order to keep you in safety."

Gratiot, rather surprised at the offer, accepted it with good grace, and the council broke up. A short while later, in private, White Crow reiterated what he had told Gratiot earlier — that his loyalties were to his own people and to the whites, but that he would maintain an aspect of friendliness and support to Black Hawk and thereby learn what the Sacs were planning, so he could pass this vital information on to Gratiot or the white war chief they called White Beaver.

Accompanied by White Crow and about two dozen other chiefs and leading warriors, including Spotted Arm, Whirling Thunder, Little Medicine Man, and Little Priest, Gratiot and his interpreter and clerk moved downriver in a little flotilla of canoes under a white flag held aloft by the Winnebagoes themselves. Two days ago, as they passed Dixon's Ferry, Gratiot paused to warn the whites there, only to find they were already well aware of the situation and very nervous about it, afraid that Black Hawk's band was going to continue up the Rock River and strike the settlement as they passed. While there, Gratiot wrote hasty letters to the secretary of war and to General Atkinson, telling them what had happened so far, of the friendly disposition of the Winnebagoes he was presently with and of his determination to continue downriver until he encountered the British Band, at which time he would endeavor to dissuade any Winnebagoes that might have joined Black Hawk. The letters were dispatched by express, and then Gratiot continued downriver with his own people and White Crow's party, arriving at Prophet's Town late that night.

In the morning their reception by Wabokieshiek's followers was very cold. Though they had been given use of this lodge in which he was still ensconced, Gratiot and Cubbage were treated with rudeness and overt suspicion, and few even paused near enough to them or long enough for Gratiot to deliver his little speech about the jeopardy they would be in if they gave their support to Black Hawk's band. With the temper of the Indians in the village growing uglier, toward noon White Crow's party erected the white flag on a pole beside the lodge "to protect our American friends," as they said. Gratiot and Cubbage were still not fearful of any personal danger, however, until two friendly Sacs who were runners for Keokuk visited them in the middle of the afternoon. The pair were Pachenoi and Wacomme, and they had been sent here with a letter from Atkinson that supposedly implored the British Band to turn back and recross the Mississippi to the Iowa country of their own volition or they would be removed by force and people would no doubt be hurt.[175] It was this pair of friendly Sac runners who informed Gratiot and Cubbage that, though the two whites were evidently not yet aware of it, they were being held prisoner here by order of Black Hawk, who was camped with his large party a couple of miles downstream.

Early the following morning — this morning — a distant chanting sound drew Gratiot and Cubbage to the doorway of their lodge and they stepped outside, joining Catherine Myott, who stood with White Crow and half a dozen of his Winnebagoes. All were looking with interest downstream. The two whites followed their gaze, and what they saw caused both to blanch. Well down this bank of the Rock River but headed their way was Black Hawk on his white stallion, leading five hundred mounted warriors. The bare upper bodies of the warriors had been liberally smeared with white clay, and some had the imprint of hands painted in black or red on chest or back. Almost all of them wore bracelets and anklets of wreathed straw, which Gratiot knew was a traditional decoration worn when members of a war party were seeking the blood of an enemy. To the irregular beat of drums, the Sac horsemen spun and whirled their mounts and then came on, moving in and out of formation, flanking, turning, reforming into a dense column, the sound of their chanting growing louder and punctuated every now and again by small groups facing in the direction of Fort Armstrong and firing their rifles into the air.

"Courage, my friend, courage," White Crow murmured, but the words, softly interpreted by Catherine, only inspired George Cubbage to abruptly turn and dash back inside the lodge. Gratiot remained in place and, desperately trying to keep his fear from showing in his expression, watched the Indians as they closed the distance. Brandishing lances and spears as well as their rifles, tomahawks, and war clubs, the shrieking warriors raced around the lodge on their snorting horses. A small group of them broke away, encircled the pole, and took down the white flag that White Crow's party had raised. They crumpled it into a ball and tossed it scornfully at Gratiot's feet. White Crow's expression did not change, but his good eye seemed to become more glitteringly intent. They then tauntingly raised a somewhat tattered British flag on the pole.

It was Gratiot who spoke first, addressing Black Hawk in English, his words interpreted into the Winnebago by Catherine. "The white flag is mine. Why have your men taken it down as they have?"

Black Hawk began speaking rapidly, but Catherine raised a hand, shaking her head. "Speak Winnebago. I do not interpret Sac well."

Black Hawk nodded and started again, speaking easily in the Winnebago tongue, with Catherine simultaneously interpreting for Gratiot. "You may be under a white flag when you are traveling, but not when you are staying in this lodge. Only the flag of our British father flies over this lodge."

Gratiot's nostrils flared. Without a word to Black Hawk he picked up the white flag, removed the British flag from the pole, tossed it carelessly on the ground, and handed the white flag to White Crow. "Tell your braves to put this back where they had it," he said levelly. White Crow grinned openly, flashing fine white teeth, and, while Black Hawk looked on without expression, told his young men to replace the white flag, which they did. Black Hawk turned and issued a guttural command in the Sac tongue to one of his warriors, who immediately leaped off his horse and approached the subagent. Gratiot braced himself, but the warrior swept past him, snatching the flag from the ground as he passed, and strode to the pole. He then very carefully mounted the British flag beside the white flag and raised the pole again so the two flags fluttered side by side. The situation was nearly ludicrous. For a long moment Black Hawk and Gratiot stared at one another, and then, as if to cool the heated tempers, there was a sudden gust of wind, a rumble of thunder, and it began to rain.

"It is not customary," Black Hawk said suddenly, "for men to let their flags fly in the rain. Is that not true?"

Stone-faced, Gratiot slowly nodded. The Sac issued an order, and the same brave who had hoisted the British flag beside the white flag now lowered them both and removed them from the pole. He very politely handed the white one to Gratiot and the British one to his leader.

"Now," Black Hawk said, his eye corners crinkled with amusement, "we will go inside and talk of important matters."

With a number of his warriors and Menakau — the Seed, his second in command, Black Hawk entered the lodge. He was followed by the Winnebago subagent and his interpreter, who were in turn followed by the dignified White Crow and several of his men. George Cubbage was cowering on his blanket on the far side away from the door. Menakau looked hard at Gratiot and then turned his gaze onto the frightened schoolteacher. He spoke swiftly in Sac, pointing first at Gratiot and then at Cubbage, with White Crow just as swiftly responding in the same tongue and shaking his head furiously in refusal. Gratiot leaned toward Catherine to ask her what was going on, but she gripped his wrist and hissed in English, "Do not speak!"

Menakau and his warriors abruptly broke into a war dance right there in the lodge, prancing in a vigorous circle, howling harsh cries and what were apparently threats at the two white men while at the same time making imaginary passes at them with knives or tomahawks. The dance lasted for ten or fifteen minutes, all during which the argument between White Crow and Menakau continued, with both the Sac and the Winnebago occasionally glancing at Black Hawk as if for support. The old Sac leader's expression remained wooden, and he made no comment. At last White Crow seemed to have prevailed. He reached into his pouch and brought forth two new plugs of tobacco, which he handed to Menakau. The war chief accepted them with poor grace and stalked out, followed by most of the Sac warriors.

Almost immediately Black Hawk began talking, this time in Winnebago through Catherine. He made no reference to what had just occurred, but only told Gratiot that two of Keokuk's runners had brought him a letter from General Atkinson and he was displeased with its contents.

"May I see it?" Gratiot asked.

"No, not now. I will show it to you when we get to our destination, which is far up Rock River."

Gratiot shook his head. "That is not the direction in which I am going."

An ugly expression sprang onto Black Hawk's face and then as quickly vanished. "You go only in the direction where and when I say. Now I will council with the Winnebagoes you have brought, and then White Crow and Wabokieshiek and I will together determine where you go and when." He turned and left the lodge, immediately followed by his remaining Sacs inside. Seeing that White Crow was preparing to follow, Gratiot quickly addressed him.

"You must do all you can, White Crow, to keep your men from joining him, and to make those of your people who are already with him to break themselves away and go off with you and remain at peace. There is only trouble ahead for them from General Atkinson's army if they do not."

White Crow considered Catherine's interpretation a moment, then nodded. He gestured to her to follow him, and the two of them left the lodge, followed by the remaining warriors. Glancing outside after them, the subagent saw to his surprise that the Indians who had surrounded the lodge had all disappeared, and he had not even heard them go.

Cubbage, still on his blanket in the shadows, spoke for the first time when Gratiot returned to his pouch and began to dig about inside for paper and pen to write a quick note to the secretary of war. "Henry," George said in a croaky, fear-filled whisper, "are we going to get out of this?"

"Of course we are," Gratiot said, glad that his own concern was not visible. "Don't worry about it." He uncorked his small inkpot, dipped the nib of his quill, and wrote swiftly on the sheet of paper he had smoothed out on the hard-packed earthen floor.

> *Apl. 26th. 1832 Black Hawk's Camp*
> *40 miles above Rock Island*

Hon. Lewis Cass,

Sir   On the 24th inst. I wrote to you from Ogee's ferry. I stated that I was on my way down the river with a few of my principal men, going to the hostile Sauks for the purpose of trying to get away all Winnebagoes whom I might find there.

I arrived here on the evening of that day and found that the whole of the hostile Indians of the various tribes collected here had determined to go up the river. I and my Winnebagoes have been unceasing in our endeavours to dissuade them from it.

This morning it was said that a part of them intend to recross the Mississippi, but that the Black Hawk and the others persist in their determination of going up Rock River. It has been the opinion of some that they intend to force their way across to Canada. I am inclined to this opinion.

When we came to this place my Indians, of their choice, hoisted a white flag. The Sauks took it down and raised an English one: I asked for an explanation. They said that I might have a flag when traveling but not here. I ordered it to be raised again. The Sauks tied theirs by the side of mine and they floated together. Then they came to my lodge and danced their war dance.

My Winnebagoes wish to go to the fort to see Gen. Atkinson, to declare to him their determination to remain at peace. In the course of the day we shall start downriver, if permitted.

I remain, sir, yours
Henry Gratiot sub agent for Winnebagoes on Rock River

Throughout the remainder of the afternoon and early evening Gratiot and Cubbage anticipated being released to continue on their own way immediately, but their spirits sank when that did not occur. After nightfall Catherine returned briefly and told them that the council was still going on and that there was much arguing over what was to be done with the two white men. As with the argument that had occurred earlier in the lodge between White Crow and Menakau, the subject was whether or not the two whites should be executed, carried off as prisoners, or allowed to leave freely. Catherine said that in the argument that had taken place in the lodge, Menakau had at first demanded that both whites be killed. Finally he had given up insisting that Gratiot be slain but had persisted in calling for the death of the white man Cubbage, whom they referred to disparagingly as a woman. It was only when White Crow had temporarily bought off Menakau with the two plugs of tobacco that the Sac war chief had agreed both men could live at least until the council decided what to do with them.

Catherine left shortly after that, promising to return as soon as the council had reached a decision, though she couldn't offer them any encouragement that the decision would be a favorable one for them. Gratiot and Cubbage couldn't sleep, and they even stopped glancing at one another, unable to stand the look of fear that each saw mirrored in the other's eyes. Just before midnight they heard the sound of many feet and went to the doorway to find that the Prophet, at the head of about forty of his men, had arrived at their lodge. Catherine was with them, and she moved from among them to stand beside the Indian subagent.

Wabokieshiek and Gratiot had known each other for many years and had become friends of a sort, but there was no friendliness in the expression of the Winnebago Prophet now as he extended some folded papers to the subagent. Gratiot looked puzzled as he accepted them.

"What is this?" he asked.

"It is the letter your General Atkinson has sent to Black Hawk. Take it back to the White Beaver and tell him to send no more like it to any of us. Tell him that the reply from Black Hawk is this: 'My heart is bad. I intend going farther up Rock River and perhaps up the Pecatonica, which our Winnebago brothers have invited us to do, and live and plant our corn among them. If the White Beaver wishes to fight us, then he can come on.' " Wabokieshiek's expression became even more grim. "You will stay here the rest of the night. In the morning Black Hawk will give you a talk with his own lips, and then you are to go away with Whirling Thunder and White Crow and this woman, and never return here again."

[*April 27, 1832 — Friday*]

The change in Black Hawk was startling. He seemed to have aged years just overnight. Where up until yesterday his demeanor had been sharp and his step surprisingly sprightly for a man nearly sixty-five, today he had been withdrawn and gloomy, decidedly disinclined to heartily encourage his followers as he always had up till now, his shoulders slumped in dejection. They had returned to the Illinois country with a total number of just over a thousand individuals. Now, counting all those that had joined them on the way upstream and when they reached Prophet's Town, their total number was virtually doubled, yet their fighting strength was below eight hundred.

All throughout this day on their laborious march upstream along the edge of Rock River, Black Hawk had repeatedly glanced back at the over two thousand Indians strung out behind him, hundreds following on their horses and many more than that dotting the surface of the stream in the vast flotilla of a hundred or more canoes, each with its capacity load of women and children and old people as well as all the band's goods. He had thought that, in order to move farther away than Prophet's Town from reach of the White Beaver's army, he would accept the invitation of the Winnebagoes to settle among their villages in the area of the Pecatonica River, following that tributary stream up to where it split into east and west branches and then following the east branch northward toward the area of Blue Mounds. But then, during last night's war dances and speeches, the Winnebago chiefs of villages in the vicinity of Blue Mounds — Whirling Thunder and Spotted Arm — had gravely and quite nervously rescinded their invitation and, as if speaking with the best interests of Black Hawk's band at heart, suggested he lead them into the difficult-to-travel, swampy upper reaches of the Rock River above Lake Koshkonong, where they would supposedly be better able to defend themselves against the attacking whites.[176] Now they were almost a lost tribe, moving purposefully up the Rock but with Black Hawk having no definite goal as a final stopping place, although his followers thought he had.

"Where have I led them?" he muttered, raising his hand high as a signal for those behind to stop.

"Did you speak, Black Hawk?" asked Black Cloud, pulling up alongside him on a chestnut mare. "Is something wrong?"

Black Hawk shook his head, glanced up at the position of the sun, and then said, "It is only a little after the middle of the day, but we will stop now. Pass the word that this is where we will camp until dawn tomorrow. Go back at once through our people and find the chiefs and head braves. There is an important council that must be held of all of them, and it cannot wait any longer." He looked at Black Cloud sharply and added, "I speak only of fourteen men, counting ourselves — the nine chiefs and five head braves as we selected them one week ago. No one else. Go."

Black Cloud frowned but nodded, wheeled his mare around, and began moving through the now stopped throng, seeking the remaining dozen he had been sent to find. He did not dally, yet it was more than an hour later before all fourteen had assembled in a secluded glade located several hundred yards ahead of the overnight encampment. Speaking little, and only as they took their places, they seated themselves in a semicircle on their blankets amid the bright wild-flowers and new grasses and lighted their pipes. Soon the quiet glade was redolent with the pleasantly acrid scent of the smoldering kinnikinnick. Although all were intensely curious as to why Black Hawk should have called a halt so early in the day and assembled them like this, not until the pipes were finished did Black Hawk rise and step onto a slight knoll that was before them. He stood facing them, letting his eyes rest briefly on each of the thirteen before he finally began to speak.

"My brothers," he said, "we have come to a bad moment — one that I had hoped we would never be forced to face. Yet, face it we must. During the winter past, while the British Band crouched near its fires on the Iowa, we received wampum from the Winnebagoes. It was war wampum, and told us that if we accept the belts, we would then be joined with them and they with us as we set out to make war against the whites and drive them from this land that was ours."

He paused and let his gaze fall briefly on Wabokieshiek and then come to rest on Neapope. "We had been lifted up," he went on, his voice a little harder, "in the belief that with the spring would come our British father with his red-coated warriors to help us in our goal to regain possession of our lands. All our people knew it was so because I had told them it was true . . . and I believed it myself. I believed it because it was told to me by Chief Neapope, who was gone from us nearly all the preceding summer and with the British at Malden. He returned and told first the Prophet, Wabokieshiek, and then me that with the greening of spring would come the British in their boats, that they would come to land at Mil-wau-kee and that many hundreds of soldiers — as many as we needed — would come with their long knives and rifles and thunder guns and aid us in ejecting the Americans who have taken our lands.

"It was because of such a wonderful promise," he went on after a slight pause, "that we received the belts of war wampum from the Winnebagoes and their promises of joining us for our great struggle if that struggle came to pass. It was because of that promise that the Potawatomies, speaking through Mawgehset, told us that when the time came to fight the Americans, *if* such a time came, they would then support us and fight beside us just as the Winnebagoes would. Some of us looked forward to that possibility and yearned for it, because we are *warriors!* Yet, there were many more who hoped it would not be necessary. We would at first return to Rock River, not to try to take back Saukenuk and our cornfields there, but to come up to Prophet's Town as we did, and there, by invitation of the Winnebago Prophet, till new fields and plant new corn and bother no one unless bothered.

"When we crossed the Mississippi I sent word to the Potawatomies at once to meet us farther up from here, which I am told they are still planning to do. But we were also told that the Winnebagoes would, *as a tribe*, unite under our cause. Now we learn from White Crow and Spotted Arm and Whirling Thunder that they disapprove of our return and the trouble it is causing, and they have taken back their invitation to us to settle on the Pecatonica. Why do you not, they say, either plant new fields at Prophet's Town as you were first invited to do and stop causing trouble to your neighbors, or else go far up this river to the swamps above Koshkonong where you can make a successful stand against enemies? But they did not say these things too strongly yet, because they, like all others, were waiting for the ships of the British to land and the red-coated army to offer us its strength."

He paused and seemed to be gathering himself to explode with the point he had been leading up to. "*But!*" he shouted, and his hand shot out, the index finger impaling Neapope with its point, "*But!* . . . there is Neapope, our second chief here under Wabokieshiek, who suddenly admits in closed council with me last night that there *is no British army coming to help us* . . . that the British had told him instead to go home and learn to live with the Americans, because there would be no more war between them. And so Neapope, having stayed away all summer, returns and councils first with the Prophet, and together they decide it would make our people and all other tribes be men again — be *warrior braves* again — if they had the belief to cling to that the strong arm of the British father was behind them. It was false. All false! We have been *deceived*, and now see us where we are!"

A wave of shock had gone across his listeners, and they stared with disbelief at Wabokieshiek and Neapope, while those two only looked straight ahead and did not speak. The shock was quickly being displaced by a searing anger, which might well have spilled over, except that Black Hawk held it in check with his next words.

"What they did was not right, but neither was it all wrong. *They* are not to blame, only we ourselves — *all* of us. We *wanted* to believe what they said. We *wanted* to feel again a pride in ourselves as warriors. And so we did, for a little while — all of us. Our people here with us," he flung out his hand in the direction of the encampment, "they, too, have felt this pride. It is what has held them together in this time of need. And so the question comes now, do we crush their minds and hearts with news of this deception? Or," he added ringingly, "do we not tell them yet? Do we wait to see if somehow the support we sought from our brother tribes is not still available to us?

"I see you looking at one another in puzzlement," he went on, "and wondering how this could be. But it *is* possible, and this is how: though the Winnebagoes have pulled away a little, they have not shut themselves up beyond reach. They are a strong tribe and greatly feared in warfare, as are the Sacs and Foxes. So, too, are the Potawatomies. And when I asked the Winnebagoes last night to continue to support us as a tribe, they did not flatly refuse. Instead they offered us this possibility: *If,* when we meet far upriver from here with the Potawatomies, if at that time we can persuade them as a tribe to join us against the Americans, then the Winnebagoes, too, as a tribe, will join us as well. When that came about, could there any longer be doubt that the rest of the Sacs and Foxes across the Mississippi would join us? Is it all not worth the effort of a little while longer to *try*?

"Let us not," Black Hawk went on, "think of punishments for the two here who deceived us. Let us think instead of the pride they instilled in us again, even if that might not have been their aim. Let us not, for the time being, tell any other person among our followers, of the deception. Let us instead allow them to continue to cling to the pride that carries them so well in the face of want. It can be only a matter of fifteen or eighteen days until we will know for sure. If, at last, at the end of that time, the Potawatomies and Winnebagoes join us, then it will have been worth this final deception by all of us here. And should those tribes refuse us and, in the end, we be left alone without any allies to aid us, then will it not be time enough to put down our arms and submit to the White Beaver, and finally go to live beyond the big river where the Americans want us to be?"

The response was strongly in the affirmative, and Black Hawk slumped faintly, exhaled deeply, and felt an unexpected gladness well up inside. He was certain that not even Keokuk could have been more eloquent. In the face of major disaster he had put across difficult points and won a short reprieve, and with it, a final vestige of hope.

[*April 27, 1832 — Friday*]

Brigadier General Henry Atkinson had finally and reluctantly come to the decision that there was no further help for it — he had to act more definitively against Black Hawk's band. His own force of regulars, though strengthened slightly by companies from Fort Crawford at Prairie du Chien and from Fort Winnebago at the Portage, remained too small to attack what was certainly a much larger Indian force, but encouraging word had been received in two letters from Governor Reynolds on Tuesday evening that he was on the move to join him with a substantial force. Early the following morning, Atkinson had written a letter to Henry Dodge and dispatched it by express to Dodgeville:

Head Qrs right wing Westn Dept
Fort Armstrong 25th April 1832

General — I received letters from Governor Reynolds last night informing me that he had ordered twelve hundred militia to Rendesvous at Bairdstown [Beardstown] on the Illinois on the 22d Inst. They are to be mounted. Besides these he has ordered out four companies of rangers which are probably by this time on the frontier. The Governor will probably bring into the field 1400 mounted men. He proposes marching to this point in order to meet supplies for his troops — although I would prefer making [a site well up] on Rock River the point of general rendesvous, still this is a good point as I find their [sic] is a good road to the prophets village on Rock River. Should it become necessary to make a movement against the Indians, of which there appears but little doubt — it will be important that a mounted force from the mineral district should act in concert with the troops that march from this place up Rock river; as, should the Indians retire up the river from their present position, their progress could be arrested by a force assembling at Dixons Ferry.

I have to request under the present aspect of affairs that you will organize as many mounted men as can be raised from your own & the settlements about you. I write to day to the commanding officer of the militia at Galena requesting him to adopt the same measures. Should the troops from the mineral district be required to take the field, I will give due notice and take measures to supply them with provisions. I send up by a steam boat to day about two hundred rifles, they will be delivered to Mr Ferguson, Indian Agent at Galena, for distribution should they be required. I have directed him to issue to you a part of them.

Atkinson's previous letter to William B. Ferguson, the rather lackluster Winnebago subagent at Galena, had been brief and direct:

Dear Sir   I have directed the commanding officer of this post to ship to your address by [the] steam boat Dove, about two hundred rifles. You will receive them and have them put in store subject to the call of the militia military authorities of Galena and General Dodge of Dodgeville. They are not to be distributed by you until their [sic] is a positive necessity for their use against threatened or actual hostility on the part of the Indians. In case they are issued, take receipts from the officers they are delivered to, specifying that they shall be returned as soon as the necessity for which they have been distributed shall cease. You will report to the commanding officer here, for the arms according to the receipts that have been sent up with them — let me hear by the return of the boat all the information you have obtained relative to the movement and position of the hostile Sac Indians.

Immediately after finishing the letter to Dodge and sending it off to Dodgeville by horseback express, General Atkinson wrote quickly to the individual whom he assumed to be commander of the militia in Galena, James M. Strode, colonel of the Jo Daviess County militia and highest-ranking militia official there:

Sir — Governor Reynolds has ordered about 1400 mounted men to Rendesvous at Bairdstown Ill river [sic] *on the 22d Inst for the purpose of marching against the hostile Indians on Rock river. He proposes in the first instance to move to the vicnity* [sic] *of this post for supplies. If it becomes necessary for him to take the field, of which there is but little doubt, he will probably reach this point by the 8th or 10th of next month as the operations against the Indians must be by the route up Rock river — a mounted force assembling at Dixons Ferry would most probably have this effect.*

I have therefore to request that you will organise [sic] *as many of the militia of your command as practicable for the object pointed out and hold them in readiness to take the field if required, of which due notice will be given, & provision made to furnish the necessary supplies. I write to day to General Dodge to the same purport as respects organising the militia of the part of the country in which he resides. I send up by* [the] *steam boat* Dove *to Mr. Ferguson Indian Agent at Galena about two hundred rifles to be issued if it should become necessary.*

General Atkinson to Coln Strode or officer Commanding the militia at Galena.

The big news of the moment for Atkinson was, of course, first the return late last night of the Indian messengers that he had sent, through Keokuk, with the message to Black Hawk to turn back, and, only an hour ago, earlier this evening, the return of Henry Gratiot from the mission upon which Atkinson had dispatched him. The subagent was accompanied by a small party of Winnebagoes, which included Whirling Thunder and White Crow. While Gratiot bathed, ate, and briefly rested, Atkinson read the full report in letter form that Gratiot had written to him, detailing the events of his dealings with the Winnebagoes at the Turtle Village and his journey with a party of those Indians under White Crow to the Prophet's Town and then the rather remarkable occurrences with Black Hawk there. Afterward, the general conversed in person with Gratiot for additional details and scheduled a talk tomorrow morning with chiefs Whirling Thunder and White Crow; he knew, through Gratiot, that they were extremely influential Winnebagoes, and that it was most likely only through their escorting of him that the subagent had been permitted to leave Prophet's Town unscathed and arrived here safely.

Now, late at night in his quarters at Fort Armstrong, Atkinson's quill pen made an almost unceasing scratching noise as he wrote a swift report to Governor Reynolds:

Sir   An express that I have sent up [the two friendly Sac messengers, Pachenoi and Wacomme] *returned from the Prophets Village yesterday and, an hour since,*

Mr. Gratiot, Indian agent, arrived here from the same place. I sent by the express a mild talk to Black Hawk, advising him to return to the west side of the Mississippi. Mr. Gratiot has brought me his answer, which is, that his heart is bad and he will not return, that if I send after him, he will fight, and that he can whip us. They, with the Prophet's Band, moved off yesterday to take a position some 15 or 20 miles above Ogees, now Dixons Ferry, where they say they will plant corn.

Mr. Gratiot considers them decidedly hostile & bent upon mischief. They state their own numbers to be 486 [warriors]. Whilst they remain on Rock River, the whole frontier, including the mineral district, will be in a state of alarm, and in danger of attack.

The position of the unfriendly Indians renders it necessary and proper that you should march by the Fort Clark route [Kellogg's Trail north from Peoria] to Dixon's Ferry on Rock River, (the crossing marked on the map as Ogees Ferry) I purpose [propose] taking a position there with the regular troops and wait your arrival, and in the mean time have provisions carried there against the arrival of your mounted force. Whether corn can be procured is a matter of doubt.

If Black Hawk's Band gains no accession of strength, they can be easily overcome. But if joined by a part only of the Winnebagoes, Kickapoos, & Pottawattamies [sic], the force will amount to 1000 or more men. Mr. Gratiot, however, is of opinion, that these tribes will not join. Still, precaution against the possibility is necessary. I can take into the field about 320 regulars; these, with the force you have ordered out, I should suppose would be sufficient. Many hands, however, make light work of a job, and there is both safety & economy in adopting such a course.

There are no beef cattle at Galena. If some could be driven on with your command, it would be advisable. I send Lieut Beall with this communication, to whom I refer you more particularly as to my views.[177] Teams are scarce at Galena but, I presume, enough can be procured to transport our Artilley [sic], munitions & provisions. As steam boats ascend the Illinois river as high as Fort Clark, you might, I presume, readily take from thence some twenty days provisions, as Wagons & teams must be abundant in the settlements on that river.

Will you assist Lt. Beall in returning with your answer as early as possible.

Atkinson signed, folded, and sealed the letter in an envelope and then, his eyes gritty from the want of sleep, wrote a final letter of the day — this one to the commander of the American Army in Washington, Major General Alexander Macomb:

General   The conduct of Black Hawk & his associates renders it necessary that I should at Once take the field and, as far as possible, prevent them from doing any mischief.

Mr. Gratiot, Indian agent, has just arrived from the Prophet's village. Black

Hawk and his party were there. Yesterday they set out in company with the Prophet's band for the purpose of taking a position on Rock river some 15 or 20 miles above Ogee's, now Dixon's Ferry, where they are determined to hold out in defiance of any force, they say, that can be sent against them. They have the British flag hoisted, under which the war dance is constantly exhibited. They must be checked at once, or the whole frontier will be in a flame.

I purpose [propose] moving by Galena and taking a position at Ogee's (Dixon's ferry) on the Fort Clark Road and await there the arrival of Governor Reynolds' mounted force, when I presume the hostile party can be put down.

Great distress is already felt on the frontier, the inhabitants abandoning their farms & falling back for safety.

P.S. — To a mild talk I sent to Black Hawk, he sends by Mr. Gratiot an answer that his heart is bad, & that he will fight any force sent against him.

Gen: Atkinson to Gen: Macomb.

[*April 28, 1832 — Saturday*]

John Dixon, his long white hair and rather hollow expression making him look much older than his forty-eight years, had been watching the procession for over an hour, and still it had not ended. Now, on reading the note that was slipped into his hand by one of the individuals passing by, he was unable to stand here watching this any longer and stepped inside his house, closed and barred the door, and immediately sat down at his accounts desk and began writing a letter.

Both ashore and on the Rock River, the Indians — more than Dixon had ever seen together at any one time — had begun passing his Rock River ferry operation shortly after sunrise this morning. They had women and children with them, as well as old people and household goods, which all gave substance to Dixon's immediate supposition that this was in no manner a war party — and yet, as the hundreds of warriors, all heavily armed, passed on horseback, staring at him and his wife balefully, he could not suppress the shudder that had momentarily racked him.

Dixon was not fluent in either the Sac or Winnebago tongue, and yet, in broken fashion and with many gesticulations, he had spoken for a short time to three of the Indians who had, early in the passage, reined up their horses together close to him. The eldest of the three, astride a fine white stallion, was an older man with sharp, commanding features. His head was bald except for a scalp lock from which depended a brass medallion and several eagle feathers. Although Dixon had never seen the man before, he knew this had to be the infamous Black Hawk himself. The Sac had raised his hand in the sign of peace, but though Dixon's initial pleasant expression had remain unchanged, he was sharply conscious of the letter presently in the inside breast pocket of his black frock coat, and his heart had suddenly begun beating much faster. Though he continued to smile pleasantly, a tremor of fear blossomed in him with such intensity that he mentally marveled at his own ability to conceal it. The second man he definitely recognized as Wabokieshiek — the Winnebago Prophet — having seen him on several occasions in the past. The third man, younger and less inclined to any display of friendliness, he did not recognize at all, but soon learned this was Neapope, one of the principal leaders of the Indians who were passing.

They spoke for several minutes — Black Hawk and Wabokieshiek patiently making every effort to make themselves understood, but Neapope saying nothing and never changing his scowling expression. Then Wabokieshiek tossed him a half-salute, and the three Indians had reined the horses away and continued moving upriver with the procession.

The letter Dixon was so hurriedly writing was addressed to the most senior officer of the militia that he knew, General Isaiah Stillman:

Dixons Ferry April 28th 1832

Genl Stillman Sir, I have a moment to say that this morning Black Hawk & his band came here & most of them have gone up the River — destination about 20 miles above this place. About 500 horses & about 100 canoes have passed this, [with it] said to be more to come. About 500 men besides women & children. they profess to be friendly, but I do not know their object they say they are going to raise corn & build a town on the pottawattimies [sic] land, whose line is within 12 miles of me on this side of the River.

I got a letter yesterday from Mr. Gratiot from the Sack [sic] village below.[178] *It was dated Black Hawk's camp 26th inst. he has gone to Rock Island. This morning I recd a slip of paper from Mr Gratiot & which was written an hour later — "War is declared, send out expresses" I have time to write no more.*

Respectfully Yr Ob Sert John Dixon

[*April 28, 1832 — Saturday*]

Atkinson sat stiffly at attention, listening carefully to Catherine Myott interpreting the opening remarks being made by the distinguished-appearing White Crow in the Fort Armstrong council chambers. He was clad in beautiful soft buckskins, the seams frilled with soft, tapered tips. The black silk band of cloth was, as usual, over his blind eye, and his shoulder-length hair was held firmly against his temples by a crimson headband.

"My Father," White Crow said, "I am in trouble, so I have come down to see you. You know me. You have heard me very often. I am now going to send my words through you to my great father in the place you call Washington." The gaze of his one good eye bored into the general's, and his next words were delivered in a very deliberate manner. "When you hear me now, I speak for all my chiefs, my braves, my children, my women.

"Father, there are very often a great many fools among us. There never has been any blood shed on our river yet. We have always" — his gaze slid to the

agents present, Henry Gratiot and Felix St. Vrain, then back to Atkinson —
"been well advised. We always listen and do all we can. Father, the Red Head
came to Prairie du Chien and gathered together all his children and told them
to bury the tomahawk.[179] I have listened to him. I have buried it, and it shall
never be raised. Father, the Great Spirit who hears knows that I tell the truth,
and it shall never be raised. We love our country. We love our father and know
that you give us good advice. We wish to raise our corn in peace. Father, the
Great Spirit made the land for the whites *and* the Indians. You wished to buy a
piece of land and we sold it to you by the instigation of our agent. I mention this,
Father, to let you know that when our agent speaks, we listen to him." He
flashed a smile at Gratiot, who dipped his head in acknowledgment of the
compliment.

"Father," White Crow went on, after adjusting the black silk cloth over his
blind eye, "I am very frank with you. I have taken General Dodge, who is my
friend, by the hand. He is like a father. This," he said, his arm sweeping up into
a point at Catherine Myott, "is Boilvin's daughter and a good interpreter who
always speaks the truth. Mr. Gratiot is our second father and always gives good
advice.[180]

"Father," White Crow continued, seeming to grow tall as he got past the usual
sort of preliminaries and homed in on one of the major points of his speech, "as
you are writing to our great father in Washington, we wish you to recommend
us. We have young men who are foolish and go on white man's ground to hunt
firewater. You have bad men on the frontier who encroach upon our grounds
and make our young men drunk and which causes these young men to do foolish
things. You must not let this be. We point them out to the notice of our great
father in Washington, who we wish will say the words that will make these men
who have the firewater stay on their own side and not disturb us anymore.

"Father, you are the master here. You see us as we are because of that —
naked and poor. You send our annuity to the fort with our name at the Portage.
We go there for it, and when we get there, the moment we receive our money
there is whiskey there in great abundance." He pointed accusingly at Atkinson.
"You *know* we are weak in this matter, and you *know* we will take the whiskey
and that we will return home a great deal worse off than when we went. If instead
of Fort Winnebago you sent our money closer to our villages, placing it in the
hands of our agent so he could bring it to us at the Four Lakes or on the
Pecatonica River, then it would do us much good. We have asked this many
times before, and our agent Gratiot has also asked this in our name, but yet the
annuity still comes to a place far away from our villages, and there the money
stays because of the men who give us whiskey in order to take it away from us,
and leave us with nothing but empty stomachs and bad dreams and anger."[181]

White Crow paused a long while, signifying that he was about to change the
subject, which he did, moving in more pertinently on the war rumblings on this
frontier. "Father, you see me here today because I heard some bad birds singing

down this Rock River from where we live." It was not necessary for him to point out to General Atkinson who the bad birds were that he was referring to. Atkinson nodded faintly in understanding, and White Crow went on. "The song they sang enticed some of our hot-blooded young men away from their mothers and fathers and wives and children. When I heard this, I came down for the purpose of taking our young men away from them, and I met them between here and my village, but they would not heed my words. All I want is our children from among them. We want nothing to do with these bad birds. Father, you must understand that this is most difficult for me, because the bad birds also send *me* tobacco painted red. It troubles me a great deal, and I am traveling all the time because of that red tobacco. I came to tell you the truth, that they have sent me this tobacco, that they are going up this river, and that they have sent to me to join them." He gave the general an odd, rather meaningful sidelong glance coupled to a half-smile. "But I will not, except" — his smile broadened — "that *you* would wish me to, that I may learn and pass on to you what is in their hearts."

White Crow paused to let that sink in, and when he continued, his voice virtually dripped with sincerity. "You may have been told that I invited them to come here and grow corn on the Pecatonica and make trouble for you, but before the Great Spirit I tell you that I did not. This British Band of Indians has gone up the river now against our will. We have told them not to, but they have not listened to us and have gone up anyway. We have told them they may not come onto Winnebago lands, where they had been planning to come." Adroitly, White Crow dumped the burden of responsibility into Atkinson's lap. "If you permit them to remain up the Rock River, then we want you to keep them away from us. If blood is spilled at our door, we can't help it. If our young men who are with the Sacs will not return with us, they must share with them what fate the Sacs bring down upon themselves. We will have nothing to do with the Sacs!"

Touching now upon the fact that there was a great deal of intertribal marriage between the Sacs and the Winnebagoes, White Crow spoke as if in admission of a crime. "Father, our blood that has mixed with them has always been very bad. Our young men who have gone to them have always been very bad to us, everywhere they have been. They have thought that this was the way they should be. We told them no, that they might come home with us and be our young men again, but that if they did not, they must then take the consequences of their decision.

"My Father, when I left the Prophet's Village to come down here, many of the bad birds there whistled words of warning — that if I came down here to talk with you, I would be hanged. But I said I have done nothing wrong, and I have not. I will follow my father in what he wishes me to do. As I was coming here yesterday I met some Sacs, and they asked me where I was going, and I said to the fort at Rock Island. They said to me, The white men will hang all Winnebagoes there. I told them I had done nothing wrong and I would go. That is the way, Father, that evil reports are sung about. They will tell you bad stories about us, but you must not believe them."

White Crow paused again for a long moment, then made a movement with his right hand, as if throwing a knife into the ground, a sure sign that he was now about to make his concluding statement.

"Father," he said, "I wish you to tell the great father that there is always clear weather between us, that we will not let storm clouds get between us and obscure our view of each other. What I have said here has been in the name of the chiefs and braves, the women and children. When we leave here, I wish you to give us a pass to show to your children, by which they will know that we are friendly." And, as always, there was that final plea for goods: "Father, you see us here before you, poor and without provisions or gunpowder. I hope you will not tell us to go away without any."

With what might almost have been described as a regal turn, White Crow went back to his place and sat down. As he did so, the older Whirling Thunder came to his feet and took the place White Crow had just vacated.

"Father," he said, his voice scratchy and faintly tremulous, "you see that I am a very old man. It is hard for me to travel, yet it was necessary that I come here with a good heart. I find the weather here is clear for us, and when I go back it will be clear at my village also. I am very thankful to you for letting your ears hear our words. From here I am going back up the river. There I shall meet your Indian children of the Black Hawk's band. Do not worry what they might say to me. I know they are fork-tongued, and I will be deaf to them. I am going back to my village, and if what I hear concerning the Sacs is not good, I will send you word. Father, the Great Spirit hears me. Although some of our tomahawks are up in the air, some are buried in the ground below. Only time will prove to you whether ours here will be raised or not. Father, I am now done. I now shake hands with you and all your children. I will send to my own children not to listen to the singing of those bad birds."

As soon as the old chief had returned to his place beside White Crow and sat down, Atkinson came to his feet, and it was evident that he was pleased with what the Winnebago chiefs had said. He nodded to them both — first to Whirling Thunder, then to White Crow — and began speaking steadily, with Catherine Myott interpreting at as regular a pace for the Indians.

"I am glad to see you," the general told them. "You did right to come here and let me know that you are friendly. You did right not to listen to Black Hawk's party. You *must not* listen to them. You must go back to your villages, plant your corn, and keep all your people together — young men and old men, women and children. You must not go out to visit those bad Sacs who are gone up the river, and you must not let those Sacs come to visit you. You must not let them settle on Winnebago lands. *All* the Winnebagoes found with the Sacs will be looked upon as enemies. I look upon you, now, as friends, and so does your great father. Now your conduct must *prove* that you are friends.

"When you get back," he went on, "you must send runners out to all your villages and give the same talk to them that I give to you. *Do not listen to the Sacs!* Stay at home and mind your own business. You heard the talk I sent to the Sacs. I told them if they did not come back, they would be sorry for their conduct. They will find what I said to them is true. The Sacs will cry a great deal before this difficulty is settled if they do not listen. I have not come here for nothing. I shall not leave this country until everything is made straight. I tell you again not to listen to those people and to have nothing to do with them. All of your people that do listen will bring a great deal of trouble on themselves.

"Your nation," Atkinson added in a sorrowful voice, "will lose everything you have — your lands, your mines, and your money — if you join the Sacs on this occasion. I give you this advice because I do not want the Winnebagoes hurt. You must listen to what I say, and everything will be good. The weather will be clear, and there will be no thorns in the path. And yes, I will give you a passport when you wish to go back to your people. You will see me again before a great while. I hope your hearts and hands may be clean, that I may then shake hands with you."

The general returned to his seat and quickly wrote a message on a sheet of paper, which his aide then handed to Gratiot, who read it quickly to Catherine Myott and then gave it to the two Winnebago chiefs. On the sheet was written:

Head Qrs right Wing Westn Dept
Fort Armstrong 28th. April 1832

This is to certify that Whirling Thunder, a Winnebago chief, White Crow, a brave [meaning war chief] & three Winnebago men have held at this place a friendly council with me today. They are directed to return to their village and have nothing to do with the Sacs on Rock River, to keep their people at home & plant their corn and live at peace with the whites. They are to send word to the other villages of the Winnebagoes to do the same. They are directed not to go among the Sacs nor let the Sacs come among them and not to suffer the Sacs to settle on Winnebago lands.

Should these people meet any white people they are to be treated kindly as long as they behave well.

H. Atkinson Br Gnl U.S. Army

[*April 30, 1832 — Monday*]

Organization of the troops and election of the officers among the militia volunteers who had rendezvoused at Beardstown had gone rather slowly, and it was not until this morning, fully forty-eight hours after his expected date of April

28 for moving the troops out toward the frontier, that Governor Reynolds issued the order to the commanding general to move them out and General Samuel Whiteside finally got them on the march.

The preceding week had been filled with a complex variety of maneuverings, positionings, elections, boisterous good-natured competitions, and a general forming of the mass of some sixteen hundred men — all but about three hundred of them mounted — to finally whip the companies into shape. The initially appointed quartermaster general early on estimated the projected expenses of the campaign — pay, subsistence, and transportation of the militia — at $88,500, and Congress had quickly granted $150,000 for the entire operation, although there were some officers who were already mumbling that the larger figure, while seemingly generous, was not nearly enough.

For most of the volunteers, even the farmers who groused about leaving their fields at such a crucial time, this whole business was a great lark — a sort of gigantic picnic of the local men's club. They drew equipment, frolicked, played practical jokes, ran races, had competitions of strength and sometimes even of intelligence, all the while existing on the items that would be the staples of their diet throughout the campaign — flour, pork, corn, and whiskey.

As usual, officers were elected from within the ranks of the companies formed. Young Abraham Lincoln had been initially elected captain of his sixty-eight-man company, with Samuel M. Thompson as his 1st lieutenant, at the first gathering of the Sangamon County volunteers. Yet, oddly enough, after he had led these horsemen forty miles to the assigned rendezvous at Beardstown, it was Sam Thompson who was named as colonel of the 4th Regiment, and Lincoln was thereafter serving under him during this initial four-week enlistment. Nevertheless, as a captain, Lincoln still had the responsibility of his own company. He was not terribly skilled at military maneuverings, and early on, while putting his men through a session of drill in a formation twenty-men wide, he came to a gate through which he wanted his men to pass to enter the adjoining field. Try as he might as his men approached the fence, Lincoln could not remember the proper command for turning the broadly marching company endwise in order to pass four abreast through the gate. He solved the problem in his own way. When they were a few steps from the gate, he called a halt and then shouted, "This company is dismissed for two minutes, when it will fall in again on the other side of the gate!"

Although Lincoln's company had formed early on after reaching the Beardstown rendezvous, it was not until the day before yesterday — on the 28th of April, the day that all the troops that had rendezvoused were finally fully organized — that they were actually mustered into the service of the State of Illinois by Colonel John J. Hardin, Illinois state inspector general and mustering officer.

Even as late as the end of that first week, additional men were showing up. Two companies of foot soldiers showed up only yesterday, and even though

Governor Reynolds was not particularly pleased to see additional men on foot, since only mounted volunteers had been called up, they were quickly formed into a battalion under the command of Major Thomas Long and dispatched under Reynolds's final order before the march of the troops began. They were sent aboard the steamship requisitioned by the government with orders to go down the Illinois and up the Mississippi to the mouth of Henderson's Creek and there to await further orders, remaining there to rendezvous on May 2 with the mounted troops who were marching by land.

Early this morning Governor John Reynolds finally issued the order to move out, and General Whiteside had started the brigade on its way — a thrilling sight of some thirteen hundred horsemen on the move in a sinuous column heading generally northward, but with no specific destination having been announced. The ground was very marshy from heavier-than-normal rains this spring, and so progress was not as swift as had been reckoned, and by the end of this first day's march, the army had stopped to camp for the night just short of fourteen miles from Beardstown on a well-selected camping area in a prairie some four miles north of the tiny frontier town of Rushville.[182] Here Reynolds issued the formal march order with destination:

Camp near Rushville 30th April 1832

To Brig. Gen. Saml Whiteside   You will march [your] Brigade with all convenient speed to the Yellow Banks on the Mississippi River the most direct Route. Shooting without order and all disorderly conduct will be prohibited in said Brigade at all times.

John Reynolds Comr in Chf &c

Immediately thereafter Whiteside issued his own general order for the troops:

Head Quarters, near Rushville
April 30, 1832

(GENERAL ORDER)
There is to be no firing of guns in the lines or encampment without permission from the field Officer under whose command the applicant may be placed; nor will any other disorderly conduct whatever be allowed in the Brigade. At 12 sounds of the Bugle, Officers and Soldiers will rise up and prepare for the business of the day; at 6 sounds they will catch horses; at 8 sounds, saddle up; at 10 sounds, parade; at 3 sounds, march; at 4 sounds, halt; at 14 sounds, Officers to attend headquarters for orders.

By order of Brig. Genl. S. Whiteside
N. Buckmaster, Brigade Major

Governor Reynolds was very pleased with himself and with his militia army. Formation may have taken a little longer than anticipated and the first day's march may have been a bit slower than he had hoped, but the army *was* on the move for Yellow Banks and Rock River at last. And it was at just about this point, as he was settling in for the night in his headquarters tent, that John Reynolds was unexpectedly confronted by an exhausted express from General Atkinson, Lieutenant Thomas J. Beall. With tightening features Reynolds read Atkinson's account of Gratiot's experience with the Black Hawk band at Prophet's Town and of the Indians' subsequent movement upriver toward Dixon's Ferry, and finally Atkinson's order that Reynolds bring the militia up not by way of the Mississippi and Rock River but on the old Kellogg's Trail to Dixon's Ferry to rendezvous with Atkinson's regulars there.

Reynolds looked at the waiting Lieutenant Beall and shook his head. "Impossible, sir," he said, shaking the letter still in his hand. "My army is already on its move to Yellow Banks. Supplies have already been requisitioned to be sent upriver by steamboat to that point to rendezvous with this force. I had advised General Atkinson of this in my last communication to him, and though conditions obviously do dictate that it would be more ideal for these troops to move directly from here to Dixon's via Peoria, that is no longer possible. I will write a letter explaining this to him and requesting that he remain at Fort Armstrong until this army can unite with him there, and, following as brief a rest as you can make do with, you will carry this message immediately back to the general. Is that clear?"

"Yes, sir," Lieutenant Beall said, uncertain whether to salute the governor or not and then doing so anyway.

"All right," Reynolds told him, "go get something to eat and some sleep. We'll have your horse seen to. The letter will be waiting for you as soon as you arise in the morning. Questions?"

"No, sir."

"Fine. Dismissed."

As soon as the regular officer was gone, Governor Reynolds wrote first a letter to General Atkinson and then a letter and official orders to one of the commanders of his rangers, Colonel David Bailey, who was already in the field with his companies near Peoria:

Camp near Rushville 30th April 1832

Col. D. Bailey   I recd this day an express from Gen Atkinson informing me that the band of Indians under Black Hawk amounting to 4 or 500 men has gone up Rock River above Dixons ferry and that these Indians are hostile.

It is quite out of my power to pursue the route which would lead direct to the Indians. We must go by the Yellow Banks for the sake of the provisions and then we will march up Rock River to the hostile party.

I inform you of the above so that you may be on the alert in the protection you will afford to the frontier and to join us on Rock River if you deem it advisable, and to act in such other manner as the good of the country may require.

Yours &c John Reynolds

The direct order to Bailey was as brief:

Rushville 30th April 1832

Col. David Bailey. You are commanded to raise fifty mounted men more out of the counties of McLean & Tazewell, and none from Peoria. Said mounted men are to be volunteers. And over all said mounted men you will take command as Major. You will start from Peoria as soon as practicable for Dixons on Rock River and range in the country near Dixons, so as to intercept any Indians of the band of the Black Hawk that may attempt to escape toward Malden. Said Major Bailey will procede [sic] towards the prophets town, from Dixons, should it [be] considered not hazardous. Major Bailey will exercise a discretionary Power over his Command, and attempt to march down Rock River so as to join the main Body

John Reynolds Com in Chief Ill Militia

[*May 1, 1832 — Tuesday*]

A prevailing fear on the frontier now was that Black Hawk would sequester his women and children in some safe place, return with his warriors to make a number of bold assaults on the white settlements, and then, before the army could retaliate, retreat by boat on Lake Michigan into Lake Huron and then down to the Detroit area and take up residence near Malden with his British friends. From there, the scenario they envisioned went on, he could mount sporadic forays into the United States, causing much death and destruction, with always an easy escape at hand for him just over the border into Canada.

This was one of the many fears plaguing Indian superintendent William Clark at the moment, and the things he had been told by messengers did not ease his fears to any extent. Now Keokuk and a number of chiefs from the friendly Sacs had come to St. Louis, becoming impatient at the continued imprisonment of the men whom they, in good faith, had left as temporary hostages until the Sacs responsible for the murders of the Menominees could be turned over. Obviously the intentions of the friendly Sacs were good, and quite as apparently it was unfair to hold their innocent people when it was not in their power to get the guilty ones away from the unfriendly Sacs and Foxes.

It was in an effort to clarify this situation for the authorities in Washington that Clark was now busily writing to the secretary of war, Lewis Cass:

Superintendency of Ind: Affairs
St. Louis May 1st: 1832

Sir, By letters received this evening from the Indian Agent at Rock Island, I am informed that the Black Hawk's party are continuing their course up Rock River, being now thirty miles above the Prophets village. Their number is estimated at 600.

I think it not improper that their intention is to join their friends in Canada, and that they will make an attempt upon the settlements before they leave us. As Genl. Atkinson is however aware of their designs, his vigilance will, no doubt, prevent the meditated blow. He is about to take a position below them, there to await the arrival of the mounted men under Governor Reynolds.

Keokuk and a number of the principal chiefs of the Sacs & Foxes have just arrived. They manifest considerable uneasiness & anxiety on account of the confinement of their people who were concerned in the Menominie [sic] affair, — three of whom were lately delivered up to Genl. Atkinson.

I have the honor to be Very respectfully, Your obt. Servt Wm Clark.

[May 1, 1832 — Tuesday]

Although Black Hawk would really have preferred that it was not so, this preliminary meeting with the Potawatomies, here where the Kishwaukee River emptied into the Rock River, was open to all in his band.[183] The hundreds of followers sat quietly about them now, listening as Neapope, Wabokieshiek, Black Hawk, and others tried to convince the visiting delegation of Potawatomies that they should support the British Band in its proposed war against the whites. But the meeting was not going well, mainly because of the continuous objections being interjected so rudely by the three chiefs from in and near the Chicago area — Chaubenee, Chechepinqua, and Sauganash.

Time after time, one or another of these three chiefs — though most often Chaubenee — interrupted to say what terrible results could be anticipated by any who joined Black Hawk and his followers in such a ridiculous endeavor. Fortunately, their presence was offset by some other Potawatomies on hand who were leaning very strongly in favor of throwing their weight behind Black Hawk. This included Mawgehset — Big Foot, chief of the huge Potawatomi village at Lake Geneva, along with a number of his chiefs and head braves, plus the delegation of three principal braves of the village of Chief Meau-eus on Indian Creek — Comee, Pukemus, and Toquamee. All the Indians of these two latter factions held an abiding hatred for the Americans. The powerful sixty-seven-year-old Potawatomi war chief Waubansee, from whom Black Hawk had greatly hoped to gain support, had not attended, though his representatives were here. And another Potawatomi chief, whose support meant the most of all, was not in attendance. This was Black Partridge, elder brother of Waubansee and principal chief of the prairie Potawatomies. Frail at the age of seventy-four, he had been unable to make the journey, but he too had sent his representatives. [184]

Black Hawk's party had arrived here yesterday and found that, in response to the runners he had sent out immediately after crossing the Mississippi River, carrying invitations to various chiefs to council with him at this place, most of those Potawatomi chiefs or their delegates were already awaiting him here. Those who were absent had shown up during the night, and so today was the day of the big council he had requested. But it had not been going well at all.

"Do you," Black Hawk had asked them early in the council, "have corn in your villages that you can spare for us? My people are nearly without food, and they are very hungry."

The chiefs and delegates responded at length in various ways to the question, but, though phrased in polite and conciliatory tones, the ultimate answers turned out to be no, they had no food to spare for the British Band, only a little to support themselves until their own crops were reaped in autumn. It was not an easy response for them to make, for the Sacs, and especially the so-called British Band Indians, were recognized as powerful warriors who were a force to be reckoned with and whom not even the mighty Dakotah Sioux or the numerous Menominees preferred to come up against alone. Yet, it was the only answer they could honestly give, and a gloomy mood settled over the large audience. It only intensified as the day progressed.

In spite of the mood, throughout the morning and afternoon of open council, Black Hawk's spies were busy among all the Indian delegates, gleaning information in whispered conversations and passing it along to him. Little by little as he sifted it, he found the elements he needed to make telling points, but these were not points he cared to make in open council with all his followers listening.

"Because," Black Hawk finally announced in late afternoon when the speakers seemed to have run out of things to contribute, "there are private matters that must be discussed only among the leaders, I hereby announce this council closed and request the chiefs and principal braves of the visiting delegations to meet with me in a short while, apart from all others."

A meager meal was provided the guests, and afterwards the nine principal chiefs and five principal braves of the British Band met with all of the important chiefs and braves of the Potawatomies in attendance — some twenty in number. Among them, though Black Hawk had tried to exclude them, were the three who were so strongly opposed to him, Chaubenee, Sauganash, and Chechepinqua.

It was these latter three who, at Black Hawk's encouragement, first addressed the private council. The trio unequivocally warned the attending Potawatomies that trying to oppose the Americans made absolutely no sense at all, and that any who agreed to support Black Hawk in such an endeavor would be considered traitors to their own tribe. It was a strong and unfortunate beginning for the three, and precisely the opening Black Hawk had been hoping for. Now the Sac leader demanded their expulsion from the remainder of the private council, stating that the three were taking powers unto themselves to speak for their tribe that they did not legally have, which all present knew was true. A vote was taken and the three were evicted with warnings, under penalty of death, not to return unless summoned.

Now Black Hawk homed in on those who remained, beginning with the three principal braves of the Indian Creek village, Pukemus, Toquamee, and Comee.

"I speak first to those here who represent the Potawatomies of the village of Chief Meau-eus. How can you people not support us when part of what we wish is merely to help you resolve the injuries you have received at the hands of the whites? Are these not the Americans who entered your territory and made their settlement without asking your permission? Are these not the Americans who threw a blockage across your stream so that the fish you need to support yourselves could not come upstream as they always had before? Are these not the Americans who, when you tried to resolve this problem yourselves, insulted you and beat you nearly to the point of death? I tell you this: if the Potawatomies of your village and those villages near you support us, we will see that you receive full vengeance and full payment for the injuries you have received from the Americans!"

Toquamee, his nose healed in a squashed manner from the beating he had received from the blacksmith named Davis at his mill site on Indian Creek, looked sharply at his companions and nodded as he saw their eyes aglint as much as his own at what Black Hawk was saying. But the Sac had gone on, and now was addressing the issue of greatest concern to the Lake Geneva Potawatomies.

"And you, Mawgehset," Black Hawk said, "whose people live on the beautiful lake only a long day's ride away from the Americans settled at Chicago — what have you to look forward to? Right now their Fort Dearborn is empty of soldiers, but it will not always be that way. Once the soldiers are again on hand there to protect the settlers, what is to stop them from spreading out, as they have often threatened to do, and take from you the lands that you love on your beautiful lakes? They *will* do this if not stopped. I promise you that if you support us, so too will we support you and see to it that the Americans are *never* able to thrust you out of your lands. Even more, *we* will thrust *them* away from the land upon which they sit, which was once yours and which, against the wishes of many of your chiefs, was sold to them."

Big Foot was nodding vigorously, fully in agreement with what Black Hawk was saying and obviously ready at this moment to throw his support behind the speaker, but Black Hawk was not ready for that yet.

"I do not wish replies from you at this time," he told them. "I only wish you to know the things I have told you already, plus this very special thing I have to say now. I have talked with the greatest war chief of the Winnebagoes, White Crow, and he is sympathetic to our aims. He has told me that he must wear the face of cooperation with the Americans so that he can in this way learn from them their plans and tell us of these so we will know what to do in our struggle. But he also assures me that if and when the Potawatomies, as a tribe, agree to support us in our present endeavor, then so too at that time will the Winnebagoes do the same. Against such combined Indian strength, how can the Americans stand? They cannot! And so I ask only that now you go home and tell your people what I have told you. Get their feelings and their wishes and then return to this place with those chiefs of your people that are not with you now. To do these things, you need six days to talk and six days to travel. To that I add one day extra, and I ask that you and the other chiefs be back at this very place thirteen days from now and tell me what your people have answered. Then we will see how long the Americans will be able to dictate to the Indians in the Indians' own country."

In the darkness only a dozen yards or so away from the private council, Chaubenee eased himself out of the hiding place in which he had been concealed and slipped unheard and unseen back to the place in the woods several hundred yards away where his companions, Sauganash and Chechepinqua, were holding all three of their horses.

"It is bad, what you heard?" Chechepinqua whispered.

"It is very bad," Chaubenee whispered back. "What is planned could be the ruin of us all. We have to leave here now and ride like the wind. I will tell you what was said as we ride, and then we must separate and warn our own people and our American friends in Chicago and other settlements."

The three quietly led their horses farther away together in the darkness, not mounting and riding off until well out of hearing of the private council, which was still in the process of winding down.

[*May 2, 1832 — Wednesday*]

In the late afternoon sun of this cloudless, almost perfect spring day along the southwestern shore of Lake Michigan, the little town of Chicago, which only hours before had been a quiet, sleepy village, was now bustling with people, and an aura of electric excitement was evident that very nearly bordered on mild panic.

A large group of the people had collected near the south gate of the long-abandoned Fort Dearborn. Before them, standing on a barrel head, a well-liked prominent citizen named Gholson Kercheval held a piece of paper high and called out loudly.

"All right, I want all of you men who just held up your hands when I called for volunteers, to line up right here and sign this paper."

He leaped down and, putting the paper on the barrel head, wrote a couple of words as a heading and then followed this with an explanatory paragraph as the men were lining up to sign their names. The men represented the majority of the male population of Chicago from the age of eighteen to fifty.

Chicago's growth had been slow but steady in the sixteen years since it had been reestablished in 1816, following the end of the War of 1812. Now there were over 150 individuals living here and a constant flow of travelers passing through. As a result, the growth of Chicago had begun to accelerate considerably.

There were a number of streets already laid out in town running compass-true to north and south, east and west, but until recently all of these streets had ended at the edge of town and only trails led away from there — not wagon trails, but footpaths that had long been the highways of the Indians. Now, for the first time, only a week ago, a regular road of consequence had been laid out leaving the town proper. It was fifty feet wide, and gave citizens clear access from the center of town to both Fort Dearborn and the Lake Michigan shore. A rough wooden bridge thrown up across the State Street slough provided easy access to the new "highway," as it was termed. There was a footbridge across the North Branch of the Chicago River just above Wolf Point, where the river's two branches converged. There were certain individuals who had taken to calling this the most important bridge within five hundred miles, because by traversing it in one direction, they could reach the ever-popular Wolf Tavern, or by crossing in the other direction, the Miller House, an establishment of overnight accommodation whose proprietors, Samuel Miller and his wife, Elizabeth — daughter of John Kinzie — had been operating the place for the past six years and who had just recently, upon complaint of the owners of Wolf Tavern, been forced to buy a license to sell the liquor they were widely known for dispensing. But the only bridge in the town over which teams and wagons could pass was the heavy log bridge over the South Branch between Randolph and Lake streets, which had been built by the Taylor brothers, Anson and Charles.[185]

The first public building had also just recently been erected, although in actuality it was somewhat more of a corral than a building, even though largely enclosed. It was called the "Estray Pen" and was to be used to hold runaway livestock until the owner could come and claim it.[186] The citizens viewed it as something of an augury for a time to come, perhaps, when Chicago might become a central point for the collecting, holding, butchering, and shipping of livestock. Two of the citizens had already expressed a plan of expanding their butchering business to one that included preserving the butchered meats in brine and shipping them to far-distant places, and there were few who doubted that the enterprising Jonas and Archibald Clybourne would do just that. And an offshoot business — a tannery — was just being started by the partners Benjamin Hall and John Miller.

Chicago's recent growth had also included a sawmill and, as a result of that establishment's output, construction of the first frame business building. A lighthouse thirty feet high was built near the lake shore and hardly finished when a second one much better than the first — ten feet higher and boasting a fourteen-inch reflector — was erected by a contractor named Samuel Jackson. An old retired trapper, Sam Lasby, became the light-keeper.

Stephen Forbes had just been elected as Cook County's first sheriff, and a new settler in town, John Watkins, established a school and became its first master. [187] John S. C. Hogan was postmaster, and last year, at age thirty, Thomas Jefferson Vance Owen had become Indian agent here.

So Chicago was definitely growing, and its citizens took no pleasure upon hearing the news brought an hour ago by Chaubenee, Sauganash, and Chechepinqua, whom they called Shabbona, Billy Caldwell, and Alexander Robinson. The measure of trust the Chicagoans had in these Indians was exemplified by the fact that not one person raised a note of doubt when the trio told of Black Hawk's band having returned to Illinois, its union with the Indians under the Winnebago Prophet, Wabokieshiek, or the combined force presently moving up the Rock River and trying to get the entire Potawatomi and Winnebago tribes to join them in a war against the Americans. Instead of disbelief, their reaction was to be galvanized into immediate self-protective action.

The three Indians had left almost at once in different directions, each to carry the news to other white settlements and Indian villages, but very quickly a dozen young men were dispatched on horses to carry this same news to all outlying settlers in the Chicago area, as far westward as the Des Plaines River Valley, encouraging all to abandon their cabins and fields and come to Chicago to take refuge in the protective confines of the abandoned Fort Dearborn.

Tom Owen, the Indian agent, extrapolating a bit on the news, at once sent an express to the town of Niles, Michigan Territory, calling for help from the Michigan militia, "due to the approach of Black Hawk and his warriors, who are already on their hostile march through Illinois, heading for Chicago and will soon be sweeping around the south end of Lake Michigan and laying waste all in their path as they endeavour to reach Canada and join their red-coated soldier friends at Fort Malden."

A large meeting of the Chicago citizenry had just finished, in which it was agreed by all present that since there was no regular army on hand, they must therefore waste no time in forming their own defensive force as a forty-member Chicago Militia. And the paper that they were now signing on the barrel head before the south gate of Fort Dearborn stated in that one brief paragraph what they had bound themselves to do:

MUSTER ROLL

May 2, 1832 — We, the undersigned, agree to submit ourselves, for the time being, to Gholson Kercheval, Captain, and George W. Dole and John S. C. Hogan, First and Second Lieutenants, as commanders of the Militia of the town of Chicago, until all apprehension of danger from the Indians may have subsided: . . . [188]

What the Chicagoans were so quickly doing was not unique. In every settlement or town that the news touched, similar actions were taken, and in an amazingly brief time the heretofore essentially defenseless communities were bristling with fortifications, local militia, and other self-protective measures. Nevertheless, each, virtually without exception, considered itself as teetering on the brink of annihilation.

[May 5, 1832 — Saturday]

At last, one month to the day after its occurrence, President Andrew Jackson, secretary of war Lewis Cass, and the American Army commander, Major General Alexander Macomb, learned of the Mississippi River crossing by Black Hawk's band from Iowa into Illinois. Several letters from General Atkinson had arrived simultaneously, and all three men were quick to express shock and outrage. They hastily conferred, at which time the president expressed the official government position. The war secretary and the commanding general then relayed the president's and their own wishes to the front, Cass in a letter to Governor Reynolds, and Macomb in a letter to General Atkinson. Wrote Macomb:

Head Quarters of the Army
Washington May 5, 1832

Sir — At this distance from the scenes of your operations it is impossible to judge of the actual state of affairs on the frontiers: but taking into consideration the conduct of the Sacs and Foxes, as represented in your several communications, the Executive has determined that something decisive must be done in regard to these Indians, especially since they have returned to their former position on Rock River in violation of their most solemn engagements and in disregard of their promises made to General Gaines last year.

You will doubtless, by the time this reaches you, have become possessed of every information necessary to enable you to judge of the actual strength of the Indians, and to decide what force may be requisite to drive them across the Mississippi.

You are then authorised [sic], should you deem it necessary, to call on the Governor of Illinois for such a force of Militia as, in addition to the regular troops under your command, will enable you to drive the Sac's [sic] and Foxes over the Mississippi, and as soon as you shall be prepared to act, you will demand of them the murderers of the Menominees, if it be ascertained that they are on the east side of the river, and order the Sacs and Foxs [sic] to recross the Mississippi. Should they refuse promptly to comply with your demands, you will forthwith attack them and force them to obedience. If, after retiring across the Mississippi, they should assume a hostile attitude, you must follow them and there demand the murderers, and if they are not delivered up as soon as practicable, you will persue [sic] and chastise [sic] the offenders until you have taken due satisfaction. In case any of their women or children should fall into your hands, it is the Presidents [sic] particular wish that they should be treated with kindness and humanity.

In the execution of these orders you will be aided by the several Departments of the Staff, which will be instructed to furnish the necessary supplies; and as it is to be presumed that due regard will be had to a just organization of the means placed at your disposal, you will not permit any waste or useless expenditure of them. You will dismiss the additional forces as soon as their services can be dispensed with.

Enclosed, I transmit for your information, a copy of a letter from the Secretary of War of this date, addressed to Governor Reynolds of Illinois, the contents of which, as far as they disclose the views of the Executive in regard to the Indians, will govern you in your conduct and proceedings.

> *I have the honor to be Sir Yours Respectfully*
> *Alxr: Macomb Major General Commanding the Army*

The enclosed letter to Governor John Reynolds from secretary of war Lewis Cass clearly indicated that there was a remarkable closeness of thought between the two high-echelon governmental employees, or that it was just easier for Macomb to very nearly copy everything Cass had written than compose his own letter. Except in two very minor respects, they were virtually duplicates. In those two matters Cass had written:

. . . It is very desirable that as much should be accomplished by the regular troops as possible, and the militia force should not exceed the amount necessary to effect the object. Of this Genl. Atkinson will judge, and your Excellency is requested to place under his orders such a militia force as he may call for. . . . Funds will be placed in the hands of the Officers of the United States to defray the necessary expenses.

So now, when the time came that General Atkinson finally received his first official response from higher authority, he could have the satisfaction of knowing that everything he had thus far done had been perfectly in line with the instructions received much after the fact.

[May 8, 1832 — Tuesday]

General Henry Atkinson was very relieved, after this prolonged period of remaining in the vicinity of Fort Armstrong on Rock Island, to be preparing at last to move out tomorrow morning on Black Hawk's trail. As the days here had turned into weeks and the weeks into a month of essentially no activity, the troops had become edgy with impatience. Early this morning he had written his official letter to the Illinois governor to receive the over sixteen hundred militia troops into federal service. The letter read:

> Head Quarters Right Wing West: Dept:
> Mouth of rock river   8th. May 1832

Sir   The attitude assumed by the band of Indians known as Black Hawk's band, and by the Winnebago Prophet & his followers, renders it necessary for the interest of the public for the service of the State troops that you now have in the field. Should you in the exercise of your official functions agree with me in the opinion, I will, so far as my authority extends as the Commdg Officer of the U.S. troops, and of this district of country, receive them into the service of the U. States.

The letter had been dispatched at once to Governor Reynolds, who was in his own headquarters tent only a few miles up Rock River at the site of Saukenuk. Reynolds had wasted no time in penning and dispatching his reply, and now, late in the forenoon, Atkinson breathed a sigh of relief as he read it:

> Camp at the Old Sac Village
> 8th. May 1832

To Brig. Gen. Atkinson
Sir.   Having been this day honoured [sic] with your requisition for all the State troops, which I have now in the field, and as I agree with you, that the good of the public requires the service of those troops in the chastisement of the hostile Indians who have invaded the State, and others, I report and deliver over to you in compliance of said requisition all the troops now organized and in the field, including mounted men, and foot, with some at this time ranging on the frontier. The proper officers will report to you the strength of the whole.

> With sincere Respect I am your Obt. Servt
> John Reynolds

Atkinson called in an orderly and directed him to go get the adjutant, Lieutenant Johnston. The orderly bobbed his head and disappeared, and Atkinson, while he waited, leaned back in his chair with fingers interlocked behind his head and closed his eyes as he mentally put into perspective the events as he knew them since his council with Whirling Thunder and White Crow.

The various parties of spies he had sent out to try to ascertain exactly where Black Hawk's band was now and what he was up to returned with confusing and highly conflicting reports: Black Hawk's band was moving overland toward the Mississippi River and preparing to cross that stream again for the supposed safety of the Iowa side; Black Hawk's band was moving northward up to Lake Winnebago, Green Bay, and beyond in an effort to escape into Canada; Black Hawk and his warriors were on the Rock River at the mouth of the Pecatonica, ready to strike a deadly blow on the settlements, while his own people were safely encamped among the Winnebagoes at Four Lakes; Black Hawk had moved to a point above Dixons for a while, where he had left his women and children, and now he had returned in strength, with increased support from other Indian factions, to the Prophet's Town area, from which location he planned to strike Galena, Apple River, Fort Armstrong, the lead mining district, and other frontier areas; Black Hawk's entire band was on the move toward Chicago, from whence it would move on to the Detroit area to join the British on the Canadian side at Malden; Black Hawk was already moving against the Illinois River settlements and would soon be hitting Ottawa, Peoria, and other frontier towns. The stories were rampant and their variations numerous. Even the Rock Island Indian agent became a part of it. Felix St. Vrain had reported to Atkinson that a Sac warrior named Poynehanesa, who had deserted from Black Hawk's band, had come in and stated that the Indians on Rock River were on the point of coming back down the river and returning to the west side of the Mississippi because they had been disappointed with the assistance they had expected from the Winnebagoes and others. St. Vrain could not, however, attest to the reliability of the report. Even Governor Reynolds had written Atkinson that a trio of his spies — John Foley, J. W. Stephenson, and William Atchison — had returned from an extensive reconnoitering expedition to report that the Indians had all dispersed among their neighbors and appeared neither warlike nor as a potential threat to inhabitants. So, in view of all these conflicting reports, at this time neither Atkinson nor Reynolds had any real idea where Black Hawk's force was actually located.

The governor had continued to move his militia army toward the mouth of Henderson Creek and Yellow Banks, frequently slowed by the muddy ground everywhere and even stalled for varying periods of time as they forded the swollen streams. They had not arrived at the mouth of Henderson Creek until May 3, and Governor Reynolds had been certain that they would find waiting for them here the steamboat *William Wallace*, which he had dispatched from Beardstown to St. Louis to get the militia's supplies and immediately bring them up the Mississippi to the mouth of Henderson Creek. Disappointment was great when they found it hadn't even arrived yet, and they were forced to break off the march and camp to await its arrival. Though the steamboat had not been there, Keokuk and a large number of his friendly Sacs had come to greet the new arrivals and put on a rousing dance for their benefit, following which Keokuk offered the services of his men in the pursuit of Black Hawk. Reynolds politely declined, but suggested Keokuk make his offer to General Atkinson.

For three full days — May 4, 5, and 6 — the mounted militia under General Whiteside had been forced to wait, before at last the steamboat showed up with the supplies and unmounted volunteers. It had been detained by having run aground several times on mud bars that had newly formed and were hidden just beneath the surface.

While waiting, Reynolds briefly considered the heated and disruptive rivalry that had developed over these past weeks between his two ranging field com-

manders, Isaiah Stillman and David Bailey. Stillman had in his battalion now
the companies of Captains Abner Eads, Japhet A. Ball, Asel F. Ball, and David
W. Barnes; Bailey's force included the companies of Captains John G. Adams,
Merritt L. Covell, James Johnson, and Robert McClure. In almost every action
Bailey undertook he found that Stillman had preceded him and in various ways
had balked him or made his way excessively difficult. Bailey's letters to the
governor had become a series of complaints and criticisms: Stillman had arrived
at Fort Clark first, and the arms, ammunition, and provisions Reynolds had
readied there for them, to be divided between them, Stillman had taken completely; Stillman had taken 150 volunteers from Peoria County, fifty of whom
were to have been Bailey's; Stillman's whole attitude was one of insulting
superiority, and in his correspondence he gave himself the title of acting commandant on the northern frontier. Without openly saying so, Stillman and
Bailey were each, in fact, contending for command of the combined troops.
When Reynolds recognized Stillman in this capacity, instead of ameliorating,
matters had only become worse, and the enduring antipathy between them was
affecting the efficiency of both.

As soon as Stillman had received Dixon's alarming letter of April 28, he had
changed his current destination from Yellow Banks to Dixon's and wrote to
Governor Reynolds:

Sir — . . . *have this moment received an express from Dixon stating that Black
Hawk with about 500 warriors passed his house . . . Henry Gratiot writes thus
War is declared, send out your expresses. . . .*

It was just after this that the first death occurred among the Illinois mounted
volunteers. As Stillman's force was en route to Dixon's, a sudden thunderstorm
swept in. A squad of men from Captain Asel F. Ball's company spurred their
horses toward a small cluster of trees, under which they intended taking shelter,
but one of them — Private Thomas Langford — remained in place on his horse
and called after the others that they were crazy to get under the trees, that they'd
be struck by lightning. No sooner had the words left his mouth than a blinding
bolt cracked from the clouds and instantly killed both Langford and his horse.

General Atkinson had made plans to move upriver with his regulars from Rock
Island to Galena and from there go directly overland on the Kellogg's Trail to
Dixon's, to meet Reynolds's force there as he had directed in his letter to the
governor. Atkinson had issued a series of orders to this end, but then had to
rescind them all when an exhausted Lieutenant Beall had returned with Reynolds's response from Rushville, stating that Atkinson's order had arrived one day
too late and that the militia was presently en route to the Yellow Banks. And
then, on Reynolds's arrival at that destination, he found the steamboat *William
Wallace* had not yet arrived and was forced to wait.

In response to Reynolds's letter of May 4 relating these matters, General Atkinson had responded to the governor from Fort Armstrong on May 5:

Sir Your letter of yesterday informing me of your arrival at Yellow Banks was received this evening.

From information recd. yesterday, on which I think reliance may be placed, it has become necessary to change the route pointed out in my last communication to reach the hostile band of Indians.

It is now stated that Black Hawk & his associates, finding after they had passed up above Dixon's Ferry that they were rejected by the Winnebagoes and Potta-wattamies [sic], & frightened by the movement of the mounted volunteers, have returned to the Prophet's Village with a view of recrossing the Mississippi. They were there three days ago and have probably been prevented from moving by the recent heavy rains. Colonel Scott, however, is in possession of all the information I have on the subject and will detail it more minutely for you.[189]

Under the present aspect of affairs, I deem it advisable that you should march your troops to the mouth of Rock River, where you will meet a further supply of provisions & corn, & where I will take occasion to consult with you as to such measures as circumstances may then require being adopted.

I have ordered back a part of the regular troops that were detached to Galena, & have been detained at the head of the rapids by the transport being aground — and I have also ordered back the boat with provisions intended for Dixon's ferry via Galena. It will be better that our supplies should be here than at Galena as we have to operate from this point, and provisions can be transported by water up Rock River in two keels and some Mackinaw [sic] boats that I have here. I have now on hand twenty days rations for two thousand men which I am in hopes will be ample for all the purposes of the campaign and, if not, more can be brought up before this quantity is consumed.

I send down the Steam Boat Java with provisions and corn to serve for your march to this point. I think it is unnecessary for you to make any further arrangement for provisions, till [sic] I see you.

Before you reach us, I will obtain information as to the position of Black Hawk.

General Atkinson enclosed with this letter to Reynolds a copy of his special order in regard to dispatching the *Java* with supplies to the Yellow Banks:

Spl. Order No. 9

Lieut. Burbank Asst. Comy Sub. will deliver to Col. Scott for the use of the militia, 35 barrels flour, 20 barrels pork, & 3 barrels Whiskey.

By order of Brig Genl. Atkinson

A. S. Johnston, Lt., A.A.A.Genl.

The general had followed this up with a brief letter of instruction to Henry Gratiot, who by this time had returned to his Indian subagency in Gratiot's Grove:

Sir: I understand the Winnebago Prophet has returned to his village, with the small band who follow him as their leader.

I have to request that you will immediately order him and his followers to remove to their own lands above the ceded territory and not to return again on pain of arrest and imprisonment.

Should he refuse to go, advise me of the fact as early as practicable.

Reynolds's force had suddenly gone from being in want for provisions to having a superabundance of them when the steamboat *Java* arrived from upstream almost coincident with the arrival of the *William Wallace* from downstream.

Yesterday, to General Atkinson's great relief, the militia had finally arrived at the mouth of Rock River, and by this time the general had received further news that caused him the embarrassment of having to change his plans once again. Some friendly Sacs had come in with the perplexing news that instead of coming down the Rock River again, Black Hawk's band was moving upstream above Dixon's. All 340 of the regulars had today been placed under direct command of the prematurely gray-haired, forty-seven-year-old Colonel Zachary Taylor and were now ready for duty, with the exception of the three companies presently en route downstream to Fort Armstrong from Galena. The militia under General Samuel Whiteside, former subordinate of Colonel Taylor during the War of 1812, had bivouacked at Saukenuk, and all that had remained to do before the whole force could set off on Black Hawk's trail was to put the militia under Atkinson's command. That process had begun when earlier today Atkinson had formally requested the militia in writing and Reynolds had officially responded in his letter of compliance. So now, with Reynolds deciding to remain with the army and being paid as a major general, and Atkinson's adjutant, Lieutenant Johnston, having arrived and gotten prepared to write, Atkinson dictated the general order that brought the whole force under his command:

Head Qrs. right Wing West. Dept.
Mouth of Rock river May 8th 1832

ORDER NO. 8

Brig. Genl. Atkinson assumes command of the Illinois State Troops now in the field, agreeably to the report of his Excellency Governor Reynolds, who has this day turned them over to duty in the Service of the United States, on a requisition made upon him to that effect. The State troops will hold themselves in readiness to move in conjunction with the regular troops at a moment's notice.

By order of Brig Genl Atkinson
[signed] A. S. Johnston Lt. & A.A.A. Genl

[*May 10, 1832 — Thursday*]

The throng of Indians sat motionless and uncharacteristically silent before Black Hawk, the hollowness of their gaze bearing mute testimony to the pangs of hunger that gripped them almost constantly these days. They had been on severe rations ever since the Potawatomies had come here to council. Since that time, select groups of men had been sent out to hunt any meat animals they could down, while groups of women and children had similarly been sent out in various directions to forage for whatever roots, grubs, frogs, crawfish, and fish they might find. A surprising amount of such food materials had been brought in, yet it was less than an adequate subsistence for well over a thousand men, women, and children.

Black Hawk's gaze moved silently across the assemblage, and then he began to speak slowly and clearly. "It had been in the minds and hearts of your leaders here," he told them, "to keep from you a discouraging development that affects us all. We had hoped the provisions we brought with us, along with those being brought in by the hunters and fishers and gleaners, would have been enough to sustain us. It is not. We can live on it for some weeks longer, perhaps, but daily we will grow weaker if new supplies cannot be obtained."

Black Hawk's tongue appeared and moistened his drying lips, and then he continued. "The discouragement that we must all now face is the fact that we have all been given false information. Our British friends in Canada are *not* coming to our aid, as we had been told. They are *not* soon to arrive in boats at Milwaukee, bringing us food and gunpowder and weapons and reinforcements, as we had been told. It was all lies, told to help hold you together in a force that could stand up to the white men."

Again he paused to lick his lips, and now there was a faint, angry undercurrent of voices from the assemblage, but it died away as Black Hawk briefly raised his hand and then continued. "Now you know the worst, and what is left to be said may make you feel better. As most of you have become aware by now, the Winnebagoes, who had promised us support, who had invited us to come up the Pecatonica and set up our village among them and plant our corn, have now backed away from that promise and turned away that invitation. The Prophet's people, though not many, remain with us, as do the strong but few Kickapoos that have become our brothers. But the Winnebagoes as a tribe have said that unless the Potawatomies as a tribe will agree to support us, they will not. So that is where we stand now. Four days from now the Potawatomies will have returned here to give us their answer. They have been badly treated by the Americans in many ways, and there is good reason to hope that they will join us. If they do, so, too, will all the Winnebagoes — we have the word of White Crow and Whirling Thunder on that — and at such time they will have provisions enough to help support us, and we will become a fighting force that can not only hold against the whites, but push them back, out and away from our country."

At last there was a degree of enthusiastic reaction from the crowd, but this, too, Black Hawk subdued with a raised hand before he continued. "While that is what we *wish* to happen and what we think and hope *will* happen, we must also at this time face what it is that we will be left to do if these things do not happen — if, most of all, the Potawatomies, four days from now, tell us that they will *not* join with us. At such a time we will then, a small force of warriors weakened by hunger, be facing an army of mounted whites three times greater than ourselves, better armed and equipped than we and with unending reserves of meat and bread. If we were only warriors alone, we would face such might without question and show them the heart of Indian warriors. But we have with us all our old people, all our women and children, all those of us who are sick or injured and must be aided, and all our belongings in the world. What then would become of these?

"No," he went on without pause, "no, my children, we could not do this. We could not bring to them, on top of hunger and want, an unbearable portion of shame and danger. So what would we do? This! My children, when and if the time comes when the Potawatomies refuse to join us and give cause for other possible allies to turn away from us, we will then have no choice but to immediately lift the white flag and surrender ourselves into the hands of the whites, realizing then for good and all that we will be sent away west of the Mississippi River and never again see these lands that hold the bones of our fathers, lands that have so long been so dear to us.

"That, then, my children," he concluded, "is where we stand now. In four days, one way or another, we will know what will be."

[*May 12, 1832 — Saturday*]

Indian Agency Chicago May 12. 1832
To His Excellency — John Reynolds Gov.
of the State of Illinois from Thomas J. V. Owen Agent

Sir   A deputation, from the United Tribes of Potawatimies [sic], *Ottowas* [sic], *& Chippeways* [sic], *waited on me this morning, and has given me assurances of the Strongest Character, of their determination to remain on terms of the most perfect peace and amity with our Government; they inform me that the Sacs are approaching towards the neighborhood of the Potowatimie* [sic] *reservation on Fox River & they fear that if the Militia pursue, that the Sacs will endeavor to* *mingle with the Potawatamies [sic], in order to save themselves from the fury of the militia, and thereby involve them (the Potowatimes [sic]) indiscriminately in the same difficulties with themselves.*

Mr. Kercheval, sub-Indian Agent, together with Mr. Caldwell (Interpreter) & Mr. Robinson, an influential man among the Indians (& the bearer of this) will proceed this morning towards Rock River with a view of directing the Indians of my Agency to remove to the East side of Fox River of the Illinois, in order that they may be out of reach of the exasperated Militia.

This deputation also informs me, that some of the principal men engaged in the Menominee massacre have been delivered over to our Government — that the Sacs are on Rock River about 30 miles above Ogee's ferry, in a state of Starvation and are anxious to recross the Mississippi but dare not descend Rock River for fear of being intercepted by the Militia & indiscriminately slaughtered without affording them an opportunity of explaining the cause of their recent movements. They aver most positively to the Potowatimes [sic] that they have no design of committing any wrong whatever towards the people of their great Father.

Of the friendship of my Indians, the United Tribes alluded to, you may rest perfectly satisfied, & it would be, not only a source of deep regret to me, but productive of the worst of consequences, should any of them unfortunately fall a sacrifice to the Militia under your command, they are now much alarmed and will endeavor to keep themselves distinct & separate from the Sac Indians, and will afford them neither aid or [sic] protection knowingly. It would be advisable for those having command of the Militia, to proceed with great caution and endeavor to discriminate between the friendly & disaffected Indians before they strike. Your knowledge of the Indian Character will enable you to see at a glance the consequences which would inevitably result from a too hasty & precipitate act of violence towards a band of friendly Indians.

With great respect I have the honor to be Your obdt Servt

Th. J. V. Owen Indn. Agent

[May 12, 1832 — Saturday]

General Samuel Whiteside was totally exhausted, as were the mounted volunteers who had followed him up the Rock River these past three days, to finally reach Dixon's Ferry and bivouac in an adjacent area that had been designated by Whiteside as Camp No. 10. So weary were the horses from these days of lunging and plunging through the muck and mire of rain-soaked and river-flooded lands adjacent to the stream that when the halt was called here, the majority of the horses stood straddle-legged, heads lowered and muscles twitching and trembling with the aftereffects of their exertions. Adding to the labors the men had faced of merely riding through the muck, they had also a large number of baggage wagons to attend to, some pulled by oxen, but most by dray horses — wagons that continually mired in the deep mud and required repeated strenuous exertions to free them. Some of the mounted companies, including that of Captain Abraham Lincoln, threw away some of their personally carried baggage, such as bedrolls and tenting materials, canteens and even weapons, in an effort to lighten the loads for their horses. None of this seemed to help very much.

As difficult as the journey from Saukenuk to Dixon's may have been for Whiteside and his fifteen hundred horsemen, which included Governor Reynolds, it was even worse for the 340 regulars and 165 unmounted militia, under direct command of Colonel Zachary Taylor, whose job it had become to transport the greater portion of the baggage, which had been loaded into the two large keelboats — one with a capacity of eighty tons, the other of thirty — and six smaller Mackinac boats. It was thought before the march was begun, probably because General Atkinson was accompanying them, that the boatmen had been assigned the plushy job, for they would be riding high and dry and comfortably in boats instead of either walking or riding horses through the incredible mud that would so plague the mounted troops. Such was not the case at all. All the boats were heavily loaded, and the muddy, turbulent Rock River was so swollen and swift with the heavy rains that had been falling, that it was impossible to row even the smaller Mackinac boats against the powerful current. Long ropes had to be attached to the bows and scores of men assigned in relays to enter the water and, with rope over shoulder and wading in water from waist-deep to chest-deep, pull the laden boats upstream foot by torturous foot against the surging strength of the current, which unceasingly attempted to pull the boats from their grip and on several occasions did just that. A team of eight or ten men on a rope for just one of the smaller Mackinac boats could last for, at best, only an hour before being utterly exhausted and forced to rest, their places taken by another team. Four to five times that many men were needed for the smaller of the keelboats, and a total of seventy regulars were constantly at work moving the larger keelboat. With those larger boats, progress was infinitely more difficult. Nor did changing from one side of the river to the other prove to be of any help; they were equally difficult.

Thus, while at first the mounted men envied those with the boats, it turned out Whiteside's horse soldiers far outdistanced the boatmen. The whole force had started upstream just after sunrise on May 10, and it had taken the horsemen over two full days — until mid-morning today — to travel the sixty-five miles to Dixon's Ferry. They would not even have made it then, except that early this morning Whiteside had given the order for most of the mounted men to move ahead as quickly as possible the remaining distance and leave the baggage wagon teams to fend for themselves and follow along as best they could. For the boatmen, now far behind, it would obviously take many days longer.

The marching orders Atkinson had issued could have been better planned. Atkinson had directed General Whiteside to lead the mounted force the thirty-five miles upstream to the Prophet's Town and if, on arrival there, Whiteside was of the opinion that it would be prudent to come up on the enemy with as little delay as possible, then he was given the discretionary power to move on. On his arrival at the Prophet's Town, Whiteside found it abandoned, with evidence of the Indians having moved upstream, so he burned the town and then, utilizing the discretionary powers he had been given, ordered the march continued right on up all the way to Dixon's Ferry, in the process quite effectively moving himself and his mounted force well beyond any significant control by General Atkinson.

Having now arrived here at Dixon's Ferry, General Whiteside's force immediately went into its Camp No. 10, groaning in the manner of all soldiers who feel put upon, especially when the word was circulated about how many straight-line miles away they were from where they had begun. A good many, of course, had volunteered from such Illinois River towns as Ottawa, Utica, La Salle, and Peru. By the route they had taken — going first to the rendezvous at Beardstown, then to Yellow Banks, then to the mouth of Rock River, and finally to here, they had traveled through unbelievably exhausting conditions for a total of about 350 miles, yet now that they were at this destination, they learned it was only just over forty miles by decent trail running southeast directly to the Illinois River communities where many had enlisted.

General Whiteside quickly learned from the militia companies already there under Majors Stillman and Bailey — who had been there for several days already — as well as the force of mounted volunteers from the mining district, under command of Colonel Henry Dodge, which had arrived only an hour or so before Whiteside, that Black Hawk's force was still about twenty-five to thirty miles upstream, presumably close to the mouth of a tributary called Old Man's Creek. Colonel Dodge's great concern at this juncture was that if Black Hawk's force was hit now and not totally defeated, it would splinter into raiding parties that would raise havoc all throughout the mining district — a possibility he did not like to contemplate. Apart from the various militia units, there were a number of other men on hand here at Dixon's, too, including James Stephenson, James Strode, Henry Gratiot, Louis Ouilmette, and William S. Hamilton.[190] These men generally confirmed the report about the present location of Black Hawk's force, but they added the ominous intelligence that these Indians appeared to be breaking into smaller parties, either to search for food or, possibly, to act as hit-and-run war parties against white settlements.[191]

General Whiteside and Governor Reynolds immediately conferred and decided between themselves that since their mounted militia had only two days' provisions left, it would be most prudent to remain resting in camp here until the remainder of Atkinson's army under Colonel Zachary Taylor came up.

It was at that point that Whiteside wrote to his commanding officer:

Head Quarters, May 12th. 1832.
Dixon's Ferry, Camp No. 10

General Atkinson

Sir I arrived here this day at 10 Oclock A.M. with the intention of pursuing the hostile Indians, but from the best information I have been able to gather, they have left their former encampment, and have dispersed in different directions. From the best information I have been able to obtain as to their movements, they were last at old mans-creek [sic], supposed to be twenty five miles above this place, on the south side of rock-river [sic]. The route being different from what we anticipated when together, with the scarcity of rations, has brought me to the conclusion to remain here & await your arrival. I will keep out scouts for the purpose of receiving information as to their present location, the better to enable you to direct our future movements.

I have the honor to be your obedient servant.
Saml. Whiteside

Though Whiteside's own mounted volunteers were exhausted, this was not the case with the two independent battalions of militia already here when he arrived, under command of Majors Stillman and Bailey. Those 341 mounted militia rangers, with an abundance of food and supplies, were well rested, impatient with their present inactivity, and extremely eager for action. The two majors, afire with enthusiasm, appealed to their superiors for permission to move out at once as an advance force on the trail of the hostiles. Again Reynolds and Whiteside conferred, and now they disagreed. Reynolds decided that it might not be so bad an idea at that. Wouldn't it be a real feather in the cap of the militia if they, without any assistance from Atkinson's regulars, managed to engage, defeat, and capture the enemy? Whiteside was not entirely opposed to showing up the regulars, but he pointed out to the governor that he had no authority to do such a thing without the consent of General Atkinson. Reynolds, in turn, pointed out that the militia was a body of state soldiers, raised by him and subject to the orders of their commander in chief, himself, and their commanding general of the militia, Whiteside. Whiteside disagreed and pointed out that the whole militia had been attached to the U.S. Army with Atkinson as commander, and therefore, Whiteside declared, he would not issue such an order. Irked but undaunted, Governor Reynolds dismissed General Whiteside and immediately sat down and wrote out the order himself, but as if ordered by Whiteside, and then summoned the brigade major, Nathaniel Buckmaster, to sign it.

HEADQUARTERS, CAMP NO. 10, DIXON'S FERRY
12th May, 1832

The troops under the command of Major Stillman, including the battalions of said Major Stillman, and Major Bailey, will forthwith proceed, with four days' rations, to the head of Old Man's Creek, where it is supposed the hostile Sac Indians are assembled, for the purpose of taking all cautious measures to coerce said Indians into submission, and report themselves to this department as soon thereafter as practicable.

By order of Brigadier Samuel Whiteside, commanding brigade of mounted volunteers.

N. BUCKMASTER
Brigade Major

Within minutes, Stillman's detachment was preparing to move out on the mission first thing tomorrow morning.

[*May 14, 1832 — Monday*]

The passage of General Atkinson's force upriver had continued to be excruciatingly slow. Today, the fifth day of their pulling the bulky keelboats and Mackinac boats upstream, they were only five miles above the burned-out ruins of the Prophet's Village — not much more than halfway to Dixon's, and the commander was just as discouraged as his men. Although his orders to Brigadier General Whiteside had given him discretionary powers to move on above the Prophet's Village, Atkinson had nonetheless expected him to stop there and wait for the rest of the army, and was disgruntled to learn Whiteside's mounted force had moved on to Dixon's. Now he had learned from their newly acquired guide, Dixon's settler Uri S. Hults, that there was another rapids ahead that almost certainly these boats his men were pulling could not negotiate. That was the reason he had called a halt and was at this moment writing to General Whiteside.

Head Quarters Right Wing West: Depart.
5 miles above Prophet's Vill: 14th. May 1832

General:

As the navigation of the river is becoming worse and strong doubts are entertained whether our large boat can cross the rapids midway between this and Dixon's, I think it best that you should move with your command down the river and meet me.[192] *I am assured that there is a good road from where you are, down the east bank of the river to this place, crossing but one small creek in the whole route. I shall set out early in the morning, and push with all speed to reach Dixon's. We shall probably get to the rapids the morning after tomorrow.*

The reasons why I desire you to fall down the river to meet me are — that you may want rations otherwise, and it is as well to move as to lie still a day or two inactive. As soon as we meet a prompt & decisive movement against the Indians

must be made When I see you, it is probable we may conclude to reduce the number of volunteers very considerably — At least to meet what may upon information be considered necessary for the exigencies of the apparent state of things. I send Mr. Hultz [sic] with this now with instructions to travel the river road that he may show you the route.
    Gen. Atkinson to Gen. Whitesides [sic]

[*May 14, 1832 — Monday*]

The detachment of militia rangers was in a much better mood today than they had been yesterday, and it was obvious that the weather was a major factor. When they left Dixon's Ferry yesterday and headed up the Rock River, accompanied by a few of the local citizens of Dixon's Ferry and even some local militia officers, such as Colonel James Strode of Galena, the skies were heavy with threatening clouds. Before the column of nearly three hundred men had gone ten miles, the heavens had opened, and they were pelted with a downpour. On orders shouted from their commanders, the men quickly set up their tents and made camp for the night, but it was a fireless camp with cold rations to eat and no one in very good spirits. Throughout much of the night the rain continued, but the skies had cleared in the morning as camp was being struck, and today had turned out to be lovely.

Major Isaiah Stillman's unexpected signal for a halt came about a half-mile after they had forded a fair-sized stream, and the column of mounted rangers strung out behind — including six ox-drawn wagons — stopped and waited. A staccato fourteen-note bugle signal brought the eight company commanders at a gallop to the head of the column, where Stillman was conferring with Major David Bailey. The 275 troopers astride their stopped horses, as well as the few civilians who were with them, were more than a little perplexed at the halt, since the sun was shining brightly and was still well over an hour from setting. It seemed to everyone much too early to be calling a halt for the day. Actually, the reason for the stop was because Major Stillman wanted some clarification about exactly where they were.

"That stream we just crossed," he asked of no one in particular, "was that Old Man's Creek?" He waited while there were some murmured discussions between the captains, followed by blank looks and shrugs. Though they were not much more than sixty crow's-flight miles north of where all eight company commanders lived, no one seemed to know for sure. "I want verbal response, gentlemen," Stillman said. "Japhet, was that Old Man's Creek?"

Captain Japhet Ball, to Stillman's left, shook his head and shrugged again. "I don't know, sir." In quick succession, similar replies were given by Captains Merritt Covell, Dave Barnes, Bob McClure, Jim Johnson, Johnny Adams, Asel Ball, and Ab Eads.

"Our orders," Stillman went on, "direct us to go only to the head of Old Man's Creek."[193]

"The trail goes on toward the northwest," Major Bailey pointed out, gesturing at the faint residue of trail they had been following, which marked the passage of Black Hawk's land force a fortnight earlier. "If what we just crossed *is* Old Man's Creek, it's obviously not where Black Hawk stopped."

Stillman considered that, and then also shrugged and remarked ambiguously, "Hard to say."

The commander stood high in his stirrups and looked about them. Since crossing the creek they had been moving through a broad low-grass prairie. At the moment, they were just in the process of passing a roughly circular grove of fairly open timber, perhaps a hundred yards in diameter, the only trees anywhere around. Beyond, to the north, the prairie continued, gradually sloping uphill and ending at a sparsely brush-dotted ridge a quarter-mile distant. There was very little underbrush beneath the trees of this grove they were passing, but rather a continuation of the lush new prairie grasses. Although Stillman was not consciously considering it as such, the grove was a site peculiarly well suited for defense: trees and logs were readily available for cover, and no one could possibly approach them from any direction without crossing indefensible wide-open stretches of slightly undulating prairie. In addition, plenty of firewood was lying about, and so this was virtually a textbook example of a campsite ideal for both defense and comfort.

"I think," Major Stillman said, settling back down in his saddle, "maybe we better figure on camping in this grove for tonight and consider whether we ought to go on or not. Give the order, Major."

David Bailey replied, "Yes, sir," although inwardly he continued to bridle at having been placed under the egotistical Stillman and forced to relay his orders. "Return to your companies," he told the captains. "This is it for today. We're camping here."

About nine hundred yards away, lying on his stomach beneath a bush on the grassy ridge, a well-muscled young Sac named Weetcho — Raccoon — watched through cupped eyes as the ten horsemen who were at the head of the stationary column but slightly off from it, abruptly broke apart, and eight of these individuals began cantering back to their places in the line.[194] In a short while the entire column was breaking apart and converging in the open grove of timber. Weetcho continued to watch as they dismounted, and when it became clear they were setting up camp, he began squirming backward, still on his stomach, until he was beyond the ridgetop and out of view of the whites. Then he came to his feet, gave a sharp whistle not unlike the evening feeding call of a bobwhite quail, and ran toward where his horse and another were tied. A second warrior, Makashenasa — Black Blanket — who was young, like Weetcho, but not so well built, came off the ridge from another direction, running as rapidly.[195] They reached the horses at nearly the same time, mounted swiftly, and moved off rapidly in a northwesterly direction toward Black Hawk's camp, five or six miles away.

[*May 14, 1832 — Monday*]

Black Hawk's expression had remained as unreadable as it had been when this second council with the Potawatomies had begun this morning, even though it was now clear that the Potawatomies as a tribe were not going to help him — in fact, might even lend their might to the Americans against him. And what this meant, of course, was that the Winnebagoes as a tribe would not help him either.

The only support he had received this day was from Chief Meau-eus, to whom he had pledged his support in resolving the difficulty Meau-eus's people were having because of the dam built across Indian Creek at the Davis Settlement. Even the bellicose Big Foot, who had proclaimed his hatred for the Americans so long and so loudly, had pulled in his horns in the face of opposition by such powers in the Potawatomi tribe as the brothers Waubansee and Black Partridge, as well as Chaubenee, Chechepinqua, and Sauganash.

Many Potawatomi chiefs had spoken during the course of this second council near the mouth of the Kishwaukee, but often they had repeated one another, and in the end, what it had come down to was this: No, we do not wish to make enemies of the powerful Americans, whom we consider our friends; no, we will not join you in any attack against the Americans, whether it be against their soldiers or against their settlers; no, we will not stand idly by and let you jeopardize our existence by doing these bad things you contemplate; yes, we will offer the strength of our arms to the Americans against you if you go to war against them; no, we will not give you corn or other food or shelter or supplies to subsist upon while you wage war; no, we will not protect you against the Dakotah Sioux and Menominees who are poised to come against you, for that is your trouble with them, not ours, and you must settle that yourselves.

There were a few exceptions, of course. Mawgehset — Big Foot — promised in an undertone to Black Hawk that he and his people would help Black Hawk in any way they could, though he must understand they could not do so openly or they would risk ostracism by the rest of the tribe. White Crow, while clearly stating that the Winnebagoes as a tribe simply could not join them in their fight or even give them aid or succor, also promised in undertones that he would continue to help by misdirecting the whites, who now trusted him, and by passing along to Black Hawk whatever intelligence he could gather about the movement or plans of the Americans. And there were still quite a number of *individual* Potawatomies and Winnebagoes and Kickapoos who would continue to support Black Hawk, as they had up until now, but such help would be without the sanction of their tribes as a whole.

By late in the afternoon, Black Hawk knew it was all over. There was no way he could oppose the whites without the support of the other tribes. He now had less than four hundred warriors to support him. Those warriors he did have were almost destitute of firearms, and the few available rifles were almost without gunpowder. He was more than ever hampered with the need to protect and provide for nearly seven hundred women, children, and elderly, who were already suffering dreadfully from hunger and sickness. He had no place left to lead his people that might be safe from the Americans, except perhaps a temporary hiding place or two that the Winnebagoes had told him about in the swamps far up the Rock River from here.

It was at that juncture that the council was sharply interrupted by the arrival of two young Sacs on horseback. The warriors galloped directly to the edge of the large gathering, and it was the more athletic of the two — young Weetcho, son of Chief Ioway — who flung himself from his mount and raced toward the council fire with the alarm.

"The Americans!" he shouted. "They are almost on us. An army of them have come!"

The unorthodox entry created momentary pandemonium, and it was several minutes before order was restored. In that brief interval the assembled Potawatomies had gathered themselves enough to announce that they were leaving at once for their own villages, that they would take no part in any sort of confrontation here, and in fact did not even care to have it known that they had been here for such a council. In an astonishingly short time, the Potawatomies had mounted their horses and fled, pausing only long enough to ascertain where the army of whites was located so they could give it wide berth as they returned to where they belonged.

The nine chiefs and four other head braves of Black Hawk's band now looked to Black Hawk, who nodded and spoke the words he had hoped he would never have to say. "We have no longer any choice," he told them. "We must now raise our white flag to them and sue for peace under whatever conditions they demand. Weetcho and Makashenasa have brought us the words that will change our lives. It is they who will return under the white flag to the Americans to bring to them the word that we bury our hatchets deep in the ground and beg peace of them."

The other chiefs were nodding and murmuring approval of this. They also approved of Black Hawk's selection of Sagano, who spoke and understood English, to accompany Weetcho and Makashenasa back to the American camp.[196] They approved of what Black Hawk instructed the two young warriors to say, which Sagano would interpret. They approved of the large white flag that was hastily rigged to a staff for Weetcho to exhibit as they approached, and under which he was to escort the chiefs of the whites back to this camp at the mouth of the Kishwaukee, if that was what the soldiers wanted. They approved of Black Hawk's orders to everyone here to pack up and be prepared to move down toward the army, if that was what the white chiefs desired. And, five minutes after the departure of Weetcho and Makashenasa, they approved of the second detachment of five warriors under a brave named Menekuk that Black Hawk ordered to mount up and, just as a precaution, to follow and watch over the deputation of three Sacs from a long distance. And, finally, they approved wholeheartedly of

Black Hawk's foresight when he ordered forty of his finest warriors to begin immediately to prepare their weapons and their horses and, despite the much greater strength of the Americans, to be ready to ride beside him and fight those Americans at an instant's notice, should it come to that.

After all, one never knew what to expect when dealing with the whites.

[*May 14, 1832 — Monday*]

Last evening, when the rain was pelting them, the rangers had quickly set up their tents and got into them and, after a meal of cold rations, had spent a soggy, uncomfortable night. Tonight, obviously, was going to be very different, and the troops were in a mood for celebration. That festive mood was not just because they had stopped to camp in this beautiful open grove of trees while the sun was still well over an hour high in the western sky.[197] Nor was it merely because this was a clean, comfortable, dry camp for a change, with already a fine hot meal in preparation at the commissary wagons. No, the principal reason for the high spirits was that, since yesterday's whiskey ration had not been consumed, and who knew what tomorrow would bring, the troops were imbibing heavily and with great gusto on the detachment's thirty-gallon liquor supply — a five-gallon keg of it in each of the six commissary wagons.

Now, with the sun low in the west, with a few fires going and numerous groups of men singing and toasting one another and getting so mellow that by this time they didn't really care whether they ate or not, it took a few moments for the sudden harsh cry that was raised at the northern side of the encampment to sink in.

"Gawww-*DAMN!* In-jins! *IN-JINS!*"

In the large encampment not everyone heard, of course, but those close to the northern perimeter of the grove looked toward the man who had raised the alarm and then followed the direction of his point toward the open prairie. In the orange glow of the sunset, three Indians — bare chested, unpainted, each with sheathed knife and tomahawk in his waistband but without firearms — were riding abreast of one another, their horses being held to a walk and no more than three or four hundred yards distant, heading directly toward the encampment. The one in the middle was holding up a stick about five feet long, to the top of which was attached a large white cloth hanging limply in the breezeless early-evening air.

Very soon the whole bivouac was in an uproar, those near the north end yelling at each other to by-god-do-something and those farther away filling the air with questions along the lines of what-the-hell's-the-ruckus-all-about. Some of the men snatched up their rifles and raced out into the prairie toward the approaching Indians, while others paused long enough to jump onto their horses, which had already been unsaddled, and ride bareback toward the three Sacs. The horses quickly passed the running men and closed the gap to the approaching trio, who abruptly stopped at the unnerving sight ahead. The mounted soldiers reached them and began to circle them closely, holding rifles high with one hand, bridles with the other, and shrieking unintelligibly. Three grasped the bridle ropes out of the hands of the Indians and began leading the horses toward the camp. More men joined them, mounted as well as running, until the three Sacs had become the nucleus of a circling torrent of men, the whole gradually moving closer to the grove.

One of the more inebriated runners stumbled and fell, accidentally firing his rifle when he hit the ground. No one was hurt by the errant ball, but the gunfire caused others to haphazardly fire their weapons too, mainly into the air, as they approached or circled. Still clutching the staff bearing the white flag, Weetcho tried to ignore the horde of yelling and shooting men. Makashenasa was clearly upset and looking about wildly. Sagano kept crying, "Wait, we talk! We talk!" but no one was listening.

"Gawww-DAMN!" a voice shouted, momentarily louder than the others. "Looky there! There's more of 'em, boys!"

Atop the grassy ridge in the distance, five Indians sat single file on their motionless horses, looking toward the activity in the prairie close to the grove. Though fully a quarter of a mile distant, they were clearly silhouetted against the sky, and instantly at least half of the twenty or more mounted men circling the Indians broke away and galloped out directly toward the five. Another ten mounted troopers erupted from the grove, some shirtless, some barefoot, some on saddled horses and some riding bareback, very nearly all armed with either rifles or horse pistols, and joined the charge. There was no formation, no organization, no control. They were merely a shouting, shrieking, cursing, whiskey-inspired mob galvanized into a disorganized group effort to do exactly what it was they had all joined this-here army to do in the first place.[198]

Those heading for the distant Indians had hardly gotten fifty yards away when one of the shots being fired near the initial three Indians was no longer randomly shot into the air. One of the militiamen who had just reached the scene, Thomas B. Reed of Captain Abner Eads's company, threw his rifle to his shoulder, took deliberate aim, and sent a lead ball larger in diameter than a thumbnail into the left forehead of Sagano in the midst of his still crying, "Wait! Wait!," smashing him off his horse and lifeless to the ground. Weetcho dropped the flag beside his dead companion and tried to wheel his horse around to escape, but reaching hands jerked him off his mount. Makashenasa did not wait to be pulled down. He leaped off, dodged through the melee of men grasping for him, and sped away faster than he had ever run before, making no attempt to dodge, even though lead balls ripped with singularly vicious hissing sounds through the grasses on both sides of him.

On the ridge, Menekuk and his four warriors could scarcely believe their eyes.[199] They had watched in amazement as the whites had rushed out upon the three Sacs approaching under the white flag, not knowing whether it meant an attack or not. When the whites merely raced round and round and the group continued toward the grove, they began to think it was just simply the way of these whites in bringing the Indian delegates to their chiefs. But then, amid the distant sounds of erratic gunfire, Menekuk saw one of the braves literally blown off his horse into an unmoving mass on the ground, while another of the three dropped the white flag and disappeared off his horse into the milling mob. Without even seeing what happened to the third, Menekuk became abruptly aware of the gang of twenty horsemen thundering across the prairie grass directly toward them.

"*Come!*" he screamed, kneeing his horse around and setting it into a gallop to the north. He heard his men coming behind him but at first did not turn around to see. Two had reacted swiftly and were only yards behind him; two, a little slower, had fallen back but now were holding their own, bent low over their horses' necks. All five were streaking with the greatest possible speed toward a distant woodland looming shiplike in the advancing dusk over the prairie. The two Sacs immediately behind Menekuk caught up nearly abreast of him as he shifted his weight and turned to look behind, just in time to hear distant shooting and see one of his companions throw up his arms and tumble disjointedly to the ground as a lead ball found its mark. It was then that he became aware of the buzzing sound as other balls whined past perilously close. One of the other warriors had pulled slightly ahead of him, bent as low as he could on his horse's back. Even as his eyes fell on the man, Menekuk saw a brilliant red furrow appear up this man's back, and there was a sound like a fist struck into a palm as the ball continued into the base of the man's skull. Somehow the Sac held on for a moment longer, but then he lurched and slid sideways off the right side of his horse.

Menekuk continued to ride, praying to Moneto to give his horse strength to continue at this terrible pace, hearing the agonized gasping of the animal as it strove to breathe past its exertions. And then the dimness of the woods was around him, and he became aware that two of his companions were still close behind. He eased the pace down slightly, letting them overtake him, and then led them in a devious route through those trees, up this ravine, around that mound, and finally on a line in the gathering darkness for the encampment near the mouth of the Kishwaukee.

Only minutes later they arrived safely, still shaken by the experience, yet somehow able to get across the details of what just occurred. There were no Potawatomies left at the camp, and everyone seemed in a haste to do whatever he was doing. Black Hawk was speaking swiftly but calmly, directing the forty previously selected warriors to mount their horses at once, similarly directing those who were left to encircle and guard and lead northward, away from this place, all their people — to make no pause until he and the chosen warriors rejoined them. Then he faced the forty, now mounted and ready and bristling with weapons, yet strangely silent.

"The war we no longer wished has been brought upon us," he rasped. "We have no more choice. They have spilled Sac blood. They have demanded our vengeance. *Now they shall have it!*"

CHAPTER VII

[*May 14, 1832 — Monday*]

WITH LITTLE MORE than half an hour of daylight remaining, the twenty pursuing rangers broke off their pursuit as the three fleeing Indians well ahead of them entered the evening gloom of the woodland. The whiskey consumed by the militiamen had made them reckless, but not so totally witless as to ride into a situation so rife with the potential of ambush.

Instead they stopped, briefly discussed the situation, then turned and went back a short distance to the dead Sac. They found him sprawled face down on the ground, a great gouge running up his back and a large hole in the base of his skull where the lead ball had entered. They chortled over their prowess and over the fact of this being "a good Injin" at last, and one of the men, who claimed to have fired the fatal shot, dismounted and inexpertly scalped the dead man, then took his tomahawk and knife from his belt and thrust them in his own. He gave the body a savage kick before remounting to ride with the others the short distance back to the first of the fleeing Indians they had killed. Shot through the spine, this one, too, was scalped and stripped of his goods. By this time the daylight was rapidly fading, and the men, heady with their triumph, were about to return to the camp when one of their number gave a yelp.

"There! By god, look! There's them three others."

The whole party turned to see three warriors, evidently without weapons, who had just emerged from a small grove of trees and were now galloping through the deepening twilight toward the prairie ridge, obviously intent on escape beyond it.

Instantly the twenty were in pursuit. Ahead, the three, almost within range, reached the ridge and disappeared beyond it. The militiamen galloped after them, but when they topped the ridge, they found themselves confronted with a mass of about twice their number of mounted Indians, who, at a cry from their leader, broke into a full charge toward them, as the three seemingly escaping Indians joined them in their rush.[200]

Stunned, then thrown into a panic, the militiamen wheeled their horses and started away, dropping their weapons in their haste to urge their horses on as the guns of the Indians began firing behind them. One soldier was hit and wounded, but managed to retain his balance. Another was hit and fell, came to his feet, and began running after his companions, only to be overtaken by the Indians and tomahawked in full flight.

In the main camp of the whites, Weetcho had been disarmed of his belt knife and tomahawk and brought roughly into the camp in the grove. In the midst of being mistreated and brokenly questioned in a mixture of Sac and English as to the whereabouts of Black Hawk's band, he had managed unexpectedly to rip loose from his captors, had snatched away his confiscated tomahawk from a startled trooper, and plunged into the dark woods, easily eluding their befuddled efforts to recapture him. The weapon in his grip restored a good measure of his self-control and confidence. He remembered the direction he had glimpsed Makashenasa running and headed that way. By the time he reached the edge of the woods, the prairie itself was becoming dark. He crouched low and sped through the grasses as fast as he could run in so awkward a manner, and had gone perhaps a hundred yards when a shadowy person rose from the grasses ahead and gripped him about the middle, bringing him to the ground. He raised his tomahawk to slash at the enemy, but then heard the frantic, grating whisper of Makashenasa ordering him to be still.

Together the two young Sacs peered over the tops of the grasses, fearful of pursuers moving toward them. Instead, they crouched even lower as they heard the thunder of hooves and the terrified cries of men — white men. In wonder they watched as the barely visible, shadowy forms of a party of mounted whites swept past, obviously terror-stricken, followed immediately by a horde of Sacs in pursuit, their own voices raised in fearsome war whoops. One of the white horsemen came directly toward them, and Weetcho rose and threw his tomahawk as the rider passed. The blade entered the man's temple, and even while he was falling Weetcho grasped the bridle of the horse and held it till it calmed slightly. Weetcho handed the bridle rope to Makashenasa and ran to the fallen trooper. A knife was sheathed in the man's belt, and he took it and scalped the man. It was his first scalp in battle, and an exultation rose in him at the knowledge that he was now a *brave!* He raced back to his companion and launched himself up onto the animal's back, snatched the bridle rope from Makashenasa's grip, and then pulled the more slightly built young man up behind him.

The whites in the principal camp heard the approaching commotion in the deepening darkness, and the noise convinced them instantly that the whole of Black Hawk's force was sweeping down on them. It did not help at all when one of the supposedly most stalwart among them, Colonel James Strode, who had accompanied the force from Dixon's as an observer, panicked and leaped onto his horse and sped through the camp heading southward. A great many of the militia took this to be a signal that all was lost, and it was now every man for himself. That initial spark of fear swiftly turned into a conflagration that turned practically the whole white force of nearly three hundred men into a panic-stricken mass of humanity. They screamed and cried, threw away their weapons, forgot their gear and supplies spread out on the ground among them, thought only of finding a horse, *any horse*, mounting it, and fleeing from this ungodly horror being launched against them. The early night became a hideous cacophony of fierce shriekings from Indian throats and horrid cries and blubberings of intensely frightened white men. There was an accompaniment of whinnying, screaming horses virtually as terrified as the men, a darkness punctuated by erratic bursts of gunfire from the weapons of the Indians, and the whole inter-spersed with the swish of disturbed grasses magnified until, to the panicky white ears, it became the swish of swords and tomahawks seeking white flesh.

For a brief time in the beginning there were coherent shouts from some of the officers, entreating their men to stop, to stand and fight, but their words were lost in the thunder of hooves and the abject terror that enveloped them. It was a total rout by some forty Indians of a white force more than seven times its size. Those militiamen in flight made no effort to stop to assess what was occurring. The ones who had found horses — which were the great majority — rode them frantically on and on into the night, pursued endlessly by the specters in their imagination far more than those in actuality, yet unable to realize this.

Near the camp, Weetcho and Makashenasa, on the horse they had captured, turned to follow their fellow Indians who had so swiftly passed them by. In moments, as they neared the creek, they heard a terrified watery thrashing and grunting ahead, and they came upon a horse that had stumbled as it galloped through the muck at the edge of the creek and had fallen in such a way that, though unhurt, it could not immediately regain its feet. Its rider was pinned by one foot under the weight of the struggling animal and was frantically trying to free himself. The two young Indians stopped their horse, and now it was Makashenasa who leaped from its back, tomahawk in hand, and raced up to the trapped white man. Before the man could bring to bear the rifle he was grasping, Makashenasa buried his tomahawk to the hilt in the back of his skull. The young Sac quickly took his own first enemy scalp, took the man's gun, managed to calm the horse and get it back on its feet again, and mounted up beside Weetcho.[201] The two *braves* once again set out after their warriors. Along the way they began to see whites lying dead who had been overtaken and killed. At last, having ridden after them for about six miles, they came up to the party of warriors returning, having given up the chase and coming back to scalp those they had downed. There were only twenty-five of them, the remaining fifteen having broken off with Black Hawk just after passing the white camp to return to their people. So, in actuality, it was only twenty-five of the Sacs, outnumbered about twelve to one, who had pursued the fleeing whites far into the night and continued to fuel the fire of their panic in one of the most disgraceful routs ever to occur to an American force.

Throughout the night the white survivors continued to flee, mostly by themselves, only with difficulty stifling the cries wedged in their throats lest they be given away by their own voices, continuing to move in solitary fashion among a horde of their fellows in similar circumstance — hearing the others and turning them in their imagination into the enemy, and so continuing to run away and away.

Even when, at last, at the end of this most hideously frightening night of their lives, the dawn broke, the fleeing militiamen continued away. Here and there as they caught sight of one another, they joined together, not as a force to stand and hold, but drawn together with a common bond of overwhelming terror that thrust them on and on without pause. A single ambition seemed to drive them — to get away, totally away — not to the remainder of their army of mounted men at Dixon's, but deliberately skirting that area because they were utterly convinced that Dixon's was where the vast Indian force attacking them was headed. Too, the fleeing men were irresistibly directed in their movement by the thought that had loomed so ironically in their minds in days past — that Dixon's was only forty miles north of where their own homes were located, and at a time such as this, no place seemed to offer greater safety than home. And so, long before a trickle of survivors began showing up in gasping panic at Dixon's, many others were already well past that frontier village and carrying the news of this incredible disaster to the areas more heavily populated with whites — the Illinois River Valley.[202]

[*May 15, 1832 — Tuesday*]

It was close to 3:00 A.M. when, in his comfortable quarters in the guest portion of the ninety-foot-long structure John Dixon had built on the bank of the Rock River adjacent to his ferry, Governor Reynolds was jarred from his sleep by a fearful pounding on his door.

"Wuh . . ." He jerked upright in bed, his heart suddenly hammering. ". . . Who is it?"

"Whiteside," came the militia general's strong voice. "We've got trouble, Governor. Bad trouble."

"Come in, come in," Reynolds called, reaching out and turning up the wick on the hurricane lamp that had been burning at low flame. The room became bathed in warm yellow light as Whiteside entered, and Reynolds squinted up at him with trepidation, knowing it was no small matter that would bring the general here at this time of night. "What's wrong, Sam? What's happened?"

"Major Stillman's detachment. Looks like it's been wiped out."

"*What!*" Reynolds came to his feet, mouth open, feeling as if he'd been punched in the stomach. "What happened?"

As the governor hurriedly dressed, Whiteside filled him in on what details he had, which thus far were few. "Three men've come in so far. Private Maxfield first.[203] He got back here about fifteen or twenty minutes ago. All three're saying the same thing. The detachment went into camp in a grove close to Old Man's Creek last evening. Just about dark, Black Hawk's bucks hit 'em in force — six, eight hundred warriors. Maybe a thousand. Maybe more. Maxfield thinks just about everybody's dead. The other two agree. It all looks pretty bad."

"Just about *everybody?*" Reynolds echoed. "Good Lord! Stillman had around three hundred men!"

Whiteside nodded and led the way to the door as they headed for the head-quarters tent where the three survivors were still being questioned. Word of the evident disaster had spread quickly, and by this time a large crowd of soldiers had gathered. They spread apart respectfully for their general and governor. Four more men had come in by this time, for a total of seven thus far, their horses pushed almost to the point of death. Whiteside called an immediate conference with his field officers and ordered them to assemble a strong mounted detach-ment for him to lead out after daybreak northeastward from Dixon's along Stillman's trace to assist any other survivors who might be coming in, to reach the battlefield and bury the dead, and to engage any hostile Indian party en-countered.

The men who had already come in were closely questioned by General Whiteside and Governor Reynolds. Each was positive he was one of the very few survivors and gave lurid descriptions of what had happened to other militiamen they knew quite well, only to have some of those very men described as dead or injured begin showing up soon afterward. The general and the governor now began to get an inkling that perhaps, while serious, this was not quite the disaster it initially appeared to be. All the survivors spoke of the terrible attack thrown against them by the Indians, but none made any mention whatever of the militia fighting back. The whole matter began to get more and more puzzling as additional men arrived on exhausted horses.

Before an hour had passed, Governor Reynolds and General Whiteside had written a joint letter and dispatched it by express downriver to General Atkinson:

Camp at Dixon's 15 May 1832

Genl. Atkinson   The party of men which I sent out to the Old Man's Creek have been defeated by the Indians. Some have returned, and we have no provi-sions so as to enable us to make persuit [sic] *after the Indians to any great extent.*

It is impossible to inform you the number slain; but it is considerable enough so to be quite serious. We are waiting the provisions.

Genl. Whiteside will march soon in the morning without provisions so as to cover the retreat, bury the dead &c.

With sincer [sic] *respect your obt. Saml. Whiteside*
John Reynolds

Another specter beyond this immediate situation was suddenly becoming very clear to Governor Reynolds. His initial feeling was that the returning survivors and the many militiamen still here at Dixon's would now be clamoring for vengeance and ready to move out with great determination to meet the enemy. He soon realized how wrong he was. An enveloping depression was settling over the troops, demoralizing them virtually to a man, and all they wanted was out. Almost all the militia had volunteered for thirty days, and that thirty-day period was close to expiring — close enough that none of the men cared to risk their necks as soldiers when in several days they would no longer even *be* soldiers. Reynolds found this a most humiliating state of affairs, and so hardly had the letter to Atkinson been dispatched when he was back in his own quarters, busily trying to circumvent an even more disastrous developing situation — an Indian war on the frontier and no manpower with which to fight it. His first communication was an order to Colonel James Strode, who was among the early survivors to return to Dixon's and who was now preparing for his return to Galena:

To Col. Strode of the 27th Regt. Ill. Mly. [sic]
You are hereby authorised [sic] *to organise* [sic] *and hold in readiness all the Militia of the County of Jo. Daviess, to march to the defence* [sic] *of the Country at any Moment on your order.*
Should it be practicable you are empowered to raise one Company of Mounted Volunteers of fifty men to elect their Officers and range on the frontier.

John Reynolds
Com in Chief Ills Mil [sic]

15th May, 1832.

In a similar vein, Reynolds wrote to Colonel Henry Dodge, who, camped out of hearing on the other side of the Rock River, had not yet heard of the defeat. The governor told him the bad news and added:

. . . you will return with your troops to the protection of the settlements. The frontier of the mining country is in danger, & they ought to Fort or secure themselves from the indians.

Immediately upon finishing, Reynolds hurriedly wrote another, longer message, this one addressed to the Citizens of Illinois, to be copied three times by his aide, with the original going to Colonel March, carried by Major Horn to St. Louis, and the remaining three to be carried all over Illinois by three trusted messengers, John A. Wakefield and Robert Blackwell of Fayette County and John Ewing of Franklin County:

Dixon's Ferry, on Rock River
May 15, 1832.

It becomes my duty to again call on you for your services in defense of your country. The State is not only invaded by the hostile Indians, but many of our citizens have been slain in battle. A detachment of mounted volunteers, about 275 in number, commanded by Major Stillman, were overpowered by hostile Indians on Sycamore Creek, distant from this place about 30 miles, and a considerable number killed. This is an act of hostility which can not be misconstrued. I am of the opinion that the Pottawottomies [sic] and Winnebagoes have joined the Sacs, and all may be considered as waging war against the United States. To subdue these Indians and drive them out of the State, it will require a force of at least 2,000 mounted volunteers, in addition to troops already in the field. I have made the necessary requisition of proper officers for the above number, and have no doubt that the citizen soldiers of the State will obey the call of their country. They will meet at Hennepin, on the Illinois River, in companies of 50 men each, on the 10th of June next, to be organized into brigades.[204]

JOHN REYNOLDS
Commander in Chief.

[*May 15, 1832 — Tuesday*]

Beneath the newly risen sun, Black Hawk watched his braves carefully place the sections of surface earth, still with buffalo grass attached, atop the graves in which had been buried the bodies of Sagano and the two other warriors. When they finished, pots of water were brought and carefully sprinkled over the grasses so they would not wilt and thus betray the fact that they had been disturbed. When they were finished, except for the dampness, there was no way of telling that this was the spot where three men had been buried. These were three, Black Hawk thought grimly, who would not be dug up by the whites, as they had a way of doing, to look for trinkets and weapons.

All the necessary words had been said, consigning these three into the great journey upon which they were now headed, toward the land where there was always plenty of game and fish and the women and children never went hungry. Now it was time to do what yet remained to be done and then be gone before the whites returned to bury their own dead, as they usually did. The bodies of the whites, already scalped, were further mangled by the angry warriors, the limbs and heads and genitals hacked off some of the dead as a warning to the whites who would soon come that this was what was in store for them, too, should they attack the Indians further.

Black Hawk now led his warriors to the grove where the soldiers had been camped. Around twenty horses had been captured and were hobbled in the prairie close by. They would, Black Hawk was certain, serve their new owners well, and their first task would be to carry burdens for the Sacs — the plunder that was scattered everywhere on the ground here, thrown wildly away by the panicked soldiers in their insane flight.

Black Hawk thought of that, and once again a feeling of wonder ran through him. He still could scarcely believe how they *ran* — how an army of maybe three hundred armed men, charged by only forty warriors at first and then twenty-five after that, had turned into witless sparrows and fled as if the evil spirit of Matchemoneto were biting at their tailfeathers! He did not look forward to fighting a war with the whites — knew in his heart that it was hopeless and they could never win. Yet, now he was encouraged, because if this was how the whites here fought, perhaps somehow, some way, after they had tasted more of Sac anger on the frontier, they would be willing to talk again about what was owed the Indians.

Kinnekonesaut — He-That-Strikes-First — the fifth head brave of the band, placed a hand on Black Hawk's shoulder. "I do not see how any of this could be," he said unbelievingly, gesturing toward the goods lying on the ground. "Moneto was surely with us."

Black Hawk nodded. "I thought," he said reflectively, "when we first began to chase them, that they really intended to stop here and turn and fight us. We expected it and were prepared to die. With them among these trees and we in the open grass, we could not have successfully attacked them if they had been only *half* as many as we. And yet they were over *ten times* our number when we chased them away from here. Kinnekonesaut, why were they like that? I have never seen palefaces with so little spirit. I expected to see them fight as the Americans did against our British brothers during the last war, but *this* party . . ." — he shoved a fist out toward the abandoned encampment — ". . . they had no such braves among them!" He shook his head. "We must pick up all they have left for us and then go back to our people and take them to the safe place White Crow told us about farther up Rock River. From there our braves can move in smaller war parties to hit the whites. Tonight I will send a first party of warriors to journey to the village of Chief Meau-eus, in whose heart it has been to support us. By the retreat of the Potawatomies from us yesterday when they heard of the whites being close, we are no longer bound to the promises we made them. Yet, I feel in my heart for the bad things the white men did to hurt the young men of the village of Chief Meau-eus and to stop the flow of their river, and so we will still try to help him."

Black Hawk cast an eye at the items his warriors were collecting. The militia's abandoned supplies being recovered would not keep his people going for very long, Black Hawk knew, but perhaps long enough to turn the tables and make it the whites who sued for peace. There were arms here — a number of pistols and hundreds of rifles and powder flasks and balls for all of them. There was the little bit of the firewater in one keg, which he ordered poured upon the ground. There were bedrolls, blankets, extra clothes, medicines, and there was what they needed most of all, *food!* The twelve oxen that had pulled the six wagons were butchered and the meat cut in strips and taken in bundles to the women for drying over fires. The wagons themselves had the spokes of their wheels knocked out, and then, since that might not be enough, the wagons themselves were burned. The hundreds of saddlebags, containing rations, were divided among the braves and draped over their own horses and the extra horses they had recovered. Before the sun was more than two hours up, they were gone — all of them — and the grove, except for the smoldering remains of the wagons and the embers of a few campfires, was empty.

[*May 15, 1832 — Tuesday*]

General Whiteside raised himself high in his saddle and looked back at the fourteen hundred mounted men at ready behind him. John and Martha Dixon stood at the doorway of their large building, Governor Reynolds beside them. Mrs. Dixon shivered — not entirely because of the chill in the air this bright morning — and her husband put his arm around her shoulders and held her close to his side. He did not glance toward the stock pen, where a mound of entrails and hides and bones was all that remained of the few stock cattle, milk cows, and oxen he had owned, which he had several hours ago freely given to the troops to help provision them for their march to the site of Stillman's Defeat. The militia had few supplies beyond that, and so there would be little more that could be accomplished on this expedition than to locate and bury the dead and, if possible, engage and disperse any Indians in the vicinity.

Of the 275 men that had been in Stillman's force, a total of 162 had thus far made it back to Camp No. 10 at Dixon's, including both Stillman himself and Major Bailey, both of whom verbally gave General Whiteside and Governor Reynolds their versions of what had occurred. That left 113 yet unaccounted for, and hope had begun to fade that very many more would come in during this day.

The only militia who were permitted to remain behind at Dixon's now were those who were incapacitated with sickness or injury, which were relatively few, and, to guard them, the exhausted militiamen who had returned during the night and were still straggling in.

With that, General Whiteside's force of fourteen hundred men, practically without provisions, moved out and headed north toward the site of Stillman's abandoned camp. During the march, they encountered, at intervals, a total of another sixty-two militiamen, all of whom, after gratefully accepting some rations and telling their stories, followed this force's back trail to Dixon's. Nevertheless, this still left fifty-one men as yet unaccounted for — a substantial number.

Throughout the march the militiamen under Whiteside were becoming increasingly vocal in their dissatisfaction at being here, and quite definite in their assertions that they would accept no further service — or orders — that would cause them to prolong their enlistments. Their most fervent wish at this point was to get their immediate unpleasant task completed and then go home. This determination increased as they approached Old Man's Creek and then the grove beyond it, with no sign of the Indians anywhere about. The first two bodies they discovered were buried where they were found. Their scalped condition did not instill in Whiteside's men any burning desire for retribution, but only deepened their depression and intensified their fear. That fear became almost palpable as, on nearing the creek, they found the mutilated bodies of nine more of their dead. Two had been beheaded, and the skin of the two severed heads had further been cut and ripped back from the underlying skull.[205] Several other bodies had gaping chest wounds and were found to have missing hearts. Most of the dead had one or more of their limbs cut off, as well as their genitals. These nine bodies — with what scattered limbs and parts of them could be found — all were carried to a central location between Old Man's Creek and the grove. Here a large common grave was dug. At its bottom, the human remains were carefully laid out and covered with blankets. A passage was read from a bible owned by one of Whiteside's men, and a prayer was offered by the general himself. Then the grave was refilled. Throughout it all, a similar thought was strong in everyone's mind: forty-one men were still missing.[206] How many of those were in this same condition or worse?

[*May 15, 1832 — Tuesday*]

General Henry Atkinson rubbed his eyes and sighed. This had been a very long day, and it wasn't over yet. He mentally berated himself for ever having let Samuel Whiteside have the discretionary power to move the mounted militia rapidly upstream beyond the Prophet's Village. Not a man given to pessimism, Atkinson nevertheless found himself wondering just what else could possibly go wrong. Almost as if in response to the unvoiced question, a voice outside his tent announced the owner as being Zachary Taylor, and Atkinson bade him enter. The stockily built officer with bristling gray moustache pushed the tent flap aside and entered from the evening gloom outside. He squinted his eyes a little against the lamplight and saluted his commander as he came to a stop.

"If you're the bearer of more bad news, Zach," the general said with a wry smile, returning the salute in an offhand way, "just turn around and leave."

The colonel smiled in return and extended his left hand, in which was an envelope. "Addressed to you, General, and I haven't opened it, so I don't know whether it's good or bad. An express just brought it in."

"From where?" Atkinson asked, reaching out for it.

"Dixon's Ferry."

The general slapped the envelope down on his portable desk and shook his head. "From Dixon's Ferry and you don't know whether it's good news or bad? How could any good news possibly come out of Dixon's today?"

Taylor shrugged and nodded in concession. The first news of the Stillman detachment disaster had reached them just after dawn today, and though Atkinson had debated about whether or not to tell his troops here on the Rock River about it, the decision had been taken out of his hands. The express had evidently let the word slip, and in moments the whole camp was talking about it in fearful whispers. As a result, although the task of pulling the boats upriver had continued, their hearts had most definitely not been in the work, and they'd made little progress today. Atkinson had expected to reach the rapids by mid-afternoon, but work had stopped for the day a couple of hours ago, and they were still three miles below the rocks.

The word that express had brought this morning was the letter signed by both Governor Reynolds and General Whiteside. And while the early-morning work on boat moving had begun, Atkinson had answered it:

> *Head Qrs. R. Wing West: Depart: 10 miles*
> *above Prophets Vill 8 O'clock 15th May 1832*

General — Your and the Governor's joint letter has just been handed to me by Mr. Ogee.

I regret to learn the defeat of the party sent out to reconnoitre the enemy. It has been impossible for us to get on faster. We hope to be within 12 or 15 miles of Dixon's to night. Not a moment shall be lost in joining you. If General Whitesides falls back for provisions you had best send down a party to night to get a supply.

> *Gen: Atkinson to Governor Reynolds:*
> *Reynolds and Gen: Whitesides.* [sic]

Throughout the day, as the men worked dispiritedly on moving the boats, General Atkinson had considered what options he had now. He was only too aware of how close to expiring were the enlistments of the militia and what was apt to occur at that fateful time. Even if more Illinois men could be encouraged to volunteer — or even be drafted, for that matter — there would still be a significant delay before a strong force could be put into motion following up Black Hawk's trail. At last he had come to a conclusion he had been holding at arm's length for a long while. It went strongly against his grain as a regular officer of the United States Army to do it, but there seemed at this juncture not to be very much choice in the matter.

For weeks the Indians presently on good terms with the Americans — the friendly Sacs and Potawatomies, the Winnebagoes north of the Wisconsin River, the Dakotah Sioux and Menominees, even the distant Chippewas and Otoes and Osages — all had offered their services in ending the problems currently being created for them by the conduct of Black Hawk and his band. Most of them, particularly the Sioux and Menominees, would like nothing better than having the full sanction of the United States to fall upon their enemies as they had long wanted to do.

All right, then, maybe that *was* the answer. Or, if not the answer, at least a *direction*. Could having the help of friendly Indians in this matter be any worse than being aided by a mob of undisciplined militia? Hadn't past experience shown time after time that regulars and militia don't mix — even when the militia were ostensibly under command of the regulars? Well, this current crop of militia had had its chance, and look what had become of it. Henry Atkinson decided here and now that the time had come to alert the various Indian agents, who were of course under federal jurisdiction, to recruit, arm, and provision the Indian forces within their agencies to help resolve this present problem.[207]

Now, with the unopened letter from the militia general, Acting Major Isaiah Stillman, before him, General Atkinson was suddenly glad he had made the decision to procure the assistance of Indian allies. As Zachary Taylor watched with an indecipherable half-smile on his lips, Atkinson tapped the envelope on the edge of the desk a time or two and then exhaled heavily and opened it. The letter, written this afternoon and making no mention whatsoever of the panic that had overwhelmed the militia detachment, was very short, and he read it swiftly, then handed it without comment to Colonel Taylor, who also read it.

Dixsons [sic] Ferry 15th May 1832

Dr Sir   You have been appraised of the defeat of the small party of men under my command by the Sac. & other indians — the whole force under Genl. Whiteside has gone to meet them & apprehensions exist that the indians will leave the ground occupied yesterday descend in canoes, & attack this place. if they should do so our force is insufficient to maintain our ground our men being fatigued & out of provision — & ammunition.

Yr. Obt. Servt. I Stillman Act. Maj com Volunteers

3 O'Clock P.M.

Colonel Taylor looked up from the letter and saw that General Atkinson was watching him closely. He returned the letter to the desktop and met the general's gaze.

"So?" Atkinson said.

"I would say," Taylor remarked slowly, "that Governor Reynolds's ranger commander is a man of noteworthy cowardice."

A faint smile tipped the general's lips. "I'll need an express in a few minutes to carry a letter to Dixon's Ferry," he said. It was a dismissal. Colonel Taylor dipped his head and left the tent without saluting. Atkinson sat motionless for a few moments and then took out a fresh sheet of paper and began to write his letter:

Head Qrs R. Wing West: Depart
Three miles below the upper rapids
15th. May 1832

General   Mr Taylor has just handed me your letter dated this afternoon. I cannot think the Indians will descend the river to night, because if Gen: White-

sides [sic] *should overtake them, & they should attempt to fall back by water, he could easily fall back also, and take a position on the bank of the river to stop their descent. Moreover it would be highly injudicious for me to separate the troops from the boats, for all the supplies both of provisions and ammunition to enable us to prosecute the campaign are on board them and, above all things, they must be preserved. If, however, against my decided opinion, the Indians should fall back and you should not find yourself able to maintain your position, it will be easy for you to fall back upon us over a good route of not more than 12 or 15 miles. As to a supply of provisions, I refer you to Mr. Taylor as to the easiest & earliest mode of obtaining them.*

 Gen: Atkinson to Gen: Stillman

[May 17, 1832 — Thursday]

"Papa," said the attractive young Sylvia Hall, as their wagon turned the bend on the two-rut trail road leading to Ottawa, "there's someone coming up ahead." Standing up as she was in the small open place of the heavily loaded wagon bed, with one hand on her father's shoulder and one on her mother's, the seventeen-year-old girl's head was higher than either of theirs.

Rachel, fifteen, and Elizabeth, eight, scrambled up beside her, spreading their feet wide to maintain their balance against the bouncing progress of the wagon. "It looks like Mr. Davis," said Elizabeth, anxious to be first to identify the horseman who had come into view from around some trees not too far ahead.

"It is," said her father. Davis, their closest neighbor in the Indian Creek Valley, was a blacksmith and easily recognizable due to his huge size. "I wonder if that old Indian brought the warning to him, too."

"Doesn't seem likely, Bill," said his wife, "if he's coming back this way instead of heading for town."

The forty-five-year-old Hall reined the team to a stop and leaned out to look backward past the load of furnishings tied in their wagon. He nodded, pleased, when he saw that his sons, John, Edward, and Greenbury, were still on their horses within a hundred yards and evidently having no trouble herding the other animals — three more horses, two mules, their dependable old milk cow, and a heifer. When he looked back to the front, William Davis was very near and just bringing his fine chestnut mare to a stop. He was holding a rifle balanced across the pommel with one huge hand, but he quickly leaned it across the crook of his left arm, which was holding the reins, and touched his right hand to the small brim of his black hat.

"Mornin', Bill," he said pleasantly, then added, "Mary Jane . . . girls. Could be you folks're going to Ottawa, too?"

"Yes," Hall said. "Evidently you saw somebody else heading in?"

Davis chuckled, but without much humor, and shook his head. "Whooo-eee! Not some — *everyone.* I was just there, and I'll tell you, I'm heading home. Never saw anything like it. People everywhere, coming in from all over. No place left to stay, anywhere. No room left in any of the houses. People're even staying in the livery stables. Setting up tents all over the place. Already swore in a town militia, and they're turning Chester Gillum's log-yard into a fort. I mean it — never saw anything like it. Indians there, too. Squaws, mostly, and I'll swear ever' one of 'em's got half a dozen kids." He paused as a thought occurred to him. "I 'spect you've got a place all lined up waiting for you, where you're aimin' to stay?"

"Well, actually, no," Hall replied. "Didn't really figure we were going to have any trouble."

"Oh, you will," Davis said. "Everyone else is, seems like." He glanced past the wagon at the approach of Hall's three sons and tossed a wave to the young men, but continued talking to their father. "Ain't going to be anyplace to pen them animals, and I really don't think you'll have much luck finding a place to stay. You've got what, nine in your family? Just like us?"

"Nine, yes," Mary Jane said, "but only eight with us now. Temperance got married, you know, and she's living 'way down in McLean County now."

"Well, our girls, Sally and Gin — Virginia — they're off visiting their grandma in St. Louis now, so we've got seven."

"William." Mary Jane turned to her husband, a note of concern in her voice now. "What are we going to do if there's no place to stay? I don't really think we should go back home, do you?"

"Well, I think maybe we better find out what the situation is now." Hall turned back to face Davis. "I guess everyone's heard about the Indians going on the warpath, and what happened up above Dixon's place — about how Stillman's rangers got ambushed and wiped out. A hundred dead, they say. Maybe two hundred. Nobody seems to know for sure, but it's a lot. After all those false alarms, it's finally happened. And some are saying they're coming this way. The Indians, I mean. We figured we'd better get into town and take along the best of our things" — he indicated the heavily loaded wagon behind him with a jerk of his thumb — "and at least try to save what we could. We got visited by that nice old Potawatomi chief from 'way up Indian Creek . . . ."

"Chaubenee," Davis put in. "I know. He comes to my place yesterday all lathered up, warning us to get into town and stay there, that Indian trouble's coming. Says in all probability they're going to make a raid on us and kill us and destroy our property. Says his village is only about thirty miles from where the massacre was — right where Sycamore Creek dumps into Rock River — so he got the news right away. Says it was bad Indians done it — Black Hawk's crowd. Says other Indians don't want no part of it, and that him an' his two sons an' a nephew were movin' off in different directions, warning the settlements on Indian and Bureau Creeks and down to the Illinois.[208] Says some others, too, up 'round Chicago are doing the same, an' along Fox River and the Des Plaines. John Henderson — you know him, don't you? Sure you do. Well, he was at my place when Chaubenee came, but John an' me, we didn't put stock in it all at first, and sent him on his way to scare other folks if that was what he had a mind t' do. But then we got to thinking about it and figured maybe we better check it out our own selves, so we made up a little party — taking along his boy Henry and all three of mine — and we took up our guns and went up to Chief Meau-eus's village, 'cause maybe you remember, I had trouble with them bucks right after we finished building the mill dam. Anyways, we got up there and the place was empty. Not a soul. Now that sort of got us a little more excited than if they was a whole bunch of 'em there, so we sent the four boys straight back to my place to guard things, an' John an' me rode right on down to Ottawa and come to find out ol' Waubansee's left his village, too. Brought all his women and children into Ottawa and left 'em there, like Meau-eus did, saying they was warned by Chaubenee, too. And then him and most of his men went off somewhere. 'Bout a dozen survivors 've come in who were with Stillman, too — all scratched and tore up from galloping through woods and fields and 'cross creeks all the way down. Stories they're tellin' are pretty bad. One thing sure — this one's no false alarm. While I was in Ottawa they sent a company of men northward looking for to help any more survivors they might come across and to see if there's any sign of hostile Indians."

"You suppose there'd be any available places to stay down in Utica?" Hall asked. Utica, somewhat smaller than Ottawa, was about ten miles farther down-river.

Davis was shaking his head even before Hall finished speaking. "Not likely. Way I hear it, word's spread so far so fast everyone's flocking in and forting up all the way down as far as Hennepin, maybe farther. I got to tell you, Bill, I ain't never seen folks so scared as they are this time."

"William, what *are* we going to do?" The alarm in Mary Jane Hall's voice was very evident as she gripped her husband's arm, and behind her the three girls were wide-eyed and huddling closer to their parents, Sylvia and Rachel with their hands protectively on Elizabeth's shoulders. Their mother glanced at them and then back at her husband and continued, "We don't have guns enough to fight off Indians! And if there's no room in town . . ." Her words trailed off.

"Hold on!" Davis raised his hand, then dropped it to steady his mare as she pranced a little. "Mary Jane, I didn't mean to get you all fretted up. There prob'ly ain't nothing much we got to worry about, so long's we all stick together. Anyway, Martha wanted me to come see you today, so meeting you saves me a trip. We want you to come and stay with us till this all blows over. We got plenty of room there and plenty of guns and enough people staying that we don't really have anything to worry about."

"Who all's there?" asked Johnny Hall, the twenty-three-year-old, moving in close on his horse and leaving twenty-one-year-old Edward and nineteen-year-old Greenbury to watch the stock, now quietly standing a few yards behind the wagon.

"Well, let's see now," Davis said, "first of all there's Martha an' me, the five boys. That's seven. An' Sally an' Gin are over at St. Louis, so they're safe enough." The five boys were William, Jr., twenty-five, Samuel, twenty-two, Alexander, sixteen, Thomas, ten, and James, seven — respectively called Bill-Too, Sam, Alex, Tommy, and Jimmie. Sally was twenty-six and Virginia — Gin — was twenty-three. "Then there's the four Petticrews, which makes eleven." William and Eleanor Petticrew, thirty-six and thirty-three respectively, and their two small sons, Charlie, six, and the baby, Tommy, only five months old. "John Henderson and his boy, Henry, will be staying with us just to give us more manpower, but the two Sarahs are staying with John's sister in Ottawa, so that makes thirteen." John Henderson was fifty-one and his wife, Sarah, a year younger. Henry was twenty-seven and their daughter, also named Sarah, was twenty-four. "Same way with the Howards," Davis continued. "Edgar and his boy, Allen, will be with us, and Mary and Ellen are with friends in Ottawa. So that's fifteen." Edgar Howard was forty, his wife, thirty-eight, their son, Allen, was seventeen, and their daughter, Ellen, was twenty. "Then there are my two hands, Bob Norris and Emery George." The two were both age twenty-four. "That's it, I guess. That makes seventeen. Then, if the eight of you come, that'll make twenty-five all told, so I reckon we sure won't have to worry about Indians bothering us any. You're going to come, ain't you?"

William Hall looked at his wife. Mary Jane hesitated and then nodded, and he squeezed her arm and looked back at Davis. "I guess, then, we are," he said, "and we thank you kindly, Bill."

Elizabeth squealed with pleasure, and both Sylvia and Rachel clapped their hands, while the three young men broke into hurrays that nearly caused the livestock to bolt.

[*May 18, 1832 — Friday*]

Black Hawk viewed the island where his band was now setting up the camp that he anticipated they would be occupying for a long time — perhaps until the Americans had suffered enough under the lead and steel of his vengeance and finally proposed peace talks. So well hidden was the high ground on the island and so highly defensible that for the first time since they had crossed the Mississippi six weeks earlier, he felt they were reasonably safe. Here only a remarkably few warriors would be able to protect the women and children against attack, should the hiding place be discovered — which was highly unlikely. What this meant was that now he was able to make maximum use of the majority of his warriors by splitting them into a number of strong war parties, one of which he would be leading himself, to sally forth and create havoc on the frontier. Not only would these war parties be able to kill many of the Americans and destroy much of what the whites had built in this country, it would also give the attackers opportunity to locate and bring away with them a variety of the provisions, equipment, supplies, food, and horses they would need in times ahead, not only to feed their hungry people in this island encampment, but to replenish their own meager supplies. And all this had become possible through the efforts of the Winnebago chief whose fidelity he had very nearly begun to doubt — White Crow.

Shortly after the Sacs left with the plunder they had gathered at the site of the incredible cowardly retreat of the whites, White Crow had rejoined them, highly impressed with Black Hawk's success and evidently far more inclined to help him now in view of that signal victory. Though White Crow admittedly still did not speak for his tribe, he assured Black Hawk and the other chiefs of the band that the news of what had occurred would cause many of the Indians who had been backing away from helping them to reverse themselves and give what aid they could short of public commitment to the band and its goals. The precipitate flight of so large a force of Americans from so few warriors, White Crow said, was already causing many Indians to wonder why they had ever been afraid of white soldiers in the first place.

Black Hawk's initial fury at the treacherous action of the whites toward his peace delegation under a white flag had been assuaged to some extent by the victory he had won, but it was a rage that was only banked, not eliminated. It would take a great deal more than this, and his vengeance could be expected in many ways before it was finally appeased. It was when they had reached the mouth of the Kishwaukee again — the women and children having long since passed beyond this point to the north, that Black Hawk dispatched his first detachment of twenty warriors from this main party with specific instructions. They were to go upstream on the Kishwaukee, leaving a bold trail for the whites to follow, should any be brave enough to come up the Rock River again after them. This would, for a time, keep the whites off the trail of the main party, which was continuing its course upstream on the Rock River; a trail that they would hide as much as possible, even though it might slow them down to do so. The war party was to continue making their clear trail, as if many more warriors than they actually were had gone this way, following the main branch of the Kishwaukee directly toward the morning sun until it reached the place near its headwaters where the river turned sharply back toward the northwest. At this point the war party would now begin to be very careful about hiding its trail. As they left the Kishwaukee here and continued to move straight in the direction they had been heading, they would in less than one mile come to a little lake that was very narrow and no more than a mile long.[209] At this point they would follow a Potawatomi trail that some had been on before — a trail leading southeast for six miles to the summer village of Waubansee on the Fox River. They would try to recruit any Indians they met to join them. A good trail would follow the west bank of the Fox River downstream, and they would follow this for thirteen miles to where they would encounter a great, dense forest called the Big Wood, which the whites feared entering.[210] Within these woods they would make their encampment, to sally forth on their raids. Included among these raids was to be a joint effort with the Potawatomies of the village of Meau-eus against the nearby settlement of whites who had so grievously harmed them.

They separated then, and the main portion with Black Hawk worked assiduously to wipe out their own trail and the one they were following, which had been made by their women and children and the warriors accompanying them. They paused to rest and sleep for only brief periods, traveling night and day, and finally overtook the leading contingent of their people about midday yesterday some four miles above the mouth of the Pecatonica, just as they were approaching the Winnebagoes' Turtle Village, where White Crow was chief.

A dog feast had been prepared for them to celebrate their great victory, and for the first time in many weeks, every member of Black Hawk's band had all he could eat. Despite that, they did not linger long here, the specter of pursuit continuing to plague them even at this time. When they left, late in the day, their numbers were augmented by nearly a score of young Winnebago warriors who were electing to go against the wishes of some of their elders and join the Sacs and Foxes in their soon-to-be-launched raids against the whites. One chief accompanied them, and only temporarily. This was White Crow, and he had come along only to show them the way to the remote hiding place where they would be safe to establish their camp.

Well into the Wisconsin country and fourteen miles upstream from the Turtle Village, they paused to rest and sleep.[211] It was dark now but they built no fires, and what little conversation they engaged in was in hushed tones, as if in fear they might be heard. In four hours they were again on the move, the flotilla of canoes skimming silently against the current and the hooves of a multitude of horses thudding in a heavy undertone of accompaniment along the east bank. A detachment of the forty men brought up the rear more slowly, working methodically and ceaselessly with bundles of limber switches, many with leaves still attached, to scrape and sweep and smooth the ground surface until the tracks the horses had left were obliterated. As dawn was breaking they passed the mouth of a large river entering from the northwest. White Crow called it Yaharaseepe, and said that a day's journey upstream on it, the river swelled mightily four times in succession to form the wide waters that were called Kegonsa and Waubesa and Monona and Mendota — the Four Lakes.[212] The river began some distance above the lakes, White Crow told Black Hawk, but it was in the area of the Four Lakes where there were important Winnebago villages, including that of the powerful Chief Spotted Arm.

Another seven miles up the Rock River beyond the Yaharaseepe, the large band of Indians reached the point where the river widened until it became the large lake seven miles long and three miles wide that White Crow called Koshkonong — The-Lake-We-Live-On. At the northern end of the lake the shorelines were extremely marshy, as was the shoreline of the Rock River above the lake, which they were continuing to follow, but White Crow took the lead and unerringly led them to a place close to where the Bark River entered from the east. The ground was even more marshy here. In a column two horses abreast now, White Crow continued leading them on a tortuous route that, while it looked little different than the surrounding ground, was firm and strong. Just yards in either direction, however, it became a marshy morass in which a horse would thrash and flounder shoulder-deep. Finally they swung close to the river again and crossed a cattail-flanked spit onto a low, flat, island some three hundred yards long and one hundred feet wide. Except for one well-hidden gravelly bank ideal for landing, the island's shoreline was a tangle of dense, bushy undergrowth that blocked the view in or out.[213]

Black Hawk watched as the canoeists beached their craft at the one open spot and then quickly unloaded them and dragged them farther ashore to make room for those still coming behind. The horsemen went into an impromptu procession in a counterclockwise fashion, stepping off on their mounts the perimeter of the island, their expressions and those of the canoeists silently expressing their satisfaction.

White Crow pulled his horse up beside Black Hawk's. "You are here," he said simply. "I can do no more now."

"For my people," replied Black Hawk, "and for myself, I thank you. Now the old people can rest."

"And the young ones fight," White Crow finished. "Now I must go from here to speak with Spotted Arm and Whirling Thunder, and you are to follow as soon as you have sent your young men where they are to go. The trail I have pointed out to you, which leads toward the sunset, will bring you to Spotted Arm's village in half a day's quick ride. The way will have been made ready for you. Farewell, my friend, until tomorrow." He rode off then, and passed out of sight through the screen of brush without a backward glance.

Well before nightfall theirs was an operating camp, and into the night Black Hawk and the other chiefs and principal warriors talked, dividing themselves into war parties and discussing where, beginning at dawn, they would go and what they would do. And late in the night, while the women and children slept, many of the warriors prayed that, for what lay ahead of them now, the Great Spirit would give them the eye of the eagle, the strength of the bear, and the wit of the wolf.

[May 18, 1832 — Friday]

John and Joseph Naper had not been having an easy time convincing the residents in and around this little settlement of theirs that the warning brought to them by the young Potawatomi chief two days ago should be taken seriously.[214] The young chief, Shata, was known to a number of them and had always been considered as much a friend to the whites as his father, Chaubenee.[215] Yet, the settlers were reluctant to abandon their homes just because an Indian had brought word that *un*friendly Indians were on the warpath and headed for this area. The Naper brothers were among the few who strongly urged that the residents pack up and head into Chicago for protection, but while it was the dominant subject of discussion, no decision had been reached until early this morning, when Barney Laughton showed up in company with a half-breed named Burrasaw and three Potawatomies.

Barney — actually Bernardus, though not too many knew this — and his brother, David, had for many years operated an Indian trading post on the South Branch of the Chicago River, an operation that they had humorously dubbed Hardscrabble. About four years ago they had sold that place and established a new trading post, which also included a tavern, about eight miles farther west at a fording place of the Des Plaines River that was often referred to as River Ford.[216] The point was, Barney Laughton knew the Indians very well, and having been warned by Sauganash and Chechepinqua of possible trouble coming, he took it seriously enough to send his wife, Sofia, and their children to Chicago while he came here to Naper's settlement to learn what they'd heard.

The men talked over the possible meaning of what seemed to be shaping up, trying to decide whether it betokened a real threat or was just another false alarm. At one point Barney turned and spoke rapidly in the Potawatomi tongue to the three Indians with him. When he turned back to the settlers, he was nodding faintly.

"They say," he told them, "that the warnings we have received are most likely true, but that the best way to know for certain would be to go to the Big Wood, where Shata has his village, and talk to him again. Two days have passed since he came to warn you, and since then he may have learned more. I'm for following that advice. I'm going to go on to Shata's village and talk to him personally. Anybody here who'd like to come along is welcome."

Both Naper brothers, along with Christopher Payne and several other settlers, joined in and rode the ten miles north-northwest to the southern edge of the Big Wood where Shata's village was located. The chief was not there, but a number of his people were, and Laughton, Burrasaw, and the three Potawatomies questioned them closely. Laughton's expression became tighter the more they talked. At last he turned to the others of the party.

"We've got trouble and there's no doubt about it," he said. "The Sacs under Black Hawk are definitely on the warpath. They wiped out a three hundred-man ranger detachment on the Rock River about forty-five miles west of here three days ago. Then they came and set up camp in the Big Wood at a place called the Blackberry Timber, about four miles north of here. As soon as it was set up, they painted themselves for war and set off down the Fox, which means they must've passed about three miles west of your settlement. Shata left to follow them without their knowing about it. The whole business is big trouble. I'd say — "

Laughton was interrupted by a nearby squaw, who, pointing at Joe Naper, several times loudly repeated the same word: "*Puckachee! Puckachee!*"

"What the devil does that mean?" Joe asked.

"It means several things," Laughton said grimly, "all pretty much the same. It means 'Be off!' or 'Go quickly!' or 'Run for your life!' It's one of the most urgent expressions in the Potawatomi tongue, and what it says, in essence, is that peril is imminent and you and your friends better get the hell out of your settlement *now!*"

The party needed no further encouragement than that. Laughton and his four men decided to wait at the village for Shata to return, but the Naper settlers had ridden home immediately, arriving here about an hour ago, in late afternoon. What they reported to the settlers was enough to convince them to leave, but they had received another warning, even more unsettling, just a short while ago, when Shata himself arrived on a horse nearly dead from exhaustion. He had not been back to his village since his departure and had come directly here at a gallop from Hollenbeck's Grove, a settlement along the Fox River just over twenty miles southwest of here.[217]

"If you wish to save your own lives," he told them, "you *must* leave now. I followed the war party to that white man's village you call Hollenbeck's. I could not tell from where I watched if any whites were killed. They may have heeded my earlier warning and gone away. It would be good if they did, because if they did not, then they are no longer alive. When I left to come here, the war party was killing all the animals and destroying all the goods and setting fire to all the buildings. Hollenbeck's is no more! Now, I must go. There are still others to be warned."

Since it was obvious that Shata's horse could not travel more than a few miles more, John Naper gave him a fresh mount, and in moments the son of Chaubenee was gone. In the short time that had passed since then, the settlers had gathered up what articles of theirs were most dear that they could carry, and now the procession, with the Naper brothers and Christopher Payne at its head, moved away from their settlement with their wives and children and headed for Chicago. A small handful of men had volunteered to stay behind and, if possible, guard the settlement and its livestock and property from destruction.

At this very moment, Chicago was already swollen with settlers who had come in for protection. Now, not only was the dilapidated, ungarrisoned Fort Dearborn filled with them, so also was every building in the town, and the Indian agent, Thomas J. V. Owen, was presently describing the situation in a letter to the governor of the Michigan Territory, George Porter. The people from the outlying cabins and settlements, he wrote:

. . . *have collected in the Garrison to the number of about 150 effective men, pretty well armed, with plenty of ammunition & Provisions, but encumbered with about 300 helpless Women & Children . . . there is reason to believe that we are in imminent danger unless relieved by the troops now in pursuit of the Sacs.*

I am much pleased to see that the Indians of this Agency have fully evinced their determination to render no aid to the Sacs whatever in this matter — they are

*now preparing to remove their families to the river Des Plaines within twelve miles
of this place for their better security in the event of an attack from the enemy. And
I have found it necessary to send them a small quantity of Provisions to prevent
their women & children from suffering. . . .*

[*May 18, 1832 — Friday*]

General Samuel Whiteside was exhausted. Worse yet, he felt frustrated.
Under his command here at Dixon's Ferry he had over a thousand men, and he
wanted nothing more than to get them mounted and on the trail of that devil,
Black Hawk, but he couldn't do so without the authorization of General Atkinson, who should have been here days ago and still wasn't. And, he grudgingly
admitted to himself, even if he had the authority, the militia under his command
had hardly shown they had the backbone to undertake any kind of offensive
measure. They were disgusted, discouraged, disgruntled. All they talked about
was their unplanted crops, the futility of this present campaign, and being
discharged so they could go home. The "fun" of Indian fighting had been very
short-lived.

The morning after burying the dead at Old Man's Creek, he had mounted his
men and followed the trail of the Indians to their camp at the mouth of the
Kishwaukee, only to find they were gone, having dumped some of their heavier
items before leaving, evidently so they could travel more swiftly, or else to make
room for the plunder they had appropriated from Stillman's campsite — maybe
both. At any rate, their trail moved off eastwardly up the Kishwaukee, and he was
inclined to follow them, but provisions were down to a dangerously low level and
the men themselves were clamoring to go back. So reluctantly he'd given the
order, expecting to find that General Atkinson had reached Dixon's with all the
provisions and supplies. He hadn't, of course, and so here they sat, still waiting
for the commander to complete a hundred-mile journey that had thus far already
taken him eight full days, and he still wasn't here. The initial high opinion he
had harbored of Atkinson's abilities had most definitely been on the wane of late.

Since returning here to Dixon's, Whiteside had not received any official report
of the debacle Stillman's detachment had suffered. Not one officer had written
him a word about it, not even Stillman, and the bits and pieces he was beginning
to glean from remarks made and conversations overheard were causing him to
suspect very strongly that there was more about that whole "withdrawal," as some
of the men termed it, than met the eye.

Atkinson was a stickler for having reports submitted to him from his commanders, and since Whiteside had only written him a few letters and no reports
at all, this evening he had been writing a lengthy account of everything that had
occurred, so far as he knew it, since separating from Atkinson at the beginning
of the march up Rock River. With a heavy sigh, Whiteside resumed writing:

*. . . Previous to my arrival at Dixons, about two hundred and sixty men had
been assembled by order of his Excellency, the Governor of Illinois, under the*

command of Majr [sic] Stillman. I was requested by his Excellency to take
command of those men, and give them marching orders, but did not feel myself
authorized to assume command, or give them any instructions whatever. Con-
trary to my wish, however, his Excellency, on the 12th, gave Major Stillman an
order to move against the hostile Indians, and take all necessary steps to reduce
them to submission. No report of the circumstances of that unfortunate affair
which took place near Sycamore Creek on the 14th. between the Indians and Majr
Stillman has yet been received, either from Majr Stillman, or any officer under his
command. He will probably report to the Governor, or to yourself. On the
morning of the 15th., as soon as I could after hearing of the disaster, I moved with
my whole Brigade to the battle ground, about 30 miles from this place, partly with
the view of burying the dead, and partly in hopes that the Indians, flushed with
victory over Majr Stillman, might be induced to risk a battle with me. I found
and buried eleven of the dead bodies of our own men, who had been cut and
mangled in a most barbarous manner. On entering the Indian Village, I found
that they had decamped in great haste, leaving most of their heavy articles, and
a large quantity of peltry &c. Our men were at this time entirely out of provisions,
and I returned to this place [Dixon's] to await your arrival and to receive further
orders.

> *I have the honor to be your obdt servt.*
> *Saml: Whiteside Brig. Genl Commanding*
> *Brigade of Mounted Volunteers.*

[May 18, 1832 — Friday]

In the dimness of the council chamber at Chief Spotted Arm's village, John
H. Kinzie waited patiently for the smoking to finish so he could address the
Winnebagoes. A council fire had been built in the middle of the hard-packed
earth that was the circular floor of this huge conical structure, and the smoke
from that fire drifted lazily upward to escape from the flapped vent at the top.

Seated beside Kinzie was his remarkably skilled interpreter, the thirty-
six-year-old half-breed Pierre Paquette. A close friendship had developed between the two since Kinzie had become Indian agent at Fort Winnebago, yet
Kinzie knew little about the man's background beyond the fact that he had been
one of the signers of the Green Bay Treaty of 1828, that he was named after his
French trader-father, and that his mother was a Winnebago woman named
Kaurayneta.[218] He did not know that Paquette's father was dead, having been
killed some years earlier by a drunken Potawatomi, nor that his mother had a
brother who was one of the most powerful chiefs among the Winnebagoes,
Kauraykawsaw — White Crow. In spite of the fact that, as on this occasion,
Kinzie had met White Crow several times, he had no idea the chief was
Paquette's uncle.

Kinzie and Paquette had journeyed here from the thirty-five-mile-distant Fort

Winnebago because Kinzie, even given the evident risk at this time when a serious Indian war had just been ignited, felt there was good reason to believe the Winnebagoes would ally themselves with the Sacs and Foxes against the Americans and that it was his duty to come and try to prevent that from occurring. Knowing only too well how swayed his charges might be over the news of Black Hawk's victory, since the Sacs and Foxes were their friends, he had made preparations over the objections of his wife, Juliette, who was very fearful he would be killed, and set out at once for Spotted Arm's village on the highest and largest of the Four Lakes, Mendota. Here on the southwestern shore, on a beautiful parklike point of land overlooking the lake, the picturesque village was located — several hundred tipis, many of which were decorated with interestingly rendered picture stories in red, black, and white paints, depicting great hunts and great battles and special occasions.[219]

At last the ceremonial smoking ended and John Kinzie rose to speak, and Pierre Paquette rose beside him and stood ready to interpret. The two-score blanket-draped Indians on hand became very still and gave him their undivided attention. In the dimness he could not see their features, but he knew they were watching him closely for any sign of nervousness or weakness, and though he was indeed nervous, he did not let it show in his expression or voice. He began by reminding them of the friendship they had enjoyed with the United States for many years and of the annuities that were faithfully paid to them at the Indian agency. He reminded them that the great father in Washington thought of them kindly as his children and wished to see no harm come to them, but that this was sadly very possible if they should listen to bad birds that might land among them and sing songs of war.

"The older and wiser chiefs know well," he went on, "the need not to offend the great father who loves them. They know the futility of attempting to stand against him, and that if they have complaints about him, he will listen to those complaints and do all he can to make things right. It is the young men who must be held closely and cautioned often, since their blood runs hot and often they do not see the pain and sorrow that lies beyond the excitement of war. It is therefore up to these wise chiefs to counsel their young men and instill in them the need to keep their hearts and minds cool and at peace."

Kinzie waited a moment until Paquette had finished, and then he sat down. Paquette remained standing, however, and now, as Chief Spotted Arm rose and began to speak, reversed his roles, interpreting into English, smoothly and only a beat or two behind the chief.

"Little Father," Spotted Arm began, referring not to Kinzie's physical size, but his place as spokesman of the great father, "we have heard your good words, and our hearts are open to you. We do not wish to go to war. Bad times have begun, and it will be a long while before they are ended, but it is our intention to keep our peace and stay in our places and take no part in these bad things. You speak the truth, for we are the older and wiser and we know well what so often lies in the hearts and minds of our young men, some of whom would not be denied this opportunity to test the strength of their arms and the quickness of their wits in combat. We promise to you that we will talk to these young men, that we will caution them and advise them that they must not do this, and that to do it they would be going against the wishes of their fathers, who want only peace. All our bands with the exception of one — that of Wabokieshiek, he whom you know as the Prophet — are intent upon remaining at peace. Over Wabokieshiek we have little control, and he is aware that if he brings wrath down upon his own head, there are none among us who will help him. But he is only one, and he has few who follow him. The great father should be informed that he speaks and acts for himself only, and not for the tribe into which he was born, though one of his parents was Sac. We here, Little Father, are determined to remain friendly with you and keep aloof from the Sacs. We had at first, in friendship, invited them to come live among us upon the Pecatonica, there to raise their corn and live in peace, but when we learned that this would distress our great father, we told them that we had taken away that invitation and that they must not come among us. That is where we stand. The Sacs have gone whither we do not know, but we are apart from them and we are at peace."

There were a few more speakers — notable among them Whirling Thunder and White Crow — who more or less echoed what Spotted Arm had said. Then Kinzie spoke again, thanking them for showing to him the goodness in their hearts. He thanked them also for their hospitality, and then he left, Paquette by his side. It was now late afternoon, and it would be long after dark before they reached Fort Winnebago.

As the Winnebagoes filed out of the great tipi and moved toward their own smaller lodges, the blanket-draped Indian who had sat beside White Crow throughout the council now walked with him and, after they had gone a short distance and were apart from the others, turned and spoke tightly.

"He was white. He was American. He was alone. He should have been killed."

"No, Black Hawk," White Crow said, an edge of sternness in his voice. "The little father of the Winnebagoes — Shawneeawkee, as we call him, after his father, whom we called the same — is our friend, as was his father. There are other white men who can be killed, but not this one. That is something you must make very clear to your warriors."[220]

They resumed their walk, continuing in silence for a distance, and then paused before the three tipis where the portion of warriors who had gone with Black Hawk were staying. White Crow reached out and put his hand on Black Hawk's shoulder. "I have told you that there are some among us who will help you where we can. I can tell you now that we are going even beyond that. Before the dawn this morning, a first war party of our young men slipped away from this village unseen. Whirling Thunder does not know this. Spotted Arm suspects it, but he does not know. They will learn of it later, when the party returns. These young men have gone out for themselves, not for the tribe. They have moved to the west and south of where we stand, to the places that are less than a day's ride from here — perhaps to the places where the white men take lead from the ground, perhaps to where they have built the road and so often travel back and forth from the Illinois to Rock Island and the Mississippi River settlements. They will not return until their scalping knives have tasted blood."

[May 18, 1832 — Friday]

Private William Durley, who had been riding in the rear beside Private Vincent Smith, thumped his heels into his horse's side, passed the other two privates in front of them, and moved up beside Sergeant Stahl, who rode in the lead beside the mail contractor. The two-abreast column had been their order of ride ever since leaving Galena this morning.

"What d'you think, Fred," Durley asked the sergeant, "we gonna reach Dixon's before dark?"

"Hell, I don't know, Bill." Stahl turned to the lanky man beside him. "What do you think, John?"

John Winters reached into his pocket and took out a heavy gold watch, flipping open the lid easily with his thumb and squinting at the hands. "Almost five o'clock now," he said. He replaced the watch in his pocket and pointed toward the large island of trees they were approaching. "That's Buffalo Grove we're coming up on now, which means we've got twelve miles to go.[221] Sure, I don't see why we wouldn't. Might be we'll even get there 'fore sunset."

"Can't be soon enough for me," called Jim Smith from behind them. "I'm tired."

"That's not news," said Redding Bennett, riding beside him. "You're always tired."

The group of six laughed at that, and in the rear, Vincent Smith slapped his leg and said, "You're stealing my thunder, Red. I been telling Brother Jim that all his life."

Durley reined in a bit and fell back to his place beside Vincent. He was tired, too, since they'd been in the saddle all day, but he was not going to complain and leave himself open to ribbing from the others as Vincent had.

The four privates and one sergeant were a detail from Captain James Stephenson's company of mounted riflemen in Galena, under command of Colonel Henry Dodge. All five were armed with rifles, and, escorting the regular mail contractor John D. Winters, they were carrying a number of dispatches themselves from Galena to General Atkinson and Governor Reynolds at Dixon's Ferry.

Just as they were beginning to enter the northwestern edge of Buffalo Grove, the attack came with devastating unexpectedness. From the knee-deep buffalo grass rimming the woods, in which they had been lying in ambush, six Winnebago warriors, their faces and upper bodies painted green to camouflage them, rose to their feet with horrendous shrieks and instantly fired all six of their rifles.

Two of the bullets missed entirely. One buzzed through the fabric on the shoulder of John Winter's coat without touching his skin. Another went through Vincent Smith's hat only the width of the ball itself above his head. Yet another grazed the back of Fred Stahl's coat. The sixth struck low in William Durley's left side and continued through his body.

The other five whites heard Durley say, "Oh, God!" and wheeled about in time to see him fall from his saddle. Instantly, making no effort to return the fire now that the Indians' weapons were empty, or to aid Durley, who was writhing facedown on the road, the five put their horses into a frantic gallop back the way they had come.

The green-painted warriors rushed to the injured man, and one, who had a sword, swung it viciously and caught Durley at the nape, very nearly severing his head. One of the Indians swiftly scalped him, held the dripping hairpiece high, and screamed in triumph, while one of the others cut off the dead man's nose. Then, still shrieking with the exultation of their victory, the six raced into the woods to where they had hidden their horses.

[*May 19, 1832 — Saturday*]

There was an air of electric tension in the encampment at Dixon's Ferry this morning, a sense of breaths being held for that order to be given which would once again plunge them into the unknown against an adversary they had quickly grown to fear, and who seemed able to move as silently, as quickly, and as undetectably as the breeze.

At last General Henry Atkinson emerged from the headquarters tent, and the tension stretched to the breaking point. Atkinson looked over the assemblage of soldiers standing beside their mounts, then glanced at Samuel Whiteside standing close to him.

"Well, General," he said, "it's been a while in coming, but now it's time. Let's go find those damned Indians."

The fact that the force had been brought into readiness so quickly was something of a tribute to Atkinson. It had been almost noon when, the day before yesterday, General Henry Atkinson and his regulars, under command of Colonel Zachary Taylor — including Major Long's battalion of foot — arrived at Dixon's Ferry, the men in a state of almost abject exhaustion from the efforts of pulling the two huge keelboats and six Mackinac boats filled with supplies all the way upriver from the Mississippi. The sound of gunfire as they approached had caused Colonel Taylor to put all the soldiers on armed alert, and it was with considerably less than good humor that Taylor and Atkinson discovered the shots had merely been a number of the militiamen shooting, not only at targets but also at one another, to see how close they could come without hitting someone.

The two officers had immediately repaired to the headquarters tent at Camp No. 10, where they held largely unsatisfactory conferences with Governor Reynolds, who was almost pathetically glad to have Atkinson here to shoulder responsibility, and General Whiteside, who kept subtly reminding Atkinson that everything that had gone wrong was the governor's fault. There had been meetings, as well, with other officers of the militia. In all these sessions there seemed to be an appalling inability on the part of everyone to give a clear, concise account of what had actually occurred in the Stillman affair. Not only were those interviewed hazy in their recollections, all gave the distinct impression of hiding information. Further, the militiamen were still clamoring for discharge, and morale was at a very low ebb. Insubordination was rampant, and the men were almost universally fractious, gloomy, and ill-tempered. The commanding general's mood changed to one of mixed emotions when he learned that Governor Reynolds had not only successfully cajoled the remaining ready-to-bolt troops of Stillman's and Bailey's battalions into remaining and continuing to protect the exposed frontier until the regulars arrived, but then had promoted Major Isaiah Stillman to Lieutenant Colonel and made him second in command of the 5th Regiment of Illinois Militia.[222]

Atkinson lost no time in ordering Colonel Taylor to begin putting matters into shape at once, and within minutes all regular and militia officers were assembled and brought to attention. They were then told in no uncertain terms to bring their units immediately to a military bearing or suffer harsh consequences. The regular officers were to direct the militia officers in all such matters. With fresh and plentiful provisions on hand again, the volunteers quickly became much more tractable. Atkinson's adjutant immediately posted the order that the general had dictated to him:

ORDER NO. 16

The frequent firing of Arms in and about the vicinity of the encampments of the different corps of the army composed of the U.S. Infy. and the State troops of Illinois now in the field compels the Comdg. Genl. to forbid a practice so dangerous to the individual members of the different corps and derogatory to the military character of well organized troops. No Officer or private, therefore, will fire again in camp or on the march without permission, or an order from the Comdg. Officer of his Regt. or company.

By order of Brig. Genl Atkinson
    (signed) A. S. Johnston A.D.C. & A.A.A.Genl.

The general had then been informed that two very influential friendly Potawatomi chiefs were waiting to see him, and he gave them an audience immediately. The two were in the company of Gholson Kercheval, captain of the militia of Chicago and subagent to Thomas Owen, who had brought a dispatch from the agent and was acting as interpreter for the two Indians, though both could speak English adequately. The Indians were introduced by both their

Indian and English names, Sauganash — Billy Caldwell — and Cheche-pinqua — Alexander Robinson. Both chiefs professed strong friendship for the Americans and declared that they would not join forces with the Sacs, abhorring what Black Hawk's force was doing, and that they had received assurances from the Winnebagoes that they, too, would have nothing to do with Black Hawk's people. They told Atkinson that he would soon be visited by Waubansee as well, who was furious over what was occurring and was organizing the warriors of the friendly Potawatomies to aid the Americans in their efforts to find and defeat Black Hawk's force. Atkinson thanked them, supplied them with provisions, and then read the letter from Owen. The Indian agent at Chicago advised him that a city militia had been established and that frightened settlers were flocking into town, putting a burden on residents. Owen had been informed that Major William Whistler, at Fort Niagara with his regulars, had been ordered to Chicago to regarrison Fort Dearborn, but had not arrived yet. In the meanwhile, reports had come in of settlements being attacked along the Fox and Du Page rivers. The situation in Chicago was growing tense — what should they do? Atkinson dashed off a brief note and gave it to Kercheval to take back with him. It said:

Sir Mr. Kircheval [sic] *will inform you of the present state of things in this quarter. I have to request that you will advise the Indians of your Agency to remain quiet, and take no part in the present difficulties, and keep me advised of any thing* [sic] *of importance in relation to the present state of hostility.*

  Genl. Atkinson to Col: Owen Indian: Agent Chicago

Finally ready to take a look at the numerous dispatches awaiting his attention, General Atkinson ordered a number of his officers to stand by as expresses for dispatches of his own that he would soon be sending out in reply. Included among the officers who were tabbed for the express duty were the two regular officers who had joined Atkinson early this morning, having come upriver from Fort Armstrong. Both had been on furlough in different locations in the South when they heard news of Black Hawk's invasion of Illinois and the military mobilization that had resulted, and both had terminated their own leaves in order to hasten back here. One was thirty-two-year-old Captain William S. Harney, who was visiting his home in Tennessee when he got the word; the other was the handsome, twenty-four-year-old West Pointer from Mississippi, Lieutenant Jefferson Davis.[223]

Among the dispatches awaiting Atkinson was a letter from Colonel Henry Dodge saying that he was in Gratiot's Grove and that:

. . . I will immediately raise as many mounted men as possible and hold the militia of this county in a state of requisition, to march when called on. I

*addressed you a few days since [and] my letter [of May 13] was opened by Govr.
Reynolds & Genl. Whitesides. The contents will no doubt be communicated to
you. The people of the Mining Country are badly prepared to receive so great a
shock as a Defeat of the Illinois Militia is calculated to produce.*

*I will endeavor to draw the settlements in immediately and if possible get the
inhabitants to fort themselves The mounted men I may be able to bring into the
field will act as an immediate cover to the settlements. If you could furnish us an
additional supply of arms it would aid us greatly in the defence of the country.
The victory obtained by the Hostile Sacks [sic] is, I fear, calculated to decide the
wavering of both Winnebagoes & Potawatomies against us. It is a most unfortunate state of things. Governor Reynolds should not have run the risque [sic] of
Defeat in the present state of our Indian relations. Could you have been permitted
to carry into effect your plans, the Menominees in concert with the Militia would
have driven out the Sacks and have settled our Indian difficulties for years to
come.*

*I would have waited [sic] your arrival, but knowing the state of the Rock River
and the difficulties you must have in ascending that river, I thought it adviseable
[sic] to return to our settlements immediately.*

*I would be thankfull [sic] to you for your advice & direction in this momentous
state of our affairs.*

I am Dear General sincerely and truly your friend

                                                  H. Dodge

Wishing that all the citizen soldiers were even half as good as Dodge, General
Atkinson put that letter close at hand to one side to be answered immediately
upon his finishing reading the dispatches. A whole packet of letters had come
from Galena, not only from militia colonel James Strode, but also from numerous residents. Strode complained about the residents and they about him. Strode
said the residents did not want to comply with his demands because they didn't
like him. The residents complained that Strode was overbearing, officious,
dictatorial, and, all too frequently, brutal when he did not get his way. As one
of the residents stated it:

*. . . Colonel Strode is a man of marked ability as a lawyer and politician, but he
is singularly lacking in any faculty for removing opposition to his domineering
spirit save by brute force, and that method in a mining camp is not calculated to
effect conciliation. We would recommend that our affairs be placed as the responsibility of our militia Captain H. Hezekiah Gear, a man of strong personality, great force of character and of commanding influence with the sturdy
miners, who has smoothed and softened the ruffled tempers of the miners suffering
from the bungled tactics of Colonel Strode.*

Atkinson summoned Captain William Harney and Lieutenant Jefferson
Davis, along with several other officers, and gave them special orders to provision

themselves and leave immediately, moving with all haste to Galena, where they would make every effort to salve the dispute between Colonel Strode and the residents, to eliminate the feelings of hostility so rampant there, and to establish defenses for the general good.

As soon as they were gone, Atkinson turned back to the correspondence at hand. There was a letter from militia colonel William S. Hamilton at his diggings in the mining district, asking what he could do to help, and so, knowing through Dodge that Hamilton was a good man, Atkinson quickly dictated a response.

Col. W. S. Hamilton of the mineral district will take command of a small reconnoitering party, proceed to Sycamore Creek on Rock River, examine the country and ascertain if practicable the position or route of the hostile Indians. Having obtained the information, they will return to these Head Quarters and report it.

By order of Brig Genl Atkinson
　　　　　　　　(signed) Albt. S. Johnston A D C & Act A.A.Genl

Beyond that there were a number of letters of descending importance that would be answered as time allowed.

Turning then to the most urgent letters to be written, Atkinson had answered that of Henry Dodge first:

Head Qrs Right Wing West: Department
Dixon's Ferry 17th. May 1832

General   Your express handed me your letter of yesterday on my arrival here to day at 12 O'clock.

I regret that Gen: Stillman was sent to reconnoitre the Indians before my arrival, & particularly the result of the encounter he had with them. It has not only encouraged the Indians, but closed the door against settling the difficulty without bloodshed. As things stand, we must try to subdue the enemy. I shall organise [sic] the forces tomorrow, and march up the river next morning. I have 320 regular troops, these with one six-pounder, & about 1200 volunteers will constitute my strength, which ought to be sufficient to effect the object before me. I think it will be best that you should organise a force for the protection of your neighbourhood [sic]. I regret that I have not a spare arm to furnish you. If you could send to Prairie du Chien you can draw from thence as many as may be necessary, which you have this my authority to do. Two Pottawattamie [sic] Chiefs are here, who came to say that the Pottawattamies will remain peaceable, and not join the Sacs. They say also that the Winnebagoes have sent to them saying that they also will not join, and advising them to the same course. How far they will be faithful it will be difficult to surmise. If you should receive any information as to the movement of the Indians, let me know it as early as practicable.

He signed it and then continued writing and dictating. The evening meal was brought to him, and he ate mechanically as he worked. Not until the evening was well advanced did he finally retire, falling asleep almost instantly. Early in the morning yesterday he was at it again, interviewing people, dictating orders, tying up loose ends, and gradually getting this military machine back in business. One of his first tasks was dictating the order for the army to begin its pursuit of Black Hawk:

> *Head Quarters right Wing West: Dept.*
> *Dixons Ferry Rock river 18th. May 1832*

ORDER NO. 17
The volunteer Illinois troops will draw ten days rations to day. Genl. White-sides Brigade will be in readiness to move in the morning. Col. Johnsons Battalion will remain at this post (Dixon's) as a corps of reserve until the return of the main army or until further orders from the Comdg. Genl.
The regular troops will move with the marching Brigade. Maj. Long will receive special instructions relative to the disposition of his Battalion. Col. Johnson will call at Genl. Head Qrs. for further instructions.
The sick will remain in Hospital at this post, and all arrangements necessary for their comfort will be made.

By order of Brig. Genl. Atkinson
        (signed) A. S. Johnston A.D.C. & A. A. A. Genl

The order to Major Long followed:

ORDER NO. 18
The Comdg. Genl deems it necessary to detach Capt. Pratts company of Foot volunteers & Capt. White's company of mounted men to Rock Island for the better security of that post. They will be held in readiness to move tomorrow morning. Special instructions will be given them before their departure.

For the remainder of the day, the camp at Dixon's Ferry was alive with activity as the army, regulars and volunteers alike, prepared for the forthcoming move up Rock River. Lieutenant Colonel Stillman and Major Bailey, who had been maintaining an unusually low profile since Atkinson's arrival, seethed at the ignominy of remaining at Dixon's to watch over the sick and injured until the army's return, and in low voices they made it clear they were sick and tired of this whole business.

This morning the activity in camp continued, as companies put themselves and their mounts in full readiness for the expedition and Atkinson, in the headquarters tent, took care of the final details. Two separate orders had yet to be given, and he dictated them to Adjutant Johnston quickly:

> *Head Qrs. right Wing west: Department*
> *Dixon's Ferry 19th. May 1832.*

ORDER NO. 19

Capt Whites & Capt. Pratts companies of Volunteers will embark this morning in the large Keel Boat under the orders of Capt. White & proceed to Fort Armstrong and report to Major Beall U.S. Army

Capt White will carry with him such of the sick & wounded of the Army as may be designated, who are to be received by the U.S. Surgeon at Fort Armstrong & afforded medical aid

By order of Brig Genl Atkinson

That order would allow the most grievously wounded from the Stillman Defeat, along with those most seriously ill, to be returned to Fort Armstrong in relative comfort and receive there the treatment that was unavailable to them here.

The second order of the day was as a result of the intelligence he had received from Gholson Kercheval and Thomas Owen of Chicago:

ORDER NO. 20

Col. Johnson will move with as little delay as possible with four of the most efficient companies now under his command, supplied with rations for six days, for the settlements on Fox & De Page [sic] rivers, reported to have been attacked by the hostile Indians, and afford the most prompt succour [sic] to the inhabitants. . . .

Finally, there was but one last letter for him to write, which he had been putting off until now — an advisory to his own commanding officer, Major General Alexander Macomb in Washington:

General   I have the honor to inform you that the regular troops reached this point on the evening of the 17th. Inst: the Illinois volunteers under Gen: Whitesides accompanied by Governor Reynolds arrived on the 12th. The hostile Indians are still before us, ascending, it is understood, this river. We proceed this morning in pursuit.

I regret to inform you that a Battalion of Rangers under Genl. Stillman, that had been ordered out by Governor Reynolds for the protection of the frontier, fell in with and were defeated by the hostile Sacs on the 14th. Inst, near the mouth of Sycamore creek, forty miles above this, with a loss of eleven men killed and a few wounded; a few Indians were also killed. I do not hold myself accountable for the movement of the force under Gen. Stillman, as they had not been placed under my command. . . .

With the final details completed by mid-morning and Major John Bliss left in command at Dixon's, Atkinson emerged from his tent, let his gaze fall across the troops in readiness, and then remarked to General Whiteside, "Well, General, it's been a while in coming, but now it's time. Let's go find those damned Indians."

[*May 19, 1832 — Saturday*]

In the study of his large house in Galena, Dr. Horatio Newhall was just finishing reading the "extra" published by the *Galenian*. It would be a good issue to send to his brother in Salem, Massachusetts, to keep him apprised of what was occurring here, since the paper was filled with the news of the Stillman Defeat, mobilization of troops, the running controversy between Colonel Strode and the residents, fortifications being established, and the pervasive fears of the isolated families who were flocking into their nearest towns and building defenses.

Forts were under construction in every major community. The one here in the center of town was being called Fort Galena, and about a dozen miles away, Apple River Fort was being built at the town of Apple River. But the majority were being erected in virtually every community farther north in the lead mining district of the southwestern Wisconsin country.[224]

The big story, of course, was Stillman's Defeat and the anger of the residents about it, exemplified by the line in this "extra" that declared, *The people here feel determined to avenge the bloody outrage on Stillman's troops.*

Dr. Newhall put the newspaper to one side of his desk and took out fresh paper. It had been several years since he'd seen Isaac, and he had gotten into the habit of writing to him regularly with all the news of the frontier. Now he dipped his pen and began in a flowing, beautifully formed cursive:

Galena   May 19th 1832

Dear Brother, . . . We had four Steam Boat arrivals yesterday, and one this morning. One from Prairie du Chien with arms, one from Rock Island with arms and Cannon, and the others from St. Louis. The Steam Boat "Dove" is impressed for the use of the town. Every man here is a soldier. A guard is stationed on every Boat to prevent able bodied men from going off. We are building a stockade in the Centre [sic] of the town, to fly to in case of emergency. We have fifty mounted riflemen, who act as rangers, making a circuit about 15 miles from town, and a guard detailed every night, of 40 men, on the skirts of the village. My Rifle & pistols are by my bedside every night. Great alarm prevails thro' [sic] the country, but I think there can be but little danger here. By the "Galenian" I send you, and by the Galenian "Extra", you will learn all the news. Except that the army have since gone out to bury the dead, and found but twelve dead, and these scalped & horridly mangled. Mr. Dougherty, who married a half breed Winnebago, and lives among them, arrived in town to day, says they notified him to remove, as his life was in danger; that the Rock River band of Winnebagoes had declared war against the U States and joined the British band of Sacks [sic]. I will inform you by postscript, what is going on. Galena is crowded with people who have flocked here for protection. I am appointed Surgeon to the Galena forces, & draw pay accordingly.

The mails are all stopped. I send this letter by S. Boat "Java" to St. Louis. I am glad the Indians have come to an open rupture: now the affair will be permanently *settled. Business of all kinds has been interrupted for several years on acct. of Indian disturbances. . . .*

Newhall stopped writing and glanced at the clock on the mantel. It was just a little after noon, and he decided to stop for a bite of lunch and get back to the letter after a while. But when he returned less than two hours later, he had an arm around the shoulders of a small boy, who was crying. He comforted the child and set him on a chair at his elbow, and then began to write again in the letter. Dr. Newhall was pale and obviously shaken, and his handwriting was less flowing than it had been:

2 o'clock P.M. *Awful news has this moment arrived. Our Express which we sent to the main army yesterday has this moment returned. It consisted of six men, fine young men who volunteered their services. When within twelve miles of Dixon's Ferry where the main army is supposed to be, they were suddenly surprised by a party of Indians, who fired on them. Mr. Durley was shot dead. He exclaimed "O God" & died. Mr. Smith had a Ball pass thro' [sic] his hat 1/2 an inch above his head. They have just arrived, all but poor Durley. He was a good young man, and of a very respectable family. He was my friend; if tears were of use I could shed them for months. I have known him for ten years. His little nephew is now at my elbow weeping for the awful death of his unkle [sic]. If there is any thing on earth I now most desire, it is to kill Indians enough to avenge the death of Durley. I have no doubt the main army is completely surrounded by Indian spies. No communication can go from them to us, or from us to them. We have satisfactory evidence of the fact. Our fort here goes on bravely. . . .*

[*May 19, 1832 — Saturday*]

Returning from Chief Rochelle's village on the Vermilion River to the village of his uncle, Chaubenee, the young Potawatomi named Pypes was pleased to see that many settlers that had been warned to gather in the towns for their mutual safety had done so. Places like Peru and La Salle, Crozier's Landing and Ottawa were filled with people busily erecting forts and keeping watch for war parties of Indians.

It was not until Pypes approached the Davis Settlement on Indian Creek that he saw, with consternation, that the settlers there had not left, and in fact had gathered there in slightly larger numbers, evidently believing this would give them strength enough to withstand an onslaught. He considered going in and warning them again, and no doubt would have done so, except that he caught the faintest glint of movement in the woods well above the settlement. Keeping close to cover, Pypes crept up and was aghast to find that a large band of war-painted Indians were entering the timber and setting up a hidden camp. Even as he watched, he saw them dispatch three groups of two young warriors each in different directions toward the settlement. It was obvious these were reconnoitering parties who would report back to the chiefs what the situation was at the settlement, how many would be opposing them there, and how best an attack could be made.

Without waiting to see more, Pypes detoured widely around them and then put his horse into a gallop toward Chaubenee's village. He was relieved to find his uncle there when he arrived and quickly explained the situation to him. There was no doubt that an attack was imminent, and so without hesitation, Chaubenee mounted his horse and set off for the Davis Settlement. It was almost dark when he arrived there and got to the Davis home unseen.

It was the big blacksmith William Davis himself who, pistol in hand, cautiously turned down the lamps before opening the door at Chaubenee's knock. Two of his older sons, John and Edward, were right behind him, rifles in hand. When he recognized Chaubenee, he stepped outside and talked with him, telling John and Edward to stay on guard. He had an idea that Chaubenee was here to warn him again, and he wanted none of the others to hear what was being said. After the last warning, the Petticrews had become progressively more nervous, and finally the family had decided to go to Ottawa. And so they had a loss of four people. Later that evening, not able to find any accommodations, the Petticrews had returned. He didn't want that happening again, and so, though now the big blacksmith listened patiently as Chaubenee earnestly explained the peril, Davis's mind was made up, and he was shaking his head before Chaubenee finished.

"Obviously you're trying to help," Davis said. "Everyone knows you're a great friend of the whites. I don't disbelieve what you're saying and that your nephew really did see some Indians skulking about, but those are just spying parties, nothing more. We've been seeing them sneaking around for months."

"But this time — "

Davis cut him off. "Listen, we've got twenty-five people here, of which fifteen are able-bodied men who can defend themselves and their families very well.

Further, there is no place left to stay in Ottawa even if we were to leave here. No," he concluded, "as I told you before, we're not going to leave here. We can take care of ourselves very well."

"You are," said Chaubenee wearily, "a very stubborn man. I hope you and those who are with you do not pay the greatest price for that stubbornness."

[*May 19, 1832 — Saturday*]

Because of the late start this morning, General Atkinson's force had traveled only twelve miles by sunset, when a halt was called and the men began setting up camp. But hardly had they stopped when an express reached them from Major John Bliss, whom Atkinson had left in charge of the encampment at Dixon's Ferry. It was staggering news. As ordered by Atkinson before leaving camp, Colonel James Johnson had led four of his militia companies away toward the valleys of the Fox and Du Page Rivers to aid the settlers there, leaving the remaining militia, now under command of Lieutenant Colonel Isaiah Stillman, to guard the sick and injured at Dixon's. A few hours later the militia packed up and left, declaring that their departure was not desertion because their enlistment period was only three days from expiring, and that by the time they reached their home territory, it would have run out. As simply as that, they had abandoned the camp and were on their way south to the Illinois River Valley. Dixon's was now virtually defenseless.

Furious at this unexpected development, General Atkinson remounted his regulars and, ordering General Whiteside to continue the pursuit of Black Hawk with his mounted militia, set off on his return to Dixon's, wondering what next would go wrong in this miserable campaign.

[*May 20, 1832 — Sunday*]

John W. Hall and his father, William, were working under the shelter of a shed adjoining the blacksmith shop on the west side. It was a very warm day, and the work they were doing on a wagon was hot. They were pleased when Davis's eldest son, Bill, brought up a bucket of cool spring water from near where he and Emery George had been at work on the mill dam. He motioned them to come to the shop where the blacksmith and Bob Norris were working, and they followed him there. At the dam they could see Emery George working, and well beyond him, nearly half a mile away on the south side of the creek, they could see the eight who were busily planting corn — Edgar Henderson and his son, Allen, Edward and Greenbury Hall, John Henderson and his son, Henry, and two of the blacksmith's sons, Sam and Alex. The elder Davis and Norris, bare-chested and sweaty at the forge, gladly laid aside their tools to join the others in a drink of the water Bill had brought.

In the large kitchen of the house sixty or seventy yards away, Martha Davis lifted the lid from the kettle and used the big wooden spoon to stir the stew a few times before bringing a taste to her mouth. She made a face and said, "Needs salt." She glanced at the woman seated at the big bench-type table, nursing her baby, and added, "Sorry for the interruption. Go on with what you were saying, Eleanor."

Eleanor Petticrew smiled as Martha dipped her fingers into the salt bowl and scattered the salt over the surface of the stew. "Oh, that's all right, Martha," she said. "Anyway, three men came into Ottawa in a tizzy from where they lived just outside town and said some Indians had burned their houses. Some others had been shot at and chased, but I don't think anyone was hurt. What I'd like to know is, How do you tell the good Indians from the bad ones? Ottawa's in a mess. People everywhere, everybody scared to death, and they have patrols out day and night and all the men walk around with guns in their hands. It gave me the shivers. I'm glad we came back here."

"Well, we're glad you came back, too, Mrs. Petticrew," said fifteen-year-old Rachel, seated on the other side of the table. She was scratching the ears of Wags, the Davises' shaggy, nondescript dog, who sat with his head resting on her leg. Beside her, eight-year-old Elizabeth Hall was drawing a picture with a piece of thin charcoal. "We were so worried about you when you left," she said. Mary Jane Hall, kneading dough in the dry sink across the kitchen, looked over her shoulder. "I'm certainly glad we came here instead of going into town. It must be awful there."

Charlie Petticrew ran into the kitchen flapping his arms like a bird. He stopped beside his mother's chair. "I'm an eagle," he announced, "and the eagle is hungry!"

"Now, Charlie," Eleanor admonished the six-year-old, "it's only four o'clock." She smiled as William Petticrew stepped into the room from the parlor, where he and seventeen-year-old Sylvia Hall had been with the two smaller Davis boys, ten-year-old Tom and seven-year-old Jimmie. He paused, leaned against the doorjamb, and grinned at his wife. Eleanor smiled back but continued talking to Charlie. "Dinner won't be ready for another hour or so. Why don't you skedaddle outside and play until —"

She was cut off by a furious barking from Wags that startled them all. The dog leaped away from Rachel and stood stiff-legged near the wall, his hackles raised, and continued to bark.

"What in the world," said Martha. She set down her spoon and wiped her hands on her apron as she went to the door.

Petticrew gasped. "Don't open that —"

It was too late. She opened the door and abruptly cried, "My God, they're here now!" They were her last words. A tomahawk struck her head, and she fell back into the kitchen without a sound.

Petticrew leaped forward, snatched up little Charlie to get him out of the way, and slammed his shoulder against the door in an attempt to get it closed. Rachel screamed and leaped to her feet, and at the same time Eleanor got up, the baby under one arm, and ran to her, standing in front of the girl protectively, her free arm reaching back and gripping the girl around the waist. Elizabeth, still clutching her charcoal, slipped under the table. Mary Jane Hall turned with the ball of dough in her hands and stood paralyzed, her mouth open.

In the shop, the five men, having quenched their thirst, were resting and talking. The piercing scream from Rachel jerked them to their feet, and John Hall, mistaking it for a war cry, said, "There are the Indians now." The big blacksmith and Norris snatched up their guns leaning against the wall nearby, and all the men rushed out of the shop and raced to the corner of the building where they could get a view of the house. The yard was alive with Indians, twenty or thirty of them, and several were on the porch trying to force their way in.

Within the kitchen, Petticrew was still struggling to get the door closed and barred, but a rifle was thrust into his chest and fired, and he fell to the floor. The Indians leaped into the room, and one held his gun muzzle so close to Eleanor's face that when he fired, her head was slammed back, her face blackened and bloody. Rachel leaped away from her, a thready scream still coming from her throat, and ran into the parlor. She almost bumped into Sylvia. The two sisters clasped hands and together they ran to their bedroom, swung the door shut, and pushed a chair against it. Then they raced to the bed and leaped onto it, pulling the big comforter over themselves, huddling together, whimpering and trembling.

Indians were streaming into the kitchen. Instantly the dog Wags had been dispatched with a single tomahawk blow as he cowered by the wall. Elizabeth gave a little cry and leaped out from under the table, grabbing the ankle of one of the Indians and biting his leg. The Indian yelped and slammed his tomahawk down on her, striking her in the neck and killing her. Little Charlie, his head crushed by a war-club blow from another Indian, sprawled atop the dog. Yet another of the warriors jerked the wailing infant, Tommy, out of his dead mother's arms. By the dry sink, Mary Jane Hall snapped out of the paralysis that gripped her and threw the ball of dough at him. It caught him harmlessly on the back of the head and dropped to the floor, but it attracted the warrior's attention. He stepped to her and slammed his bloody tomahawk into her temple; then, shrieking fiercely, raced outside with the baby, holding him by one ankle. He swung the child around his head several times and then slammed him into a tree stump close by, crushing his head.

All of this had happened in mere instants. The five men from the blacksmith shop heard only the screams and shots from inside the house and saw the death of the child, and then the elder Davis and Norris fired at the Indians, but none fell. Around twenty shots from the Indians came in response. John Hall heard a gasp and turned. His father was on his back on the ground, a hole in the left center of his chest, his lips mouthing a prayer almost inaudibly. Even as John knelt beside him, William Hall died.

John looked around and caught a glimpse of Norris and William Davis, Jr., just rounding the back corner of the shed at a dead run and, well out into the field, the big blacksmith racing toward the nearest timber, his rifle still in his grip. William Davis looked back just in time to catch John's glance and shouted, "Take care!" and plunged on. Hearing a shriek, he turned to find a number of the Indians climbing the rail fence between the house and the shop and running toward him. He leaped to his feet and ran toward the creek, which was only twenty yards away. A couple of shots buzzed close to him, and as he ran he saw Emery George swimming frantically across the mill pond, but the young hand was not fast enough. A flurry of shots came, and George screamed before disappearing beneath the surface. Closer to him, just below the dam, John saw Bob Norris climbing out of the creek on the far side. The man dropped as more shots sounded from behind young Hall, but he couldn't tell whether Norris had been hit or had merely ducked. Far beyond in the field, the men planting corn had now begun to scatter, but more Indians were boiling from the woods to their right. The whites turned to the left and plunged on toward more woods in that direction.

The elder William Davis had nearly reached the woods when six Indians on horses emerged from it and galloped toward him. He changed direction, running on a course parallel to the edge of the woods, but they easily overtook him, and the big blacksmith went down under tomahawk blows. Back at the creek, his twenty-five-year-old son, Bill, slipped unseen into the water, plastered his head with mud, and closely hugging the high, steep bank, moved slowly downstream.

John Hall, too, reached the creek some thirty yards below the dam and threw himself over the twelve-foot-high embankment, but he landed on earth and rocks at the base, momentarily stunning himself. As the Indians appeared above, he gathered a deep breath and threw himself into the water. Shots were fired and he sensed the balls ripping through the water close to his head, but he swam to the bottom and then continued to swim and pull himself along, moving downstream. His chest began to burn with the need for air, and still he continued to move, finally coming up with concentrated slowness fifty feet from where he entered and still close to the steep embankment. Two Indians were on the bank behind, looking out across the water, expecting him to surface toward the other side. He inhaled deeply and sank again, continuing along the embankment. As his breath began to fail again, he rose cautiously and found he was out of sight of the Indians around a slight bend. Scattered shots were still being fired, but nowhere near him at the moment. He was able to take three or four good breaths and once again submerged. At the end of this breath he found a clump of driftwood branches against the bank, and shouldered his way inside until he could barely see out and he was sure no one could see in. He grasped a handful of mud from the bank and smeared his face and hair hurriedly with it, and then lowered until only that portion of his head from the nostrils up was exposed. He was in that position when Bill Davis, his head a muddy boulder moving slowly along the shoreline, joined him, and they nearly wept with joy at being reunited.

Inside the house the Indians rushed into the parlor and found the ten-year-old,

Tom Davis, who had snatched a rifle from over the mantel and was holding it leveled toward the doorway. He pulled the trigger and the hammer sparked on the flint, but the gun was unloaded. A tomahawk whirred across the room and struck him in the stomach. He went down with a sharp cry, and instantly an Indian was on him and cut his throat. On the sofa, seven-year-old Jimmie huddled in a ball, too terrified even to whimper. One of the Indians snatched him up under his arm, but did not kill him.

In the cornfield, Edward and Greenbury Hall raced together toward a stand of timber and, reaching it, plunged out of sight. A hundred yards from them, John Henderson and his son, Henry, along with Edgar Howard and his son, Allen, also reached the timber and vanished into the woods. The remaining two who had been working in the cornfield with them were not so lucky. The brothers Sam and Alex Davis had run in another direction, toward a different grove of trees, only to be cut off by several Indians on horseback.

Sam jerked to a halt, threw up his rifle, and pulled the trigger, but the rifle misfired, and he went down under two shots sent his way. Alex, having lost his weapon, changed direction and ran frantically away, but the horses pounded up behind him, and he was dropped by a tomahawk blow. Both were scalped, stripped, and mutilated, including the severing of their genitals.

Back inside the house, the Indians had easily forced the bedroom door open and four of them, two to each of the girls, dragged Sylvia and Rachel out of the house. They were hustled to the rail fence, thrown to the ground beside little Jimmie, and left to huddle there under guard of two warriors.

Indians were everywhere now, forty or fifty of them, rushing about, piling up to take with them those items they wanted, such as firearms and food stores. Others were starting to destroy the little settlement, smashing windows, breaking furniture, generally rampaging through everything. Still others dragged the dead from inside the house out into the dooryard, stripped and scalped them, and then, in their frenzy of victory and hatred, got ropes from the shop and hung them by their feet from low branches of the huge old oak beside the house. With tomahawks they struck the bodies repeatedly, and with knives they sliced into their flesh, until the remains of all were hardly recognizable. One, with a sword found inside the house, slashed furiously at the bodies, beheading and dismembering several. All the stock and fowl were killed and the dam broken in. And, at last, the shed, mill, blacksmith shop, and house were set afire.[225]

Sylvia, Rachel, and Jimmie, unable to watch, continued to huddle, their heads together, crying together as they faced the ground, but then they were roughly jerked to their feet and forced to walk toward a distant woodland to the north, more than a mile from the house. They moved swiftly, and Jimmie was forced to run to keep up. Before long he was unable to match the pace and fell back. He was struck by an Indian from behind to hurry him up, but he only stumbled and fell. Two of the Indians then grabbed his hands and held them in opposite directions, arms outstretched. A third approached with a rifle and aimed it at the center of his chest. The little boy was frightened, but he was no longer crying. The shot struck him in mid chest, and he slumped in death. His scalp was taken, and then the two horrified sisters were hustled along even faster.

When they reached the woods, they entered it and came to a clearing where the Indian horses were being held. There were also a number already there from the Davis stable, and Sylvia and Rachel recognized some horses from neighboring farms. In a short time, their destruction and mayhem completed at the house, the remainder of the Indians came, all of them bearing plunder of some kind. They tied these goods to their horses and then put the two teenaged girls on horses in the midst of them and started north. The girls could now see that the full number of Indians in the party was around seventy.

The procession moved at a steady, rapid pace, with numerous scouts ranging out and back constantly to guard against attack by interception or pursuit. The Indians were largely Potawatomies from the villages of Big Foot and Meau-eus, along with a number of Sacs from Black Hawk's band, plus a scattering of Winnebagoes that had joined them on their way south.

In this way, the horses of the girls occasionally being lashed from behind, they traveled well into the night, until at last they stopped for a two-hour rest. No longer fearful of being followed or attacked, the Indians built a large fire and did ritual scalp dances around it, stamping and prancing and singing their victory songs while waving and shaking in the faces of the girls the scalps that had been taken. They ended the ceremony by pitching into the fire the severed breasts of the dead women and genitals of the men.[226] After this they ate and slept.

It was nearly midnight when the whole party roused, remounted, and, again with the Hall girls on horses in their midst, continued on their journey north. The two Potawatomies who were in charge of this party were Toquamee and Comee, who had finally consummated their long-harbored desire for revenge on the blacksmith William Davis.[227]

[*May 21, 1832 — Monday*]

Militia colonel James Strode, in his customary megalomanic manner, had decided that the population of Galena, while no doubt frightened about the Indian threat, especially since the death of William Durley, just were simply not well enough prepared in case of attack. The stockade in the center of town was not yet finished, and the work on it was being accomplished in a lackadaisical manner. The people simply weren't prepared for a real invasion by the Indians. To prove this point, he felt nothing would suffice as well toward this end as holding an attack drill. Unfortunately, he neglected to tell any other person in Galena that it was merely a drill.

At 2:00 A.M. he shot off a rifle and two pistols and then rang the town's alarm bell long and loud. To every militiamen who appeared he shouted, "We're under attack! *Indians!* Get everyone in the stockade. We're under attack!"

The word spread immediately, and the fear that resulted was immense. The possibility of such attack had been on everyone's mind, and now, evidently, in the dead of night it had come. In a short time the entire town was awake. Crying women, clutching babies in their arms and clad in nightwear, rushed barefoot from their homes to the safety of the stockade. Men in underwear ran back and forth, rifles in hand, helping those slower or more hampered with illness or injury get to the fortification. Old Widow Gleason, hearing a militiaman clump up her steps to warn her, thought it was Indians entering, leaped from a first-floor window to the ground, and managed to get to her feet and begin running, but her heart gave out and she fell dead.

Throughout the remainder of the hours of darkness the militiamen ranged back and forth at the town's perimeter, seeking the attacking enemy, but found nothing. By daylight, when the night guard was summoned and questioned and none had seen any Indians anywhere or knew anything of the attack, Strode was called to account for the alarm.

To the intense anger of all the townspeople, he told them it had merely been a drill to show them the dreadful state of their unpreparedness. He announced something else as well. He had decided that since the town was obviously not going to protect itself adequately unless forced to do so, he was declaring martial law.

During the time from the alarm until dawn, while the whole town had been busy eluding shadows and getting themselves into the safety of the stockade in the center of town, Strode had been very busy in his quarters writing out this declaration:

The force of uncontrollable circumstances, added to the approbation of the public, openly expressed, has induced me to declare, for the time being, MILITARY RULE. I am aware that it is an expedient seldom ventured upon, and the greatest danger from it is its too long continuance. Therefore, we must improve the brief time given ourselves to accomplish a large undertaking. To-day [sic] every man who cannot produce a certificate of exemption from the Surgeon of the 27th Regiment of Illinois Militia is to labor from 9 o'clock A.M. *to 6 o'clock* P.M. *on the stockade now erecting for the safety of our fellow citizens; and those who disobey this necessary injunction shall be punished with the utmost severity.*

And further, all and every person whatsoever, who shall sell or give to any person spirituous liquors until 7 o'clock P.M., *shall be punished as a court martial shall determine. And all persons who shall fire guns without positive orders, unless while standing guard to give alarm, shall stand one hour on a pivot, supported by bayonets. And all persons who disobey the commands of those whose charge it is to erect block-houses, batteries and stockade work now in progress, shall be dealt with in the same manner.*

Done at my headquarters in Galena, the 21st day of May, 1832.

J. M. Strode, Colonel Comd'g 27th Ill. Militia

Living up to his reputation, James Strode continued to be a very unpopular individual in Galena.

[*May 21, 1832 — Monday*]

The city of Ottawa on the Illinois River was in a state of uproar throughout the night as, beginning in the evening, the survivors of the attack on the Davis Settlement in Indian Creek continued to come in. The Hall brothers, John, Edward, and Greenbury, came in, as did William Davis, Jr., John and Henry Henderson, and Edgar and Allen Howard. So far as anyone knew, these eight were the only survivors of the twenty-five people who had been on hand when the Indians struck.

By morning, a strong company of men had been raised and set out nervously to check for survivors, ready to bolt in an instant back toward town if the Indians were still there. Instead, they encountered a group of the survivors of Stillman's Defeat, who had camped within four miles of the Indian Creek massacre. The party urged the soldiers to join with them and help them, but the soldiers, still fleeing from the horror they imagined at their heels, would not and simply turned their backs and rode off toward Ottawa. The party continued toward the Davis Settlement, even more apprehensively than before. They found no Indians, but the tracks of scores of them. The fires in the buildings had burned down to piles of smoldering embers, and everywhere there was devastation.

The condition of the bodies that were found made many of the men weep or become sick. The worst to view were the women, hanging by their feet from the trees and terribly mutilated, and the children, hacked to pieces and scattered on the grounds. Morosely, fearfully, they gathered up the remains, and while a common grave was dug by some, others began moving about searching for those still missing, which included Robert Norris, Emery George, Sam, Alex, and Jimmie Davis and their father, William, and Sylvia and Rachel Hall.

They found William Davis, Sr., first, in the open field close to the woods he had tried to reach. His youngest son, Jimmie, was found north of that, also in the prairie, but with the trails from him heading toward the distant woods. They followed that trail to where it entered the woods and did not dare go farther, but they did find a strip of cloth that, they hoped desperately, one of the girls had torn from her dress to leave as a marker. The body of Emery George was found wedged against the debris of the destroyed dam. He had been shot in the head, and was the only one found thus far who had not been scalped and mutilated. Robert Norris was found just south of the creek and, finally, Sam and Alex at the edge of the cornfield near the woodland on the far west. But of the seventeen- and fifteen-year-old Hall girls no trace could be found, and all were convinced they had been carried away as prisoners rather than slain.

The found bodies were brought to the remains of the settlement and there gently laid in the common grave with the others. There were no blankets with which to cover them, so pieces of unburned or only charred planks from the outbuildings were brought and used to cover them as best as could be done. The grave was filled and a prayer quickly said, after which the party returned with all speed to Ottawa.

The town was horrified at the reports of the returned men, revolted at the descriptions of what they found and angered beyond any fury previously known. They were ripe for what young Bill Davis had to say when he mounted a wagon bed and addressed them.

"I, for one," he said loudly, "will prepare to leave tomorrow morning on the trail of the Indians that did these terrible things. I want to rescue the Hall sisters if that is at all possible. And I want *very much* to avenge the awful deaths of so many of our friends and relatives. I will go alone, if necessary, but I will welcome any who have the strength and courage to join me." Even before he finished speaking, John Hall, eldest brother of the missing sisters, climbed up on the wagon beside young Davis, signifying his determination to join the rescue attempt.

Almost two-score men volunteered to accompany them, and as if to atone for previous behavior, half a dozen of these were members of Stillman's defeated troops.

CHAPTER VIII

[*May 22, 1832 — Tuesday*]

MAJOR GENERAL Alexander Macomb, commander of the United States Army, was thoroughly frustrated by the lack of reliable communication being received from the western frontier. His irritability over General Atkinson's failure to send him frequent and detailed reports of what was going on there was increasing to the point where he was prepared to do something drastic about it. The brief, rather testy letter he wrote now to Atkinson conveyed some degree of his feelings:

Head Quarters of the Army
Washington 22 May 1832

Sir: It is understood that Black Hawk, and his associates, finding that the Potawatomies and Winnebagoes are unwilling to join them in their contemplated hostilities, have determined to surrender the murderers of the Menominees, and to retreat across the Mississippi.

The character of Black Hawk is such that no confidence can be placed in what he may promise, nor is there any security for his better conduct in the future. It is therefore the President's order that Black Hawk be demanded of his associates, with other hostages, and if his band continue embodied or refuse to deliver him up with the hostages required, that you attack and disperse them, taking if possible, Black Hawk, and a sufficient number of prisoners.

It is firmly believed that unless energetic measures are taken at this time with Black Hawk and his band, the same outrages on the frontiers of Illinois will be repeated annually to the great annoyance and disquiet of the frontier settlements, attended with endless expense to the United States.

I have the honor to be respectfully Sir,
Your obedient servant
Al: Macomb Major General

[*May 23, 1832 — Wednesday*]

General Henry Atkinson was still plagued by the sense of frustration that had gripped him so long. Trying to find and come to grips with the Indians under Black Hawk was like trying to come to grips with ghosts. They seemed to appear without warning wherever the army wasn't. When the army followed a trail, the trail, however bold it began, ultimately faded away and eventually disappeared, as if one by one the members of the party were being sucked off into some sort of void. Yet here and there all over the frontier the attacks were not only occurring, they were growing in number and severity. To keep the men busy who were presently here at Dixon's Ferry, he had ordered Major John Bliss to take charge of constructing a fort, which they would call Fort Dixon. That work was well under way, though far from completion.

Expresses were being received from all over with complaints of what was occurring. Attacks had occurred on settlements near the mouth of Plum River, some thirty miles downriver on the Mississippi from Galena, where property was burned, horses stolen, and stock killed. A letter from Oliver Kellogg complained that when he had returned to Kellogg's Grove after a trip, he had found that all his buildings there on the Peoria-Galena Road — which most people were still calling Kellogg's Trail — had been burned and everything destroyed. It was a substantial loss, since in addition to his own house, there were a couple of log cabins that served as store and tavern, a large barn, and a stage-house, which consisted of seven buildings for travelers, each seven feet high, ten feet wide, and sixteen feet long, and all of them sided with basswood bark. He reported having seen only one Indian, who had immediately disappeared in the grove to the north. Much farther to the east, the settlers of the Fox and Du Page river valleys were complaining of attacks on their properties, as were settlers in La Salle County near Ottawa. The facts were glaringly and gallingly evident. The Indians were very effectively where the troops were not, even though Atkinson continued to send detachments in the direction of such incidents. And as yet, he knew nothing of the massacre at Indian Creek.

The major detachment of fourteen hundred mounted militia under General Whiteside pursued the trail of the Indians up Sycamore Creek a long distance, and finally came to where the Indians had camped. Here they found residue of some of the plunder taken from Stillman's Defeat, as well as several of the scalps of the men killed there, which had been hung, in warning, on branches where the following troops would discover them.

Then had come humiliating news. A smaller detachment under command of Captain Elijah Iles ascertained beyond doubt that the trail of the Indians, which first led east and then south, had been a ruse meant to divert the army from overtaking the march of the main army and people of Black Hawk, who had evidently continued northward, up Rock River — a trail, according to Iles, ". . . *which the Indians have covered with remarkable cleverness.*"

The already obvious undercurrent of dissatisfaction among the militia had grown stronger, to such extent that Governor Reynolds called a conference of all the captains and asked for a vote as to what should be done. The result was so clearly in favor of going home that General Whiteside, in his wrath, declared he would no longer lead them except to be discharged. With that the army, then at the headwaters of Sycamore Creek, after pillaging the temporarily deserted village of Chief Chaubenee, headed for the Fox River to follow it to its junction with the Illinois, where the men were assured they would be given their discharges.

Hanging as a constant specter over everything these days was the matter of the Indians who as yet had not raised the tomahawk against the whites. There was good evidence that such a condition could not last. As the letter to Atkinson written at Prairie du Chien three days ago put it:

> *U.S. Indian Agency at Prairie du Chien.*
> *May. 20. 1832. 10 OClock at night.*

Br. Genl. H. Atkinson,

Sir, The S. Boat "Dove" arrived here to night, about an hour since, and leaves in the morn'g. early for Galena It brings us no further news from you, than was recd. formerly by the "W. Wallace" 6 or 7 days past. I am greatly surprised that no further accounts have reached here, and that nothing certain has been recd. as to the present position of the Indians.

About 10 or 12 days past the Sioux of Wabasha's band was [sic] here, and after much persuation [sic] agreed to return and be quiet until their G. F. [Great Father, the President] should settle their differens [sic] with the Saccs [sic] & Foxes. The Menomines [sic] also reluctantly did the same except 3 men. And nearly all have left and gone up with the Sioux.

I am now apprehensive from some movements of the Winnebeagoes [sic] of the Wisconsin that they are becoming dissatisfieed [sic] and that they will join the Saccs & Foxes if aney [sic] further unfavourable affair takes place between the Inds. & the whites: Indeed I consider that the descision [sic] of all the Winnebeagoes mentioned will be to join them; but if beaten, they will be verry [sic] frindly [sic] to the whites. The only portion of these Inds. under my Agency are those on the Wisconsin. The other Winnebeagoes of my Agency on the upper Mississippi I have no fear of. They will stand firm to the U.S.

I this morning at 8 oClock [sic] dispatched three men in a small fast running bark Canoe to examine the position, and see what the Winnebegoes [sic] of the Wisconsin are doing, and should they find them quiet, the Express will proceed to the portage, to which place I gave them letters. It will take them 3-4 days to go & 2 to return. The moment I am advised I will acquaint you with all that I may learn. We are here preparing for the worst. The opinings [sic] of the Fort have been

*closed by wooden pickets, and the works put in as good a state of defence as could
be in so short a period. . . .*

                              Yours respectfully Jos M. Street U.S. Ind. Agt.

Meanwhile, the situation in the Fox and Du Page river valleys remained very
tense. The group under John and Joseph Naper, who had headed for Chicago,
had reached their destination without problem. They found that the panic was
widespread and that settlers were pouring in from all quarters, but not until the
arrival of the Naper settlement refugees was reliable news of the approach of the
Indians received. A new shock wave went through the assemblage as they learned
of the destruction of the settlement at Hollenbeck's Grove. Although word had
been received that a force of U.S. regulars had been ordered to regarrison Fort
Dearborn, that force had not yet arrived, and the populace was extremely fearful.
One of the very real concerns was how long food supplies could last with this
rapidly burgeoning population. Thus far the Chicago butchers John Noble and
his sons and the Clybourne brothers, Archibald and Jonas, had kept up with the
demand and provided all the meat needed, but that couldn't last too long.

A company of thirty men had immediately been raised under Captain Jesse
Brown and Lieutenant Richard J. Hamilton to go out and range the country for
a week in an effort to find and engage the hostile Indians and escort to Chicago
any settlers needing their help. Twelve of those who had just come in from the
Naper settlement were part of the company, including the Naper brothers,
Christopher Payne, Baley Hobson, Alanson Sweet, Israel Blodgett, and Robert
Strong. Leaving a volunteer force of several hundred still at Chicago, Brown's
company moved out. At Laughton's place on the Des Plaines, they found
everything normal, and much to the relief of those from the Naper settlement,
their property and goods had not been touched. They moved on, and when they
reached Plainfield, eleven miles south, they found that the settlers, who had
elected to remain there, had built a fort of rough logs erected around the cabin
of the Reverend S. R. Beggs. The little fortification was being called Fort Beggs,
and all the men on hand were under command of their elected captain, Chester
Smith. At the strong recommendation of Captain Brown, they agreed to abandon Fort Beggs and head for Chicago.

Going on toward the southwest, they came next to the cabin of Abraham
Holderman, adjacent to an island of trees sometimes called Holderman's Grove,
and found it had been only slightly fortified. The women and children had
already been escorted to safety at Chicago, and the men who remained included
Holderman himself along with his neighbors, Ezra Kellogg and Samuel Cummings. Here, too, were gathered the refugees of the Hollenbeck settlement, the
Hollenbeck brothers, Clark and George, William Harris, Ezra Ackley, and
Patrick Cunningham. Also on hand was a Dunkard preacher en route to visit the
family of his brother, Aaron, who lived at Hollenbeck's Grove — the magnifi-
cently black-bearded Reverend Adam Payne.[228] Stopping off at Holderman's to

visit his stepson, Sam Cummings, the Reverend Payne was disturbed to learn of the destruction of the Hollenbeck's Grove settlement, but was relieved to learn that a few days before that affair, his brother had taken his family to the safety of Ottawa.

Captain Brown and his men remained at Holderman's overnight and listened carefully as the Hollenbecks related the destruction of their settlement, including the Hollenbeck store and the eight houses that had been there. The men had seen the Indians coming and fled, but all were certain they'd have been killed if the Indians had pursued. Fortunately, a supply of whiskey was discovered by the Indians in the store before they burned it down, and they had concentrated on drinking that first, so the settlers had escaped.

In the morning, an express from Ottawa en route to Chicago paused at the cabin and delivered the stunning news of the massacre that had occurred at the Davis Settlement at Indian Creek, some twenty miles to the west. Captain Brown, immediately mounting up his company to continue toward Ottawa, urged the men at Holderman's to leave the dubious safety of this poorly fortified cabin and head for Chicago at once, but the advice was refused — at first. Less than an hour after Brown's departure, however, though the Holderman's Grove settlers were determined to remain at the fortified cabin and protect their property, all but one of the Hollenbeck's Grove settlers decided they would, after all, go on to Chicago. The Reverend Payne was the exception, declaring that he had decided to go on to Ottawa to visit others of his kin, which had been the object of this visit to Illinois. Sam Cummings begged his stepfather to go to Chicago with the others or stay here at Holderman's with them, but he refused.

"I don't see why you didn't ride on with Captain Brown's company then," Cummings complained. "You'd've been a lot safer. But if you feel you've *got* to go to Ottawa, then at least take a gun to protect yourself."

The preacher shook his head. "I have three things to keep me safe — a very fine bay mare who, I doubt not, can outrun any Indian horse, a fine brass spyglass, with which I can observe the surrounding country and observe approaching danger long before it reaches me, and, most of all, my Bible. Rest your fears — I walk with the Lord and He protects me. He always has."

With the misgivings of the three settlers he was leaving, the Reverend Adam Payne put his fine bay mare in motion on the two-rut wagon road leading toward Ottawa. He had not traveled more than an hour when, as he approached a small grove, half a dozen Indians on foot stepped out of the trees no more than thirty yards ahead. Rejecting the instant impulse to turn and flee, knowing it would invite attack, the preacher raised his hand in greeting. An arrow whistled in and thumped into his chest. Stunned, his hand gripped the shaft of the arrow still projecting and he began to lean forward. Before he could fall, two more arrows struck him in the body, and he was dead before he hit the ground, the reins still clenched in his left hand.

The Indians approached easily on foot, so as not to startle the already frightened horse into flight. One snatched the reins, and the others now yelped in triumph as they scalped him and cut away the skin of his chin to take the long black beard.[229]

Less than an hour later, Samuel Cummings, who had glimpsed what appeared to be his stepfather returning on the same mare, unbarred the door of Holderman's little fortified cabin and rushed out with Abraham Holderman and Ezra Kellogg to greet him and find out why he was returning. Though they had been aware of the approach of no one else, they rounded the edge of the cabin to find themselves in the midst of Indians. In seconds, all three were dead. In only minutes more, their mangled remains and burning cabin were all that remained, their horses and goods having been taken by the attackers, including the Indian still wearing the black trousers, coat, and hat in which the Reverend Adam Payne had been clad.

Captain Jesse Brown's company, unaware of what had occurred behind them, rode directly to Ottawa without incident and arrived to find the town still deeply shocked over the disaster that had occurred only twelve miles to the north. The companies of Illinois 5th Regiment Militia under Colonel James Johnson that had been sent out by General Atkinson had arrived just yesterday afternoon and had heard with dismay an abundance of garbled stories of the Indian Creek massacre. Captain Brown presented himself to Colonel Johnson, who had just completed writing a report to General Atkinson of the massacre. After reporting where his company had been, along with details of the Hollenbeck's Grove attack that they had gotten from the survivors at Holderman's, Brown cleared his throat a bit self-consciously.

"Sir, we are a small company of thirty men, and there is some fear among us that on our return to Chicago, which we plan to begin tomorrow morning, we may be attacked. I would like to officially request of you an escort to that place."

Johnson was shaking his head before Brown finished.

"Can't do it, Captain," he said. "We have our orders from General Atkinson, and I can't just detach men to escort you. However, let me call for some volunteers from the militia here unattached to my command and see what we can come up with."

The word went out, and within an hour Major David Bailey, survivor of Stillman's Defeat and deserter from Dixon's in the absence of Atkinson, agreed to accompany Brown's company with a detachment of a dozen of his men who were anxious to reach Chicago.

[*May 23, 1832 — Wednesday*]

The Rachel and Sylvia Hall of late this afternoon bore little resemblance to the pretty, well-groomed girls they had been almost three days ago. The long black hair of the fifteen-year-old was tangled and filthy, matted with bits of leaves and branches and debris, though her curved comb was still wedged in it. Her original clothing that had become torn and clotted with the mud and muck of numerous creek crossings, had been taken from her, and she now wore a white calico dress with ruffles around the hem. Her shredded stockings had been discarded and her shoes were now on bare feet, her ankles severely crisscrossed with the weals and scratches of brambles.

Seventeen-year-old Sylvia had fared about the same. Her hair, blond and shorter than her sister's, had not taken so much punishment, but it too was clotted with debris and stringy with mud. The clothing she had been wearing when captured had become as badly ripped and tattered as her sister's and had been replaced with a dress of blue calico. She, too, wore her shoes over bare feet, and in addition to scratches on her ankles and arms, she had a substantial bruise over one cheekbone where she had collided with a low branch in the darkness that first night.

The huge lake they had passed on their left an hour or so ago had now become a river again, its waters much clearer than previously and more swift in its progress. The shoreline had changed, too, from being mostly interspersed prairie and woodland trail within sight of the river waters to now a sloppy, mucky passage through marshy areas that seemed endless, the mud from the hooves of the horses ahead often flicking up to spatter them even more.

"Are we never to stop, Syl," muttered Rachel in a croaky voice. "Are we just going to keep riding forever. I'm so tired I could die."

Sylvia shook her head and winced at the pain it caused her. "I don't know, Rachel. I thought when the river turned into a lake we'd stop, but they just keep going and going." She was close to tears again and bit her lip to fight them back, then went on crossly. "And you stop talking about dying. We're not going to die, do you understand? We're not!"

They fell into silence again, no longer crinkling their noses at the smell of the mounted Indians who continued to press close to them from ahead and behind, aware that they themselves probably smelled nearly as bad. Occasionally the one who commanded the others, he with the misshapen nose and a scar on his face, would rein in close and try to talk to them, but they could not understand, although by pointing at his own chest and saying a single word, they came to know that his name was Toquamee. Several of the fresh scalps had been strung together and tied to hang beneath his rifle barrel, one of which was long and blond and could be no one else's than little Elizabeth's. The girls had learned to avert their eyes from it, lest they go again into a paroxysm of vomiting, as had struck them both when they first recognized it.

Both tried to make their minds blank, to avoid thinking of the horror and devastation of three days ago, but repeatedly the ugly thoughts returned to haunt and shake them.

After that first rest stop of some two hours they had made the first night — when the Indians had danced in their awful way and had shaken the bloody scalps in their faces, and then slept while their guarded captives moaned in their misery — the whole party had remounted and moved on through the night.

Without further pause to rest or refresh, they had pressed on until about sunrise, when Rachel made signs that she had to get down to relieve herself. For the first time they realized there were some Indian women in the party. Toquamee yelled some words, and the procession paused. Immediately one of the squaws, a medium-sized woman of about thirty, rode up and stopped near them. Her hair, which was evidently long, disappeared into the collar of her buckskin blouse. Toquamee said more words, and the squaw, expressionless, dismounted. She stepped to Rachel's horse and pointed at her and the ground, signifying she should dismount. Rachel did, nearly falling as her feet hit the ground. At gestures from the squaw, she stepped off into the bushes. As she squatted, the squaw turned and went back toward the column, and Rachel was alone. She had fleetingly thought of trying to run away or hide, but knew they would find her, knew as well she could not abandon Sylvia, even if she could get away. As she started back, the Indian woman stepped into view from behind a nearby tree. There was a slight smile on her face. She spoke a few words to Toquamee and then rode off toward the rear. When Rachel attempted to mount, her horse was pulled away from her, and she was made to walk alongside Sylvia's horse for a long distance. Even when they came to a sluggish, muddy creek, she was not allowed to remount and had to wade across in the muck and roily water, which at one point reached waist depth. After a while, when her legs began to fail her, she was permitted to get back on her horse and ride. Finally, an hour or so after midday, they had stopped inside a peculiar circle of bushes in the midst of a prairie, with a line of timber well to the east.[230]

The girls had found it difficult to dismount, so stiff were they. They also feared that as soon as they were on the ground, they would be tomahawked and scalped. That hadn't occurred. A number of the Indians stayed on their horses as a guard and took posts at intervals around them. The Indians' horses were allowed to graze while a fire was built, and a quantity of beans and acorns were tossed into a pot and roasted as one of the warriors stirred them constantly with a stick until they were nearly blackened. Oddly enough, the girls found the smell almost inviting. The Indians ate the roasted kernels with evident relish and gave the girls some on a concave piece of bark. They nibbled on the blackened pieces and were able to swallow some of it after vigorous chewing. The acorns were rather bitter, and the beans, which had a better taste, were harder than parched corn. Neither of the girls thought she could sleep, but both did, almost immediately after eating the little they had. Two hours later they were shaken awake and made to remount for the ride to continue.

Just after they started again, around twenty of the Indians in the party galloped off toward the west. The main party continued generally northward, and after nearly an hour the group that had split away came back holding their spears and bows at the ready, as if they had been used or were soon to be used on someone in pursuit. The party began riding at a more rapid pace, and the girls became very afraid again, fearful that if a party of whites came up behind or intercepted the Indians, they would be killed so the Indians could escape more swiftly. A great deal of conversation passed among the Indians as they rode, but gradually the tension eased, and after riding at the rapid pace for an hour, the party slowed and the weapons were put away.

Near sundown they stopped again, this time for the night. Bundles of skins and cloths were opened and numerous wigwams set up. A large fire was built, and the Indians sprinkled a mixture of tobacco and dried corn into the flames. Toquamee then placed some into the hands of the girls and indicated they should do likewise. Not knowing what the ritual meant, they did so.

"What do you suppose that was all about?" Sylvia said, as they were signaled to sit down together perhaps thirty feet from the fire.

Rachel shook her head. "I don't know. Maybe it's supposed to show they were successful in whatever it was they did."

The supper prepared was more substantial by far than previously, probably because now it was the squaws who cooked. As nearly as the girls could estimate, there were eight or nine women with the party, and three of these did the cooking. Dried slices of meat were broken into small pieces and cooked in a pot holding just enough water to cover them. Dried corn was pounded into a mash and then tossed into the water of another large pot and cooked into a thick gruel. After a while the meat was added to this and the whole cooked some more. Coffee was boiled in a copper kettle. Both girls found it strange when they were the first to be given wooden bowls filled with the food mixture and wooden ladles with which to eat it. When they began to eat, the Indians filled other bowls similarly and ate the meal. Despite their hunger, the girls did not relish what they ate.

"Needs salt," Rachel said. Then, remembering these were some of the last words her mother ever spoke, she burst into tears, and it was a while before they subsided and she could resume eating. When the meal was finished, a squaw took their bowls and ladles and disappeared with them. A dance began, this one more sedate than the scalp dance, the men moving eerily about in a shuffling circle around the fire, the sweat on their bare chests glinting in the firelight and the darkness irregularly pierced by one or another erupting in a high-pitched cry. Occasionally the dancers raised their knees high in exaggerated steps with head thrown back, and often they bowed low at the waist with arms akimbo and feet stamping in miniature steps as they turned round and round while orbiting the fire.

Abruptly and unceremoniously the dance broke up. The girls were led to a small wigwam that had been set up. There was sufficient room for the two of them, but hardly enough for the two squaws who also crowded in and lay down on either side of them. They slept, but only fitfully, hearing the other Indians moving around considerably all through the night. At dawn's light they were roused, not well rested, and given a breakfast identical to their supper.

They had expected to move on again, but instead a circle of ground was cleared about thirty feet in diameter and a slender pole about twenty-five feet high erected in the center. Nearby twenty spears were pushed into the ground, blunt end down and flint tip up, and on top of these were placed the scalps of the whites. Rachel felt the gorge rising in her throat, but Sylvia gripped her hand and the feeling passed, and they watched what followed as if mesmerized. There were not scalps enough for all the spears, but on those that were empty, human hearts were impaled.

Toquamee and other warriors shouted orders, and squaws came forward with small bowls and painted the girls alike — one side of the face scarlet, the other black. The girls, fearing the worst, were then led toward the center and made to sit on a blanket close to the center pole, with just enough room between them and the pole for a person to pass. Then the warriors began dancing around them, this time with spears in hand, occasionally jabbing them toward the girls but more often driving them savagely into the ground point first, as if stabbing an enemy.

"Are we going to die now, Sylvia?" Rachel murmured in a quaking voice.

"No," Sylvia replied, though not knowing. "No! You've got to believe we're not going to die. Don't look down at the ground. Keep your head high. Don't cry. And please, Rachel, don't throw up. Just hang onto my hand and watch."

So hard did Rachel grip that Sylvia could feel the bite of her nails, but she didn't pull her hand away. Together they watched a more formal version of the scalp dance, and finally, after half an hour of this, two older squaws came and helped them up and led them away to a wigwam a little larger than that in which they had spent the night, which was now nowhere to be seen. Inside the wigwam, the Indian women used basins of water and rough pieces of cloth to scrub the paint off the faces of the girls. It hurt their skin, but neither girl made any sound of complaint.

Once again the camp was struck and they moved on northward, now going at a much slower pace and constantly being joined by other Indians until the girls thought they were everywhere. Both girls were exhausted — drained physically as well as emotionally — and neither gave evidence of being much concerned when they were separated and rode in different parts of the party, each flanked by two squaws. At times of rest, which were more frequent now, Sylvia and Rachel were allowed to be together, although their four guardian squaws stayed close to them at all times.

The ground over which they traveled that afternoon — yesterday — was rough, barren prairie land for the most part, although they did cross several creeks and one large river at a fording place. When they stopped for the night, the atmosphere was much more relaxed.[231] The food, though not appreciably different, tasted better, and they were given lumps of maple sugar to eat, as much as they wanted. It was one of the best things they had ever tasted. Wigwams were erected again, and this night, though the men danced again about the fire, the girls were not required to be in the midst of it. As the short dance was ending,

Toquamee issued some commands and the girls were taken to one of the larger of the small wigwams by the four squaws. Inside, their clothing was taken from them and, a bundle being opened, they were given dresses that appeared never to have been worn before, the smaller one white calico with ruffles and the other plain but pretty blue calico. Despite their fear of their captors, they were pleased, and wondered aloud to each other where the dresses had come from. The squaws, after throwing away their shredded stockings, tried to throw away their shoes as well and give them moccasins to wear, but the girls reclaimed the shoes and refused the moccasins. One of the squaws pulled the comb from Rachel's hair and threw it away, but Rachel became irate.

"My mother gave me that comb!" she flared, knowing they couldn't understand her but having to speak anyway. "You're not just going to throw it away." She went and retrieved it, and the Indian women, smiling at each other, did not stop her.

As they felt their new dresses and reveled in the cleanliness of them, they suddenly stopped and stared at one another. As if a switch had been thrown, it occurred to both sisters simultaneously that it seemed they were not going to be killed by their captors. It had been such a sword overhanging them, such a deadly, omnipresent threat, that their minds and bodies alike had been drawn tight with anticipatory dread ever since their capture. Now, for the first time, it seemed that threat had been eliminated. They burst into tears, fled into each other's arms, and stood there a long while, crying uncontrollably, while the squaws frowned and muttered among themselves, unable to understand what had caused such an outburst of emotion. And, with the lifting of the weight of peril from their own shoulders, the tragedy of the loss of their family and friends crashed down even harder upon them. It was a considerable time before they were able to stop their weeping.

Later, clad in their new dresses and feeling somewhat better, considering the circumstances, they saw a much-ornamented Indian man speaking with Toquamee. The unfamiliar Indian was tall and clad in fine buckskins. A large brass medallion hung around his neck and a cluster of red-tipped eagle feathers hung from a full head of black, loose-falling, shoulder-length hair, which in itself was significant, since most of the warriors they had seen had all or at least part of their hair plucked out. He wore calf-high moccasins with fur edging and decorated with colored beads and porcupine quills set in geometric designs. Slanted over his left eye was a black cloth. His whole bearing was one of authority, and it was obvious that even though Toquamee seemed to be in a heated discussion with him, he also managed to exude an aura of great respect toward him.

"Who is that man?" Sylvia asked one of the squaws impulsively. "A chief of some kind?"

The squaw shook her head, not understanding. Sylvia tried again. She pointed at Toquamee and said, "Toquamee?"

The squaw grinned and nodded. "Uhh," she replied, "Toquamee!"

Sylvia pointed at the more resplendent individual. "Who? Who is that?"

The squaw did not understand the words, but she understood the inflection and the point. She bobbed her head and grinned again. *"Kawraykawsawkaw,"* she said. *"Shai su okamawo kitchi Kawraykawsawkaw."* — White Crow. He is War Chief White Crow.

Sylvia shook her head, and though the squaw tried several times more, the girl could not make her mouth move to form the proper sounds for the name as the squaw made them. But she leaned toward Rachel and murmured, "I'll bet that's the big chief of them all."

They continued to watch Toquamee in conversation with the man they took to be a chief and wondered why the two kept looking at them and occasionally pointing their way, and why Toquamee seemed so agitated. But eventually the squaws herded them into the wigwam for the night — all four squaws staying inside the structure with them — and their wonderings went unresolved.

They had been awakened this morning at dawn and, after a hasty, unsatisfying meal, had broken camp, mounted, and ridden off, again to the north. There had been no sign of the impressive Indian who had been arguing with Toquamee. The pace was somewhat faster again and the riding through a variety of terrain — first largely prairie country, then becoming more timbered, at least near the river, and finally, as they neared the head of Lake Koshkonong this afternoon, the ground had become very marshy.

Now, well above the lake, they moved into the marshiest area yet encountered and their line became single file much of the time, winding and turning through a difficult morass until abruptly a turn to the left brought them to more solid footing, though marsh waters were on each side. And finally they moved into an area of open higher ground some three hundred yards long and one hundred feet wide, all but surrounded by a growth of dense bushes.

Side by side now, both Sylvia and Rachel gasped aloud as they saw what lay before them — an Indian encampment of great size, filling almost the entire open area. Hundreds of wigwams were here, and many hundreds more women and children and old people. It took the girls a little while to realize that there were very few young or mature men on hand. As if magnetically drawn, their eyes went to the largest of the wigwams and to the two men standing before it. One was the fine-looking Indian they had seen at the camp last night with the black cloth over his eye. The other was a much older man with sharp nose and shiny bald head from which grew a single scalp lock. His eyes were piercing and they were staring at them, and there was no doubt in the mind of either of the sisters that this was a very powerful man.

The squaw Sylvia had tried to question last night moved up beside them. She pointed at the two men. *"Oti okemas,"* she announced proudly. *"Kawraykaw-sawkaw etla Makataimeshekiakiak!"* — Great chiefs. White Crow and Black Hawk!

[*May 23, 1832 — Wednesday*]

In his usual sneaky way of doing things that in the long run would be primarily beneficial to himself, Colonel James Strode was still busy writing letters. The one he wrote last night to the secretary of war, bypassing any chain of command and going over the heads of all his superiors, including Governor Reynolds and General Atkinson, was clever in the way it subtly indicated that he was a superb and wonderful soldier and just as subtly castigated those he wished shown in a bad light, such as Reynolds and Atkinson. The letter he was working on this evening, to Reynolds, was giving no indication of the letter written to the secretary of war, but again showed himself to be a wonderful tactician and commander while at the same time toadying to the governor with that same cunning degree of subtlety.

Last night's letter stressed all those points predicated to make the reader see the situation — and the present general leadership — in the worst light:

Galena May 22. 1832

To the Hon. Lewis Cass Secretary of War.

Sir,   The peculiar & alarming condition, in which we are at this time placed, has induced me to address you by the bearer, Mr. Mills. It is not at my individual instance, that he is despached [sic], but by the counsel & advice of a board of officers & the expressed wishes of the most respectable gentlemen in the place & vicinity. Benjamin Mills Esq. the gentleman, who bears this, is of the highest standing & respectability, & being a citizen of the town & having a personal knowledge of our necessities & exposure to danger, has been fully authorised [sic] to make to the proper authority, a developement [sic] in detail, of every occurrence which has already transpired, as well as of the circumstances which have hedged us in with danger & imposed upon us the necessity of making this representation, to the head of the War Department.[232] The immediate departure of the boat in which he goes prevents me from doing it at large. Genl Atkinson the commander of the U.S. military forces is in the field, seventy five [sic] or eighty miles distant. The Executive of our State is with him, and we can not without a larger protecting force than can be prudently spared from this place, hold communication with either of them. Our mails have been intercepted. The Military garrisons at Prairie du Chien, Rock Island, & Jefferson Barracks have sent out the last soldier that can be spared from them, & in this dilemma, there is no one possessing the means, if they were invested with the discretionary power to afford us protection. We have therefore thought it proper to apply to you for a Government force to be stationed at this place, until the termination of the present hostilities. This Section of the State is invaded by powerful detachments of Indian Warriors of the Sac, Fox, Winebago [sic] & Potawamie [sic] & part of the Kickapoo Nations. A Skirmish took place on the evening of the 14th. Inst. between a small detachment

of the Illinois Militia, consisting of about 250, under the command of Genl
Stillman & about 300 Indians, in which the latter were successfull [sic]. The
actual loss on both sides is uncertain. We know of but twelve killed on our side
& an equal number Wounded. There are however some missing. I was in this
skirmish as a volunteer in Capt. Eads' Company, being then on my passage
through the country. We request you most earnestly to despatch an adequate force
to this place for its present means of defence [sic] are wholly inadequate to its
protection. I beg leave also to refer you, to a communication, made yesterday to
the President of the United States by Col. Wm Campbell & others.[233] The defence
of the country is left almost exclusively to me by reason of my commission under
the Executive of this State, with means entirely inadequate to the object

It is proper that I should add that Mr Mills has been selected as the bearer of
this message on account of his personal acquaintance with the country & its
present condition & his ability to explain satisfactorily any matters that may be
inquired of him concerning us. We have given him assurance that the government
will afford him a suitable compensation for this service and hope that, considering
the dangerous crisis of our affairs & our necessity for speedy aid, which we have
no other present means of procuring, as well as the duty of the Government to
protect & defend us, you may be inclined to ratify this assurance.

I have the honor to be with great respect Your obedient Servant
James M Strode Col. commg 27th Regt Ill. Militia.

The letter that Strode was presently writing to Governor Reynolds was much
more optimistic, and took credit for all the supposedly wonderful things being
done for the defense of Galena. And to Reynolds, Strode was his usual fawning
self:

Head Quarters 27h. Regt. Ills Ma.
Galena May 23rd. 1832.

To His Excellency John Reynolds Govr. of the State of Illinois
Sir   I arrived here on the evening of the 16th. Inst. but the news of the Kish
wauke [sic] battle had preceeded [sic] my arrival.[234] terror had seized all the
citizens of our country. I forthwith proceeded to obey your instructions to me
before my departure from your camp. I have organized one company of mounted
volunteer Rangers consisting of 75 men well armed & equiped [sic] commanded by
Capt. J. W. Stephenson and seven Militia companies, four of whom have been
employed in the Town of Galena in the construction of a Stockade work and Block
Houses for the defence and protection of this important point. Also I have detailed
thirty men under the command and direction of Lieut. J B R Gardenier of the
United States Infantry as a company of Artillery, who have been imployed [sic]
up to this time in the erection of a Block House on a commanding point to be used
as a battery, which will be finished in a few days. I have procured a piece of

Artillery from Rock Island of a six pound caliber with the appropriate carriage and munitions, which will be under the command of Lieut. Gardenier. We expect to have it, and the stockade finished in three more days, which it is believed will be sufficient to sustain this place from any attack of the Indians however formidable it may be. All intercourse with the settlements & country below by land is cut off. I have in consequence of this fact detained a Steam Boat here in the public service to enable us to transmit important inteligence [sic] to the country above and below, it being the only means left for the transmission of any inteligence [sic] whatever. On the evening of the 18t. [sic] Inst. I detailed five men from Capt. Stephensons Company to accompany the mail contractor with an express to yours and Genl. Atkinson's Head Quarters, but unfortunately as this party entered the North side of Buffaloe [sic] Grove, (twelve miles north of Dixons on the public road,) they were fired upon by a party of Indians. And one valuable man killed, and three others shot through their cloths [sic] they were compelled to retreat to this place without effecting the object of their expedition.²³⁵ on the evening of the 21t. Inst. the Indians attacked a Block house at the mouth of Plum River situated on the Bank of the Mississippi, but were repulsed.²³⁶ We have recd. inteligence [sic] of Indian sign within a few miles of this place, as also a few Indian scouts have been seen who made their escape. We have information derived from what we believe to be an authentic source that the Pottowatomies [sic] and Winnebagoes have made and are now making common cause with the Sac's [sic] & Foxes they lost Two Chiefs in the battle of Kish wau ke [sic]. By unanimous wish of the citizens loudly expressed martial law was proclaimed during the construction of the public works for defence on the morning of the 21t. Inst. after which it will abate. We have sent to Prare du chien [sic] and Rock Island requisitions for arms, but have not been able to procure enough to arm half our people; and we have sent a requisition to Jefferson Barracks for more by the Stam [sic] Boat Java which left here yesterday morning for St. Louis. I wish you to confer with Genl. Atkinson if your Judgment accords with mine to take myself and troops under his command for the future or (at least during the present immergency) [sic] as I have no doubt the present service requires commanders of more experience and higher rank: but I feel anxious to contribute all the service I can for the public weal, and if you prefer it, continue under your direction and command, but it has been suggested to me that the General government would more freely concur in what has and will be done in this quarter for the necessary defence of the people, if it were under the direction and superintendance [sic] of a general officer of the US. army.

David G. Bates the gentleman intrusted [sic] with this dispatch is a person of high respectability, by whom I hope yourself and Genl. Atkinson will forward to me, such orders and directions as you and he deem propper [sic] and whatever items of inteligence has [sic] been omitted in this dispatch will be supplied by him

I have the Honor to be yours respectfully

J. M. Strode Col Commdg. 27th. Regt. Ills. Mila.

[*May 24, 1832 — Thursday*]

The seven men eating their breakfast around the fire three miles west of the small camp they had made last night were still very subdued with the unpleasant duty they had performed yesterday.

"I knew Bill Durley pretty well," said Aaron Hawley. "Nice young feller. Quiet. Never hurt nobody, ever I heard about. Think he was 'sposed to get married come June. Damn' shame, that's what it was."

"War is always a damned shame," Felix St. Vrain said. "Seems as if it's always the nice ones who get killed."

"Yeah, I know what you mean," spoke up William Hale. "Strode and Stillman are still livin', ain't they?"

The heavy-handed attempt at humor did not go over well at all. There was no laughter, and the men fell silent for a time. The four who had not yet spoken were Alexander Higginbotham, John Fowler, Aquilla Floyd, and Thomas Kenney. They, along with Hale, were all from the lead mining district. Hawley, who used to live in Galena, now had a place near the Pecatonica River some five miles from William Hamilton's diggings. The tall, dark-haired Indian agent now lived at Rock Island, and except for him, all in this party were on their way home, following an absence of several weeks.

Long before the hostilities had broken out, those six had been joined by Hawley's friend Chester Sage, and all had set out together for Sangamon County on a cattle-buying trip. They'd made a number of purchases and had begun driving the animals back, when, as they passed Fort Clark in Peoria, they learned of Stillman's Defeat and the outbreak of Indian war. Immediately they left the cattle there under the care of Sage and set out for home, moving up the Illinois River to Kellogg's Trail and following that north. They had arrived at Dixon's Ferry without incident, stayed overnight, and left there two days ago to resume their journey to Galena.

It was close to noon when they approached Buffalo Grove. Keeping well on the alert, with their rifles in hand, they continued through the grove on the public road and were very relieved when they reached the northwest side without having encountered Indians. The relief was short-lived. Hardly had they left the trees when they encountered a grotesquely mutilated and bloated body on the edge of the road. Obviously it had been there for days, yet the men looked about fearfully before they dismounted. It was Hawley who turned over the facedown body. The scalp was gone and the nose badly slashed. The movement of the remains caused the nearly severed head to turn enough that he was able to see the features, and he jerked back.

"My God," he gasped, "that's Bill Durley!"

"Let's get the hell out of here!" Hale shouted, already remounting. "We gotta tell someone about this."

"Let's get back to Dixon's," Higginbotham said, adding, "Fast!"

And so they had. They reported their grisly find to General Atkinson, who listened with a dour expression. It was the first report that had come of the death there, and once again the grip of frustration in fighting such an enemy wrenched his insides. He asked the six what their plans were now.

"Well, it was likely four-five days ago Durley was killed," Fowler replied, "so the Indians wouldn't likely be hanging around there. We didn't see any fresh sign of 'em. I guess we'll just head on toward Gratiot's Grove and Hamilton's and tell them the news if they haven't heard about it yet."

"I'd like Mr. St. Vrain to go along with you, if you don't mind," the general said.

"Certainly," Higginbotham nodded. "Actually, if you want to send an armed escort, we won't object."

Atkinson smiled faintly. "I wish I could, but I'm too short of men here. If you wouldn't mind waiting until I get some dispatches prepared . . ." He left the unfinished question hanging.

"We'll wait," Aquilla Floyd said.

"Excellent. I presume you'll take on the task of burying young Durley when you get back to that point?"

With understandable reluctance, the men agreed they would do so. After breakfasting in the camp yesterday morning, they waited for Felix St. Vrain to join them with the dispatches. There were messages for Colonel Dodge and Henry Gratiot in the mining district, and from there he was to go to Galena with more messages before finally heading down the Mississippi to Fort Armstrong on Rock Island. As soon as he arrived, they set off. A spade furnished by Atkinson was lashed to Aaron Hawley's saddle.

As they had done the day before, they approached Buffalo Grove cautiously with weapons at the ready, but again they traversed the woods without incident. Durley's body was exactly as they had left it. They let it remain where it was and stepped upwind half a dozen yards and set to digging a grave. With the seven men taking turns at it, the work went swiftly. They put Durley's remains in a piece of light canvas shrouding that Atkinson had provided and placed them gently in the grave. Higginbotham spoke a brief prayer, and then they remounted and hastened away on the road leading toward Galena. It was not too many miles before they would reach the trail that went north to the mining district settlements.

The late start away from Dixon's and the delay to bury Durley left not much time for traveling. By sunset they had gone only another fifteen miles northwest, and here they stopped to make camp. At dawn today they arose and set off, having decided to get a few miles behind them before stopping for breakfast. Three miles from their camp they had stopped.

Now, with their breakfast completed and the gear packed and stowed on their horses again, they set off. They had gone no more than a mile when Felix St. Vrain sucked in his breath sharply and said, "Oh-oh."

They stopped immediately. A party of about thirty Indians had just come into sight from within the large stand of trees they all recognized as Kellogg's Grove, where the trail they would have taken went north. All were armed, and they were well within gunshot range.

"Easy, boys," St. Vrain said in a steady undertone. "Don't panic. Keep your guns down. For God's sake, don't try to make a run for it. Stay calm. I think we'll be all right. They'll know me."

The Indians, exhibiting no signs of friendship, continued approaching, and as they came close enough to see their features, St. Vrain visibly relaxed and blew out a gust of air.

"We're all right," he said, still speaking softly. "The one leading is an old Sac friend of mine, Mugateh — Little Bear. That's the Prophet, Wabokieshiek, beside him. I know him very well too. That's his brother, Atako, on his left. The one on the far right is Manatoka, Winnebago. There are Toagra and Nausaunay — Winnebagoes too.[237] Only a few Sacs among them. I think we're all right."

St. Vrain moved ahead of the others a little, holding up his hand in a sign of peace. The Indians, now only twenty yards away, gave no similar sign. St. Vrain moved toward them even more. The hand he had held up, he now outstretched toward Little Bear.

"Mugateh," he said heartily. "I hope you are well. We have not met in too long. Wabokieshiek, Atako, I greet you."

Mugateh stared at him a moment and then made a slashing motion with his hand toward the outstretched hand, simultaneously issuing a guttural command: *"Tsi heaibe!"* — Kill them!

To the consternation of his companions, St. Vrain wheeled his horse around, slammed his heels hard in the animal's sides, and bent low over the saddle as his mount plunged into a gallop. "Ride!" he shouted. "Scatter! *Ride!*"

The party broke apart instantly, all except John Fowler, who didn't react quickly enough. Several shots were fired, and he was flung from his saddle as if he had been swatted by an invisible hand. More shots, and St. Vrain, already twenty yards away, screamed and fell from his saddle as the balls found their mark.

The Indians broke apart, instantly in pursuit. Shots were sent whistling at all the men in flight, but none were hit, nor were their horses. Six or seven warriors zeroed in on Bill Hale, whose horse was not a good runner. In just under a mile they overtook and downed him with tomahawks.

Aaron Hawley had galloped off to the north, instinctively heading toward the Pecatonica settlements. Several Indians thundered after him, but Hawley's horse was noted for its speed. He was nicely outdistancing his pursuers when he leaped his horse into a creek. The water was shallow, but the muck on the bottom was deep. His horse became badly mired, and as he struggled to get free, the howling Indians pounded up. He leaped from the saddle and surged to shore, gained the other side, and began to run, but was struck in the back by two balls and killed.

Kenney, Floyd, and Higginbotham had been fortunate. They had separated to a certain extent, but when they looked back they saw they were not yet being pursued and they drew together, continuing to ride at an all-out gallop. Turning again, Higginbotham saw that four or five had taken up the pursuit, but they were now well back. The three whites rode as they had never ridden before. Twice they entered wooded areas on the line of their flight, changed direction in the midst of the woods, and exited where it would not have been expected. The pursuing Indians soon gave up and turned back.[238]

The riderless horses were captured. The dead were all scalped and their weapons and goods taken. Even their clothing was taken from them. For St. Vrain there was a further indignity. His hands and feet were cut off and then his chest was opened and the heart removed. From hand to hand it went, as the warriors in turn tore chunks from it with their teeth and chewed and swallowed in ritualistic frenzy.[239]

[*May 25, 1832 — Friday*]

It was with understandable nervousness that the fifty mounted volunteers from the mining district, under the general command of Colonel Henry Dodge, rode into Spotted Arm's village, Kaukishkaka, this morning. Yet, that apprehension was well hidden, and the men rode in a precise four-abreast column behind their two company commanders, Captain James H. Gentry and Captain John H. Rountree. Riding beside Dodge was the subagent, Henry Gratiot. Directly behind them was Catherine Myott, the Winnebago interpreter.

The village the force was entering was located on this picturesque point of land on the southwest side of Lake Mendota. It was teeming with Winnebagoes, who eyed the arrivals with a certain amount of contained suspicion and nervousness.[240]

Four of the principal chiefs — White Crow, Whirling Thunder, Spotted Arm, and Little Priest — came forward, and Dodge recognized them all: White Crow, the handsome man with the black silk cloth angled across his left eye; Whirling Thunder, a short, thickset man of about thirty-five, whose customary morose, rather sullen expression seemed to underline his reputation for cruelty; Spotted Arm, the genial chief, who was about sixty, stoop-shouldered and with poor physique; and Little Priest, who was about the same age as Whirling Thunder, but no more than six or seven inches over five feet tall, his appearance fierce and uninviting, his eyes extremely dark and piercing. Dodge greeted the four chiefs individually and spoke to them through his interpreter, Catherine Myott. They responded with questions. Why was he here with so many armed men, and what did he want?

"We want to council immediately," Dodge told them, "on a matter of great importance for your entire tribe."

The three conversed in undertones for a moment and then White Crow responded, telling Dodge that a council would be called at once. Spotted Arm called three young men to him and instructed them, and these three then sprinted off through the large village as criers, calling aloud for the chiefs and subchiefs and principal braves to assemble for council. Among other chiefs who congregated were Silver, Old Turtle, and Little Black.

Within half an hour, in a grassy area outdoors with his men standing together a short distance behind him, Dodge was addressing them, telling them very forcefully that the great father in Washington was displeased with them, and that his war chief here in this land, White Beaver — General Atkinson — wished to know in no uncertain terms where the Winnebagoes stood in the war in progress. If they were not supporting Black Hawk, then why was he hiding in their lands? Why was he able to send his parties out to attack the whites with what seemed to be the approval of the Winnebagoes? Why were groups of Winnebagoes themselves apparently going out in small parties to kill or commit depredations? Why were certain Winnebagoes joining in the war parties going out? Had the Winnebagoes declared war on the whites without ever stating openly that they had done so? Were they women, that they had to hide behind the actions of Black Hawk? It was time now, Dodge told them sternly, for them to declare themselves in these matters that were affecting everyone in this country.

It was White Crow who replied, and the deference paid him by the other chiefs and principal braves was indicative of his stature in the tribe. They were not, he said, permitting Black Hawk to hide in their lands. They had, in fact, rescinded a previous invitation for him to come here with his people. If he was hiding in their lands, White Crow said — and Dodge was convinced of his sincerity — he knew nothing about it. The Sacs were not sending out war parties with Winnebago approval, so far as he knew. The Winnebagoes had stated to both White Beaver and Shawneeawkee — the Indian agent from Fort Winnebago, John Kinzie — that they wished to remain neutral in this matter between the whites and the Sacs. That was the official tribal policy in this matter. Unfortunately, there were hot-blooded young men who yearned to test themselves in war, and though they had warned all the young men against this, some had chosen to go out in little groups or to attach themselves to Sac parties and try to earn their feathers. Such individuals were treated with harshness when they returned and made to realize that what they had done was wrong and would not be tolerated. But some, he said, had chosen to become part of Wabokieshiek's band, who were allied to the hostile Sacs. The Winnebagoes had not declared war against the whites and had no intention of doing so, and they were not women hiding behind the Sacs.

Dodge spoke again, warning them of the dangers to themselves if in any way they aided, abetted, or counseled the Sacs or gave them shelter or food. The Sacs, he told them, were liars and traitors who only wished to draw the Winnebagoes into the war to draw attention away from their own actions and in this way escape, leaving the Winnebagoes to bear the brunt of the punishment when the whites finally won the war, as they eventually must, despite the seeming cowardice in the recent action at Old Man's Creek where twelve Americans had been killed.

Chief after chief arose to speak, each giving assurances that they were peaceful, not at war with the whites and not planning to be. Yet, despite the talks, Dodge was not entirely sure they were telling the truth. Little Priest he did not trust at all, and Whirling Thunder was nearly in the same category. He wanted to trust White Crow, but was becoming uncertain that the chief was speaking the truth.

When the council broke up, White Crow asked to speak to him and Henry Gratiot privately. The two Americans, curious, agreed. The three, along with Catherine Myott, withdrew to one side.

"You have heard," White Crow began, "of the attack made by Potawatomies and Sacs on the Indian River settlement of whites?"

Dodge's expression turned grim. "We have," he said. "Fifteen people killed — women and little children cut to bits. What kind of bravery does that take?"

"It was a very bad thing," White Crow agreed, shaking his head sadly. "The Indians involved were very angry, and what they did, they did from the anger in their hearts."

"That's no excuse to smash babies against tree trunks and cut off the arms and legs of older children and women! Those who were guilty will be hunted down and punished." When White Crow made no comment, he realized there was something very specific the one-eyed chief wanted to tell him, and his interruptions were not helping. "Go on," he said.

"Two older girls were taken away in that affair," White Crow said. "It may be in my power to get them away from those who have them, if I could offer them something in trade that they want more. If this can be done, would you wish it?"

"Yes, we would," Gratiot said instantly.

"What would you give?"

"That I do not know. It would have to be discussed with General Atkinson."

"There is not time enough," White Crow said. "Those who have them may kill them if too much time passes."

"How much would be needed?" Dodge asked.

"Horses, first. Three for each of the girls. And money. A thousand dollars for each. Six horses, two thousand dollars."

"We can't auth —" Gratiot began, but he was cut off by Dodge, who gripped his arm and spoke quickly.

"It will be paid," Dodge said, "if I have to pay it myself. You and a few of your people return with us to where I live. I will give the horses and half of the money to you. The other half is to be paid when the girls are placed in our hands."

White Crow considered this and nodded. "We will come with you," he said. "But keep this strongly in your mind. I have not approached those who have the girls with such an idea. They may not wish to give them up. I can only try, but do not be surprised if I fail."

"We understand that," Gratiot said. "Where are the girls now?"

"I cannot tell you that. I saw them for a short time when they were brought near my village, but they were taken away from there."

"Can you find them again?" Dodge asked.

"I think yes, that is possible."

"Then do it. Find them. Pay the ransom and then bring them to us. How much time will you need?"

"Six days? Seven? Eight?" White Crow shrugged.

"Bring the girls to us nine days from today."

"*If* we get them, we do not dare bring them very far toward you, lest we are seen by whites who kill *us* trying to rescue them from us." White Crow was firm.

Dodge nodded. "I can understand that. All right, nine days from today bring them to the Blue Mounds. A small fort has been made there. We will come there from where we are and you will come there from where you are, and you will give us the girls."

"It will be done," White Crow said, "*if* we can get the girls. If we do not arrive, it is because we could not get them. I will go now and get my horse and those who will come with me to where you live."

"Well," Gratiot said as they walked toward their own horses, "what do you think?"

"I think White Crow is a slick individual," Dodge said, "and I don't trust him as far as I can throw him. But, for the moment, we don't have any choice."

[*May 26, 1832 — Saturday*]

The company of men under Captain Jesse Brown returned to Chicago after an absence of five days, bringing with them a number of refugees from the settlements. By this time Chicago was so crowded that all accommodations had been taken, and people were crowded two or three families to a single room. The old Fort Dearborn was full as well, and latecomers were making temporary quarters in rude shanties that had been haphazardly thrown together. No one was comfortable, and no one was very happy about the present situation.

The arrival of the company under Captain Brown threw the entire town into an uproar. A special town meeting was called on the parade ground within Fort Dearborn and the full account of their absence was related. The people were stunned at the news of the destruction the company had found at Hollenbeck's Grove, dismayed and horrified at what had happened at Indian Creek, and then terrified even more when Brown related what had occurred on their way home. The little settlement at Holderman's Grove had been in good shape when they passed through on the way to Ottawa, but on their return there they had found the body of the preacher, Adam Payne, along the road and the Holderman's Grove fortification destroyed, its defenders slain. They had hurried on to Fort Beggs, and those who were there elected to abandon the place and come with them to Chicago.

The war was coming closer and closer to Chicago; the population was on the thin edge of panic and wondered when, if ever, the regulars would reach here to regarrison Fort Dearborn. The commander of the Chicago Militia, Captain John S. C. Hogan, wrote hurriedly to Detroit asking that three hundred militiamen be sent at once to aid them, then wrote another brief letter, this one to secretary of war Lewis Cass:

Hon Lewis Cass

Sir   From the alarm that arose from reports from Rock River, the Inhabitants of this place formed a Voluntary Military association on the 18 Inst for the purpose of defence [sic], and which I have the Honor to command. Since that time the Post has been filled with refugees from the country in every direction, flying from scenes of bloodshed and devastation unsurpassed in the history of Indian warfare in the western country. From the opportune arrival of a Vessel with supplies of provisions for the anticipated reoccupation of this Fort, they have been prevented from suffering the most severe want if not from actual starvation. I have considered it necessary to issue rations to them, and continue to do it at the rate of Eight hundred daily — and the number is increasing. I trust the speedy arrival of the U.S. Troops will relieve me of this arduous duty. I have the honor to be

With great respect Your Obt. humble servant
John S. C. Hogan Capt. Ill Militia Comg Fort Dearborn

[*May 27, 1832 — Sunday*]

General Henry Atkinson felt as if he were suspended from a rope, stretching out in various directions and never able to get a purchase on anything. Little hit-and-run attacks seemed to be occurring everywhere across the state from the Mississippi to near Chicago, yet without any major force being reported toward which he could direct his army's energies. The present whereabouts of Black Hawk was a complete mystery. Everyone had ideas about where he'd taken his people, but no one had proof. Some of the stories had the women and children back in Iowa country, while others had them in Canada.

Messages and letters were being received from all directions, mostly complaints about Indian attacks — cabin burnings, stock killed, even poultry shot, as if in target practice. Everyone wanted help, but usually the damage was already done and the Indians far away from the site before he even learned of it.

The greatest aggravation, aside from not knowing the true whereabouts of Black Hawk's band, was having had no word at all from General Whiteside and Governor Reynolds. By now, it seemed to him, they should have overtaken Black Hawk's force and engaged the hostiles, but there was no word or even rumor of this having occurred.

Three days ago, Atkinson had written a letter and sent it express to Governor Reynolds:

Head Quarters Right Wing w. Dept.
Dixon's ferry May 24th. 1832

Dear Sir   I have just received from Peoria by express a packet of letters and
newspapers for you, and others for myself. I forward yours. I have received also a
letter from Lieut. Holmes Asst. Com: of Sub: informing me that he had arrived
at Peoria on board Steam Boat Caroline on his way to Hennopen [sic] with
60,000 rations of provisions for the troops where they would be landed. From other
letters received, I am informed that there is an express on the way from St. Louis
with instructions for us from the Department of War instructing us to pursue,
punish, and drive the Sacs out of the Country.

I am very much in hopes that General Whitesides [sic] will fall in with the Sacs
and succeed in overcoming them. I am informed by express from Col: Johnson who
is at Ottaway [sic] that the hostile Indians are assembling in the Great Woods on
Fox River, some 45 miles from Chicago; that a War party of 25 or 30 made an
attack on some families . . . on a branch of Fox River, fifteen miles above
Ottaway, and killed fifteen men, women and children, and captured two young
females, it is supposed, as they are still missing. Should you not fall in with the
Indians (which it is all important Genl: Whitesides should if possible) it will be
best to fall down towards the supplies, taking some position for the protection of
the frontier.

I shall, as soon as I learn the position of the Indians, put the regular troops in
motion to act with you against them should it be necessary; yet it is of the utmost
importance that this point should be occupied to prevent the Sacs from falling
back and reoccupying this river. I must order some of the volunteer corps to relieve
the regulars; these operations however will depend on further information from
you as to the position & movement of the Sacs. I learn from Lieut Holmes that
the militia are turning out with fresh spirit under your late requisition, & that a
company of volunteers may be expected from St. Louis to join us. I sent out
yesterday and buried a man that had been killed and scalped on the Galena road.

Gen. Atkinson to Governor Reynolds

One of the letters Atkinson had received as part of the express from Peoria was
from General Macomb, which he answered the following day:

Genl Atkinson to the General-in-Chief.
Head Qrs. Right Wing West Dept
Dixons Ferry   May 25th 1832

General—I had the honor to receive your letter of instructions of the 5th Instant
last evening by an express from St. Louis, directing the course to be pursued in
relation to the hostile conduct of the disaffected Sacs and Foxes Indians.
. . . I expect to hear this evening, or in the morning, of the operations of the

mounted force under General Whitesides [sic] and should not circumstances be favourable I shall move at once to the mouth of the Fox River & take measures to pursue the Enemy who are supposed to be in the Great Woods on Fox River some forty miles above its mouth. The exigencies of the case requires the movement, but in making it, I shall leave this river open, which is very much to be regretted as the Indians may fall back and occupy the swamps below us. Besides, it will leave the mineral district liable to attack — perhaps I may not be obliged to make the movement.

The unfortunate rencounter [sic] between the Rangers & the Indians has deranged my plans. I was desirous & had all my arrangements to make a decisive stroke with a force in numbers to insure success, and prevent the disaffected of other tribes from joining the Enemy. Under existing circumstances it is difficult to say what accession the enemy may gain & it may protract the War many days.

The force now in the field might be sufficient to accomplish the object before us, but I am confident it cannot be retained but a few days: Hence I fear I shall have to depend upon the State troops which have been called out by the Governor to rendezvous at Hennepin on the 10h [sic] of next month.

As far as my judgment and ability will allow your instructions will be fully complied with.

Enclosed are several papers which will show that the disaffected Indians have been fully warned of the necessity of re-crossing the Mississippi & their refusal to do so.

General Atkinson followed this with another letter to Governor Reynolds, giving him instructions in regard to the militia:

Head Quarters Right Wing West Depart.
Dixon's Ferry   May 25th. 1832

Dear Sir   An express reached me last evening from St. Louis [with] instructions from the Depart: of War and the General in Chief bringing also a packet addressed to you by the Secretary of War which I send herewith. A copy of the Secretary's letters to you has been furnished me. Upon the subject of these communications I have to remark that our operations have accorded the views of the Government, thus far, altho' anticipating them, but as there is a probability that the term for which the present volunteer force is bound to serve, will expire before the object before us can be accomplished, I have to require agreeably to my instructions from the Depart. of War, that you will, if the present military force cannot be kept in the field, supply their place as early as practicable with a force of two thousand militia, a thousand of whom at least to be mounted. I prefer that 600 or 800 should act on foot as riflemen and Infantry This force to assemble at Hennopen [sic] and be held in service as long as the law will authorize, unless sooner discharged. I will take occasion as soon as I ascertain the position and state *of things relative to the hostile Indians, to see and arrange with you every thing as to prospective operations.*

I deem it very important to hold this position for the present unless the presence of the regular troops should be required by pressing circumstances to act elsewhere, in which case they will promptly be put in motion. If the position of the hostile Indians is such as to justify a movement against them with our combined forces, I will immediately abandon this place and join you provided the volunteers under Gen: Whitesides [sic] can be prevailed upon to continue in the service a short time longer. If they cannot, our further operations must be suspended, till a new force can be organized.

I have some hopes however that Gen: Whitesides will have been enabled to make a successful stroke against the enemy, or that he will yet overtake and overcome him. Having written to you yesterday by express, I will close this communication with a request that you will keep me advised with every thing relative to our present object.

Gen: Atkinson to Gov: Reynolds

The following day — yesterday — Atkinson finally took the step he had been reluctant to take, but now, because of the nebulous availability of the militia, he felt he had no other choice. It was time to bring into the field some of the Indians who had been offering their services against the Sacs and Foxes and whatever other Indians might be aiding them. The man he wanted to put in charge of the Indians was Colonel William Hamilton from the mining district, who had volunteered for this job and who was presently here at Dixon's. He dictated the orders through his adjutant:

> *Liut [sic] Albt. St. Johnston. A.D. Camp &c to Col Hamilton*
> *Head Qrs: Right Wing West Dept. Dixons ferry 26th. May 1832*

Sir, You will repair to Prairie du chien [sic] without delay, collect the Sioux and Menominees in that section of the country, and march them to this point to cooperate with the U.S. Troops against the hostile Indians.
> *By order of Brigr Genl Atkinson*
> *(signed) Albt. S Johnston A D Camp & A.A.A.G*

This was followed by an allied letter to the Indian agent at Prairie du Chien, Joseph M. Street:

Dixon's Ferry, Rock River 26th. May 1832

Sir   I have to request that you will send me at this place with as little delay as possible as many Menominee & Sioux Indians as can be collected within a striking distance of Prairie du Chien. I want to employ them in conjunction with the troops against the Sac and Fox Indians, who are now somewhere forty or fifty miles above us in a state of War against the whites.

I understand the Menominees to the number of three hundred warriors, who were a few days ago with you, are anxious to take part with us. Do encourage them to do so, and promise them rations, blankets, pay &c. I have written to Captain Loomis to furnish them some arms if they can be spared & ammunition. If there are none at Prairie du Chien, I must procure some in this quarter.

Colonel: Hamilton, who has volunteered his services to lead the Indians to this place, will hand you this letter, and if the Menominees and Sioux can [be] prevailed upon to come, will perform the duty. I have to desire that Mr. Marsh may be sent with Col: Hamilton & the Indians, & an interpreter of the Menominee language.[241] I need not say how glad I should be to see you, also, but I suppose you cannot, under present exigencies, be spared from your agency.

We are engaged in a war that may last many weeks, & perhaps months. I am authorized to call upon the Governor of Illinois for such militia force as may be necessary to subdue the hostile Indians. The Menominees will draw rations of pork, flour, and corn at Fort Crawford to last them to this place

I shall rely on your known ability and patriotic feelings in accomplishing the object requested of you.

I refer you to Col: Hamilton for the state of things here.

Gen: Atkinson to Gen: Street. Ind: Agent.

A third letter in this vein was dictated to the commanding officer of Fort Crawford, Captain Gustavus Loomis:

Dixon's ferry Rock river 26th. May 1832.

Sir   I have requested General Street to send to me as many Menominee and Sioux Warriors as can be collected with despatch [sic] to operate in conjunction with the troops against hostile Sacs and Foxes. Should the Menominees and Sioux require some arms and ammunition I have to direct that they may be furnished from the Depot at Fort Crawford — also five days rations or more to last them to this place.

I have not time to give you an account of the posture of affairs in this quarter, but refer you to Col Hamilton who goes up to conduct the Indians to this place, and who understands the state of affairs with us.

Gen: Atkinson to Capt. Loomis.

Two more letters of similar content followed, one to Captain Joseph Plympton, commander of Fort Winnebago, and another to General Hugh Brady, who was at that post the last Atkinson had heard.

Early this morning, William Davis, Jr., and John W. Hall, two of the young men who had so miraculously survived the attack at the Davis Settlement on Indian Creek, arrived and presented themselves to the general, giving him full details of that terrible affair. They were grim young men, and John Hall concluded their remarks with an impassioned plea.

"General," he said, "we believe my sisters, Sylvia and Rachel, are still alive and with the Indians. It is our intention to try to rescue them if we can. We plan to follow the Indians to wherever they are and get the girls away."

General Atkinson sighed and shook his head. "That," he said, "would be foolhardy in the extreme. Believe me, I sympathize fully with how you feel and want to help effect that rescue in any way possible. But I cannot at this time send an escort with you, and the idea of the two of you, brave though you may be, facing the entire hostile band of Indians to effect the rescue is foolish and would almost certainly result in your both being killed, and perhaps, Mr. Hall, your sisters as well. There are two men, however, who are most likely to be able to help you, because of their many years of association with the Winnebagoes — the Indian agent Henry Gratiot and Colonel Henry Dodge. Both are in the mineral district, and if you will wait, I will write a letter to Mr. Gratiot authorizing him, in the name of the United States, to ask their Winnebago friends to try to ransom the girls from their captors. If you will carry that letter to him, it may help."

The two young men agreed, thanked him, and left to rest and have something to eat before departing again. Atkinson immediately sat down at his desk and swiftly wrote the letter.

General Atkinson to H. Gratiot Esqr
Head Qrs. Right Wing W D Dixons Ferry May 27th 1832

Sir   In the attack of the Sac Indians on the Settlements, on a branch of Fox River . . . fifteen Men, Women, and Children were killed, & two young women were taken prisoners. This heartrending occurrence should not only call forth our sympathies but urge us to relieve the Sufferers.

You will therefore proceed to the Turtle Village or send someone of confidence, & prevail on the head Chiefs and Braves of the Winnebagoes there to go over to the hostile Sacs and endeavour to ransom the Prisoners — offer the Winnebagoes a large reward to effect the object $500 or $1000 for each.

I expected to have heard from you before this.

Atkinson gave the letter to his aide with instructions to hand it to Davis and Hall and give them directions for getting to Gratiot's Grove. When the aide left, he sank back in his chair, weary of all the paperwork involved in running a war. One important letter yet remained for him to write, and he had deliberately put it off until last. Having learned of the actions of Colonel James Strode at Galena, he had become furious at what the man had taken upon himself and had wanted to allow himself some time for his own temper to cool to some degree. Nevertheless, still considerably rankled by the man's effrontery and overt megalomania, he wrote:

Genl Atkinson to Colo Strode

Head Quarters Righht [sic] *Wing West Dept*
Dixons Ferry 27th. May 1832

Sir, I have received by the hands of Mr Bates your letter of the 23rd. inst: addressed to Governor Reynolds and myself.

As I have not called upon the authorities of Galena for a military force to be employed in the service of the U States, I cannot assume command over the Troops organized by you, nor take upon my self any responsibility for the expences [sic] *incurred. Yet I cannot but admonish you against the course you have adopted, of declaring martial law, pressing individual property, coercing personal labor, hiring Steam Boats by the day &c &c involving an expence* [sic] *that will not, I am sure, be assumed or sanctioned by the government.*

(signed) H. Atkinson: Brigr Genl U.S.A.

[*May 27, 1832 — Sunday*]

The disgruntled Illinois State Militia force, which had been sent by General Atkinson to follow the supposed trail of Black Hawk's force, had been signally unsuccessful. At first, discipline was virtually nonexistent, and matters got so out of hand that General Samuel Whiteside had to issue a stern order:

Head Quarters may 24th. 1832

General orders
The great disorder in the Brigade occasioned by the mens [sic] *quiting* [sic] *their places in the line and stattering* [sic] *over the country renders absolutely necessary to inflict punishment on every one who violates orders in that particular: Colonels of Regiments and Majors of Separate battalions will require that every man shall keep his place in the ranks, if the individual is able to march and if not he will obtain permission of his captain to march in the rear of the army. all foot men will march with Majr Long's battalion. Should any man attempt to pass out of the army on either flank, or should be found out without permission they will be taken into custody of the guard, and if he be an officer will immediately be arrested. The officer of the day will be particularly charged with the execution of this order.*

By order of the Brig. Genl.
N. Buckmaster Brig Maj

Not far into their march, a verbal order had been given to the militia by Governor Reynolds giving them leave to pillage any Indian town encountered.

Growing ever more surly and uncooperative, the volunteers, having lost the trail of Black Hawk's detachment twenty miles or more into their march, had continued following Sycamore Creek upstream until they came to the Potawatomi villages under Chief Chaubenee, which had been temporarily abandoned. For their protection, Chaubenee had sent his people to the peaceful villages near Chicago while he, his son, and his nephew made their grueling rides to warn outlying settlers. While the detachment of regulars under Colonel Zachary Taylor remained in ranks and watched disapprovingly, the much larger militia force systematically pillaged the Indian towns, taking anything that caught their eye. While doing so, they discovered a frail old Potawatomi man who had elected not to leave. This was the first Indian they had encountered, and instantly a cry arose to kill him.

The unarmed old Potawatomi protested that he was a friend of the Americans, and to prove it he produced from inside his garment an old safe-conduct pass, badly faded and tattered but still legible, which he had received from General Lewis Cass during the closing months of the War of 1812.

"The letter's a forgery," shouted a short, disreputable-looking private. "Let's kill 'im."

"Make an example of him!" cried another.

"He's a spy," bellowed a third. "Run him through!"

"Shoot the bastard!" yelled a fourth.

Others were chiming in with similar incitements when a stern voice rose above the others. "*Stop!* You men back off! He's harmless, and no one's killing him."

The words had come from their company commander, Captain Abraham Lincoln. His face was flushed with anger as he stepped between the cringing Potawatomi and the soldiers. "It must not be," he shouted. "We will *not* kill this man."

"You're a damn' coward, Lincoln!" a voice cried out, instantly seconded by others.

Lincoln smiled mirthlessly, curled his hands into fists at his sides, and replied, "If any man here thinks I am a coward, let him test it right now!"

"Damn you, Lincoln," complained the short soldier who had first raised the cry against the old Indian, "you're bigger'n we are."

Lincoln gave him a scornful look and then let his eyes move across the men of his company as he spoke. "You can guard against that very easily," he said. "Any of you. Choose your weapons."

Grumbling, the men began breaking away and moving off. Captain Lincoln escorted the Indian to General Whiteside, who questioned him briefly, then wrote him out a fresh safe-conduct pass and let him go. But, disgruntled at having lost the trail of the hostiles and believing they had gone north, Whiteside gave in to the complaints of his men and headed them down the Fox River to its mouth on the Illinois River, where Ottawa was situated.

They arrived there the following day, May 25, and at once the army went into
camp, anticipating the immediate discharge they had been promised by Governor Reynolds. But General Whiteside was not quite finished with them. At once
he issued an order:

Headquarters May 25, 1832

Special Order. Col. DeWitt (and other officers):
*You are hereby commanded forthwith to cause an inquiry and search of regi-
ments in your line and report the articles of any description taken by the men at
the Paw Paw and the Indian villages on Sycamore Creek belonging to the Indians,
by whom taken, with the supposed value of such articles, to headquarters this
evening.*

By order of Brig. Gen. Whiteside
N. Buckmaster, Brigade Major.

To more howls of complaint from the men, who would not be given their
discharges until the order was complied with, all articles that could be located
that were stolen from the villages — corn, beans, maple sugar, beaver traps,
rifles, tomahawks, knives, kettles, skins, and other items — were confiscated
during the next two days and set aside to be returned to the Indians. While this
was occurring, the commanders were catching up on their correspondence.
Governor Reynolds, anxious to be away from this campaign entirely, wrote a
brief letter to General Atkinson:

Camp at Ottawa 26th May 1832

Gen Atkinson
*Dear Sir   I recd this day a letter from the Secy of War informing me that the
power of judging and acting in the defence [sic] of this state had been given to you
exclusively, so that I have decided on my course. I must therefore inform you that
I will furnish you with militia men as you may deem expedient.*
*I would suggest to you that the army here will be discharged, and that perhaps
a corps of four or five companies ought to be organized for the protection of the
frontier until the militia I have called out arrive. If you deem it right please inform
me before I leave here and I will organize them.*
I shall return to Belleville in a few days.
I have the honor to be Your obt servant.

John Reynolds Gov. of Illinois.

General Whiteside, too, having received a communication from General
Atkinson, wrote to him today in a slightly testy manner, chafing a bit under the

admonition Atkinson had written at the lack of reports from his field commanders:

Camp at the Mouth of Fox River May 27th, 1832

Genl. H. Atkinson

Sir   I received your communications of the 24th. and 25th. by express, this day. I would have informed you of my movements earlier if anything of importance had occurred.

In pursuance of your special order on the 22d. Inst. I moved with the Brigade of Mounted Volunteers under my command, up Sycamore Creek, by slow marches, sending our scouts in every direction to scour the country and obtain information of the position and movements of the hostile band of Sacs & Foxes. On the 23d. Inst. I found a trail which I followed to a small Indian Village on Sycamore Creek, where our spies found a number of scalps of men, women and children, but I could find no evidence that any large body of Indians had collected near the place, or that there was any reasonable hope of finding them by a farther pursuit eastwardly.[242] This village had been entirely deserted for several days.

Supposing, from the information I had received, by express, that the hostile band had crossed over to the Fox River of Illinois, I marched southwardly up one of the branches of Sycamore Creek, to its source, and then by way of the Papau [Paw Paw] Grove to this place. The Putawatomie [sic] Indians who inhabited the Villages on the route, had left them, and probably removed to the eastern side of Fox River for safety.

The troops under my command having been mustered into service for no particular length of time; and having entered the service on a very short notice under the impression that they would be retained only about three or four weeks, have become impatient and anxious to return home.

His Excellency, Governor Reynolds has made a call for two thousand men, to rendezvous at Hennepin, on the Illinois River, the 10th of June next, and the Volunteers under my command will, probably, by his order, be mustered out of service at this place in a few days. You will be enabled to judge from the information you already possess, what will be the situation of the frontier on this river, between this time and the 10th. of June, & can take such steps as may be in your power for its protection. The troops under the command of Col. Johnson, were at this point on my arrival, engaged in building a fort opposite the mouth of Fox River, for the protection of the settlers in the immediate neighbourhood, but most of his men are leaving him for their respective places of residence, so that there will be no person to defend the place but the inhabitants, amounting to about forty or fifty effective men. . . .[243]

I have the honor to be Yr obt servt.

Saml. Whiteside Br. Genl.
Commanding Brigade of Mounted Volunteers

Today, with the confiscation of many of the stolen Indian articles that had been recovered, the mounted volunteers under General Whiteside were mustered out of the service by Brigade Major Nathaniel Buckmaster. Before being given their discharge, the men were exhorted to reenlist for a period of twenty days, which would give the new volunteer force, already being pulled together under Governor Reynolds's order, time to get assembled and organized before the frontier was left defenseless. Despite the guaranteed short term of the enlistment, only one man in four agreed to reenlist. Those three hundred who did were formed into six companies commanded by Samuel Smith of Greene County, Benjamin James of Bond County, Elijah Iles and George McFadden of Sangamon County, William C. Rawls of Schuyler County, and Adam W. Snyder of St. Clair County. Abraham Lincoln, unable to secure enough men to reenlist under him as their company commander, accepted his discharge and immediately reenlisted as a private in the company of his friend, Elijah Iles.

Late in the evening, Colonel Zachary Taylor also wrote to Atkinson, giving many of the same details Whiteside had written about, but adding details of value to his commander:

. . . *All the trails we fel* [sic] *in with were going north, no doubt to the head waters of Rock River, or some where near lake Michigan; I do not beleive* [sic] *we were in reach of or* [in] *striking distance* [of] *any number of hostile Indian* [sic] *from the time we left r. River* [sic] *untill* [sic] *we reache* [sic] *this place, as the militia were scattered in small numbers in our rear for 10 or 15 miles daily without being molested, or so far as I can ascertain without having a single horse stolen. . . .*

. . . I have just recd. a letter from Lt. Holms informing me that he was at the foot of the rapids of the Illinois (the head of navigation) with a Steam Boat & 60,000 rations, where he was erecting a block hous [sic] *for their protection.*[244] *I shall drop down to that place tomorrow & remain untill I hear from you which I expect will be by the return of the express, when I hope you will deem it for the interest of the service to order me to join you, at which time I will enter more particularly into our movements &c, since I saw you.*

I write on my knee at ten oclock [sic] *by very little light, & am fearful what I have written will barely, if at all, be inteligable* [sic]. *My respects to the officers of your command & accept Genl, not only my best wishes for your health &c but for the honourable termination of the perplexing & difficult duty that has been assigned you*

Your Friend Sincerely Z. Taylor

At this same hour, sixteen miles northeast of St. Louis in the town of Edwardsville, Illinois, Harriet Buckmaster, wife of Illinois Militia Brigade Major Nathaniel Buckmaster, was writing him a letter that put into words what many of the Illinois citizens were pondering:

Edwardsville, May 27th, 1832

Dear Husband,

You say in your last letter you think you shall be at home in a few weeks. I hope you will be dismissed and get home soon. I would like to know why the Soldiers are coming back one, two and three at a time. If they come away without leave, I should be glad to see them whipped all the way back. Some come sick. Some, their eyes hurt with [gun] powder, &c, but we do not hear much complaint from them after they get here. I think you had better — all of you — stub your toe, prick your fingers, or something of the kind, and come home. . . . I am almost of the opinion that the most of these men that come down here are runaways and cowards. If we were foolish enough to believe one-half of what we hear, we would be frightened every day. . . . I got a letter out of the [Post] office directed to you from your brother John. Took the liberty of breaking the seal and reading it. They have received your letter — written a short time after our marriage — at last, and are all well. We have but a few moments ago locked up a man in the Cell. He was brought here from Alton for threatening a person's life and, since dark, there has been three more brought here from that place, one for committing a crime in St. Clair. I never had a very good opinion of Alton. I detest the place and all the people (but a few) that are in it. Grandma sends her love to you. We are all well. For my part, I never had better health in my life than I have had for a few weeks past. All I want now is to have you get home safe. Yes, I want all that are out on this expedition to come back. And fetch Black Hawk with you. I would keep him willingly for a short time. Would by far rather have him than Alton trash. . . . Remember me to all inquiring friends and accept the best wishes of your

Affectionate wife Harriet Buckmaster

P.S. I want you to get home as soon as you can, for I have something to tell you.[245]

[*May 28, 1832 — Monday*]

White Crow and Whirling Thunder, with Catherine Myott beside them, interpreting where necessary, had been speaking with the leaders of Black Hawk's band at the hidden camp for more than four hours. White Crow, his blind eye covered by the black silk cloth tied obliquely across his head, had spoken most, though Whirling Thunder frequently interjected his concurrence with what White Crow was saying. Black Hawk had said little, and only occasional comments or questions came from Neapope and Wesheet and the other eight Indian leaders seated about the council fire.

Thirty yards away, the Hall girls — Sylvia and Rachel — were standing together fearfully, aware that the talking concerned them but having no idea what it all meant. Their new calico dresses were no longer as crisp and neat as they had been and were now smudged with smears of grease or charcoal and showed little rips here and there. Many other Indians stood or moved about on the expanse of this island haven, though quietly, respecting the seriousness of the council in progress. The four squaws who had been the omnipresent guardians of the girls were within a few feet of them, sitting quietly and straining to hear what was being said. A dozen feet from the white girls stood the only three of their captors they recognized — the scar-faced and broken-nosed Potawatomi warrior named Toquamee and his two friends, Pukemus and Comee. The faces of all three were set in harsh lines, and occasionally they glanced malevolently at the girls.

There had been only one interruption in the flow of the council — about an hour after its commencement — when a party of six Indians arrived. One was the Prophet, Wabokieskiek, and beside him was Mugateh — Little Bear. They rode their horses to the edge of the council ring and waited patiently until Black Hawk recognized them and bade them speak.

"We have struck a strong blow!" Mugateh said loudly. "We have killed four whites at the island of trees the whites call Kellogg's. We took the scalps of all, and we wish to do our scalp dance with them."

Black Hawk nodded, pleased. "It is good news," he said, "but you seem to have other news you are holding back." He turned his gaze slightly to the Prophet and dipped his head for him to speak.

"There were six," Wabokieshiek said proudly, "of which we killed four. Three were messengers. One was the American father of Keokuk!"

"St. Vrain?" Black Hawk said, surprised. "You killed St. Vrain?"

"I personally killed none of them," Wabokieshiek admitted, "but our party killed four. Keokuk's white father was one of those. They have his scalp and wish to dance over it tonight."

The leaders sitting in their circle were generally pleased, yet Black Hawk's expression did not become lighter. If any possibility of negotiating a peace with the Americans had still existed, it was now extinguished. He felt no grief at the death of the Indian agent, since St. Vrain had always chosen to side with Keokuk in his decisions. Yet, he knew St. Vrain to have been a courageous man, and the death of a courageous man was always a matter of some sorrow.

Black Hawk shook his head. "We are in council here. I will have no dancing in this camp. If you wish to camp apart a little distance from us, you may have your dance. Mugateh and those with him should go there now. Wabokieshiek, as first chief, should remain in this council."

The Prophet dismounted and let Mugateh and his men lead his horse away as he took his place in the council circle. Towaunonne — the Trader — who was one of those in the circle, spoke swiftly then, bringing Wabokieshiek up to date on what the council had been discussing. When he finished, White Crow resumed speaking.

At last the council ended, and Menakau — the Seed — barked out an order. Immediately the four guardian squaws came to their feet. Two kept Rachel in place, while the other pair took Sylvia by the arms and led her thirty yards away, to where Whirling Thunder, White Crow, and Catherine Myott were standing. As Sylvia approached, she saw that his good eye was locked on her and there was a faint smile on his lips. He murmured a few words, and immediately Catherine put them into English.

"White Crow says, Do not be afraid. You will be going with him soon."

Sylvia's brows pinched together. "What about my sister?" she asked.

"The other will stay here with the Sacs who took her."

"No!" The words were sharp and determined. "I will not go without Rachel. Either we both go or we both stay. Tell him that."

White Crow and Whirling Thunder laughed aloud and nodded to one another. White Crow turned and faced the chiefs clustered about Black Hawk, all of whom were watching them.

"Brothers!" he said loudly. "I find I have more to say. I have told you how important it is to the Americans that these girls who were taken captive be brought back to them. They have offered a very large reward for them. Horses and five hundred dollars each." He did not tell them the whites had offered a thousand dollars each; after all, he himself deserved remuneration for his efforts in these tricky and dangerous negotiations. He went on smoothly: "Five hundred dollars each — a *thousand* dollars. It is a great deal. You had thought you would go but halfway on this, accepting half of what they offered and keeping half of the two girls. But as this older one has just told me, they are sisters and they must be together. Either they go together or they stay together, but it must be together. Half will not do. I have told you of the reward you will receive for this. If you keep both, the anger of the whites will be even greater and their search for you more determined, and they will think that I have failed them and that I do not have your trust and that what I tell them cannot be trusted. If both come with me, I will pay you what the whites have told me I can and you will have horses and money, and more than that, the whites will trust me even more than before. They will believe the false stories I will bring to them, and I will better be able to know their plans to bring them to you. Is not having these things better than having them? You need the horses and you need the money to provide for your hungry people. Is it better to have two young white women, or is it better to have horses and a thousand dollars' worth of food and supplies to continue your struggle against the whites?"

There was a prolonged discussion among the leaders of the Black Hawk Band, and then Wabokieshiek spoke.

"Take them both then, and give us what you have promised."

Whirling Thunder smiled broadly and stepped away toward where Rachel was being held. He disengaged her from the squaws who flanked her and led her to where Sylvia still stood with White Crow and Catherine. As the interpreter and the two young women stood apart a little, the Sac and Winnebago chiefs in the band approached, and there was a great deal of hand-shaking and head-nodding. Then the chiefs separated and went to their own wigwams. Toquamee and

Comee, however, approached and stood grim-faced at a short distance, looking from White Crow to the girls and back again.

Toquamee reached to his waist and pulled out a large knife. "I took them," he said. "Now you have talked them into your hands, but I will not let them go without keeping a part of them."

Whirling Thunder stepped back a little, but the finely dressed White Crow remained close to the girls, his own right hand resting on the haft of his belt knife. Without expression he watched as Toquamee stepped to Rachel and in one fluid movement cut off a large lock of her hair over the right ear, then another from the back of her head. He stuffed the tresses in his waistband. Then Comee stepped up to Sylvia and cut off a lock of her long hair just over her right eye.

When Comee stepped back a few paces, Toquamee spoke. He was still holding the knife menacingly, and his left hand rested on the tresses in his belt. "You have them now," he said, "but we will have them back. In three or four days."

"You are on Winnebago lands now," White Crow replied evenly. "Your chiefs have agreed to send them with me. You will not get them back."

Toquamee shook his head. "I am Potawatomi. These chiefs," he flung out a hand to take in the encampment, "are Winnebago and Sac and Fox. They are not my chiefs. I will take these two back."

"If you try," White Crow replied levelly, "your hair will decorate a Winnebago lance."

Toquamee glared at him angrily a moment, then thrust his knife back into his waistband, spun on his heel, and strode away, Comee close behind.

White Crow spoke softly to Whirling Thunder, then to Catherine. In turn, Catherine spoke to the girls, who still had no good idea what was going on. "We go to the horses now. You will come with us. If not, you will both die. Come."

She followed the two Winnebago chiefs who were moving off now, and after a glance at one another, the two girls gripped each other's hand and followed.

"Where are we going now, Sylvia?" Rachel murmured.

"I don't know," the older girl replied, "but we don't have much choice, do we?"

[*May 28, 1832 — Monday*]

The sense of imminent panic continued to build at Galena as the three survivors of the attack on the St. Vrain party finally reached the town after encountering and eluding several more parties of Indians. The shock wave produced by the death of Indian agent St. Vrain and the three messengers had the entire population in a state of extreme anxiety.

Even before the return of those survivors two days ago, Galena lawyer Benjamin Mills had written of the state of matters in this frontier outpost town to Indian supervisor William Clark in St. Louis.[246] Not a terribly courageous man,

Mills had had enough of Galena and its growing problems and was preparing to bail out:

May 25th

Sir   Since I saw you, I find the Boat is about to set off in which I must start for Louisville. I regret it because I would make this little note more in detail. But as it is, let me say in the first place we have every evidence that the Winnebagoes have joined the hostile Sacs, that wandering parties of both are scouring the country for depredation & slaughter, that the public roads are waylaid.

As proofs: Not a Scout from the Whites goes out without seeing more or less Indians. A late one was surprised & had one killed & two others narrowly escaped — private habitations has [sic] been assailed by them, the mail intercepted and the carrier probably killed. At Galena we are too remote from Govr Reynolds or Genl Atkinson to wait their direction or advice before we act.

In very great haste I am with Respect Yrs &c
B. Mills

Colonel James Strode continued to be active in the town and, not yet having received his reprimand from General Atkinson, continued to serve as dictator of Galena, even to the point of giving orders to the regulars stationed here. Immediately after the return of the survivors of the St. Vrain party, he wrote to Atkinson:

Head Quarters 27th. Regt. Ills. Mila. Galena

Sir   I avail myself of the present opportunity to communicate to you the situation of our affairs here. I have in pursuance of the orders from Govr. Reynolds mounted a company of mounted volunteer Rangers consisting of seventy-five effective men, from which corps I detailed 25 men with dispatches directed to yourself and Govr. Reynolds on the morning of the 24th Inst. under charge of D. G. Bates & Fred Dixon, with directions to bring from you such commands and directions as you think proper to make. I also received orders from Govr. Reynolds to organise [sic] this Regt. and hold it in readiness to march to the defence [sic] of the country at any moment on my order which I have done. I have requested the assistance of Liut. [sic] Gardenier of U.S. Infantry in this emergency. He has constructed a Block house on a commanding point to be used as a Battery, and I have taken the liberty to undertake the construction of a stockade work with Block houses which became necessary by force of public opinion, for the safety and maintenance of this important point in any contingency, and was compelled also to gratify the public demand by declaring martial law during the progress of the public works. . . . The express you started by Mr. F. St. Vrain, Kinney [Kenney], Fowler, Holley [Hawley], Hale & others, near Kelloggs old place were attacked by 30 Indians in day light on the prairie Fowler was seen to fall and Hales horse was seen without its rider and St. Vrain was heard to have made an exclamation. It is believed by Kinny [sic] and the other man [Higginbotham] who detailed to me the particulars that three of their seven were killed. We have no other facts worth your notice: Capt. J W Stephenson, the Gentleman entrusted with this dispatch, will communicate to you such particulars as are within his knowledge. He [is a] gentleman of high respectability as a citizen and active, useful and ifficient [sic] as an officer.

I have the honor to be with great respect Your Obedt Servt.
J. M Strode Col. Commd'g 27th. Regt. Ills. Mila.

Whatever letters were being written to General Atkinson now, however, would take longer to catch up to him. Shortly after sunrise today, leaving Major John Bliss to command at Fort Dixon, which was presently under construction, Atkinson left with a small force to establish a new headquarters at Fort Johnson on the Illinois River across from Ottawa and the mouth of the Fox River.

In St. Louis, William Clark had just received from Benjamin Mills and several others the appalling news of the attack on the party at Kellogg's Grove and the apparent death of St. Vrain and three others. A letter had also been received from secretary of war Lewis Cass that indicated without subtlety how angered the government was over this Black Hawk situation. Cass had written:

. . . Unless this [Black Hawk] party submit unconditionally, and surrender hostages for their good conduct, we shall only encourage this spirit of disaffection, and it will spread among the other tribes, till we are involved in a general Indian war. Every dictate of prudence and humanity requires that the predisposition for hostilities so long manifested by this band should now be effectually checked. Year after year our frontier may be exposed, the settlers driven in with the loss of their crops and to their entire ruin, the people harassed by continued militia calls, heavy expenses entailed upon the government, and our standing and influence with the Indians destroyed, unless an example is now made, the effect of which will be lasting. Under these circumstances the President has directed that operations be continued against the party of Black Hawk, unless they submit unconditionally to the demand General Atkinson is authorized to make. . . .

Clark shook his head, imagining the fuel he was heaping on the fires of wrath already raging in Washington with the letters he was preparing to dispatch now to Secretary Cass. He had written:

. . . Provisions for Genl. Atkinson's army have been taken up the Illinois River to the foot of the rapids near Vermillion [sic], which is about 40 miles from Dickson's [sic] Ferry, where the army was at the last accounts. One of the Steamboats has returned and brings the following statement of facts: The Indians killed three

families on the 20th, consisting of 15 men, women, and children, about 25 miles from the rapids, on Indian Creek, a branch of Fox River; — Two young ladies not found, supposed to be taken prisoners. The number of Indians about 30 — believed to be Pottawattamies [sic]. *One man has been found killed near Buffalo Grove, supposed to be a mail contractor. The out settlements are breaking up, much distressed for want of provisions.*

It is reported that a large collection of Indians are in the Big Woods of Fox River; these, I suspect, are the Illinois and Fox River bands. I do not believe that any of the Missouri bands will join the hostile Sacs. . . . I am informed that Mr. St. Vrain, the Indian Agent for the Sacs & Foxes, was killed by a small party of those Indians — said to be from Black Hawk's Band. There were 5 or 6 others in company with him, one or two of whom are said to have been killed also. . . . By the same Boat there arrived a deputation from the friendly portion of the Sac & Fox Tribes now on their lands west of the Mississippi, consisting of Pashepaho, the head of the Sac Tribe, and three other chiefs. They came for the purpose of representing their perilous situation, placed as they are at the mercy of those Indians whose jealousy & hatred they have aroused in consequence of their refusal to join them, on the one side, and by the inveterate hostility of the Illinois militia who consider & view them all as enemies, on the other side. They state that an attack was contemplated some days since, on Taomin's [Taimah's] Village, by a volunteer company of about 30 men who had settled on the Demoine [Des Moines] River, but which they now believe is abandoned for the present. Yet, as threats have been made by some of the Militia against Keokuk's people, they ask the protection of the U. States. As it is believed the Sac Agent is killed, and it is necessary that an active, zealous & efficient Agent be constantly near those Tribes to advise them & watch over their conduct, and learn & report their movements &c, I have, in order to obviate the numberless difficulties which must arise from the want of an Agent among the Tribes in question, temporarily appointed Mr. Pilcher, and directed him to proceed with all possible despatch to the Sac & Fox Agency, to take possession of the public property, with directions to visit the different villages of the friendly Sacs & Foxes & learn their movements &c. . . . [247] *The Sac chiefs now here inform me that a part of the Winnebagoes, Puttowattamies* [sic] & *Kickapoos of Illinois had joined the British party of Sacs & Foxes. . . . In that event, the force of the enemy will be near 1500 of the best warriors, which will require a considerable force to subdue & drive out of the country, should they make a stand, and which is strongly indicated by the murders & depredations committed at different points. Genl. Atkinson's army does not, in my opinion, exceed 1300 effective men (Regulars & militia.)*

[May 29, 1832 — Tuesday]

Now in the custody of White Crow and Whirling Thunder and, if guarded at all, only by occasional glances from Catherine Myott, Sylvia and Rachel Hall still had no idea what lay ahead. Though Catherine spoke English, she was disinclined to answer their questions, saying only that they would know what White Crow wished them to know when he was ready.

The girls had expected that they would be taken away from the hidden island camp of Black Hawk right away yesterday when they were put in the custody of the Winnebago chiefs, but they had only moved to a large wigwam and remained there throughout the night with the two chiefs and their interpreter, though a group of sixteen Winnebago warriors spent the night sleeping about their small fire just outside the wigwam.

Early this morning they had risen and, as usual, were permitted to go to the river's edge and its adjacent shrubbery to perform their toilet. Since, for the first time, they were all by themselves, they contemplated fleeing, but the river was swift and deep, and neither trusted her own swimming ability enough to make the attempt. Besides, where would they go if they *did* manage to cross the river? They were obviously deep in Indian territory somewhere and would surely be tracked down and caught again almost immediately. Besides, both had a feeling that their lot had improved considerably, now that they were with the Winnebagoes. When they returned to the wigwam, they ate a better breakfast than usual, prepared for them and Whirling Thunder and White Crow by Catherine. A short time later White Crow removed from his pack a long-necked dry gourd about twice the size of his two fists bunched together. He jiggled it and the girls could hear the loud rattle of several pebbles inside, though they could see no opening in the gourd where the stones might have been inserted.

White Crow, gourd in hand, left their wigwam, and the girls stood outside the doorway with Catherine and watched, fascinated and wondering, as he went from wigwam to campfire to wigwam throughout the camp. At each wigwam he stood before the open door, rattled the gourd vigorously, and then spoke briefly — a speech that sounded to the girls like a lecture. At each campfire with families grouped around it, he walked in a circle about the fire, rattling the gourd continuously until he returned to his starting place, then seemed to make the same short speech. It took him nearly three hours to cover the entire island encampment before he finally returned to where the girls were. He spoke with Whirling Thunder and Catherine briefly, retied the black silk band covering his blind eye, and then went outside, mounted his horse, and rode off with half a dozen of his men following.

All day long the Indians in camp moved about their duties, the men repairing their equipment and sharpening knives and tomahawks, the women dying clothes or washing them, working rawhide into chamois-soft doeskin or coarser buckskin, and scrounging in the marshy shallows of the island, searching for frogs or anything else edible. Their available food resources were obviously dwindling rapidly, and nothing was wasted.

Just after nightfall White Crow returned. The others having eaten, Catherine quickly prepared a bowl of meat and beans for him, which he ate methodically, seemingly lost in thought. But when finished, he set aside the bowl and let his gaze fall full upon his two captives. He surprised them immensely by abruptly addressing them in passable English.

"You are Sylvia Hall and Rebecca Hall."

It was not a question, but both girls nodded and Rachel said, "Yes, we are. I'm Rachel."

"Are your mother and father alive?"

Sylvia bit her lip, and Rachel shook her head and replied softly. "I saw our mother killed in the attack. Later I saw a scalp that I know was my father's hair, and I believe he is dead too. And our sister. And our brothers."

White Crow brushed a speck of food from his brightly decorated shirt and sighed. "It is bad," he said, "when such things happen. War is not a good thing."

"It wasn't *war*," Sylvia flared. "It was murder! They just came and murdered everyone!"

White Crow shrugged sympathetically. "You have had a bad time," he said, "but I have something to say that will make you feel better. When the sun comes up tomorrow, I am going to take you to your own people."

CHAPTER IX

[*May 30, 1832 — Wednesday*]

IN THE MIDST of the party of Winnebagoes, Sylvia and Rachel Hall rode steadily at an easy pace. The party stopped at intervals to rest, and it seemed to the girls that mounted Indian messengers, presumably all of them Winnebagoes under White Crow and Whirling Thunder, were always coming and going. In the evening they reached a stream that Catherine Myott told the girls was called the Yahara — River-of-the-Four-Lakes. Here they found three families camped, evidently awaiting them, and joined them. A wigwam was erected for the girls and Catherine, and when they returned from cleaning up at the river bank, they found that several other wigwams had been raised and a meal laid out.

The two girls squealed with delight at their first glimpse of the food. This was not the usual Indian fare they had been eating since their captivity. Here there were potatoes baked over coals, loaves of good bread, and pickled pork, along with steaming hot coffee. The girls relished the meal and ate heartier than they had at any time during the past ten days. They paid little attention to the fact that White Crow and Whirling Thunder sat somewhat apart, their heads together in conversation. Occasionally they glanced grimly toward the darkness surrounding the camp.

Less than an hour after they turned in, the girls were awakened by loud, angry talk. With Catherine beside them, they peeped from the doorway and saw White Crow and Whirling Thunder, along with their men, standing in a cluster near the fire. They were being confronted by a dozen horsemen, ten well-armed Potawatomi warriors under Toquamee and Comee. The two warrior leaders were speaking harshly, making fierce gesticulations that were obviously threats.

"What is it?" Sylvia asked Catherine, suddenly very frightened. "What's happening?"

"It is the warriors who captured you. They have come to demand you be given back to them, so that you can be killed, as they say it is their right to do. They are telling White Crow that if he does not give you up to them, they will take you by force and kill anyone who tries to stop them."

The girls gasped and clung to one another as they continued to watch. White Crow shook his head and spoke angrily at Toquamee, and the argument became more heated. Abruptly Toquamee lifted his rifle and pointed it toward White Crow. At this, Whirling Thunder raised his hand and barked a harsh command. From the darkness a circle of thirty Winnebago warriors stepped into view, bristling with weapons leveled at the Potawatomies. It was a tense moment.

White Crow spoke coldly, and in the wigwam, Catherine interpreted for the girls. "Look well at the hand Whirling Thunder has raised," he said. "Should he drop it, you would all be dead in that moment. We will not kill you, because Black Hawk needs all the strength of men he can get, but you will go from here now and you will remember what I say here. Your faces are known, *all* of you, and if you come near us or any Winnebago village again, you will be killed on sight. Go now, while you can."

Toquamee and Comee stared at White Crow and heard their own men stirring nervously behind them. Without a word, the two reined their horses around and moved away through their own men, who parted to let them pass and then fell in behind them. In moments the darkness swallowed them up.

Catherine let the flap drop back in place and directed the girls to return to their pallets and sleep. "There is no more to fear," she told them. "They will not return. Ever."[248]

[*May 31, 1832 — Thursday*]

The general war fever continued to build throughout the frontier, augmented by the public proclamation issued by Governor Reynolds that declared that the state had been invaded by "powerful detachments of Sacs, Foxes, Winnebagoes, and Potawatomies and that all tribes were to be considered hostile," and further inflamed by editorials in various frontier newspapers, such as *The Galenian*, that called for "a war of extermination until there shall be no Indian (*with his scalp on*) left in the north part of Illinois."

The army under General Atkinson had virtually disintegrated, and he was left at Fort Johnson across from Ottawa with a skeleton force barely enough to make limited patrols and to guard supplies. Aware that he, after a long and honorable career in the United States Army, might well be on the brink of losing the war, Atkinson tried to cover his flanks by writing to General Macomb:

Perhaps there have not been at any time stronger grounds for apprehending a combined war on the part of the Indians, nor could there be a greater alarm or more distress on the frontier.

Also, in his desire to start making a positive showing against the hostile Indians, immediately upon receiving a report from Thomas Owen in Chicago, carried to him by Sauganash — Billy Caldwell — Atkinson wrote a hasty reply for Caldwell to take back with him, a letter relating bitterly that the militia force had largely failed in doing anything thus far beyond taking flight at shadows. He added:

. . . the Governor, on his arrival here, discharged the Militia, retaining only six companies who afterwards volunteered for 20 days. These, since my arrival here on the 28th inst. have been organized into a Regt. I am not for the present able to do more than hold my position on the Rock River to keep the hostile Indians from occupying it, and this position, to keep them from committing further murders in this quarter.

I have called upon the Governor of Illinois by the authority of the President for three thousand Militia (who are to be mostly mounted) to rendezvous at this place on the 12th of next month. As orders for the assemblage of 2000 was given by the Govr. on the 14th Inst. to assemble at Hennepin on the 10th. June, I shall probably be enabled by the 15th June to organize a force to march against the Indians.

I was anxious to hear where the Pottawatomies [sic] were and, as respects their feelings & temper with regard to the war between the Sac & Fox Indians & the whites. Mr. Caldwell informs me that all those who resided in this part of the country are now in the neighborhood of Chicago and that the [Potawatomi] Nation are willing to join us against the Sacs & Foxes. I am much pleased that they are disposed to adopt this course, as under existing circumstances, they could hardly do otherwise than take sides and it is altogether important we should know which. With the regular troops I have on the Rock River, the Militia of Illinois, & some 300 Menominee Indians that I have sent for, and will most probably join me in the neighborhood of Prairie du Chien, I shall, I think, be able to take the field by the 15th to the 17th of next month and drive all the hostile Indians from the country. I am desirous, however, to employ the Potawatomies who know the country occupied by the enemy, and would therefore, besides using their arms in aiding us, be of very great importance. Will you ascertain what number I can depend upon to join me and if they would come to this place and move with us. The reason that I propose for their joining here is that I could more readily furnish them with provisions, such as corn and some meat. Should they agree to join, I want them here about the 15th June.

A variety of grisly rumors continued to spread widely, creating an ever-rising sense of panic in the white population, and those settlers who, until now, had dared to remain on their farms or in their isolated cabins, gave in to the fear and fled to the nearest large towns, which were themselves fortified and protected by local militia groups. As one of Atkinson's officers wrote in a letter:

. . . The alarm and distress on the frontier cannot be described; it is heart rending to see the women and children in an agony of fear, fleeing their homes and hearths, to seek what they imagine is a brief respite from death.

A flood of letters descended on Washington relating to President Jackson, secretary of war Lewis Cass, and others a horrendous succession of atrocities and describing northern Illinois as being "full of scenes of bloodshed and devastation unsurpassed in the history of Indian warfare in the western country." Only a few of such reports were based on actual occurrences, and those few were universally grossly exaggerated. Nevertheless, the patience of President Andrew Jackson was wearing very thin, and in the temporary absence from Washington of Secretary Cass, he directed acting secretary of war John Robb to reprimand Atkinson for his inactivity and his failure to send regular reports.

Word of threatened attacks on Chicago reached the town of Niles on the St. Joseph River upstream from Lake Michigan, and immediately a local militia force was raised to go to the aid of that settlement, some of the sixty men mounted but most on foot. During the march, the little force heard that Chicago was in no danger but that they themselves definitely were, because General Atkinson had seventeen thousand soldiers and was pressing the Indians directly toward them. They immediately lost courage, became mutinous, and turned back, only to be intercepted by a larger force of two hundred volunteers of the Michigan State Militia marching to the same destination from Detroit under command of Major General John R. Williams, president of the Bank of Michigan and one of the first trustees of the University of Michigan. The whole force was put into camp at a stockade that had been thrown up at the Door Prairie, there to assess the situation and decide on whether to proceed to Chicago or not.[249] They remained here over a week and finally moved on again to arrive in Chicago today.

The specter of the Fort Dearborn Massacre a score of years earlier was haunting the local population, and even while Atkinson was writing to Indian agent Thomas Owen, Colonel Owen was raising a force of ninety-five Indians to serve with a scout battalion and aid in the defense of Chicago should it become necessary, as everyone expected it would. The commander of the Indians was to be Sauganash — Billy Caldwell — with the post of second-in-command given to Chechepinqua — Alexander Robinson. Among the sixteen other chiefs with command positions were Wabansi, Shawnese, White Pigeon, Mzhikteno, and Pile-of-Lead. The United States regulars requisitioned from Niagara had still not reached that place to reestablish Fort Dearborn as a government post, and on his arrival General Williams decided to remain there and protect the citizenry until the regulars did arrive. While the majority of the citizens were relieved, food was growing very scarce. All the meat that had been donated by butcher Archibald Clybourne had been used up, and had it not been for the arrival of 150 head of cattle driven up from the Sangamon District by John and Mark Noble, the population in Chicago, now five times larger than normal, would have suffered.

The war, if such it could be called, was now almost two months old, and thus far the effectiveness of the whites in combating the relatively small and miserably equipped and supplied Indians under Black Hawk had left much to be desired. There seemed little likelihood of improvement in the near future.

[June 3, 1832 — Sunday]

Colonel Henry Dodge rode at the head of his volunteer force of close to sixty well-armed, grim-faced men as they approached within a mile or two of James Morrison's Grove, which was as frequently called Porter's Grove. They were a tough crew, these men that had been handpicked by Dodge and whipped into an elite force of Indian fighters. Though they rode in an easy manner, there was a subtle alertness about them that indicated they were ready for anything — an aura of strength and determination that very clearly conveyed itself to the more than two dozen Indians riding in their midst.

"Looks like we made it, Colonel Dodge," said the young man riding beside him. "I'd begun to think we were never going to get away from Blue Mounds Fort."[250]

Dodge smiled at Peter Parkinson, Jr., the seventeen-year-old son of one of his lieutenants. "I had no doubt of it, Peter. None at all."

The militia colonel's response was accurate so far as he was concerned, but there were a number of men in his command who, several times over the past twenty-four hours, had wondered if perhaps Dodge had bitten off somewhat more than he could chew.

The smile lingered on Dodge's face as he thought of the unusual events in which they had been so deeply involved. Henry Dodge had been recruiting more men to his force a couple of days ago in Morrison's Grove — which was where young Peter Parkinson had enlisted — when word had come in by Indian runner that Chief White Crow had rescued the Hall girls and would return them to Dodge at Spotted Arm's village, where he was at that time. Dodge knew better than to ride into that stronghold with his little force, experienced Indian fighters though they were, and had immediately sent the runner back with a counter-proposal that he would indeed meet White Crow and accept the return of the girls, but not at Spotted Arm's village. Instead, he instructed the flamboyant one-eyed Winnebago chief to meet him, as they had originally agreed to do, at Blue Mounds the following day — on June 3.

After the runner departed, Dodge had sent an express to Gratiot's Grove to alert the Indian subagent and ask him to meet them at Morrison's Grove on June 4 and to bring along the remainder of the ransom payment that would be due White Crow, as well as whatever men could be spared to accompany him. He also sent an express to the miners still at Blue Mounds and told them to get prepared but to treat the Winnebago party cordially when the Indians arrived. From Ebenezer Brigham he obtained a fine, large steer to take along as a gift.

Dodge had his own men see to their weapons and get everything in readiness for any sort of eventuality, and the men busied themselves toward this end throughout the remainder of the day. They were all ready for the expedition by sunrise yesterday, but Dodge had deliberately held off departure until noon, preferring to let the Indians arrive first at Blue Mounds and establish their camp.

The ride to Blue Mounds had taken less than two hours and the party of Winnebagoes were there when they arrived; some fifty warriors and numerous chiefs Dodge recognized — White Crow, Whirling Thunder, Spotted Arm, Little Priest, Old Soldier, Swallow, Broken Shoulder, and Big Man — had already set up their camp. A single large wigwam had been set up in the meadow that had been selected as the campsite. Dodge halted his force a hundred yards from them and directed his men to dismount but to keep alert without appearing to be ready to fight a battle. He then left his weapons behind and, with young Parkinson walking behind him leading the steer, walked into the Indian encampment. Private Parkinson was very nervous, but Dodge was very much at ease, pausing to greet various of the warriors as he passed them, shaking hands with a few, smiling and acting as if this were the most usual thing in the world. He finally stopped a few feet before the chiefs, who were standing together, waiting.

Catherine Myott immediately moved up beside them to interpret, and Dodge smiled at her.

"I sort of expected you'd be here, Catherine," he said. "Good to see you."

The interpreter had looked at him steadily, and the corners of her eyes crinkled faintly as she spoke. "It takes a very brave man to walk without weapons among bears. Or a fool."

He grinned. "Hidden teeth are often more to be feared than those that are bared," he said.

She smiled then but said nothing more, and Dodge turned his attention to the other chiefs. In turn he greeted and shook hands with them, then turned his attention back to White Crow, who was clad in beautifully worked buckskin and extravagant ornamentation, the black silk cloth as usual tied diagonally across his blind eye. Dodge indicated Parkinson and the steer behind him. "We have brought you and your party a gift of welcome," he said.

White Crow smiled and turned slightly to order a warrior to take possession of it. The warrior took the tether from Parkinson's grasp and led the animal a short distance away near a fire. At a further nod from White Crow, the animal was butchered on the spot, and immediately a crowd of warriors and a few squaws began preparing the steer to roast it. Dodge turned his attention back to White Crow.

"You have the two girls with you who were captured at Indian Creek." It was not a question, and Catherine did not interpret it as such.

"We have," White Crow replied.

"I would like to see that they are well and talk with them before we talk," Dodge told him.

The one-eyed chief nodded. "Come."

He led the way to the centrally located wigwam and held aside the flap for Dodge to enter. Seated on a mat, a heavily built squaw standing beside them, were Sylvia and Rachel Hall. For an instant the girls stared uncomprehendingly at Dodge, and then they scrambled to their feet and leaped to him, throwing their arms around him and hugging him tightly, sobbing in relief.

He patted them a bit awkwardly and finally sat down with them and listened while they related the events of their captivity. Dodge was especially interested in how White Crow had thwarted Toquamee and Comee in their effort to take the girls back by force.

"The next morning after that," Sylvia went on, "we moved out and traveled through land that was not so marshy as where we were before, and the trees were bigger and farther apart. Later in the day we came to some big lakes, and we went between two of them to the biggest Indian village we ever saw, right on the shore of the biggest lake."

"Spotted Arm's village," Dodge commented.

"I guess," Sylvia said, then continued. "We stayed there a couple of days, and then at sunrise today we set out again, heading west, but with about twice as many as were with us before. About the middle of the morning we saw some old tracks of a wagon."

"Yes," Rachel put in, "and we were so excited! It was the first indication we had that the Indians might really be taking us home, as they said they were. Then we began seeing more signs of civilization. When we were about a mile from here, White Crow took my handkerchief, even though it was pretty dirty, and tied it to the end of a pole and held it up as we approached." Some men came out of the buildings and waved and the Indians waved back, but though White Crow and some of the others rode up to them and talked to them for a little while, they didn't let us come close to them. They just put us in here, and we waited until you came. Are you really going to take us home now?"

Dodge nodded. "Soon. We have to talk to them first, but don't worry. You're safe now."

Colonel Dodge returned outside and spoke with the chiefs for a long while, telling them quietly but firmly that if there was any thought in their minds to join the hostile Indians or even aid them through providing them food or a safe place to stay, they should put such thought aside, as this would make them enemies of the whites, and they would have to pay the same price that Black Hawk's people would eventually have to pay.

Spotted Arm's nostrils flared during Catherine's interpretation of Dodge's remarks, and the friendly aspect of the other chiefs diminished. Dodge noted it but pretended not to, and to take the sting out of his words he added, "It is with pleasure that we note you seem to have no inclinations in that direction and that the girls you have brought to us are well. Today you will have your feast" — he indicated the steer, which now was being roasted directly on the coals. "As for tonight, some of the cabins here are empty because of those who have left them until these present troubles are over. There is room for all of you within their shelter, and you are invited to use them. Tomorrow we will council. That is all I have to say for now."

Dodge, giving the chiefs no opportunity to respond, turned and walked back toward his men, Parkinson close behind him. At his orders, the militia moved into the Blue Mounds community and settled down for the night inside Blue Mounds Fort and several of the cabins adjacent to it. Some distance away, they could see the chiefs inspecting the cabins Dodge had designated for their use. A certain tension remained among everyone. Dodge ordered his men to try to get some rest, but to sleep on their weapons and be prepared to rise quickly for any emergency that might present itself. Dodge himself finally turned in a considerable while after darkness had fallen. Close to midnight he was awakened by the sound of running feet, and the door to his quarters was thrown open. It was Captain Bion Gratiot — brother of the Indian subagent — who entered, the words tumbling from him in an almost unintelligible rush.

"Colonel Dodge, get up! *Get up!* We've got to prepare for action immediately. The Indians are going to attack! They're . . ."

"Easy, son, easy," Dodge said evenly, coming to a sitting position on his bunk and beginning to get dressed. "Calm down and tell me what's happened."

With an effort, Bion Gratiot calmed down and related what he thought was the presage to an attack. The Indians had, he told Dodge, in violation of the courtesy and respect Dodge had afforded them, abandoned the cabins they had been assigned to and had gone well out into the darkness and made camp there. Captain Gratiot said that since he understood their tongue, he went out to watch them, and had found White Crow addressing them before a fire. He said he had listened to them.

"Did they know you were there?" Dodge asked, pulling on his boots over his trouser legs.

"Yes. I made no secret of it, and they didn't seem to care at all that I was there. White Crow just went on telling them that Colonel Dodge was no great shakes as a fighter and that if Black Hawk came across him he would chop Dodge's force to bits, as he had done with the soft-shelled Stillman and his much larger force. I don't know exactly what he means by 'soft-shelled,' but it was no compliment."

Dodge quickly explained to him that it was a reference to the crawfish found in the streams and lakes. Hard-shelled and with fierce pincers, it was able to defend itself well against enemies, but at those times when it outgrew its shell and shed it for a larger one, the new shell was as soft as butter for some time afterward, and it was while it was soft-shelled that the crawfish was most vulnerable.

"Well," Gratiot went on, as if this proved his point, "White Crow called the whites — all of them — a soft-shelled breed who can't stand up before the yell of the Indians, nor can they stand the tomahawk or spear. He said when the spear is thrust at them they squawk like ducks and run to stick their heads in the bushes like turkeys or quail. Then he turned and pointed right at me and told me I had better quit you and go home and stay there."

"Was that it?" Dodge asked when Captain Gratiot lapsed into silence. "Is that all it took to alarm you?"

"Well, no, not exactly," the militia officer responded, somewhat miffed at Dodge's apparent lack of concern. "The whole bunch of them were very surly. They were sharpening their knives and tomahawks and running whetstones over the heads of their spears and talking in whispers so I couldn't overhear. Finally, a couple of the young men rode off toward Four Lakes, and I'm sure they went to get more warriors. Taking all these things into consideration, along with my knowledge of the Winnebagoes," Captain Gratiot concluded with some degree of self-importance, "I don't think there's any doubt about it. They're planning to attack before dawn. I think we'd better prepare for the worst."

"Don't worry, Captain," Dodge said, coming to his feet. "I assure you, nothing's going to happen. But I think it might be worthwhile for me to take some steps to insure this by letting White Crow know we're not of Stillman's soft-shelled breed. Come along."

They left the cabin, and Dodge summoned his officer of the guard, along with six of the men on guard. The eight, with Dodge leading the way, walked straight to where Captain Gratiot directed. A large number of Indians were gathered around the fire, and the chiefs were still there. All seemed startled at Dodge's appearance, and those in his path looked toward their chiefs and then gave way before him. He looked neither left nor right as they parted, but walked directly to the chiefs and stopped in front of them.

"White Crow," he said, with Bion Gratiot interpreting, "you have shown your faith and friendliness to the Americans by rescuing the Hall girls and bringing them here, so I find it hard to understand why you are comparing us now to those soldiers defeated by Black Hawk's party near the Kishwaukee. We, here, are *not* a soft-shelled breed. You indicate you have come here in good faith. You still have the Hall girls, which proves my good faith in you, as we could have taken them away from you. I will now ask you to prove your good faith — you and five of these chiefs with you — by coming with me now to a cabin, where we are close to each other. I and my guards will stay with you until tomorrow's council."

With some reluctance, White Crow and the five chiefs Dodge designated — Whirling Thunder, Old Soldier, Spotted Arm, Big Man, and Little Priest — let themselves be escorted by Dodge's guard to the cabin he mentioned. Dodge told them they would sleep here and that he would sleep here with them. He ordered that a strong guard be placed around the cabin and that a double guard be placed around the entire camp. Having done this, he made himself comfortable and quickly fell asleep, still unarmed, amid the five chiefs.

This morning he had another surprise for the chiefs. "We will have our council today as promised," he told them, "but not here. The agent Henry Gratiot, whom you know, is waiting at Porter's Grove, eight miles west of here, to council and to give you the rest of the reward that you have earned. We will leave for there at once. The chiefs will ride inside the formation of my soldiers, and the Hall girls will ride inside the formation of your warriors. In that way we will know we can trust one another."

Again there were grumblings and harsh looks, but Dodge ignored them and gave the orders for the men to mount up and the march to begin. And now they were approaching Porter's Grove, where the council would be held. As they entered the settlement, they were met by a small corps of men with Henry Gratiot at their head. The subagent greeted each of the chiefs in turn, along with many of the principal braves. Then Henry Dodge and Henry Gratiot, as the two principals for the whites, led the chiefs and principal braves to where the council was to be held, in the clearing adjacent to the fortified cabin. The majority of the soldiers and Indians remained apart in two separate groups nearby, eyeing each other suspiciously, and both groups ready for anything. It took nearly two hours for the food Gratiot had readied to be passed around and for the pipes to be smoked.

White Crow spoke first, his words being interpreted by Catherine Myott. As was customary at such councils, there were preliminary remarks to be made, and White Crow went into a long rambling talk, establishing his place in the tribe, describing the relations with the whites, and giving an account from his perspective of the events leading to the present war. At last he came to the point — the Hall girls. He told how they had ransomed them, how at first the Sacs were only going to give them one of the girls, but how they had managed to get both, and of the following trouble with Toquamee and Comee. Then he bade a warrior bring the two captives to him, which was done without delay, the girls coming to a stop to one side.

"My Fathers," he went on, pointing at the girls, "here are our two white sisters that we got from the Sacs. We have brought them here and we take their hands and we give them into the hands of our sister here, Mrs. Myott, for we know her and that she is true, and when she speaks to you for us, or to us for you, we perfectly understand each other, and so she must take our two white sisters and give them to the whites, to whom they belong.

"My Fathers," he concluded, "we take by the hand these two white sisters which we have brought to you. We have saved their lives, for they were to be killed by the Sacs" — the eyes of Sylvia and Rachel widened as Catherine Myott interpreted this — "and all we ask of you is that you will not put us or our children in the same situation that these young white sisters were, for we have brought you these white sisters to prove to you that we are friends of the Americans."

When Dodge made his reply, he spoke in a gentle and friendly manner. "Our friends the Winnebagoes, you have succeeded in getting the female prisoners, and your treatment of them, as admitted by the girls themselves, has been noble, kind, and humane. No men, either civilized or savage, could have acted with more delicacy of feeling than you have done on this occasion. You deserve and have well earned the highest reward, offered by General Atkinson, for this important service."

Dodge allowed his gaze to slide across the chiefs, and abruptly his voice became colder. "We have advised you to leave that part of your country occupied by the Sacs, but you say the Sacs have driven *you* and that your situation is a dangerous one, the Sacs remaining encamped so near to you. Yet our ears have heard that you are selling horses to them for cash taken from our people, murdered by those very Sacs on the highways. It should not be, and will be hereafter considered by us as your aiding and assisting the Sacs to continue the war against us. We advise you to bring your families immediately within the range of our settlements, that all communication between you and the Sacs should be cut off, otherwise suspicion will rest on you, and the lives of your people will be in danger. The United States is about to engage the Menominees and Sioux to help them in the war against the Sacs. The warriors of those tribes will be in the field in only a few days, and it will be very hard for them and us to discriminate between you and our enemies.

"In a few days more," he went on, his voice harsh now, "there will be two thousand mounted men in the field who will revenge the blood of our people that has been spilled by the Sacs. Nothing but death and destruction await them. They are faithless to all treaties, governed by none of the just principles that regulate the intercourse of one nation with another. Their hands are covered with the blood of their own agent, who had been selected by their great father, the president, to attend to all their wants, and who had been uniformly kind and good to them. The Sacs have abandoned their nation and country. They hope to collect the disaffected of all the Indian nations, the restless and discontented of the Winnebagoes, the Potawatomies, and the Kickapoos, and subsist by murdering and robbing our people. How can our government make a treaty with them? What pledge can they have from the Sacs that they will be faithful to engagements they may have with us? I will tell you — justice, sound policy, and the example that has now become necessary to give us a lasting peace with all the nations of Indians with whom we have treaties, have rendered it necessary that this band of Sacs should be exterminated. They will be killed like the pirates of the sea. The hand of every man should be against them, because they are the enemies of all mankind."

Dodge looked at his listeners, and they stared back at him soberly, but none made any sound. The white leader nodded as if to himself and spoke again, no less harshly. "Now I will ask some questions, and I want the answers to them. From you, White Crow. You profess to being our friend. We'll see. If you don't answer my questions truthfully, I will order that you be shot. How far are the encampments of the Sacs from those of the Winnebagoes?"

White Crow studied Dodge and realized that this was indeed no soft-shelled American. The white leader's eyes told him he meant what he said, whatever the cost. The one-eyed chief decided at that moment that he was not going to put himself or his party in jeopardy to protect the Sacs, and he nodded. "Close by. When the Winnebagoes move, the Sacs follow and camp close by them." At least that, he thought, ought to give the Americans pause about marching into Winnebago territory.

"How many horses have the Winnebagoes sold to the Sacs altogether?"

"Ten given for the young women and two sold by us. We did not think it any harm when we did so."

"Where, at this time, is the Winnebago Prophet and the one hundred Winnebagoes who were with him?"

White Crow shook his head as if he didn't know, then thought better of it and replied. "Wabokieshiek and his son are with the Sacs, but the half-breed Winnebagoes are all with us, both men and women. But we have sent away all the Sacs, men and women alike, who were with us."

"How many Potawatomies are with the Sacs?"

"The Potawatomies have taken all their men and women from among them, and they have sent all the Sacs that were with them back to their own people. During the battle with the soft-shelled soldiers" — the words came out contemptuously — "four Sac women ran to the Potawatomies, but the Potawatomies told them to go back, that they would have nothing to do with them."

Dodge nodded faintly and asked, "How many Kickapoos are with the Sacs?"

White Crow shrugged eloquently. "Who can know? There were seventeen lodges of the Kickapoos who joined Black Hawk. I would guess the number of men as about thirty or forty."

"How many Sacs, Winnebagoes, Potawatomies, and Kickapoos are there altogether at the Sac encampment?"

"A thousand persons, altogether. Three hundred and eighty are Sac warriors. About a hundred Kickapoos. The rest are Fox and half-breed Winnebagoes and Potawatomies. Of them all, seven or eight hundred are men, but the old men and braves stay at home. They tell the young men to go out and kill and take all they can."

Again Dodge nodded, as if this confirmed what he had estimated. "How many horses are at the Sac encampment?"

"About a thousand, I think. Maybe even more."

Dodge stared steadily into White Crow's one good eye. Now for the most important question of all. "Where is Black Hawk's hidden camp?"

White Crow hesitated for several beats, then replied in a low voice. "On the Rock River about forty miles above the Turtle Village, at the mouth of Bark River."[251] When Dodge did not ask any more questions immediately, White Crow went on in a conciliatory tone of voice. "My Fathers, I want your advice. I do not want blood spilled on our ground. There is something, I do not know whether it is right or wrong, and you must tell us. The Sacs want us to give them a piece of land, and we are willing to lay them off a piece in the prairies. When they go to it, we will come and tell you where they are, and you may then go and do with them as you please. Tell us, Fathers, is it right for us to entrap them in that way?"

Dodge appeared to consider this, but before he could reply, White Crow went on. "My Fathers, one of our men named Sheoshook lost his wife. She died, and it is our custom that when one of our friends dies, we sell something in order to mourn for him, and this man sold a horse to the Sac for the money. Here it is, and we give it to you, Father Dodge." He took a small pouch from his belt and passed it to Dodge, continuing to speak as he did so. "My Father, I speak the truth before all these people and wish what I say to go before our great father, the president. You see me and our chiefs and braves before you. We are all happy, and we will do what you tell us. You invite us to come in and stay with you, and we will do so until this business is settled. We have among us some who are half-breeds and cannot speak Winnebago, and these may stay or go where they please, but I will bring in all of my own band who speak Winnebago. I want to go back and arrange the business with the Sacs. I will take them to the place I spoke to you of. You must appoint a day, and I will meet your army and you may surround them. I will take you to them, and you can kill them all. Tell me if you wish me to do it or not."

Still there was no answer from Dodge, and White Crow seemed to be growing more and more nervous, as if afraid Dodge would live up to his threat to shoot him here and now. He moistened his lips and went on: "The Potawatomies, Ottawas, and Chippewas are one people. We have had a talk with them. We have agreed to abandon our country and give it up to the Sacs in order that the whites may come into our country and kill them, for we want them exterminated. The Ottawas and Chippewas have already removed to their agent, and we will do the same. Among the Sacs is our blood, and the blood of all the nations, but we will do whatever you say."

White Crow glanced toward the Hall sisters and then back at Dodge and Gratiot. "My Fathers, when we bought the two prisoners from the Sacs, they told us that if we brought the women to the whites we would all be put in jail, but we told them we were coming to our brothers and had nothing to fear. You will soon be writing to our great father, the president. We wish you to tell him that all this difficulty is caused by the Sacs, and we shall withdraw entirely from our country until the war between the whites and Sacs is ended, but in doing so we shall lose all our corn, and we request the president to give us something in the fall to support us in the winter, for we shall raise no corn or anything else. When the land is cleared of the Sacs, we want to return home." White Crow folded his arms across his chest, indicating he was finished speaking.

Again Dodge let his gaze swing back and forth across the Indians before he replied. His voice was firm, but not so harsh as previously. "My friends," he said, "you ask me if it would be right to give the Sacs an encampment on your ground for the purpose of betraying them to us, or of placing them in a situation on high ground where we could surround and take them. I answer that when any people come on your ground and drive you from your villages, you have the right to kill them. The Sacs are a band of renegade outlaws who should be killed wherever they are to be found. The government, by their war chief, General Atkinson, will employ the Menominee and Sioux against the Sacs, and my advice to you is to join them and to kill and plunder the Sacs to remunerate yourselves for the losses you have sustained by them. But I will send General Atkinson this talk, and he will tell you also what to do. He will have two thousand men mounted and all the people of this country ready to move against them.

"Now we are nearly finished here. We are pleased at your return of the Hall sisters, and the remainder of the payment will be made to you in full through order of General Atkinson, relayed to you by Colonel Gratiot. There is peace between us, and yet, in our hearts, we feel there is waiting only an opportunity for you to turn your back on what you have told us and go to Black Hawk's aid. To prevent this and to show your good faith, we wish you to leave with us five of your people — at least three of them chiefs. You need not fear for them. They will be cared for and treated well until it is deemed proper to return them to you."

The chiefs discussed this in murmured tones, and then White Crow spoke a final time. "To show our good faith, we will do as you ask," he said. "Those we will leave among you are my son and the son of Chief Broken Shoulder, as well as Chiefs Spotted Arm, Big Man, and Whirling Thunder. Mark this final word well. If in the slightest way any harm should come to any of them, the hand of every Indian will turn against you."

Within a quarter-hour the entire complement of Indians, with the exception of the five hostages, had galloped off eastward. And the Hall sisters, Rachel and Sylvia, were free at last.[252]

[*June 4, 1832 — Monday*]

Joseph M. Street, the Indian agent at Prairie du Chien, fully expected the cooperation of the Sioux and Menominee to aid the Americans in their war against Black Hawk's band, but he was more than a little surprised when a delegation of Winnebagoes from the Crosse Prairie showed up under the leadership of their chief, Waucon Decorah, offering their services in the same pursuit.[253] Oldest and most powerful of all the Winnebago chiefs, Decorah, as he was most often addressed, had a dignified manner and commanded respect from all his people. He had fine Roman features, and from his bald head fell one single lock of long, gray hair. His clothing was natural, finely made buckskins and doeskin with very little ornamentation of any kind. He spoke to the Winnebago agent for over an hour before leaving with a stream of devoted followers behind him.

In the letter he was presently writing to Colonel Henry Dodge, the delight Joseph Street was experiencing in this circumstance of Indians volunteering to fight against Black Hawk was clearly evident. He was presently, Street wrote:

. . . engaged (under the orders of Genl Atkinson) in endeavours [sic] *to procure and forward as large a force of Sioux & Menominee Indians as could be readily assembled, and much of my time up to the present moment is exclusively devoted to the attainment of this object. The express* [was] *dispatched* [to the tribes] *within an hour of the arrival of Genl. A's express, and I shall expect 2 or 300 Sioux here on tomorrow even'g. There is* [sic] *41 Menominee Warriors in readiness and waiting to descend with the Sioux to Genl. Atkinson. Many Winnebagoes are suing to go. I have uniformly said to them, "do as you please. Your Great Father no longer restrains you. Like a kind father to his red children, when they were killing each other he tried to make peace between them, and desired you not to go to war The Sacs & Foxes refused to hear his words and disobeyed his commands. They came over upon his lands and disturbed his white children. This he will not suffer. And he has placed his army between them & the Mississippi, who are watching to prevent their return. Gnl. Dodge & the men under his command is* [sic] *watching from Rock River to the Wisconsin to prevent their return this way, and men are marching from Illinois who will follow them up Rock River and kill them all. Your Great Father now considers them the common enemies of all mankind & means to pen them up and kill them all. . . . You ask to be permitted to go to war and drive them out. Do so. I no longer restrain you. Some of your people south of the Wisconsin are suspected of giving help to the Sacs & Foxes. Prove that you are 'true men' and friends to the white people by driving these disturbers of the peace of our country out of your land or hide them beneath the ground. I repeat, your Great Father, no longer able to keep them at peace, has penned them up, and intends to kill them all. His men from a distance will not know you from the Sacs & Foxes, and if you are found together many of your people may be killed by mistake. But turn your hands against them and aid in subduing these wolves and you will be safe, and prove your friendship to the whites and your love of peace & quiet. Do therefore as you please.*

[June 10, 1832 — Sunday]

General Henry Atkinson at Fort Johnson on the Illinois River seethed at the delay involved in the efforts to raise another three thousand militia to make an assault on Black Hawk's force. True to his promise, Governor Reynolds had issued orders to the various Illinois counties for the raising of such a state force, but the date of rendezvous for these troops was June 15, and little could be done prior to that time except accumulate the requisite war supplies at Fort Wilbourn.

Adding to the frustration was his inability to ascertain the whereabouts of Black Hawk. Reports came in almost daily with supposed intelligence that Black Hawk was here or there or somewhere else, but all had proven incorrect, and so, while Atkinson anguished over it all at Fort Johnson, little hit-and-run bands of hostile Indians continued to rampage with seeming impunity across the frontier. No word had been received from Galena in an inordinately long time, and Atkinson became convinced that if the communication could be reopened he would learn concrete information about the Indian situation. A first effort to do this had resulted in failure. Before the militia had been mustered out, the company of Captain Adam W. Snyder had been ordered to report to Colonel Zachary Taylor at Fort Dixon on Rock River to receive orders. When they got there, Colonel Taylor read the dispatches from Atkinson and then gave Captain Snyder orders to continue to Galena, but at this Snyder's company had balked. Word had just reached Dixon of the attack on St. Vrain's party and the death of the Sac agent and others. Only days remained until their enlistment expired, and Snyder's men simply refused to undertake the mission and returned to Ottawa in time to be mustered out. Atkinson was furious, but he hadn't given up on the project, and so he called in Captain Elijah Iles, commander of one of the companies that had just reenlisted for a period of twenty days to remain and protect the settlers until new troops could be assembled.

The company of Captain Iles seemed particularly suited for a dangerous mission, since it was largely made up of privates who were former generals, colonels, captains, and other distinguished men from the disbanded militia companies, such as the former General James D. Henry, who had served as a regular army lieutenant under General Winfield Scott in the War of 1812 and saw action in the battle of Lundy's Lane and several other battles. Another was the former Captain Abraham Lincoln, who had been one of the first to reenlist for the twenty-day service. All had been mustered in by a West Point graduate who was now serving as adjutant of the new company, Lieutenant Robert Anderson.

It was nearly sunset on June 4 when Captain Elijah Iles presented himself to General Atkinson at headquarters. He came to attention and saluted smartly. "Reporting as ordered, sir!"

Atkinson returned the salute and directed the militia captain to stand at ease. "Captain," he went on, "you have some very distinguished fighting men in your company. How would they feel about undertaking a mission that could prove to be hazardous?"

Iles's eyes glittered with anticipation. "I believe, sir," he said, "that they would leap at the opportunity."

"I thought so. How many men do you have now, and how long would it take them to prepare to ride?"

"The present muster is fifty men, General. They're well equipped and eager, but they're getting rusty from inactivity. We would need no more than one day of preparation."

"Excellent. Here's what I have in mind." Atkinson then explained the urgent need to reopen the communication with Galena and assess, if possible, the Indian presence between here and there. "You would travel from here to Fort Dixon on the Rock River, where you would deliver dispatches to Colonel Taylor, and from there follow the Kellogg's Trail — or the Galena-Peoria Road, as I believe it's being called now — to Galena, again with dispatches to deliver and with the view of conferring with military and civilian authorities to ascertain their present situation. Every effort should be made to discover, from those who may have solid knowledge, the present whereabouts of Black Hawk's principal encampment before the new troops arrive here."

"Nothing would please us better than such an expedition, General. We could leave here first thing in the morning the day after tomorrow."

"I'll have the orders drawn," the general said. "Thank you, Captain."

The special order was dictated and posted first thing the next morning:

> *Head Qrs. right Wing West. Dept*
> *Ottoway* [sic] *June 5th. 1832*

Spl. Order No. 16.

Capt. Isles' [sic] company of mounted Volunteers will be in readiness to move from camp tomorrow morning on an excursion of several days. Capt. Isles will call on the Genl. for Special instructions.

By order of Brig Genl Atkinson
> *(signed) A. S. Johnston, A.D.C. & A.A.A. Genl.*

The day was spent by Captain Iles's troops enthusiastically readying themselves and their equipment, molding balls and fitting new flints to their rifles, and with the captain conferring with the general. Wishing to be as little encumbered as possible, the men decided to take nothing along that could be dispensed with. Each man had only his rifle, a blanket, tin cup, coffee, canteen, a wallet of bread, and some fat side of meat to be boiled or eaten raw. Two of Iles's men, who had gone down to Fort Wilbourn at the foot of the Illinois Rapids to aid in loading the army's supplies into smaller boats and bringing them up had not yet returned as expected, and it was decided not to wait for them. The actual marching order was posted the following morning only minutes before the forty-eight-man company headed out:

Spl. Order No. 17

Capt Isles [sic] *of the mounted Volunteers will march this morning with his company to Dixon's Ferry Rock river, & report to Col. Taylor & receive his orders.*

Capt Isles with his command will return to this place in nine or ten days, should not important matters connected with the public service prevent it.

By order of Brig. Genl Atkinson

The first night out, the company camped about twenty-five miles northeast of Ottawa, just after crossing Big Bureau Creek.[254] The next day, assuming the Indian risk greater, they traveled at a slower and more watchful pace and finally arrived at Dixon's at seven o'clock in the evening. They looked across the Rock River and groaned when they saw the poor excuse for a fort that had been erected there by Major John Bliss — a small, low, uncomfortable structure built largely of squares of prairie sod.

Colonel Taylor was informed by the guard of the detachment's arrival and sent over a lieutenant in a canoe to ferry its commanding officer over. Iles told the officer that he appreciated the offer, but that he would not come with him immediately. "Please tell Colonel Taylor that I will be over as soon as I get my men settled. We're going to camp beside a good spring I know of about a half-mile upstream."

Later, true to his word and accompanied by Private Henry, Iles crossed over to the fort and found that Colonel Taylor was a bit piqued that the detachment had not come across to camp with him, since they would have been safer here.

"Colonel," Captain Iles said, smiling to take the sting out of his words, "we feel just as safe where we are as we would be quartered in a one-horse fort, but that's not really the reason we camped out. I know what my orders are that General Atkinson has sent to you in this pouch" — he handed it to the officer — "and I really prefer testing the mettle of my men before embarking them on that possibly perilous mission."

"And perilous it may well be," Taylor agreed. "Since the murder of the men along Kellogg's Trail, all communication with Galena has been cut off, and chances are the road is still being watched. I want you to proceed toward Galena and will have your orders ready for you in the morning. For now, if you wish to camp at the spring, so be it. What can I provide for you and your men? Do you need arms, ammunition, powder? What about horses?"

"Thank you, Colonel, but our equipment is good. We'll trouble you only for some coffee, side meat, and bread."

In the morning, joined by John Dixon, who had sent his family under guard to Galena for safety, Iles crossed his company over the river and reported to Colonel Taylor. The orders had been drawn and called for the detachment to collect and bury the remains of the St. Vrain party and then proceed to Galena, making a careful search for signs of Indians, especially with a view to finding out if they were planning to escape out of the area by crossing the Mississippi below Galena, and also trying to ascertain their present whereabouts. Colonel Taylor also assigned one of his regular officers, Lieutenant John Harris, to go with the party.

They started off at once, their ride made easier by being able to put all their wallets of corn and other food in the four-horse wagon John Dixon was driving. They were still in sight of Fort Dixon when Captain Iles detailed six men to ride lookout — two to the right, two to the left, and two in front, all six to remain in view of the main body and remain out until camp was made for the night. Watchful for Indian sign, they followed Kellogg's Trail, and all went well until sundown, when they paused to make camp just after crossing a ravine. The flank scouts came in immediately, and in moments the two advance scouts came thundering back toward them.

"Indians! *Indians!*"

The whole company leaped to their feet and, able to see a long distance ahead on the road, could make out a large body of men on horses coming their way. They scrambled back below the shelter of the ravine that crossed the road, and John Dixon, the last one in, took a final look before dropping into cover.

"They're Injins, all right," he said, his white beard bobbing excitedly.

Iles ordered the horses moved far to one side, out of sight in some brush cloaking the little valley, and then stationed his men at intervals in the ravine, comforted by the fact that they would not be able to be seen by the approaching party until the riders were within thirty feet. With this accomplished, Captain Iles went to Private Henry.

"General," he said, "would you like to take command?"

The former officer smiled and shook his head. "No, but thanks for asking. Stand at your post." Still grinning, Henry moved from one man to another, talking to each in a low voice and bolstering his spirits. A peek by Dixon over the edge of the ravine at the riders still approaching in the faltering daylight was enough to send him sliding back down to the bottom with words hissing from his mouth. "My God, there must be two hundred of them!"

Lieutenant Harris, U.S. Army, had armed himself with two holstered pistols, two horse pistols in his belt, and was carrying a double-barreled shotgun in both hands. He ran up and down the line, occasionally saying the same words: "Captain, we're going to catch hell!" At last, at a sharp word from Private Lincoln to settle down because he was unnerving everyone, he stopped in one place and two or three times picked his flints and reprimed his weapons. When finally finished, he moved along the line slowly and, seeing the men calm and ready at their posts after having received the encouragement from Henry, moved up beside Iles and said, "Captain, we are safe. We can whip five hundred Indians!"

It was not until the riders, unaware of the hidden company, topped the ridge at the edge of the ravine, only thirty feet distant, that Iles recognized Colonel Henry Dodge. Instantly Iles shouted to his men, who had rifles aimed.

"Hold your fire! They're militia."

There was consternation at first on both sides, with horses rearing and weapons being drawn, but then they settled down, and Iles's company let out a great cheer of relief. Not a man in the ravine had thought he would live to see the sunrise.

They made their camp and talked long into the night, Dodge reporting that he was en route from Galena to Dixon's to find out what had happened to the army, since no word had been received for the past ten days. Dodge told them that only a few hours before, his party, which included Colonel Stephenson and his company of militia from Galena, had found and buried the mutilated bodies of St. Vrain, Fowler, and Hale near Kellogg's Grove, though they had not been able to locate the body of Hawley.[255] Burial of the unfortunate dead had been Stephenson's mission, and with the grisly chore accomplished, Stephenson's company had remained with Dodge's party to locate and report to General Atkinson. Dodge also told Iles of the Porter's Grove council with the Winnebagoes and the final rescue of the two Hall girls. He said he was en route to General Atkinson to report this and other matters, not the least of which was intelligence of the whereabouts of Black Hawk's principal camp at the mouth of the Bark River.

In the morning the two groups separated, and the company of Captain Iles was again on the march for Galena. Before noon, just as they passed into a grove of trees, the two advance scouts galloped back to the company and reported a sighting of Indians.

"Where?" Iles demanded.

"Right there, dammit! Can't you see 'em?"

Iles followed the line of their point to the right and saw two of his own scouts — one of them wearing a red shirt — trying to catch an Indian pony they had encountered. The two had been involved in Stillman's Defeat, and since their horses were weak and it was easier for them to march out of the column, Iles had detailed them to ride with the front guard, where they would not have to keep in formation. Having lost the Indian horse, the pair came back to the column a little sheepishly.

Captain Iles shook his head disgustedly. "You two," he told the pair, "can ride in the rear from now on and drop back as far as you want. You two," he indicated the advance guard, "can get back in formation." He then selected two other privates, one of them Abraham Lincoln, to ride as advance guard, and the march continued.

Late in the afternoon yesterday, some fifteen miles from Galena, the company reached the Apple River settlement, where one of the principal structures had been converted into a fort.[256] They found the stockade filled with women and children, along with only a handful of men, and everyone in a state bordering on panic. Just a couple of hours earlier two of the men, who had been working in the field, had been fired on by Indians and then chased into the stockade. The inhabitants all expected a major attack and insisted that Captain Iles's company stay inside the stockade with them for the night. Iles gently refused — it would simply have been altogether too crowded — and instead they camped for the night about a hundred yards away. Private Henry, whom the men insisted on calling General, drilled the men all night, so that at any time they might be called, they would leap to their feet and stand in two lines, with the front ready to fire and fall back to reload while the second stepped up and took their places. The defense action was practiced several times during the night, and the men got very little sleep.

A careful scouting early this morning showed no sign of Indians anywhere in the vicinity, so the company took its leave and continued to Galena. Now, well before noon, they rode into Galena to the cheers of the populace.

[June 12, 1832 — Tuesday]

"Just what in hell is going on out there?" President Andrew Jackson stormed. "I want to know why we haven't heard from him, and I want you to tell him that in no uncertain terms! Understood?"

"Yes, Mr. President." Acting secretary of war John Robb gathered up his papers and stood. "I'll see to it immediately, sir."

Less than ten minutes later, in his own office, Robb was pacing back and forth and dictating so rapid a heated stream of words to General Henry Atkinson that his secretary was having difficulty keeping up.

Department of War, June 12, 1832

Sir, Information has reached the Department, from Dixon's Ferry, Hennepin, Rock Island, Chicago, Detroit, Galena, Prairie du Chien, and St. Louis, of the movements, depredations, and murders committed by the hostile Indians upon the frontiers, but nothing has been received from you, upon the subject of your movements with the regular and militia forces under your command, since the 10th. of May, when you report your force to be 340 regulars, 165 foot volunteers, and 1500 mounted men. If you have written subsequently, your communications have not been received.[257]

I am directed by the President to say that he views with utter astonishment and deep regret the state of things. Orders were forwarded to you on the 5th. of May to call upon the Governor of Illinois for such a force as you might deem necessary to drive the Indians across the river and, if they would not surrender the murderers of the Menominees or assumed a hostile attitude after having recrossed, to forthwith attack and chastise them.

If the information received at the Department is to be relied upon, (and your report of the 10th. May in which you state your numerical forces to be 2000 corroborates the statements) a force sufficient has been acting with you in the field for some days past to have effected the object of your expedition. From the instructions given and the measures adopted by the Department and the Governor of Illinois, the President had a right to anticipate promptness and decision of action and a speedy and effectual termination of Indian hostilities, and the capture or death of Black Hawk, the principal agent in the work of death and desolation. Some one is to blame in this matter, but upon whom it is to fall is at present unknown to the Department.

It was expected that you would have despatched [sic] expresses daily from your Head Quarters to the nearest and safest point of communication, and have kept the Department advised of your movements, and the state of affairs in the region of country where you were called to act.

The President is at a loss to account for this remissness, especially as letters from the seat of war and its vicinity are almost daily received, from the agents of the Government and others, one of which, dated the 21st. of May at Prairie du Chien, contains this remarkable sentence: "Is it not strange that no official communication has reached this post from Genl. A. or Govr. R. since the battle near Dixon's Ferry — all is rumour [sic] and report."

The President directs your particular attention to the subject of this communication and instructs me to say that Black Hawk and his party must *be chastised, and a speedy and honorable termination put to this war which will hereafter deter others from the like unprovoked hostilities by Indians upon our frontiers.*

I have &c, &c (signed) John Robb Actg. Secy of War

Genl. H. Atkinson, Illinois, Via St. Louis.

[*June 13, 1832 — Wednesday*]

Keokuk was uncomfortable in the fact that he had even crossed the Mississippi River, and his state of mind was in no way improved by the malevolent looks he had received from the whites at Rock Island — soldiers and civilians alike — as he had made his way to the Sac Indian Agency office to speak with St. Vrain's temporary replacement, Joshua Pilcher. He had been speaking to Pilcher for fifteen minutes and was irritated that this man let so little of what he felt appear in his expression that it was impossible to read him or have a clue to what he might be thinking.

"I have only this much more to say to you," Keokuk said firmly. "I and my people are Sacs, and we have had nothing to do with this present trouble lighted by Black Hawk and those who have joined him. We tried to prevent this, but we failed. We tried to dissuade him, but we failed. We invited him to live with us across the river, but he refused. What has been done is on his head, not ours. You have been invaded not by Sacs, who are your friends, but by Black Hawk and his band, who are no longer connected to us. We now wash our hands of it and leave your army to squash him. There is nothing more we can do. We leave now to hunt for the rest of the summer at the starting waters of the Nichnabatona and the Nondowa and the Au Boyer."[258]

[June 14, 1832 — Thursday]

Black Hawk was depressed at how his Indian allies were gradually pulling away from him. In the face of the continued success by the raiding parties and the total ineffectuality of any white men they had encountered, that they should be drawing away from him was incomprehensible. Yet, he had to admit he believed the reports of spies, that many of the Indians he had counted upon, particularly the Potawatomies, were moving closer to the white settlements, where they would be safe and not drawn into the conflict.

True, there were those who were remaining faithful, and these were extremely important to him — notably the Winnebagoes who were supporting him openly under the Prophet, Wabokieshiek, and those supporting him covertly under White Crow. Without their continued aid, he would have a difficult — perhaps impossible — time of it. His mood was not improved when he thought of his people on the Rock River island at the mouth of Bark River. Their hunger was getting worse each day, and there was simply not food enough to be found anywhere near the encampment. They had taken to digging for roots and eating grubs and grasshoppers and worms to supplement their diet, and still it was not enough. They had begun to kill the horses and eat them, despite his order that if they did so, the perpetrators would be killed. Yet, what were they to do? They were hungry and sick and weak, and their eyes, if not their tongues, blamed him for the predicament in which they now existed.

Word had come that the detested Menominees and Sioux, who had been prevented by the whites from fighting the Americans, were now being encouraged by those very whites to join them against Black Hawk's band. Worse, some of his allies — some of the Winnebagoes and most of the Potawatomies — were also offering to take up the hatchet against them.

What was needed, Black Hawk decided, were some strong blows against the whites, stronger than any thus far. Blows that would not only destroy the enemy and raise Black Hawk's prestige among the tribes, but that would also provide his people with the type of plunder they most needed now — meat and grain. And perhaps just such a blow was shaping up today.

Black Hawk and two of his minor chiefs, Toogranau and Koonay, were leading ten of his young warriors on a raid.[259] None of the young men had as yet earned the eagle feather of a brave for having killed an enemy. Today, the Great Spirit willing, they might have that opportunity.

These thirteen Sacs were being guided along the Pecatonica River by two Winnebago chiefs — White Crow and a village chief named Chaetar, who had long been Black Hawk's friend.[260] It had been agreed among them that White

Crow and Chaetar would only lead them to the whites against whom the attack would be made, but once the objective was sighted, they would slip away and return toward Four Lakes. As for Black Hawk and Toogranau, they too would move off just before the attack began, heading back for their island encampment. This would leave Koonay, a tall, seasoned fighter of about fifty, to actually lead the young men, armed only with tomahawks, knives, and war clubs, to the attack. Koonay had tomahawk and knife, but except to defend himself, he would not strike. This was the day for the young men. After the successful fight they envisioned, the plan was for Koonay to lead them to other settlements for more attacks.

The war party was following the Pecatonica upstream and soon came to an area of very fertile, level bottoms that were under cultivation, where two settlers named Omri Spafford and Francis Spencer had established a farm. It was no more than six miles southeast of the small stockade called Fort Hamilton.[261] These farmers, along with a number of others, Black Hawk's guides told him, had been working in these fields every day, and they would undoubtedly be here today.

They were. From a hill some distance off, the members of the war party looked down at six men wielding hoes in the black earth of a cornfield. The six, who had been spending their nights in the safety of Fort Hamilton, had ridden down from there early this morning to cultivate the crops. Besides Spafford and Spencer, there were hired hands named Bennett Million, Abraham Searles, James McIlwaine, and John Bull. Their horses were tied in the shade near the edge of the cultivated field.

White Crow touched Black Hawk's shoulder, nodded when Black Hawk looked at him, and then he and Chaetar moved away. Black Hawk and Toogranau remained where they were and watched approvingly as Koonay stealthily led the young men toward their quarry, they perfectly mimicking his movements.

Within minutes, the eleven were peering at the six whites from a screen of bushes along the river only thirty yards away. Twenty yards beyond the whites, six flintlock rifles were leaning against a large boulder on the other edge of the cornfield close to the horses. A couple of jugs also rested on the ground close to the big rock.

Koonay held his charges in place with hand signals and waited. For nearly twenty minutes they waited, until finally Omri Spafford wiped his brow with a cloth and lowered himself to the ground with a grunt, motioning the others to do likewise. All but one did. The exception was young Bennett Million, who walked to the boulder and picked up one of the jugs by the finger hole, then brought it back to the others. Just as he reached them, Koonay gave a chopping signal with his hand, and all eleven Sacs burst from cover, shrieking their war cry.

From his vantage point with Toogranau, Black Hawk nodded approvingly.

Koonay's strategy of waiting until the men sat down was well thought out. Precious moments were lost as the farmers leaped to their feet to dash toward their weapons, but the attackers were upon them before they could reach the rifles. There was a wild melee of swinging arms and shrieks and cries. Two of the men, Spencer and Million, split off, angling away from the action toward the river, but in different directions. They were a hundred feet or more away before three of the young warriors broke off in pursuit. The remaining four whites lay dead amid the spears of new corn, and Koonay stood apart, watching proudly as the eight young warriors scalped the bodies and mutilated them in ritualistic frenzy.

On the distant hill, Black Hawk was grinning. "They have done well, those new braves," he said. He started away, and Toogranau fell in beside him. "We will take the horses with us and tell these fine young braves that we will hold a dance of celebration for them when they return to our camp."

[June 15, 1832 — Friday]

General Henry Atkinson looked better than he had for quite a few weeks past. Part of the reason was that the militia force of three thousand men he so desperately needed was rapidly assembling here on the Illinois River and would soon be organized, equipped, and in condition to march. An even stronger reason, however, was the fact that he was finally getting a line on where the elusive Black Hawk had established his secret camp.

As more and more of the new volunteers came in, Atkinson had realized that having them rendezvous at Ottawa was pointless. A vast amount of supplies had been brought from St. Louis up the Illinois River as far as the steamboats could bring them, which was at the foot of the Illinois Rapids, and deposited at Fort Wilbourn at Peru, Illinois. That installation was no more distant from Dixon's than Ottawa, and so it was foolish to transfer all the goods from the steamboats to Fort Wilbourn and then reload them in smaller boats to be transported to Fort Johnson across from Ottawa. The trail to Dixon's from Peru — called the Peru Road — was every bit as good as that from Ottawa to Dixon's, and so, accordingly, Atkinson had moved his headquarters three days ago to Fort Wilbourn and the assembling troops were redirected here. It would take four or five days after the rendezvous date of today to elect officers and shape the army into its brigades, regiments, battalions, and companies, but once that was accomplished, the thrust after Black Hawk could begin.

The direction of such a thrust was now clear to the commanding general. Despite the fact that reports from Chicago indicated that small parties of Sacs still hovered in the Big Woods area along the Fox River, Atkinson had become convinced that these were merely annoyances, and that Black Hawk's principal band was far from there, well up the Rock River. His pinpointing of Black Hawk's present encampment location came as the result of two letters he received, and of the arrival at Fort Johnson — the day before headquarters was moved downriver — of Colonel Henry Dodge with his news of the rescue of the Hall sisters and his council with the Winnebagoes.

The first letter had come from Captain Joseph Plympton, commanding officer at Fort Winnebago, who had written on June 5:

Sir, I have the honor to inform you that an Indian has just arrived from Rock River who reports that the hostile Sac & Fox Indians, about 300 strong, are at a place on Rock River called "Where they peal [sic] the Bark," 10 or 50 miles above [Lake] Koshkonong — in a thick & swampy country — where they say they are determined to make a stand. . . .

The second letter, dated two days later from that same post, had been written by John H. Kinzie, the Winnebago subagent stationed there:

Sub-Indian Agency, Fort Winnebago, June 7, 1832

Sir, In haste I enclose for your information a letter sent to the Winnebagoes of Upper Rock River by the Winnebago Chiefs in this vicinity. They seem determined to prevent the hostile Indians from encroaching any further on their lands, and say they will kill every one who shall cross the line of demarcation they intend to establish. This will be somewhere in the vicinity of Muddy Lake, east from this and distant about 60 miles. Muddy Lake is about 10 or 15 miles north of the place on Rock River called "where they peel the bark" The country thereabouts and to the eastward of it is very swampy and thickly timbered. A compy. of Infty. has just arrived from Green Bay.

Very respectfully, Sir, Yo. Obt Sevt Jno H. Kinzie

The triangulation of Black Hawk's location seemed to become complete, however, on the arrival here on June 11 of Colonel Dodge, who brought with him a copy of the speech he had made to the Winnebagoes, including the questions he had asked and their replies — especially that final, pertinent question about Black Hawk's present whereabouts, and White Crow's answer that his camp was on an island in the Rock River at the mouth of the Bark River. At last Atkinson had a target!

Dodge, having reported to Atkinson on June 11, was anxious to start back the same day to continue his patrols and urge the further erection of fortifications in the mining district, but the general had him wait long enough for him to write to the Winnebagoes, Henry Gratiot, and Colonel Zachary Taylor. He was very pleased with Dodge's report and felt that perhaps his accomplishments at Blue Mounds and Porter's Grove might help Colonel Taylor overcome to some degree the rather dim view that crusty regular held of the militia generally. When Atkinson had sent Taylor back with the small force of regulars to command at Dixon's and to rely on the militia to help keep that quarter safe, Taylor had characteristically sniffed and commented, "The more I see of the militia, the less confidence I have in their effecting anything of importance, and therefore tremble not only for the safety of the frontiers, but for the reputations of those who command them."

Within a couple of hours after finishing his report, Dodge was leading his company back again toward Dixon's and Gratiot's Grove. The written "talk" he carried from Atkinson to the Indians was rather remarkable:

To Whirling Thunder & the Crow.
The other Chiefs and Braves of the Winnebago Nation

Brothers, Your talk has been brought to me by our friend General Dodge. It gives me great pleasure to hear that your hearts are good, and that you hold your white Brothers fast by the hand Continue to keep the chain bright between us. Let no thorns grow up in the path and both you and us [sic] will be happy.

Do not listen to the Sacs, they are bad men and shall be punished before I leave the country. I am coming with a great Army. You must take up the hatchet and join us The Sioux, Menominees and Pottowattomies [sic] are our friends. They will go with us against the Sacs. Our friend Genl. Dodge and Mr Gratiot will tell you when to raise the hatchet — be still until you receive my words through them. You may promise the Sacs a piece of land to deceive them in the way you propose in your talk with Genl. Dodge. Keep the Sacs deceived about every thing till we are ready to strike them.

The letter Dodge was carrying back with him to Henry Gratiot was only a brief message, but it touched on the genesis of Atkinson's plan:

Sir, I have reced. [sic] your letter of the 6th Inst. by Genl: Dodge. Obtaining the ransom of the two female captives from the hostile Sacs is a source of great gratification to the whole community & an object that I had at heart above all things. . . .

I have sent a talk to the Winebagoes which Genl Dodge will shew [sic] you. Impress upon them the propriety and the truth of my remarks, and engage them to comply with my advice.

When we take the field it will be necessary for you to accompany some part of the Troops with the woman who interprets for the Winebagoes. I shall probably put a strong force under Genl: Dodge, to operate on one side of the [river?] while I am operating on the other. You can therefore with safety go with him. Genl Dodge will inform you of things here.

(signed) H Atkinson Brigr Genl U.S. Army.

General Atkinson's letter to Zachary Taylor was more encouraging than any he had written him since Taylor's return to Dixon's Ferry:

Colonel, . . . I approve of the measures you have taken relative to taking a position on the road towards Gratiot's and of employing the volunteers to scour the country. Keep this operation up till I join you, which will, I think, be in ten days at the furthest. Request Capts Snyder & Isles [sic] to continue in service with their companies till my arrival at Dixon's.

The Militia of Illinois are now coming in and it is probable we shall organize a force of more than Two Thousand in 5 or 6 days, when we shall set out and join you at your position on Rock River. The position of the enemy has decided me on this course of operations. None of them are in the Great Woods on the Fox River. Therefore, retain the Indian allies with you. The cattle about Dixon's may serve in part for their subsistance [sic] till I send a drove over from this place, which are now being collected and will as soon as possible be dispatched. Besides, I shall take over a large supply of provisions when the Army moves.

I shall employ some hundred or two of Pottowattomies [sic] to move with me against the Sacs, not so much on account of their strength, but to make them a party in the war. . . .

(signed) H. Atkinson, Brigr Genl US Army

P.S.   Should you think the Sioux and Menominees can be used to advantage by Colo [sic] Hamilton in the Mineral District till my arrival, send them over. I understand beef cattle can be obtained at or about Gratiot's for them. H. A.

Yesterday, to prepare the Chicago area Winnebagoes for their role in the forthcoming push against Black Hawk, Atkinson wrote to Thomas J. V. Owen, the Indian agent at Fort Dearborn:

Head Qrs. of the Army of the Frontier
Fort Deposit, near Ottaway [sic] 14th, June

Dear Sir, . . . The young ladies who were made captive by the Sacs have been ransomed by the Winebagoes [sic] and delivered over to Gnl. [sic] Dodge and Mr Gratiot Sub Agent.

I have the same advice from Genl. Dodge who came over to see me a day or two since, that you have recd. from the Pottowattomies [sic] chiefs as to the position of the hostile Indians. It is their stronghold from whence they issue in small parties to commit depredations.

The Illinois Militia have arrived and we are now organizing an Army and shall take the field in two or three days. We have more than 3000 Militia besides 14 Companies of Regular Troops. With these we can certainly rid the country of the enemy. I shall keep a force about Ottaway whilst I am operating on Rock River.

I wish the Pottowattomies under Caldwell [Sauganash] and Robinson [Chechepinqua] to join me at Dixon's in about six or seven days. . . .

Today, with Fort Wilbourn and its surroundings a vast mustering-in camp for the new issue of militia just called up, Atkinson had just received an express from Colonel Taylor:

> Camp at Dixon's Ferry of Rock River
> June 13, 1832

Genl   Your communication of the 11th inst. by Genl Dodge came safe to hand yesterday morning, & I can assure you that I was truly gratified to learn that the militia were coming in, & I truly hope that enough will join to bring the war to a successful termination sooner than you calculate on.

Col. Hamilton got here last night with a Winabago [sic] & four Menominees, having left about 165 Sioux's [sic] & Menominees at Buffalo Grove, 12 miles from this place on the Galena Road. He left here this morning & will take a position with them in the vicinity of the hostile Indians for the purpose of cutting off any small parties that may attempt to leave or join them from the west side of the Mississippi, or elsewhere, take female prisoners if practicable, steal their horses, & distress them in every possible manner. This I thought preferable to keeping them here inactive, & eating up our provisions. Col. H. has promised to communicate promptly anything of importance that may transpire which may be necessary for you to know, particularly in relation to the movements of the enemy. I have directed him to procure flour at Galena & beef in the Mining District for the subsisting [sic] of his Indians.

Col. Henry [Pvt./Gen. James D. Henry] with Capt. Iles' company returned a few hours since from Galena. They report signs of small parties of hostile Indians which are daily made between this & that place, who occasionally burn the houses which the inhabitants have left, besides stealing horses & committing other depredations. On Saturday last they took 12 or 15 horses from Apple River, part of them out of the ploughs, the owners having made their escape. From all I can learn, they are more anxious to get horses than to take scalps, which induces me to believe they will attempt to make their escape from us through the country in some direction or other if it is possible for them to do so. Col. Henry represents [that] the citizens at & about Galena [are] in such a complete state of alarm that you need not expect them to take any steps or measures to prevent them from recrossing the Mississippi, even were they to pass in sight of their doors. Majr Riley is now with 2 companies at Kellogg's Old Place [Kellogg's Grove] about 18 miles from the settlements on Apple River, & Capt Smith's company of the 1st [1st Infantry] is at Buffalo Grove where they will remain until you are ready to move against the enemy; & I hope they will be able to protect the persons & property of the people of Galena & its vicinity, as well as to put a stop to the passing of Indians between the Mississippi & headwaters of Rock River. Capt Snider [sic] with his company is with Majr. R's command, but I expect they will return here by the 15th or 16th inst., as he informed me before he marched that the time for which his compy. [sic] volunteered to serve would expire then, & he drew rations to serve that period. I do not expect his company can be prevailed upon to serve longer; I will, however, try & prevail on them to do so.

My respects to all the gentlemen of the army with you, & accept, Genl, the assurances of my esteem & respect.

In the midst of the preparations in and around Fort Wilbourn, a bit of ironic amusement made its rounds in a copy of a letter written by Isaiah Stillman to the editor of the *Sangamo Journal* in Springfield, Illinois:

Dear Sir: Having been permitted to return to this place [Canton, Illinois] for the purpose of assisting to organize a Battalion of Rangers to march on the frontiers, in my hurry and bustle of business, I have only time to say that I have been informed by credible authority that representations have been made to the citizens of Sangamo and elsewhere, that the men under my command, on the 14th were defeated by fifty-nine Indians. This report has been circulated by a few deserters, who broke from our ranks at the first appearance of danger, and further circulated by some of our sapient wiseacres and electioneering demagogues. Testimony will hereafter show that our enemy consisted of more than five hundred Indians, well armed and equipped.

Our men conducted with prudence and firmness, and I regret that officers and men, who have been considered brave in the battles of Tippecanoe, Bridgewater, Chippewa, &c., should be disgraced in consequence of misrepresentation and falsehood. Maj. Stephenson, together with several gentlemen from Galena, who volunteered as privates, have received the same censure as ourselves: Maj. S., to my knowledge, was engaged and conducted in a manner that would have done credit to a veteran soldier.

Thirty-four Indians, from the best account, were killed.

Yours, &c. I. Stillman.

[June 15, 1832 — Friday]

Ebenezer Brigham of Blue Mounds was relieved. When the two miners named George Force and Emerson Green had been killed in ambush late yesterday afternoon, everyone thought it was the prelude to a major assault on the little fortification here that the miners had built. Force had been a lieutenant in the militia and Green a private, and the rest of the local militia members were very upset and nervous. Then Colonel Henry Dodge had shown up this morning with a company of his rangers, having just returned to the Mining District from a grueling tour in the saddle that had taken them to Galena and Dixon's Ferry and Ottawa, then back again; a tour made nerve-racking by having found and buried the bodies of the unfortunate members of the St. Vrain party near

Kellogg's Grove. Much of Dodge's force, when it had returned to Gratiot's Grove, had been temporarily dismissed, to go to their own fortified stations in order to rest and get fresh supplies and fresh horses before Dodge would assemble them again for another round of ranging the Mining District for the enemy skulking about. Dodge himself had gone to Dodgeville with this small company that had remained with him, then had come here to Blue Mounds from there. And despite their weariness, Dodge's rangers had helped bury the two miners, who had been shot and scalped less than a mile from Blue Mounds Fort.

Just two hours ago, Dodge had finished his final inspection of the defenses at Brigham's mine and was impressed with their sturdiness. He expressed the opinion that a few men within the fortification could easily hold off quite a few attackers. When he lifted himself into his saddle to join the rest of his company, waiting a short distance off, he looked down at the powerfully built Ebenezer Brigham.

"It's well deserving of the name Blue Mounds Fort, Eb," he said. "Keep up the good work and stay alert. I'm convinced we won't have peace with this bandit collection of Indians until we've killed them right up to their dens." He had then grinned as he reined his horse around. "Keep your hair on!"

Dodge had kneed his horse toward the others, and the whole column set off on the road leading southwest toward Fort Hamilton, where his scattered ranger companies had been instructed to rendezvous with him again. Brigham had watched them go, hoping that any Indians in hiding nearby had seen them too, and would avoid any more incursions here like the one that had taken the lives of Force and Green yesterday.

Now, in mid-afternoon, Brigham sent two of his employees, Benjamin Smith and William Griffith Aubrey — who was a lieutenant of the local militia — to the spring about a mile north to bring back some fresh water for the other miners to drink. The deaths of their fellow miners still very heavy in their minds, the two young men had armed themselves well, each with a pistol, Smith additionally with an old standard flintlock and Aubrey with a new U.S. Yaeger.[262]

As they approached the spring, Smith thought his mare was favoring her left front hoof and got down to check it. With his knife he picked out a pebble that had lodged under the shoe. He then remained afoot and began leading his horse by the reins for the remaining short distance, following Aubrey, who was still in the saddle, holding his horse to an easy walk.

In the bushes just beyond the spring, six Winnebago Indians crouched in concealment. They were under command of two braves named Hunkquat — He-Who-Has-Seen-the-Chief — and Wauzeeree — North Wind.[263] Hunkquat, a lean, wolfish individual, barked a harsh command and the Indians fired. Aubrey took two of the balls through his body and cried out as he was slammed from the saddle, the reins still gripped in his left hand. Smith felt the passage of a ball through the side of his shirt and instantly dropped the reins and leaped away. His pistol fell from his belt into the dirt, but he managed to hold onto his rifle as he plunged into the nearby bushes and raced back toward the fort as fast as he had ever run. When he cleared the bushes he glanced back and saw the six Indians clustered around Lieutenant Aubrey, but none chasing him. Two, however, raised their rifles and fired at him, but both balls missed, and he plunged on.

The alarm was raised immediately, and within a few minutes a squad of twenty heavily armed men galloped to the site. They found Aubrey lying on his side in the path some thirty feet from the spring, but a swift search indicated the Indians had vanished. The men dismounted and inspected Aubrey's body for signs of life. The two rifle balls had entered his body, one in the left side, one high on the right shoulder, but neither wound mortal. Yet, Aubrey was dead. So hurried had the attackers been to get away that they hadn't even scalped him, although he had been severely stabbed in the neck with a spear — evidently the intended killing stroke — and his rifle was gone, as were both horses and both pistols.[264]

"Damned Sacs!" one of the men said bitterly, then broke into a stream of curses.

"They weren't Sacs," said Benjamin Smith. "Their heads weren't shaved. They were those damned treacherous Winnebagoes!"[265]

[*June 16, 1832 — Saturday*]

Colonel Henry Dodge and two of his rangers were within a mile of Fort Hamilton. Expecting the worst, all three had their guns at the ready. There was good reason for their caution.

Word of a tragic attack by the Indians had intercepted him yesterday only an hour after he left Blue Mounds. The express, a gangly red-haired youth named David Worth, had come from Captain Robert C. Hoard, one of the principal smelterers of the area at Fort Defiance. That small stockade had been built on the Daniel Parkinson farm, five miles southeast of Mineral Point. The report was that five men had been killed the day before by an Indian war party several miles below Fort Hamilton, along the Pecatonica River. A young man named Bennett Million, who was evidently the only survivor, had managed to escape the Indians and reach Fort Defiance on the headwaters of Otter Creek, about fourteen miles from where the attack had taken place. Chased by the Indians, he had taken at least two lead balls through his clothing, though they had barely grazed his skin, and had finally eluded them by four times swimming across the Pecatonica and, bypassing Fort Hamilton, which he thought might have been taken by the Sacs, made his way to Fort Defiance, which he had reached in the middle of the night.

Dodge had immediately dispatched a detachment of his remaining rangers, under Captain James H. Gentry, to go to Fort Hamilton at double speed, to render aid if necessary. If the fort was secure, then Gentry's detachment was to continue to the scene of the attack and bury the dead, then try to ascertain the number and movement of the enemy and return to Fort Hamilton to meet him there.

Dodge, with those left of his command, stopped briefly at Mineral Point to alert the miners there to possible danger. He rejected the offer of one of the miners there to ride to Dodgeville and take Dodge's wife to safety in Galena.

"Someone already suggested that," he said, a note of pride in his voice, "but my wife refused. She said, 'My husband and sons are between me and the Indians. I am safe so long as they live.' And, gentlemen, my sons and I fully intend to stay alive."

The detour to Mineral Point took several hours, after which Dodge set off late in the day for Fort Hamilton with his small force. At nightfall, still an hour or so away from Fort Hamilton, they camped at Fretwell's diggings under a double guard.

First thing in the morning today, while his rangers prepared their breakfast, Dodge rode on with just two of his men, giving the others orders to follow as soon as possible. It was close to 8:00 A.M. when the three approached to within a mile of Fort Hamilton, at which point a movement just ahead caused them to jolt to a halt, weapons at the ready. A rider came into view from behind a screen of trees, but it was only one of the miners of the area, a sturdy German individual whom Dodge recognized as Henry Appel. They paused and spoke together for a minute, Dodge pointing out the danger the miner could be in, traveling alone this far from the fort.

"Ach, I know," he said. "I haf been in fort zince alarm vas zounded. I go to mine cabin now only to get blankets und come back quick!"

"Good enough," Dodge said. "Keep alert and hurry back."

Dodge and his men spurred their horses into a gallop toward the fort as Appel continued riding toward his cabin, which the rangers had passed a short time before. The three militiamen were close to the fort, when, from well behind them, they heard three shots.

"Probably Captain Gentry's men doing some target shooting," Dodge murmured. They continued to the fort and were just dismounting when there was the sound of drumming hooves, and Henry Appel's horse galloped toward them. It faltered as it neared them, and they could see that there was blood all over the saddle. A ball had passed through the top part of the horse's head and punctured one of its ears.

Dodge raced into the fort shouting the alarm, saw Captain Gentry's detachment there, and called for the officers to get their men armed and mounted immediately. Most of the horses were unsaddled and the men themselves not yet really pulled together for the day. A short time later, Dodge's remaining men came in. While they were preparing, Dodge conferred with Gentry and learned that late yesterday the detachment, guided by Bennett Million, had found the site of the attack and the scalped and otherwise mutilated bodies of four men — Omri Spafford, Abraham Searles, John Bull, and James McIlwaine. Of Francis

Spencer no trace could be found, and from young Million's account of the attack, it was presumed Spencer was dead and his body would be found some time later.[266] The bodies were hastily buried, and the detachment scouted around until they found the tracks of the Indians, all of them evidently afoot, heading northeast toward the East Branch of the Pecatonica. The assumption was, until the shooting this morning, that the Indians had disappeared back into the wilderness from which they had come. Now it seemed likely that they had circled back to the vicinity of Fort Hamilton and struck again.

Dodge circulated among the men as they made their final preparations, urging them to greater speed and firing them up with an almost constant stream of rhetoric. Finally, about half an hour after his arrival, with a strong detachment left behind to guard the citizens at Fort Hamilton, twenty-nine men were mounted and grimly ready to move out after the war party.[267]

"They've only got a thirty-minute head start on us, boys," Dodge cried, "and as far as we know, they don't have horses. I'm sure we can catch and kill every damned one!"

There was a yell of approval, and Dodge smiled grimly. He drew out his sword and held it high. "I *intend* to overtake them before I stop. Mark what I'm saying — I *will* overtake them before I stop, and when I do, I'll charge them with sword in hand, no matter how many there are! If there are any here who won't follow me in doing this, I want them to fall out right now. I want no cowards with me!"

Not a man moved back as the whole group burst into approving cries and shouts to get started. "All right, then," Dodge said, "we're committed to it." He stood high in his saddle and shouted, "Forwaaaard!" and broke into a gallop, the twenty-nine thundering close behind. About a half-mile from where he had briefly encountered Henry Appel, Captain Gentry's horse developed a severe limp. Moments later they found the stocky miner's body. Appel's scalp was gone and his body badly mutilated by random tomahawk blows and spear thrusts. Since Gentry could ride no farther, he volunteered to get back to the fort and bring out a burial detail to inter the remains. Dodge nodded and thundered on, the company at his heels.

The Indians, clearly on foot, had scattered at first to confuse pursuit, but they had converged again several hundred yards east, and once the trail was picked up, it was plain enough to follow easily. Soon it entered a large prairie, near the center of which was an extensive thicket of almost impenetrable brush, prickly ash, and fallen timber, all cloaked with wild grapevines and averaging about ten feet in height. There was no way to know if the Indians were still in it. Dodge's men glanced at one another nervously. If the Indians were hiding in there, it was big trouble. It would be hard to see a man standing only ten feet away.

"Boys," Dodge told them, "I don't think they're in there. It's what they want us to think, so we'll lose a lot of time thrashing about in there trying to find 'em. We'll split up here. You six" — he pointed to the men — "go around to the right and watch for any Indian sign coming out. You six" — he pointed to others —

"go around to the left. The rest of you, follow me through on the trail. If you find a trail coming out, signal. We'll all meet on the back side. Watch sharp now!"

They split apart, the two squads circling and Dodge's group plunging directly into the thicket. Among those who went to the right were Privates Samuel Black and Peter Parkinson, who both lived at Willow Springs near Fort Defiance and who had become close friends. Black, who had no family here, had more or less attached himself to the Parkinsons, and he and Peter had become inseparable friends, though Peter had a difficult time understanding Sam's moods, which regularly fluctuated between high spirits and black depressions. Now, as they rode slowly around the fringe of the thicket, staring at the ground for the trail of the Indians, Samuel was chatting constantly and laughing a great deal at his own wit.

"I don't know what you're so cheerful about, Sam," Peter complained. "I've got a bad feeling we're going to smell gunpowder before this is over. You realize if we catch up with those Indians, we're going to have to fight them, no matter how many there are. But that's okay," he added with bravado, "because no matter what we get into, I'm going to come out of it just fine."

"Maybe you are, but I'm not," Sam said, then laughed again. "Nope, if we go into battle — and I'm sure we will — I'm going to get killed. Mark my words."

Peter thought he was joking, but then saw he wasn't, and became very serious. "Look, Sam, if you've really got a presentiment you're going to be killed, let me find some kind of excuse to keep you out of the battle. You know, we could make your horse get lame or have you take a fall and get hurt or something."

Sam Black shook his head. "Nope. Thanks, Peter, but I couldn't do that. I'd rather be killed than have the word go back to my mother in Ohio that I was a coward."

They fell into an uncomfortable silence then and continued watching the grasses. Their job was fairly easy compared to that of the group under Dodge. The trail was much harder to follow inside, but they pushed along with considerable effort and were near the far side when there came a yell from the group on the right. Sam Black had discovered the tracks they sought. The squad that had circled left was at this point only a few hundred yards away, and they quickly galloped up to them. Moments later, Dodge's group burst out of the thicket nearby. The trail exiting the thicket was very clear now, with no effort having been made to hide it — weeds bent over and broken down from the passage of a file of men on foot. The Indians! They were headed directly east toward the East Branch of the Pecatonica. Once again the pursuit went forward at high speed, very nearly in single file itself and extending back from Dodge for a quarter-mile or more.

In less than four miles they topped a low hill and caught their first glimpse of the quarry — a string of eleven Sacs far ahead, trotting at a surprisingly casual pace through a broad prairie and heading toward the far-distant banks and scattered brush that marked the meandering course of the Pecatonica. The leader of the group, a tall man of about thirty, was visibly egging the others on, often running backward, talking to them and encouraging them after him with motions of his arms.

The course the Indians were taking led them to a small tributary stream of the Pecatonica with very steep banks. The Sacs had no trouble scrambling down one side and up the other, but the pursuers had to dismount and coax their horses down, across, and up the other side with considerable difficulty. Some of their guns got wet and had to be discharged and wiped dry and reloaded. While so engaged, four or five of the Indians managed to circle around and, from a considerable distance, get a few shots off at the whites with the weapons they had taken from the Spafford party. A return fire from Dodge's men, however, sent them running back to the others, with no one on either side hurt.

The small stream crossing had delayed the pursuers enough to let the Indians reach the Pecatonica, where they slid down the very steep and rugged bank to the water, swam across in the midst of a horseshoe bend, and came up on shore on the other side in the midst of the horseshoe, a circular area about one hundred acres in extent. Here there was a bit more cover, along with several oxbow ponds, the residue of river course changes long ago.

Dodge was familiar with the area, and also knew of a fording place at the upper arm of the horseshoe bend. He led his men at a full gallop to that point, and they thrashed across, cutting off the escape of the Indians through the "mouth" of the horseshoe. Now the Sacs were boxed in, unable to retreat across the river again due to the steepness of the bank they had descended. Dodge immediately ordered four men to keep watch from atop slight hills at the narrow mouth of the bend to prevent the Indians from slipping past, then ordered his party to dismount. They left their horses with a four-man guard, and the remaining twenty men advanced on foot behind Dodge. They finally glimpsed where the Sacs had taken refuge, on the edge of one of the oxbow ponds, behind a six-foot embankment where they were crouched to make their stand. Separating the militia from them was a grassy clearing no more than forty feet square.

Keeping to cover, Dodge advanced with his men to the edge of the clearing until they were no more than thirty or forty feet away from the hidden Indians, who evidently felt the clearing was enough to deter a direct charge, where the whites would be exposed to their fire. They underestimated Dodge. He spread out his remaining twenty men in an extended line, ten to each side and himself in the center, his adjutant, Lieutenant Charles Bracken, to his immediate right.

"This is it, men," the colonel said, and, sword in hand, began the advance across the clearing. The line of men moved boldly, if somewhat apprehensively, into the clearing. When they reached about the midway point, the Sacs opened fire. Three privates were struck and mortally wounded. Two balls, either of which would have been fatal, hit Samuel Wells in the chest and throat. F. Montaville Morris was shot through the heart. Samuel Black, hardly an arm's length from Peter Parkinson, was shot in the head.

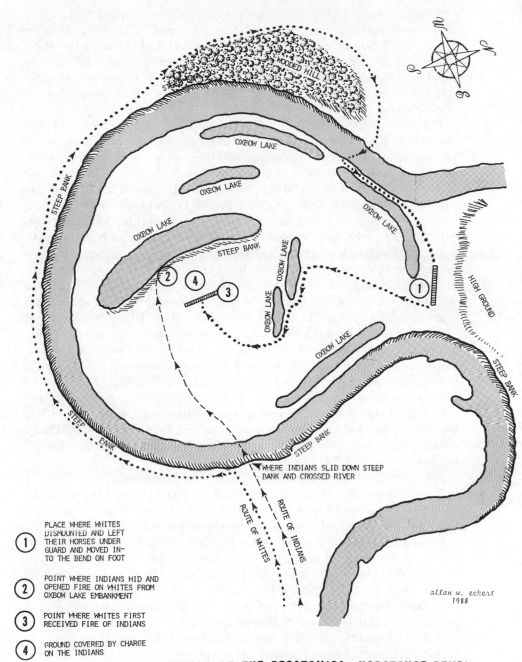

WOODED HILL

OXBOW LAKE

OXBOW LAKE

OXBOW LAKE

STEEP BANK

OXBOW LAKE

STEEP BANK

OXBOW LAKE

OXBOW LAKE

OXBOW LAKE

STEEP BANK

HIGH GROUND

STEEP BANK

STEEP BANK

STEEP BANK

STEEP BANK

WHERE INDIANS SLID DOWN STEEP
BANK AND CROSSED RIVER

ROUTE OF WHITES

ROUTE OF INDIANS

ROUTE OF WHITES

allan w. eckert
1988

① PLACE WHERE WHITES
DISMOUNTED AND LEFT
THEIR HORSES UNDER
GUARD AND MOVED IN-
TO THE BEND ON FOOT

② POINT WHERE INDIANS HID AND
OPENED FIRE ON WHITES FROM
OXBOW LAKE EMBANKMENT

③ POINT WHERE WHITES FIRST
RECEIVED FIRE OF INDIANS

④ GROUND COVERED BY CHARGE
ON THE INDIANS

BATTLE OF THE PECATONICA (HORSESHOE BEND)

"Charge!" shouted Dodge, his sword uplifted, and the rangers broke into a wild run, brandishing their weapons. Almost blinded by tears for his fallen friend, Peter Parkinson raced forward with the others. Within instants the whites were within ten feet of the now partially visible Indians, and the militia opened fire at what they could see of the enemy. It silenced some, but not all. A second volley from the Sacs dropped Private Thomas Jenkins with a serious, but not mortal, wound.

The whites plunged over the low rise and pounced upon the Sacs, and from this point on it was a fierce hand-to-hand battle, with bayonets and rifle butts and a couple of swords against tomahawks, war clubs, spears, and knives, the whole punctuated with the clang of steel against steel, with screams of anger and triumph and cries of pain and fear, along with the terrible meaty sound of weapons colliding with flesh and bone. Private Levin Leach, his rifle having been fired, glimpsed a young warrior thrusting a spear at him. He dropped his gun and grabbed the sharp, napped flint head of the spear in his bare hands and hung on. The Sac kept jerking and thrusting the weapon, trying to drive it through Leach's body, but the private hung on grimly, all the while his hands being severely lacerated. Finally Leach jerked hard on the spear and pulled the Sac off balance so that he fell. Instantly Leach scooped up his rifle where it had fallen and drove his bayonet through the Indian's chest, killing him.

Several yards away the Indian leader, Koonay, was hastily reloading after having put his first shot into one of the privates. Colonel Dodge, a few yards away with bloodied sword in hand, saw him raising the weapon and shouted to Lieutenant Bracken, who was close by but looking the other way. "Here's one — kill him!" Even as Bracken was turning, Koonay pointed the rifle at him and pulled the trigger, but the hammer snapped without igniting the powder. He dropped the gun and jerked his knife from his belt, then leaped toward Dodge with a savage cry, but Dodge drew a pistol from his belt and shot him through the head.[268]

"There, by God!" Dodge exclaimed. "I've killed him myself!"

In an amazingly short time — which seemed much longer to the participants — it was all over. Eleven Sacs lay dead, and those that had slain them were slicing away the topknots of hair from their otherwise bald scalps.[269]

Leaving the bodies of the Sacs where they fell, Dodge's men collected their own dead and wounded and put them on horses. Privates Samuel Wells and F. Montaville Morris were both dead. Private Samuel Black had a severe head wound where a ball had entered just over his ear. It had not penetrated to the brain but had fractured the skull, and though still alive, he was unconscious and evidently in bad shape. Peter Parkinson mounted his horse and had other men lift the limp form of young Black up to him, determined to carry him all the way back in his arms.[270] Private Thomas Jenkins had been shot through the shoulder, but was able to ride on his own. Henry Dodge led his triumphant little force back to Fort Hamilton, where they found that within an hour of their departure,

Colonel William Hamilton had arrived with a party of Sioux and Menominees brought from Prairie du Chien. Dodge ordered all the Sac scalps turned over to the Indian allies, who were delighted with the gift of these trophies from their slain enemies. The Sioux and Menominees almost immediately went to the site of the skirmish — which some of the men were already calling the Battle of the Pecatonica and others were calling the Battle of Horseshoe Bend — cut the bodies of the eleven dead Indians into bits, and held a war dance around them.

Finally alone in quarters at Fort Hamilton, Colonel Dodge wrote out a hasty but gratifying report:

Hamilton Fort June 16th 1832

Sir   Our men buried the five men killed at Spaffords [sic] Farm before my arrival at this place. The Indians killed a man in less than ½ mile from this place. I instantly pursued them with 29 mounted men. I came in sight of them in about 2½ miles and pursued them into a bend of the Petittotica [sic]. I dismounted my men, linked my horses, left four men in charge of them and advanced at open order under trail arms until I came up with them. I had placed on the hills 4 pointers to prevent their escape. 21 of us advanced on the Indians. We received their full fire by which three of our men fell, severely wounded. I instantly ordered a charge on them, which was obeyed with the greatest promptitude. In less than half a minute we killed the whole party, consisting of eleven men, and got their scalps.

Col Hamilton arrived here with his Indians. His party, added to Decary's [Decorah's] party will make about 200 men who will be engaged under their leaders in ranging the country so as to cover this position as well as the fort at the Mounds.

I shall return home today. Should anything take place of moment, send me an express immediately.

H Dodge Col Commanding

Dodge put his pen aside and leaned back, rubbing his eyes with his knuckles and yawning hugely. He felt very good for the first time in quite a long while.

The Americans finally had a victory to flaunt, and they cared not a whit that it would quickly assume an importance far out of proportion to its value in the war. They had, prior to now, had virtually nothing to crow about, and they meant to make the most of it. With this victory, the whites could no longer be assumed by the Indians to be a soft-shelled breed.

[*June 17, 1832 — Sunday*]

At virtually the same time Colonel Henry Dodge was setting out yesterday to pursue the Sacs in the vicinity of Fort Hamilton, some twenty-two miles to the south, a similar pursuit had been mounted by Captain Adam Snyder at Kellogg's

Grove. Now, with yesterday's action behind, Snyder was writing his report to Bennett Riley:

Kellogg's Grove 17th June 1832

To Major B. Riley. U.S. Army comdg at Kellogg's Grove.

Sir   On the morning of the 16th, with forty three men, I commenced the pursuit of some Indians who came in the vicinity of our camp to steal our horses & who succeeded in stealing one of Mr. Kellogg's. About one mile from the Grove the trails shewed [sic] there were a considerable number of Indians near us. After pursuing some considerable length of time, we discovered that four were in company with the stolen horse. We rapidly pursued these about 20 miles in the direction of the Mississippi River, where we suddenly lost the trail. After some search it was found. We had pursued them so hotly that they left the horse & part of their breakfast. After a short rest we made rapid pursuit again & about ten miles from this place we overtook a party of them & killed four of them, they having returned in this direction. In this skirmish one of my company was mortally wounded. I then took up my return march, which was very slow in consequence of the wounded man having to be carried on a litter. When within about four miles from this place, a party of five of my men went down to a branch on the left to get water & were fired upon by a large party of Indians. They killed two of the five & wounded a third. They immediately commenced firing on us in a body. At this time many of the men were on foot & without guns in consequence of the litter, which was carried by eight men, frequently relieved. The men were for the moment thrown in complete confusion, & retreated a short distance, where I succeeded in rallying and forming. We then commenced firing on them & maintained our ground for a considerable time. The Indians shewed no disposition to follow us. The number of the Indians was thought by most of the men to exceed 100. My own opinion was there was not more than fifty or sixty. About one half were mounted and the others on foot. I do not know the number of Indians we killed in the last skirmish. I am only certain of one. My loss is three killed and one slightly wounded.

I am respectfully your most obedient servant

A. W. Snyder Captain Illinois M. Volunteers

Names of men killed & wounded:
   Killed: William B. Meckumsum, Benjamin Scott, Benjamin McDaniel

   Wounded: J. M. McTyre Cornelius

[*June 18, 1832 — Monday*]

The party of five men and a boy of sixteen had congratulated themselves heartily yesterday upon reaching the cabin belonging to Ament J. Hodges, less than ten miles north of Hennepin near Big Bureau Creek.[271] Ever since crossing the Illinois River just above Hennepin, all of them had been exceedingly nervous. All, that is, with the exception of the youth, Ziba Dimmick, who looked upon this excursion as a lark and had been disappointed that none of the many shadows they had jumped at on the journey had been Indians. He had carried his own brand-new flintlock and yearned for an opportunity to use it on the redskins.

The others of the party — Elijah Phillips, Sylvester Brigham, Jim Forristall, Aaron Gunn, and Hodges, wanted nothing to do with the Indians. This was especially true of Ament Hodges, who suspected he was probably on the Potawatomies' list of people to attack, simply because he had built his cabin nearer to one of their sugar camps than they liked and because he had shot one of their dogs that had come sniffing about his cabin.

It was Hodges's nervousness about going back where the Potawatomies might still be skulking about that had prompted him to hire the other four men to go with him. Safety in numbers, he always figured. Actually, he and the Dimmick boy alone could have rounded up the few cows he'd left running loose about the cabin when he'd fled to Hennepin following the Indian Creek massacre.

They had checked the cabin thoroughly and found that nothing had been bothered, and decided that the Indians must all be a lot farther north and probably wouldn't come back this close to the Illinois River again, what with so many militia being mustered in so close to here at Fort Wilbourn. In an hour's search they had located all four of the cows and brought them back to the cabin, planning only to pause long enough to eat their lunch and then return to Hennepin.

While the six were eating — Dimmick listening wide-eyed while the men told their tall tales of hand-to-hand fights with the Indians or hair's-breadth escapes they'd made — a heavy thunderstorm came up. After the initial booming and roaring of the elements had passed, the clouds continued to drop a steady downpour, and as it continued into the early evening, they had decided to remain here overnight and start back in the morning.

Late in the night, Phillips had awakened to the sound of his horse whinnying and stamping outside and got up to see what was the matter. There was no longer any sound of rain and, in fact, the moon was brightly shining, as he noted by peeping through a crack in the door. His limited vision of the outside showed his horse stamping nervously, but since none of the other five horses or four cows seemed nervous or upset, he decided to go out to his gelding and see what was wrong. He had unbarred the cabin door, opened it, and stepped outside.

Instantly the crash of several shots had shattered the night air. Two lead balls plunged through Elijah Phillips's chest, one passing through the heart, and he had flopped dead on the threshold.

The other men leaped up and quickly dragged the body inside, slammed and barred the door, and thrust their rifle barrels through the chinks in the logs.

Deprived of the scalp and fearful of exposing themselves to rifle fire while trying to steal the horses and cows, the Indians outside howled in fury and sent a few more shots into the logs, but not knowing how many armed men were inside, they melted off into the night.

Throughout the night those inside the cabin kept their vigil, and the more Ziba Dimmick looked at the stiffening body on the floor lying in its large coagulating pool of blood, the more the enormity of what had occurred crashed home on him. He was certain the Indians were still outside, patiently waiting for the door to be opened again so they could kill more. Maybe they'd even set the place afire.

Now daylight had come, and peer as they might through the chinks, no one could see a sign of life except for their own horses and Hodges's cows. At last they decided that one of them should slip out, get on his horse, and ride back to Hennepin for help. As to who that someone was to be, they took a vote.

Sixteen-year-old Ziba Dimmick won — or lost, depending upon the outlook. In any event, he was elected to make the ride. Fearful of letting his own terror show, he rechecked the load and prime in his gun and, taking a deep breath, slipped out of the cabin toward the horses. There were no shots, no yells, nothing, yet he was sure that at least half a hundred Indian eyes were staring at him and a variety of weapons, from rifles and bows and arrows to tomahawks and war clubs, ready to be used against him.

His plan had been to try to slip away quietly, but as soon as he had untied his horse, he leaped onto its back and sent it off into a thundering gallop to the south. Just short of two hours later, still dripping from swimming his mount across the Illinois, he reported his story to militia officials. A company of militia about to be discharged volunteered to go check things out.

"Want to go with us, boy?" called one of the men as they mounted up.

"Not me!" young Dimmick said. "I ain't never goin' north of the Illinois River again in my whole life!"

[*June 18, 1832 — Monday*]

The report being written by Colonel Henry Dodge to General Henry Atkinson about the fight with the Sacs on the Pecatonica River was one of the longest he had ever penned, yet he wanted to be sure Atkinson was presented with all the details. Above and beyond that, he had reached the point where there was no more to say about the skirmish but considerably more to say in regard to the Indian allies, and so, after reading over what he had already written, he resumed writing in the new vein:

. . . Colonel Hamilton had arrived with the Indians about one hour after our defeat of the hostile Sacks [sic]. *The friendly Indians appeared delighted with the scalps. They went to the ground where the Indians were killed and literally cut*

them to pieces. On the 17th, early in the morning, Mr Gratiott [sic] and myself had a talk with Waucond [Waucon] Decary [Decorah] (who is in English called Snakeskin) of the Wisconsin. You may recollect that Genl Street in his letter to me which I left with you stated that Decarry [sic] had agreed to raise the hatchet against the Sacks and that he would watch their movements in the direction of the head of Rock River. He had not proceeded up the Wisconsin higher than opposite the East Blue Mound, which is about 55 miles below Fort Winnebago. I invited Decarry to go to Colonel Hamilton's and see Mr Gratiott and the woman, their interpreter, and where I would communicate your talk to them. Decarry and his band arrived at Colonel Hamilton's in time to see the man killed by the Sacks on the road. The next morning Gratiott and myself considered the Winnebagoes [sic] from Prairie Le Cross entirely under the direction of Col Hamilton and that we had nothing to do with them. After hearing your talk, Decarry said his people would unite with us to fight the Sacs; that they were pleased that we had killed a party of them; that when he left home he was not prepared for a long trip; that he wished to return to the Wisconsin for the purpose of getting as many warriors as possible to join him; that the Sacks had killed his daughter and that he would join the whites in killing them up; that he wanted new moccasins for his men and some other preparations to make; that he would be ready before the whites to take the field; that the principal men would meet Gratiott and myself at my house and have a perfect understanding in a few days with us. He prepared to start when it was discovered the Winnebagoes from Prairie La Cross were determined to follow him. The Sioux appeared discontented and said they would go also. They told Mr Marsh in my presence that he had hurried them from their homes; that there was no provision made for their families; that their moccasins were worn out; that he had told them that they were to be used merely for Spies & Flankers; that they were not to be put to hard fighting. Marsh told them their families would be provided for by Genl. Street; that he had promised to do so and would not disappoint them; that they should have new moccasins; that they should be used as Spies. I told them that we could kill the Sacks [and] we wanted them to assist us in finding them. It appeared they were determined to go, & about seventy or eighty of them accompanied the Winnebagoes. I was extremely anxious to retain them. They would have acted as Spies and would have kept the enemy in a state of check while we were recruiting our horses for the expedition. Whether the Indians will return or not, I am at a loss to say. The Winnebagoes make solemn promises. I hope they will not deceive us, as we are doing everything in our power to conciliate them. Decarry says the whole of the Rock River Indians are over the Wisconsin; that they have left the Sacks the entire possession of the country; that they are now high up the Rock River where there is but little for them to live on & must perish for want. That I cannot believe. I have been told there is fish in great abundance upon which alone they can no doubt subsist. Gratiott & myself have sent Whirling Thunder and the Spotted Arm, and the three young men who accompanied them, with a confidential man by the name of Emile. He is a Frenchman who has traded for nine years with them. He was directed to proceed on and ascertain, if possible, where the Sacks were encamped and return as early as possible. If the Winnebagoes have all left the country, it will be difficult for him to get information on this important subject. The Winnabagoes [sic] *must know where the Socks* [sic] *are and I will endeavor to ascertain that fact (if possible) and communicate to you all the information I may be able to procure on that subject. If you could spare about three companies of mounted men to assist us in the protection of the Frontier, it would render us a very important service at this moment. The horses I have had in service one month want recruiting* [recuperation] *to prepare them for the expedition. The grazing is good and they would recruit much in six or eight days.*

The importance of the subjects connected with this communication must make my apology to you for its length.

> *I am, Dear General, with Sentiments of Regard and Esteem,*
> *Your Friend and Obedient Servant*
> *H Dodge Col Commanding Michigan Militia*

[June 18, 1832 — Monday]

The raiding party of six Sac braves was being led by Kinnekonesaut — He-That-Strikes-First — and he realized that his men were at this point so exhausted that they must find a place to stop and make their stand against the pursuing whites. So closely pushed were they that the heavy rain, which might have been a blessing in other circumstances by obliterating their trail, had been only a continued aggravation. The ten horses they had stolen from the Apple River settlement had become increasingly balky, and precious time had been lost in keeping them together as the raiding party attempted to get them back to Black Hawk's encampment.

When the enemy finally pulled to within two miles behind and came into clear view for the first time, Kinnekonesaut was concerned at the size of the party. He counted them as they streamed out of a woodland into a prairie and saw there were twenty-six of them, and it was obvious by their gesticulations that they had simultaneously caught sight of Kinnekonesaut's party.

The Sac leader, without slackening the pace, stood high on his horse's back and saw, a half-mile ahead, a small but dense thicket of trees and brush perched like an island in the midst of the prairie. It was the only possible haven, and he dropped back astraddle his pony and urged his followers toward it, noting with some degree of satisfaction that at least his men would be able to fire against the enemy when they were overtaken; each of the Sacs still had his square of oiled buckskin snugly wrapped around the breech of his flintlock rifle, to keep his powder dry from the drumming rain.

[REPORT OF ILLINOIS STATE MILITIA CAPTAIN JAMES W. STEPHENSON CONCERNING THE BATTLE OF WADDAM'S GROVE:

Apple River, June 19, 1832

Dear Sir: — The night we left Galena, ten more horses were stolen from this place; some of them from the stables within 30 yards of the Apple River Fort. I took the trail the next morning before sunrise with the command I had with me, consisting of 12 men, together with some of the fort's members, and pursued them to a point beyond Yellow Creek about 12 miles east of Kellogg's Grove, where we overtook the gentlemen.[272] *They were about two miles off when we first saw them. Before we got within firing distance they reached the woods. . . .]*

The stolen horses balked as the party under Kinnekonesaut entered the heavily overgrown, acre-sized thicket, and it was only with the concerted effort of all six mounted Indians that they were able to force the animals some twenty yards into the thicket to a copse where the undergrowth was not quite so thick as elsewhere. Kinnekonesaut left Stump-on-Fire to guard the captive horses while he moved on horseback a short distance to the right with the other four. They tied their horses another ten feet or so deeper in the thicket and then moved back to a position fifty or sixty feet from the edge of the clearing. Here Kinnekonesaut placed them into position at intervals of about ten feet. So dense was the cover that they were all but hidden from one another. Each of the braves carefully checked the load and the powder charge of his weapon and charged the pan with fresh, dry powder from his horn. Then they waited.

[. . . we kept close upon them for some miles when, perceiving they would be overtaken, they detached and entered one of the largest and most difficult thickets to pass through you have ever seen . . .]

Kinnekonesaut, who had crept back close enough to the edge of the thicket to observe, saw the pursuing Americans thunder up and come to a halt close to where the trail of his party entered the thicket. Some of the white men were talking loudly, argumentatively, apparently in objection to pushing into such a seemingly impenetrable jungle of growth, but their leader silenced them, gave them time to check and recharge their weapons, and then ordered a charge into the thicket.

As the whites yelled fiercely and began forcing their horses to thrust their way in, Kinnekonesaut slipped back to where the other five were hidden. For the whites, almost instantly the cover closed so completely around them that they could hardly see one another, let alone a hidden enemy. When the horsemen were little more than ten yards into the thicket — and because of their height in their saddles over the low, dense growth — Kinnekonesaut and his braves began to catch fleeting glimpses of them. Realizing that they themselves were still hidden from view, Kinnekonesaut screamed out an order to fire, and the five Sacs fired in a staggered manner as they sighted the approaching horsemen.

The noise of the rifle fire was deafening, and though the whites fired back instantly, they were firing blindly toward the sound of the Indians and entirely without effect. Immediately the whites turned and thrashed back out of the thicket, with one less man than they had when they entered — Private Michael Lovell had caught a ball in midchest and lay dead in the dense carpet of brush.

The Sacs had swiftly reloaded, and again Kinnekonesaut crept to within spying distance. He saw them arguing among themselves, and he was sure that at this point they would fall back a little and merely surround the thicket to box the Indians in, and while the majority waited to down any Indians attempting to escape, would send just a few skilled men in on foot to seek out and kill or dislodge the Indians. Instead, he was amazed to see them all dismount and leave their horses in the charge of several of their men, and then the remainder, after reloading, taking a stance to charge the thicket on foot in a group. Once again, as the whites ran together toward the thicket, Kinnekonesaut drew back to his men, and they waited.

The whites on foot were somewhat harder to see than when they had been mounted, but the five defenders kept their eyes on the thrashing sound of their passage as they approached and soon began catching momentary views of them, this time much closer. Again Kinnekonesaut gave his yell, and again the staggered shots of the defenders resounded. Some of the whites returned the fire, again firing at sound rather than at sighting, and again their shots were wild and ineffective, except for one ball that miraculously sped thirty or forty feet through the tangle without being deflected and buried itself in the hip of one of the stolen horses being tended by Stump-on-Fire. The animal screamed and reared wildly, broke away, and bulled a passage back out to the open prairie.

The whites, their own weapons needing reloading, broke and fled back into the open again, once more leaving behind one of their men, Private Stephen P. Howard, who was shot through the head and instantly killed. In addition, a ball had passed through the thick muscle at the right base of Private Edwin Welch's neck just above the shoulder, and, dazed and bleeding badly, he was helped back into the prairie by a companion. Kinnekonesaut followed, and from his screened vantage point watched them once again argue about what to do now. The orders of their commander prevailed, and when their reloading had been accomplished, he led them back to the edge of the thicket and then ordered them down on their hands and knees to crawl into the thicket and thus be out of sight of the enemy as they approached.

Unbelieving, Kinnekonesaut slipped back to his people to wait and, in doing so, missed seeing a further action of two of the attackers. The scream of the injured horse had not gone unnoticed by them, nor the point at which it had plunged out of the thicket. The two were Privates Thomas Sublette and John

Waites, and they entered the thicket about four feet apart at the point where the wounded horse had emerged.

Back with his men, Kinnekonesaut watched closely. There was less noise made by the attackers this time, but soon he began to see the swaying of brush above the forms of the whites who were crawling in toward them. He silently pointed these out to his braves, and each selected a specific movement of brush to concentrate upon. As soon as the first man — Private Charles Eames — broke into view, hardly more than ten feet away, Kinnekonesaut fired, putting a bullet through his brain.[273] The other braves fired at the base of the moving brush. Two of the shots missed, but one ripped through the left side of Captain Stephenson, creating an extremely painful but not mortal wound.

With only a shot or two fired among themselves, the whites leaped to their feet and scrambled away to the open again. Off to the side, in the little copse where the horses were under the guard of Stump-on-Fire, the two whites had appeared. Stump-on-Fire raised his rifle and pulled the trigger. His gunpowder had become damp, and the flint created only a flash in the pan. Before he could recover and just as the firing broke out among the others, Private Waites leaped forward and plunged his bayonet about three inches into Stump-on-Fire's chest. The Sac gasped and gripped the bayonet and rifle barrel strongly to keep it from being pushed farther in by another lunge. As the two men struggled, Private Sublette ran in from the side, grasped Stump-on-Fire's topknot, and jerked his head back, at the same time slashing his throat with a finely honed butcher knife. A great gout of blood burst forth as the jugular was severed. He fell to his knees and then onto his back, moved spastically a few times, and then died. Waites jerked his bayonet free, and then he and Sublette drove the horses back out into the prairie, where the exhausted animals moved to where the militia's horses were standing, and here they gathered and stood trembling.

Peering from cover, Kinnekonesaut was astonished to see the whites making hasty preparations to withdraw. His gaze narrowed, however, when he saw the horses they had worked so hard to steal trotting over to those of the militia and mingling with them. Stump-on-Fire! He drew back into the thicket and moved as swiftly as possible to the copse. Solemnly, he took the fallen brave's knife and tomahawk from his belt and looked for his rifle, but it was gone. He gently closed the open, staring eyes of his companion and moved quickly back to the others. With a few whispered words he led them back to their horses, which they untied and led laboriously through the thicket to the back side. Looking out carefully, they saw no one. At a signal from Kinnekonesaut they mounted and galloped off northeastward through the prairie grasses toward a distant line of timber.

[. . . *we tried every possible way to drive them therefrom, but all was unsuccessful — such as charging them on horseback, then part on foot and part on horseback, then by trying to crawl upon them. Finally I saw the only chance was to dismount and all to charge on foot — our boys went into the thicket under full charge like men. We got in the midst of the Indians before one fired. Here we had a pretty close fight. Altho' the guns on both sides were discharged frequently, there was not a single fire made at the distance of more than thirty feet from the object aimed at either from the Indians or ourselves. We got into such close quarters as to be constrained to use the bayonet and butcher's knife We killed five or six of the damned scoundrels, and lost three of our own men. George [Charles] Eames, L. P. [Stephen P.] Howard and Michael Lovel [Lovell] were shot dead. There were more Indians in this brush than I had supposed there were. We got from them all the horses except one on which one of them made his escape. One of our horses was shot Another was so sick that he could not be moved When we commenced on these boys, we were perhaps the most perfectly drowned set you ever saw, having ridden the whole day in incessant rain. I would suggest the propriety of collecting all your mounted men, and sending them to bury these dead soldiers as early as possible. . . .]*[274]

CHAPTER X

[*June 18, 1832 — Monday*]

I N HIS OFFICE at the Department of War in Washington, D.C., secretary of war Lewis Cass was just completing one of the longest and busiest days he had ever spent in this office. Over the weekend he had an interminable succession of conferences with the president, members of the Cabinet, members of Congress, the adjutant general, numerous military field officers, and other individuals. Now, late in the evening of this mid-June Monday, he was just finishing the extremely important letters and orders that he had been dictating since early this morning.

He leaned back in his chair, yawning and stretching hugely. Grueling though the day had been, he actually felt better than he had felt for a considerable while. At last the agonizingly slow wheels of government had begun to move. At long last President Andrew Jackson — undoubtedly with an eye toward political maneuvering, since he would be running for reelection this coming fall — had reached the saturation point with halfway measures in the Black Hawk War.

"I will tolerate no further procrastination on the part of our generals in the field," the president had stormed, "nor will I condone the pusillanimous conduct of the volunteers!"

The secretary of war felt a twinge of pity for General Atkinson — a good man, if a bit conservative, who was obviously caught in the grip of circumstance. Having had the experience many times himself of trying to run a military operation where militia were involved, Cass could sympathize fully with the frustrations that were always engendered. Added to that, of course, was the abysmal state of communications. Atkinson's letters of May 25 and May 30 had finally been received here just a few days ago in the same dispatch. Why, he wondered, as he had scores of times before, was it necessary to depend on a form of communication where important missives were either lost or delayed for weeks? Why couldn't someone develop some means of swift and sure communication so that, in time of war like this, relevant strategies could be formulated with up-to-the-moment information and important orders relayed instantly? Cass had no way of knowing that just over two hundred miles to the north of where he was sitting, an art professor at New York University was at this very moment deeply immersed in developing just such a means of communication. His name: Samuel F. B. Morse.

Following the numerous conferences, the secretary of war had written to Major General Winfield Scott, presently stationed in New York:

Sir, You will proceed without delay to Chicago & assume the command of the regular troops & militia in the service of the United States, operating upon the frontiers of Illinois, Indiana & Michigan, against the hostile Indians.

A disaffected band of Sacs & Foxes, now probably increased by individuals from other tribes, have engaged in hostilities against the United States, & are spreading alarm & devastation over the frontiers of Illinois & the adjacent country. Gen. Atkinson, with the regular troops at his disposal, was ordered some time since to Rock River, where he was stationed at the last advices. Gov. Reynolds, of Illinois, had called out a considerable detachment of the militia of that State, which had repaired to the scene of operations, but had claimed & received their discharge, with a small exception, before any impression had been made upon the enemy. You will perceive, by the copies of the letters herewith enclosed, that Gov. Reynolds had ordered out a farther [sic] detachment of 3000 men, to rendezvous upon the frontier on the 10th ins [sic]. Gen. Atkinson has probably, at this time, upwards of 400 regular troops, & it is hoped, that with this combined force, he will be able to subdue the enemy without loss of time. . . . But as the theatre of this warfare is remote, & the accounts of the force & operations of the Indians are various & conflicting, it is difficult for the Department to form a correct estimate of the amount of troops which may be necessary to effect the objects of the government. The nature of the warfare is so distressing to the whole frontier that every principle of policy & humanity requires it should be brought to a termination without delay. As little should be left to the contingencies of such a campaign as possible, & the President is desirous of guarding against any reverses which, tho' they are not anticipated, may yet happen.

The orders, which will be transmitted to you from the Adjutant General's office, will shew [sic] you the amount of the regular force, which will be placed at your disposal, & the stations from which they will be withdrawn.[275] *The various staff departments have been instructed to communicate to you the arrangements which have been made for the transportation & subsistence of the troops, & generally, for all the facilities, which your operations may require.*

It is hoped that the force already upon that frontier, and that which is now ordered, will be found sufficient to subdue & chastise the Indians. In addition to this, a bill has just passed Congress, providing for raising 600 mounted men, to serve one year. This corps will be enlisted & organised [sic] without delay & ordered to the scene of action.[276] Should circumstances, however, require any additional force, you are authorised [sic] to call upon the Governors of Missouri, Illinois, Indiana & Michigan for such an amount as you may find necessary. The Executive of these States & the Executive of Michigan have been requested to supply any call you may make. But no militia will be received into service for a shorter period than three months from the time of their arrival at the place of rendezvous, to be disbanded previously if their services should be no longer required. The enormous expense & the utter inefficiency of the troops, when shorter periods are permitted, render this regulation indispensable.

On your arrival at Chicago, should you find peace not established, you will take the control of all the operations against the Indians, & pursue & subdue them. In the discharge of the duties enjoined by these instructions, you will not regard the boundary line of your department, but will carry on your operations wherever necessary, whether in the Eastern or Western department. You will communicate immediately with Gen. Atkinson & give him such orders as you may find necessary.

The Indians, at the last accounts, had sought refuge in the swamps & fastnesses of the Rock River, whence they were issuing, probably in small parties, & spreading alarm & devastation over the frontiers. As they will be enclosed between the forces under your immediate command & those under Gen. Atkinson, a combined movement will be necessary, which is more dreaded by the Indians than any attack upon a single point can be. The frontier also will be better protected & these murderous incursions prevented.

It is the desire of the President that you march against & attack them, wherever they may be. Nor will you suspend your operations till they are effectually subdued. Let no truce be granted till the Black Hawk is surrendered, if he survive the contest, together with some of the principal warriors, & such a number of the murderers of the Menominees as may be sufficient for the purpose of example and justice. The murderers will be surrendered to the civil authorities of the proper district in Michigan, & the other persons will be confined at one of the military posts as hostages for the conduct of their friends.

If the main body of any of the tribes possessing the country east of the Mississippi have joined in these hostilities, no peace will be granted to them but upon the condition of their abandoning all claim to such country & removing to any district west of that river, which may be assigned to them by the government. And this stipulation will form the basis of any arrangement you make with them. If, however, disaffected individuals only living in this region should be found engaged in hostilities, you will not interfere with the possessory right of the tribe to which such individuals belong. But these persons will not be suffered to remain in their present place of residence. They must migrate west of the Mississippi to such district as may be selected for them. It is indispensable to the future security of the frontier, & to a just & proper influence over the Indians, that not an individual who has participated in these outrages should be permitted to remain east of the Mississippi. On the termination of hostilities, arrangements will be made immediately for their departure, & hostages for the faithful performance of the condition will be required.

It is very desirable that the whole country between Lake Michigan & the Mississippi, & south of the Ouisconsin [sic], should be freed from the Indians; and with this in view, you will endeavor to prevail upon the friendly or neutral Chiefs of those tribes, if such there be, who have not principally been engaged in these hostilities, to cede their claims & to remove west of the Mississippi. Reasonable stipulations respecting temporary annuities, subsistence, &c, similar to those recently made in treaties with the Southwestern Indians, may be granted to them. If any considerable proportion, tho' not a majority, of the tribes east of the Mississippi & west of Lake Michigan should have taken up arms against the United States, the same proportion of the country possessed by them will be required; the boundaries to be amicably arranged with those who have not engaged in this warfare. This measure is not only just in itself, as the United States agree to provide them another country, but it is required by a due regard to the future. If their government is so weak that the disaffected cannot be restrained, the tribe has no right to object to a division of interest, for the purposes of peace, which was allowed, if not created by themselves, for the purposes of war. Besides, if this aggression passes by without some effectual preventative, our frontiers will still be exposed to the same calamity & the spirit of disaffection will extend to the other tribes.

This Department cannot judge what proportion of the Sacs & Foxes is engaged in this conflict, but whatever it may be, the principles above stated will apply to them. If the principal authorities of these tribes are in arms, no peace will be made till they are entirely cut off from the Mississippi by a strip of from 50 to 100 miles in width, as the country belonging to them may allow, taking into view their numbers & the advantages for cultivation & hunting, so as not to distress them for the means of subsistence. You can, however, if necessary from the nature of the country, give them an assurance that the Government will, on being satisfied of its inadequacy, add to it, either by giving them an adjoining district or land in some other quarter. But [at] any rate, the hostile party will be removed from the Mississippi and their just proportion of the country transferred to the United States. Neither annuities nor any other favorable stipulation will be granted to the hostile Indians, with the exception of the assurance of a country, sufficient for their support. The friendly Indians will be treated with great kindness and, where stipulations with them are necessary, they will be made in a spirit of humanity and just liberality. But, if possible, it would be desirable to induce Keokuk & the other friendly Sacs & Foxes to relinquish their right to any of the country upon the Mississippi. By this measure, the probability of future difficulties would be removed & the frontier greatly strengthened.

Should you find, on your arrival in Chicago, that the difficulties in that quarter are over and no farther [sic] *operations are required, you will give the necessary orders for the troops to resume the several stations whence they have been taken. Should you think that a display of force under your command would be useful in its effects upon the Indians, you will continue there with the regular troops & report the circumstances to this Department.*

You will be careful that the militia are regularly mustered into service and that there is not an undue proportion of officers to men. The preservation of the public property will require the most vigilant attention, and the President has entire confidence that your operations will be conducted with every regard to economy, which the great objects of peace & security committed to you will permit.

I am Sir, Very respectfully Your obt Svt.
(signed) Lewis Cass

P.S. It is essential that the places of rendezvous of the militia should be [as] *near the frontier as possible.*

Lewis Cass considered what he had written to General Scott and was satisfied with it. With nine regular army companies of artillery, eleven of infantry, plus an additional 208 recruits from the harbor of New York — making up a grand total of 1,258 regulars — along with whatever requisition of men he wished to make from the militias of three states and one territory, Scott should have no difficulty subduing the enemy.

After writing instructions to the governors of Missouri, Illinois, Indiana, and the Michigan Territory as to their obligations in this respect should Scott call upon them for support, Cass then turned his attention to letters directed to Atkinson's immediate superior, General Edmund Gaines, to the United States commissary general, George Gibson, and to the Indian superintendent in St. Louis, William Clark, whose letter he concluded with:

. . . The U.S. will not suspend their operations till the Black Hawk & his party are reduced to unconditional submission, and such a lesson taught to them as will secure their future good conduct & [which] *will reach every tribe east of the Rocky Mountains. Tell them their only chance of preservation is to remain quiet, & that course I trust they will take. If their countrymen now feel the justice of the United States, they must attribute their calamity to the unprovoked aggressions & cruelties of which they have been guilty.*

Finally, after many hours of dictation, and having used the skills of four expert secretaries in the process, Lewis Cass reluctantly turned his attention to the letter he had most dreaded writing — the one to General Henry Atkinson, whom he truly liked. It was one he would write in his own hand, rather than dictate, and though he sat at his desk and pondered long over it before beginning, he could devise no way to soften the blow and realized that beating around the bush would only prolong the agony of his friend and himself. The letter he finally wrote was brief and unemotional, with the only indication of his sensitivity toward Atkinson apparent in his signature. He wrote:

Sir, During my absence of a few days from the department, your letters of May 25th and 30th were received.

I appreciate the embarrassments under which you labour [sic] in consequence of the discharge of the Illinois militia and the present inadequacy of your force. The strength of the hostile Indians and their plan of operation are unknown here, but it is obvious that the frontier is in a state of danger and much alarm. The President is determined that the most vigorous measures shall be taken to terminate the existing difficulties and, with this view, Maj. Gen. Scott has been ordered to repair to Chicago, with a considerable body of regular troops, to assume the general command of the operations against the hostile Indians. By a combined movement from that place and from your position with the means now provided, I trust this warfare will soon end. I transmit you herewith a copy of the instructions given to Gen. Scott and, so far as respects any arrangements with the Indians which circumstances may require you to make before his arrival, you will please be guided by the views therein stated. The accompanying order of the Adjutant General will shew [sic] you the accession which has been ordered to your own force as well as the general outlines of the plan.

With much respect, I am, Sir, Your ob Servt.,
Lew Cass

[*June 19, 1832 — Tuesday*]

Major General Winfield Scott was reading one of a number of publications stacked on the low table beside his chair. As were the others, the pamphlet he was absorbed in at the moment was a medical article; and, also as were the others, it was concerned with the symptoms, onset, and treatment of the dread disease that was currently scourging Europe, the Asiatic cholera — a particularly virulent strain so devastating that often a victim who had been hale and hearty upon rising in the morning would be dead by evening.

As a young man growing up in Virginia, Scott had once harbored medical aspirations that were almost on a par with his leaning toward military leadership. Whether to be a physician or an officer was a question that had plagued him for nearly a year. At last he had made his decision and entered the army as a captain twenty-four years ago, at the age of twenty-two. He had never for a moment regretted that a military life had swayed him most. Nor did he harbor any bitterness at the fact that, four years ago, he had been passed over as commanding general of the army in favor of Alexander Macomb. The reason, he knew, was not only because of frequent stormy conflicts with officers of higher rank, but equally because of his strong — and usually justified — opinions, which had the effect of causing subordinate officers to consider him overbearing, condescending, and arrogant. He was unabashedly outspoken in criticism where he felt it was merited — a trait that had even gotten him suspended from the army for a while, because of a decidedly indiscreet criticism of General James Wilkinson's role in the Aaron Burr conspiracy. But while these might have been marks against him, none could deny that he was a superb general with an uncanny ability to assess situations swiftly and make exactly the right decisions. That was the reason he had been commanding general of the Eastern Department of the United States Army for the past eleven years.

Yet, despite his love of the career he chose, he had never lost an abiding interest in matters medical and had a remarkable knowledge in the field for one never academically schooled in the art and practice of medicine. His current interest in the Asiatic cholera had been the outgrowth of discussions about it with his surgeon friend here in New York, Dr. Thomas G. Mower, who had studied the disease firsthand a year ago in France.

Both General Scott and Dr. Mower were appalled at how surprisingly few people in America were even aware of the choleric plague sweeping Europe, even though tens of thousands had already perished under its onslaught and there was evidently no end in sight. So far as had been determined, the disease had its genesis in India, where it had sprung into being as a deadly scythe cutting a vast swath through the population for two or three years before making its appearance in the great Turkestan region and then spreading into the Balkans and thence throughout Europe.

Winfield Scott was of the opinion — an opinion singularly unpopular — that eventually the disease would find its way across the Atlantic and strike North America. He hoped that would never occur, but unlike certain fellow officers and acquaintances who were palliative toward the problem and sometimes even scornful of his concern, he felt he was being pragmatic rather than pessimistic in his belief. It was that very pragmatism that inspired him to borrow these publications from Dr. Mower in order to absorb whatever he could about the disease, including the pitifully few, and too often ineffective, methods of prescribed treatment.

Rapt in the treatise he was presently reading, Scott suddenly became aware that a light tapping on his door had grown into an imperative rapping. He set the publication aside and strode to the entry. A nervous lieutenant saluted smartly, apologized for disturbing him, and then handed him an official packet that had just arrived from secretary of war Lewis Cass. Scott thanked him and closed the door, then opened the pouch.

An hour later, having absorbed the contents of what Cass had sent him, the general stood for a long while at the latticed windows of his study, staring unseeingly at the twilight stealthily infiltrating the multitude of ships riding at anchor in New York Harbor. When he turned away, there were two matters that dominated his thoughts. The first was transportation for his troops. An army that had to march overland with its equipment for hundreds of miles in order to reach the enemy was apt to be unfit for battle when it got there. Scott meant to keep the marching to a minimum.

Around the middle of last March he had been privileged to read some correspondence that had passed between Major Henry Whiting at Buffalo and Scott's friend and fellow Virginian Major General Thomas Jesup, the present quartermaster general of the United States Army, who was in Washington. In that correspondence, Jesup and Whiting had discussed the possibility of transporting troops and war supplies to the west via steamboats on the Great Lakes — boats that could take on their cargo and passengers at the mouth of Lake Erie and follow that lake westward to its mouth, then up the Detroit River to Lake St. Clair, then upstream farther still from there on the St. Clair River into Lake Huron. From that point the steamboats could go north to the Mackinac Straits and then, theoretically, into Lake Michigan and southward to Chicago.

The problem, which had been pointed out in Major Whiting's early letters, was that no steamships had ever gone to the head of Lake Michigan, and even if they could make it there, the sandbars directly off Chicago were·extremely treacherous, prohibiting a landing. Whiting had gone on to say that no steamboats were available for such a voyage except at an exorbitant price, and added that, indeed, without means of obtaining wood for fuel at the head of Lake Michigan, such a project would probably be out of the question. Later, however, Jesup had written again to say that if someone were foolhardy enough to make such an attempt, there were four steamboats on Lakes Erie and Huron that could be put to such service, for a price. These were the steamers named *Henry Clay*, *Sheldon Thompson*, *William Penn*, and *Superior*.

The coincidence had not been lost on Scott that in the packet he had received from Washington today had been included a brief note from Quartermaster General Jesup, who told Scott:

. . . You may rely, confidently, on every aid which the means or credit of this department can afford. I wish you success, health & happiness.

Tomorrow, Scott decided, he would write to both Cass and Jesup, requesting Cass to have orders cut for all the troops that were being assigned to him from along the Atlantic seaboard and the Great Lakes to rendezvous at Buffalo instead of Chicago, there to be transported by steamboat to Chicago, "where they may arrive rested and eager to meet the rigors of pursuing the hostile Indians through the wilderness." The letter to Jesup would be an official request for the government to hire the services of the four steamers.

The second matter strong in General Scott's mind at this moment encouraged him to leave his quarters and take a carriage to the quarters of Dr. Tom Mower. The surgeon answered the door himself on the summons of the ornate brass knocker, and his craggy features softened in a smile when he saw it was Scott.

"Well, General, this is a pleasant surprise. Come in and have something to warm your throat. What brings you here this time of the evening?"

"Cholera," Scott replied. Over brandy and cigars he explained to Dr. Mower what his orders entailed. "We're going to have a great many men together in a small area," he said. "It isn't likely that the Asiatic cholera will appear on this continent by then, but I don't want to leave anything to chance. I want you to put together for me all the medicines and medical supplies I might need for treating the disease if it did break out sometime during the course of this campaign."

"I can do that," Tom Mower nodded, "but it won't be cheap. Do I bill the quartermaster general?"

"No," Scott said quietly, "you'll bill me. I'm doing this strictly on my own."

[*June 20, 1832 — Wednesday*]

For the refugees who had crowded into Chicago, many of them tightly quartered within Fort Dearborn, the arrival eight days ago of Major General John R. Williams with his detachment of one hundred Michigan Territory militiamen was cause for celebration and great relief. He immediately placed Colonel Edward Brooks in command of Fort Dearborn until such time as the regulars arrived to regarrison the fort. And on the day after Williams's arrival, he received an express with news that Major William Whistler, with his detachment of regulars from Fort Niagara, had left Detroit by sailing ship for Chicago on June 3 and thus should be arriving there soon. The mantle of gloom that had prevailed over the populace, residents and transients alike, was dispelled, and an almost festive mood arose. It was a bit premature, because the danger was by no means past.

Four days later, on June 16, only twenty-eight miles west of Chicago, a war party of some twenty Sacs attacked a squad of soldiers from Fort Payne at Joseph Naper's settlement. The soldiers had been detailed to go out to cut and haul shingles for the roof of the Fort Payne blockhouse. They were busily at work only a mile and a half from the fort when they were fired upon. Private William Brown, of Captain Morgan L. Payne's company of mounted volunteers, was shot through the temple and died instantly. When a stronger detachment returned to the scene a short while later, the Indians were gone, and Brown had been scalped and mutilated.[277] As soon as the news reached Chicago, General Williams ordered Colonel Brooks with a detachment of thirty-five men to the scene to assist in defense there until recalled.

Another surge of relief was experienced when the ship carrying Major William Whistler and his one hundred regulars of Companies G and I of the U.S. 2nd Infantry arrived three days ago and anchored just beyond the great sandbars off Chicago. It was something of a *déjà vu* for Whistler, who twenty-nine years earlier had helped his father, Captain John Whistler, build the original Fort

Dearborn, at which the senior Whistler had become first commanding officer. The newly arrived troops, under direction of Lieutenant Julius J. B. Kingsbury, were landed in small boats, with the officers and their families scheduled to disembark last. However, during the landing, a severe storm arose, which halted the process. For three days the storm raged, and it was not until this morning that Major Whistler and the other officers and their wives and children were able to come ashore.

The new Fort Dearborn commander did not endear himself to the Michigan volunteers. He allowed some of the refugees to remain within the security of the fort, but ordered the militia troops out to make room for the regulars. With a considerable amount of grumbling, the Michigan volunteers left the fort and set up their own camp some twelve miles north, along the Lake Michigan shoreline near what was called Grosse Point.[278]

One of the Illinois militiamen, Private Stephen Mack, viewed with irony the fluctuating moods of the soldiers and citizens in the Chicago area, and expressed himself in this vein in a letter written to his sister, Lovicy Cooper:

Dear Sister: I have been out on one expedition against the Sauke [sic] Indians since my last letter, but we could not find them where we expected and were obliged to return and wait for reinforcements to enable us to penetrate further [sic] into the country. General Atkinson will be on the move again in a few days and General J. R. Williams (now at this place) will probably move on to his assistance. In that case I shall join him with a few volunteer riflemen from this place. You need be under no apprehension on my account, for I can assure you that all of the accounts that you receive from the seat of war are greatly exaggerated. It is really amusing to me, who sees all the operations and knows perhaps better than almost anyone the real danger, to read the accounts of maneuvers of the enemy never thought of by them, and of battles never fought. And then to sit down and listen to the remarks of the raw Yankees who have lately emigrated to this country, one would think that Napoleon Bonaparte had risen from the grave and presented himself in the person of the Blackhawk [sic] and that the spirit of his millions of heroes were concentrated in the 5 or 600 warriors led by that chief. I by no means wish to undervalue our enemies, [for] they are brave and subtle and it may be dangerous to encounter them without an overpowering force, but I can by no means approve of the tardy operations of our chief officers, for it gives time to the nimble-footed Indians to ravage our frontier settlements and bathe their hands in the blood of helpless women and unsuspecting infants. Had more prompt measures been pursued in the commencement, I have no doubt but many lives would have been spared, and we should have been at this moment in the full enjoyment of peace. . . .

[*June 21, 1832 — Thursday*]

Though it had taken longer than General Henry Atkinson anticipated to get the three thousand militia troops mustered into the service of the United States and then organized into their units, the job was nearly done now, and he anticipated moving his headquarters back to Dixon's Ferry within the next few days.

The confusion of so many men converging on the Illinois River at Fort Wilbourn was staggering, and there were many problems to iron out, large and small. The New York editor and poet William Cullen Bryant, who was passing through the area on tour, wrote:

> *. . . They were a hard-looking set of men, unkempt and unshaved and apparently eager to make war, but there are many delays and the settlers complain that these citizen soldiers are too often making war upon their pigs and chickens than upon the Indians.*

The unauthorized sale of liquor by civilians (and some militia men) to newly mustered-in troops, along with the unauthorized discharge of firearms, prompted General Atkinson to issue his General Order No. 35, specifically prohibiting those practices. For his own part, not yet having received the news that command of the war was being transferred to General Scott, Atkinson had, several days ago, written optimistically to General Macomb in Washington that:

> *. . . I have a Militia force of three thousand men and about four hundred regular troops. With these I cannot fail to put an end in a short time to the perplexed state of Indian hostility in this quarter. Should, however, the Sacs elude us and recross the Mississippi, I will pursue them forthwith and never cease till they are annihilated or fully and severely punished and subdued. . . .*

Among the matters Atkinson had to attend to was the killing of a settler — Elijah Phillips — in the uncomfortably nearby area of Big Bureau Creek. The general had immediately issued a special order to this effect:

> *Head Qrs Army of the Frontier*
> *Fort Wilborn* [sic] *June 19th. 1832*

Spl. Order No. 26

Major [John] *Dement will proceed with his Battalion of Spies this morning to the Bureau Woods in the direction where the Indians killed a white man yesterday morning & where Indian signs have since been seen.*

He will scour the woods in the direction of Dixon's Ferry, & if he falls upon any such trail pursue it while there is a prospect of overtaking the enemy & spare them not should they be come up with.

After performing the above duty, Major Dement will join the regular troops at Dixon's & report to Col. Taylor.

> *By order of Brig Genl. Atkinson.*

In the organization of troops at Fort Wilbourn since then, three brigades had been organized and the three officers now commanding them had been elected by virtually unanimous vote of the militiamen. The generals of the first, second, and third brigades were, respectively, Alexander Posey, Milton K. Alexander, and — once again in a commanding role — James D. Henry. These units were further organized regimentally and then into companies.[279]

There was a momentary alarm when a party of ninety Potawatomi warriors showed up, and it was possible that they might have been fired on by trigger-happy recruits, except that they had women and children with them. It was soon ascertained that they had arrived under command of Waubansee, Chaubenee, Aptakisic, and Sauganash — the latter two better known respectively to the whites as Half Day and Billy Caldwell — to lend their services to the army.[280] The four chiefs presented themselves to Atkinson, who welcomed them with genuine warmth. When they asked, with Sauganash serving as interpreter, where their women and children were to be lodged and cared for during the time the warriors were acting in conjunction with the army, Atkinson had their families placed in the recently abandoned village of Waubansee at the mouth of the Fox River, across from Ottawa, with a guard to protect them and rations allotted to them.

Yesterday, with the brigades fully formed and their units organized, Atkinson sent Brigadier General Posey's 1st Brigade to Dixon's Ferry to arrive there coincident with Major Dement's spy battalion and to await there the rest of the army, which would be following soon. Traveling with Posey's brigade was the independent company of Captain Jacob M. Early, in which Abraham Lincoln had just enlisted as a private — his third enlistment of this campaign — following his discharge after the twenty-day enlistment.

[*June 22, 1832 — Friday*]

Black Hawk was deeply shaken and saddened by the deaths of the ten young warriors and their leader, Koonay, in the fight against Colonel Dodge on the Pecatonica. He was greatly angered by the atrocities committed on the corpses of those men by the Sioux and Menominees who had been brought to Fort Hamilton. But there was an unexpected benefit. He had thought, when first he learned of the tragedy, that it would undermine his prestige among the Winnebagoes presently allied to him, and that they would abandon him. Actually, the penetration of the Sioux and Menominees into their country to aid the whites had angered them too, and the atrocities committed on Black Hawk's people had engendered their sympathy as well as their wrath, and thus the tenuous bond between themselves and Black Hawk remained intact — strained, perhaps, but as yet unbroken.

The successes of most of his raiding parties, which had been bringing in much-needed horses and some small food supplies, were very gratifying to Black Hawk, but he had not lost sight of his plan to launch some stronger forays against fortified white positions. To this end, he had prepared a ritual dog feast in his hidden encampment yesterday, with White Crow and the recently released hostages, Whirling Thunder and Spotted Arm, as honored guests. This dog feast, in which a live white dog was hung by its hind legs from a painted pole and disemboweled, was a ceremony meant to invoke the blessing of the Great Spirit on their next endeavor. The Winnebago chiefs being honored had reaffirmed their friendship for Black Hawk and his people and their sympathy for the struggle in which they were engaged, though at the same time pointed out that the vigilance of the whites made it increasingly difficult for them to aid the Sacs as much as they had been doing until now, or as much as they might wish in the days and weeks to come.

In the flickering light of the campfire last night, Black Hawk had stood before his assembled warriors and their families and raised high his medicine bags, one in each hand. He turned slowly in a complete circle and, when facing them again, spoke fervently.

"Braves and Warriors! This is the medicine bag of our forefather, Mukataquet — the grandfather of my father and the father of the Sac nation. Mukataquet handed it down to Nanamake — the father of my father and a great war chief who successfully raised his tomahawk against all the nations of the lakes and all the nations of the plains. Nanamake passed it on to my father, Pyesa, who carried it proudly in battle and who, in turn, passed it on to me as he lay dying from the fatal bite of a Cherokee arrow. This medicine bag has never been dishonored, and it will not be disgraced now."

Now, in the first light of day, with two hundred warriors, in full war paint and bristling with weapons, ready to follow him, Black Hawk again spoke to them, which they did not expect.

"Last night," he told them, "I dreamed a dream!"

Immediately there was an expectant hush over the assemblage. Dreams were extremely important signs. Was this dream that had filled Black Hawk's sleep a portent or an omen? They subconsciously leaned toward him, so as to miss no word when he spoke again.

"In my dream," Black Hawk continued, "I directed my course toward the sunset, and at the end of three days of easy travel and two nights of good rest, we arrived at a place where the Americans were hiding behind strong walls. We fought them, and when it was finished, we feasted! The enemy had fallen before us!"

There was a roar of delight and enthusiasm from the men, and Black Hawk waited patiently for it to die away of its own accord. Then he looked from one side to the other of them and smiled.

"We go there now. That place is *Moscohocoynak!*" — Apple River.

[*June 24, 1832 — Sunday*]

The four-man express from Galena, carrying missives from Colonel James Strode and others to General Atkinson, had left the mining town shortly before noon. The party included Frederick Dixon, a visiting Kentuckian named Edmund Welsh, a young man of eighteen named David Kirkpatrick, and one of Strode's militia privates, W. George Hercleroad.[281] On approaching Apple River Fort some two hours later, they waved as they passed seventeen women and young children collecting wild strawberries along the nearby creek. Without pause, they continued to the fort, a hundred yards or so beyond.

Inside Apple River Fort they reported to the commanding officer, Captain Clack Stone, who was guarding the place with fewer than twenty of his men, the remainder being on detached service. They took a little refreshment and passed along what little news they had, telling Stone that while the skies were clear here, it had been raining when they left Galena, and they had discharged their flintlocks to test them against the dampness. Three had reloaded at once, but Welsh had decided to wait until they stopped here at Apple River. Now he carefully reloaded, and they were ready to go on.

The four set out eastward on Kellogg's Trail, and had gotten no more than three hundred yards from the fort when about two dozen Sac Indians rose up from where they were hiding in the grass some distance away and fired toward them. Only one bullet found its mark.

Welsh, who had pulled some yards ahead of the other three, was knocked from his horse by a ball that passed through his thigh. With the Indians rushing upon him to take his scalp, he rose to a sitting position and fired his rifle at them, which had three distinct effects. It momentarily made the Indians duck down in the tall grass, it alerted the women on the other side of Apple River Fort to drop what they were doing and rush pell-mell for the security of the stockade, and it also frightened Welsh's horse into a panicky gallop back toward the little Apple River settlement.

To their credit, Welsh's companions did not flee. Instead, at Dixon's shout of "Come on, boys!" they came up to their fallen comrade with rifles pointed to shoot at any enemy who showed himself. When several of the Indians rose, they pulled their triggers. All three weapons snapped without firing, the gunpowder having become dampened in the moist air since leaving Galena. Dixon reined up beside Welsh and, with Hercleroad's help, pulled the injured man up behind himself. The Indians had stopped and were looking back strangely, but when the three feinted with their rifles, began racing away.

The men turned their horses and galloped back to the fort, arriving just as the last of the women and children fled inside. The stockaded gate was closed and barred, and Captain Stone's men peered over the walls, expecting to see the Indians who had attacked coming back for a charge. Instead, they were in time to see them pass out of sight over a brushy knoll.

Welsh's wound was being treated by some of the women and found to be a clean entry and exit, with no bone breakage involved nor any major blood vessels cut — painful but not serious.

"Something's crazy here," Clack Stone said, shaking his head in puzzlement.

There must've been more'n twenty of 'em. They must've realized your guns snapped when you didn't shoot. So how come they didn't rush the four of you? How come they ran off?"

Frederick Dixon straightened, a light dawning in his expression. "I got me a hunch," he said slowly, "that they figgered the whole militia comp'ny was in here, and that you was gonna come bustin' out to rescue us and chase them all t'hell-an'-gone. Betcha they wasn't nothin' but bait. That's why they acted so queerlike. Reckon they's two-three times that many waitin' in ambush just t'other side that little hill."

"*Injins coming!*" shouted one of the privates on the parapet. "Oh, my God," he added, "*look* at 'em all!"

The distant sounds of savage Indian shrieks carried to them all, and those on the parapets saw a wall of what appeared to be a couple of hundred Indians on horseback charging toward them. The guards fired too soon, when the attackers were still largely out of range, and no bullet found its mark. The following lull in defensive shooting, in order to reload, allowed the Indians to gallop unscathed into the settlement and take refuge behind cabins, outbuildings, hog pens, wagons, troughs, and whatever other cover they could find, from which they began a steady firing at the fort.

Inside the fort, Elizabeth Armstrong, wife of one of the militiamen on detached duty, took a command position among the women. She quickly divided them into two squads — one to mold bullets and the other to reload the flintlocks of the defenders as they were fired.

About half an hour into the siege, Private Hercleroad, who had taken a position on the parapet, peered through a crack between the pickets and glimpsed the movement of one of the Indians. Checking his load to make sure his own rifle was well primed, he raised up to where he could see clearly over the wall. The Indian was still in sight, and Hercleroad took careful aim. He was just beginning to squeeze the trigger when his head was snapped back violently by a ball that struck him directly between the eyebrows, traveled through his brain, and burst apart the back of his skull, killing him instantly. At almost the same moment, Private James Nutting took a ball through his upper right arm.

After the siege had continued for an hour, only a small number of the attackers continued firing at the stockade, while the remainder went on a rampage of destruction in the surrounding settlement. They shot chickens and hogs, smashed furniture and mirrors, set cabins and outbuildings afire, and finally withdrew, driving before them around thirty head of cattle and twenty or more horses.

Inside Apple River Fort, the defenders kept a close vigil. Late in the afternoon, Frederick Dixon volunteered to make an attempt to ride to Galena to give the alarm and bring back help. He mounted his horse, and the gate was opened just enough for him to ride through. Immediately he put his horse into a gallop on the Galena Road. In a short while he was gone from sight, and the defenders were relieved that no shots had been heard.

Young David Kirkpatrick harbored a growing fear that Dixon would be ambushed out of their hearing. If he'd been ambushed and the Indians returned to renew the siege, Apple River Fort might fall. He decided he would ride toward Galena as well, though by a more circuitous route than Dixon had taken. As dusk was beginning to gather, the young man slipped out on horseback as Dixon had done and, keeping clear of the road, was soon swallowed up in the gloom of a grove of trees to the west.

[*June 25, 1832 — Monday*]

Black Hawk and his warriors were jubilant. The attack on Apple River Fort yesterday had been a distinct success. Not one Indian had been hurt in the slightest, much less killed, and it was certain that at least three of the whites had been shot, including the one who had been shot first outside the fort. Not only that, they had gotten away with a supply of flour and foodstuffs, along with a score of horses and thirty head of cattle. As Black Hawk had dreamed it, so it had come to pass. And now, only an hour or so past midnight, there was the prospect ahead of an even greater triumph.

The celebration had been brief, interrupted as it was by the news of the large group of Americans camped to the east of them, but that was of little moment. A much greater victory celebration could well be in store.

Black Hawk had been disappointed yesterday when the ruse to draw the soldiers into an ambush had failed, yet now that very same ruse could be attempted again. Fearful that white warriors would come upon seeing the smoke of the burning buildings at Apple River Fort, Black Hawk had led his men away toward the southeast along the road leading to Rock Island. After a half-hour's travel, he left the trail at an angle to the west, to give the impression to any who might follow that they were headed for the Mississippi with the intention of seeking safety on the other side. In a stand of timber they began to circle, carefully obliterating their tracks. When they had again encountered the road to Rock Island, so carefully had they disguised their passage that only the most excruciatingly close inspection could have detected that they were now moving northeast, heading toward Kellogg's Grove.

Some five miles away from that point, they had finally stopped to feast and rest. The cattle and horses they had taken were restless, and lest their sounds and movements be detected, Black Hawk had selected ten young men to drive them and an additional forty seasoned men to precede and flank them as guards as they continued to move the animals in as direct a line as possible toward their hidden encampment above Lake Koshkonong. Those who had been detailed for this task were disappointed at not being able to stay with the main body, but there was no argument or grumbling among them as they set out to follow the orders of their chief.

The 150 who remained had then continued their feast, some of them snatching naps as they wearied during the revelry. Then, one of the braves that had been sent as a flanking guard with the group that had left, returned with his horse in a lather. The Sacs crowded around him as he told Black Hawk and the other chiefs that as they had neared the island of trees called Kellogg's Grove, they had seen the winking of campfires from far off. They had detoured quietly around the place, but several of them, including the one who was now speaking, had slipped in close to investigate. There were soldiers, he told them — one hundred of those who all wore the same kind of clothes and fifty more of those who dressed in the clothes of settlers. The soldiers had some guards posted, but they and the ones they were guarding seemed not overly alert.

Black Hawk's dark eyes glittered, and he rubbed one hand across his bald dome. "Perhaps," he said, "the Great Spirit has meant for us to do much more to the whites than He revealed to me in my dream. The trap we failed to catch the whites in at the fort yesterday, we will try again today."

[June 25, 1832 — Monday]

Colonel James Strode wrote swiftly to General Atkinson. The first part of the letter recounted what he had been able to reconstruct of the attack on Apple River Fort from the versions told him by Frederick Dixon and David Kirkpatrick, both of whom had managed to reach Galena safely, though Kirkpatrick five or six hours after Dixon. Now, commenting about the Sacs who had attacked the fort, Strode finished the letter:

. . . Their trail led into the Rock River road, followed it some distance [southward], thence tacked to the right obliquely and made in toward the Mississippi. The sign was large. The present location of the Indians is uncertain.

I sent two mounted volunteer companies commanded by Captains Stephenson and Craig early this morning to succour [sic] the Fort, and remove all the women and children to this place, but the most of the people are disposed to sustain the place and I think it right. The horse companies have just returned, nothing occurred. Dixon, a man well acquainted with the Indian character and customs, is convinced that they are near there now in large force. The seat of war is manifestly in this neighborhood at present.

Yrs, &c J. M. Strode

[June 25, 1832 — Monday]

Militia Major John Dement was angry with the way he had been so cavalierly treated by Colonel Zachary Taylor. That was the regulars for you, he thought. They had no consideration for the militia at all. If it had been his own regulars who had just come in from a grueling scour of the wild country, looking for Indians, Dement had no doubt that the colonel would have given them plenty of time to rest and refresh themselves before sending them out again. But not if the detachment were militia. No, sir! Small wonder, Dement thought, that his father-in-law, Colonel Henry Dodge, had expressed contempt for so many of the officers in the United States Army.

So here they were, camped only a stone's throw from the burned-out, skeletal remains of the cabins of Kellogg's Old Camp and fairly close to where the St. Vrain party had been so tragically struck down. And only minutes ago they had received a somewhat dubious report that a large party of Indians had crossed the road not far from here, a report which they'd be checking out immediately after the men finished their breakfast. After yesterday's thorough scout with no sign of them, now this. Damned Sacs! They were like ghosts the way they appeared and disappeared. No wonder his men were grumbling.

While his men were rising from their blankets, relieving themselves, brewing coffee, and fixing some vittles to wolf down, Dement reviewed the events that had brought them all to this miserable situation.

When General Atkinson had given him orders to lead his spy battalion up toward the Big Bureau Creek Valley, where Elijah Phillips had been killed, in an effort to pick up the trail of the Indians, his men had high hopes they would find them. The orders were clear: there was no mercy to be shown, they were to overtake and kill them all. Trouble was, the rains they'd had subsequent to the settler's death had wiped out any trace of the Indians, and so, in accordance with their orders, they had moved on to Dixon's Ferry — searching for fresh Indian sign as they went, but finding none — and finally reported to Colonel Taylor in his ridiculous little mud fort at Dixon's. And Taylor had immediately ordered Dement and his fifty-man force to join with two companies of regulars and go some forty miles northwest, establish his base of operations in the vicinity of Kellogg's Grove, and range the country in the direction of Hamilton's and Gratiot's and Galena for fresh Indian sign. He was ordered to stay there until General Atkinson arrived at Dixon's with the main army.

Though rankled at the colonel's seeming insensitivity, Major Dement had nonetheless held his tongue and followed orders. They had arrived here about thirty-six hours ago, in the evening of Saturday, June 23. Still following orders, the next morning — yesterday — Dement and his men, each with less than a dozen rounds of ammunition, searched the surrounding country scrupulously for some eight hours and found no fresh Indian sign. He'd improved his camp last night and warned his men to keep sharply alert so long as they were in this place, then posted sentries to be rotated at three-hour intervals.

Some while before dawn this morning, an express messenger from Gratiot's Grove, en route to Dixon's, came into the camp in a very excited state and reported that about five miles northwest of here he had encountered a major Indian trail of what was apparently a couple of hundred horsemen or more that seemed to be heading for the Mississippi River. Unaware that it was the trail Black Hawk's party had made on its way to attack Apple River Fort — or even that the fort had been attacked — he was certain it was the Sacs trying to reach safety west of the big river.

Major Dement had immediately named one of his men as his own express to accompany the Gratiot's messenger at double speed to Dixon's and relay the intelligence to Colonel Taylor, as well as to General Posey, who should have arrived at Dixon's by now. As daybreak shot the eastern horizon with streaks of light, Dement ordered those men roused who were not already awake. When all were up and assembled, he gave them instructions. They were all to remain here in camp until the sun was well up, during which interval they were to take care of personal needs, eat their breakfast, and carefully see to their weapons. When these matters had been accomplished, a detachment of ten men would ride as an advance guard to the formation of twenty-five horsemen Dement himself would lead in the direction of the reported Indian trail. The remainder of his battalion were to make a circuit around the encampment at a distance of a quarter-mile to look for fresh Indian sign. On returning, they were to leave their horses saddled and be ready to act on any contingency that might arise.

Now, about an hour since the express was sent off toward Dixon's, Major Dement's men were ready and eager to move out on the assignment. Dement ordered the detachments to mount and, putting out the ten-man advance guard to precede his body of men by about half a mile, set out in a northwesterly direction on Kellogg's Trail.

They had traveled no more than a mile and a half from the main camp when the advance guard caught sight of seven seemingly unarmed Indians on horseback a short distance ahead of them. The Indians seemed shocked at being discovered and immediately broke into a gallop toward a grove of trees a quarter-mile distant. Instantly the advance guard threw caution to the wind and plunged into furious pursuit.

Well behind them, Dement saw what was happening and cursed savagely. "Damned fools!" he snarled. "Can't they see it's the same stunt that was pulled on Stillman? Come on! We've got to help them."

He kicked his horse into a gallop, the detachment close behind, and headed after his guards. He groaned aloud as he saw them near the trees, saw the pursued Indians vanish into the timber, and saw close to 150 mounted Sacs in full war paint burst from hiding in the trees at the advance guard, a fusillade of gunfire directed at the whites. Half of the advance guard fell in that first moment, and the remaining five wheeled practically in mid stride and were now thundering at top speed back toward the detachment, the triumphantly howling Sacs perilously close behind.[282]

"Come on, boys," Dement cried again, "we've got to save them!"

As the gap between them closed, Dement, who knew some of the Sacs from treaty councils he'd attended at Rock Island, caught glimpses of Black Hawk as well as Chiefs Neapope, Weesheet, and Chekokalauko. As the desperate chase continued, the Indians spread out like a funnel behind the white riders and, as the guards dashed into their midst, Dement screamed at the whole complement of his men to wheel and make for the main camp. The two companies of regulars there were the only hope of getting out of this with their scalps intact. But by this time the mouth of the funnel was closing in on them.

Streaking to the front of his party, Dement led them to what appeared to be the thinnest portion of the Indian line and literally bulled his way through them, dodging tomahawk blows and spear thrusts. Though bent low over his horse's neck, Dement vaguely felt the passage of it as a thrown lance arrowed through that narrow gap and clipped away a small chunk of his horse's mane and flesh in its flight. A short distance away, the paymaster of Major Dement's spy battalion, Zadock Casey, who was the present lieutenant governor of Illinois, was struck by a ball that passed through his lower leg and into the abdomen of his horse. It seemed no one would get through the encircling Indians alive, yet they all managed to break through and pounded onward toward the main camp.

Though riding as fast as they'd ever ridden, for Dement and his men it seemed to take forever to cover that mere mile and a half back to the camp. Dement groaned aloud in relief as he saw that the remainder of his men and the regulars ahead of them had moved closer to the ruins of the cabins and were waiting outside the clutter, crouched and ready to admit their fellows and then batter the enemy with their gunfire. In a moment more they were among them and flinging themselves from their saddles to join those afoot in the fight as the Indians swept around them and the burned ruins in a great encircling ring.

The firing was very hot on both sides, and the motionless air quickly filled with a throat-searing haze of smoke, while eyes burned and watered from powder flash. Oddly, only two more Americans were shot, and neither of these was killed. Lieutenant Tramel Ewing had a lead ball pass through his thigh, and Private Marcus Randolph took a ball high in his left buttock. Despite his wound, Lieutenant Tramel Ewing, whose horse was known to be one of the fastest in service, volunteered to make a dash for Dixon's Ferry in an effort to hasten relief to this point. With some reluctance, Major Dement agreed. When there came a momentary break in the Indian line, Tramel shot through it at great speed. A few Indians from the main body of warriors fell in behind him in pursuit, but he so quickly pulled away from them that within a half-mile the pursuers gave up and came back.[283] Several Sacs were shot off their horses, including Patchetowart — the Liar — fourth principal brave of the Black Hawk band, who had been on the white stallion.[284] The cacophony of the battle was almost beyond belief — a terrible blend of the horrendous shrieks of the Indians and fierce cries of the whites mingled with the screams of horses caught in the crossfire, and the whole punctuated by the frightful crash of gunfire.[285]

The bodies of the multitude of dead horses lying about were scant cover for the regulars and militia, and gradually they began moving more into the somewhat sturdier cover that the ruined cabins and what once passed as a blockhouse provided, hiding behind blackened logs and soot-stained remains of stone chimneys and fireplaces. Though the white and Indian forces were closely matched in numbers, abruptly, amazingly, the Indians began to fall away, now that the advantage was no longer theirs and they realized they had become more exposed than their intended quarry. The firing from the soldiers became more sporadic as one after another of the men ran out of ammunition. Dement prayed the Indians would not realize this was what was happening.

"Choose your targets carefully!" Major Dement ordered. "No more shooting at random. We can't afford it. Let them come as close as you dare before firing. We've got to make every shot count, or we're as good as dead."

The Sacs moved gradually into the grove sixty or seventy yards away, and now the contest became one of careful sniping, watching closely for the inadvertently exposed arm or leg or body into which a lead ball could be sent. Hour after hour the fight continued under these altered conditions, and Dement was certain that Black Hawk was deliberately maintaining a holding action until nightfall, when he could gather his warriors for a rush in force.

Close to six o'clock in the evening, the firing on the part of the Indians suddenly ceased. Anticipating a trick, Dement held his men in place, waiting, watching. And then they heard it. A distant rumble like faraway thunder seemed to rise from the very ground and vibrate in their legs and bodies. They stared at one another, expecting the worst, prepared to see a thousand savage warriors sweeping down on them on horseback in a mass attack from which they could not possibly escape.

It was indeed the thunder of horses' hooves, but not with Indians on their backs. To the almost hysterical cheers of the battle-weary regulars and militia alike, the approaching First Brigade, under Brigadier General Alexander Posey, came into view.[286]

[*June 25, 1832 — Monday*]

General Atkinson was in a quandary.

The past few days had been extremely busy, moving his various units forward from Fort Wilbourn to Dixon's Ferry and other places. The Third Brigade's First Regiment under Colonel Samuel Matthews was sent to remain at Ottawa and guard the inhabitants from the annoying little hit-and-run attacks the Indians continued making in the area and which still had the populace on edge. As Governor Reynolds had so succinctly stated it three days ago in a letter to Ninian Edwards, *"Blood flows here on a small scale tolerably fast."*

Atkinson had sent General Posey's brigade here to Dixon's first, and General Alexander's soon followed. Atkinson himself had left the Illinois River with General Henry's brigade, but he had moved on into Dixon's first, and Henry's would arrive tonight. Dixon's was alive with troops, and everything seemed in readiness for the immediate push he planned up the Rock River toward the point above Lake Koshkonong where, according to all the intelligence he'd been receiving, Black Hawk had made his main encampment. Command of this post at Dixon's had already been transferred from Colonel Taylor to General Brady so that Taylor could accompany him on the march.

But then had come some problems. The large number of Indians Colonel Hamilton had brought into the field to assist the army had grown impatient at the army's slowness to do anything and had gone home, except for twenty Menominees. And then, shortly after Atkinson's arrival at Dixon's, two expresses had come in bearing word of the large fresh Indian trail that had been discovered, evidently heading toward the Mississippi River, and General Posey was ordered to march to Kellogg's Grove to join Major Dement's spy battalion and check it out with all due speed.

At 2:00 P.M. the wounded Lieutenant Tramel Ewing arrived with his account of the major attack being launched against Dement's detachment at Kellogg's Grove, and of General Posey hastening in that direction to render aid.

So the dilemma facing Atkinson now involved a number of factors that would strongly influence the direction in which he moved his troops. Was Black Hawk's principal camp still far up the Rock River? Did the large fresh Indian trail that had been discovered mean that Black Hawk was moving his people away with the intent of crossing the Mississippi in the vicinity of Plum River? Or was that trail merely the trail of the large body of Indians with whom Major Dement was presently engaged at Kellogg's Grove?

The plan of operation that had seemed so clear to General Henry Atkinson only a few hours ago now was no longer clear at all. *Where was Black Hawk?*

[*June 26, 1832 — Tuesday*]

The appearance of the large force of soldiers that had come to the rescue of the brave white chief at Kellogg's Grove had unnerved Black Hawk. He realized immediately that General Atkinson was once again on the move and was convinced that the soldiers he saw were only a small part of the force the White Beaver would be setting against him.

The loss of his good and dependable friend, Patchetowart, as well as Chief Chekokalauko, had moved him deeply, and he was morose and taciturn as he led his warriors throughout the night on their move back toward Lake Koshkonong. The plan he had long been considering, he now embarked upon. He had given orders to his men to leave a trail that would look as if it had been deliberately obliterated, yet which would still be legible with difficulty. This time he wanted the enemy to follow him, because this time he intended setting up a deadly ambush for the army of White Beaver to fall into.

Black Hawk set a grueling pace for his men, stopping to rest only occasionally and briefly. They had emerged from Kellogg's Grove timber out of sight of either the men they had been fighting or those coming to their aid, and set a course due east until they encountered Yellow Creek in about three miles. The Indian trail that they found paralleling its downstream course led them, in fifteen miles more, to where the creek emptied into the Pecatonica River, reaching this point at nightfall. Here the trail became even broader, and they followed it downstream along the Pecatonica at a slightly slower but nevertheless steady pace to where it emptied into the Rock River only a few miles below White Crow's Turtle Village.

White Crow was absent from the village when they arrived there this morning, and though the Winnebagoes there welcomed and fed them and encouraged them to rest a while, a noticeable coolness prevailed. Black Hawk was not quite sure why this should be, but he made no comment about it, and less than an hour after their arrival they were on the move again heading up Rock River.

Now, twenty-four hours after having left Kellogg's Grove, they had arrived at the head of Lake Koshkonong. Seven miles above was his principal encampment, but they were going no farther today. Here, at the northwestern point of the lake, the trail was broad and open, but a short distance away on both sides, that level terrain gave way to a jumble of rocks cloaked with brush rising high on both sides. Here a thousand warriors could crouch unseen and, from each side, lay down a withering fire against an army moving through on the trail below, where there was little cover to lend protection from such an attack. Here was where Black Hawk planned to ambush the army of General Atkinson when it arrived.

[*June 28, 1832 — Thursday*]

In his temporary headquarters at Buffalo, Major General Winfield Scott grimly studied the reports he had been receiving. From what he could gather, what they faced here at the rendezvous point — as well as at the points of landfall they would make later — was a race with nature. The Asiatic cholera, so long confined to Europe, had finally made its appearance in Quebec. From there it had spread rapidly to Montreal and then southward to Albany. The disease had moved westward in Canada as well, and one of the letters on his desk reported the alarming intelligence that an outbreak had just occurred only fifty miles from here, at Little York.[287] Obviously, very soon it would reach Buffalo, and Scott viewed it as imperative that his assembling troops be aboard the steamships and en route to Chicago before the malady made its appearance here. To this end he ordered his aide, William DeHart, to write to all the field commanders converging on this place. The letter DeHart had just completed to Colonel Abraham Eustis was typical:

Head Quarters. Buffaloe [sic]. *June 28, 1832*

Sir. The Major Genl Commanding has instructed me to call to your attention the great necessity which exists to use every precaution to guard against the introduction of disease, especially the cholera, among the troops under your command, whilst on their way to Chicago. There seems to be but little doubt that this plague has extended as far as Little York in U[pper] Canada, & will in all probability continue its progress along the upper lakes. It is therefore recommended that during the voyage, the most efficacious disinfecting agents should be freely used, especially the Chloride of lime, or Soda, and the general confides in your discretion and vigilance to use all means which may avert so great a calamity. . . .

[*June 29, 1832 — Friday*]

General Henry Atkinson had made his decision. Right or wrong, it was a course of action he meant to pursue to whatever conclusion it would bring. Yesterday, at noon, he started his army away from Dixon's Ferry and up the Rock River. To General Posey, presently at Fort Hamilton, he sent an order to attach his brigade to Colonel Dodge's troops and rendezvous with him at Lake Koshkonong. A dispatch to General Alexander ordered him to move his brigade at once to rendezvous with him on the Rock River at the mouth of what he called Sycamore Creek, but which was actually the Kishwaukee River. Colonel Fry's regiment of General James's brigade was sent as an advance detachment to meet there the seventy-five Potawatomi warriors who had assembled at the Kishwaukee under Sauganash and Chaubenee to aid him in his advance on Black Hawk's stronghold. Fry was told to equip the Indian allies with white headbands to be worn at all times, in order to tell friendly Indians from hostiles.

Reports received from the field indicated that a few outrages were still being committed by hostiles throughout the area — such as the murder of settlers Joseph Boxley and John Thompson at Sinsinawa Mound.[288] The westward-moving trail of the perpetrators was followed by a small force of militia, but it ended after four miles at the east bank of the Mississippi River, and scraped marks in the river mud on shore indicated they had entered canoes and probably fled to the Iowa side.

Now, as orders were given for the first night's camp of this march, General Atkinson thought it ironic that they were camping very close to where Stillman's Defeat had occurred what seemed a lifetime ago, yet it had been only six weeks earlier. This present operation, Atkinson thought grimly, was going to have a considerably different outcome.

[*July 1, 1832 — Sunday*]

Black Hawk looked with a stony expression over the island encampment. The littered nature of it bespoke volumes, since normally his people were extremely fastidious in their habits. Now the whole camp area was strewn with the bones of cattle and horses, the remains of saddle packs and bits of torn paper and food containers, the ashes of fires that had consumed most of the canoes for food-cooking heat, since they were too weak to go out and collect firewood. His people sat or moved about lethargically amid the debris, unseeing of it in their misery. The talons of hunger once more tore at their stomachs and minds, and once again, in defiance of his order, they had begun killing the horses needed so desperately to finish this campaign and ultimately remove them to safety; yet he could not blame them. They had become gaunt and hollowed-eyed over these weeks of privation, and a great many were sick — some to the point of death.

Soon, he thought, very soon, this would be ended. The white army was on its way upstream, its pace having quickened upon the discovery of the trail he had left for them to find; an intriguing trail that irresistibly beckoned them on, because it seemed the Indians had so assiduously attempted to hide it. A few days more at most and they would be here, and following that, he would lead these poor wretches who trusted him to safety west of the great river.

Black Hawk summoned a trusted warrior to his side and told him to send out however many young men it would take to act as runners to reach all the small war parties that were still out. The message they were to deliver was for all braves and warriors to return at once to the main encampment.

It was time for the trap to be sprung.

[*July 3, 1832 — Tuesday*]

The proud new steamboat *Warrior* had arrived only yesterday on its first passage up the Mississippi River from St. Louis to Galena. The citizens flocked out to see it and marvel at its improvements over the earlier models. One such citizen, after his visit aboard, was so impressed that he immediately wrote a letter about it to the editor of the *Galenian*, and today that letter was published:

Mr Editor: — I have just been on board of the steam boat Warrior, and am highly delighted that our western waters have gained such an acquisition. She has a splendid barge attached to the larboard side which has two cabins; the gentlemen's in front is thirty-two feet and a half long, with sixteen berths. The keel of the barge is 105 feet long; that of the Boat bearing the boiler 111. The boat is elegantly fitted up, and the accommodations excellent. The boat is commanded by Capt. Throckmorton, & owned by Mr. Wm. Hempstead of Galena; and the public owes him their best wishes for his exertions in placing this beautiful vessel upon our western waters.

In his cabin aboard the *Warrior*, Captain John Throckmorton was just completing his log entry when there was a firm rapping on his door.

"Enter."

An officer of the United States Army stepped in. "Good day, sir. Excuse me for bothering you. I am Lieutenant Theophilus Holmes. I have been ordered to hand you this."

He extended an envelope, which Throckmorton accepted and looked at curiously. There were no other markings on it than his own name. He looked up at the officer.

"What is it, Lieutenant?"

"An official government order, sir. It's a requisition placing the steamboat *Warrior* into government service for the war effort."

Throckmorton's nostrils flared, and he glanced down at the envelope still in his hand. "And if I refuse to accept it?"

"Then, sir, I'm afraid this vessel will be confiscated. It is vital in the present emergency, sir."

Throckmorton remained silent a moment and then tossed the envelope onto his small desk. "Who's to captain her?"

"It is hoped, Captain Throckmorton," Holmes said, "you will stay on as skipper, along with your crew in their various capacities. The government will recompense you for such services. But you will not be conscripted. If you prefer not to remain, the government has men experienced enough in river navigation to take over."

"Nobody else is operating this boat, son," Throckmorton grated. "No one but me."

"Very good, sir. I take it this means you accept the requisition?"

"I guess I do."

"Thank you, sir. In the envelope you'll find your first orders. You are to proceed immediately to Fort Crawford to load a cargo of munitions of war, provisions, and other government necessaries, at which time you will be given further orders."

At this very moment, about fifty river miles upstream at Prairie du Chien, eight men were just now affixing their signatures to a letter of appreciation to Colonel Henry Dodge:

Sir; The undersigned, citizens of Prairie du Chien, have witnessed, with feelings of high respect and admiration, the patriotic exertions which you have made for the defence [sic] of our frontier against the cruelties of savage warfare. Fully appreciating the nature and motives of the bold and energetic course of conduct which you have pursued in behalf of our suffering country, we send you by Capt. Jas. B. Estes, a double-barrelled [sic] gun, which we hope you will accept as a small testimony of the high estimation in which we hold your character as an officer and a citizen.

We are, with sentiments of high respect and esteem, Your most obt. Servts.

> (signed) J. M. Street, T. P. Burnett, W. M. Read, H. L. Dousman, Michael Brisbois, M. B. W. Brisbois, Jean Brunet, J. Brisbois

[*July 3, 1832 — Tuesday*]

General Henry Atkinson heard the order being relayed to halt and camp and smiled faintly. The waters of Lake Koshkonong rippled into a surface of sparkling diamonds to their left, and the general experienced that sense of rising excitement inside that he had felt before when closing in on an enemy.

"I'll have you soon, Mr. Black Hawk Chief," he murmured, then glanced about to see if anyone had heard him, but no one was close to him at the moment.

The decision to establish camp here when it was not yet even noon had been judiciously made, and not merely to allow time for the brigades of Generals Alexander and Posey to rendezvous with them. Advance scouts had come in from close to the top of the lake, some three or four miles north, and reported that the point where the general had reached was the last ground they had passed that was high and dry enough for a decent camp. Beyond that point it became progressively more swampy, and there was no place to camp at all. Besides, they had encountered a phenomenal increase in Indian sign, not just of passage but of foraging, which meant the main encampment of Black Hawk's band was probably not too far off. That was when Atkinson had ordered the flankers and advance guard in and called the halt.

The march up the Rock River from the mouth of the Kishwaukee, which Atkinson still thought of as Sycamore Creek, had been essentially without incident. The friendly Potawatomi force under the combined leadership of Waubansee, Chaubenee, and Sauganash had been camped there waiting for them, but they kept largely to themselves when the march resumed. The pulses of the soldiers had begun racing when, at the mouth of the Pecatonica, the army encountered indisputable evidence of the passage of a party of from 150 to two hundred mounted Indians heading up the Rock River. The trail was several days old, and there appeared to have been an effort made to disguise it, but that effort had failed, undoubtedly due to the haste with which the Indians had been traveling.

On June 30 Atkinson's force, which at that time had been composed essentially of the brigade under General Henry and the regulars under Colonel Taylor, had reached the Turtle Village, where White Crow was chief, but it had been abandoned in the face of the approaching troops. Atkinson had found this a little strange, in view of the fact that White Crow's people were considered friendly and the one-eyed chief himself had been instrumental in helping the Americans, not only in ransoming the Hall girls from the Sacs but in pointing the way to Black Hawk's hidden camp. He wound up considering the evacuation of the village as having been a prudent effort by White Crow to avoid contact with Black Hawk's people on the one hand, and on the other, unfortunate accidents on the part of trigger-happy soldiers who might consider any Indian in this remote region as being hostile.

The movement upstream from that point on had been made slowly and with great care. The advance guard had been doubled and the weapons of all the troops were kept primed and ready for any exigency. On July 2 the army had camped at the outlet of Lake Koshkonong, where the large body of water, fed far above by the Rock River, narrowed sharply and became the Rock River once again. Traces of what seemed to be a hastily abandoned Sac camp were found here, along with a few scalps of whites hanging from branches as if in warning. The camp was maintained here longer than usual — until this morning, in fact — while strong detachments of scouts had scoured the area in all directions. All they found were a few Winnebagoes, who were questioned closely but gave vague and contradictory stories concerning the whereabouts of Black Hawk. Actually, the only thing they agreed on was that White Crow's people had gone to Spotted Arm's village at Four Lakes to "get out of the way." An effort was made to hire several of the Winnebagoes as guides, but they refused and were finally released. [289]

It was just at sunset last evening that Captains William Gordon and Peter Menard arrived from General Alexander's brigade. The brigade, they said, coming in this direction on Atkinson's order to rendezvous with the main army, had gone into camp about twenty miles west of them and would be forming a junction with the main army some time the following day. They had investigated the Plum River area close to the Mississippi River, and no sign had been found of any large body of Indians having crossed. To the contrary, on the march from there to here, they had crossed a number of Indian trails, some small, some substantial, but all of them were headed in a northeasterly direction. Atkinson had been delighted that his gamble to continue to ascend the Rock River had paid off. As yet there had been no word from the combined force of General Posey's brigade and Colonel Dodge's rangers, but Atkinson expected them very soon.

General Atkinson felt very good. Black Hawk was nearly in his grasp, and there was little danger that he and his people could outdistance them now. After all, the main encampment of the hostiles obviously included the women and children and elderly who had originally gone up the Rock River with him. How far or fast could the Sac leader travel when encumbered by them? Tomorrow morning, he decided, he would send out major detachments to try to pinpoint at last the main encampment of Black Hawk.

[July 4, 1832 — Wednesday]

White Crow smoked his pipe quietly, exhibiting no trace of the roiling emotions within his mind — a paradoxical combination of high anticipation and gnawing fear. Seated beside him in the wigwam, Black Hawk stared at the small cook-fire, as if hoping to see in its glow a vision of comfort from the Great Spirit.

The first threads of dawn's light were beginning to lace the eastern sky now, and from outside came the subdued commotion of the Sacs packing up their goods and preparing to move out as soon as Black Hawk should give the command. The events of the past twelve hours had been momentous, and White Crow considered them as the wisp of smoke from his pipe tomahawk curled lazily upward.

When he had arrived in the early evening yesterday at the place where Black Hawk was planning his great ambush of the White Beaver's army, he had been impressed at what preparations had been made. The majority of Black Hawk's scattered war parties had come in, and he now had a force of some 325 warriors assembled here. They were already secreted in their hiding places in the rocky prominences overlooking the trail, and even knowing they were there, White Crow had been able to detect no sign of them as he passed through the defile. Black Hawk had emerged to meet him, an aura of confidence emanating from him and the glint in his eyes attesting to his eagerness to spring this great trap on the whites. They had moved to a nearby hidden copse, and it was there, beneath the shade of a sugar maple, that White Crow had burst Black Hawk's bubble of enthusiasm.

The Sac leader was well aware that Atkinson's force had stopped and made camp at the midpoint of the eastern shore of Lake Koshkonong, no more than five miles from this place, and he expected the ambush would occur sometime tomorrow, at which time he was sure they would wipe out a fair portion of the near-one-thousand men the White Beaver had led there. But Black Hawk's expression clouded and then became stony as he listened to the news White Crow brought.

The one-eyed chief had at first remarked on his genuine admiration for the brilliant ambush Black Hawk had set. It was indeed a trap that had every potential of doing exactly what it was set up to do. But, White Crow had gone on, suppose instead of a thousand men, the white chief of soldiers had close to *three* thousand? That, unfortunately, was the case.

On the march to join the White Beaver, he told Black Hawk, was another force of whites a thousand strong under another white chief, which was coming from the southwest in the vicinity of Plum River and was now within twenty miles of uniting with Atkinson. In the morning they would move around the bottom of Lake Koshkonong, and the White Beaver would wait until they had joined him before the army advanced to this ambush point.

His plan in shambles, already Black Hawk had an alternative to attempt, and he spoke as White Crow paused. "Then I must do what I have always kept in the back of my mind to do in the event that flight became the only answer. I will abandon this trap and go to my camp at once and lead them as fast as we can travel toward the sunset, until I have taken them safely across the Mississippi."

White Crow shook his head and then adjusted the black silk scarf angled over his blind eye. "That is no longer possible, Black Hawk," he said soberly. "You would be cut off and wiped out. There is yet *another* army of white soldiers, the same size as the other two, which is also moving to unite with them. This one is coming from the west and north, from the place of the lead mines close to Four Lakes, and they would cross your trail and follow it like wolves. And to make it even worse, Colonel Dodge and all his warriors are with them."

"I would wait till they passed and then cross their trail, rather than let them cross mine."

"No!" White Crow was emphatic. "You cannot. The army that Colonel

Dodge is with is not directing itself to go around the bottom of the lake. It is closer for them to come over the top of the lake to make the union with the White Beaver, which will lead them through this very place. They could not fail to see where you had gone and follow at once."

A glaze had come over Black Hawk's eyes at that point, and for once he had no idea what he could do now to avoid the pincers that were gradually closing on him and his people. White Crow smiled and reached out his hand, placing it on Black Hawk's arm.

"All is not lost, my friend. Listen well."

The Winnebago chief then went on to lay out in verbal detail a brilliant maneuver. Black Hawk was to call his warriors out of their hiding places here at once. When all were assembled, they would ride — White Crow and his guard of five Winnebagoes with them — back eastward to where the Rock River became Lake Koshkonong. They would cross the river at that point, and the whole party, with the exception of White Crow and his five men, would move upstream along the east bank, going directly to Black Hawk's hidden island encampment at the mouth of Bark River. While they were doing that, White Crow's party would carefully move south along the east shore of the lake until, in the darkness, they were close to the White Beaver's camp. Here they would leave sign that the whites could not fail to find in the morning, which would lead them directly to Black Hawk's warrior trail going upstream from the head of the lake.

"As soon as my party has left those signs," White Crow went on, "we will turn back and come directly to your camp. You will have your people prepared to move out as soon as the sky has become light, but you will have them separated into two groups, and this is why." White Crow then went on to explain that one of the groups should be all but fifty of Black Hawk's warriors, those fifty to remain with Black Hawk, and the other group would be the women, children, sick, wounded, and elderly.

The large party of some three hundred warriors, White Crow had continued, would then, making no effort to conceal their trail, move up the south bank of Bark River three miles, to the first creek that enters from the south. They were to move up this smaller creek until, in less than two miles more, they came to the place where the creek they were following was formed by two smaller creeks. [290] Here they were to stop and build many campfires, so that to the whites who would follow their trail, it would seem as if this were where Black Hawk's secret camp had been.

The second group, led by Black Hawk and guided by White Crow, would move as fast as their age and health would permit, going up the east side of the Rock River. The fifty warriors who were to stay with this group were to follow at their rear, meticulously wiping out every trace of this passage, which was why they were waiting here until daylight, in order to be able to see to disguise this trail. White Crow would lead them to where, just above the first large bend of the Rock River, there was an Indian ford. Here they would cross to the west side of the river, which they would continue following upstream for twenty miles to where the Rock River suddenly curved back to the south and a smaller stream the Winnebagoes called Shawneeawtheepi — Silver River — entered from the north.[291]

At this point, White Crow told Black Hawk, they would cross to the east side of the Shawneeawtheepi, where they would find a good Indian trail, which they would follow northeast for seven miles to a place called Broken Tree, where a gigantic old oak had many years before lost its top half to a bolt of lightning.[292] Here, a very faint trail leading north would take them a final six miles, to the Rock River again, which at that point emptied out of a lake the Winnebagoes called Sinnissippi.[293] Here the Rock River tumbled over huge rocks in a narrow defile called simply the Rapids. Adjacent to the Rapids was an area of high ground surrounded by rocks and in turn surrounded by swamp, and it was on that high ground, even better hidden than this place where they were now sitting, that Black Hawk's new encampment would be made, well out of the reach of the great armies closing in on them.

Black Hawk had nodded. It was a masterful plan, but one thing still bothered him. "What of my warriors who go up Bark River to make the false trail and the false camp?"

"Once the fires have been built and heaped with wood," White Crow said, "they will leave them to burn out by themselves, and move straight toward the rising sun, again making no effort to hide their trail. Soon they will come again to Bark River, which they will continue to follow upstream to the east until it suddenly turns north where a large creek we call Scuppernong enters. From here they will go eastward up the Scuppernong, which soon becomes a great marsh into which their trail will go and then vanish. In the midst of the marsh they will turn and go north, and when they leave the marsh they must conceal their track for the first mile. After that they can ride rapidly north until they reach the great Winnebago trail that joins Mil-wau-kee in the east to Four Lakes in the west. They will follow it west until it crosses Rock River and the trail we followed going north. From here they will follow our trail to the new hidden camp. That is my whole plan for you. I can do no more."

Black Hawk had gripped his shoulders and, with the glint of tears in his eyes, spoke in a voice close to breaking. "It is a good plan. We could ask no more. The Sacs have no greater friend than White Crow."

"Do not forget Whirling Thunder," White Crow said, "who is at this moment leading Colonel Dodge and the army he is with to this very spot, so the whites will continue to trust us."[294]

In moments, then, Black Hawk had given the orders. His warriors came out of their hiding places in the rocks and quickly brought up their horses, which had been hidden a little distance away. They all struck out immediately to the east, and as soon as they had crossed the Rock River just above where it emptied into

Lake Koshkonong, Black Hawk and his men turned east. It was by this time nightfall.

"Now we have our job to do," White Crow had said then to the five Winnebago braves who had remained with him. They were Chikakemakaw, who was Chief Spotted Arm's brother; Hunkqua — One-Who-Has-Seen-the-Chief; Houkmenunkaw — Sitting Chief; Waukeeaunskaw and his son, Waukeeska; and Moychenunkaw.[295] The latter was ordered to remain here with the horses and await their return.

White Crow did not wish to carry a gun, but the remaining four braves carefully charged their weapons with fresh, dry gunpowder from their horns and then prepared to walk, each with one hand covering the hammer and pan so the charge would not be jarred away or dampened by dew. The one among them who was most familiar with the dim trail they would follow was Houkmenunkaw — Sitting Chief — and so White Crow directed him to take the lead. Moving in single file with the silence of wraiths in the darkness, the six Winnebagoes followed the trail southward along the lake shore until, after nearly three miles, Houkmenunkaw abruptly halted. Instantly sensing it, the others stopped soundlessly.

From no more than ten feet ahead came the faintest sound of humming, barely within the limits of audibility. The partial moon had not yet risen, but under the starlight, their eyes now well accustomed to the darkness, the Indians could just make out the shadowy form of a standing sentry's head and shoulders projecting above and beyond the deeper shade of a dense tree. He was gazing out over the waters of the placid lake, very softly humming the notes of a little song his mother often sang to him when he was a toddler.

Houkmenunkaw raised his rifle, aimed down the barrel at the faint silhouette of the sentry's head, and thumbed the hammer back to full draw. The harsh double-click would have sent a more seasoned soldier into a dive for cover, but the young sentry made the fatal mistake of merely turning sharply toward the sound. In that split instant, Houkmenunkaw found his aim and pulled the trigger. The blast was deafeningly loud, and the sentry's head snapped back as if struck by a gigantic club.[296]

Instantly the five Indians, no longer concerned with silence, were racing back the way they had come, their moccasined feet thudding and splashing and crackling branches. Within fifteen minutes they were back at their horses and mounted, following with ease the broad trail left by Black Hawk and his warriors.

White Crow was not concerned that there would be pursuit. The White Beaver would read this as an effort to snare a pursuing detachment in an ambush and, wisely, would simply strengthen his guard and wait for morning to make whatever move he thought best.

They had not mentioned to Black Hawk what kind of sign they had left that would encourage the whites to follow and discover the trail of the warriors, and not until now, with his people ready to move and split into the two groups, did he put the question in his mind into words.

"You are certain," he asked White Crow, "that the sign you left for the whites will draw them to this place so that they will follow the trail of my warriors?"

"I am certain," White Crow replied with a smile.

[July 8, 1832 — Sunday]

Throughout the night just past and the early hours this morning, the steamboat *Sheldon Thompson* had been chugging its way north on Lake Huron. Off the port side of the ship, the five-mile-distant coastline of the Michigan Territory continued to slide past as a vague, dark line on the western horizon. The weather had been holding extremely well, and the churning of the great, canopied sidewheels of the steamer in the reasonably calm water left a foamy trail that stretched far behind the vessel.

It was midmorning, and Major General Winfield Scott had still not emerged from his tiny cabin adjacent to that of the skipper, Captain Aaron Walker. Nor was he in any hurry to do so. Except for the exercise of stretching one's legs, there was precious little to do on deck. He continued his reading of one of the medical books that had been loaned to him by his New York surgeon friend, Dr. Thomas Mower. This one was devoted to the detection and treatment of virulent diseases. The book had been published quite a few years previously, and there was nothing in it about the specific strain called Asiatic cholera, but there was a passage about cholera in general that he was finding fascinating:

. . . In every case of Cholera, one of the earliest symptoms is a purging of a slightly cloudy watery fluid, like the rinsings of a milk bucket or the residue water in which rice has been boiled. As soon as possible following this first manifestation of the disease, the patient should be given a dosage of no less than 20 grains of the purgative mercurous chloride (Calomel), which should be combined with one-quarter to one-half grain of Opium to aide the stomach in retaining it for a time. Should this not result in a purge within four hours time, another dose of similar strength should be administered. This will produce a bilious discharge from the bowels. If the diarrhoea is yellow, black, green or brown, either the patient does not have Cholera or, if he does have it, it is a mild manifestation from which he will recover safely. Beware of the administration of too great or too frequent an administration of this prescription to a patient, but there is little danger if it is taken in reason. . . .

General Scott looked up with a faint frown of annoyance as there came a discreet tapping on his door. He reached over, turned the curved brass lever that disengaged the latch, and swung the door open.

Sergeant John Heyl immediately snapped to attention and brought up his arm in a smart salute. "Captain Johnson's compliments, sir," he said briskly. "The captain wonders if you'd care to join him on deck at the bow. We've just begun to get our first glimpse of Bois Blanc ahead."

Bois Blanc Island, named by the first French explorers here after the great forest of birches, whose pale trunks rose like whitewashed pickets all over the face of the island, marked the eastern approach to the Straits of Mackinac, through which flowed the waters of Lake Michigan on their long journey to the Atlantic.

As Scott approached the two officers standing on the foredeck looking toward the distant bulk of the island, Lieutenant James W. Penrose came to attention and saluted, as, a moment later, did Captain Philip Johnson.

"Gentlemen," said Scott affably, returning their salute. "Well, now" — he inclined his head toward the land mass — "there's a welcome sight. We'll evidently soon be passing into Lake Michigan."

"Yes, sir," said Penrose. "I wish Mary was on deck to see it, but she's not feeling her best this morning." Both Penrose and Johnson had brought their wives and children along on this voyage, planning to leave them in quarters at Fort Dearborn during their absence on the march against Black Hawk.

"Same with my wife," chuckled Johnson. "Good thing we joined the army instead of the navy. I don't think either one was cut to be a mariner's wife."

The general and lieutenant joined Captain Johnson in his laughter, and as it died away, Johnson was first to speak again. "I'll have to admit, General, I've not been able to shake my concern until we caught sight of Bois Blanc. Now that feeling's lifted, and I really think we've outrun it."

"Yes," Scott said in a rather clipped manner. "Perhaps. I do hope you're correct, Captain." He turned his gaze toward the island, looming faintly closer now, and the two glanced at one another, taking it as a dismissal.

Penrose cleared his throat softly and said, "Guess we'd better check on our families, sir."

Both junior officers saluted and turned away with a crisp about-face, but Scott neither returned their salute nor responded. The captain's remark had brought to mind again all too freshly the fearful events that had occurred at Detroit and afterward.

Scott's force had embarked from Buffalo on the four steamships laden with war cargo, the report just received still filling their minds. The Asiatic cholera, which had already begun to ravage Quebec, Montreal, Little York, and Albany, had broken out in New York City, and within six hours of its initial appearance there, scores were stricken and four had already died. One question was paramount in everyone's mind all the way up the length of Lake Erie: Had they eluded the disease? It seemed they had, when all were still hale as they steamed into the western end of Lake Erie. Not as heavily laden with cargo as her three sister ships, the *Henry Clay* had easily outdistanced them and reached the mouth of the Detroit River some twenty hours ahead of them, in the early evening on

July 4. Yet, just as the *Henry Clay* was angling in toward the dock at Detroit, a soldier doubled over with symptoms undeniably choleric.

The skipper wisely diverted his approach within mere yards of the dock and moved offshore a distance to drop anchor. By the next evening, when the other three boats came upriver and began heading in toward the Detroit dockage, the stricken soldier was being ravaged by an uncontrollable fever and a number of others had begun showing symptoms. The *Sheldon Thompson* moved up to within thirty yards of the *Henry Clay*, and as soon as the nature of the problem was relayed in a stentorian voice by the first officer, General Scott took action. In an effort to spare Detroit from an epidemic, he had the order called over to his officer in charge aboard the *Henry Clay*, Major David E. Twiggs, for the steamboat to proceed upstream another mile and dock at Belle Isle, where it would be serviced with medicines and other supplies by a small boat from Scott's ship. As soon as this was accomplished, the *Henry Clay* was to continue without further stop into Lake St. Clair, then up the St. Clair River into Lake Huron. They were to go directly to Bois Blanc Island and, if the disease aboard had continued to spread, to remain there.

Thus far the *Sheldon Thompson* and *William Penn* had been unaffected, but the trailing *Superior* hove to nearby with the frightening report that a number of men were already down with cholera and the crew was in a mutinous state. With difficulty, Scott prevailed upon the skipper not to land at Detroit, but he declined to anchor at Belle Isle and adamantly refused to steam on to Bois Blanc. He finally agreed to anchor a little apart from the *Sheldon Thompson* and *William Penn* and then, in the morning, proceed with them in their upstream passage at least as far as the head of the St. Clair River. At that point he had every intention of putting in to Fort Gratiot just below the entry to Lake Huron.

By the next morning, July 6, Detroit was reporting that the first cases of Asiatic cholera had been detected among the citizenry. The three steamboats weighed anchor at once and began the upstream passage, the *William Penn* quickly falling behind, as it had agreed to tow a schooner up to the entry to Lake Huron. As they came up to Belle Isle, the *Henry Clay* upped anchor and fell in with them.

The *Sheldon Thompson* was leading by a considerable margin when it pulled in at Fort Gratiot, whose commanding officer was Major Point. Scott dropped off the several companies of men he had brought as reinforcement for Fort Gratiot and quickly reembarked. As they began moving around a headland and into Lake Huron, Scott glanced back in time to see the *Superior* just pulling into the dockage the *Sheldon Thompson* had vacated.[297] And though they had seen nothing of any of the sister ships since hitting the open waters of the lake, Scott felt sure they were still coming along, far to the rear.

Now, steeped in these melancholy thoughts, Major General Winfield Scott hardly took notice that they had entered the passage where Pointe Aux Pins was off the starboard beam and Pointe au Sable was off the port beam. In fact, though

Sergeant Heyl had come up and was speaking to him, he wasn't even aware of it until the noncommissioned officer tugged at his sleeve.

"Uh . . . yes. What is it, Sergeant?"

"Regret having to tell you this, General," Heyl said, his voice trembling, "but the surgeon has just reported three cases of cholera aboard."

[*July 10, 1832 — Tuesday*]

General Atkinson had daily been sliding back into that state of depression and frustration that had plagued him in the early part of the campaign against Black Hawk. Once again the wily Sac leader had vanished like some sort of phantom in this difficult country of swamps and bogs and sinkholes.

Since the arrival here in the area of Lake Koshkonong of his force of regulars under Colonel Taylor in concert with General Henry's brigade, and the subsequent union with the brigades of Generals Posey and Alexander along with Dodge's rangers, little of consequence had been accomplished. Numerous detachments had been sent out in all directions to scour the surroundings for the enemy, but to little avail.

The morning after the sentry was shot, Colonel Fry had been sent to follow whatever trail could be found, along with the independent spy battalion of Captain Early, of which Private Lincoln was a member. Colonel Fry had had no difficulty in locating and reporting the site where a great ambush had been prepared and then mysteriously abandoned. Suspicion of White Crow giving aid to the enemy and treacherously attempting to lead the whites into a trap began to grow, though there was no proof. Fry's detachment had also located the abandoned island refuge of Black Hawk, where the Sacs had no doubt made their camp for a long while, but it showed signs of having been abandoned two days earlier. Captain Early's company, in its explorations, had found what appeared to have been a subsequent major camp of Black Hawk's people up a tributary creek of the Bark River, some seven or eight miles due east of Atkinson's camp on Lake Koshkonong, but which could be reached only by a laborious journey of about double that mileage by going up the Rock River to the Bark River, then up the latter to a smaller creek, and finally up that smaller creek to the junction of two others. Again, all they found was an empty campground with the residue of many fires, but no enemy. The trail of the departing Indians had been followed eastward until it vanished in a swamp, and once again no one knew where the Indians were. A suspicion began to grow that instead of making for the Mississippi River with his people to escape into Iowa country, Black Hawk might be leading them to the shores of Lake Michigan and then northward into Canada, where the army could not pursue. Once again, the frustration of being unable to pinpoint the location of the enemy was gnawing at the foundations of discipline among the troops.

Provisions had begun to be very scarce and nerves tightly drawn. The officer of the day, Captain Dunn, was mistakenly taken for an Indian and shot and nearly killed by one of the sentries. Governor Reynolds and his staff, who had once again accompanied the militia to the scene of action, were quickly disenchanted with the whole business and today had left to return to his gubernatorial activities in Belleville.

There was a great weariness among the troops from endless slogging through bogs and marshes. Sinkholes were a common problem, and many of the searchers, including Private Abraham Lincoln and his friend, George Harrison, lost horses in them.[298] Every effort in all directions was proving fruitless, and though each supposed new bit of intelligence brought in by the spy companies or Indian scouts under White Crow was investigated thoroughly, none proved fruitful toward locating the new whereabouts of Black Hawk.

The big concern for General Atkinson was the alarming waste of provisions and the growing want for them in the army. To ease the situation, he first discharged all the Indian allies with him, who were doing little except consuming provisions at an alarming rate. The sole exception was his retention of the one-eyed White Crow as a guide and scout, along with a handful of his warriors. Atkinson also detached General Posey's brigade with orders to march to Fort Hamilton and remain there to await further orders, and in the meanwhile, to guard the Mining District, to escort any supply trains passing through, and to keep alert to intercept and engage Black Hawk's band if it should try to escape toward the Mississippi.

At about the same time, to alleviate the food shortage in the army, he dispatched the brigades of General Henry and General Alexander, along with Dodge's rangers, to Fort Winnebago, which had now become a supply depot, with about one hundred packhorses, to return with them loaded with another twelve days' worth of provisions for the army. No one noticed that when White Crow learned of the preparations of over two thousand of the men for their departure, he quickly retired to where the several wigwams were located that his small party had set up. Inside one of these, with a warrior standing guard outside in case anyone should come near, he went into urgent conference with a warrior of about twenty-five who had just arrived that morning. The young man, whose name was White Pawnee, listened carefully to the instructions being given to him, and when they were finished and had risen, he and White Crow had gripped one another's shoulders and then embraced warmly. A few minutes after the Winnebago chief left the wigwam and returned to the whites, White Pawnee quietly led his horse into some heavy cover nearby and, unseen by the whites, mounted and rode rapidly in the direction of Fort Winnebago.

Today the enlistment of the independent companies expired — those, including the one Abraham Lincoln was in, that had immediately reenlisted following the first mustering-out of the militia in Ottawa. No longer needing them in the service, Atkinson ordered them mustered out, and in the forenoon they had started home, accompanying a detachment under Colonel Ewing that was taking the sick and wounded back to Dixon's Ferry. From that point, Atkinson had directed, the mustered-out militiamen would have to find their own way back to their homes.

Dissatisfaction prevailed, and to keep his men busy to some extent, when all searches for Black Hawk's whereabouts were proving fruitless, Atkinson moved his main camp up closer to the mouth of the Bark River and ordered the construction of a stockade, which was called Fort Koshkonong.[299] It was placed under command of Captain Gideon Lowe.

General Atkinson had finally received the orders turning command of the present theater of war over to General Winfield Scott and censuring Atkinson for his poor communications with the War Department and his relative inactivity against the hostile Indians. As he commented in his immediate reply to secretary of war Lewis Cass:

. . . I regret that my letters should have been delayed on their passage, as well on account of the information they contained to the Dept. of War as that it should have given the President dissatisfaction and cause of censuring my conduct. I have written, although not daily, as often as I had anything to communicate that I thought would be of any interest to the Dept of War. . . .

To General Scott he wrote with good grace:

. . . I had been advised by the Secr [sic] of War of your approach with a large body of Troops to put an end to this perplexing and difficult Indian War. I am gratified at the measure adopted by the government in this instance and particularly as you are placed in General command. . . .

Finally, only a few moments ago, Atkinson had completed writing a letter to the commanding general of the United States Army, Lieutenant General Alexander Macomb, in which he said, in part:

. . . after being baffled on his [the enemy's] trail through swamps for the last three days, I have been compelled to suspend my operations for the want of supplies. The Mounted Troops move today for the nearest depot for provisions, whilst the regular Troops take post on Rock River till their return, some five days hence, when I shall again move after the enemy. . . . I find, upon search, that the enemy, instead of halting in the first swamp above us, seem to have fled precipitately . . . it will be extremely difficult to overtake them. . . .

[*July 10, 1832 — Tuesday*]

The new camp being occupied by Black Hawk and his people on the Rock River at the mouth of Sinnissippi was, as White Crow said it would be, ideal in many particulars. It was extremely isolated and unlikely to be found; if found, it was a highly defensible position. The fly in the ointment turned out to be that there was even less food here than had been available at the island camp far below, and his people were suffering from extreme want. A few of the more feeble among the infants, elderly, and wounded had died, each being given the traditional funeral rituals, yet in a manner that underlined the hollow desperation growing among them all. With each passing day their strength was failing. The detachment of warriors that had laid down the false trail for the whites had finally rejoined them, and though all were gratified to see them, their presence put an even greater demand on the extremely limited supplies. Only two of the original hundreds of canoes remained, the others having been burned for firewood at the island camp and here. Black Hawk had come to the reluctant conclusion that very soon his followers would not even be physically *able* to move, much less mount offense or defense against the whites.

Now, seated by his fire with Neapope and others of the chiefs of his band, they were discussing what to do. When the discussion was over, there was little joy or lightening of spirits over the only real option left open to them at this point. It was Black Hawk himself who summed up the situation and the final decision to the encampment at large.

"My people," he said loudly, "we have been deserted by our allies and we have no food. We grow ever more weak, not only in our ability to fight, but in our ability to even move. We now are left with only four hundred warriors to defend us in whatever lies ahead. We are better able to defend ourselves here than anywhere in the open, yet we gradually become weaker the longer we remain here. So we have decided. We will wait here only a few more days, and if we are not discovered and attacked by the army of the White Beaver by then, we will set out away from here in the direction of the sunset and try to reach the Mississippi and the safety we will be able to find on the other side."

[*July 11, 1832 — Wednesday*]

A considerable commotion arose from the soldiers gathered on the deck of the anchored steamboat *Sheldon Thompson*, looking downward over the rain into the water below. Grim-faced, Major General Winfield Scott strode toward them, and the babble of their intermingled, hysterical exclamations became more audible and understandable as separate comments issued in concert.

"Oh, hell, *look* at them — they're waving at us!"

"My god! Oh, my god, they're still alive!"

"An omen, that's what it is. We're all going to die!"

"Hail Mary, full of grace . . ."

"Oh . . . they're ghosts . . . *ghosts!*"

On and on they went, and Scott shook his head and began shouldering his way through the men. They objected until they turned and saw who it was. They parted before him, their babble fading into an apprehensive silence. The general stopped at the rail and looked down toward the water. The only change in his stern visage was the sudden twitching of a jaw muscle. At length he turned from the rail and let his gaze pass over the troops, recognizing in their expressions a mixture of fear and loathing and superstitious dread, not directed at him but as a reaction to what they — and he — had just witnessed. His moving gaze paused when he saw the skipper of the *Sheldon Thompson* looking down at him from the wheelhouse some distance away.

"Captain Walker," he said loudly, "I want this boat moved at once to a different anchorage."

His expression was frozen in grim lines as he returned his gaze to what had upset the men. He felt sick inside, and the events of the past two days flooded his mind in a montage of horror.

It had been close to 10:00 A.M., at the eastern edge of the Straits of Mackinac, that the initial symptoms of Asiatic cholera had been detected in three of his men. By 2:00 P.M., when they had neared the western edge of the straits, those initial symptoms had turned into fevers of such intensity that all three were now delirious, and five more had begun exhibiting symptoms. The four companies of troops aboard were all but petrified with fear.

As they had steamed around Waugoshance Point and angled southward in Lake Michigan, matters became worse. More of the men abruptly doubled over with instant pain so unbearable that they could not even walk to their berths and had to be carried, writhing in agony.

Some two hours later, as they were passing the Manitou Islands, the private first stricken with the disease abruptly died in a paroxysm of pain. By this time others had gone into the stage of intense fevers, and still more were beginning to show the first symptoms. Had the *Sheldon Thompson* been within sight of shore, almost certainly many of the panic-stricken soldiers on board would have leaped and swum to get away.

As soon as the harassed surgeon — the only medic aboard — determined that the first soldier was dead, he lurched away with his own eyes bulging in fear and staggered to his isolated bunk, where, from his baggage, he extracted a bottle of whiskey and drank so much so rapidly that he was rendered wholly incapable of helping anyone.

General Scott was summoned, and, viewing with disgust the semiconscious doctor sprawled across his bunk, spoke aloud but softly in words heavy with contempt. "You ought to die!" Wasting no more time with him, he turned his attention to administering medications to those who were suffering, desperately trying to do all those things to help that he had discussed in New York with Dr. Mower, along with anything he'd been able to glean from the medical texts.

Orderly sergeant John Heyl had appeared within moments at the commander's side and began to assist, anticipating the general's needs and doing whatever it was possible for him to do in order to help, from mopping up messes of vile-smelling vomit to bathing fevered brows with cool Lake Michigan water in buckets. Few men aboard volunteered to help, fearful of coming anywhere near the afflicted, and Sergeant Heyl had soon given up requesting volunteers and took direct action.

Stepping out on the deck, he strode to the nearest group of privates. "You six men," he ordered, pointing them out, "come with me."

No one moved, and Heyl's brows drew down. *"Now!"* he snarled. "You have only one other choice, which is to swim to shore, because I will *by god* throw your asses overboard. Which is it?"

Heyl was a big man, fully capable of carrying out his threat, and there was no doubt in his demeanor that he would do exactly as he said. The six privates had reluctantly followed him back into the bunking lounge that had become the hospital. With the blood draining from their faces, they watched woodenly as Sergeant Heyl wrapped the body of the dead soldier tightly in his own blanket and then ordered the men to find weights and tie them with short lengths of cord to the ankles, knees, waist, and neck. It was done hastily, and then, at his directions, the body was carried to the nearest rail. Sergeant Heyl bent his head and, with only the words, "Take this poor soldier home, Lord . . . amen," gave the wrapped figure a shove and committed it to the depths.

Throughout the remainder of the day and night of July 9 the *Sheldon Thompson* had continued steaming toward Chicago, the smoke from her funnels settling close over the water as if becoming a misty shroud for those who had died and then been wrapped, weighted, and dropped overboard. Captain Johnson and Lieutenant Penrose had remained closeted with their families and out of sight throughout most of this time, while General Scott and Sergeant Heyl, both exhibiting the strain of their unstinting efforts, continued to treat, console, clean, and encourage the dozens now stricken. The steerage was by that time filled with as many patients as it could hold, and victims of new cases were being laid on folded blankets on the deck.

Just as they had approached to within sight of the shoreline at Chicago, close to sunset yesterday, Sergeant Heyl, moving across the deck from one patient to another, suddenly fell to the planking as if he'd been struck a severe blow by someone, yet no one was near him at the moment. No one came to his aid, and after a moment he came groggily to his feet and tried to walk. He felt his legs from the knees down becoming very stiff, and attempted to run vigorously in place to restore his circulation. It didn't help, but the symptoms abruptly changed. The pounding of his own pulse drummed in his ears, and a surge of nausea gripped him. He felt a wave of intense cold move upward from his feet and legs into his body and arms. His limbs cramped, and he bent over with a grunt as he felt a pain in his stomach like the thrust of a sword. He fell again, and this time did not get up. Within a few minutes his hands had curled into grotesque claws in reaction to the agonizing cramps stiffening them. Vaguely, he felt someone pick him up and carry him inside the steerage and, in his haze of pain, saw that it was General Scott. He tried to smile and say, "Well, I've got it, haven't I?" but the smile didn't form, and no words issued. He was distantly aware that the commander used his foot to push a dead soldier out of a bunk and onto the floor, and there was the dim sensation of gently being laid down. For a minute or two there occurred a period of almost painless lucidity, and he told the general what he had experienced. Then the pain returned, intensified, and he lapsed into unconsciousness.

By the time the *Sheldon Thompson* had neared Chicago at about dusk, sixteen men had already died and had been consigned to the deep. Still more cases were breaking out, and the total number of men aboard who were infected was then seventy-seven. Captain Aaron Walker had eased his ship slowly and carefully through the unfamiliar waters toward where a number of sailing ships were moored about five hundred yards offshore, which indicated it would be a safe place to anchor for the night. On shore in the gathering twilight could be seen the tiny figures of a great many people converging to watch the wondrous sight of a type of ship many had never before seen.

Standing at the rail were General Scott and his aide, Lieutenant Sumner. The general shook his head sadly. "They realize they're witnessing history this evening," he murmured. "The first steamboat ever to reach the head of Lake Michigan. They no doubt consider it a great historical event, not only for Chicago, but for Great Lakes navigation. I don't think they'll be so pleased when they learn what we have aboard." He shook his head again, and then his manner became brisk. "Captain Walker has put his yawl at our disposal, so the moment we anchor I want you to go ashore with my compliments to Major Whistler at Fort Dearborn. Advise him of our problem aboard, and tell him that he has until sunrise to move all civilians out of the fort. At that time we will begin moving our afflicted men ashore in small boats and bring them into the fort, which will be converted into a temporary hospital. The garrison is also ordered to leave the fort and make camp a respectable distance away. Also, request of Major Whistler that he please have accommodations set aside for me at a lodging house or some other place within the town proper, not at the fort."

By this time the *Sheldon Thompson* had slowed and stopped within hailing distance of the other ships. The anchor was lowered in fifteen feet of water, and immediately calls of welcome and requests to visit were called over to them from the other vessels. Captain Walker immediately responded in a heavy voice that carried well. "Do not attempt to come to this ship. We have cholera aboard."

The speed with which every one of the sailing vessels hoisted anchor and moved a long way off underlined the almost uncontrollable terror that the proximity of cholera engendered among mariners.

During the night, as the *Sheldon Thompson* rode at anchor, three more of the afflicted had died, raising the death total to nineteen. Early on, the business of wrapping the bodies in blankets before weighting them and dropping them overboard had been given up as time-consuming and pointless, and soon even finding weights heavy enough to hold the bodies down had become a problem.

As a result, the three who died during this night each had a weight tied to the ankles only, and they had been dropped overboard with little ceremony.

Now, in the morning light, having given Captain Walker the order to hoist anchor and move the ship from this spot, General Scott continued to stand at the rail, morosely looking at what had so greatly disturbed the men who were still clustered nearby. The water was extremely clear. Suspended in it were the bodies of the three men who had been dropped overboard last night, held in an upright position by the weights that had been tied to their ankles. Their heads lolled gruesomely, and their arms waved freely in the water with the action of the slight currents, moving in such a way that there was the macabre illusion that they were beckoning to those still on board. One of the three was a soldier who had won the respect and admiration of all on board, orderly sergeant John Heyl.

[July 15, 1832 — Sunday]

Colonel Henry Dodge, sitting astride his horse under the noonday sun next to General James D. Henry, swiveled in his saddle and looked back over the four regiments of mounted men stretched out behind them. They were still forming into their column for the ride ahead, and despite his lingering skepticism over what the Winnebago woman had told him, he still felt a sense of anticipation. It was all probably something she'd dreamed up, or a story deliberately contrived to point them in the wrong direction, but what if it were the truth? He smiled to himself. Strange how things worked out sometimes. If he hadn't led his men through that god-awful shortcut and had gone instead with the brigades, she would have been gone long before their arrival.

Her name was Tuckwahqueeg Sorra — Autumn Sister — but was addressed by those of her party merely as Sorra. Dodge had encountered her a short time after his arrival here at Fort Winnebago three days ago. Although he and his rangers had left General Atkinson's headquarters encampment on Rock River at the same time as the two thousand men comprising the brigades of Generals Alexander and Henry, shortly after their march had begun Dodge had split away from the brigades to take what he called a shortcut, which, he explained to his men, might cut as much as half a day off the eighty-mile ride through the wilderness. Henry and Alexander had declined to go that way, because Dodge had admitted it would be rough going in some parts. His own men, however, had urged him to lead on and they would follow.

Actually, it had cut a full eighteen hours off the ride, but they had arrived at Fort Winnebago very exhausted, their clothing torn, their flesh scratched and gouged, their horses badly spent from the unbelievable stretches of briars, thorn trees, thickets, treacherous rocky defiles, and other brutal terrain he'd led them through. The men had actually cheered at breaking into sight of Fort Winnebago, and as they walked their weary horses in the last few hundred yards, a good bit of semiserious bantering had gone on between the men and himself, the upshot of which was that if he planned on going back the way he had come, he'd be going alone, because they were going to collectively retire from his command.

At the fort, while the men took care of their horses and then themselves, Dodge had reported to the commanding officer, Captain Joseph Plympton, handing him the packet of dispatches sent by General Atkinson. The officer looked them over and then nodded.

"I was beginning to wonder when the general was going to send for some of the supplies that have been brought here," he said. "Twelve days' provisions on a hundred packhorses, you say? We'll take care of it. Give me a minute and I'll be right back. Then we'll exchange some news."

He left and conferred briefly with his adjutant, telling him what supplies should be prepared to be loaded on the packhorses when they arrived with the two approaching brigades. He also gave the order for the fort's bakers to prepare bread for Dodge's men and those of the brigades to arrive.

Dodge and Plympton then talked for over two hours, each filling in the other on the events in his own scope of affairs. During their discussion they observed the Winnebago Indian agent, John H. Kinzie, walking by. Plympton caught his attention and invited him to join them. Kinzie did so, and it was not long before the agent mentioned that his interpreter, Pierre Paquette, had just that morning told him there was a squaw at the fort, with a party of Winnebagoes under Chief Man-eater, who claimed to know the whereabouts of Black Hawk. Dodge became very interested and questioned Kinzie at length. It seemed that Man-eater's village was near the area where Black Hawk's hidden camp was allegedly located, and not wishing to get caught in the middle when the white army eventually caught up with the Sacs, they had stopped at Fort Winnebago on their way farther north for safety until the danger was passed. Dodge asked to meet the woman and speak with her through Paquette, to which Kinzie readily agreed.

The woman was Sorra, a heavy squaw of about forty, with enormous pendulous breasts partially visible through the rips and tears of her tattered blue calico trade dress. She had only one visible tooth, and long stringy hair that was beginning to turn gray. Seated on the ground a little distance from her party, she was vigorously rubbing the palms of her hands together for no apparent reason.

The ranger colonel and the interpreter squatted close to her, at which she giggled and took a greasy lock of her hair between finger and thumb and began twisting it. Paquette introduced Dodge and Sorra to one another, and then was kept busy interpreting in both directions as the two conversed animatedly. The old woman laughed frequently, exposing the single yellowed incisor protruding from lumpy, discolored gums.

Seemingly incapable of nonmovement, Sorra scratched and sniffed and bobbed her head as she spoke. What she told Dodge in an excruciatingly roundabout way boiled down to this: Black Hawk had fooled the whites into thinking he was far to the east of Lake Koshkonong and heading for Lake Michigan. Actually, she said, he and his Sacs — including not only the warriors but all their families as well — had established a camp at what the people of

Man-eater's village called the Rapids. That place was located at the mouth of Sinnissippi Lake, some forty miles north of Lake Koshkonong. They did not think the whites could find them, but if they did, Black Hawk's warriors would fight them in that place, where, because of the terrain they occupied, they would have a great advantage over a much larger enemy force. But, Sorra added, Black Hawk's people were very hungry, and there was little food where they were. She then went on to explain to Dodge exactly how to get there. Then she lapsed into silence, scratching and squirming.

"Ask her," Dodge directed Paquette, "how it is she came by this information."

Paquette put the question to her, and Sorra immediately responded with a string of words, then howled with laughter, holding her enormous stomach and rocking back and forth, the great breasts swinging alarmingly beneath the thread-bare fabric of her calico. Paquette was grinning broadly as he turned back to face Dodge.

"She says she was told by a young Sac brave who was very much in love with her because of her great beauty."

Dodge laughed aloud and then tried to ask more questions, but Sorra had evidently decided she had said enough and would say nothing more. Soon she got up and rejoined her party. In a few minutes more, Man-eater's party had moved out to the north, Sorra bringing up the rear, using both hands to scratch her bouncing buttocks.

The next morning the brigades of Alexander and Henry arrived, planning to rest overnight, load up in the morning, and start back immediately. Atkinson's orders had been explicit. They were to return with the provisions by the fastest, most direct route. Fate, however, delayed them. During the night, for some reason never discovered, their more than two thousand horses suddenly panicked and stampeded over the camp. No one was killed, but there were a few minor injuries among the men, a great deal of equipment damaged, and two precious days lost in recapturing the scattered horses.

Dodge told General Henry what he had learned from Sorra and expressed his eagerness to return to Atkinson via a detour to the Rapids to check out her story. Henry did not reply at once. He cupped his chin and stepped several yards away, thinking. Then he returned and they discussed it at greater length. Though both men were inclined to disbelieve the tale that had been told by Sorra, yet there was an intriguing sense to the story. Henry called a council of all officers of the rank of captain and above in both brigades and directed Dodge to retell the story for their benefit.

"Gentlemen," Henry said when the ranger colonel was finished, "I am inclined to disbelieve the tale. Yet, if it turned out to be true and we missed this opportunity, we could delay the termination of the war by months and cause many lives to be needlessly lost. In such a case, we would be hard put to forgive ourselves. Therefore, I have decided to detour with my brigade and accompany Colonel Dodge to investigate it. General Alexander?"

"Absolutely not, sir!" Milton K. Alexander was indignant. "You seem to have forgotten our orders from General Atkinson to return by the fastest and most direct route. What you propose could delay us two or three days. I will not disobey the commander's order."

"Sir!" It was Lieutenant Colonel Jeremiah Smith, second in command under Colonel Jacob Fry of the Second Regiment of Henry's Third Brigade.

"You have something to add, Colonel Smith?"

"Yes, sir, I do. I agree with General Alexander. You cannot put your subordinate officers in the position of ignoring General Atkinson's express directive." There were some *sotto voce* murmurs of agreement from other officers of Henry's Third Brigade, but they were stilled instantly at the general's stony glare.

"In such a circumstance as this, Colonel," Henry replied icily, "I can and I fully intend to." He turned his attention back to the Second Brigade commander. "General Alexander, you're certain you won't accompany us?"

"Quite certain."

"Very well," Henry said in a more normal tone. "That being the case, the provisions for General Atkinson do not necessarily have to be delayed any further. Do you have any objection to leading all the packhorses in your column?"

"No objection."

"Excellent. Then that's settled. We leave at noon tomorrow, you your way, we our way."

Last night, Pierre Paquette presented himself to General Henry and Colonel Dodge and said a party of a dozen Winnebagoes had just arrived and learned of the plan to march on Black Hawk's alleged hiding place. All twelve wished to accompany the expedition, and one of them supposedly knew exactly where the Rapids was and could act as guide. Henry and Dodge glanced at one another, and Dodge nodded faintly.

"Tell your Winnebagoes we would be pleased to have them join us, Paquette," Henry said.

Paquette flashed stark white teeth in a broad grin and turned to leave, but stopped and turned back when Colonel Dodge spoke his name.

"Who is it, Paquette? The one who says he can lead us to the Rapids?"

"His name is White Pawnee," the interpreter said, then added, "You do not know him, Colonel, but his father is a great chief and you know him well."

"All right, then, who is his father?"

"He is the chief with one eye. My uncle, White Crow."

Now it was noon, and astride his horse beside Henry and waiting for the general to give the command for the march to begin, Dodge saw the commander suddenly wheel his mount around and face a horseman from the rear approaching at a canter. It was the Second Regiment commander, Colonel Fry. In his hand he carried a folded paper. He reined up close to the general and saluted, then extended the paper in a manner that could only be construed as apologetic.

Henry accepted it but did not open it immediately. He did not seem surprised, but he looked at Fry questioningly. The regimental commander cleared his throat self-consciously and looked at Henry directly. "It's a formal remonstrance, General," he said, "instituted by Colonel Smith, who requested that I show it to you and then present it to General Atkinson on our return. Eight officers — four of the Second Regiment, two of the Fourth Regiment, and one each of the First and Third — have signed it as a formal protest against embarking on the course you propose."

Henry gave a faint nod and opened the paper, glanced at it briefly, and looked up again. "Your signature is not on this document, Colonel Fry."

"No, sir, it most certainly is not. I have no sympathy with it. To the contrary, I am bitterly opposed to such an action."

"Summon these men forward, Colonel," Henry said. "I would like you to return with them."

"Yes, sir." Fry saluted again, reined his horse around, and cantered toward the rear. Henry remained in place without speaking to Dodge or looking at him. The ranger colonel decided he wouldn't make any bets on what was going to happen now. A formal remonstrance was extremely serious, only a step removed from mutiny. Not only could it have grave consequences for James D. Henry when he returned to Atkinson, at this moment it could well demoralize his entire command and frustrate his plans.

Within five minutes Colonel Fry returned, the eight officers riding in a column of twos behind him. They formed themselves in a flank line facing General Henry when they stopped. Most of them looked more than a little uncomfortable. Lieutenant Colonel Smith wore an aspect of defiance. Without speaking, Henry made eye contact with each man in turn before resting his attention on the Second Regiment commander again.

"Colonel Fry," he said in a perfectly normal, conversational voice, "place these eight gentlemen under arrest. Escort them to the rear and place them in the custody of Colonel Collins of the Fourth Regiment, who is hereby charged with escorting them to General Atkinson for trial, at which, I have no doubt, they will be shot for disobedience in the face of the enemy."

"Sir." It was Lieutenant Colonel Smith. He looked stricken. "Would the general permit me a few moments to retire and consult with my fellow officers who have signed this document?"

Henry dipped his head. "Permission granted, Colonel."

The eight moved off twenty yards and stopped their horses beneath the branches of a gigantic gnarled oak. They began speaking in hushed, urgent tones to one another, frequently gesticulating, obviously monumentally upset. In less than ten minutes, during which time Henry, Fry, and Dodge had neither moved nor spoken, they came back. Lieutenant Colonel Jeremiah Smith saluted.

"Sir. Permission to speak?" At Henry's nod, he went on. "Sir, we — all of us, without reservation — wish to beg the general's pardon. We did not fully consider the gravity of our action nor the full import of the document when we signed it. We request with utmost humility that the document be returned to us for suitable disposal of same, if that meets with the general's approval."

General Henry was still for a moment. Then he raised the folded paper and tore it in half three times. "Gentlemen," he said, letting the pieces flutter from his hand onto the ground, "I have no idea what document you refer to. If the officers present will please return to their places in the column, we have a war to fight."

The officers, with expressions of men reprieved from the gallows after the noose had already been tightened, galloped toward the rear, followed somewhat more sedately by Colonel Jacob Fry. Only then did General Henry allow the faintest trace of the smile that was in his eyes to quirk his lips.

"Well, Colonel," he said to Dodge, falling in beside him again, "let's go see if we can find this rascal Black Hawk."

[*July 15, 1832 — Sunday*]

From: *John Norvell, citizen of Detroit*
To: *Robert Norris, editor of the Philadelphia Inquirer*

Dear Sir — The cholera continues to prevail in this city. Between thirty and forty cases, in all, have occurred; and of these about eighteen have resulted in death. Most of the others are convalescent; the remainder doubtful. Facts and experience have fully demonstrated here, that the disease is not contagious, but epidemic, and that undue excitement and fear exercise an active agency in producing the mortality among its subjects. The town is almost deserted by its laboring inhabitants; and the countenances of the remaining citizens, with some few exceptions, exhibit marks of unusual depression and melancholy. This is greatly to be lamented. The effect is unhappy. With every determination to resist the mental contagion, I occasionally find myself just in the act of yielding to it. My family have, so far, entirely escaped. How long this exemption may continue, I know not; but I do not let the idea of dread to prevail among them, and believe that, up to this moment, they have not known what apprehension on the subject was.

I regret to add, that the intelligence from the regular troops is disastrous. Of the three companies of artillery under Colonel Twiggs, and two or three more companies of infantry with them, few remain. These troops, you will recollect, landed from the steamboat Henry Clay *below Fort Gratiot. A great number of them will be swept off by the disease. Nearly all the others have deserted. Of the deserters, scattered all over the country, some have died in the woods, and their bodies have been devoured by wolves. I use the language of a gallant young officer. Others have taken their flight to the world of spirits, without a companion to close their eyes, or console the last moments of their existence. Their straggling survivors are occasionally seen marching, some of them know not whither, with their knapsacks on their backs, shunned by the terrified inhabitants, as the source of a mortal pestilence. The dead bodies of the deserters are literally strewed along the road between here and fort Gratiot. No one dares give them relief, not even a cup of water. A person on his way from fort Gratiot here, passed six lying groaning with the agonies of the cholera, under one tree, and saw one corpse by the road side, half eaten up by the hogs. Col. Twiggs himself, and surgeon Everett, have both been attacked, and are very low. They were still living at the latest accounts from Fort Gratiot, and sanguine hopes were entertained of their recovery. No other officers have yet been assailed, except lieut. Joseph Clay of the 4th Infantry. He was 25 when he died at fort Gratiot on July 8.*

You will remember that the troops under Colonel Cummings, several of whom died here, embarked on board the steamboat William Penn on Saturday last for Chicago. The sickness among them increased as they proceeded to Fort Gratiot, and became so great by the time they arrived there, that they were disembarked, and have returned to the vicinity of this city, and encamped at Springwells, about three miles below town. Seventeen or eighteen of them have died, and some still remain sick, probably never to recover. One half of the command of General Scott, ordered to Chicago by the lakes, will never reach him; a large portion of them dying; a still larger number of them deserting from an overwhelming dread of the disease, and the residue obliged to march back. This is a gloomy picture; but it is literally true.

We have intelligence from the scene of Indian war, yesterday and this morning. Gen. Dodge, near Galena, had encountered a banditti of savages, consisting of twelve, and killed every man of them, scalping eleven. Captain Stephenson, near the same place, had encountered another body of them, and killed six or seven, losing three of his own men. The fight was close and desperate, the instruments of the sanguinary contest being chiefly bayonets, knives and tomahawks. The most unfavorable part of the war intelligence is that Black Hawk, with the main Indian army, had retreated to west of the Mississippi, where it will be difficult to take him. It is to be hoped that peace will never be made with him, or any of his hostile allies, until they are placed beyond the possibility of committing another depredation or massacre. The frontier inhabitants have become exceedingly exasperated; and many of them, without knowing the real situation of Gen. Atkinson, have blamed his apparently slow movements. I have no doubt that he has, under the circumstances, acted for the best.

Yours truly, John Norvell

[July 16, 1832 — Monday]

General Winfield Scott had always had little patience for any field officer who failed or was inordinately delayed in the execution of an operation and then made an effort to place the blame for this failure or delay on the vagaries of nature. Yet now, for the first time in his long military career, he was finding himself utterly and completely balked by just such a vagary.

He had begun dictating this letter to the secretary of war well before midnight, on completion of other letters he had begun to dictate before nightfall. Thus, when he paused now and glanced out of the window, he was astounded to see that it was growing light outside. At his pause, Lieutenant Hannibal Day, relieved momentarily of the interminable writing, took the opportunity to put down his pen and vigorously massage his right hand with his left. General Scott turned and saw him doing this and smiled. The young lieutenant was one of Major Whistler's officers of the Fort Dearborn garrison, and had offered his services to the general shortly after the commander's temporary headquarters had been set up here on the north side of the Chicago River opposite the fort. Scott had accepted the offer, not expecting too much, and had been more than impressed by the ability of the young man and the enormous help he had been.

"A long night, lieutenant," Scott said gently. "I do apologize. I hadn't really thought this would take so long. You'll be happy to learn we're nearly finished."

Lieutenant Day nodded, then grinned a little sheepishly. "This last one," he admitted, "really has been the longest letter I've ever had dictated to me."

Scott chuckled. "Let's take a little break for a cup of coffee, and then we'll conclude."

The two men were silent over the beverage, the lieutenant settling back more comfortably in his chair, respecting the fact that the commanding general was steeped in thought. This long stint of work had begun with a letter to Governor Reynolds and then had been succeeded by several others — to General Atkinson on the Rock River, to Major Whiting in Detroit, and to the commanding officers at Forts Howard, Mackinac, Winnebago, and Armstrong. And finally, this present extensive report to secretary of war Lewis Cass.

The letter to Governor Reynolds had set the stage for those that followed:

> *Head Quarters North Western Army*
> *Chicago, July 15, 1832*

> *Sir,   To prevent or to correct the exaggerations of rumour* [sic] *in respect to the existence of cholera at this place, I address myself to your Excellency. Four steamers were engaged at Buffalo to transport United States' troops & supplies to Chicago. In the headmost of these boats, the* Sheldon Thompson, *I, with my staff & four companies, a part of Col. Eustis's command, arrived here on the night of the 10th, instant. On the 8th. all on board were in high health & spirits; but* [by] *the next morning six cases of undoubted cholera presented themselves. The disease rapidly spread itself for the next three days. About 120 persons have been affected more or less with it; fifty have died and forty are convalescent. The few new cases which have occurred, since the 12th. have been of a milder type.*

> *The whole of the infected battalion is confined to the limits of Fort Dearborn —*

the former garrison — Major Whistler & two companies having, before the land-
ing, marched out & encamped at a safe distance.

Most of the inhabitants fled from this place on hearing that we had brought the
cholera with us; but finding that the few remaining & Major Whistler's command
remain uninfected, the citizens are inspired with confidence & are, many of them,
returning.

Humanity & policy have equally dictated the measures I have adopted to
prevent the spread of the disease; & with a view to ulterior operations, in the field,
I have separated myself & my staff from the fort & the region of probable infection.

I am now waiting the arrival of the three other steamers with troops & supplies,
the Henry Clay, the Superior, & the Wm. Penn. I Have received no news from
either [sic] since my departure from Detroit, the 5th. instant. It is probable that
one or more of them will arrive here with cholera on board. If so the same sanitary
measures will be adopted in respect to the infected troops on their landing. The
sick will be placed in hospital & the well encamped apart. By constantly sepa-
rating the one from the other, & keeping the whole from battalions & detachments
which have not had the disease, a portion may, after some weeks, be so thoroughly
disinfected as to be allowed to take the field.

Under a late act of Congress six companies of Rangers are to be raised &
marched to this place. General Dodge of Michigan is appointed Major of the
battalion, & I have seen the names of the captains; but I do not know where to
address them. I am afraid that the reports, from this place, in respect to cholera,
may seriously retard the raising of this force. I wish, therefore, that your Excel-
lency would give publicity to the measures I have adopted to prevent the spread of
the disease, & of my determination not to allow any junction or communication
between the uninfected & infected troops. The war is not at an end, & may not
be brought to a close in some time. The Rangers may reach the theater of
operations in time to give the final blow. As they approach me, say at this place,
I shall take care of their health & general wants.

I write in great haste, & may not have time to cause my letter to be copied. It
will be put into some post office in the South.

I have the honor to be, yr. Excellency's most obt. servt.
Winfield Scott.

The other letters that had followed had touched or elaborated on a variety of
detail not expressly covered in the letter to the governor:

• On receiving General Scott's order, via Captain Sumner, to evacuate his
garrison from Fort Dearborn before sunrise, Major William Whistler had roused
his two companies of United States troops and marched them in the darkness to
a point up the lakeshore some two miles north of the fort, and there established
a camp.[300]

• The Chicago residents, along with the refugees from the surrounding areas who were here to find safety from Indian war parties, on learning of cholera aboard the *Sheldon Thompson* and the fact that the troops were to be landed the next morning, had fled with precipitate haste, in terror of the disease that was considered a much deadlier and far more insidious enemy than the Indians. With but a few exceptions, all had left with their families to outlying places of refuge — some to Laughton's, some to Grosse Point, some to Wentworth's. Many of the vacated structures in Chicago, such as Mark Beaubien's Tavern — which had accommodations for four families of travelers — were taken over by the uninfected families of officers from the *Sheldon Thompson* immediately after landing.

• The sailing boats that had fled their anchorage on learning of the disease had gone far out into Lake Michigan, almost out of sight, but after a while they began returning and resumed their anchorage, though none of them closer than a hearty hailing distance to the *Sheldon Thompson*. Two of these, schooners carrying supplies for the troops, were ordered by Scott to proceed immediately to Fort Howard at Green Bay, those supplies to be transshipped at once to Fort Winnebago for the use of General Atkinson's forces.[301]

• All the blankets and other bedding aboard the *Sheldon Thompson* that were the property of the boat were taken into Fort Dearborn by order of General Scott for use of the sick, for which General Scott provided Captain Walker a draft for the purchase of new bedding, since he did not want the diseased bedding brought back aboard his boat.

• The lack of timber severely hampered the efforts of Captain Aaron Walker of the *Sheldon Thompson* to find fuel to burn aboard his vessel on the way back, and in order to fill this need he had purchased a roofless log building that was being used as a stable, along with a rail fence enclosing three acres close by, and this wood was cut into proper lengths and loaded aboard the boat, which finally weighed anchor and started back toward the Straits of Mackinac yesterday.

• By the end of the first full day ashore at Chicago — July 11 — there had been a total of nineteen deaths among Scott's force, along with seventy-seven presently suffering with the disease in the Fort Dearborn hospital, these latter including Scott's right-hand man, acting assistant adjutant general, Captain P. H. Galt, along with Lieutenant W. A. Thornton, Lieutenant William Maynadier, and a recent West Point graduate who was close to death, Lieutenant Franklin McDuffey.

• During the night of July 11, new cases of the disease had appeared, and six more deaths occurred before daylight.

• By the end of the second full day ashore — July 12 — a total of eighteen men had died in Fort Dearborn, and these were taken just short of two miles southwest of the fort and buried, the earth removed from one grave used to fill in the previous one until all were interred. The burials were without coffin or shroud except that each body was wrapped in the blanket on which the individual was lying when he died. No marker was raised over these graves.[302]

• During the day yesterday, Lieutenant Gustav Brown and Captain John Monroe had died — and after the letter to Governor Reynolds was finished, a few hours ago, word had been brought that Lieutenant Franklin McDuffey had finally died.

• As he wrote in his letter to Henry Atkinson, should all hope fail Scott of marching an effective force to the war front, he would still join General Atkinson in person, but he was prepared first to wait until he had definite intelligence in regard to the troops who were supposed to be here from the other steamboats.

• The initial business attended to by General Scott upon disembarking from the *Sheldon Thompson* was the issuance of two general orders:

ORDERS NO. 2

The care of all will first be directed to the accommodation, comfort & cure of the sick, both officers & men.

In lodging & providing for these it will be recollected that other detachments are expected which may unhappily have suffered as much from the ravages of the cholera as the detachment now landing.

This fear will be taken into consideration by the commanding officer of the first battalion of artillery in distributing his sick officers & men in the limited quarters of Fort Dearborn.

When the sick, as they successively arrive, are comfortably lodged, the well *will next be quartered; but as soon as tents are received, the whole, except* sick *in* hospital *will be encamped on ground which will be designated.*

It is desirable that the well, as far as may be practicable, should be immediately separated from the Sick — except attendants left with the latter. The commanding officer of the Fort will, accordingly, cause the barn, belonging to the United States, to be cleaned out as a barrack for the well men.

Large boxes, as well as barrels, containing general supplies for the army, may be left on the outside of the Fort, for the present, & until the quartermaster's & commissary's departments can find, or construct shelter for such articles; but smaller boxes, parcels or cases being liable to be lost or pilfered, must be promptly stored on being landed.

If sentinels should be needed for the protection of the supplies they will be furnished by the commanding officer of the Fort on the requisition of the staff department having charge of the supplies.

Requisitions strictly within the General Regulations of the Army will be complied with, by the staff, on the signatures of commanding officers of battalions & separate companies. All extraordinary requisitions [should] be presented to the assistant adjutant general, or an aide-de-camp, for the approbation of the commanding general.

Requisitions for ordnance & ordnance stores will be submitted to the comman-
dant-in-chief of artillery, for his signature.

WINFIELD SCOTT

The next general order was explicitly designed to soothe the fears of the populace and to encourage their communication with the commanding general:

ORDERS NO. 3
It is of the utmost importance that the inhabitants of the neighborhood be preserved from Cholera. The Commanding General cannot obtain information nor send off expresses unless he can have free communication with the inhabitants. For this purpose he has kept at a distance from Fort Dearborn to satisfy himself that he is free from infection & to impart that Confidence to others.

The officers & men at Fort Dearborn, for these important reasons, will take care not to mix with the inhabitants of the Country; but on the contrary warn off such as may approach them. Walks in solitary places will, it is hoped, be found sufficient.

By order of Major Genl Scott
W. C. DeHart Aide-de-Camp.

Finally, at 11:40 P.M., Scott had begun dictating, and now, with the sun on the verge of rising, sixteen pages had been completed and they were not yet finished. This, of course, was the long report to secretary of war Lewis Cass, which covered many of the items contained in the other letters, but also expounded on other matters:

. . . I learn now that Lieut Col Twiggs, the Commanding Officer on board the Henry Clay, *and whom I passed two miles above Detroit on the 5th., has taken upon himself the high, and in my opinion unwarrantable responsibility, of landing the troops from that Boat one mile below Fort Gratiot, and of abandoning the voyage to this place because a few cases of Cholera had occurred among the men. From his letter to me of the 7th. inst. via Detroit, and the express, it does not appear that there was any difficulty in standing on made by the Master or Crew, but that that Officer took upon himself the responsibility on account of "the rapid spread of the Cholera" — that is, four deaths and eight new cases in three days, among more than, I think, 370 men! . . .*

The example of Lieut Col. Twiggs may have a fatal influence on the other detachments which were to have come by the Superior *and* William Penn, *besides infecting, by proximity, the four companies in Fort Gratiot, if they had not taken the seeds of Cholera before. . . .*

Yesterday, under the apprehension (from the nonappearance of the Clay) *that a panic had seized the crews of some or all of the steamers, and possibly some of* the Commanders of the Troops in the rear, I wrote instructions to all the detachments, whether afloat or ashore, to proceed hither by any means in their power or that of the Quarter Master's Department. Those letters went off last night by the return of the Sheldon Thompson. One of them was addressed to Brigr Genl Brooke, commanding at Fort Mackinac, respecting the two companies of the 5th. Infantry.

I further wrote by the express sent off on the 12th. to Detroit, to say that if any accident should prevent the general supplies from coming up in the Superior or in the Penn, it was my wish that Major Whiting should adopt other prompt means of sending, at least, a portion of the Hospital stores & medicines. Some essential articles under this general head are already wanting and others are in danger of being soon exhausted. Col. Eustis, by my desire, will write again to Major Whiting on this subject, specifying the articles of more immediate necessity. Should all the detachments behind arrive, there is great reason to fear that all will be more or less reduced by cholera. The uninfected, if there should [be] such, shall be kept at a safe distance from the infected, and from the latter the sick from time to time separated from the well. Some further time will then be necessary to disinfect the latter, or at least the clothing in use, before it would be safe to permit such detachments to form a junction with the forces of Brigadier Genl Atkinson, the Rangers, or other troops. Perhaps I may be able to dispense with the field services of all suspected detachments; but on this point, I am not able at the moment to speak positively. It is almost certain that if Troops suspected of Cholera were to approach Volunteers or Rangers, there would be a general disbandment of the Volunteers, if not of the Rangers. . . .

Genl Atkinson's two letters to me dated respectively the 9th. & 11th. inst. will sufficiently explain the present state of the war. It is infinitely mortifying to me and to all the Officers here that we are by a stroke of Providence unable to march immediately to the theatre of operations. As soon as I am relieved of my anxieties for the troops now afflicted with cholera and disembarrassed in respect to the detachments in the rear, I shall, with any healthy and unsuspected body of men I can collect, march upon the enemy and form a junction with Genl Atkinson or cooperate with him. . . . So far all who came with me have been unintimidated by the presence of Cholera, and many of us have left families exposed to this greatest of enemies. Nevertheless, the survivors are all anxious to march to battle the moment we may do so with advantage to the country.

Out of 190 men, we have lost fifty-one. . . . Seventy men are yet sick, of whom at least forty are decidedly convalescent; and so are all the remaining officers who have had the Cholera. The few new cases which occurred yesterday and the day before, are generally of a milder type. Today there has been no new case and but one death. We shall, however, lose a few more men. The morale of the survivors of every class is yet unbroken. Major Whistler's detachment and the few inhabitants who are in the village remain uninfected.

I wrote to Genl Atkinson fully apprising him of my situation and prospects here *on the 12th instant, so that he might prosecute his own plans without any immediate reliance on the forces which were expected to arrive here. . . .*

Now, General Scott, beginning to doze in his chair, snapped erect when his head nodded and shook himself to clear his mind of the sleepiness attempting to engulf him. He looked over at Lieutenant Hannibal Day and saw him sound asleep with his head lolling back and snoring gently. He rose and touched his secretary on the shoulder. Lieutenant Day came awake instantly, flustered that he had allowed himself to drop off.

"Not much to go, Lieutenant," Scott said. "Let's get it finished, and then we can go to bed and get some real sleep."

Day said, "Yes, sir," found his place on the paper before him, dipped his quill, and poised there, ready to begin. Scott, who had moved to the window, stood there a moment looking at Fort Dearborn bathed in new sunlight slanting in from across Lake Michigan, then turned around and resumed his interrupted dictation.

A few of the inhabitants have returned here, but not the Indian agent, Mr. Owen. He went off on the 11th. and is not expected back while there is any danger from Cholera. He would have been a great resource to me in obtaining information as to the temper and designs of the Pottawattamies [sic] and other Indians. I am at a loss to whom to apply for information on this head.

The Officers of the Staff remaining with me are Col Eustis (as Commandant in Chief of Artillery), Captain Mackay [sic], Lieut Sumner, and Major Kirby, paymaster. We are quartered in the upper part of the Village. The Quarter Master and Commissary of Subsistence are fully occupied with their own immediate duties. Col Eustis is always ready to give his assistance in any way and in every thing. Major Kirby is my principal dependence as a military secretary and he is now aided by Lieut Day, a young Officer of merit from Major Whistler's command. [Lieutenant Day found himself blushing, and Scott smiled but went on without pause.] *I have myself so much manual labor to perform in the way of writing, notwithstanding the assistance derived from these three officers, that I have but little leisure for thought.*

Brevet Lieut Col Worth, Brevet Capt James Monroe, and Lt. Dehart [sic], all of my staff, have been ordered to the East. Every one of them from sickness and debility, being incapable of labour [sic] of any sort. I was satisfied that I should have buried them all if they had remained here much longer. Capt Galt is still in hospital, and if he should be well enough in a short time to resume his bureau duties, he would still have to undergo a process of disinfection in respect to his clothes, before it would be prudent either in regard to the inhabitants or myself for him to join me. Lieut Tupper of the U.S. Marines came with the express-rider this evening from the interior of Michigan to volunteer his services for the field. He was not deterred by the reports of Cholera which he met on the road. I am sorry that I have no duty to assign him.

General Scott suddenly yawned and stretched expansively. "This is ridiculous, Lieutenant. Let's get some breakfast and a nap, and we can finish this letter later today."

"Yes, sir, sounds fine." Lieutenant Day was not at all displeased.

[*July 17, 1832 — Tuesday*]

Black Hawk had made his decision. It was a great risk, but there was no longer any choice. This camp at the Rapids of Rock River was a good hiding place and very defensible, but there was no food to be had, and his people were starving. Whatever cattle and foodstuffs the warriors from raiding parties had brought in had long since been consumed, and since none of the raiding parties were out anymore, there was no hope of precious food supplies being brought in. The only hope left was to gather their waning strength, use what horses they had for the transportation of the sick and weak and elderly, carry the few remaining canoes with them for crossing streams, and strike out with all possible speed for the Mississippi River.

The irony of it all was not lost on the Sac leader. There was no longer any vestige of hope that they could remain east of the Mississippi in the land that was rightfully theirs. They were now in the position of wishing desperately that they were back in the Iowa country, where they could have remained without difficulty, yet on which they had turned their backs to come here. They had paid a price far greater than Black Hawk had envisioned, and the debt was as yet unsettled. There could well be an infinitely greater price to be paid in the days ahead if they did not reach the Mississippi River before they were discovered.

It would have been Black Hawk's choice to move his people by way of the wilderness, where the possibility of detection would be reduced, but Black Hawk did not know this country well enough to attempt it. White Crow had not returned, and they had no guide. Their only hope would be to return to the great east-west trail of the Winnebagoes, which ran from Mil-wau-kee on a nearly direct line westward to the Four Lakes. It would be easier traveling, but far more dangerous. From Four Lakes they could strike directly for the Wisconsin River, cross it into the wild country beyond, and then reach the Mississippi somewhere many miles above Prairie du Chien.

So now, once again, they were packed and ready to go. Many of the horses were now rigged with travois to which blankets had been affixed and upon which those who were not capable of walking at all would ride. Still, many of the very weak who should ride would have to walk, and this would be hard on them as well as more dangerous, because it would slow down the whole procession greatly.

On a more personal level, Black Hawk still had the devotion of his followers.

Their respect for him as a war chief had slipped considerably over these weeks, but if he were able to get them safely back to Iowa, their love for him would be even greater, and he would be highly honored among them and continue to be their chief so long as he drew breath.

Black Hawk raised his arm, and instantly there were yips and cries from watchful braves to silence the din of the multitude who waited.

"Now we start again," Black Hawk said in a loud voice, "but we are no longer running away. Now we are running *to*. We are running to our home, where we will be safe from the whites."

There were loud cries of approval, and then the whole procession began to move.

CHAPTER XI

[*July 18, 1832 — Wednesday*]

T WO HOURS after nightfall, the camp of the combined commands of
General James D. Henry and Colonel Henry Dodge was thrown into
momentary confusion by a sudden burst of gunfire from the sentries. In moments, those who had retired for the night were on their feet and those still
awake, including Dodge and Henry, were standing ready with their weapons.

"Now what?" General Henry gritted, and Dodge shifted uncomfortably, sensing that the commander's question was more an indirect criticism of him than
anything else. Actually, he couldn't blame the general for being testy. Their
impromptu expedition toward the Rapids of Rock River had been extremely
rough going and had taken far longer than anticipated, in part because quite a
few horses had given out, leaving their riders to walk or run alongside the
mounted men. Frequent detours had become necessary due to the swampy
nature of the ground, which had developed into a series of amazingly extensive
marshes.

Around noon today, after three days of slow, rigorous travel and two nights of
uncomfortable camping since their departure from Fort Winnebago, they still
hadn't reached their destination. Finally, at General Henry's clipped order,
Dodge had summoned the interpreter and demanded to know if their guide,
White Pawnee, was deliberately delaying them by leading them on a roundabout
route.

Pierre Paquette had shrugged. "If the Rapids was an easy place to get to," he
said logically, "Black Hawk would not have gone there to hide from the Americans. You cannot hold my cousin White Pawnee responsible for a land that is
difficult to march through."

The white leaders weren't too sure of that, but a short time later they reached the all-but-abandoned village of Chief Man-eater, and Paquette questioned two old Winnebagoes who were still there.[303] The three spoke at length, and then Paquette turned and reported to Henry and Dodge.

"They say the Rapids is only a short distance from here, but that it will do you no good to go there. They say Black Hawk and his people were there for some time but they have gone now, to an area where there will be more food for them to eat. They say the Sacs were very hungry."

"When did Black Hawk leave, and where has he gone?" General Henry asked, obviously irritated.

Paquette questioned the pair again and listened while they replied. "They said," he told the general, "that the Sacs left yesterday and they have gone north, a half-day's journey, to the Cranberry lake, where they say there are many ducks and geese to hunt and many fish to catch, so they no longer need to be hungry."[304]

A small detachment was sent immediately to investigate and within two hours returned with confirmation: Black Hawk had obviously made his camp there for some time, but it was deserted now. Evidently the two old Winnebagoes were telling the truth, and the growing exasperation among the soldiers was abruptly changed to jubilation. A significant glance of intermingled relief and pleasure had passed at that moment between General Henry and Colonel Dodge. They had been vindicated in their gamble to find Black Hawk.

A council of the officers had been held at once and the decision made without opposition to camp here for the night, then take up the trail first thing in the morning and engage the Sacs the moment they overtook them. With this decision made, two of the detachments' adjutants — D. H. Merriman of the 4th Regiment and William W. Woodbridge of Dodge's rangers — volunteered to leave at once to report their discovery to General Atkinson. From the party of Winnebagoes that had accompanied them here, Paquette selected a minor chief named Little Thunder to guide the two adjutants the remaining forty miles to Atkinson's camp. The three men left immediately.

Now had come the alarm in the darkness, and the majority believed they were under attack. In a short while, however, it became clear there was no danger. The gunfire had been by two sentries, who fortunately had missed in their efforts to shoot the intruders who thundered into the camp — the two adjutants led by Little Thunder. All three were very excited, and gradually their story came out, as Merriman and Woodbridge reported to their commanders and Paquette interpreted for Little Thunder.

The three men had traveled southward for a dozen miles or more when, just at dusk, they had encountered a broad, fresh trail of many Indians heading due west. After studying it for several moments, Little Thunder had become very excited, gesturing and talking rapidly. The two officers, who knew none of the Winnebago tongue, had been unable to understand him. They wanted to continue to Atkinson's camp to report this, but, in evident exasperation, Little

Thunder had suddenly galloped his horse back in the direction from which they had come. The officers, knowing they would be lost without his guidance, and with night coming on, had no choice but to follow him. They had tried to warn him not to risk galloping into camp without their first identifying themselves from a distance, but to no avail. They were fortunate in not having been killed by the sentries when they arrived.

Now, after talking with Little Thunder at length, Paquette turned to the commanders. "He says the trail they found was one of many horses, but equally of many who are without horses and must walk. He says that there are also many marks of travois, which indicates that quite a few in the party are too ill to either ride a horse or walk. He says there is no doubt that it is the trail of Black Hawk, who is most certainly on his way to the Mississippi River with all his people."

By this time the two old Winnebagoes who had told them Black Hawk had gone north to the Cranberry lake were brought to the headquarters tent by General Henry's brigade inspector, Major Murray McConnel. He had caught the two trying to slip away in the darkness. With Paquette's help, the pair were questioned and finally admitted that they had lied in order to give Black Hawk and his people a chance to escape. The two were placed under guard, and the officers assembled for another council.

"Gentlemen," General Henry told them, "advise your commands to get all the rest they can tonight. At sunrise we march south to intercept Black Hawk's trail, which we will follow until we have caught him."

[July 19, 1832 — Thursday]

In the light of dawn, Black Hawk moved stiffly among his people, his muscles aching from yesterday's long walk. Though he could have ridden, he had chosen to walk as an example for those who were required to do so, and as hard as it had been on him at age sixty-five, there were many of his followers for whom the twenty-five-mile march had been even more difficult. Doggedly, with only one major pause during the entire day, they had followed their two Winnebago guides, the Prophet, Wabokieshiek, and Wampanoset.

Black Hawk had chosen this camping place for the night just after they had struck the main east-west Winnebago trail that ran all the way from Mil-wau-kee on the shore of Lake Michigan westward to Spotted Arm's village at Four Lakes.[305] In the fading light of day they had turned westward on the trail, and in a short time had come to the Indian fording place of the Crawfish River. In the gloom of twilight they had crossed over, and here, on the west side of the river, they had made their camp; a cold camp, because Black Hawk had allowed no fires to be built lest they be spotted by roving patrols from General Atkinson.

Now, as he walked through the camp murmuring words of encouragement to all as they were preparing for this new day's march, he paused at the sight of a withered old Sac who, five decades ago, had been a fellow warrior of Black Hawk's father, Pyesa. His name was Caukeecamac, and his face was smeared with a mixture of mud and black paint — the sign of death.[306] As Black Hawk approached, Caukeecamac came to his feet with difficulty and pointed morosely at the blanket-enshrouded figure on the ground, beside which he had been sitting.

"It is my wife, Black Hawk," he said in a voice made reedy by age and emotion. "She was hungry to the point of death when we began our walk yesterday. I had to help her often. Her bones were old and her flesh was cold and I had to help her often. The cold of the water as we went through it last night, with no fire to warm her on the other side, was too much. I held her to me during the night, but the Great Spirit touched her, and she is gone."

"Old friend, I am sorry for you and her." Black Hawk put his hand on Caukeecamac's shoulder. "I will have young men dig a grave where you may lay her before we leave."

"That will be good," the old man said. "Then you can leave, but I will go no farther. I am sick, and I am too old and weary to run anymore. I will stay by my wife. That is my place."

Black Hawk stood silently a moment and then nodded. He selected several young men, who quickly dug a shallow grave, into which they placed the body of Caukeecamac's wife, and gently covered her over.

Within minutes the Sacs were on the move again, following the Winnebago trail to the west. Behind them, Caukeecamac sat beside the mound of freshly turned earth, facing toward the river, toward the east — toward the direction from which the whites would come.

[July 19, 1832 — Thursday]

Abraham Lincoln, sitting in his own chair in his own home in his own town of New Salem, Illinois, opened his copy of the *Sangamo Journal* and skimmed the various columns until he found what he was seeking. He read the brief article quickly and then leaned back and stretched his long legs out before him, smiling broadly.

It was good to be home again, to be away from the discomfort and privations of the frontier, always with the potential of death lurking close by. He had not been sorry when his third and final enlistment in this present Black Hawk War had expired and was not tempted to reenlist yet again, feeling he'd put in his service well and faithfully, even if he hadn't come under enemy fire.

After reaching Dixon's Ferry in company with Colonel Ewing's detachment, he and his close friend, George Harrison, had set out afoot on their own to the south. When they reached Peoria, they pooled their meager funds and bought a canoe to continue downriver, Lincoln fashioning a paddle out of a piece of old planking. Just below Pekin they overtook a couple of men making their way downriver on a large log raft, who hailed the returning militiamen to join them aboard for some food. Not having eaten anything except the most meager of rations since leaving General Atkinson's force, they accepted gladly and devoured with unseemly greed the meal that was provided — eggs, fish, cornbread with butter, and hot coffee — while they passed on what news they had from the front.

Lincoln and Harrison soon bade their river acquaintances farewell and continued paddling downriver to Havana, the seat of Mason County. Here they sold the canoe without difficulty for as much as they had paid for it and walked the rest of the way southeast to New Salem, just a little over twenty miles.[307]

On his arrival he happened to read a back issue of the *Sangamo Journal* that carried an article listing the names of Sangamon County candidates for political office who had served in the militia. He was not pleased when he found that his own name was not on the list, since he was an announced candidate for the Illinois legislature when he enlisted. Without even resting a day, he had gone at once to the offices of the publisher and demanded a correction be made.

That was the reason he had smiled when he picked up today's issue of the newspaper. The statement it carried was:

Some weeks ago we gave a list of those candidates of this county (omitting by accident the name of Captain Lincoln, of New Salem) who were on the frontier, periling their lives in the service of their country.

[*July 19, 1832 — Thursday*]

The downpour was one of the heaviest thunderstorms most of the men in the combined force of General Henry and Colonel Dodge could remember, and now it was obvious they would have to camp for the night here instead of overtaking the Indians as they had hoped.

Early this morning, while the men were preparing for the march, Dodge had hastily written a note to General Atkinson, to be carried by the same two officers who had found Black Hawk's trail yesterday. Again the pair would be led by Little Thunder, and would separate from the main column when it followed the Indian trail southwest while they continued straight south along the Rock River. The letter jubilantly informed the general that they had discovered the trail of Black Hawk's retreat and were in pursuit.

So they were. With greater alacrity than this force had moved in a considerable while, they ate a hasty breakfast, made their preparations, and moved out. In order to travel as swiftly as possible, they left behind every possible item of which they could disencumber themselves — five baggage wagons, excess food supplies, extraneous camp equipage, extra saddle gear from horses that had died or been lost on the way to the Rapids, sutler's stores, even blankets from those who felt they could do without.

With many of the men on foot at this point — their gear tightly stowed in packs carried on their shoulder — the best speed they could achieve was no swifter than a fast walk, yet they knew it would be faster than Black Hawk's people could move if, as Little Thunder had maintained, many of them, too, were afoot and they were hampered with the transportation of sick or injured people as well as little children and the elderly.

At the point where they intercepted the trail of Black Hawk, where the two adjutants would separate from them to carry their dispatches of yesterday to General Atkinson, General Henry called a brief halt and swiftly wrote a further message for them to carry, advising the commander of what they had done today to this point, concluding with the comment:

We will continue our pursuit until prudence dictates otherwise. We are now on the trail.

As the march was resumed on the trail, which was now estimated to be no more than eighteen or twenty hours old, they were soon further encouraged when they saw where the Indians, obviously suffering from hunger, had peeled the bark from trees to chew on it and had dug up indian potatoes and other roots for the questionable nutriment they could derive from them. So desperate a body of people could hardly elude them for long.

When General Henry saw the men on foot beginning to flag, he reined up and turned over his mount to one of these men and continued forward at a strong pace afoot. Instantly, all down the line, other mounted officers did the same. Over creeks, through fields and forests, across bogs and swamps where they sometimes had to wade chest-deep in mucky water, they followed the trail laid down by Black Hawk's band. Rough going though it was, there were few serious complaints, because hour by hour the trail was growing fresher.

On several occasions they had encountered straggling Winnebagoes who had deserted Black Hawk and now, weaponless, contrite, and wishing to atone for their poor judgment in having joined the Sacs in the first place, offered all the information they could to help the whites. Black Hawk's band, they said, was in desperate straits, weakening so fast that they would soon no longer be able to travel. And, most heartening to the pursuers, they were only a few hours ahead of the whites at this point.

When the column had reached Rock Lake, the trail followed the east shore, and they with it. Threatening clouds had been filling the sky, and now, late in the day, it was certain they would soon be drenched. It happened near the southeastern end of the lake, just as Black Hawk's trail merged with the great Winnebago trail and turned west on it. They had gained an advantage and, almost simultaneously, a restraint. Though the route had become much easier to travel, the skies suddenly opened in a veritable gush of rain.

They had crossed at the fording place of the Crawfish River, and among the first to reach the opposite side was Dr. Addison Philleo, physician and editor of *The Galenian*. He was also among the first to see the old Indian sitting on the low mound of earth that was turning to mud; an Indian whose head was bald except for a single scalp lock of long, gray hair; an Indian weary beyond the point of movement and without weapon or hope; an Indian whose physical appearance and dress identified him unquestionably for what he was.

A Sac!

Instantly Philleo and several others of the militia who saw the Indian threw their rifles to their shoulders and fired in ragged concert. The old man was slammed backward, sprawling face-up in death across the low muddy mound. Philleo shouted he was first to fire and rushed to the dead man and scalped him, holding the grisly trophy high in one hand as he danced a little jig. [308]

The column had completed its crossing of Crawfish River and continued westward on the trail in the driving downpour. With the rain, the temperature had plummeted, and those who had left their blankets behind cursed themselves for their foolishness. Nightfall overtook them, and the utter darkness, uneased by illumination of moon or stars, increased their difficulties and fear as ominous blue-white flashes of lightning all but blinded them and the crack of phenomenal thunder threatened to burst their eardrums. The acrid stench of ozone hung heavy around them.

At last, a few minutes ago, when they were four or five miles west of Crawfish River, General Henry had raised his hand and called a halt. To carry on in such conditions was insanity. The order was relayed to take or make whatever shelter was possible.

"Tomorrow, Colonel Dodge," he said, the rain dribbling from his chin in a steady rivulet, "almost *surely* tomorrow! Black Hawk will be in our grasp."

[July 19, 1832 — Thursday]

Black Hawk's people had fallen bone-weary to the ground when at last, shortly after the great rain had begun, he had called a halt on the west bank of the stream the Winnebagoes called Koulakau. [309] Now, having slept only about four hours, the camp was jerked into wakefulness by the arrival of one of their rear guards just before midnight.

They had not traveled far today, despite the good Winnebago trail they had been following. Since leaving Caukeecamac sitting beside the grave of his wife early this morning, they had come only fifteen miles, and it had been a dreadful march. Several more of his old people had died or simply dropped out of the procession, unable to travel farther and resigned to their fate. Two of the more severely wounded warriors had also died, but there had no longer been time or inclination for death rites, and they had been laid gently off the trail where, perhaps, they would not be found and mutilated. Slower and slower they had moved as the day progressed, knowing that sooner or later their trail would be found by the whites and followed, yet unable to encourage any greater speed from their bodies. The trail behind them had become littered with the items they had dropped — personal belongings, mainly, keepsakes that they had borne with them ever since returning across the Mississippi. Now they had little meaning for their owners, many of whom had already raised their croaky voices briefly in death chant. Bit by bit, they were being stripped by circumstance of all they had held dear, yet somehow it no longer mattered so much as it once had.

There were still those who could function well — the young warriors and braves whose energy and determination seemed limitless. It was they who carried the only items they dared not cast aside — the several canoes, their knives and tomahawks and war clubs, their flintlocks and ammunition. Even the last of their corn, which had been preserved in large skin bags, was nearly gone. In the midst of the starvation, until today, they still had not touched it, for those kernels were their key to the future, the seeds so imperative for planting the fields of this land to which they had returned. But in their present desperation, they had begun to eat it, because they had finally realized these yellow kernels would never experience the life-kindling fall of the rain and the sweet taste of good soil in which to sprout.

Now, in the midst of this cold and dreadfully rainy night, the rear guard had rushed into camp with fearful cries that startled them all into wakefulness.

"Black Hawk! *Black Hawk!* The white warriors are behind us!"

The guard paused briefly to question a brave who had come to his feet and then continued rushing in the direction where it had been pointed out that the Sac leader lay trying to rest. Black Hawk came out from beneath the dubious shelter he had rigged against the driving rain, a blanket draped over a bush and an adjacent low tree branch.

"How close?" he asked as the guard pounded up to him and stopped, gasping for breath. "How many?"

"Two hours. Three, perhaps. Seven hundred men, maybe eight hundred. Many have no horses, but they are close. They have stopped to camp only an hour this side of where we ourselves stopped last night. They will be here in the morning."

"But we will not be," Black Hawk told him. He raised his voice against the drumming of the rain. "Rise up. We leave this place now. Wabokieshiek and the young warrior Wampanoset, who assists him in guiding us, says we are but two hours' easy walk from Spotted Arm's village, where we will receive good food and supplies and horses — and men to help us fight our white enemy. Rise! We leave at once."

[*July 20, 1832 — Friday*]

In his temporary quarters in Chicago, Major General Winfield Scott fumed at the stroke of fate that was keeping him locked in place here. A total of fifty-nine of his men had died since the outbreak of Asiatic cholera and fifty were still ill, though twenty-eight of these were convalescent. The disease was clearly subsiding, and those of his force and Major Whistler's who were well could now conceivably be ready to move in a day or so, except for the galling lack of medical supplies and tents. And now, it might be all too late. The letter he'd just received from General Atkinson indicated that his force had finally dislodged Black Hawk from his hiding place and was in full pursuit. There was a good possibility that it would all be over before Scott could even get his men into the field. As Scott put it in his letter to secretary of war Lewis Cass:

. . . I enclose a copy of a letter, dated the 17th., this moment received, from Brigadier General Atkinson. Also a copy of a previous one from him dated the 11th.

Private letters received from his camp represent a general want of confidence in the Illinois volunteers. I hope, in a day or two, they will have redeemed their character. . . . I cannot dwell on the situation of the troops ordered to rendezvous here, and on my own individual prospects of service and utility, without feeling a pang which it would be useless, if practicable, to describe.

The Penn, which was reported to have left Fort Gratiot with two companies of Artillery (landed there from the Thompson) and which was to have brought up two companies of the 5th Infy., ought to have been here the day before yesterday, or yesterday at the latest She has not arrived, and even if she should come, all on board will probably be sick, as the false movement of Lieut. Col: Cummings's detachment in her, from Detroit, no doubt infected the boat itself. But what is worse, I know, from Detroit, she will bring no tents, no spare medicines and hospital stores, — nothing, in short, which we, here, already want, and the want of which will be increased by her arrival.

It may be asked — how did it happen that the four companies of Artillery, here, came without tents? At Detroit, the Thompson, being comparatively a small boat and with six companies on board, with myself and most of the general staff, Colonel Eustis and the master thought it best to lighten her by leaving all extra baggage and the tents of the six companies Being informed of this, I followed the example and left many articles of my own, essential to me in the field. These things, we supposed, would follow us in a day or two in the larger boats and, till their arrival, we expected to bivouac here. All were then in high health and spirits. The general supplies from New York, Philadelphia, Watervliet, &c had not then arrived at Detroit — such as tents, medicines, hospital stores, ordnance stores &c I had sent orders in advance for Major Whistler to encamp his command and mark out a camp for the troops on their way to Chicago. We found him, for the want of tents, still in the fort. He was immediately ordered out to make room for the sick detachment, and he, with the families of his officers and the two companies, bivouacked at, I trust, a safe distance from the fort or the hospital.

I have before reported why we landed two companies from the Thompson at Fort Gratiot. The master solemnly protested against entering on Lake Huron without further lightening his boat. The weather was also, then, very hot and, altho' cholera, so far as I knew or believed, had not manifested itself among us, we were not (knowing the disease had broke [sic] out in the Clay) without some slight fears on this head.

Thus it happened we stood on from Fort Gratiot with four companies only, and *from Detroit, without tents, with a medicine chest equal to ordinary wants for six companies, say three months; with subsistence for twenty days, and about 24 rounds of cartridges per man. Even the woolen pantaloons and vests of the battalion were left in tierces at Detroit, to lighten the load.*

We found here an abundant supply of flour, pork, lied corn [lyed corn: hominy], *some salt, beans, candles, soap and vinegar; but the greater part, of the smaller parts of rations, is still below — particularly the vinegar. One hundred and twenty head of beef cattle, on the hoof, are soon expected, and we may have musket cartridges sufficient for 500 men for a campaign. All other essentials, necessaries and comforts are below and Major Whiting writes (under date the 14th) that he doubts whether a steam boat or sail vessel can be engaged to come hither.*

. . . We have given up all hope of the arrival of a healthy detachment of regular infantry . . . tents would be essential to them here, as in the field. I say essential — here, because if I were to put a detachment in the houses of this village, the inhabitants would take and spread the cholera thro'out the country and thus prevent the U.S. Rangers from coming in this direction, if not drive every volunteer out of the field. It is impossible for me, in this place, to detail all the measures I have put in practice to guard against those evils. Suffice it to say, the inhabitants and Major Whistler's command are, so far, uninfected, and I take care to spread the fact near and far, orally and by letters.

Major Whistler reports, today, sixty-three bayonets for duty — the battalion of Artillery, in the fort or hospital, eighty-one Col. Eustis hands me this paragraph: —

"The health of the batalion [sic] *of Artillery is evidently improving and the progress of the cholera is checked. In the last four days there have occurred 11 new cases and ten deaths The sick report is reduced from 70 to 50, of whom 28 are decidedly convalescent. The new cases are more mild than those of previous occurrence. There are now, for duty, 81 non-commissioned officers and Privates, and five musicians The four companies, on leaving Detroit, counted about 190 enlisted men — 59 have died, and 4 were left sick at Mackinaw* [sic]. *Fifty remain sick, and 86 enlisted men for duty."*

Many Officers have been more or less affected by the cholera. Two only have died — brevet 2nd lieutenants Gustavus Brown and McDuffie [McDuffey]. *The others have got well or are getting better — Dr. Macomb continuing the most afflicted of the number. Consequently we have but one medical officer for duty — Dr. De Camp. A private physician* [Dr. Elijah Dewey Harmon] *has been engaged to attend the few ordinary cases in Major Whistler's camp. He refused to enter the cholera hospital.*

I have established a sort of Lazaretto, or intermediate hospital, for convalescents, over the river opposite to the fort, and given permission to the well and convalescents to stroll on the lake shore in the same direction: if we had tents, that scheme of disinfection might be considerably extended. The few inhabitants of the village who had remained, or have returned, have been warned not to go in that direction.

I have thus given a rapid view of our wants and supplies, and of our prospects. Nothing can be more deplorable than the latter contrasted with the high expectations of the government (and my own) ten days since. It remains for me to say what, under my melancholy circumstances, I may do or attempt.

The war against the enemy, actually in the field, is not over and may not be concluded in many weeks — perhaps months. Other tribes, too, may, if a decisive blow be not soon struck, take part against us. The Pottawatimies [sic] are believed to be friendly, and a part, at least, of the Winnebagoes. The Indian Agent, Mr. Owen, having fled from the cholera, I have but very imperfect means of judging of the temper and dispositions of those tribes. I suppose, however, neither may be expected to join in hostilities against us in a short time.

I have written to General Atkinson to pursue his own plans according to his own discretion, and upon his own responsibility, till I can join or approach him — that is, be in a situation to take upon myself the chief direction within the immediate theatre of active operations. It would be manifestly improper for me, at this distance & with my inferior knowledge of the country and the enemy, to take upon myself the direction of his movements. And here I am bound, in candour [sic] to say, that my confidence in that officer's zeal, talents and judgment, tho' heretofore high, has not been in the least abated by the protraction of the campaign he is engaged in. The character of the country and the enemy have lengthened out the war, together with the nature of the principal part of the force under his command. These considerations being taken into view, I do not know — I cannot flatter myself that I might have done better. Nevertheless, as a new General may, for the moment, inspire more zeal and confidence, I am most anxious to make the trial. . . .

[July 20, 1832 — Friday]

The reception Black Hawk and his bedraggled, exhausted party met with well before dawn when they arrived at Spotted Arm's village was hardly what he expected. In no uncertain terms, Spotted Arm and his chiefs informed the Sacs that they would not be allowed to stay here. If they did so, with the Americans coming quickly behind them, it would be interpreted as showing that the Winnebagoes here had allied themselves to the Sacs, which could mean that this beautiful village on the southwest side of Lake Mendota would be destroyed. Spotted Arm was not willing to take this chance.

"We do sympathize with you and your people," Spotted Arm told Black Hawk, "and we are sorry for the condition you are in. We are prepared to give you some food and blankets to help you, along with some gunpowder and lead, but you must not stay here. You must move on."

So they had, until they were several miles beyond Spotted Arm's village and close to the point where a stream entered the southwesternmost corner of Lake

Mendota, and here Black Hawk called a halt.[310] The persistent, cold, drizzling rain had sapped them of the will to go on, and Black Hawk finally had to give in to their demands for a stop; they were simply too exhausted to go any farther today without rest.

Throughout the day they rested here, taking shelter in the number of tents Spotted Arm had given them and greedily devouring the limited amount of food he had provided. Though Black Hawk had hoped to lead them on toward the Wisconsin River later in the evening, they could not go without rest, and he became increasingly nervous the longer they remained here. Spies that he had sent back on their own trail to report on the advance of the Americans and to hamper them as much as possible, returned at intervals with unnerving reports. Though the Americans, too, were having difficulties with fatigue and had lost many of their horses because of the rapid pace, yet they kept coming, slogging on determinedly through the fields and forests and marshes on the trail of the Sacs. Occasional firing at them by the spies had caused delays for them, because each time they had paused to set up their battle lines, anticipating an all-out attack. Each time, when it had not occurred, they had resumed their march and pressed on.

Finally, as dusk was closing in, one of the scouts, who had been shot at by the whites when he came too close, reported that the Americans were now approaching the northeast end of Lake Monona and were at this point no more than eight or ten miles behind Black Hawk. Two of the scout's companions had been shot and killed. A council of the chiefs and principal braves was called, and it was decided that an ambush had to be set in the narrow part of the trail they had traversed between Lake Monona and Lake Mendota.

It was Black Hawk himself who, at close to sunset, led the large detachment of warriors back to this point and carefully deployed them behind trees and logs, rocks and brush.[311] Here, cold and wet in the gathering darkness, the small but desperately determined Indian force was ready, at Black Hawk's signal, to fire on the Americans when they had entered well into the trap.

[July 20, 1832 — Friday]

General James D. Henry and Colonel Henry Dodge were not pleased with how slowly their march was progressing. Both now regretted that they had pushed their men and horses so furiously early in this pursuit of the retreating Black Hawk. Now they were paying the price. Scores of horses had given out in today's march. Some of these could be rested by merely being led without packs or riders, but others were beyond recovery and could travel no farther without days of rest and good graze. These they had reluctantly left behind. For each of those, yet another man was left afoot, and despite the frequent trading-off of places with those who were riding, the pace of the army, hampered by the persisting cold drizzle and resultant mud underfoot, had slowed considerably, to little more than a slow human walk.

Even though they were heartened by the number of items belonging to the Indians that they were continually finding along the trail they were following — pots, kettles, mats, and tattered blankets — their pace had not quickened appreciably. Further, they had lost precious time on three occasions when rifle fire directed at them seemed to betoken an assault and they formed themselves into battle lines. Several times they had returned fire, and once, just before sunset, two out of three warriors who had come too close had been killed, and then scalped and mutilated as the troops came up to where they had fallen.

Close to sunset, however, the commanders realized that to push the troops any harder to catch up today would not only dangerously weaken them, it would leave them unfit to fight a battle. Their guides, Paquette and White Pawnee, were strongly urging against a passage through the narrows in the dusk or darkness. So now, about a quarter of a mile northeast of Lake Monona, just before entering the long spit of land separating that lake from Lake Mendota, they stopped to camp for the night.[312] A strong guard was set out, and for the first time since the pursuit began, General Henry allowed the men to build fires and cook a hot meal.

"Tomorrow, by God," he muttered, more to himself than to Dodge, "we will engage the enemy!"

[*July 21, 1832 — Saturday*]

General Henry Atkinson was in a state of grim exultation. It seemed the fates had yesterday handed him a wholly unexpected opportunity for vindication.

Early yesterday, as he had broken camp a dozen miles above the mouth of Bark River and had begun moving his army up to Rock River to attempt to attack Black Hawk from the rear while the detachment of General Henry and Colonel Dodge struck him from the front, had come the urgent express from General Henry and Colonel Dodge. It had brought the welcome intelligence that their detachment had discovered the fresh trail of the enemy heading for the Mississippi; that Black Hawk and his Sacs had finally been flushed from their hiding place, and that Henry and Dodge were in full pursuit.

General Atkinson had immediately ordered his force turned around and, as the order was obeyed, hastily wrote a letter to Henry and Dodge and sent it off by express:

> *Genl Atkinson To Genl's Henry & Dodge*
> *Head Qrs 1st division of the North westn* [sic]
> *Army — Camp 12 Miles above the Mouth of*
> *White Water* [Bark River] *July 20, 1832*

To Genls Henry & Dodge,   I have received by express your letters of yesterday, informing me of your having discovered a Trail indicating the movement of the main body of the enemy S.W. of you [and of] *your purpose of pursuing with a*

view [of] overtaking & subduing them. I have to urge and direct that you will
press on with all haste and never lose sight of the object till the enemy is overtaken,
defeated &, if possible, captured.

I was on my march to dislodge the enemy should he have been found in the
position he occupied a few days since. I shall now fall back to the mouth of White
Water with the Regulars and part of Allexanders [sic] Brigade, sending however
two hundred mounted men & some Indians to ascertain whether all the enemy's
force have crossed Rock River.

If I can possibly come up with you in the pursuit, I shall do so with the regulars
& some mounted Troops.

Throughout the day yesterday the march down the Rock River had continued,
and in the evening they made camp at the foot of Lake Koshkonong. It was here
that the second urgent express of the day had arrived, but this one from the
opposite direction. It was a message from Major General Scott, imparting the
horrible intelligence of his force having been crippled by a cholera epidemic and
now required to make an indefinite stop at Fort Dearborn. Scott had ordered
Atkinson to carry on with his prosecution of the war as he thought best and under
his own responsibility.

Now, with his force in its final preparations for the day's march across country
to the west, Atkinson hurriedly dictated a message to be carried to Chicago
immediately:

> *Genl Atkinson to Genl Scott*
> *Head Qrs of the Division of the Army on Rock*
> *River Camp, below Lake Cosconong [sic]*

Sir,   I had the honour [sic] of receiving your letter of the 18th Inst: last night
by express. I had just returned from an excursion up the swamp with the regular
Troops and Allexander's [sic] Brigade, whither I had been with a view of cooper-
ating with Henry and Dodge, who were on the opposite side of Rock River seeking
the enemy. At day break yesterday morning I received letters from them stating
that the whole body of the enemy had left the swamps and were making their way
towards the Mississippi, that they were on the enemy's trail and would pursue
with all speed and with an expectation of overtaking and subduing them.

I am now on the march with the regulars and part of Alexander's Brigade,
following the same direction, and although I shall not get up to participate in the
first conflict, I may be in time to close the affair.

Besides, should the enemy, contrary to expectation, elude pursuit and cross the
Mississippi, I shall be in place to act. In the latter event I shall so dispose of the
regular Troops and Militia as may seem best calculated to prevent any act of
hostility on the river frontier till your arrival or advice. In the meantime I will
discharge such part of the Volunteers as may seem least efficient.

I can hardly think it possible the enemy can reach & cross the river before he is overtaken. Henry and Dodge have with them 800 picked Mounted Men divested of all heavy baggage. They are only one day's march in his rear with a distance of 100 miles or five days ordinary march yet for him to make.

To guard against being deceived on receiving the information from Genl's Henry and Dodge of the movement of the enemy, I have detached McHenry's light Battallion [sic] with a small body of Pottowattomies [sic] and two Winebago [sic] guides accompanied by Maj. Morgan, to the position known to have been recently occupied by the enemy, to ascertain with certainty if he had moved off entirely. The Winebago guides have overtaken us and report the enemy to have disappeared.

I think you may calculate with a certainty of having nothing to do on this side of the Mississippi, as the enemy has crossed over, or will be subdued before he reaches that point. The result I shall probably know today, and will communicate with you by express immediately.

I mentioned in my last that I had thrown up a stockade and block houses on Rock River at the mouth of White Water creek six miles above Lake Coshconong [sic], for the security of the sick and our supplies. I have left it Garrisoned by one company of the 5th. Regmt. under Capt. Lowe & for the present a Batallion [sic] of volunteers [under Lt. Col. Powell H. Sharp] is encamped near it. There is, in depot there, about 17,000 rations. . . .

[*July 21, 1832 — Saturday*]

Black Hawk's sour expression had changed little throughout today's difficult forced march, but the heavy rage that had bloomed in his heart early this morning at discovering the duplicity of the Winnebagoes — the one-eyed White Crow in particular — had remained with him ever since.

Through virtually superhuman effort, since before dawn Black Hawk had led his people some twenty miles from the camp where they had spent the night west of Spotted Arm's village. When, an hour after darkness had fallen last night, the Americans had still not shown up to fall into the carefully set ambush, Black Hawk had sent some of his spies back to check on where they were and what they were doing. They quickly reported back that the Americans had gone into a fire-camp some two miles east of the ambush site and would apparently remain there until morning. Leaving spies to watch the whites, Black Hawk had broken up the ambush and led his warriors back to the camp at the southwestern end of Lake Mendota and ordered them to sleep fast and well, that they would be on the march for a hard day's journey beginning an hour before dawn.

It was while they were in the camp last night that White Crow and a minor Winnebago chief named Bull Head had appeared on fresh horses they had procured at Spotted Arm's village, and they were leading an extra horse with them. The riderless horse, they said, was for their chief Little Priest, who, with seventeen of his young men, was presently guiding the Sacs toward the Wisconsin River. Black Hawk had been very pleased to see them, yet disappointed that they had not brought a body of fresh Winnebago warriors with them to help fight the Americans, should his Sacs be overtaken. White Crow had merely smiled and said that just such a body of Winnebago warriors was coming to aid them and would arrive before dawn. Gratified, Black Hawk had turned in, and, for the first time since the retreat toward the Mississippi began, had slept well and uninterruptedly for five hours.

When the Sac leader had aroused early this morning, however, he had been informed that not only had the promised force of Winnebago warriors not shown up, but that during the night White Crow, Bull Head, and Little Priest, along with all seventeen of Little Priest's men, had slipped away, and from things White Crow had said after Black Hawk had retired, it was altogether possible they were on their way to join the Americans to guide them directly to the Sacs.

Now, only a couple of hours after midday, Black Hawk's band had reached the Wisconsin River. He had wanted them to cross over immediately, but so many were so utterly exhausted by the past eight or nine hours of hard marching without pause that they simply could not make the crossing at once. Reluctantly, Black Hawk ordered that camp be made on the south shore of the river.[313] At once Black Hawk had held council with the leaders.

"I cannot believe, my brothers," he told them, "that the Americans behind us will not come up to us today before our people are rested enough to cross the river. We must prepare for such an eventuality. We have only the few canoes we have carried so far, and so it will take us many hours to get all our old people and the women and children across in safety. We will start to do that as soon as they have rested a little, but in the meantime I want sixty of our warriors who are most fit and able to fight to return to the high hills we passed a short while ago. There they are to hide and wait for the whites to come, as they will. When they do, this party is to attack them and hold them long enough for those of our people to cross who have not yet been taken to the other side. I ask now for one of our leaders to ride at the head of these sixty warriors, to return to the high hills and there act as a rear guard to engage the enemy when he comes. Who among you will lead these men?"

"I will do it," said a deep voice. "I owe it to you, Black Hawk."

The man who had spoken stepped forward. He was a tall and lanky individual about forty-five years old. He was familiar to everyone present because, shortly after Black Hawk's band had crossed the Mississippi in early April, he had been named the band's second principal chief under Wabokieshiek. This was the Sac Indian who had been Black Hawk's closest friend for many years, and still was, despite the fact that, since his lie about the British coming to Mil-wau-kee to help them, Black Hawk no longer fully trusted him. Now he was apparently intent upon making amends.

The Sac leader turned and looked at him, and then reached out and gripped the man's shoulder.

"Yes," Black Hawk said, smiling for the first time in many days, "I think we will be able to rely on you, Neapope."

[*July 21, 1832 — Saturday*]

Chief Neapope had formulated his plan as he rode back to the hills with his sixty warriors. Black Hawk's band, he had concluded, was finished. The whites would soon be upon them, and though the Sacs would fight, how could they hope to stand against so much stronger an enemy? Yet, aware of the stubborn nature of Black Hawk, he knew the Sac leader would egg them on and on until there were no more of his warriors left alive to fight. Perhaps there was honor in such a course, but to the pragmatic Neapope, life itself was considerably preferable to posthumous honor.

As soon as he and his rear guard had reached the summit of the highest of the hills through which they had passed an hour or so earlier, he had spread the warriors out to watch for the approach of the Americans. Neapope himself remained atop the hill, and from here, looking toward the river a quarter-mile distant, he soon saw the few canoes beginning to make their way across the strong current of the Wisconsin. With them went numbers of horses, each crossing with two riders and, like the canoes, returning each time with only one. Time after time they crossed, and gradually the group of people on the far shore became larger; yet, as Black Hawk had pointed out, it would take many hours to get them all safely across.

Now it was midafternoon, and one of the guards who had been stationed farthest to the rear ran up to him, then collapsed to the ground, gasping to catch his breath.

"Neapope," he panted, "they are coming!"

"Tell the others to prepare to fight them when they enter the hills," Neapope said.

The warrior shook his head. "No, they are not coming through the hills. They seem to know we are waiting for them here. They are circling around to the north on the low ground."

Neapope was quiet for a moment. Then he sighed deeply. "Take one other with you," he said, "and go tell Black Hawk what is happening. Tell him the other warriors must come to cut them off from the lower side and we here will move down on them from the heights to catch them between us. Tell him it is our only hope. Hurry!"

The warrior came to his feet and ran in a disjointed way downhill toward the river. As he passed a hidden warrior he called to the man, who fell in beside him, and together they ran toward the river. Glancing occasionally away toward the low area to the north where the whites would appear, Neapope watched his two young men surge through the marsh area, sprint across a broad area of higher sandy ground and then rush into Black Hawk's camp on the south shore of the Wisconsin.

Within minutes, all but a small handful of Black Hawk's warriors were rushing toward the string of low hills stretching from the foot of Neapope's high hill toward the river. It was a good location to meet the enemy. Here the warriors would have a marsh at their rear in which to take refuge if retreat became necessary. For the actual fighting, they would be atop the timbered hills, where there was good hiding and from which position they would be looking down on a ravine of sorts essentially free of cover, which the whites would have to pass in their advance.

Very soon now, Neapope knew, they would be clashing with the whites. Even with the excellent cover the warriors had, their chances of holding the whites in this place for very long were remote. And when the time came, as surely it must, for the Sacs to fall back, then he would put his own plan into operation.

[*July 21, 1832 — Saturday*]

In the middle of the afternoon, with the all-day drizzle showing no sign of letting up, a small party of advance scouts under Captain Joseph Dickson thundered back to the main column of men under General James D. Henry and Colonel Henry Dodge. The news they brought was electrifying: Black Hawk's people were only a few miles ahead and were evidently attempting a crossing of the Wisconsin River. Immediately the entire white force was urged into the fastest advance it could manage, which was really not very fast at all, because the day had been a difficult one.

Shortly after daybreak this morning, the Americans were up and on the move, immediately fording the river connecting Lake Mendota with Lake Monona. The narrow, brushy strip of land separating the two lakes was so ideally a place for an ambush, that the size of the advance guard had been doubled and the main body moved forward in the spread-out line of battle formation. Very quickly they came to the place where the ambush had been set up by Black Hawk during the night and then abandoned. The trail led to where the main encampment had been, near the mouth of a small stream entering the southwestern point of Lake Mendota.

Here, with the enemy obviously in full retreat again as a body, the American troops were pulled together and took up the pursuit as a tight-knit body, moving faster than their wearied mounts could bear. Before the middle of the afternoon, over forty horses of the Americans had given out, and their riders were forced to continue on foot, tossing away such equipment as camping and cooking gear, just as the Indians they were pursuing had been doing.

Within the first few hours of the ride, six Sacs — all of them old men who could no longer maintain the pace of the retreating Indians and had slumped to the ground to stoically await whatever fate would bring — were overtaken and captured. There was precious little information of value that the old Indians had to impart, and no one raised any serious objection when they were summarily shot and scalped and their bodies left lying in the trail as a warning to other Indians in the neighborhood.

Now, with the warning of the advance guard fresh in their minds that the Indians were in hiding on the brushy heights of the hills encountered just before the Wisconsin River, the main advance was wisely diverted by General Henry and Colonel Dodge away from the trail leading into the midst of the treacherous hills. As they reached the place where a ravine split the ground ahead and snaked its way toward the river, they were fired upon by the rear guard of the Indians. Not knowing whether this was Black Hawk's main body of warriors or merely a rear guard, the whites fell back a little, took cover, and returned fire.

[*"Hold them! Drive them back!" The orders of Neapope were relayed from warrior to warrior, and they grimly held their ground and, when propitious moments came, burst from cover and drove the whites back.*]

Three times in succession the attack by the Indians held the whites in place and then drove them back a short distance, each time with a few casualties on each side but with the action otherwise indecisive for either side. Eventually, however, it became clear to the whites that the force harassing them was in fact a rear guard and not the main body of warriors. As this became apparent, the whites met the brief charges of the Indians with stronger resistance easily and drove them back into hiding.

[*As the whites pushed them ever harder toward where the river crossing was being made, Neapope urged his rear guard to hold fast, that the remainder of the warriors had been sent for, yet little by little they were driven back from the heights overlooking the ravine and into the tall marsh grasses beyond, and here, at last, the main body of warriors led by Black Hawk appeared to reinforce them.*]

As the afternoon dwindled into early evening, the slow advance of the whites encountered a considerably stronger resistance, and it quickly became obvious that the rear guard of the Sacs, with whom they had been skirmishing, had been strongly reinforced, and heavier fighting broke out. Here Henry and Dodge dismounted their men, leaving the horses under the care of every tenth man, and advanced from this point on foot. The heavier resistance continued, and there were a few casualties fairly evenly distributed on both sides.

Now a distinct caution had settled over the whites, and with good reason — not only were their horses fatigued virtually beyond further usefulness, their ammunition had dwindled to an alarming point, and the weapons of many of the men were useful only because of the bayonets that had been attached. Gradually the Indians gave way and fell back into cover that was even more dangerous for the whites to advance into — heavy grasses, often as deep as six feet, in which the Indians were successfully hiding and engaging the whites in deadly hand-to-hand combat.

As the sun began to set, Henry and Dodge pulled their men back into a defensive line and called a council of officers. The consensus was that, with so

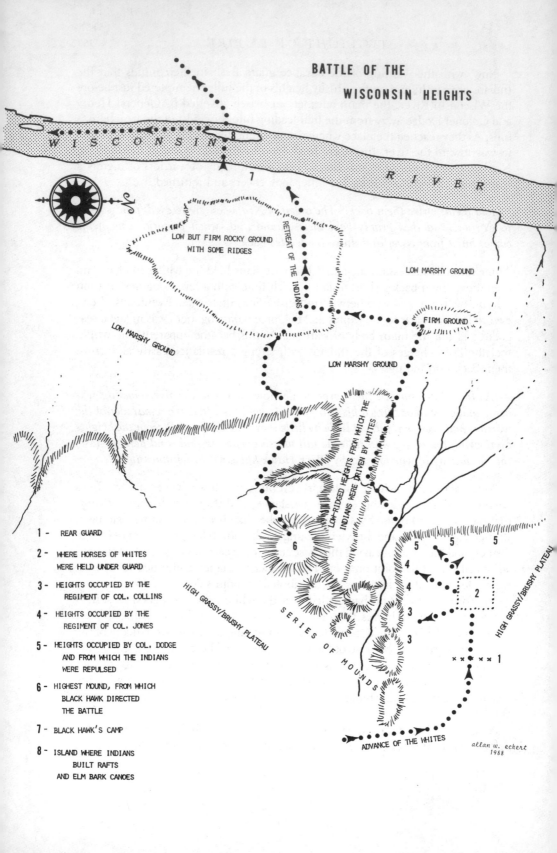

BATTLE OF THE
WISCONSIN HEIGHTS

WISCONSIN RIVER

LOW BUT FIRM ROCKY GROUND
WITH SOME RIDGES

LOW MARSHY GROUND

RETREAT OF THE INDIANS

FIRM GROUND

LOW MARSHY GROUND

LOW MARSHY GROUND

LOW-RIDGED HEIGHTS FROM WHICH THE
INDIANS WERE DRIVEN BY WHITES

HIGH GRASSY/BRUSHY PLATEAU

SERIES OF MOUNDS

HIGH GRASSY/BRUSHY PLATEAU

1 - REAR GUARD

2 - WHERE HORSES OF WHITES
     WERE HELD UNDER GUARD

3 - HEIGHTS OCCUPIED BY THE
     REGIMENT OF COL. COLLINS

4 - HEIGHTS OCCUPIED BY THE
     REGIMENT OF COL. JONES

5 - HEIGHTS OCCUPIED BY COL. DODGE
     AND FROM WHICH THE INDIANS
     WERE REPULSED

6 - HIGHEST MOUND, FROM WHICH
     BLACK HAWK DIRECTED
     THE BATTLE

7 - BLACK HAWK'S CAMP

8 - ISLAND WHERE INDIANS
     BUILT RAFTS
     AND ELM BARK CANOES

ADVANCE OF THE WHITES

allan w. eckert
1988

little daylight remaining — it was 8:00 P.M. now — and the Indians in hiding in such dangerous cover, with the remaining horses of the whites all but useless and their ammunition all but depleted, it was virtually suicide to attack the Sacs further today; even if they pushed on, it would be dark before they could reach the Indian encampment. Besides which, many of the weapons were fouled with the moisture and mud and would disastrously malfunction if the action were continued. With this in mind, Henry and Dodge ordered their force back to a strongly defensible location, where they established a battle camp, putting out a heavy guard. It was here that Paquette and White Crow and their small party of Winnebagoes, who had fought well beside the whites in this day's action, announced that they were returning to Spotted Arm's village to get fresh horses for themselves and to return with a stronger force of Winnebago warriors to assist the whites.

A role call was taken among the whites to ascertain what amount of casualties they had sustained. The casualties were amazingly light. A single private — Thomas J. Short, a volunteer in the company of Captain Josiah Briggs, 3rd Regiment of the 3rd Brigade — had been killed, and four others — Meredith S. McMillion, James Thompson, Armstead Jones, and Joseph R. Young — had suffered crippling wounds.

[As the whites fell back a little and formed themselves into a heavily guarded battle camp, the main body of Indians under Black Hawk also withdrew back to the river crossing to help those still remaining to get to the other side, while Neapope and the rear guard remained to hold the position. Four prominent chiefs had been killed in the action — Meeneekau, Machakeet, Ninnamakee, and the elder Weesheet — along with thirty-one warriors, and about two dozen other warriors were injured.][314]

The militiamen not on guard duty slept on their primed weapons, ready in an instant to rise and defend themselves. General Henry and Colonel Dodge, however, along with their principal officers, got little sleep. They talked far into the night and reluctantly came to a difficult decision. Their force had one day's rations remaining, along with only enough ammunition to sustain, perhaps, one more decisive onslaught by the Indians. The Indians were obviously crossing the Wisconsin River, and if pursuit was to be continued, they would have to get across the river too, and they had nowhere near enough tools to build the rafts they would require for the crossing.

[Neapope and his few chiefs remaining took stock of what strength they had remaining, and it was frighteningly little. Their gunpowder was all but depleted, their food virtually nonexistent. Two courses only remained open for them — continued retreat as swiftly as possible, with the specter of faster pursuit by the whites overhanging them, or surrender.]

The decision reached by the white officers was that they would remain here on the field throughout the night, and in the morning, advance on what Indians remained in Black Hawk's camp on this side of the river and engage them in combat until they were all wiped out. It was strongly believed that, while the majority of Black Hawk's people were probably crossing the river to continue overland to the Mississippi River, some could conceivably be heading down the Wisconsin in canoes that one of the old Indians captured during the day said they had with them. Accordingly, well before dawn, while General Henry was writing a report to General Atkinson, Colonel Dodge selected Captain James B. Estes as an express to carry, on the best horses remaining, an urgent message to Prairie du Chien to alert both Captain Gustavus Loomis at Fort Crawford and Joseph Street at the Indian Agency there of what had happened. After a brief account of the battle, Dodge continued:

. . . *From their crippled situation, I think we must overtake them unless they descend the Wisconsin by water. If you could place a field-piece immediately on the Wisconsin that would command the river, you might prevent their escape by water.*

General Atkinson will arrive at the Blue Mounds on the 24th, with the regulars and a brigade of mounted men. I will cross the Wisconsin to-morrow, and should the enemy retreat by land, he will probably attempt crossing some twenty miles above Prairie du Chien; in that event the mounted men would want some boats for the transportation of their arms, ammunition, and provisions. If you could procure for us some Mackinaw [sic] boats, in that event, as well as some provision supplies, it would greatly facilitate our views. Excuse great haste.

I am, with great respect, your obedient servant,
H. Dodge, Col-Com. Michigan Mounted Volunteers.[315]

The journey overland on horseback to Prairie du Chien would be about ninety miles and would be accomplished with greater speed than the canoes could make, even with the current behind them, since the winding course of the river made the journey for them from twenty to thirty miles farther. At the same time, the Fort Crawford commander was advised to patrol the Mississippi River upstream from Prairie du Chien and try to intercept those Indians believed to be traveling overland in an effort to reach and cross the Mississippi.

[Some two hours after darkness had fallen and an uneasy quiet was prevailing, Neapope, without discussing his plan with anyone other than a warrior who stayed beside him constantly, climbed to the top of the highest knoll and there, in the stillness of the night, cupped his mouth and called out loudly toward the Americans.

"Winnebagoes who are with the white men, hear me! Give my words that I

speak now to the chiefs of the white warriors. Tell them this: White Chiefs, Black Hawk does not wish to fight you any more. He wishes peace with you on the terms that you may set. Black Hawk has forced us into a war that his women and children did not want. We are weak and starving. Give us the signal that we may safely do so, and we will lay down our weapons and deliver ourselves into your hands. Or let us go in peace and we will cross the Mississippi River and never again return east of the river. Listen to us! Hear our words! We can fight you no longer. Give us the assurance that we may turn ourselves into your hands in safety and we will do so now! Give us the assurance that we may go in peace across the great river, and we will do so now!"

The rear guard warriors under Neapope were astounded at his utterances, and believing that he had received instructions from Black Hawk to say these things, they were greatly discouraged. They waited to hear the response of the whites, but there was none, and about an hour later Neapope again raised his voice with the same entreaty. Again there was no response.]

In the camp of the whites, the officers and men heard clearly the stentorian voice of Neapope in the night, calling out from the high hill, but with Paquette and White Crow gone and no one left to interpret, they had no idea what he was saying and took his words to be no more than encouragement of a chief — presumably Black Hawk — to his warriors. After the second such message there was a long silence, and then, only an hour before dawn, the same voice rose again in the same way and finally lapsed into unbroken silence.

Neapope had let the silence that enveloped the hills stretch out a long while after his second call, and it was only an hour before dawn when, for a third time, Neapope called out and once more the whites did not reply. But by now the word had passed among the warriors of the rear guard that what Neapope was proposing to the whites was being done on his own, not with the direction or concurrence of Black Hawk, and they were appalled. They confronted him and told him they would not abandon Black Hawk, and with the single exception of the warrior who was always with Neapope, they turned their backs on this second chief of their band and slipped away in the final darkness of night to where Black Hawk's people were just finishing their crossing of the Wisconsin, and they crossed with them. And Neapope, abandoning Black Hawk and his own people, also slipped away, heading toward a Winnebago village where he had made arrangements to be safely hidden from the whites if his plan of surrender had failed.

[July 22, 1832 — Sunday]

On the wooded island in the Wisconsin River that lay within mere yards of the far shore, the men, women, and children of Black Hawk's band who had gathered since the crossing was begun yesterday were now, in the first light of dawn, putting the finishing touches to their feverish handiwork of the night. In these fifteen or sixteen hours of work, the bark of a dozen large elms had been stripped from just above ground level to a height of ten or fifteen feet. Peeled away from the trees and placed upon the ground, the tubes of bark, with the slit side up, were crudely but securely lashed together with rawhide strips and limber willow switches. Then sturdy lengths of branches three feet long had been cut and placed at intervals in the slit, holding the sides apart, until the tubes of bark were transformed into makeshift canoes. The tarlike resins of pines were speared inside the fore and aft to keep water from seeping in.

Placed in the water one by one as they were finished, more resins were smeared in them as leaks were discovered and sealed, until now they were reasonably leak-free. Scooplike pieces of bark were given to children who would ride in them with their mothers or grandparents, and their job would be to constantly bail out any water that might seep in as the downstream journey progressed.

In addition to the makeshift canoes, a large raft had been made of dry lengths of driftwood bound together with sinews and covered with skins. Such a craft could float with a considerable load aboard, but it could not withstand any rough water. Fortunately, there were no rapids between this point and the mouth of the Wisconsin.

So now, by the first creeping light of new day in the east, the Sacs had three good canoes, each capable of holding up to ten adults, plus the twelve makeshift canoes, in which six or seven could ride, plus the large, crude raft that could carry perhaps fifteen adults. Any individuals who could possibly continue the overland flight would do so. Those who could not would float from this point the roughly one hundred miles to the mouth of the river, and from there across the Mississippi to the supposed safety of the Iowa shore.

For Black Hawk to send any of his people downstream this way was a calculated risk, but one that had to be taken. Several of the elderly had already died of starvation, exhaustion, and exposure, and many of those remaining alive had so little strength remaining that they could not travel any longer by land. There would be great risk that some of these boats might swamp and their occupants drown, since many could not swim at all or were not strong enough to swim in such a current. There was the even greater risk that they would be cut off by their enemies somewhere along the way, and, should this occur, the only hope was that because they were noncombatants, they would be allowed to go on in peace. All those who would float downstream — the majority of the children up to eight years of age, the majority of women with small children, virtually all of the elderly who were incapacitated by weakness — were now ready to set off downstream.

In the gloom of the morning twilight they were carefully lifted aboard by the strong younger warriors standing in waist-deep water. They had no paddles, but a few in each boat were provided with flat pieces of bark to help with the maneuvering, or with long sticks to push away from shorelines or obstructions they might approach. It would be a long and difficult journey with only a moderate chance for their survival, but better than continuing on land on a journey in which certainly the majority would succumb.

Few words were spoken as the odd flotilla carrying close to one hundred individuals was gently thrust into the current and swept downstream. Amazingly, none of the boats tipped or swamped, and in less than a quarter-hour, all had disappeared beyond a bend in the river.

Black Hawk then called before him all who remained — the chiefs and braves and warriors who still retained some degree of their strength, about a quarter of whom were still mounted on horses that could, at this stage, do little more than walk.

"When we came east of the Mississippi," he told them, "we came because we were assured by our second chief, Neapope, that our British friends would come in great numbers in boats to Mil-wau-kee and there they would aid us in our struggle. Too late we learned that Neapope had betrayed us with lies. Yet, we forgave him, for he did what he did in the belief that perhaps they would help us when they saw how other tribes allied themselves to us in our struggle against the Americans. But the other tribes were afraid and remained neutral or even turned against us, and we were left with only what small strength we had among ourselves. Now, once again, Neapope has betrayed us. In the night he called to the Americans in my name and offered our surrender to them, and when it was not accepted, he abandoned us and fled with one other to some distant place where he will be safe from the danger that still faces us all. He is dishonored among us, and should we survive, he must eventually face our wrath for what he has done."

Black Hawk fell silent for a time, and no one spoke as the sounds of awakening birds filled the air. At last he dipped his head once and said, "With those who are weak gone on by water, we are now left to travel at a faster speed to the great river." He raised his right arm high. "The Americans will be at our heels, and so now we must move quickly. And so now" — he dropped his arm quickly in a point to the west — "we go on!"

[*July 22, 1832 — Sunday*]

At last it was a day dawning without rain, and in the light of the new sun, the militia force of General Henry and Colonel Dodge stared at the deserted encampment of Black Hawk on the south bank of the Wisconsin. Whatever heavy baggage had remained to the Sacs had been left behind, pots and other cooking equipment, lodge poles, bundles of skins, broken weapons. The enemy had obviously crossed over the river here, and a scouting party sent across soon returned with the intelligence that evidently a sizable portion of the Sacs had gone downriver in makeshift boats constructed from the bark of elm trees that had been stripped. These were evidently those who could no longer travel well by land. Another portion, larger still, had gone on by land, as evidenced by hoofprints and moccasined footprints.

Another meeting of the officers was held, and despite Dodge's remark in his letter to Captain Loomis that they would cross the river tomorrow in pursuit of the enemy, it was now clear to them all that they simply did not have the strength or supplies to do so, especially in the essentially unknown country northwest of the Wisconsin River. Instead, the decision was now made to construct litters for the injured men and then head immediately to Blue Mounds, some twenty miles south of here, where fresh horses and supplies could be obtained from the supply train that had been sent there on General Atkinson's orders.

The pursuit of Black Hawk might be delayed, but it would definitely continue.

[*July 22, 1832 — Sunday*]

Under the skilled guidance of her master, Captain John Throckmorton, the steamboat *Warrior* had arrived on the west side of the Mississippi River about one hundred miles upstream from Prairie du Chien. Stretched out on the west bank of the Mississippi here was the immense village of the powerful Dakotah Sioux chief Wabasha.[316] It was specifically because of Wabasha and his Sioux that the *Warrior* had come here.

Since being impressed into military service, the *Warrior* had encountered nothing in its patrolling up and down the Mississippi between Fort Armstrong at Rock Island and Fort Crawford at Prairie du Chien that was any more noteworthy than a drifting log. It was at the latter fort that Captain Throckmorton had finally been given the assignment of ferrying a military detachment upstream to this point.

The mission had come about after the Fort Crawford commander, Captain Gustavus Loomis, had finished a meeting with the Indian agent at Prairie du Chien, Joseph Street. Street had received a message that the Sacs under Black Hawk might be headed toward the Mississippi and it was necessary, if at all possible, to prevent the band from crossing over. The *Warrior* was, of course, patrolling the Mississippi, but the steamboat could not be everywhere at once. Could Captain Loomis send a detachment of soldiers with an official request to Chief Wabasha to have his Sioux warriors take up a patrol of the river from his village down to Prairie du Chien to report any sighting of the Sacs attempting to get across? Loomis, decidedly bored with this post and irked at being stationed more or less out of touch with events of the Black Hawk War thus far, immediately fell in with the idea. He immediately summoned Lieutenants James W. Kingsbury and Theophilus H. Holmes to him. They were to undertake the mission requested by Street, taking with them aboard the *Warrior* fifteen regulars and six militiamen. In addition to recruiting Wabasha's help, they were to keep alert for the Sacs and engage any of the hostile Indians they might intercept.

No sign of hostiles had been seen on the upriver journey. The meeting between Chief Wabasha and the two lieutenants had gone well. Anxious to help in any way to destroy the Sacs, Wabasha dispatched over 150 of his warriors in four parties, to begin the on-shore patrol requested — two on the west side of the Mississippi, two on the east. Three days ago they had begun their patrol, spreading themselves out not only along both shorelines of the river, but also at intervals several miles inland to watch for fresh sign.

Now, with a new load of firewood aboard for the boilers, Captain Throckmorton gave the order to cast off, and the return journey of the *Warrior* to Prairie du Chien was begun.

[*July 23, 1832 — Monday*]

Lieutenant Hannibal Day, still assigned to Major General Winfield Scott as his secretary, hesitated with his pen poised just above the paper, waiting for the commanding general to begin his dictation of the letter to secretary of war Lewis Cass.

Over the past fortnight Lieutenant Day had developed a keen sense of devotion, even respectful affection, toward this general who was so concerned for the welfare of his men and the citizens, this officer who was so anxious to prosecute the war and yet so thwarted in his efforts. The events of these awful days had aged the general noticeably, and just when it seemed things were beginning to improve, once again fate was intervening disastrously.

"Are you ready, Lieutenant?" Winfield Scott asked, turning from the window through which he had been gazing across the river at Fort Dearborn.

"I'm ready, General," Day said, dipping the pen nib and shaking it gently to dislodge the excess.

"Excellent. We're going to be moving along rapidly. If I go too fast, just speak up and slow me down. Here we go."

The general began speaking in a steady tone, pausing briefly at the end of each sentence to give the lieutenant a chance to keep pace. The young officer's pen flew across the pages in precise, legible lines as the general dictated:

Sir My last report was dated the 19th. instant. Nothing has since been received from Brigr general Atkinson.

It has never been my professional habit to imagine or create difficulties, but rather to suppress & to overcome them. I have, however, in this expedition (I may not call it campaign) *been so baffled & crippled by the hand of Providence, as to be left almost without the possibility of doing good, and may, by the slightest error, do an infinite deal of harm. The nature of this danger will be seen in the sequel.*

I have reported again and again that I had put in practice all the means in my power to overcome the Cholera and to prevent its spread among the troops and inhabitants in this region of the country. Those measures were successful beyond hope, up to the date of my last report in which I stated my intention of marching about the 25th., with sixty-three regulars and Captain Orr's company of Indiana mounted volunteers. I had determined upon this march without waiting for many essentials usually required for troops of the firmest health — such as tents, canteens, and an abundant supply of medicines and hospital stores. Horses and some wagons were (and are) expected up, together with beef on the hoof, by that time. New difficulties, however, have occurred which may defeat that particular purpose, and perhaps all hope of active operations from this place for many weeks.

Three citizens have died in and about this village under symptoms believed by a private physician and the inhabitants to be those of the Cholera, and this morning three of Major Whistler's command have been sent to the Fort with that disease. (A fourth and fifth are reported whilst I write.) One of the first belonged to the little guard kept at Head Quarters (in the upper part of the village) since the 12th. and which was sent back to Major Whistler yesterday, in perfect health.

The steamboat Wm. Penn, no longer expected (since the 19th.) arrived yesterday morning with two companies of Artillery (those left at Fort Gratiot) and two of the 5th Infantry. We had, at first, the joyous report that the Cholera was not on board. This seemed to us, ashore, almost a miracle, as the Artillery had been landed at Fort Gratiot from our boat, and we knew that Lieut. Colonel Cumming's [sic] infected detachment had been more than a day in the Penn from Detroit. I was on the beach. Not a death had occurred; but on enquiring of the surgeon (Dr. Finley, who overtook the Penn in the St. Clair River, being on his way to Green Bay or the Sault) I learned that there were two suspicious cases on board — which, on his advice, I ordered to be sent immediately to the Cholera hospital (the Fort.) Dr. DeCamp, the surgeon on duty in the Fort, reports one of these a clear case of cholera, and I learn, unofficially whilst writing, that the man is dead. . . .

. . . I am still of opinion, from all that I can learn, that volunteers (perhaps, Rangers) will neither approach troops infected with Cholera, nor suffer such as are suspected of that disease to approach them, and hence the greatest difficulty in my position. I must either remain inactive here, when all who are able are desirous to march and fight, or join Brigadier General Atkinson with the near probability of driving away all his mounted volunteers, when mounted men are essential in operations against a mounted enemy. We may, also, by joining him, infect with the dreaded disease, his regular force and thus destroy all hope of subduing the hostile Indians for an indefinite period. On the other hand, I have no prospect of obtaining a sufficient force, in some time, with which to march against the enemy without joining him. . . . one of Captain Russell's company, that got ashore the day before yesterday, sickened last night and is dead this morning. Of the two sick, first landed, one died yesterday, and the other may recover — all three clear cases of Cholera. . . . We have heard of the death of surgeon Everett, whom I had put in orders as medical director. He marched with me during the late war, but I have no time to indulge in private grief. His high professional standing and excellence as a man will cause his death to be universally regretted in the

army. . . . No officer has died here since my last report. Brevet 2nd lieutenant
Ury is the only one remaining seriously ill. . . .

[*July 27, 1832 — Friday*]

Captain Gustavus Loomis was ecstatic with the realization that the war had
finally reached Prairie du Chien, and he was by-God making the most of it.
Although he had been sitting inactively here at Fort Crawford for a very long
time, feeling sorry for himself at being out of the field of action, now it seemed
all that was past.

As soon as Captain James Estes appeared at Prairie du Chien as an express
from Colonel Dodge, the Fort Crawford commanding officer had been galvanized into action. He was very pleased with himself at having earlier sent the
steamboat *Warrior* up to Wabasha's village to get the assistance of the Sioux, and
delighted that there were suddenly many more preparations he could make right
here in the Prairie du Chien area in view of the shifting theater of war.

Immediately after reading the message Captain Estes had brought from Colonel Dodge and then conversing with him for a while, he had repaired with Estes
from the fort to the mouth of the Wisconsin to see if there were any suitable place
near Jean Baptiste Brunet's ferry crossing where a piece of artillery could be
mounted. It was as they had been making this inspection that the steamboat
Enterprise hove into view from downriver and soon docked. She was carrying a
most welcome two companies of the 4th Infantry as a reinforcement for Fort
Crawford.

Loomis had immediately stationed a picket of eight men at Brunet's Ferry.
Then, placing the newly arrived Lieutenant Joseph Ritner of the 4th Infantry in
charge of a detachment of twenty-five well-armed soldiers, he had stationed
them aboard a large flatboat mounted with a six-pounder cannon and ordered
them to take anchorage in the midst of the Wisconsin River, ready to fire at any
hostiles who might appear from upstream.

The *Enterprise* and the remainder of the 4th Infantry Captain Loomis had
then ordered up the Mississippi as far as La Crosse. Their instructions were to
stop at all the Winnebago villages along the river and order the Indians at each
to take their canoes and go down to Prairie du Chien, issuing a stern warning that
any canoes left behind would be destroyed. As soon as they had returned from
this mission, he ordered the steamboat to run a regular twenty-five-mile patrol
downstream on the Mississippi from the mouth of the Wisconsin to the mining
community of Cassville, then back up again to the Wisconsin.

Loomis had also put a squad of five men in a canoe and sent them well up the
Wisconsin to watch for the approach of any Sacs and Foxes coming downstream
by watercraft. If any were seen, they were to assess the numbers and, not
engaging them or letting themselves be seen, turn back at once to the ferry, the
flatboat, and Prairie du Chien to announce the approach at each stop so full

preparations could be made for an attack. After a few fruitless days of watching, however, the squad had returned.

A number of Menominees who had arrived here several days before, having been recruited in the Green Bay area by Colonel Samuel Stambaugh, were counciling with Joseph Street at the Prairie du Chien Indian Agency when Captain Estes arrived. Loomis had quickly prevailed upon Street to have Colonel Stambaugh lead them out and let them range outward to the north and east from Prairie du Chien to watch for any sign of the retreating Sacs and Foxes.

And now, having established this web of traps meant to prevent the fleeing Sacs and Foxes from crossing the Mississippi, Captain Gustavus Loomis positioned himself, spiderlike, in his quarters at Fort Crawford to await the news that the quarry had become ensnared.

[*July 28, 1832 — Saturday*]

Under the light of the new sun, General Henry Atkinson watched with pleasure as his force of thirteen hundred selected men began to break up their night's camp on the northwest bank of the Wisconsin and form themselves into their proper marching order. Now, he thought, if only Black Hawk didn't pull another of his vanishing tricks, they would soon have the Sacs in their grasp.

These past days had been a time of anxious preparation, assembling supplies and fuming at the delay this occasioned. Atkinson feared that the fleeing Black Hawk would take advantage of the respite to slip away one more time, yet he was determined not to take up the march again until they were fully prepared to follow it to the conclusion and wrap up this war once and for all.

It was four days ago — the afternoon of July 24, following a three-day forced march — that Atkinson and his regulars under Colonel Zachary Taylor, along with General Milton K. Alexander's brigade of mounted militia, arrived at Blue Mounds and found the recuperating force under General Henry and Colonel Dodge awaiting them. Expresses had already brought the news of the engagement at the Wisconsin Heights, yet now the stories were told again and again, reviving the spirits of those who had gone through it, firing the imaginations of those who had not yet had the opportunity to taste battle.

Having constructed litters for their injured men, Henry and Dodge had spent the remainder of that day after the battle at the scene of their triumph and then marched wearily to Blue Mounds the following day to await Atkinson's arrival there. Immediately upon reaching Blue Mounds, Dodge and Henry learned that General Posey's brigade, on orders from General Atkinson, had established a camp on the south shore of the Wisconsin sixteen miles northwest of this place at the abandoned community called Helena, long ago built by makers of lead shot, which could be shipped by water easily from this point.[317] Posey's force had arrived at Helena — about twelve miles downstream from where the Battle of Wisconsin Heights had been fought — only an hour or so after the makeshift flotilla of Sac and Fox women, children, elderly, and ailing had passed by that spot.

Realizing that Atkinson would soon reach Blue Mounds and take up the pursuit of Black Hawk, Dodge sent an express to General Posey, along with a good supply of axes and augers, requesting that he use the logs of the abandoned buildings at Helena to make a number of rafts for the ferrying of the army's baggage, supplies, and equipment across the Wisconsin River at that point when Atkinson's army again took up the march.

Because of their own forced march, General Atkinson's force was itself exhausted upon reaching Blue Mounds, and much as they longed to get on with the pursuit of Black Hawk, they welcomed a chance to rest for a day and reprovision, consoling themselves with the fact that their quarry was weaker and more exhausted than themselves, as well as deeply disheartened and virtually without provisions of any kind.

Upon his arrival at Blue Mounds, General Atkinson learned that Governor Reynolds had finally wearied of this Indian war business and had left with his staff to return to St. Louis and, finally, to his headquarters at Belleville, Illinois. The governor's withdrawal from the field did not discommode Atkinson in the least, and he hardly gave it a passing thought as he turned his attention to other details of a more pressing nature. Atkinson was more concerned with the possibility of Black Hawk's eluding him again and the urgency of getting back on his trail as quickly as possible. Even his report to General Winfield Scott, considering the good news he had to impart, was brief almost to the point of terseness:

Head Qrs of the Division of the North West
Army west of the Rock River, Blue Mounds
Michigan Territory 25th July 1832

Sir, I have the honor to report to you that General Henry with his brigade, accompanied by Genl Dodge with a Battalion of Michigan volunteers, who were as I informed you by letter on the 21st. Inst., detached in pursuit of the enemy, succeeded by forced marches in coming up with him on the banks of the Ouisconsin [sic] opposite to this place on the evening of the 21st Inst: and immediately made an attack upon him which resulted in his [the enemy's] defeat with a loss of thirty five men killed and, it is presumed, a much larger number wounded, as he was seen during the action bearing them off — our loss amounts to but one man killed & seven wounded. Night coming on, our Troops were called back and the enemy saved from entire destruction, and he passed over to an Island where he had, and was in the act, of sending Women and Children [downstream]. Henry and Dodge remained on the ground the succeeding day & night and part of the next day, but were unable to renew the attack in consequence of the entire absence [of] boats, canoes, or the means of constructing rafts to cross to the Island. They fell back to this place on the evening of the 23rd. for a supply of Provisions, where

*I joined them last evening with the regular Troops and part of Alexander's Brigade
after a forced march of three days from Cosconong* [sic].

*I shall move this morning with my whole force to a point on the Ouisconsin
sixteen miles below, where we shall endeavour* [sic] *to cross the* [river] *by Rafts or
some other means and if possible overtake the enemy and subdue him, although
we are worn down with fatigue and privation. He must be much crippled, and is
suffering for subsistence.*

*The Troops under Henry & Dodge behaved with the greatest gallantry, resisting
a charge of the enemy's Cavalry, and in turn charged him at every point with the
greatest promptness and success, to which may be attributed the very small loss
they sustained.*

(signed) H Atkinson Brigr. Genl U.S. Army

Appalled at the practice of the militia to take scalps from the Indians, General
Atkinson had issued an order prohibiting such a barbaric act, much to the
disappointment of many of the volunteers. At least one young lieutenant, intent
on procuring such a trophy from this war, devised a plan to circumvent the
commander's order. The officer in question was Lewis Clark, son of the Indian
superintendent, William Clark, who wrote to his father in St. Louis:

*. . . I figure that if I kill a Red Rascal, before the Indian dies I will have his head
off. Then, having his noodle in my hands and free of any charges of mutilation,
I can take the scalp off with impunity. . . .*

After a full day of rest and reprovisioning, General Atkinson put his army in
motion again, and within twenty-four hours had assembled them on the south
bank of the Wisconsin at the ruins of Helena. A number of rafts had already been
constructed by General Posey's force, and more were hurriedly constructed as
the commander dictated another General Order:

*Head Qrs 1st Army Corps North West Army
Ouisconsin River at Helena 26th July 1832*

ORDER NO. 64

*All the U.S. Infy for duty at this place except forty men including the sick, one
hundred & fifty mounted men of Brig Genl. Posey's Brigade of Ill. mounted
Volunteers, four hundred of Brig Genl. Alexander's, four hundred of Brig. Genl.
Henry's & the mounted Michigan Volunteers under the command of Genl.
Dodge, will be in readiness to cross the Ouisconsin river at sun rise tomorrow, well
supplied with ammunition & provided with provisions for eight days (including
the rations on hand) which will be drawn this evening.*

The remainder of the Ill. mounted Volunteers not required for active service, will be encamped for two days at this place, under the command of the Senior Officer of their respective Corps, who may be left with them. At the expiration of that time, unless they should receive other orders, they will be marched to Fort Hamilton.

The Quarter Master's Dept. will furnish transportation for the sick & provisions. All the baggage wagons will be left at this place.

 By order of Brig. Genl. Atkinson

   (signed) Albt. S. Johnston A.D.Camp & A.A.A. Genl.

The commander followed up that order with another that he had been meaning to dictate earlier, but had not had the time. Now he did so:

ORDER NO. 65

The Comdg. General takes great pleasure in announcing to the army the result of the action between the Volunteer troops under Genls. Henry & Dodge, and the enemy on the evening of the 21st inst. After a forced march of 40 miles these brave troops came up with the enemy on the bank of the Ouisconsin and immediately attacked & dispersed him with a loss of thirty five killed & many wounded, incurring on their own part a loss of only one man killed & Seven wounded.

Night coming on, our Troops were recalled & the enemy saved from entire destruction, & enabled to throw himself across the river, some bark canoes having been provided for his transportation.

Both Officers & men are reported to have behaved with such determined bravery that no individual distinction could justly be made. Hence the thanks of the Comdg. Genl are due to all, which he offers with much gratification.

The enemy is yet in the country & further effort is necessary to chastise & subdue him. The Troops are now under marching orders for this purpose, and the Comdg. Genl. looks to every Officer & Man to do his duty with promptitude & cheerfulness, and in this expectation he is convinced he will not be disappointed.

 By order of Brig. Genl. Atkinson

   (signed) Albt. S. Johnston A.D.Camp & A.A.A. Genl.

The crossing of the Wisconsin River took all day yesterday, and a camp was set up on the bank to get everything in readiness for the march this morning. While the crossing was in progress, General Atkinson wrote hasty letters to General Scott in Chicago and to the commander of Fort Crawford at Prairie du Chien, the former to be carried to Chicago by the Potawatomi chief Sauganash — Billy Caldwell — and the latter to be carried express to Captain Loomis at Prairie du Chien by Cut Nose, a minor chief of the Menominees who had joined the Americans with some of his fellows.

In the letter to General Scott, Atkinson wrote:

Head Qrs. division of the North Western Army
On Ouisconsin river, Helena July 27th. 1832

General.   I arrived here yesterday from the Blue Mounds and we are now in the act of crossing the river with a select body of men consisting of regulars & volunteers amounting to thirteen hundred. The tardiness and difficulty of crossing on rafts will detain us all of tomorrow and will give the enemy five days the start of us, a most unfortunate circumstance, but unavoidable. The trail of the enemy leads up the country between this river and the Mississippi. He intends making his way to the Chippaways [sic], or crossing the Mississippi — probably the latter. He appears to be in a distressed situation for subsistence & to facilitate his movements has thrown away kittles [sic], skins &c. — comforts to an Indian — and he must be much crippled in his recent conflict with the volunteers. I am in hopes, notwithstanding our delay, to be enabled to overtake him, if he does not cross the Mississippi, in six days. This excursion before us must end our active operations for some time, as all the horses of the volunteers, as well as pack and officer's horses, are worn down.

It would be well that you should cross over to the Mississippi as early as practicable, as in the event of our not closing the War in the pending exertion, an organization of a new force must take place.

I send this letter by Mr. Caldwell, a chief of the Pottiwattime [sic] nation, and Waponce, a war chief. I commend them to your notice as worthy of confidence. To the former I refer you for any information relative to his tribe you may wish to acquire. He is a gentleman of education and intelligence.

General Dodge is with me in command of the Michigan Volunteers. He has accepted of the appointment of Commandant of the Corps of Rangers.

With great respect, Sir, I have the honor to be Your Mo. ob. Svt.
H. Atkinson B. Gn. US. army.

The letter to the Fort Crawford commander was more succinct:

Head Qrs. Division of the North Westn Army,
(Helena) On Ouisconsin River July 27th. 1832

To Captn Loomis

Sir,   I send down Cut-Nose, a Menominie [sic] Indian to apprize [sic] you of our arrival at this place yesterday . . . we are now crossing the river to fall on the enemy's trail, with a hope of overtaking him. His course leads north and his intention supposed to be to reach the Chippways [sic], or cross the Mississippi some forty miles above Prairie du Chien. You can be in no danger, crippled and disheartened as he must be. Yet, be vigilant.

I expect to be at the Prairie soon with the Troops. I am too much engaged to write to both you & Genl Street. Shew [sic] him this letter as addressed to you both.

(signed) H. Atkinson Brigr Genl U.S. Army

Since writing the within, Genl Dodge has handed me your letter of the 25th. Inst.
I wish some of the Menomonies [sic] and Sioux could be thrown ahead of the Sacs,
as I fear they have such a start on us we shall not be able to overtake them.
Continue your operations till I hear from you again.

Now, at last, all preparations completed, the command was given and the
large force started out, marching in three parallel columns and angling just a
little west of due north, and keeping a sharp eye out for the trail of Black Hawk's
Sacs, which they anticipated finding quickly.

Within an hour the trail was discovered, heading generally northwest. Word
of the discovery spread rapidly through the column and the spirits of the men
soared, and there was about them almost the sense that they were hounds who
had caught the scent of their quarry and were breaking into hot pursuit. For
twelve or fourteen miles more they followed over very difficult country — up or
around steep hills, through narrow defiles, over grassy knolls, into forests, and
through densely brushy terrain — until they reached a place where the trail of
the Sacs had turned to move upstream along the Pine river, where they gratefully
stopped to make camp for the night. [318]

[*July 29, 1832 — Sunday*]

In the week that they had been drifting downstream with the current of the
Wisconsin River, the nearly one hundred women, children, elderly, and injured
of the Sacs and Foxes had encountered no one. Still suffering greatly with
weakness and the need of food, they had drawn up to shore each night and slept
along the banks. A few birds — passenger pigeons and bobwhite quail — had
been brought down by the boys and few men among them who could still hunt
with bow and arrow, and some fish were caught. These, along with some frogs
and crayfish, berries and roots, had made up their diet since their departure from
the main band moving across country under Black Hawk.

Several of the party had died during this water passage — two warriors who
had succumbed to their wounds and three elderly people who could no longer
tolerate the fatigue and exposure. Yet, despite these hardships, despite the sorrow
weighing so heavily in their hearts and minds over the loss of loved ones in the
Wisconsin Heights battle, their spirits had gradually been rising. In only a few
hours more they would reach the Mississippi River, and once across, they were
all certain, things would be better. There would be food and rest and safety, and
eventually they would be reunited with their husbands, fathers, brothers, and
uncles who were still in the field trying to escape the pursuing Americans.

There could be grave danger ahead, they knew, since the mouth of the
Wisconsin lay only three miles from Fort Crawford, and it was because of this
that they had waited until nightfall this evening to continue the slow downriver
float. They would have a better chance to float past undetected under the cover
of night, and they were further encouraged when, just before midnight, they

became enshrouded in a light fog. As their dozen bark canoes, three regular canoes, and large raft neared the mouth of the river, they became utterly silent, not even dipping the pieces of bark that had served as paddles, for fear of the sound being detected.

Now, two and a half hours after midnight, they were just approaching the mouth of the river when, only yards ahead of them, a huge, dark bulk became visible. Those Indians with makeshift paddles began using them frantically to move out of sight in the foggy darkness, but they were too close, and almost simultaneously came the cries of several men as the Indians became visible to the soldiers aboard the flatboat anchored in the middle of the river.

"Fire!" shouted Lieutenant Joseph Ritner. "Fire, dammit!"

The blasts of rifle fire and the thunderous boom of the six-pounder shattered the stillness of the night. There were screams and hoarse cries and splashes as the Sacs and Foxes tried to escape the murderous attack. The flimsy makeshift canoes of elm bark had all capsized with the exertions of their passengers to get away. Many Indians were killed in that first firing, and scores of others tried to swim to shore, but at least two dozen could not swim well enough and drowned.

The only craft of the Indians with any chance to escape was one of the three large canoes that had been so laboriously carried overland from the hidden encampment at the Rapids of the Rock River to the Wisconsin. Unlike the other two, miraculously it had not been punctured by grapeshot or bullets. Those aboard paddled with frenzied strokes of bark, hands, and sticks, making their way past the big boat and out into the current of the Mississippi. With Lieutenant Ritner shouting orders above the continuing gunfire, the flatboat weighed anchor and tried to pursue the three large canoes, containing about thirty Indians. Twice the larger boat ran aground on sandbars, and by the time they were freely in the Mississippi River's current, the canoes were out of sight downstream but still audible as their occupants continued splashing the water to get away. The flatboat followed for a mile or two, but finally gave up and returned to the mouth of the Wisconsin.

At the scene of the attack, the bodies of fifteen men and about the same number of women and children were fished from the waters. Thirty-two women and children and four old men still alive were captured and taken under guard to Fort Crawford.

For the two dozen or more who managed to reach shore and stagger away in the darkness, the danger had not ended. The party of Menominees who had been ranging out from Prairie du Chien under Colonel Stambaugh were nearby and rushed to the scene upon hearing the first gunfire. As they encountered the survivors of the river attack, they methodically killed them with knives and tomahawks and war clubs, remembering only too clearly the deaths of the twenty-six unarmed Menominees at the hands of the Sacs in this same area last fall. So, of the Sacs and Foxes who had actually made it ashore after the attack on the river, only ten managed to hide and survive the deadly aftermath.

At long last, the Menominees had taken their vengeance.

[*July 29, 1832 — Sunday*]

Major General Winfield Scott smiled at Lieutenant Hannibal Day and said, "Well, Lieutenant, since this will be the last communication you will be writing for me in the foreseeable future, before we begin I want you to know how deeply I appreciate the service you have been to me throughout this difficult time."

Lieutenant Day flushed and grinned. "It hasn't been easy, General Scott," he admitted, "but I wouldn't have missed it for the world. I rather suspect I'm going to find it somewhat boring duty when I return to Major Whistler's command later today."

"And *I* suspect, sir," Scott rejoined, "that no matter what you do in this man's army, you will excel and advance rapidly and far. I intend to write Major Whistler a note of appreciation for his lending me your services and my own personal recommendation for your promotion." He cleared his throat. "Now, then, before we become maudlin, let's get this last matter taken care of."

"Yes, sir!" Day, still grinning, dipped his pen and immediately began writing swiftly as Scott spoke in his usual measured tones of dictation:

> *Head Qrs. North Western Army.*
> *Chicago. July 29th., 1832*

To Colonel Abraham Eustis.

Sir   I leave you in the immediate command of all troops here & expected here. Should you move before the arrival of Major Payne's detachment [from Fort Gratiot], you will leave him instructions to follow. So will you give, or leave, instructions for companies of Rangers which may be within your reach, or which may approach this place, after your departure, to take the same general route which I shall now designate.

From a letter just received from the Secretary of War, I find it is his opinion, on account of the Cholera, that the movements of the detachments infected with that disease should not be precipitated. You are fully aware of my own policy to guard against the spread of the calamity. I shall, therefore, leave you the same discretion which I have heretofore exercised myself on this critical subject; but hope by the arrival of Lieut. Col. Cummings' small detachment, if not before, it may be deemed safe, in respect to humanity & the good of the service, for you to take up the line of march.

I shall personally, with my small party, proceed rapidly to Galena & Fort Crawford, via Dixon's Ferry.[319] *You will, with all the forces except the sick and invalids, take the same general route for Galena, where you will find further instructions from me.*[320] *Enquire at the Post-Office at that place — if there be, as I suppose, one there.*

I wish all the troops that march hence to take with them subsistence for not less than twenty-five, nor more than forty, days; & the horses as much forage as may be convenient. Spare tents, canteens, havresacks [sic] & nose bags, for the use of

the troops on the Mississippi would be extremely desirable. Some of each, I hope,
you may bring with you; but, as I know your baggage train will be limited, I will
not specify numbers. The same remarks might be extended to essential medicines
& hospital stores, & I will ask you specifically to bring with you one or two extra
hospital tents.

You will, as long as new cases of Cholera shall happen to occur here, or on the
march, take all proper measures to avoid a junction with the Rangers or Volun-
teers; but long before you reach the Mississippi, I trust your Battalions will cease
to be suspected of Cholera.

I have kept you, up to this time, so fully acquainted with my correspondence &
views, with all authorities & on all subjects, & my confidence in your intelligence,
zeal, & abilities is so great, that I deem it superfluous to say more to you at
present. I know well that I leave the public interests in safe & able hands.

I remain, Sir, With great respect, Yr. Most Obedt. Sert. [sic]
                    (signed) Winfield Scott.

Within half an hour of finishing the letter, General Scott, mounted on a fine chestnut gelding, turned his eyes westward and raised his hand as a signal to the small party behind him, prepared to lead them out of Chicago, where he had arrived nineteen days earlier — an interval during which his force had suffered over two hundred individual attacks of cholera and sixty-eight deaths.

"Well, gentlemen," he said, dropping his arm as he spoke, "it's time we go fight a war."

[*July 31, 1832 — Tuesday*]

Though haste was essential in their continued move toward the Mississippi River, Black Hawk's band paused in the midst of a beautiful leafy bower, and there they gently placed on the ground the body of Chief Ioway, who had toppled dead from his horse a few minutes ago. He had complained not at all about the bullet wound low in his side, received during the Battle of Wisconsin Heights. It had bled considerably at first, but after being doctored with herbs and stuffed with the down plucked from the breast of a buzzard, it had seemed to give him little trouble.

Throughout these days of traveling cross-country, he had ridden his flagging horse as well as any of the others, and none in the party but himself knew how weak he was becoming and that, while the outward bleeding had been stanched, his lifeblood had continued leaking away into his body cavity. Then, just as they entered this glade, he suddenly leaned sideways and fell to the ground. He was dead before anyone reached him, perhaps before striking the ground.

Gently, respectfully, the warriors laid him out, his head toward the rising sun, his arms along his sides, his feet together. The squaws who still rode with them carefully painted him in the manner of a war chief riding to battle, and then just as carefully and gently built a neat, conical monument formed of logs and leafy branches over his body. To the uppermost of these logs, Black Hawk attached the eagle feather he removed from his own scalp lock.

"Yesterday," Black Hawk said to the encircling warriors, women, and young people still with him, "Chief Ioway told me he had had a vision. He said he had seen himself dead before the sunset of this day, but he had also seen us arrive the day after at the Mississippi, and no one would see us arrive. His vision was true as to himself. It will also be true in regard to us."

He placed his hand on the wooden monument. "Sleep well, Ioway," he said softly. Then he remounted his horse and led his warriors to the west, toward the Mississippi River, less than a full day's ride ahead of them.

[*August 1, 1832 — Wednesday*]

Head Qrs. North Western Army
Dixon's Ferry Augt. 1, 1832

To Brigr Genl Henry Atkinson

Sir: I received by express, at Chicago, on the evening of the 28th. ultimo, your letter of the 25th giving me the pleasing intelligence of the affair of the 21st. in which generals Henry & Dodge obtained a victory over the hostile Indians & succeeded in driving them across the Wisconsin. I congratulate you on the results of the affair; and deeming it highly honourable [sic] to you, the generals before named, & the mounted men who were engaged, I lost no time in forwarding copies of your letter — one to the Secretary of War, now at Detroit, & one to the War Department.

I set out on the morning of the 29th, with Captains Galt & Bache, & Lieutenant Maynadier (all of my staff) to join you, or the troops nearest in pursuit of the enemy, via this place & Galena, or Fort Hamilton. It is believed here that you are now at the latter place, & I address this letter accordingly. I shall proceed early tomorrow, & expect to reach Galena the next day. My wish is to see you as early as practicable, or to hear from you, if public duty should prevent your coming directly to me, — on the general state of the war, the position of the enemy, the number of troops in pursuit of him, the subsistence in depot, &c &c.

Colonel Eustis, at the head of about 400 regular infantry, probably left Chicago this morning, with orders to march upon Galena, leaving behind only the sick & invalids. Major Thompson, with two companies of the 2nd Infantry, arrived by land on the 28th; Lieutenant Colonel Cummings was expected, with a small detachment, by yesterday, & Major Payne by the 10th instant. All the troops which have marched, or which are to follow Col. Eustis, will take from Chicago subsistence for from twenty-five to forty days — most probably for thirty days. No precise route to Galena was prescribed to Col. Eustis, but I think it probable he will pass by the mouth of the Peeketonike [Pecatonica] *& Fort Hamilton.*

The troops had but few new cases of cholera among them, from the date of my last letter to you up to my departure, & most of those yielded readily to medical treatment. We supposed that not a new case would occur on the march — particularly after the second day.

On the supposition that the enemy were, all, across the Wisconsin, that it would be necessary (to farther pursuit) to organize new supplies, & in a great measure new troops (The Rangers) I sent orders from Fort Payne or Naper's, to discharge the regiment of volunteers stationed at Forts Wilbourn & Johnson & am about to discharge all the volunteers found here. I hope to find you have done the same thing in respect to the larger portion of the mounted force immediately with you.

I may early proceed from Galena to Fort Hamilton, particularly if the public service should render it inconvenient for you to join me at the former place; but I deem it important to be for a few days within the reach of the Mississippi with a view to correspondence with the administrative departments of the army, the Governor of Missouri, Rangers &c.

If you should not be at Fort Hamilton as report represents, nor near it, this letter may be slow in finding you. I shall however write again from Galena with better intelligence of your position & movements.

I have the honour [sic] *to be, Sir, Very respectfully Ymost* [sic] *Ob. Sert.*
Winfield Scott

P.S.   Should [you] *be in fact on or near the Wisconsin, instead of Fort Hamilton, I shall advance rapidly after a halt of a day or two at Galena, to join you at Fort C*[rawford] *or at some point on the Wisconsin.*

[*August 1, 1832 — Wednesday*]

At last they had arrived!

Black Hawk felt a swell of exultation rise in his breast as he viewed the half-mile expanse of the great Mississippi River spread out before them under the midday sun, only a short distance below the mouth of the Bad Axe River.[321] And, just as Chief Ioway had predicted, no one was there to see their arrival. Now all that remained was to quickly get his band across and to the safety of the far side.

The Prophet, Wabokieshiek, had been the one to direct them to this point, and he had assured Black Hawk and the other chiefs that there would be a whole flotilla of canoes drawn up on shore there for their use. And so there had been, for a while. But then Captain Loomis had sent his stern warning to the Winnebagoes along the river to come down to Prairie du Chien in their canoes and that any such boats left behind would be smashed. The Mississippi River Winnebagoes were very desirous of having the Sacs leave their country, but now, with Black Hawk's band clearly on the run and a large white force coming up behind him, they were afraid of giving any indication of having provided aid to the enemies of the whites. Accordingly, they had removed the thirty canoes that had been drawn up on the bank here for Black Hawk's arrival and took them down to Prairie du Chien, rather than have them destroyed. The only exceptions were three medium-sized canoes that, along with a log raft, had been drawn farther up into the bushes and allowed to remain where they were, hidden from sight of anyone passing on the river.

Black Hawk's people found the canoes and raft quickly and brought them to the water's edge, but felt a great disappointment at how few there were. There were no elm trees anywhere nearby from which to strip the bark and build more of the makeshift canoes, and with only these three canoes available, it would take days for the band — still numbering close to five hundred — to be ferried across in relays, and there was not that much time. Many of their horses had been killed and eaten to ward off starvation, and those that were left were extremely weak and could not possibly carry riders across the broad river, more than a half-mile wide at this point. It was, in fact, doubtful that many could swim across at all, even if free of all encumbrances.

Now, to make matters even worse, rear guard scouts had just brought word that the white army was closing fast behind them and would surely be upon them by midday tomorrow. Black Hawk immediately ordered a guard of twenty hand-picked warriors to climb the high bluffs on their back trail and watch for the approaching white army. When the rear guard was engaged by the whites, the twenty warriors were to retreat northwestward, hopefully to decoy the whites away from where the band was located and close to the mouth of the Bad Axe.

The ferrying of canoeloads of his people across the Mississippi was commenced, and though eighteen could go across at one time — six to each canoe — only twelve could be deposited on the far shore, since two men were required for the paddling of each of the three canoes. Moreover, it took the better part of an hour to make the journey across and back. There simply wouldn't be time enough, and a resurgence of the fear settled over them all as they crouched on shore and anxiously watched the inadequate ferrying process continue.

The raft was loaded with women and a number of the smaller children who were still with them. All the women were equipped with pieces of bark to use as paddles and gradually move the cumbersome craft across the river. They realized it would no doubt be many miles downstream before they reached the opposite shore, but at least they would reach safety. It didn't happen that way. Dangerously overloaded, the raft moved out into the current and was swept downstream. By the time they were swept out of sight of the others, they were no more than a few hundred yards offshore. A great snag projected from the water far ahead — a whole tree that had toppled into the water when a steep bank had caved in and had finally lodged here with its snaggly roots projecting above the water like a great spider waiting to snare them. The women rushed to one side of the raft to try to paddle it away from the imminent collision, and instead the shifting of their weight caused the raft to upend, dumping its entire complement of screaming passengers into the water. Almost all were drowned.

For three hours the tedious ferrying of the Indians continued, but with each transit taking such a very long time, the three canoes were only in midstream with the fourth crossing when those in the boats shrieked with alarm and pointed upstream. The paddlers began working with a frenzy they had not exhibited before, and the three boats surged rapidly toward the far shore.

At first those on shore could not see what had alarmed those in the canoes, but then they were stunned to see an enormous steamboat appear around a bend upstream, belching heavy smoke and churning the water to a froth.

Black Hawk looked at his people crowded on the sandbar here, and saw some 450 Indians — weak, exhausted, alarmed, some beginning to scramble into hiding in the riverine growth but many more resolutely awaiting his command. He shook his head and glanced at Makatauauquat — Black Cloud — standing close to him.

"Our people can run no farther, Black Cloud," he said. "It is over. I will surrender myself to them and beg them to let the rest go in peace."

"I will surrender myself with you, Black Hawk," replied the third principal brave of the band.

Black Hawk nodded and turned to a woman standing close by. She was Kishkasshoi, half-Sac and half-Fox, a daughter of Wapello and niece of Quashquame.[322] "Quickly," he said to her, "go find me a stick and tie a white cloth on the end of it and bring it to me. I take pity on the women and children, and I will shake hands with the Americans."

[*August 1, 1832 — Wednesday*]

Captain John Throckmorton, in the wheelhouse of the steamboat *Warrior*, was first to see the three canoes in the water far ahead. Beyond question, they were Indians crossing, and probably part of Black Hawk's band. He immediately rang the bell in a general quarters signal and spun the wheel slightly to establish a more direct course of interception with the boats.

The twenty crew members of the *Warrior* leaped to their posts without hesitation, and the few soldiers not at this moment on deck quickly appeared from within the two cabins. As they had done in their drills numerous times before, the soldiers rushed with those already on deck, weapons ready, to battle positions along the forward rails. Three civilians on board, A. E. Hough, James G. Soulard, and the owner of the *Warrior*, William Hempstead, also came on deck with weapons but were sensible enough to stay well back and out of the way. Lieutenants James Kingsbury and Theophilus Holmes moved back and forth past their detachment of fifteen regulars and six volunteers, issuing crisp orders to the riflemen and directing the three artillery privates to ready the six-pounder. Then they joined the Winnebago interpreter, Wabakawsawkaw — White Cheeks — standing at the bow.[323]

Abruptly Captain Throckmorton spun the wheel, and the 111-foot steamboat shuddered as she responded to the demand and began angling toward the eastern shoreline. Lieutenant Kingsbury turned in surprise and looked toward the wheelhouse, then followed the direction of the skipper's point. On shore was a great crowd of Indians, some of them already moving into cover, but others remaining in view.

"They're raising a white flag, Lieutenant Holmes," one of the privates called. "Looks like they want to surrender."

On shore they could see one of the Indians, obviously a Sac because of his plucked dome and single scalp lock, lift high a stick to which was attached a limp piece of white cloth.

"It's a damned trap," growled one of the volunteers. "Look how many are going into the bushes. They just want to get us in close to make an attack."

"And what about them in the canoes?" another of the soldiers pointed out anxiously. "They're getting away."

"Silence!" barked Kingsbury. "Wabasha's warriors will take care of any that reach the other side. As for you men, keep down behind that rail as much as possible and keep ready. Artillery, canister load and keep a bearing on those Indians on shore." He looked over his shoulder toward the wheelhouse, and Captain Throckmorton anticipated his question.

"I'm going to stand to about sixty-seventy yards offshore, Lieutenant," the skipper said. "Looks like they want to talk, and I reckon we better find out what they've got to say before any shooting starts."

The first mate of the *Warrior*, Samuel Berson, grinned up at his superior. "Looks like we're in for some fun, Cap'n," he chuckled. "Tol' you we'd be fightin' redskins 'fore it was over."

Throckmorton scowled as he powered down the *Warrior*. "I tell you what, Sam," he said, "there is no fun in fighting Indians. Not ever! Now you boys look sharp."

The *Warrior* slowly closed the gap separating them from the Indians on shore. Far out across the river, the three canoes filled with Indians had by this time just reached the west shore, and the Indians aboard were leaping out to join the near-forty others who were peering from cover at what was occurring, relieved that the great smoke-boat of the whites had not come after them, but concerned for the rest of their party.

"Soon as we stop, White Cheeks," directed Kingsbury, "call to them. Find out if they have a chief with them. Or if Black Hawk's there."

As the rumble of the engines became muted, the thrashing of the paddle wheels ceased, and the anchor was dropped, White Cheeks called out loudly toward shore in the Winnebago tongue. As soon as he finished, a younger warrior close to the one with the flag shouted a response, and then the bald

Indian on shore stuck his flag stick in the sand and cupped his mouth. He also shouted an extended string of words.

White Cheeks turned to the officer. "I ask first if any talk Winnebago tongue. He who answer first say he is Wawkonchawkoohaw, the one called the Sac. Say he is first son of the Prophet, Wabokieshiek. He say yes, they have chiefs, and yes, Black Hawk is with them. He say Black Hawk holds flag, but Black Hawk can talk Winnebago and would say own words."

"That was Black Hawk who answered next?"

"Yes." White Cheeks nodded. "Black Hawk. He say he want his people be let go in peace. He say Black Cloud, third principal brave, stand beside him. He say he and Black Cloud surrender their own selves to Americans if their people be let go in peace 'cross river."

"Tell Black Hawk and Black Cloud to come aboard in one of their canoes," Kingsbury ordered.

White Cheeks called out again and listened to the response, then turned to the lieutenant, shaking his head.

"Black Hawk say no have canoe. Only three on other side river. He say you send small boat to shore, get them. If Americans do, he say he and Black Cloud come to smoke-boat without weapons, shake hands with Americans."

"T'hell with that!" shouted the volunteer who had spoken before. "It's a trap, by God!"

Lieutenant Kingsbury hesitated a moment and then dipped his head toward the artillerists. "Fire!" he said.

Instantly the heavy boom of the six-pounder sent a shrieking array of canister grapeshot into their midst. In moments the sandbar was littered with dead and wounded, and those still unhurt were rapidly disappearing into the brush. At once the twenty-one soldiers raised themselves above the rail, aimed, and fired their rifles. Chaos erupted on shore among the two hundred or more Indians still clustered together. Many fell dead or screaming with injuries, while others began running or scrambling for cover. One of those killed in the first fire was Black Cloud, who slumped to the sand at Black Hawk's feet. Even as the Indians broke into flight for cover, another burst of rifle fire came from the steamboat and then the blast of the cannon again. Hoarse commands could be heard among the bushes on shore, and then, at last, a hail of rifle fire was sent toward the *Warrior*.

A lead ball slammed through the bulkhead of the wheelhouse and smashed out the window on the opposite side, narrowly missing Captain Throckmorton's head in its passage. Another ball punched through the slatted wood rail and buried itself in the calf of one of the privates. Numerous other shots were striking the hull and bulkheads, and more windows were shattered.

Nine or ten times more the six-pounder boomed, and each time more Indians screamed as the vicious grapeshot raked the sandbar and ripped through the vegetation in which the Sacs and Foxes had taken cover. The wounded who were still exposed squirmed into heavy cover, some getting help from their fellows, and soon there was no sign of a live Indian anywhere.

For over an hour longer the fight continued, until Throckmorton was advised by the third mate that their supply of wood was running low, and if they were going to make it safely downriver the remaining forty miles to Prairie du Chien, they'd better leave soon. With dusk soon to be coming on, Throckmorton agreed and gave the order to weigh anchor. As this was being done, he viewed the shore through his telescope and counted twenty-three Indians dead on the sand or partially in the brush.

The smoke rising from the funnels became thicker, and the paddle wheels began to turn. Slowly the *Warrior* began to ease around and then gradually picked up speed. Within minutes the steamboat had passed around a bend in the river and gone out of sight of where the encounter had taken place.

[*August 1, 1832 — Wednesday*]

Black Hawk's face was deeply lined as he stood before his people in the gathering dusk. For nearly an hour he had been talking to them, consoling them for the losses suffered only hours earlier with the attack by the Americans aboard the smoke-boat, entreating them to give up on the hopeless idea of trying any further to get safely across the Mississippi in the three canoes, which had now come back to their side of the river, imploring them to follow him again to take up the march, as he was prepared to do within the hour, and head north into the territory of their allies, the Chippewas. For the most part, he spoke into ears that would not hear.

The majority of the Sacs and Foxes and few Kickapoos and Winnebagoes still with them wanted only to resume the crossing by canoe and get as many people across as possible throughout the night and during the day tomorrow before the whites could arrive. If they worked hard at it, perhaps even all of them could make it across to safety.

Black Hawk only shook his head. "We are finished," he told them glumly. "We have no food, almost no powder and lead. We are weak and tired and hungry. Our eighth chief, Pamaho, who was with the canoes when they last crossed over, has fled into the darkness on the other side, and he is no longer of us. So what remains to us, with only these three small canoes left as a means of escape? You wish to continue crossing. That is foolish. No more than a very small portion of you could possibly get across before the whites would be on us, and then we would be doomed. Our only hope lies among the Chippewas, and it is there I plan to go. A few of our Winnebago friends have agreed to guide us, though they will not stay with us once we have reached our destination. I ask one final time: Are there none here who will go with me?"

There were a few. Wabokieshiek and his lodge, plus the warriors and families of four other lodges, agreed to join him. In the end a total of forty-six individuals took their places behind Black Hawk. In addition to Wabokieshiek, there was Chief Keokaqua and the fifth chief of the band, Chokepashepahio — Little Stabbing Chief — plus eight warriors and thirty-five women and children.

The small group and the much larger group stared at each other for a long moment, and then, without a further word passing between them, Black Hawk strode away, his little knot of followers strung out behind him. All were soon lost to sight in the brush. [324]

It was the younger Weesheet — Sturgeon Head — who finally broke the silence that hung over those who had remained behind. The fourth chief of the now all-but-disintegrated band, he stepped to a small rise before them, mounted it, and faced them. When he spoke, his voice was heavy with anger and bitterness.

"Now they have brought us to ruin, now that they have lost us our women and children and all that we had. Now that they have done these things, now they have run to save their own lives. Well, we here will continue to do as we planned. We will continue as long as we can to take our people over the river. And when at last the white warriors come up to us, we will fight them until the last of our strength and will is gone. We can do no less than that, nor no more."

[*August 1, 1832 — Wednesday*]

General Henry Atkinson looked out over the camp and felt a wave of admiration for these men who pressed on so grimly with the task at hand; men who had pushed themselves to the limit with hardly a murmur of complaint. A dozen, a score, half a hundred of their horses had given out, yet those left on foot kept pace with the column over terrain that was often very difficult.

The march had begun this morning at sunrise, and by 10:00 A.M. they had crossed the Kickapoo River — a heartening landmark, since it meant they were at that point less than twenty-five miles from the Mississippi River. Throughout the day they continued to march, once passing a wooden burial edifice over the body of a man gaudily painted and garlanded and who was evidently a chief. The structure was torn down, and despite the new prohibitive regulations, the dead man's scalp lock was cut away. Here and there other bodies were discovered — usually old people or those who had died of wounds. The very tracks of the Indians they were pursuing indicated the unutterable fatigue they were undergoing, yet somehow they had managed to go on. Somehow, just knowing the Indians were more exhausted and hungrier than they gave the army the will to continue without complaint. There was great hope they would catch up to the enemy before the day ended, but they did not.

At dusk, when Atkinson estimated they were about eight to ten miles distant from the Mississippi, a halt was called to camp. The only water supply nearby was a small spring located at the base of a steep cut in the hill they were crossing. In order to get water, the weary men had to climb down the treacherous face of the cut, fill their canteens, and climb back up.

Now, with darkness closing around them and the men preparing their meal, General Atkinson regretted what he was about to do, but he hoped the men would realize the necessity of it. The Indians were obviously at or close to the Mississippi River by this time and would be attempting to get across by any possible means. Hopefully they had no boats, but he remembered only too well how they had cut elm bark and made a whole fleet of canoes in a short time to send part of their band downstream on the Wisconsin. If they had been able to do it there, chances were they could do the same here in order to cross the Mississippi. Thus, it was necessary to come up to them as quickly as possible, before the escape could be effected. It was at that point that Atkinson had made his decision, and now he summoned his adjutant, Lieutenant Albert S. Johnston.

"I have a letter I want you to write, Lieutenant, to the commanding officer at Fort Crawford." He then went on to explain what the letter should contain and directed him, as soon as it was written, to send it by special express — three horses for the same rider, he to lead two and ride one, alternating on their backs to make the best possible time in reaching Prairie du Chien, which was some thirty to thirty-five miles south. "By the time you finish writing the letter and sending off the express, the men will be finishing their meal. You will at that point make a round of the camp and pass the order, in my name, that we will rise and begin our final move to the Mississippi at two o'clock in the morning."

In less than half an hour, the express, leading his two spare horses, left the camp on his way to Prairie du Chien and Fort Crawford. The letter he carried was brief but urgent:

> *Liut* [sic] *Johnston. A D Camp To Capt Loomis*
> *Head Qrs: 1st. Army Corps North Westn*
> *Army Camp, One day's march, Northwest of*
> *Kickepoo* [sic] *river 1st. August 1832*

Sir, The Commanding General directs me to inform you that we are encamped near the camp occupied by the enemy last night, and the Troops under his command will march against him at 2 O.C. Tomorrow morning. The General expects to overtake the enemy early in the day tomorrow on the banks of the Mississippi.

They have been hard pressed by the Troops. Their route from the Ouisconsin is strewed with dead generally from wounds received in the battle of the Ouisconsin, and they suffer much for provisions — they subsist entirely on Horse flesh.

The General directs that the moment you receive this note, you will lose no time in sending a Steam boat up the River opposite this point — put on board 60 barrels of Flour & 30 barrels of Pork, a six-pounder with a sufficient quantity of fixed ammunition & 5000 rounds of musket Cartridges.

(signed) Albt. S. Johnston. Aid-De-Camp & AAA Genl

[*August 2, 1832 — Thursday*]

At 2:00 A.M. the strident, staccato notes of the bugle jerked the men of Atkinson's army out of their sleep and they rose in the darkness, moaning and groaning with the aches in their muscles. Hasty breakfasts were prepared, horses rounded up and saddled, and within an hour the army was on the move, except for a number of volunteers who were still having difficulty rounding up their horses in the dark and were given the order to follow as soon as possible.

For several hours the column walked their horses carefully through the unfamiliar terrain and neared their quarry just as the dim gray light of dawn began filtering through the fog overhanging the Mississippi. At this point, a couple of miles from the river itself, the bluffs on which they were approaching were heavily timbered before giving way to nearly sheer drops of three hundred feet to the narrow river bottoms. As they emerged from a heavy stand of timber and began passing through a relatively open area before reaching another dense timber growth, the twenty-warrior rear guard that Black Hawk had stationed there the previous day opened fire on them. Had they held their fire a little longer, the results could have been punishing to the Americans, but they fired too soon, and at so great a range in the misty, poor visibility of early daylight that not a single ball found its target.

Instantly, believing the attack had come from Black Hawk's main force, the army moved into its prearranged battle formation and began advancing in five columns — General Henry's brigade on the far left, Dodge's volunteers next, the regulars under General Atkinson moving directly up the center, General Posey's force to the right of them, and on the far right, General Alexander's brigade.

Immediately upon firing, the twenty warriors retreated toward the north, slipping and sliding down into a steep ravine and following it downstream toward its junction with the Bad Axe River just above its mouth at the Mississippi, drawing Alexander's brigade in cautious pursuit, as was intended. The other four battle columns continued forward on their course, however, and within an hour some of Colonel Ewing's spies, attached to Henry's brigade, discovered the main trail of the Sacs was farther south than the direction in which the decoys were leading Alexander.

Immediately recognizing the strategy of the decoys, General Henry led his men along the trail Ewing had discovered. The trail moved down a steep but relatively easy descent to the base of the bluff, which it took the brigade almost an hour to finish negotiating. Here, where the trail followed more level ground toward the river, it was heavily timbered, cloaked with underbrush and cluttered with driftwood from Mississippi River floods of the past — a setting ripe for ambush. General Henry studied the situation and then dismounted his force and put the horses under heavy guard. He then called for a squad of eight men to volunteer to take the lead, in order, if an ambush had been laid, to draw the enemy's fire. It was a suicide mission, and yet, without hesitation, eight Chicago men of the Cook County volunteer company of Captain Harry Boardman stepped forward to accept the assignment.

THE BATTLE OF BAD AXE

BAD AXE CREEK

MISSISSIPPI RIVER

300' HIGH BLUFFS
ALL COVERED WITH
HIGH GRASSES AND
WOODS WITH FALLEN
TIMBER

ALEXANDER'S ADVANCE

POSEY'S ADVANCE

ATKINSON'S ADVANCE

DODGE'S ADVANCE

HENRY'S ADVANCE

allan w. eckert
1988

Within a few minutes the squad was moving out warily through the dangerous terrain. In less than five hundred yards they walked right into the ambush that had been suspected, and in the first fire of the enemy's rifles, all eight were killed — 1st Sgt. Russell Rose, Dexter Graves, Jonathan Smith, Rufus Brown, Pierce Hawley, William Rogers, Stephen Scott, and the captain's own younger brother, Jonathan Boardman. Instantly Henry charged up, leading three hundred of his men, and drove the Indians back with a fierce bayonet charge, moving from tree to tree toward the more open area of heavy brush, deep grasses, and sand between the timber and the shore.

Within another quarter-hour they were in the midst of the main body of some three hundred Sac, Fox, and Kickapoo warriors, as well as nearly a hundred women and children. Henry immediately dispatched his brigade major, Murray McConnel, back to Atkinson with the news that the main body of Indians had been discovered and help was needed. Even as McConnel left, a desperate fight broke out, and the initial scattering of rifle fire became virtually a barrage, accompanied by the hoarse yells of the attackers and the fierce shrieks of the defending warriors. A number of the women scooped up their small children and fled to the river, where they leaped in and tried to escape. Some were swept downstream and came ashore safely there, but a number of them could not swim well enough and were drowned.

It was fully an hour after the ambush of Henry's squad before Alexander's and Atkinson's wings burst onto the scene, Alexander pushing the decoy warriors ahead of him from the north, Atkinson and part of Dodge's force, guided by Major McConnel, coming in behind Henry. Posey's force, almost directly over them atop the bluff, found the three-hundred-foot drop at this point so sheer that it could not be attempted, and he was forced to turn his men back and follow the rim of the drop-off southeastward, searching for a place to come down safely.

Caught between the left and right wings of the army, with the sheer bluffs to the east and the river to the west, the Indians had no escape and could only fight with intense desperation despite their weakness from hunger and exhaustion. When their remaining ammunition was quickly expended, they fought with tomahawks and bows, lances and war clubs and knives. Lieutenant Robert Anderson saw a frightened Sac woman of about nineteen standing in the deep grasses with a little girl of about four in her arms. Even as he saw her, a rifle ball passed through the little girl's right elbow and into her mother's breast, killing her. The woman fell, pinning the screaming child beneath her, and as the tide of battle carried him on, Anderson could not shake the tragic picture from his mind.

To the north, from near the mouth of Bad Axe Creek, Alexander's brigade charged their horses into the melee. The front of the column stopped and took cover as the firing became heavy there, but the mounted men in the rear were still approaching at a walk. Bringing up the rear was Private Aaron Payne, whose brother Adam, the Dunkard preacher, had been killed by Indians in May near Hollenbeck's Grove. As they began moving out of the timber and into the open, he caught sight of an Indian woman and her little boy of about eight crouched behind a tree, trying to hide from the attackers. Thoughts of his dead brother filled his mind and he was tempted to shoot them, but then he decided he could not do that to such harmless people and rode on. He had not gone more than eight or ten yards farther when the boy scrambled to his feet with a rifle in his hands and fired at Payne. The two balls with which the gun had been loaded entered his back close to the spine, and he cried out as he toppled from his horse. His fellow rangers spun around and thundered back to the squaw and boy, riddling them both with gunfire.

It was now close to 10:00 A.M., and some of the warriors made it to a stretch of marshy shoreline and attempted to surge through a broad slough to a low willow island several hundred yards away. Once again the fates were against them. The steamboat *Warrior*, with a stronger force aboard, steamed into view. The big boat would have been here much sooner, but the heavy fog overlying the river had delayed its departure from Prairie du Chien. Now, seeing a sizable number of the Indians surging through the morass to the island, Captain John Throckmorton bore down on them, and in the first burst of its cannon, killed three of the warriors. Then it methodically raked the willow island from end to end with canister shots, killing many more. The cannon blasts abruptly held fire as a detachment of volunteers from Henry's and Dodge's forces made a wild dash through the slough, gained the willow island, and swept it end to end in a fierce bayonet charge, in some instances shooting Indians out of the trees up which they had climbed to escape detection. Askaiah, one of the Menominee warriors attached to Dodge's command, was part of that charge on the willow island. As two Sacs were shot out of a tree, Askaiah sprang forward, knife in hand, to scalp them, and was himself shot and killed by one of the volunteers who mistook him for a Sac. Some of the Indians tried to swim the long distance across the river. A number of these — including Patchetowart, fourth principal brave of the band — were shot as they swam. Others drowned in the attempt. A very few made it across the wide expanse of muddy current. One of these, Nanisa, the twenty-five-year-old sister of Black Cloud, realized that there could be no escape for anyone who merely tried to hide. Wrapping her infant son in a blanket, she led one of the horses to the river and whipped it with a willow switch to force it into the water and to swim for the far shore. Clenching the blanket in her teeth so the infant's head would be above water, she gripped the horse's tail fiercely in both hands and held on as the animal swam all the way to the western shore.

The whole battle scene became pandemonium as Indians were killed indiscriminately wherever found, of whatever age or sex, and the carnage increased as the remnants of strength of the warriors failed them. The soldiers fired at virtually anything that moved, killing women and children as they sought to hide in the bushes or burrow out of sight in the sand. More and more were being killed by sharpshooters as they took to the water and attempted to escape by swimming. The whole scene quickly took on more the aspect of a massacre than an actual battle. Private John A. Wakefield found himself rooted in place, almost blinded by tears, as he stared at a little group of Indian children ranging in age from about three to eight, screaming and crying with the wounds they had received.[325]

Gradually the gunshots became fewer, and then finally ceased altogether as the battle ended. Lieutenant Robert Anderson, still with the image of the slain Sac woman and her wounded child in mind, made his way back to where the incident had occurred. At first he couldn't find them, but then a faint whimpering drew him to the correct place, and he carefully pulled the dead mother off her baby and carried the child to where a field hospital had been set up and left her there for care.[326]

The statistics spoke volumes. Twenty-one soldiers had been killed and seven wounded, but some 350 Indian men, women, and children were killed — 150 of these shot or bayoneted on the shore or the willow islands, scores of others shot or drowned as they attempted to swim the broad river.[327] Forty or fifty of the Indian horses were recovered as well.

The American wounded were loaded aboard the steamboat *Warrior* and taken to Prairie du Chien for treatment, and one of them, 2nd Lieutenant Samuel Bowman, died on the deck of the boat en route. Beside him, on his stomach, lay Private Aaron Payne, the two bullet holes in his back only temporarily cauterized prior to anticipated surgery when he was finally hospitalized.[328] Thirty-six women and children prisoners were also on board, under heavy guard, to be imprisoned and interrogated.

For the very few that managed to swim the river and reach the western shore, the safety they found among those that had crossed earlier by canoe was short-lived. As they set out morosely to attempt to join their fellow Sacs under the peaceful Keokuk, they were set upon by a party of one hundred of Wabasha's Sioux warriors, and the great majority were slaughtered. Among this number was the fifth principal brave of the band, Kinnekonesaut — He-That-Strikes-First.

A search was made for Black Hawk or his body; when it was not located, some of the captives were questioned through interpreters, and it was clearly ascertained that the Sac leader, along with Wabokieshiek and a party of nearly fifty, composed mainly of women, had fled the night before. Though it was stated he had headed northward, toward the territory of the Chippewas, General Atkinson was not entirely sure that the wily Sac leader had not gotten across the river. Nevertheless, the commander had no intention of ordering his weary troops to try to pursue Black Hawk, although he immediately dispatched an express to Keokuk in the Iowa country with a demand to be relayed to the hostile fugitives: If they would surrender, they had Atkinson's promise that all but a few hostages would be released.

There were many odds and ends to be taken care of in the days ahead — wounded to be treated, fugitives, including Black Hawk, to capture and bring to justice, reports to be written, troops to be discharged and allowed to go home, Indian prisoners to be interrogated — but these matters were, at the moment, far from consideration by the troops. To all the soldiers on this piece of remote river bottom on the Mississippi River, one thought was predominant, one fact was manifestly clear: the Black Hawk War had ended with this battle.

EPILOGUE

[*October 3, 1838 — Monday*]

ONE of General Henry Atkinson's first actions upon his return to Prairie du Chien after the Battle of Bad Axe was a hasty letter written to Major Thomas J. Beall at Fort Armstrong on Rock Island:

Sir   On the morning of the 2nd Inst. we came up with the enemy on the left bank of this River, opposite the mouth of Ioway [the Upper Iowa River], *attacked and defeated him with great loss on his part & a comparatively small one on ours. The remnant of the Sacs succeeded in crossing the river, disheartened & perishing. They will, it is expected, try to get upon the Ioway, or fall down and join Keokuck* [Keokuk] *& Wapelto* [Wapello] *with a view of surrendering themselves up.*

I have to request that you will order Keokuck to send a party to the remaining part of Black Hawk's band, and demand that the principal men remaining be surrendered up as hostages and the band itself divided between Keokuck's and Wapelto's bands.

More than 300 of Black Hawk's band have [been] *killed, and we have about 70 women and children prisoners, which I shall keep to coerce the hostile party to terms. Should they not comply, they will be immediately pursued till they are killed or subdued.*

I expect to fall down to Fort Armstrong with the Troops in five or six days, when I expect to have, through Keokuk, the determination of Black Hawk's party.

Let me hear by the return of the Boat relative to the subject of this letter.

(*signed*) H. Atkinson Brigr Genl. U.S. Army

On the day after the battle, the Indian agent at Prairie du Chien wrote a report to General Atkinson in which he said:

The moment we heard of the battle, of Genl. Dodge, and that some were escaping by the Wiskonsin [sic] I collected the Winnebeagoes [sic] & the Menominees & sent them out to guard the river and take all they could prisoners & bring them to me. They obeyed immediately and have evry [sic] day brought in some prisoners since they first went out.

The Winnebeagoes have brought in 24 prisoners, of which 3 are Warriors, nine [actually 11] women & 10 children. The men are all deld. [delivered] into the Fort, the rest are with the Winnebeagoes. The Winnebeagoes in the [mean-] time have killed & scalped seven men.

The Menomins [sic] have killed & scalped five men, and brought in 12 prisoners — 1 man, 3 women, & 8 children — two of the Menominee prisoners are wounded and one Winnebeagoe prisoner — one dangerously.

The Menominees have not lost a man — but the Winnebeagoes [sic] had a fine warrior shot by a Sac yesterday.[329]

Two Sacs had passed round the guard in the Wiskonsin by land and made a small raft below the mouth of the Wiskonsin and crossed to the west of the Mississippi. Two Winnebeagoes followed after them, found the raft and took their trail. The Sacs turned on them unexpectedly in the bushes and shot one Winniebeagoe [sic] dead. The other escaped to his canoe & got off with the news. The Winnebeagoes go to bury him this morning & pursue the Sac.

For the first few days, the most important matter, apart from the care of the wounded, was following and capturing the survivors who had gotten away. One of the first Sacs of significance to be brought in was captured by Wabasha's Sioux — the second chief of the Black Hawk band, Neapope, who professed to know nothing about the whereabouts of Black Hawk and revealed that it was he who, at the Battle of Wisconsin Heights, had called to the whites and tried to surrender the whole of his band. Neapope was fortunate to have been taken alive, since in the first seventy-two hours after the battle the Sioux overtook and slew sixty-eight Sacs and Foxes and brought in twenty-two women and children as prisoners. Among those the Sioux killed, on the banks of the Cedar River in Iowa, was the ninth chief of Black Hawk's band, Towaunonne — the Trader. Only one important chief had eluded them, and this was the fourth chief of the band, the younger Weesheet — Sturgeon Head.

Within just a few days, Major General Winfield Scott, who had arrived at Galena the day after the Battle of Bad Axe, finally took over as commanding general of the army. He had missed the Black Hawk War, it was true, but he had survived a much more dangerous war against Asiatic cholera. Of the 850 men that had left Buffalo with him for the West, 190 had died, 180 had deserted — mostly in the Detroit area, and of which many subsequently had died — and the entire force had been reduced by the insidious enemy to less than two hundred effective men. Nor had Scott truly left it behind. Within a week of his arrival, cholera had raised its ugly head at Fort Armstrong, and over the next three weeks

140 men had been stricken with the disease, of which twenty-six had quickly died. Galena and Prairie du Chien were affected as well, but to a lesser degree.

On his arrival at the front, Scott had quickly held meetings with Atkinson, and receiving his full report, he ordered the weary volunteer troops discharged and directed the grateful brigadier general to return to his wonderfully prosaic duties at Fort Jefferson, where he was greatly pleased to be reunited at last with his family.

The troops themselves had remained at the site of the Battle of Bad Axe for only a day and a half, and then the regulars were transported on the steamboat *Warrior* to Prairie du Chien, while the volunteers made their way there overland, on horseback. While mildly grousing at having to ride back on horses while the regulars were traveling in comfort by water, the volunteers were delighted upon arriving at Fort Crawford to learn that the following morning most of them would march for Dixon's Ferry, where they would be discharged and could go home — that for any further operations General Scott, now headquartered at Fort Crawford, would depend upon the rangers and U.S. Infantry.

Only two days after the Battle of Bad Axe, the town of Chicago, having undergone its first official U.S. survey, by James Thompson, received its first official geographical location, and the jubilant residents were certain that now Chicago was on its way to eventually becoming a great city. There was solid basis for this belief, and it was not merely the establishment of the first public education and Sunday school there that created such a conviction. While the troops had been moving back and forth through the valley of the Rock River and the lower Wisconsin area of Michigan Territory, they were not oblivious to their surroundings. Now, with time to reflect, they remembered very clearly the great beauty of the land they had traversed — the splendid rolling hills and great forests, the lovely lakes and timbered groves, the rich black earth, the wonderfully extensive prairies that, under judicious plows, could become bountiful farmlands. And certainly there were more lead mines to be dug in the mining district, more smelteries to be built, more commerce to be established in a land that now, free of Indian threat, was like a ripe plum for the plucking — and a great many of these men were already making plans to come back and stake their claims on these government lands. Nor were they the only ones. A flood of publications were soon published, extolling the wonders of this fertile, lovely land that — now, or soon to be, under the complete control of the United States — would be open for development. And soon, it was rumored, that beautiful country above Illinois would be taken out of the jurisdiction of the Territory of Michigan and instituted, instead, as the Territory of Wisconsin, with ultimate statehood not all that far in the future — another ripe plum for those with a political bent who had not done quite so well in their own state or territory.

The war had brought the Americans great rewards of their own for the price they had paid. The total loss in American lives, including the settlers killed at various places, was some 250 individuals, and the entire war cost was somewhere in the vicinity of two million dollars. It was a very small price to pay for the grand domain that was now open to them as a result of the war — a war that had suddenly given enormous impetus to the settlement and development of the Wisconsin Territory, which was finally established four years later. Soldiers returning to the Eastern Seaboard brought with them glowing stories of the richness of the northwestern Illinois and southwestern Wisconsin lands, their beautiful prairies, great forests, glorious, gemlike glacial lakes, and vast mineral wealth, and soon there was a veritable migration of easterners into these lands, aided by the establishment of regularly scheduled steamboat runs from Buffalo to Chicago by the *Daniel Webster*, the *Monroe*, the *Anthony Wayne*, the *Columbus*, and the *Bunker Hill*, to name only a few.

All the prisoners who had been collected at Fort Crawford were, within a fortnight, transported down to Rock Island and incarcerated at Fort Armstrong while the fugitive Sacs and Foxes were still being sought. The prisoner Neapope was confined with them in the Fort Armstrong stockade on August 20, and during one of the first interrogations he underwent, he declared with a show of pious contrition, "For myself, I have no vices — I do not smoke or drink — and I cannot think what could have led me into such bad roads as I have been traveling as I now find." Before long, all of them were taken farther downriver and imprisoned at Jefferson Barracks as hostages to be held until the Indians finally found Black Hawk and turned him over to the American authorities.

It was General Joseph Street at Prairie du Chien who put into motion the Indians he was sure would eventually capture the fugitive Black Hawk. Two days after the Battle of Bad Axe, and holding forth promises of great reward, he employed the two powerful Winnebago chiefs Chaetar and the One-Eyed Decorah to find and bring in Black Hawk. Aware that there were murmurs circulating among the whites that they had helped Black Hawk to some extent during the war, they solemnly denied the charges and assured the agent that, to prove to him they were innocent, they would return with Black Hawk in bondage or else never return again themselves.

All the Indians, as it was turning out, were finding that the war had been very disadvantageous to them. Despite the fact that — with the single exception of the attack at Indian Creek — the Potawatomies had been not merely loyal but extremely helpful to the Americans, Governor Reynolds labeled them as allies of the Sacs and Foxes and stirred up great resentment toward them among many of the whites. Yet, there were those who realized the significance of what they had done, Chaubenee in particular, who had ridden three horses to death just in his effort to warn the Americans of the approaching danger. In the Chicago area, as well as the Des Plaines River Valley and the Fox River Valley, Chaubenee was welcomed to enter any store, take whatever he fancied, and go his way. He was welcomed as well in any hotel or restaurant, where he could eat his fill without having to pay, and later he was free to ride on trains whenever and to wherever he wished at no charge. Despite this individual recognition, the Potawatomies were generally treated poorly. The same held true for the Winnebagoes, whose duplicity in the war was to some extent now laid bare. White Crow, who had effected the rescue of the Hall girls, had earned for himself a thousand dollars in the transaction, but it was a bitter reward in view of the fact that his own beloved son, White Pawnee, had been slain by the Sioux for aiding the Sacs and Foxes.

Other tribes, who had thought throwing their weight on the side of the United States against the hostile Indians would guarantee their lands to them, quickly found themselves in the position of having to give in to the demands of the United States government that a new treaty be drawn up. It was to be a treaty in which they would cede their claims to *any* lands east of the Mississippi River in exchange for reservations that would be set aside for them far west of the great river, and annuities that would be meant to sustain them until they were again functioning as a well-organized tribe. As with many treaties in the past, it dealt with only a portion of the tribes involved, overlooking entirely the rights of those who were ignored. A case in point was the Winnebagoes. Although the Indian lands on the Fox River and Lake Winnebago were to be forfeited to the whites by the terms of the treaty, none of the Winnebago chiefs of the many villages in those areas were invited to the treaty.

The first of the treaties had been scheduled for September 10 at Rock Island, but the outbreak of cholera postponed this for some days. When it was finally held, the Winnebagoes were forced to cede all their lands in the Wisconsin country south of a line from Green Bay, down the Fox River of Wisconsin to the portage at Fort Winnebago, then down the Wisconsin River from there to the Mississippi. For this they were to receive a much less valuable piece of land, plus an annuity of ten thousand dollars for twenty-seven years. For faithful services rendered to the United States, the Fort Armstrong interpreter, Antoine LeClaire, was presented with two sections of land. Alexander Robinson — Chechepinqua — was granted an increase in his lifetime annuity of two hundred dollars, raising it to five hundred dollars each year — an annuity he took far longer than the government expected, since he lived to the age of 110 and finally died in 1872.

The friendly Sacs were also brought to treat at Rock Island and were summarily forced to agree to never come east of the Mississippi River again, and to insure this, they had to cede some eight million acres of land west of the Mississippi — a strip of land fifty miles wide inland from the west shore of the Mississippi River all the way from the Minnesota country to the Missouri Territory — and they had to agree that they would never again "reside, plant, fish, or hunt, on any portion of the ceded lands." And at the treaty with the Sacs, General Scott had the audacity to elevate Keokuk to the rank of principal chief of all the Sacs, a station he could never have been entitled to by tribal law.

In a succession of treaties, the Potawatomies wound up giving to the United States all their lands in Illinois, Indiana, and Michigan and agreeing to let themselves be moved far west of the Mississippi. Similar treaties were being held elsewhere, the object being the removal of *all* Indians east of the Mississippi to reserves established for them west of the great river. On the following October 14, for example, the Chickasaws were required to cede all the lands east of the Mississippi.

In the midst of all these matters, Andrew Jackson, with Martin Van Buren as his running mate, was reelected president of the United States, winning 219 electoral votes against the forty-nine won by his Kentucky opponent, Henry Clay.

And what of Black Hawk in all this? On the night of the steamboat *Warrior* attack on his people, he had fled with the handful of followers who chose to go with him, but even by them and his Winnebago guides he was soon largely abandoned as a great manhunt was launched by the various tribes to find him. Soon, of the forty-six who had started out with him, he was left only with his son, Nasheweskaka — Loud Thunder — and two chiefs, the Prophet, Wabokieshiek, and Chokepashepaho — Little Stabbing Chief.[330] There would no longer be the safety among the Chippewas that he had envisioned, and so he moved through the forests of the Lemonweir River Valley and then into the hundreds of caves and crannies of the towering rock formations of the Dalles of the Wisconsin River. For a while they hid at the Seven Mile Bluff. From here he could see the surrounding countryside for several miles and be early warned of the approach of any searchers. It was from here that he sent out those few still with him to look for food and to try to determine if any of their Winnebago friends were anywhere nearby. When they returned, it was with the report that Indians were coming, and it was not known whether they were friends or foes. Their best security lay in separating.

Wabokieshiek took refuge among the chimney rocks at the east end of the bluff and was shortly afterward captured by the Winnebagoes on Black River and taken to Prairie du Chien and imprisoned. Little Stabbing Chief was captured when he went out to look for food, and he, too, was taken to Prairie du Chien. Along with his son, Black Hawk held out longer, in a place that he left with his name — Black Hawk's Nest. It was not a haven for long. At dusk one evening, he discovered that his pursuers had made a camp at the base of the very cliff where he had taken refuge. In the darkness he crept down toward them and found to his delight that they were his friends, Chaetar and the One-eyed Decorah. He was on the point of joining them when he overheard them talking about capturing him, and so he returned to his hiding place, alerted his son, and the two of them fled to the west. The two Winnebagoes quickly found his trail, however, and pursued him relentlessly for three days, until they caught up to them when they took refuge in a wigwam at a Winnebago village close to the Mississippi. At this point they offered no resistance, and Black Hawk merely held out his hands together so he could be bound.

Chaeter and One-eyed Decorah appeared with Black Hawk, Wabokieshiek,

Loud Thunder, and Little Stabbing Chief at Prairie du Chien on August 27 and turned their captives over to the Indian agent, Joseph Street, who in turn delivered them into the hands of Lieutenant Colonel Zachary Taylor, then commanding at Fort Crawford. Chaetar and One-eyed Decorah were given a reward of 20 good horses for their accomplishment. On the morning of August 29, Black Hawk, in chains, along with twenty-six other Sac and Fox prisoners, was sent downriver aboard the steamboat *Winnebago* to Rock Island, accompanied by Joseph Street and a military guard commanded by a bright young lieutenant named Jefferson Davis.[331] On the way downstream, the *Winnebago* stopped briefly at Galena, where great crowds were attracted when word spread of the notable prisoners aboard, but Lieutenant Jefferson Davis would not allow any visitors inside the quarters where the prisoners were being held.

Leaving Galena, they continued down to Rock Island. Their orders were to turn the prisoners over to General Scott at Fort Armstrong, but on their arrival they discovered by shouts from shore that cholera had broken out. The *Winnebago*'s skipper refused to land, and when General Scott himself came out in a small boat, the skipper refused to let him board his ship. The frustrated general was not pleased, and gruffly ordered Lieutenant Davis to continue with his prisoners downriver to Jefferson Barracks below St. Louis, where the other Sac and Fox prisoners of war had already been taken.

At the mouth of the Iowa River, the *Winnebago* stopped briefly to release some of the hostages that were not on the list — a number of women and children and the three small sons of Chief Taome. They were ordered to go to Keokuk's village, where they would live hereafter. The remainder of the journey downriver to Jefferson Barracks was uneventful, but their arrival created even more of a stir than the previous arrival of other prisoners, including Neapope.

General Atkinson immediately ordered all the prisoners placed in well-guarded confinement and the principals fitted with heavy ankle irons. Black Hawk took great offense at this, and in a letter he dictated he said:

> *We are now confined to the barracks and forced to wear ball and chain. This is extremely mortifying and altogether useless. Is the White Beaver [Atkinson] afraid I will break out of his barracks and run away? Or is he ordered to inflict this punishment upon me? If I had taken him prisoner on the field of battle, I would not have wounded his feelings so much by such treatment, knowing that a brave war chief would prefer death to dishonor. But I do not blame the White Beaver for the course he pursues, as it is the custom among the white soldiers, and I suppose is a part of his duty.*

Soon Jefferson Barracks had become a popular stopping place for notables passing through the country, all of whom wanted to view, interview, or sketch the illustrious Sac who had made war on the United States. One of these was the artist George Catlin, who made portrait sketches of Black Hawk, Neapope, Wabokieshiek, and others of the incarcerated Indian leaders, from which later he would paint portraits in oils. Another visitor was Maximilian, Prince of Wied-Neuwied, who was touring the American West expressly to see the Indian tribes. Washington Irving showed up and talked with the chiefs through an interpreter, and then wrote to a friend:

> . . . a forlorn crew, emaciated and dejected — the redoubtable chieftain himself a meagre [sic] old man upwards of seventy. He has, however, a fine head, a Roman style of face, and a prepossessing countenance.

In March 1833, a delegation of twenty-one chiefs and principal braves of the Sac and Fox tribes, led by Keokuk, came to Jefferson Barracks and presented a petition to General Atkinson:

> We, the undersigned Chiefs and Braves of the Sac and Fox tribes of Indians assembled in council at Jefferson Barracks on the 26th day of March, 1833, request our father, General Atkinson, to intercede with our Great Father, the President, for the release from confinement of the following named individuals of our nation captured during the last summer, viz.: Black Hawk and his two sons, Nasheweskaka and Nacaiite, Toway, Tashepakio, Pamaho, Ashquasape, Atarko, Neapope, Wabokieshiek. We bind ourselves for the good behavior of the afore-mentioned prisoners.
>
> Signed at Jefferson Barracks on the 16th [sic] day of March, 1833, in the presence of M. S. Davenport, Agent; Clifton Wharton, Capt., U.S. Dragoons; Albert S. Johnson [sic], Lieut., 6th Inf.; Antoine LeClaire, Interpreter; Thomas Noel, Capt., 6th inf.
>
> (signed with their marks by:)
> Keokuk, Naotuck, Wakoma, Peachenoa, Makene, Sakatonapeso, Natoaqua, Weshekuckkaaskuk, Nachemis, Apenose, Nanekapoetuck, Wapekawka, Watuppena, Quakaose, Keskekatates, Naquahekit, Mashquake, Kakaquemote, Wakoshashe, Tuakataquot, Shekokalako.

Atkinson could not comply, because he had only just learned that the government had other plans. He had just been handed a letter by Indian superintendent William Clark, who had received it from the United States commissioner of Indian affairs, Elbert Herring:

> The Secretary of War considers it expedient that Black Hawk, The Prophet, Neapope and Weesheet, together with not exceeding four others to be selected by yourself and Genl. Atkinson, and now confined as hostages at Jefferson Barracks,

should be conducted to this place, in the vicinity of which they can be kept with less danger of escape, and with more comfort to themselves. . . .

Conducted to Washington, where they arrived on April 24, the captive Indians named in the letter — with the exception of Weesheet, who had pneumonia — plus Pamaho and Nasheweskaka and a son of Wabokieshiek, were taken for a brief audience with President Andrew Jackson. After the introductions, the president had little to say to them, but he did ask the question, "Why did you do such a foolish thing as to make war on the United States?"

"I am Wabokieshiek," said the Prophet, speaking first, since he was the titular chief of the Black Hawk band, "and I say to the great father that we expected to return immediately to our people. The war in which we have been involved was occasioned by our attempting to raise provisions on our own lands, or where we thought we had a right to do so. We have lost many of our people, as have the whites. Our tribes and families are now exposed to the attacks of our enemies, the Sioux and the Menominees. We hope, therefore, to be permitted to return home to take care of them."

Then it was Black Hawk's turn. "Great Father," he said, "I am a man and you are another. We did not expect to conquer the whites. They had too many horses and too many men. I took up the hatchet, for my part, to revenge injuries that my people could no longer endure. Had I borne them longer without striking, my people would have said, 'Black Hawk is a woman, he is too old to be a chief, he is no Sac.' I thought of these things, and this caused me to raise the war whoop. I say no more of it — it is known to you. Keokuk once was here. You took him by the hand and, when he wished to return to his home, you were willing. Black Hawk expects that, like Keokuk, we shall be permitted to return, too."

"That is something yet to be decided upon," President Jackson replied. "You will be provided with clothing and food, and for now, you will be confined. How long this confinement will last will depend on the conduct of your people on the frontier."

Within a few hours, the Indians were taken away to Fort Monroe, where, no longer required to wear irons, they were given the freedom of the post but could not leave. They were immediately treated very kindly by the fort's commander, Colonel Abraham Eustis. That evening, Elbert Herring, acting on orders from secretary of war Lewis Cass, wrote a brief note to William Clark and Henry Atkinson:

You will be pleased to inform Keokuk that Black Hawk and his five associates . . . arrived here in health and are kindly treated — that there is no intention to injure them, that powerful reasons demand their detention at present, and at the proper time they will be liberated and returned to their country.

Herring concluded his letter by saying that it would be up to Clark and Atkinson as to when the prisoners could be reasonably released back into their tribes without endangering the lives of the American settlers on the frontiers.

Clark received the letter on May 14 and replied immediately:

. . . I feel satisfied that all of the least reflection among the Sacs & Foxes are fully impressed with the utter folly & hopelessness of contending against the arms of the U States with any combinations the Indians are capable of forming. I therefore think that the Sac prisoners confined at Fortress Monroe may be restored to their friends and country without affecting the interest or safety of our citizens; and their release will not only be hailed with thankfulness by their own immediate family & friends, but will also be a gratifying proof to Keokuk and other friendly Chiefs of the confidence placed by the Government in their good faith & intentions. . . .

Clark concluded by saying that he strongly felt the Indians should be brought back by way of Baltimore, Philadelphia, and New York, that they might see how futile it would be to ever again make war on so powerful a country as the United States.

In his reply, six days later, Atkinson agreed that the Indians should be brought back home, but requested that they be turned over to Keokuk, ". . . *in order that they may be made to feel a dependence on the Chiefs for their release . . . ,*" and further, that the prisoners should be brought back in a series of visits to the principal Eastern cities so that they could see the might of the United States and realize how foolish any further resistance would be.

The recommendations of Clark and Atkinson were taken immediately. The six Indians were released from Fort Monroe on the evening of June 4, and on leaving, escorted by Brevet Major John Garland, Black Hawk shook hands with Colonel Eustis. "We have buried the tomahawk," the old Sac said, "and the sound of the rifle will hereafter only bring death to the deer and buffalo. The memory of your friendship will remain until the Great Spirit says it is time for Black Hawk to sing his death-song."

Major Garland, leading the erstwhile prisoners, who had suddenly become tourist celebrities, took them for a visit of the Gosport Navy Yard at Norfolk, Virginia, where they were given a tour of the impressive seventy-four-gun warship *Delaware*, then lodged them at the Norfolk Hotel for the night. A crowd had gathered in the street, and, prevailed upon by Garland to say a few words to them, Black Hawk went out on the balcony and spoke a single sentence: "We will go home now, with peace in our hearts toward our white brothers, and our actions hereafter will be more satisfactory to you."

The next morning the party, already greatly impressed at the incredible size and strength of the United States, embarked up the length of Chesapeake Bay to Baltimore on the steamboat *Columbus*. It was planned to continue from there immediately to Philadelphia, but the voyage had made Black Hawk ill, and so they took lodging at the Fountain Inn on Light Street. Here the lionization they had been receiving suddenly ended. Word spread of their presence and again a crowd gathered, but this time an ugly one that remembered only too well the soldiers who were killed in the recent war. For their own safety, Major Garland slipped them out a back door and took them three miles south to Fort McHenry. Later in the evening they were taken to a theater where the play *Jim Crow* was being presented, and they found that in his box across from theirs was President Andrew Jackson. When the play was concluded, the president rose and bowed to the crowds who applauded him, and then introduced the Indian visitors. Again the crowd applauded, and this time it was Wabokieshiek who responded through their interpreter.

"I would cheerfully take you all by the hand," he said pleasantly, "but you are too numerous. But to you we pledge ourselves, as representatives of our nation, never again to wage war with the white men of America, and do sincerely hope you will keep back the rifle on your part, while on ours, we will bury the tomahawk in the earth."

As they moved out of the theater, President Jackson walked up to Black Hawk and shook hands with him, saying he had heard of the Indian leader's illness and hoped he was feeling better. Black Hawk responded that he was, indeed, feeling much better, and he thanked the president for their release from detention. Andrew Jackson quirked a bristly eyebrow and looked at Black Hawk directly. He seemed about to say something, but instead merely shook his head faintly, and then invited Black Hawk and his companions to meet with him again at his quarters the next morning before his departure.

The meeting took place as the president requested, and this time he was a little less cordial than the evening before. "When I saw you in Washington," Jackson told them, letting his penetrating glance settle on each in turn and then come to rest on Black Hawk, "I told you that you had behaved very badly in raising the tomahawk against the white people and killing men, women, and children upon the frontier. Your conduct last year compelled me to send my warriors against you, and your people were defeated with great loss and your men surrendered, to be kept till I should be satisfied that you would not try to do any more injury. I told you I would inquire whether your people wished you to return, and whether, if you did return, there would be any danger to the frontier. General Clark and General Atkinson, whom you know, have informed me that Keokuk, your principal chief" — Black Hawk started and then scowled at this — "and the rest of your people are anxious you should return, and Keokuk has asked me to send you back. Your chiefs have pledged themselves for your good conduct, and I have given instructions that you should be taken to your own country.

"Major Garland, who is with you, will conduct you through some of our towns. You will see the strength of the white people. You will see that our young men are as numerous as the leaves in the woods. What can you do against us?

You may kill a few women and children, but such a force would soon be sent against you as would destroy your whole tribe. Let the red men hunt and take care of their families, but I hope they will not again raise their hands against their white brethren. We do not wish to injure you. We desire your prosperity and improvement. But," — and now Jackson's voice became very hard and cold — "if you again plunge your knives into the breasts of our people, I shall send a force that will severely punish you for all your cruelties. When you go back, listen to the counsels of Keokuk and the other friendly chiefs. Bury the tomahawk and live in peace with the frontiers." Startlingly, he suddenly smiled broadly as he extended his hand to Black Hawk. "And I pray the Great Spirit to give you a smooth path and a fair sky to return."

Black Hawk accepted his hand and shook it briefly, then nodded. "My Father," he said, "my ears are open to your words. I am glad to hear them. I am glad to go back to my people. I want to see my family. I did not behave well last summer. I ought not to have taken up the tomahawk, but my people have suffered a great deal. When I get back I will remember your words. I will not go to war again. I will live in peace. I shall hold you by the hand."

They saw some more sights in Baltimore before leaving, and next were escorted by Major Garland to Philadelphia and lodged at the Congress Hall Hotel. The size of the city and the impressiveness of its monuments amazed them. And now it began to seem to them that the great white father was omnipresent, because here was Andrew Jackson again, riding in a parade of horsemen through the streets of Philadelphia to the cheers of tens of thousands of people. In turn Garland took them to the Philadelphia Mint, so they could see how coins were made, and from there to the Fairmount Waterworks, so they could see how the needs of all these thousands of people for water were being met. He also took them to the Cherry Hill Prison, so they could see how white men punished their own miscreants. Again they were in a city where, during the four-day stay, they were made celebrities, and numerous invitations came for them to attend teas and dinners and the theater, some of which were accepted, though Black Hawk steadfastly refused to issue the bloodcurdling war whoop of the Sacs for the amusement of the gatherings. Not surprisingly, the newspapers found the party to be of sustaining front-page interest, and had soon dubbed Black Hawk's son with the name Tommy Hawk.

On their last afternoon in that city, there was a large military parade, with such a display of might that Black Hawk was again impelled to address the crowd that assembled that evening under the hotel balcony.

"Why did we go to war against the United States?" he said, when the throng had hushed to hear him. "I will tell you. The whites first made a treaty with their feather pens and had some of our minor people sign it. Then they waited a long time before they finally came, and, saying they had bought it from us, began to take the lands upon which we grow our corn and in which our fathers are buried. My heart grew bitter against the whites, and my hands strong. I dug up the tomahawk and led my warriors to fight. I fought hard. I was no coward. Much blood was shed. But the white men were mighty. They were as many as the leaves of the forest. I and my people failed. I am sorry the tomahawk was raised. I have been a prisoner. I see the strength of the white men. They are many — *very* many. The Indians are but few. They are not cowards. They are brave, but they are few. While the Great Spirit above keeps my heart as it now is, I will be the white man's friend. I will remain in peace. I will go to my people and speak good of the white man. I will tell them that they are as the leaves of the forest, very many and very strong, and that I will fight no more against them."

In New York the presence of the Indian party made no less an impression on the citizens than it had in Philadelphia, and society vied within itself to be host to these quaint, blanket-swathed people from the western wilderness. When at last they left New York, having canceled a proposed trip to Boston, they started up the Hudson River in a steamboat, and along the way Major Garland pointed out to Black Hawk the United States Military Academy at West Point and explained what was done there.

Intrigued, Black Hawk told the officer, "We have a national dance to make our warriors — where the old warriors recount to their young men what they have done, to stimulate them to go and do likewise. It surprises me that you have a place of national dance for your young men, as I did not think the whites understood our way of making braves."

Another ugly reception met them at Albany, and it was only through the heroic efforts of Major Garland that they managed to escape by taking a carriage to Schenectady. From there they continued their journey to Buffalo via the Mohawk River and Erie Canal, arriving at the eastern end of Lake Erie on June 28. It was from Buffalo that Major John Garland wrote to secretary of war Lewis Cass on June 30:

> . . . *Since I took charge of the Indian prisoners at Fort Monroe I met with kind and hospitable people until my arrival at Albany where, for the first time, the party were unduly assailed by a mob assembled to witness the landing of Black Hawk. The sight was really appalling, both from the number of the mob and its ruffian-like appearance. I fortunately met with some few gentlemen, with whose assistance the party reached a carriage in safety. The driver, however, was pelted with brickbats in trying to force his way through the crowd. I determined under all circumstances of the case to make a speedy retreat and accordingly drove, under cover of dark, to Schenecktady [sic] where we arrived with whole bones and empty pockets, for in passing through the crowd of Albany ruffians, my wallet containing $100 was extracted from its hiding place by some dexterous cut-purse [pickpocket]. This unpleasant affair caused me to move more rapidly through the country than I had intended to do. The people of the towns and villages do not appear satisfied with the rapidity of my movement. The fact is, both the Indians and myself are heartily tired of crowds. . . .*

At last Major Garland made arrangements for transporting his Indian charges to Green Bay and got them aboard the steamboat to begin their journey through the Great Lakes. Among the passengers was William Armiger Scripps, the famed publisher of London, on his way to visit relatives in the American West. He was quite taken by Black Hawk and his party, and late that evening wrote in his diary:

Black Hawk was dressed in a short blue frock coat, white hat and red leggins tied around below the knee with garters. . . . His shirt not very clean. . . . His nose perforated very wide between the nostrils, so as to give it the appearance of the upper and under mandibles of a hawk. He wears light colored leather gloves, and [carries] a walking stick with a tassel. . . . His son likes to make great use of a silver toothpick . . . [and he] . . . has many ornaments about him and little bells that jingle as he walks.

A short stay was made in Detroit, but once again affairs became ugly when Black Hawk and the other five Indians of his party were hanged and burned in effigy in the streets. They stopped just as briefly to visit at Mackinac and then finally reached Green Bay. From here the journey became a frontier voyage by canoes that the Indians were more accustomed to, moving upstream to Lake Winnebago. From there the Fox River of Wisconsin was followed upstream to the portage at Fort Winnebago, then down the Wisconsin to its mouth at Prairie du Chien. Since this was where Wabokieshiek and his adopted son lived, they were released here in the custody of Joseph Street, and the remaining four were taken down the Mississippi River by Major Garland to Fort Armstrong on Rock Island. And there, at last, on July 30, following a grand council held by Garland with Keokuk, Wapello, and other friendly chiefs of the Sac and Fox tribes, Black Hawk, his son Nasheweskaka, Pamaho, and Neapope were released into the guardianship of Keokuk — the ultimate ignominy for Black Hawk, which he never quite overcame.

Determined to live up to his word given to the president of the United States, Black Hawk put up his wigwam and lived quietly at Keokuk's village on the Iowa River for many years. At last a small reservation was set apart expressly for him and the few devoted followers who were still with him. It was located on the Des Moines River in the northeast corner of Davis County, and it was here that Black Hawk built his house.

Finally, today — October 3, 1838 — at the age of seventy-one years, Black Hawk died quietly in his sleep, and he was buried beneath a fine old oak tree five hundred yards from where he died.[332] The words he had spoken less than a year before to a group of whites at a holiday celebration now became a fitting epitaph.

Rock River was a beautiful country. I liked my town, my cornfields, and the home of my people. I fought for them.

AMPLIFICATION NOTES

The following are amplification notes keyed numerically to the text through the entire volume. Simply find the number below that corresponds to the superscripted number in the text.

1. Kneebingkeemewoin is pronounced Nee-bing-KEE-mee-woyn.
2. Pyesa is pronounced Pie-EE-sah.
3. The spelling of Sac has many variations, including Saulk, Saulkie, Sauk, Saukie, Saque, Sock, Sockey, Sackie, Sauc, and others. For simplicity and ease of pronunciation, the simplest form — Sac — will be used in this volume.
4. The pronunciation of the names of Pyesa's forebears is as follows: Kiakukiak is Kye-ah-KOO-kee-ak; Nanamakee is Nah-nuh-MACK-kee; Mukataquet is Muck-ah-TOK-kwet.
5. The center of the village of Saukenuk — pronounced SAC-eh-nook — although erroneously shown on some maps as being located on the south bank of the Rock River, was actually on the north bank of that stream, some three miles upstream from its mouth at the Mississippi River, and the entire village was situated in what is the present city of Rock Island in Rock Island County, Illinois. The village was centered at the foot of a small rapids, on the site of present Black Hawk State Park, opposite Vandruff Island and directly across the Rock River from present Milan, Illinois.
6. Almost from the beginning, the word "Sparrow" was dropped from the child's name and he was simply called Black Hawk. His Sac name has been spelled with many variations, including not only the most common, Makataimeshekiakiak — pronounced Mack-uh-TYE-me-she-KEE-uh-kee-ack — but also Macataimeshekakiak, Maccitamichicakack, Makataishekiakiak, Mama-tawaimeshekaka, Makatawimeshekaka, Makatawimeshekka, Muccatamichacakiq, Muckcata-mechecaca. In addition, he was often referred to by a number of familial terms, including Father of Nasheweskaka, Father of Wathemetha, Grandson of Kiakukiak, Great-Grandnephew of Namah, Great-Grandnephew of Paukahummawa, Great-Grandnephew of Sturgeon, Great-Grandnephew of Sun Fish, Great-Grandson of Nanamakee, Great-Grandson of Thunder, Great-Great-Grandson of Mukataquet, Seed-of-the-Thunders.
7. The Bay of Bad Smells is present Green Bay, Wisconsin. It was also often referred to as Stinking Bay. These references to smell had to do with the large number of winter-killed fish that often washed up on the shores as soon as the ice was out in spring. They would rot there, and the stench was at times very bad.
8. Name pronunciations: Namah is Nuh-MAH; Paukahummawa is PAW-Kuh-hum-MAH-wuh.
9. Name pronunciations: Koweeth is Koh-WEETH; Nothamukano is No-thah-MUCK-uh-no.
10. An account of the final conflict between the Iroquois Confederacy and the whites may be found in another volume of The Winning of America Series entitled *Wilderness Empire*.
11. Wisconsin, initially spelled in the way of the French traders, Ouisconsin (or Quisconsing), is a word of Chippewa derivation but of unclear meaning. The Wisconsin River was referred to

by the Winnebago chief named Snakeskin (Waukonhaka) as the Neekounts-Sara, meaning Gathering River, which is a reference to "a river having many children" (or tributaries).

12. The Indians from as far east as the Hudson Valley and as far west as the Rocky Mountains referred to the Mississippi River as "the Grandmother of Rivers," but no evidence has been discovered to indicate that they ever called it "the Father of Rivers," which appears to be an appellation originated by the whites, probably the British. More frequently the Indians referred to it as the Mississippi, meaning "Big River." Derivation of Mississippi is traced most specifically to the Ottawa tongue, in which it is *Misses Sepe*. Variations of this in other dialects are *Metha Sepe* (Shawnee), *Meche Sepe* (Kickapoo), *Mecha Sapo* (Sac), *Mecha Sapua* (Menominee), and *Meze-Zebe* (Chippewa). In these variations, the first word means Big or Large, the second means River. Oddly enough, the Winnebagoes referred to it as *Nekoonts Hahtakah* — again, the two words meaning Large and River. The Sioux, on the other hand, called it *Wapta-Tonga*, with the two words once more signifying Big and River.

13. The council in question was held in June 1764 at Niagara and presided over by North American Indian supervisor Sir William Johnson.

14. Full details of Pontiac's War and his assassination may be found in The Winning of America Series volume entitled *The Conquerors*.

15. Name pronunciation: Kataka is Kuh-TOK-kuh.

16. Greater details of Harrison's early career and St. Clair's terrible defeat, as well as the Battle of Fallen Timbers, won by Anthony Wayne's army, and the opening of the Ohio Territory, can be found in another volume of The Winning of America Series entitled *The Frontiersmen*.

17. The community that grew up with the establishment of Fort Washington on the north bank of the Ohio River very quickly became a thriving metropolis that was first named Losantiville and then, at the behest of Governor/General Arthur St. Clair, who was a member of the Society of Cincinnatus, renamed Cincinnati. With the signing of the Treaty of Greenville in 1795, Ft. Washington's value as a strategic western outpost began to wane.

18. Pronunciation of Chiryskata is Cheer-ee-SKAH-tuh.

19. The 828,000-square-mile Louisiana Purchase, consummated in 1803, doubled the size of the existing United States, extending its borders westward to the Rocky Mountains. Because French foreign minister Charles de Tallyrand recognized that France's grip on Saint Dominique was tenuous and funds were desperately needed to finance Napoleon's continued military maneuverings, he broke the terms of the three-year-old Treaty of Idlefonso, which dictated that France could transfer it to no other power than Spain. In meetings with the U.S. minister Robert Livingston — who was, without consent of Congress, acting as an agent of President Jefferson in the highly secret negotiation — Tallyrand sold the vast territory to the United States for eighty million francs — equivalent to fifteen million dollars. Such an uproar was created in the United States by the unilateral move on the part of the president that both Massachusetts and New York protested to the point where they threatened to secede from the United States.

20. George Rogers Clark's Kaskaskia campaign and subsequent taking of the entire Illinois and Indiana countries during the Revolutionary War is detailed in The Winning of America Series volume entitled *The Frontiersmen*.

21. The Two Rivers area, one of the most favored fall hunting areas of the Sac and Fox tribes, was located in the vicinity of and westward from Palmyra, Marion County, Missouri.

22. This settlement was located on the north bank of the Cuivre River — also erroneously called the Quiver River or Cover River in some historical accounts — near the site of present Old Monroe, Missouri. This river forms the boundary between present Lincoln and St. Charles counties.

23. Ludwig van Beethoven's compositions were among those by European composers that had become very popular in the cultural centers of the United States at this time. Half a century after it was first published in March 1802, Beethoven's *Sonata Quasi una Fantasia* was dubbed *Moonlight Sonata* by music critic Ludwig Rellstab — the name by which it has been more familiarly known ever since.

24. Those boundaries encompassed the present State of Louisiana.

25. Governmental clerks and offices had been in a process of transferring to the new capital all summer and early autumn, but it was with the convening of Congress here on November 17, 1800, that Washington, D.C., had officially replaced Philadelphia as the United States capital.

26. The development of Chicago and its Fort Dearborn, resulting in the ultimate Fort Dearborn massacre, is detailed in The Winning of America Series volume entitled *Gateway to Empire*.

27. President Jefferson had invited the famed botanist William Bartram to accompany the expedition as chief scientist, but Bartram, then sixty-five years old and becoming frail, declined.

28. Pronunciation of Michikiniqua is Mish-ee-KIN-ee-kwa.

29. The material used in the calumet was a very fine-grained, compact, partially metamorphosed clay that is now commonly called pipestone, but known to geologists as catlinite — named after the American Indian artist, George Catlin, who, at considerable personal risk from certain Indians who tried to prevent his doing so, visited these Indian quarries in 1836. These quarries, still being worked today (along with several other deposits of the same material discovered since), are operated exclusively by the Indians of the area and cannot be exploited commercially by anyone else.

30. The pronunciation of Keokuk is KEE-oh-kuk.

31. The pronunciation of Hashequarhiqua is HAH-she-kwar-HEE-kwa. The name, in English, is Bear.

32. General James Wilkinson's appointment as governor of the Territory of Louisiana was finally dated March 11, 1805, eight days after an Act of Congress changed the *District* of Louisiana to the *Territory* of Louisiana, which was to operate under a governor, a secretary, and three federal judges.

33. Major James Bruff was so alarmed at the reaction among the other tribes that he wrote to General Wilkinson:
    The favoritism of the United States toward the Osage has excited the jealousy & hatred of the other nations to such a degree that I am apprehensive of the consequences if large presents are not made to them also.

34. Quashquame's name is pronounced Kwash-KWA-mee, which, in English, means Jumping Fish. His Indian name has also been spelled in various documents and accounts as Quashquama and Quashquahing. Pashepaho's English name is the Stabber or, actually, more accurately, the Fish-Stabber, but he has also been called the Gigger, sometimes erroneously spelled Giger (and thereupon erroneously pronounced Gy-ger). His Indian name, pronounced Puh-SHEP-ah-ho, has also been spelled Pashepahoe, Pashipaho, Pishkenawer, and Pecha Paho. Outchequaha's name, pronounced Whut-chee-KWE-ha, means, in English, Sunfish (or Sun Fish), though he was not the Sun Fish who was an uncle of Black Hawk. The name Outchequaha has also been spelled as Outchequaka. For Hashequarhiqua, see Note no. 31.

35. This Sac chief's name, pronounced Lay-OW-wah, has also been written Laiyuva and Layouvois.

36. A number of modern accounts portray the five Sacs who signed the treaty as being a band of Sac Indians who were wintering near St. Louis. That, of course, is wholly in error.

37. Although the Sac and Fox tribes were a close confederacy in times of war, their association was more nominal than actual in peacetime, with much jealousy and mild squabbling occurring between them. Generally speaking, the Foxes followed the lead of the Sacs in matters where their confederation was concerned. The Foxes primarily occupied the Iowa side of the Mississippi and were numerically smaller than the Sacs, so they were thus conciliatory to a greater degree to the whites. Population estimates for the two tribes in 1804 was 5,800 Sacs and 2,100 Foxes.

38. Following is the full text of the November 3, 1804, Treaty of St. Louis:

    Articles of a Treaty, made at St. Louis, in the district of Louisiana, between William Henry Harrison, Governor of the Indiana Territory and the District of Louisiana, Superintendent of Indian Affairs for the said Territory and District and Commissioner plenipotentiary of the United States, for concluding any treaty or treaties which may be found necessary with any of the Northwestern tribes of Indians, on the one part; and the Chiefs and head men of the united Sac and Fox tribes on the other part.

    Article 1. The United States receive the united Sac and Fox tribes into their friendship and protection and the said tribes agree to consider themselves under the protection of the United States, and no other power whatsoever.

    Art. 2. The General boundary line between the land of the United States and the said

Indian tribes shall be as follows, to wit: Beginning at a point on the Missouri River opposite to the mouth of the Gasconade River; thence in a direct course so as to strike the River Jeffreon, at the distance of 30 miles from its mouth and down the said Jeffreon to the Mississippi; thence up the Mississippi to the mouth of the Ouisconsing River, and up the same to a point which shall be 36 miles in a direct line from the mouth of the said river, thence by a direct line to a point where the Fox River (a branch of the Illinois) leaves the small Lake called Sagaeqan; thence down the Fox River to the Illinois River, and down the same to the Mississippi. [NOTE: *The term in Article 2 of the Treaty stated as "the River Jeffreon" was actually supposed to have been written as "the Two Rivers." Two Rivers refers to the present North River and South River of Marion County, Missouri, which empty into the Mississippi River within a quarter-mile of one another. The point given as being on the River Jeffreon "at the distance of 30 miles from its mouth" gives an approximate location on the North River near the present town of Bethel in Shelby County, Missouri.*] And the said tribes, for and in consideration of the friendship and protection of the United States, which is now extended to them, of the goods (to the value of two thousand two hundred and thirty-four dollars and fifty cents) which are now delivered, and of the annuity hereinafter stipulated to be paid, do hereby cede and relinquish forever, to the United States, all the lands included within the above described boundary.

Art. 3. In consideration of the cession and relinquishment on land made in the preceding article, the United States will deliver to the said tribes, at the town of St. Louis, or some other convenient place on the Mississippi, yearly and every year, goods suited to the circumstance of the Indians of the value of one thousand dollars (six hundred of which are intended for the Sacs and four hundred for the Foxes), reckoning that value at the first cost of the goods in the City or place in the United States, where they shall be procured. And if the said tribes shall hereafter at an annual delivery of the goods aforesaid, desire that a part of their annuity should be furnished in domestic animals, implements of husbandry, and other utensils, convenient for them, or in compensation to useful artificers, who may reside with or near them, and be employed for their benefit, the same shall, at the subsequent annual delivery, be furnished accordingly.

Art. 4. The United States will never interrupt the said tribes in the possession of the lands, which they rightfully claim, but will, on the contrary, protect them in the quiet enjoyment of the same against their own citizens and against all other white persons, who may intrude upon them. And the said tribes do hereby engage that they will never sell their lands, or any part thereof, to any sovereign power but the United States, nor to the citizens or subjects of any other sovereign power, nor to the citizens of the United States.

Art. 5. Lest the friendship which is now established between the United States and the said Indian Tribes should be interrupted by the misconduct of individuals, it is hereby agreed that for injuries done by individuals no private revenge or retaliation shall take place, but instead thereof, complaint shall be made by the party injured to the other by the said tribe, or either of them, to the superintendent of Indian affairs, or one of his deputies; and by the superintendent, or other person appointed by the President, to the Chiefs of the said tribes. And it shall be the duty of the said chiefs, upon complaint being made, as aforesaid, to deliver up the person, or persons, against whom the complaint is made, to the end that he or they may be punished agreeably to the laws of the state or territory where the offence may have been committed. And, in like manner, if any robbery, violence or murder shall be committed on any Indian, or Indians, belonging to the said tribes, or either of them, the person or persons so offending shall be tried, and, if found guilty, punished in the like manner as if the injury had been done to a white man. And, it is further agreed, that the chiefs of the said tribes shall, to the utmost of their power, exert themselves to recover horses or other property which may be stolen from any citizen or citizens of the United States by any individual or individuals of their tribes. And the property so recovered shall be forthwith delivered to the superintendent or other person authorized to receive it that it may be restored to the proper owner. And in cases where the exertions of the chiefs shall be ineffectual in recovering the stolen property, as aforesaid, if sufficient proof can be obtained, that such property was actually stolen by any Indian or Indians belonging to the said tribes, or either of them, the United States may deduct from the annuity of the said tribes, a sum equal to the value of the property which has been stolen. And the United States hereby guarantee to any Indian or Indians of the said tribes a full indemnification for any horse, or other property which may be stolen from them, by any of their citizens, provided that the property so stolen cannot be recovered, and that sufficient proof is produced that it was actually stolen by a citizen of the United States.

Art. 6. If any citizen of the United States, or any other white person, should form a settlement, upon the lands which are the property of the Sac and Fox tribes, upon complaint being made thereof, to the superintendent, or other person having charge of the affairs of the Indians, such intruders shall forthwith be removed.

Art. 7. As long as the lands which are now ceded to the United States remain their property, the Indians belonging to the said tribes shall enjoy the privilege of living and hunting upon them.

Art. 8. As the laws of the United States regulating trade and intercourse with the Indian tribes are already extended to the country inhabited by the Sauks and Foxes, and as it is provided by those laws, that no person shall reside as a trader, in the Indian country, without a license, under the hand and seal of the Superintendent of Indian Affairs, or other person appointed for the purpose by the President; the said tribes do promise and agree that they will not suffer any trader to reside amongst them without such license, and that they will, from time to time, give notice to the Superintendent, or to the Agent, for their tribes, of all the traders that may be in their country.

Art. 9. In order to put a stop to the abuses and impositions, which are practiced upon the said tribes by the private traders, the United States will, at a convenient time, establish a trading house, or factory, where the individuals of the said tribes can be supplied with goods at a more reasonable rate than they have been accustomed to procure them.

Art. 10. In order to evince the sincerity of their friendship and affection for the United States, and a respectful deference for their advice, by an act which will not only be acceptable to them, but by the Common Father of all the nations of the Earth, the said tribes do, hereby solemnly promise and agree that they will put an end to the bloody war which has heretofore raged between their tribes and those of the great and little Osages. And for the purpose of burying the tomahawk and renewing the friendly intercourse between themselves and the Osages, a meeting of their respective Chiefs shall take place, at which, under the directions of the above named Commissioner, or the Agent of Indian affairs residing at St. Louis, an adjustment of all their differences shall be made and peace established, upon a firm and lasting basis.

Act. 11. As it is probable that the Government of the United States will establish a Military Post at, or near the mouth, of the Ouisconsing River, and as the land on the lower side of the River may not be suitable for that purpose, the said tribes hereby agree, that a Fort may be built, either on the upper side of the Ouisconsing, or on the right bank of the Mississippi, as the one or the other may be found most convenient; and a tract of land not exceeding two miles square, shall be given for that purpose. And the said tribes do further agree, that they will at all times, allow to traders and other persons traveling through their country, under the authority of the United States, a free and safe passage for themselves and their property of every description. And that for such passage, they shall at no time, and on no account whatever, be subject to any toll or exaction.

Art. 12. This treaty shall take effect and be obligatory on the contracting parties, as soon as the same shall have been ratified by the President, by and with the advice and consent of the Senate of the United States.

In testimony whereof, the said William Henry Harrison, and the Chiefs and headmen of the said Sac and Fox tribes, have hereunto set their hands and affixed their seals. Done at Saint Louis, in the District of Louisiana, on the third day of November, One Thousand Eight Hundred and Four, and of the independence of the United States the Twenty-Ninth.

Additional Article. It is agreed that nothing in this treaty contained shall affect the claim of any individual or individuals, who may have obtained grants of Land from the Spanish Government and which are not included within the general boundary line laid down in this treaty: PROVIDED, that such grant have at any time been made known to the said tribes and recognized by them.

WILLIAM HENRY HARRISON, [L.S.]
LAYOWVOIS, or LAIYUVA, [L.S.]
         His (X) *Mark.*
PASHEPAHO, or THE STABBER, [L.S.]
         His (X) *Mark.*
QUASHQUAME, or JUMPING FISH, [L.S.]
         His (X) *Mark.*
OUTCHEQUAHA, or SUN FISH, [L.S.]
         His (X) *Mark.*
HASHEQUARHIQUA, or THE BEAR, [L.S.]
         His (X) *Mark.*

In presence of
WM. PRINCE, *Sec'y to the Commissioner.*
JOHN GRIFFIN, *one of the judges of the Indiana Territory.*
J. BRUFF, *Maj. Art'ry, U.S.*
AMOS STODDARD, *Capt. Corps of Artillerists.*
P. CHOUTEAU, *Agent de la haute Louisiana pour le department Sauvage.*
CH. GRATIOT.
AUG. CHOUTEAU.
VIGO S. WARREL, *Lieut. U.S. Artillery.*
D. DELAUNEY.
Sworn Interpreters:

JOS. BARRON.
HYPOLITE BOLEN   *His* (X) *Mark.*

[*Note: the additional article of this treaty was added by Harrison to benefit his friend and host, Auguste Chouteau, who had extensive property holdings under Spanish grants in the area of the cession.*]

39. Not only were the five Sac Indians who signed the treaty not qualified or authorized to sign for either Sac or Fox tribe, no Fox Indian was on hand or consulted (although in some accounts one of the five is identified as a Fox chief), and a substantial strip of land at the northern end of the cession belonged to the Chippewas and Winnebagoes, not the Sac or Fox. This latter error was later admitted by the United States, and that portion of land was ceded back to those Wisconsin tribes.

40. The St. Louis Treaty of November 3, 1804, was ratified by the United States Congress on January 25, 1805.

41. The pronunciation of Tecumseh is Tuh-CUM-sa, although it is often incorrectly pronounced Tuh-CUM-see. The pronunciation of Tengskwatawa is Teng-skwah-TAH-wah, although it is often incorrectly pronounced Tens-SQUAT-uh-wuh.

42. The pronunciation of Nasheweskaka is Nuh-SHE-wuh-SKAH-kuh.

43. The pronunciation of Wacome is Wah-KOH-mee.

44. Details of Tecumseh's rise to power, his betrayal by his brother, and his own ultimate death at the Battle of the Thames in Canada are presented in detail in The Winning of America Series volume entitled *The Frontiersmen.*

45. At this time the Winnebagoes occupied the territory largely bordered on south, north, west, and east by, respectively, the Rock River, the Wisconsin River, the Mississippi River, and Lake Michigan; the Potawatomies were directly southeast of them, extending southward to central Illinois and eastward to Indiana, although most of the Indian boundaries at this time were in a general state of flux, depending upon pressures from whites and other tribes.

46. William Clark, after his triumphant return from the Lewis and Clark expedition, had first been appointed to the position of Indian superintendent for the western tribes, but when the governor of the Missouri Territory, Benjamin Howard, stepped out of that office to become commanding general of the United States Army's western department, Clark had been named to take his place, and the duties of Indian superintendent had been incorporated into the office of governor.

47. The fort was originally built in 1808 by a small force of men under Lieutenant Alpha Kingsley, on the site of the present city of Fort Madison in Lee County, Iowa.

48. This was the establishment of the federal highway later to be designated as U.S. Route 40, which is still partially in existence and now partially traversed by Interstate Route 70.
49. Fort Dearborn was named after U.S. secretary of war Henry Dearborn. The minute-by-minute details of the massacre that occurred there on August 15, 1812, are chronicled in The Winning of America Series volume entitled *Gateway to Empire*.
50. Fort Crawford was named after President Madison's new secretary of war, William H. Crawford.
51. Fort Edwards was located two miles northeast of present Warsaw and three miles southwest of present Hamilton, in Hancock County, Illinois, directly across the Mississippi from present Keokuk, Iowa.
52. In this treaty of May 13, 1816, the chiefs and principal warriors, evidently without fully realizing the ramifications of their signing, wholly confirmed the illegally obtained and completed Treaty of St. Louis of November 1804. That the Sacs really didn't understand what they were signing is underlined by the comment made by Black Hawk much later in his autobiography, in which he says, regarding this 1816 treaty: "Here, for the first time, I touched the goose quill to the treaty — not knowing, however, that, by that act, I consented to give away my village. Had that been explained to me, I should have opposed it, and never would have signed their treaty. . . ."
53. Rock Island, three miles long and three-fourths of a mile wide, is presently the site of the Rock Island Arsenal. Fort Armstrong, named after secretary of war John Armstrong, as originally built, was about 270 feet square and had three blockhouses (each with a six-pounder cannon), barracks and officers' quarters sufficient for three full companies, a well-built stone powder magazine, and a two-story, twenty-eight-foot-long commanding officer's quarters with two one-story, fifteen-foot wings.
54. The St. Peters River was later renamed Minnesota River. It took five years — until 1824 — to complete the fort built on this site, an installation first called Fort St. Anthony and subsequently renamed Fort Snelling, after the officer who had come to finish construction of the extravagant installation, Colonel Josiah Snelling.
55. It was to Antoine LeClaire that Black Hawk eventually dictated his autobiography — a document that tends to be rather self-biased and misleading in respect to what actually occurred. In 1829, prior to the Black Hawk War, LeClaire, as half-Indian, was granted a section of land at present Moline, Illinois. In 1832, after the Black Hawk War, he was granted two more sections of land. George Davenport was an Englishman who had served the United States in the War of 1812. As soon as the war ended, he had begun trading with the Indians both as an independent and as a representative for the American Fur Company. The Indians liked him and treated him well because of his consistently fair treatment of them. During the Black Hawk War he was appointed by Illinois governor John Reynolds as acting quartermaster general in the Illinois Militia, with the rank of colonel. In partnership with Antoine LeClaire and on land that LeClaire had sold to him, Davenport and others founded the city of Davenport, Iowa. In 1845, George Davenport was murdered by robbers who broke into his home one night.
56. The Two Rivers are the North River and South River in Marion County, Missouri, from the Mississippi River southeastward. Black Hawk's traditional fall and winter hunting camp was located near the site of the present Marion County seat, Palmyra, but the hunting often extended as far southwestward as the present Woodland and Ely areas.
57. A number of mines had been established by the Indians among the rich lead deposits in southwestern Wisconsin, northwestern Illinois, and east-central Iowa. These deposits had been attracting many whites, some of whom bought land from the Indians to mine the valuable mineral, while others simply squatted on the land and defied the Indians.
58. The exact location of this campsite is not definitely known, but it was probably the same camp he had used on occasion in years past, located in present Adair County, Missouri, near the site of the present town of Brashear.
59. Neapope's name has quite often been spelled Napope, and actually appears on different treaties spelled both ways. A less-often-encountered spelling is Nahpope. The correct pronunciation is Nya-POPE, which in English means Broth.
60. Bad Thunder — sometimes erroneously identified as Black Thunder — was one of the principal civil chiefs of the Sac tribe and the undisputed head of the so-called British Band, though Black Hawk acted almost in the role of prime minister to him and it was unheard of that Bad

Thunder would oppose the wishes of Black Hawk in anything. Ioway and Namoett, too, were civil chiefs, but they acquiesced to whatever Black Hawk wanted.

61. Variously called Winnebago Prophet's Town, Prophet's Town, and Wabokieshiek's Town, this large, disreputable village was more an Indian outlaw community than anything else. Its population was primarily Winnebagoes, but there were many other tribes represented here as well. The town had become a gathering point for dissidents of various tribes and even outcast whites. It was located on the south bank of the Rock River about thirty-eight miles upstream from the Mississippi, just a mile below where present Five Mile Branch empties into the Rock River, on the site of present Prophetstown in Whiteside County, Illinois. The Burlington Northern Railroad actually bisects the old Indian village site.

62. A man of about twenty-six years at this time, Wabokieshiek — pronounced Wah-bow-KEY-sheek — was also called the Winnebago Prophet or just the Prophet. His name was also variously spelled was Wabakeeshic, Wabckcshccck, and Wabeqezheick. The literal translation of his name is White Cloud, meaning Blindness, because the white cloud referred to in this terminology is the white haze of the cataract over the eye. Wabokieshiek was a half-Sac, half-Winnebago medicine man who had claimed to have experienced a number of visions in which, he said, it was proclaimed that he should become a prophet to his people and their associated tribes. He may have been influenced in this by Tecumseh's younger brother, Tenskwatawa, the famed Shawnee Prophet, who was similarly more or less a renegade, self-proclaimed prophet and for some time enjoyed enormous power among the Northwest Territory tribes. Though a heavy drinker, Wabokieshiek gained a surprising amount of prestige among the tribes of northern Illinois and southern Wisconsin. Like Black Hawk, he leaned heavily toward the British and disliked Americans intensely.

63. The river originally called Fever River is the present Galena River of Jo Daviess County, Illinois, which empties into the Mississippi River just below Galena.

64. Topenebe, in a highly drunken condition, was killed in a fall from his horse during the autumn of 1826.

65. The government blacksmith shop was established two years later in Chicago. Aiding Lewis Cass as commissioner in these negotiations was Solomon Sibley, while Henry Rowe Schoolcraft acted as secretary. The Indian agent on hand for the Potawatomies was Alexander Wolcott, aided by his subagent, John Kinzie, while the factor was Jacob Varnum.

66. The pronunciation of Wabeshaw is WAW-buh-shaw; Pamoske is pronounced Pee-MOS-kee.

67. The pronunciation of Mawgehset is MAW-guh-set; his village initially had been located at the southwestern end of Lake Geneva, Wisconsin, on the site of the present town of Fontana, but at this time it was located at the east end of Lake Geneva about a mile west of the site of present Big Foot Beach State Park, in present Walworth County, Wisconsin, just north of the Illinois line.

68. The pronunciation of Wekau is WEE-kaw; that of Chichonsic is Chee-CHON-sick.

69. The name Gagnier (pronounced Gan-yea) has erroneously been spelled Ganzier in some accounts.

70. Louisa Gagnier survived her injuries and grew to womanhood.

71. Jefferson Barracks had been established by General Atkinson in 1826 as a military post on a bluff overlooking the Mississippi River ten miles south of St. Louis. The quarters, first constructed as temporary log barracks, were replaced by permanent stone barracks beginning in 1827.

72. The new village that had been established for the Sacs by Pashepaho was located on the bank of the Iowa River near the site of present Wapello, in Louisa County, Iowa.

73. Site of present Muscatine, Iowa.

74. Black Partridge has variously been known by the Indian names of Mukaytaywuzuk (pronounced Muh-KAY-tay-wuh-zook) and Nanaloibi (pronounced Nah-nuh-LOY-bee) and is thought to have been born in 1758. He was instrumental in saving the Kinzie family from destruction during the Fort Dearborn Massacre of 1812 (see the author's *Gateway to Empire* volume of The Winning of America Series). His brother, seven years younger (1765), was named Waubansee (pronounced Waw-BAN-see), and he, too, was generally a friend of the Americans, although he served long and well as war chief of the prairie Potawatomies. Waubansee's name has also appeared in various historical documents as Waubaunsee, Waubunsee, Wabunsi, Waubaunse, and Wabansi. Two different English meanings are noted for

his Potawatomi name — A-Little-Eastern-Light and He-Causes-Paleness-in-Enemies, the first probably being the actual meaning of Waubansee and the latter likely to have been a nickname bestowed when he became war chief. Sauganash is pronounced SAW-guh-nash, and though this is the name usually used for him, it was not his true name. Born at Detroit about 1778 as the son of an Ottawa chief's daughter and British officer Captain William Caldwell, he was called Billy by his father — later becoming known as Billy Caldwell — and Tequitoh by the Ottawas, that name meaning Straight Tree. However, because of his closeness to the whites all his life, especially the British during his formative years, he was dubbed Sauganash by the Ottawas, which meant the Englishman. Chechepinqua (pronounced Chee-chee-PIN-kwa) was also known by the name of the Scots trader Alexander Robinson, who sired him with an Ottawa woman. His Indian name means, in English, Tame Rattlesnake. Like Sauganash, Black Partridge, and Chaubenee, Chechepinqua was for many years a close friend of the Kinzie family in Chicago.

75. Fourteen tracts of land were reserved from the ceded territories and from other government lands, these tracts assigned to individual Indians. One of two sections at Gros Point (present Wilmette, Illinois) went to Antoine Ouilmette on behalf of his wife, who was a full-blooded Potawatomi. Ouilmette himself received eight hundred dollars for his losses during the War of 1812. The heirs of John Kinzie, also for losses incurred during the War of 1812, received thirty-five hundred dollars. Eleven tracts of land went to mixed-bloods, including Chaubenee (two sections), Sauganash (two and a half sections), and Chechepinqua (two sections). Sauganash's sections were on the North Branch Chicago River six miles above its junction with the main river (in the area where present Irving Park Avenue crosses the river). Sauganash sold this land not too long after it was awarded to him. Chechepinqua's two sections were on the Des Plaines River near Des Plaines, Illinois. Chaubenee requested that his two sections be so located as to include his old home and council house at the Paw Paw Grove. By direction of Major Langham, who was then surveyor general of Illinois and Missouri, a survey and plat of the reservation was made by a deputy surveyor, and Chaubenee felt assured that the home that he and his family had occupied for so many years was secure to them forever.

76. Pronunciation of Panoahah is Puh-NOAH-huh.

77. This confluence is in the vicinity of Wedron, Illinois, in La Salle County.

78. The smaller creek entering from the north was Little Indian Creek, almost exactly midway between the towns of Baker and Serena.

79. The pronunciation of Meau-eus is MO-ee-yus.

80. The pronunciation of Toquamee is Toe-KWA-me, also known by the name of Degwagek, and his name in English was Autumn; pronunciation of Comee is KO-me, who was also known as Okama, which means Leader.

81. This ferry was located on the site of present Dixon, Illinois, in Lee County. At least one source of this period states that the name Ogee is pronounced Oz-ha, but other sources show the spelling not only correctly as Ogee but also as Ogie and Ohgee, indicating that they were spelled phonetically, and if so, then the correct pronunciation was very probably Oh-gee.

82. Actually, Dixon's health improved so much that he ultimately reached the age of ninety-two and outlived all twelve of his children.

83. The site of Kellogg's Grove, which was also known as the Burr Oak Grove and later Timm's Grove, was located just under fifteen miles west and slightly north of present Freemont, Illinois, just over a mile northwest of the present village of Kent and virtually on the county line of Stephenson and Jo Daviess counties, Illinois, very close to where the county line is crossed by the Chicago & Northwestern Railroad tracks. An historical marker has been erected here.

84. John Dixon's physiognomy was remarkably similar to that of the well-known western character actor Walter Brennan.

85. This former community of Boyd's Grove was located not far from the site of present Depue in Bureau County, Illinois.

86. Site of present Dixon, Lee County, Illinois.

87. Gratiot's Grove was located along the Pecatonica River at the site of present Gratiot in Lafayette County, Wisconsin.

88. The name of Chief Pamoske, pronounced Puh-MAH-skee, has variously been spelled as Pamoski, Peemashkee, Peearmaski, Peamashka, Pashasakay, Peahmuska, Piemosky, Pianosky,

and Pierremaskkin — all generally meaning The-Fox-Blowing-His-Horn. He was the son of Chief Pymanshebt — sometimes spelled Pie-Man-Shee or Pyamaskiwa — which translates in English to Little Tornado or Twister or, sometimes, Whirlwind — who had presided over the Dubuque's Mines village until his death by natural causes around 1796. Pamoske was the Fox chief most responsible for preventing the whites from taking over the lead mines developed by Julien Dubuque after Dubuque's death in 1810. The name of Allotah was pronounced Al-LOW-tuh. His English name of Morgan was adopted by him, according to a story prevalent at this time, after he had been befriended in his youth by a British trader named Morgan.

89. The Fox village, established about 1780 in the vicinity of the Dubuque Mines, was located on the west shore of the Mississippi just south of the mouth of Catfish Creek, just south of present Dubuque, Iowa.

90. These Indians allegedly came from the Sioux village located on the site of present Winona, Minnesota.

91. Wabasha is pronounced Waw-BASH-uh. It has also been spelled Waubasha, Wapasha, and Waupasha. He was known to the French as La Feuille, to the British as the Leaf or Falling Leaf, and to the Americans as Red Leaf. Though noted historically for his advocacy of peace, Wabasha was also a fighter of renown and had led his warriors on many successful forays for the past three decades. This particular Wabasha should not be confused with the one who preceded him or the one who followed. The first Wabasha gained renown as a warrior chief during the period of the American Revolution. The one-eyed Wabasha was his son, who was born about 1773 in the Winona village. This second Wabasha was held in great respect, especially in his later years, by members of his own tribe and others. One peculiarity for which he was noted was rarely being seen anywhere without his pipe-bearer. Another was the fact that when he attended peace councils, he always spoke sitting down, because he was too great a man to have to stand before any other, unless the council involved the presence of the president of the United States or the Indian superintendent, William Clark. In later years he was a strong advocate of peace, believing that his tribe could only survive by remaining at peace with the other tribes and with the encroaching whites. His son, the third Wabasha, took over leadership of the village at the death of his father and remained there until removal of these Sioux in 1853. The last historical mention of him was his residence on the Niobrara Reservation in 1872. Some historians contend that the second Wabasha was not the leader of this party that deceived and attacked the Fox peace party on May 5, 1830, but existing evidence seems to indicate that he was most likely the leader of the Sioux war party on this occasion. Although Wynkoop Warner was the man most blamed for this entire affair, the maneuverings of John Marsh, subagent to the Sioux, who was also at Prairie du Chien, was probably as much or more to blame. [See also Note no. 241.]

92. The pronunciation of Minnetana is MINN-nee-TAH-nuh; pronunciation for Masheptah is Muh-SHEP-tuh.

93. Thomas Loraine McKenney had been appointed in 1824, at age thirty-nine, to be the first head of the Bureau of Indian Affairs, an office that had been created on March 11 that year by secretary of war John C. Calhoun. McKenney wrote several important books about the American West, including three folio volumes of Indian portraits he produced in conjunction with James Hall under the title A *History of the Indian Tribes of North America, with Biographical Sketches and Anecdotes of the Principal Chiefs.*

94. Pronunciation of Katice is Kuh-TEESE.

95. On the morning after the massacre of the Foxes, the body of Chief Pamoske was further degraded by the Sioux: a metal hook on one end of a rope was stuck in his mouth, as if he were a fish that had been caught, and the other end was tied around his neck. The rope was then attached at its midpoint to a horse, and the chief's body was dragged all the way into Prairie du Chien for the Sioux victory celebration, which was witnessed and described in full by Elizabeth Therese Baird, daughter of one of Prairie du Chien's primary American pioneers, Henry Monroe Fisher.

96. The bill in question referred to the Sacs and Foxes *only*, excluding from its provisions any of those tribes previously covered in treaties.

97. Traders Farnham and Davenport may have coached the Indians on what to ask for in this portion of the negotiations. Certainly the two traders were themselves eager to see such a deal

consummated, and when it appeared to be falling through, they even agreed to settle the Indian debt owed them for a flat forty thousand dollars, but Clark and his commissioners would have no part of it.

98. His full name was Felix de Hault de Lassus et de Luziere, of Bouchain in Hainault, which was in the north of France. The older man, last of a long line of gentlemen in his family who had held governmental office of the highest importance and trust, was a Knight of the Grand Cross of the Royal Order of St. Michael at the time he had been forced to leave France during the so-called Reign of Terror, and that was when he had come to North America with his family and settled in Spanish territory. His eldest son eventually became Governor de Lassus of Upper Louisiana, and the brother of the governor, Jacques St. Vrain, was an officer in the French Navy as well as the father of two sons, Ceran and Felix.

99. Marie St. Vrain was the former Marie Pauline Gregoire, daughter of Charles Cyril Gregoire of France.

100. Thomas Forsyth was extremely upset at being fired and never got over his bitterness at being so summarily discharged without any direct reason ever being given to him for the action. So exalted was his opinion of himself that he often claimed in later years that the Black Hawk War would never have taken place had he remained in office. A year and a half after his discharge, when the Black Hawk War was just breaking out, Forsyth had written about the matter to the U.S. representative from Missouri, William H. Ashley, as follows:

St. Louis May 8th, 1832

Dear Sir You know that I have always been at a loss to know why I was removed from Office, and what were the charges alleged against me and from what source those charges came, but I have lately had some light thrown on that subject. I have always had good reasons to believe that Genl. Clark was inimical to me, but I was much asstonished [sic] *when I heard the nature of the Charges which it is said he made against me at Washington. There is a Major Campble* [sic] *United States agent for the lead mines at Fever River, he informed a friend of mine sometime ago at Galena, that it was currently reported at Washington City, that G[eneral] Clark had Charged me with being friendly and holding communication with the British in Canada, that I sent letters by Indians visiting there or in short that I was a Traitor to the United States, and that this was the cause of my dismissal. Major C—— asked my friend if I could have acted thus. My friend told him that it was the most outrageous and unfounded charge that was ever made by one man against another. Now my good Sir is this not too grievous to be borne, you have known me for the last twenty years, you know also the services I rendered during the last war* [the War of 1812], *you were on the frontier at this place, we frequently met at Genl. Howards, you had an opportunity of knowing every thing that was going on then. I appeal to you if those charges are not most outrageous, unjust and untrue. It is hard that I should suffer under such calumnies. Justice to myself demands that I should know if such charges were made against me by Genl Clark. Therefore, would you be good enough and endeavor to find out wether* [sic] *what Major Campbel* [sic] *told my friend is true, or put me on some track to ascertaining, by so doing you will confer a favour on an injured man, could I get any proof that G[eneral] Clark has made those charges aginst* [sic] *me, I will publish it with some more of his foul deeds to the world. It is stated that the Indian disturbances this year and last will cost the Government between 2 & 300,000 dollars, all of this enormous expense might have been saved and the Indians living quietly on their lands had G[eneral] Clark taken my advise* [sic] *according to my letter to him dated April 30th 1830* [a letter in which Forsyth advocated to Clark a show of military force at Rock Island, which he claimed might encourage the British Band to leave Saukenuk], *he never answered my letter, therefore my advise* [sic] *was not heeded. Conscious Sir of having done my duty to my country, of having risqued* [sic] *my life to relieve the defenceless* [sic] *frontier from Savage Massacre during the war, and of always endeavouring to sustain the character of an honest man, those things are extremely* [sic] *mortifying to my feelings, to relieve my feelings and vindicate my reputation, which is as dear to any man as life, I hope will be a sufficient apology for obtruding myself upon your notice. I should be much pleased to hear from you, should you have any leisure from the arduous duties which you must have to attend to.*

I am &c T.F.
General William H. Ashley
PERSONAL
H. Representatives, Washington City

101. The first Chicago River bridge was built at what became the Randolph Street crossing. The platting was done by civil engineer James Thompson, and the legal location was Section 9, Township 39, Range 14. The individual lots were being sold at from ten to sixty dollars apiece.

102. This road ran from Prairie du Chien to present Portage, Wisconsin, on the north side of the Wisconsin River, essentially along the trace of present State Route 60 to Prairie du Sac in Sauk County and then continuing along the north side of the river on State Route 78 to directly across the river from present Portage in Columbia County.

103. Because of the unusually poor grammar, spelling, and punctuation in the original of the petition, the author has taken the liberty of cleaning it up for readability's sake, though no change in context has been made.

104. The injured man referred to was Loudon L. Case, but it later turned out that he had been injured in an altercation with Winnebago Indians from Wabokieshiek's village, not far from the Prophet's Town.

105. At this time the agent was, of course, Felix St. Vrain, and the commanding officer of Fort Armstrong on Rock Island was Captain John Bliss, who was commanding Company D and Company H of the U.S. Third Infantry.

106. In order of signing, the petitioners were: John Wells, Bengamen [sic] F. Pike, Henry Mc knel [sic], Albert Wells, Griffith Aubrey, Thomas Gardner, Joshua Vandruff, Samuel Vandruff, John S. Bain, Horace Cook, David B. Hale, Joel Thompson, Joel Wells Ju [sic], John W. Spencer, Joseph Danforth, Wm. T. Brashar, Jonah H. Case, Charles H. Case, Samuel Wells, Charle [sic] French, Benjamin Goble, Gentry McGee, Jno. Barrell, Wm. Henry, Aratus Kent, Levi Wells, Joel Wells, Michael Bartlit [sic], Huntington Wells, Thomas Davis, Thomas Levitt, William H. sams [sic], Charles French, Uri [sic] S. Hults, Eri [sic] Wells, Asaph Wells, George V. Miller, Edwad [sic] Varner.

107. A native of Culpeper County, Virginia, Edmund Pendleton Gaines had entered the United States Army as a lieutenant at the age of eighteen in 1795. Although he left the army on "extended leave" for several years and practiced law in the Mississippi Territory, he returned to military service and in 1807 was promoted to the rank of captain. President Madison, in 1811, appointed him major of infantry. During the War of 1812 he was seriously wounded while defending Fort Erie, and the gallantry of his actions there resulted in his being promoted to brigadier general with a major general's brevet. In 1817 he had served under General Andrew Jackson in the campaign against the Creek and Seminole Indians, and in 1821 was himself placed in charge of the Army's Western Department.

108. At this time companies of the U.S. 1st Infantry were in garrison at Fort Crawford in Prairie du Chien under command of Colonel Willoughby Morgan.

109. The pronunciation of Kinnekonesaut is Kin-ee-KON-ee-SAWT; it has often been spelled Akiniconisot.

110. The treaties referred to by General Gaines were those that were consummated on November 3, 1804; May 13, 1816; and August 19, 1825; but he did not fully quote the second article in question. When the War of 1812 ended, the United States engaged in an exchange of lands with the Potawatomies, giving them a portion of land between the Rock River and the Mississippi River, which had been ceded by the Sac and Fox in 1804, and getting as the United States' part of the exchange certain property in the area of Chicago. By 1825 the Indian population within the ceded area was largely Winnebago, and in the second article of the treaty that year, the Sac and Fox (though not Black Hawk and other concerned members of the tribe) relinquished what claims they had to land east of the Mississippi River "to the tribes interested therein," but not, as Gaines implied here, to the United States. The question of legality of the transactions in all three of those treaties has always been in contention.

111. General Gaines here uses the same questionable logic in the option he gives the Indians, that since they cannot stay on the land that has been sold by the United States, they *must* go west of the Mississippi, conveniently bypassing the fact that the greater portion of the so-called ceded land east of the Mississippi was still unsold and unoccupied by whites, thus making it still land that the Sac and Fox had every right to live and hunt upon by the terms of the very treaty the Americans kept throwing up to them.

112. The second treaty, consummated on May 13, 1816, was nothing more than a simple peace treaty that was negotiated between the United States and the Sac and Fox at the close of the War of 1812, and it involved no additional annuities for these Indians.

113. Gaines here refers to a sum of one thousand dollars granted by the Treaty of November 3, 1804, another one thousand dollars granted by the Treaty of August 4, 1824, for the cession of lands of Missouri, and a final six thousand dollars for the Sac and Fox portion of the strip of neutral ground across Iowa that was ceded by them and the Sioux in the Treaty of July 15, 1830.

114. The pronunciation of Cheetochena is Chee-TOTCH-en-nuh; while that of Quiltohame is Quill-toe-HOM-me.

115. Henry Gratiot had been appointed subagent to the Rock River Winnebagoes three months before, on March 7. At the moment, he was still using his home at the settlement called Gratiot's Grove — present Gratiot, Wisconsin — as his headquarters, but the location where the agency was ultimately established was on the east side of Sugar Creek — now the Sugar River — on Winnebago land in the Michigan Territory. It was six to eight miles from White Breast's village and the same distance from where the Sugar River emptied into the Pecatonica River.

116. Thomas C. Legate, a native of Massachusetts, was commissioned second lieutenant in the U.S. Third Artillery in 1812. He was discharged in 1815 but then reinstated a few months later. In 1821 he transferred to the U.S. Second Artillery and subsequently became assigned to the Ordnance Department as superintendent of the lead mines at Galena, a position he continued to hold until his resignation in 1836, after which he made his home in Galena as a civilian.

117. The two chiefs who died during this mission were Ioway and Namoett; the survivor was Kinnekonesaut. This Chief Ioway who died on the trip is sometimes confused with the second Chief Ioway — possibly a son of the first — who became seventh chief of Black Hawk's band when it was formally organized on April 20, 1832 [q.v.].

118. John Jacob Astor's Columbia River fur headquarters, Astoria, at present Astoria, Oregon, had been captured by the British.

119. The Treaty of July 15, 1830.

120. The "Red Banks" was more often, and more properly, called the "Lower Yellow Banks," and was located at the site of present Oquawka, Henderson County, Illinois.

121. The reference here is to Fox chief Pamoske, slain along with seventeen others near Prairie du Chien while en route to the peace conference there, as earlier chronicled.

122. The skipper of the *Winnebago* was a civilian resident of Galena named Captain P. Hunt.

123. The "slough" Lieutenant McCall refers to here and elsewhere in his letters is evidently not only an abundance of small, low, grassy islands through which the steamboat had to wend its way in its passage, but primarily a low, marshy shoreline area located on the Illinois side of the river downstream from the mouth of the Rock River to opposite present Muscatine, Iowa. The *Winnebago* had, under General Gaines's orders soon taken up a regular patrol back and forth through the sloughs rather than be allowed to become vulnerable by lying very long at anchor in any one place.

124. The "point of concentration" Lieutenant McCall refers to here was where General Gaines had a small blockhouse constructed on the site of what is presently the little town of Andalusia, four miles downstream from the mouth of the Rock River.

125. At this time, Saukenuk's lodges were mainly concentrated near the Rock River shoreline, but the town was still very large and covered an extensive area, so there were lodges, wigwams, and houses here and there adjacent to and within the cornfields that followed the slope of the land upward east of the trail (and roughly on the same line as present Ninth Street) from the Rock River to Fort Armstrong. Ravines had eroded at various places in the rise in the ground eastward from Ninth Street, as well as the bluff presently called Black Hawk's Watch Tower. In essence, Saukenuk was on a sort of "step" of the land, with the terrain west of the village a prairie that gently dropped to the bank of the Mississippi and the terrain east of the village becoming a continuous slope rising gently from the prairie, and it was on this gentle slope that the majority of the Sac cornfields were located.

126. The site of this rendezvous was approximately one hundred miles upstream on the Illinois River from its mouth at the Mississippi, in present Cass County at the site of present Beardstown.

127. The personnel involved in these military matters were as follows: The First Regiment's staff officers were Col. James D. Henry, Lt. Col. Jacob Fry, Maj. John T. Stuart, Adj. Thomas

Collins, Qtrmstr. Edward Jones, and Paymaster Thomas M. Neale, while the commanders of the regiment's seven companies were Captains Thomas Carlin, William F. Elkin, John Lorton, Achilles Morris, Samuel Pierce [sometimes spelled Pearce], Adam Smith, and Samuel Smith. The Second Regiment's staff officers included Col. Daniel Lieb, Maj. Nathaniel Butler, and Qtrmstr. William Jordan, while the seven company commanders were Captains George Bristow, William Gillham, John Haines, Hiram Kincaid, Henry Mathews, William Weatherford, and Alexander Wells. The staff officers of the Spy Battalion were Maj. Samuel Whiteside, Adj. Samuel F. Kendle, Qtrmstr. John S. Greathouse, Paymaster P. H. Winchester, and Armorer John F. Gillham, with the four company commanders being Captains William Miller, Solomon Preuitt, Erastus Wheeler, and William B. Whiteside. Staff officers of the Odd Battalion were Maj. Nathaniel Buckmaster, Adj. James Semple, Qtrmstr. David Wright (with Qtrmstr. Sgt. John H. Blackwell), Paymaster Joseph Gillespie, Surgeon Charles Higbee (Surgeon's Mate Richard Roman), and Armorer John Krupp. The three company commanders were Captains John Loraine, Solomon Miller, and William Moore.

128. The "hidden place" that Black Hawk mentioned was a natural basin close to the river but hidden from view of passersby on the water. It was located twelve miles downstream from Rock Island, almost exactly midway between the present communities of Buffalo and Montpelier in the southwestern corner of present Scott County, Iowa.

129. In the letter-writing style of this period, the term *ultimo* refers to the preceding month, *instant* refers to the current month, and *proximo* refers to the upcoming month. Duncan's Illinois militia force, shown here by McCall as being composed of fifteen hundred mounted men, was actually sixteen hundred men.

130. The route taken by the Illinois militia from the rendezvous at Beardstown to Rock Island was essentially as follows: approximately on the path of present U.S. 67 from Beardstown to Rushville to Macomb to Monmouth. From there the route took them almost due northwest across Cedar Fork to Little York, then north across Henderson River on approximately the trace of State Route 94 to Aledo. The route followed an Indian trail from there, crossing Edwards River at a place called Army Ford, about 2.5 miles southeast of present Millersburg, then north by north-northeast to Andalusia on the Mississippi River bank just southwest of the mouth of Rock River.

131. Marching from Fort Armstrong were the regulars under First Lieutenant John W. Spencer and the volunteer ranger company under Captain Benjamin F. Pike. They marched south toward Saukenuk along the course now followed by Ninth Street and then turned east at what is now about Thirty-first Avenue, following this course to the top of the bluff, at which point they again turned south in the direction of Black Hawk's Watch Tower.

132. General Gaines was later the object of some extremely sharp criticism, evidently to some degree justified, from the militia for the indiscriminate and frightful use of artillery directed in a perilous manner toward the Illinois troops, and for a general sense of confusion that prevailed in both militia and regular troop movements. The trail followed by the militia approaching from the south crossed the Rock River's south channel at present Milan to Vandruff's Island. The trail traversed the lower end of the island to another ford that crossed the main channel of Rock River near where the present railroad bridge and U.S. 67 cross over. High water, however, forced the volunteers to cross at another ford that was located farther upstream a half mile, near the eastern end of Vandruff's Island.

133. It is important to point out what great significance was entailed among the Sac and Fox by possession of a grizzly bear claw necklace. Such necklaces were generally made of the enormous yellow-striped claws of the grizzly, along with pieces of river otter fur. There were two versions of the necklace, the more common of which was composed of claws whose base had been perforated for stringing on a piece of strong rawhide thong, around which, between the claws, was wrapped in spiral manner an otter fur that had been cut into strips. Each of the bear claws then had a second perforation made in it at about its midway point, through which it was strung again with a strong rawhide thong, and then threaded on this thong between each of the claws, to keep them apart, was a large glass bead, usually blue. Hanging down from the back of the necklace, very often with the tip of the tail nearly touching the ground, was a complete prime otter skin, finely tanned to great suppleness and with the fur side out. Attached at intervals to both the claw necklace and the skin were wampum medallions, into which were woven intricate and very significant symbols. The second type of grizzly bear necklace was

essentially like the first except that the strips of otter skin separating the claws were not wrapped in spiral fashion, but rather in lengthwise segments that were sewn together on the underside. This was usually done when fewer claws were on the necklace than in the former case. In either version, anywhere from a minimum of twenty to a maximum of forty grizzly bear claws were used to make a necklace. Such a necklace was one of the most prized possessions in the Sac and Fox culture, because it was far more than merely a beautiful and impressive ornamentation; the difficulty involved in getting the claws — they were *never* an item of trade — was what made them so significant and so valuable. There were only two ways in which such a necklace could be procured, and both were exceptionally dangerous. In the first, the warrior journeyed westward through enemy territory to where the bears lived, risking capture by hostile Indians, then finding and killing a bear, often only with a spear and knife, and removing its claws to bring home with him to be strung into a necklace there. The second method was every bit as dangerous as the first, perhaps even more so. The warrior had to slip into enemy Indian territory, usually in the territory of the fierce Cheyennes, Arapahoes, Rees, Blackfeet, Crows, or Dakotah Sioux, locate an Indian who was wearing such a necklace (which in itself indicated that that warrior was uncommonly brave and skilled), and then kill that warrior in hand-to-hand combat and take the necklace from him or die in the attempt. Obviously, then, owning a grizzly bear claw necklace was a mark of incredible prestige among the Sac and Fox tribes, as well as others.

134.   The Indian signers of the treaty, exactly as spelled and in the order of their signing, as well as the witnesses who signed after them, are as follows:

SAC CHIEFS
Pash-e-pa-ho — Stabbing Chief — his X mark
Washut — Sturgeon Head — his X mark
Cha-kee-pax-he-pa-ho — Little Stabbing Chief — his X mark
Chik-a-ka-la-ko — Turtle Shell — his X mark
Pem-e-see — The One That Flies — his X mark

SAC WARRIORS AND BRAVES
Ma-ca-la-mich-i-ca-tak — The Black Hawk — his X mark
Men-a-con — The Seed — his X mark
Ka-ke-ka-ma — All Fish — his X mark
Nee-peek — Water — his X mark
A-sam-e-saw — One That Flies Too Fast — his X mark
Pan-see-na-nee — Man Who Pounces — his X mark
Wa-wap-o-la-sa — White Walker — his X mark
Wa-pa-qunt — White Hare — his X mark
Ke-o-sa-tah — Walker — his X mark

FOX CHIEFS
Wa-pa-la — The Prince — his X mark
Kee-tee-see — The Eagle — his X mark
Pa-we-sheek — One Who Sifts Through — his X mark
Na-mee — One Who Has Gone — his X mark

FOX BRAVES AND WARRIORS
Al-lo-tah — Morgan — his X mark
Ka-ka-kew — The Crow — his X mark
She-she-qua-nas — Little Gourd — his X mark
Koe-ko-skee — One Who Knows — his X mark
Ta-ko-na — The Prisoner — his X mark
Na-kis-ka-wa — One Who Meets — his X mark
Pa-ma-ke-tah — One Who Waits — his X mark
To-po-kia — Night — his X mark
Mo-lan-sat — Made Hairless One — his X mark
Ka-ka-me-ka-peo — Sits in Grease — his X mark

WITNESSES
Joseph M. Street, U.S. Indian Agent at Prairie du Chien
W. Morgan, Colonel 1st Infantry
J. Bliss, Brevet Major 1st Infantry
Geo. A. McCall, aid-de-camp [sic] to Maj.-Gen. Gaines
Sam'l Whiteside
Felix St. Vrain, Indian Agent
John S. Greathouse
M. K. Alexander
A. S. West
Antoine LeClaire, Interpreter
Jos. Danforth
Dan S. Witter
Benj. F. Pike

135. The Jumping Fish (Quashquame) and the Stabbing Chief (Pashepaho), though Sac chiefs through heredity, had lost their chieftainship and leadership voices in the tribe, for the most part as a punishment for having signed the treaty of 1804, which had caused the majority of the Sac and Fox problems afterward. They were still called chiefs and still had some leadership duties, but in a very limited capacity.

136. McCall became a little confused here and combined the name of the Indian agent, Felix St. Vrain, with that of the Indian interpreter, Antoine LeClaire.

137. Reynolds here refers, of course, to Prophet's Town, the village of the Winnebago half-blood, Wabokieshiek.

138. At first it was reported that twenty-three of the Menominees had been killed, but this figure was increased later by the death of some of those who were wounded. At the September 5 council at Fort Armstrong, the correct number of twenty-six was given.

139. There is some confusion in regard to exactly who the settlers were who were at the William Davis settlement at this time, but the records do show that among them were Mr. and Mrs. John H. Henderson and children; Mr. and Mrs. Allen Howard and family; Emery George (shown as Henry George in some accounts); Robert Norris; Mr. and Mrs. William Petticrew and small child and babe in arms; Mr. and Mrs. William Hall and family (including wife, Jane Rebecca, daughters Elizabeth, eight, Rachel, fifteen, and Sylvia, seventeen, and sons John W., twenty-three, Edward, twenty-one, and Greenbury, nineteen); Mr. and Mrs. William Davis and family (nine members, including wife, Martha, sons William Jr., Alexander, and Jimmie and daughter Temperance Cutwright and three other children).

140. The Potawatomi village known as Meau-eus Town (pronounced MO-ee-yus Town) was located on the north bank of Big Indian Creek approximately four miles southeast of present Earlville, La Salle County, Illinois.

141. Chaubenee — whose name means the Coalburner — was once the righthand man of Tecumseh, during the period of Tecumseh's rise to power and right up to the time of Tecumseh's death at the Battle of the Thames in Ontario in 1813. (For details of Chaubenee's career and his important connection with Tecumseh and afterward, see The Winning of America Series volumes entitled *The Frontiersmen* and *Gateway to Empire*.) Following that, and in accordance to directions he had previously received from Tecumseh, Chaubenee had espoused the cause of the Americans among his own tribesmen and other tribes, saying that it was inevitable that the Americans should prevail and that it was only by working *with* them that the Potawatomies (or other tribes) could salvage anything of their culture, dignity, and possessions. As a result, he had become a great favorite of the Americans and often acted as liaison between the whites and the tribes. He had moved his village site numerous times in the past. Once, prior to the War of 1812, it had been located within the present city limits of Chicago, along the South Branch of the Chicago River six miles above Wolf Point, where North and South branches joined. Another Chaubenee village site, just after that war, was located on the Vermilion River a few miles above its mouth at the Illinois River only a bit over three miles south of present La Salle, Illinois. Yet another village site of his was established on the site of present Paw Paw in present Lee County, Illinois, and though this site was eventually aban-

doned as a town site, Chaubenee retained his claim on the land and was eventually granted this land by the whites for his services to them (see below). However, the site of his village at this time — a village the whites called Shabbona's Town — was approximately twenty river miles upstream on Big Indian Creek from the site of Meau-eus Town, just southeast of the site of present Shabbona Grove, De Kalb County, Illinois, at the point where the Chicago & Northwestern Railroad bridge spans the creek. Chaubenee (pronounced Shaw-BEE-nee and ultimately adulterated phonetically to Shabbona by the whites) at this time owned (see Note no. 75) two sections of land on the upper waters of one of the tributaries of Big Indian Creek, seven straight-line miles southwest of Shabbona Grove, at the site of present Paw Paw in southeastern Lee County, Illinois.

142. Pukemus is pronounced Poo-KEE-muss.

143. This reference to the Chippewas did not mean the Chippewas were part of the confederation planning to attack the Sac and Fox Indians, since that involved only the Sioux and Menominees. However, for many years tensions had been strong between the Menominees and the Chippewas, to the north of them. Fearful of being attacked from the rear by the Chippewas if they concentrated on the southward attack against the Sacs, the Menominees negated this possibility by making a peace with the Chippewas.

144. The differentiation between the Mississippi River Sacs and the Missouri Sacs should be clarified here: a splinter group known as the Sac of the Missouri at this time numbered about six hundred individuals and had maintained a generally separate identity from the rest of the tribe since their separation from it during the War of 1812, at which time Clark had encouraged them to leave the Mississippi Valley and settle on the Little Moniteau River in Missouri, where they were provided for by the U.S. factor, John W. Johnson. But not very long ago the Rock River Sacs raised a threat against the agency, which resulted in Johnson returning to St. Louis and many of the Missouri Sacs returning to the Rock River region. So few Missouri Sacs remained there at the time of this invitation to make war that the refusal was of little consequence.

145. Many historical accounts state that Black Hawk's party that crossed the Mississippi River on April 5 was composed of about two thousand individuals, but a close examination of the number who died or were killed or captured during the campaign and afterward more closely supports the figure of around one thousand. Atkinson reported there were about five hundred warriors of the Sac and Fox, plus contingents of Kickapoos and Winnebagoes. Former Sac and Fox subagent John Connolly estimated the number of men and boys as four hundred, while Thomas Forsyth, who was probably most familiar with the actual size of the tribe, estimated the number of Sac and Fox warriors as being 368, plus about one hundred Kickapoo warriors. His Sac and Fox estimate seems very close to the mark, but the Kickapoo estimate, based on the twelve lodges of Kickapoos that joined Black Hawk, seems a bit high, and half that number is more likely.

146. The Four Lakes, as the region was called at this time, was the site of present Madison, Wisconsin. The four lakes themselves, often simply called First, Second, Third, and Fourth lakes are, respectively, the present lakes named Kegonsa, Waubesa, Monona, and Mendota, all of them connected by the Yahara River or, as it was called at this time, the River of the Four Lakes, which empties into the Rock River just below the town of Fulton in Rock County, Wisconsin. The capital city is situated on the strip of land between Monona and Mendota.

147. The river referred to by the whites at this time as Sycamore Creek (or River) was the present South Branch of the Kishwaukee River, which empties into the Rock River just over seven miles downstream on Rock River from the center of present Rockford, Winnebago County, Illinois, and three miles west of New Milford, Illinois, as well as seven miles upstream from the mouth of present Stillman's Creek. [See also Note no. 183.]

148. This crossing of the Mississippi River by Black Hawk's band took place close to the mouth of the Iowa River on the west bank and in the area called the Upper Yellowbanks on the east side, near the site of present New Boston in Mercer County, Illinois.

149. Companies E, C, and K, under Major Bennet Riley, commander of the 6th Regiment, were assigned to the steamship *Enterprise*. Companies I, D, and G, under Captain Zalmon C. Palmer, were assigned to the *Chieftain*.

150. A shako was a stiff military hat with a narrow brim in front, a high crown, a metal insignia plate in front enclosed by braid, and topped by a stiffly upright plume.

151. The April 10, 1832, *Missouri Republican* in St. Louis carried the following brief notice: *The 6th Regiment, U.S. Infantry, under Brig. General Henry Atkinson left Jefferson Barracks on Sunday, April 8, in the steamboats Enterprise and Chieftain. Eighteen other officers are in the party and they include Bvt. Maj. Bennet Riley; Capts. Zalmon C. Palmer, Henry Smith, Thomas Noel, Jason Rogers, and George C. Hutter; Lts. Asa Richardson, Joseph Van Swearingen, Albert Sidney Johnston (assistant adjutant general), Joseph Donaldson Searight, Nathaniel Jackson Eaton (acting commissary of subsistence), Thomas Ludwell Alexander (adjutant of detachment), Thomas Jefferson Royster, John Suthpin Van Derveer, James Seymour Williams, and Washington Wheelwright (ordnance officer); Surgeon William Carr Lane; and Maj. Thomas Wright (paymaster).*

152. The two steamboats did not arrive at Rock Island at the same time, as some accounts have claimed. Nor was General Atkinson aboard the *Chieftain* when he arrived, even though this is what is portrayed in some accounts. According to Atkinson's adjutant, Lieutenant Albert Johnston, the commanding general arrived at Rock Island aboard the *Enterprise* at midnight on April 12.

153. The reference is to Colonel Willoughby Morgan of the 1st Infantry, a native of Virginia, who had been stationed at Fort Crawford at Prairie du Chien for sixteen years until his sudden death from acute gastroenteritis just nine days before this council. He was commanding officer of Fort Crawford at the time of his death. General Atkinson had received a letter from the adjutant of the 1st Infantry, John J. Abercrombie, dated April 4 at Fort Crawford, which said, in part: *Genl. I was directed yesterday by Colonel Morgan to write to you, & request you send to this post an asst. Surgeon to assist Doctr. Beaumont in his duties; in consequence of his very feeble state of health nearly the whole of the Doctors time was engrossed by himself. The necessity however no longer exists — with deep regret I must now announce the painful intelligence of the Col's Death! He departed this life about half after eight O'clock this morning. . . .*

154. The pronunciation of Pankeene is PAHN-key-nay.

155. The pronunciation of Natauetaheka is Nuh-TAW-et-tuh-HEE-kuh.

156. Apenose is pronounced APP-puh-knoss. Taimah is pronounced TY-muh. The Fox village of Taimah at Flint Hill is the site of present Burlington, Iowa.

157. General Atkinson made an error here. The crossing was at the *Upper* Yellowbanks, which was located at present New Boston, rather than at Yellow Banks, which was eighteen miles farther downriver on the Mississippi at present Oquawka.

158. Why Atkinson chose to deliberately state he had not detained any of the chiefs when, in fact, he had done just that, is not clear. It may be that his intention was to remove any restraints on them once the runner was well on his way to Morgan's village. If so, he did not follow through with that intention.

159. A third tavern license was issued for three dollars to one Russell E. Heacock, who lived outside the Chicago town limits some five miles up the South Branch of the Chicago River and called his place Heacock Point. The property was located at Section 32, Township 39, Range 14 (a couple of blocks south of present Cermak Road and about midway between Halsted and Ashland avenues), and the license allowed Heacock to keep a tavern at his residence.

160. For sake of example, some of the price controls set were as follows: a pint of wine, rum, or brandy was to be sold for thirty-seven and a half cents. (At this time the U.S. issue of dimes and half-dimes was not in circulation, and so computation of all price amounts less than one dollar was on the basis of the Spanish coin valued at twelve and a half cents, known as the York Shilling in New York or the Nine Pence in New England.) Each pint of gin was to be sold for thirty-one and a quarter cents, each pint of whiskey for eighteen and a quarter cents, and each pint of cider or beer for six and a quarter cents. Lodging per individual per night was twelve and a half cents, with an additional charge of the same amount for each breakfast or supper consumed, and dinner cost set at thirty-seven and a half cents. A horse could be fed for twenty-five cents and kept overnight for fifty cents.

161. The original Laughton store was situated at the place that had long been called Hardscrabble; a second store or trading post, combined with a tavern, was operated later by the Laughton brothers in the present Chicago suburb of Riverside.

162. At the next sitting of the commissioners, the individual appointed to serve as first official ferryman for Chicago was Mark Beaubien.

163. Mawgehset — Big Foot — a volatile and domineering chief, had been so named because his right foot was half again as large as his left, due to a congenital defect.

164. The commanding officer of Fort Winnebago was Lieutenant Colonel Enos Cutler of the 5th Infantry, but he was absent at this time and throughout all of the Black Hawk War, and Captain Joseph Plympton had been left temporarily in charge.

165. This is the same Zachary Taylor who subsequently, due to his gallant services as a U.S. Army general, became president of the United States.

166. Kakekukanuck is pronounced Kay-kee-KOOK-uh-nuk. Wameykay is pronounced Wah-MAY-kay. Poyekakanumeta is pronounced Poh-ye-KAY-kah-new-MAY-tuh.

167. Kauraykawsawkaw is pronounced Kaw-RAKE-uh-SAW-kaw. The name has also been spelled Kawraywawsaw.

168. White Crow's town, most often called the Turtle Village, was located on the site of present Beloit, Wisconsin.

169. Whirling Thunder's name in the Winnebago tongue was Waukaunweekaw, pronounced Waw-KAWN-we-kaw. Spotted Arm's name was Manaketchumpkau, pronounced Man-uh-KEE-tshump-kaw. The Liar's Winnebago name was Pashetowart, pronounced PASH-she-toe-wort.

170. Pronunciations include Pamisseu as Pah-MISS-soo, Weesheet as WEE-eh-sheet, Choke-pashepaho as CHO-kee-PASH-uh-puh-ho, Pamaho as PAM-uh-ho, and Towaunonne as TO-wuh-NUN-nee.

171. Pronunciations include Menakau as MEN-uh-cow, Makatauauquat as Mack-uh-TAW-aw-kwat, and Kinnekonesaut as KIN-nee-CONE-nee-sawt.

172. Isaiah Stillman was born in Massachusetts in 1792 and had come to Sangamon County, Illinois, when he was thirty-two years old. In 1830 he moved to Fulton County and became a merchant in the town of Canton, as well as colonel of the 32nd (Fulton County) Regiment of the State Militia. He became Fulton County treasurer in 1831 and on October 15 of that year was elected brigadier general of the 5th Brigade, 1st Division, Illinois Militia, although his commission was not actually issued until January 10, 1833. Pursuant to Governor Reynolds's order of April 16, 1832, Stillman had recruited to his battalion the companies of David W. Barnes and Asel F. Ball of Fulton County, as well as that of Captain Abner Eads of Peoria County, and was currently protectively ranging the countryside eastward from the Mississippi River.

173. The *"damage on the Frontier"* of which Reynolds speaks was at this time merely the damage incurred through abandonment of farms by settlers.

174. George Cubbage is believed to have been a New Jersey man who came to Gratiot's Grove in 1830 or earlier. He established the first school in Scales Mound Township of Jo Daviess County. Catherine Myott was one of two half-breed children sired by the former Winnebago Indian agent at Prairie du Chien, Nicholas Boilvin, who had died in 1827 following sixteen years of being agent to the Winnebagoes. Her brother, Nicholas, had been raised more as an Indian than a white and was presently a Winnebago tribesman in good standing. There were evidently some other siblings, but their identity is clouded, and Catherine Myott had virtually no contact with them. Catherine, who was not yet twenty at this time, was the widow of a white settler about whom very little is known. She was often used as an interpreter by various agents and subagents because of her fluency in both English and the Winnebago tongue.

175. Pachenoi is pronounced PASH-uh-noy. Wacomme is pronounced WOK-uh-mee.

176. Lake Koshkonong in the southwest corner of Jefferson County, Wisconsin. The name Koshkonong means The-Lake-We-Live-On.

177. Lieutenant (soon Major) Thomas J. Beall of the 1st Infantry.

178. Dixon here refers to Prophet's Town, which was located approximately twenty-seven river miles downstream on the Rock from Dixon's Ferry.

179. White Crow's reference to the Red Head meant Indian supervisor William Clark, who had been a commissioner for both the treaties negotiated with the Winnebagoes at Prairie du Chien — in 1825 and in 1830. Although they signed the treaty of August 19, 1825, they did not attend the treaty of July 15, 1830. Still, they were present at the negotiations at this latter treaty and had signed an earlier document (July 10 — but never ratified by Congress) in which they pledged themselves to "a firm and lasting peace" and reaffirmed the provisions of the treaty of 1825, to which they had put their hands.

180. By calling Henry Gratiot their "second father," White Crow was merely pointing out that they were aware that he was the subagent and not the top Winnebago agent, who was, of course, John H. Kinzie, at Fort Winnebago.

181. Less than a year before — on October 15, 1831 — Henry Gratiot had petitioned William Clark to have the Winnebago annuity paid to the tribe in their own country instead of at Fort Winnebago, where unscrupulous traders and liquor dealers were handy at bilking the Indians out of what they had received in return for whiskey that was often watered down as much as twenty to one.

182. The campsite for the army at the end of the first day's march was in present Schuyler County, Illinois, about four miles north of Rushville and just under five miles southeast of present Littleton, and about the same distance west-southwest of the present town of Ray.

183. A great deal of confusion exists in today's historical accounts as to exactly where Black Hawk held his two councils with the Potawatomies in relation to where Isaiah Stillman made his camp. Some have placed those councils at the confluence of the present South Branch of the Kishwaukee River (then known as Sycamore Creek) and the North Branch of the Kishwaukee River, approximately two miles south and just a little west of the present town of Cherry Valley. Some have located the site at the point of land two miles due west of present Morristown, where present Killbuck Creek empties into the Kishwaukee. Neither of those locations is correct. The actual site was on the south bank of the Kishwaukee River at its mouth, right where it empties into the Rock River, this location in present Winnebago County, Illinois (close to the Ogle County border), being almost exactly five miles north-northeast of where Stillman's force camped on the evening of May 14, 1832, on the north side of the present Least River at the site of the present town of Stillman Valley in Ogle County, Illinois.

184. Waubansee at this time still maintained the same village he had since before the War of 1812, located a few hundred yards up the Fox River from the site of present Fox River Grove in McHenry County, Illinois, but this was his summer village now. His winter village, which he and his people were occupying at this time — and on the verge of leaving in favor of the summer village about fifty miles north — was on the point of land where the Fox River emptied into the Illinois River directly across the mouth of the Fox River from present Ottawa, Illinois, where his people had a close and friendly relationship with the white residents of Ottawa. His elder brother Black Partridge, however, had moved his village several times since its location had been at Wolf Point in the Chicago area, where the North and South branches of the Chicago River converged. His present village was located near the site of the present city of Sycamore in DeKalb County, Illinois; actually, 2.6 miles northwest of Sycamore at the point where present South Branch splits, going upstream southwardly to DeKalb and southeastwardly to the north side of Sycamore.

185. The log bridge had been built at a cost of $486.20, and two hundred dollars of that amount had been paid by the Potawatomies for the right to take advantage of the easier access to town that it would give for the many Indian villagers living to the west.

186. Bids had been taken for construction of the Estray Pen, and the lowest bid made was twenty dollars. However, only twelve dollars was ever paid, because the construction had not been completed according to what was called for in the contract.

187. When Billy Caldwell, the well-liked and highly respected half-breed who was also known as Sauganash, learned of the establishment of this school, he was very impressed and pleased. His own early schooling in the Detroit area had given him a great advantage over Indian youths his age at that time, and so he gave public notice in all the Indian villages within a half-day's drive that he would buy the books and clothing and pay the tuition of all Indian children who would attend the school, provided they would put aside their native garb and dress like the white children. There was, unfortunately, not one acceptance of his generous offer.

188. In addition to the Chicago Militia officers, Captain Gholson Kercheval, First Lieutenant George W. Dole, and Second Lieutenant John S. C. Hogan, the remaining thirty-seven who signed up were, in order of signing, Richard J. Hamilton, Jesse B. Brown, Isaac Harmon, Samuel Miller, John F. Herndon, Benjamin Harris, S. T. Gage, Rufus Brown, Jeremiah Smith, Herman S. Bond, William Smith, Isaac D. Harmon, Joseph Laframboise, Henry Boucha, Claude LaFramboise, J. W. Zarley, David Wade, William Bond, Samuel Ellis, Jeddiah [sic] Woolley, George H. Walker, A. W. Taylor, James Kinzie, David Pemeton, James Ginsday, Samuel Debaif, John Wellmaker, William H. Adams, James T. Osborne, E. D.

Harmon, Charles Moselle, Francis Labaque, Michael Ouilmette, Christopher Shedaker, David McKee, Ezra Bond, and Robert Thompson.

189. This was Colonel John W. Scott, whom Atkinson was returning to Reynolds with his letter. Scott had been staying at Rock Island ever since arriving there with Governor Reynolds's letter to Atkinson of April 22.

190. Colonel Dodge's volunteer force of some fifty men from the mining district had as its captain James H. Gentry. Colonel Dodge's own son, Henry L. Dodge, had been elected the company's first lieutenant, while a son-in-law of Dodge, Paschal Bequette, was second lieutenant. Charles Bracken was aide-de-camp to Colonel Dodge. William S. Hamilton, a settler in the mining district, was the son of Alexander Hamilton, who had been killed in a duel with Aaron Burr twenty-eight years earlier. Louis Ouilmette was a scion of the noted Antoine Ouilmette family of the Chicago area, from whom the present suburb of Wilmette got its name.

191. The stream then known by the name of Old Man's Creek has been mistakenly identified as present Kyte River or Least River, but this is incorrect. Old Man's Creek, which is known today as Stillman's Creek, sometimes called Stillman's Run, empties into the Rock River just over twelve miles farther upstream than Kyte River, which empties into Rock River at present Daysville, which is nineteen river miles upstream from present Dixon. Stillman's Creek empties into Rock River from the east, just one mile upstream from the present town of Byron, which is on the opposite side of the river. This, of course, was still eight miles downstream — five straight-line miles — from the mouth of the Kishwaukee, where Black Hawk's people had been encamped and where the Indian councils were held.

192. There are three significant series of rapids on the Rock River; the first located three to four miles above the mouth and immediately below the site of Saukenuk; the second some twelve to fifteen miles below Dixon, between present Sterling and Rock Falls; the third just below the mouth of the Pecatonica River near the present village of Rockton.

193. The creek Stillman's force had just crossed was, indeed, the stream known at that time as Old Man's Creek and presently as Stillman's Creek. Their crossing of it was at the site of the present village of Stillman Valley.

194. Weetcho is pronounced We-ETCH-oh. He is believed to have been the son of Ioway, seventh of the nine chiefs of Black Hawk's band.

195. Makashenasa is pronounced Mack-uh-SHEN-ah-suh.

196. Sagano — meaning He-Walks-Straight-Ahead — is pronounced SAH-guh-no.

197. This grove of trees where the detachment had made its camp ultimately came to be known as White Rock Grove.

198. It may be significant that it was later this year when the United States Army abolished its traditional daily liquor ration for soldiers.

199. Menekuk — meaning He-Who-Cries-Loud — is pronounced MEE-nuh-kuk.

200. In his autobiography, Black Hawk, concerning this action, says that he and his men were, at this point, ready to die to avenge their fellows, and that ". . . *I gave another yell, and ordered my brave warriors to* charge *upon them* — *expecting that we would all be killed! They did* charge! *Every man rushed and fired.* . . ."

201. There is reasonable evidence to suggest that the man killed in the creek area by Makashenasa after being pinned by his fallen horse was Gideon Munson, a government scout.

202. There is probably no battle or skirmish in the annals of American military action in which a greater variety of versions have been told than in the matter of this action, which became known as Stillman's Defeat or Stillman's Run. The ignominy of what occurred so deeply filled the survivors with shame for their cowardice that practically everyone involved made up a different story to tell to justify the precipitate flight of the eight companies of militia rangers. The very variety of the stories is what defeats them and bears evidence to their falsity, for few coincide in practically any respect. Some accounts have the attacking force of Indians very heavily armed and numbering over eight hundred warriors. Within four days of the incident, most residents of the Illinois River Valley had been convinced through the accounts of survivors who showed up amongst them that the attacking force of Indians numbered two thousand bloodthirsty warriors, and to prove that, it was allegedly later discovered that ". . . *the trees where we were encamped were found to contain six to ten bullets each.*" Quite a few accounts emphasize all out of proportion the ambush, if so it can be termed, of the twenty horsemen who chased the five Indians and killed and scalped two of them. (Some accounts,

perhaps rightfully, place the commander of the commissary, Samuel Hackleton of Lewiston, Fulton county, as the leader of that chase.) Only a few of the accounts admit to the murder of one of the trio of Sacs in the initial peace delegation. A large number of the accounts bring close scrutiny to the matter of the whiskey drunk by the militiamen prior to the action, by the fervent denials that it had anything to do with the matter. Some accounts flatly state there was no drinking whatever, others that there was some, yet others that there was a great deal but that it did not really affect those who imbibed. One account says there was one barrel, but it contained only two gallons of whiskey. The fact remains that the report of the commissar prior to the detachment's departure from Dixon's shows that a full barrel of whiskey (thirty gallons) was included in the ratio of one full keg per each of the six commissary wagons. This is, surprisingly, corroborated to a degree by Black Hawk himself in his autobiography, in which, while describing the things his people found in the abandoned camp of the whites, he states: ". . . We found, also, a variety of saddle-bags (which I distributed among my braves), and a small quantity of whiskey, and some little barrels that had contained this bad medicine, but they were empty. . . ." Many accounts appeared weeks and months after the skirmish in newspapers as eyewitness accounts from the survivors, virtually all of which made every effort to justify the panic-induced horror that the fleeing militiamen experienced. Quite a few state that once the attack began, the other two Sacs who made up the initial white-flag deputation were executed while being held captive, evidently mixing this fanciful story with the actual death of the two who were killed from the party of five being pursued at the beginning of the action. Identification of Thomas Reed as the slayer of Sagano is accurate. In the spirit of imputing heroism to their leaders, one account (in the Sangamo Journal, Springfield, Illinois, June 14, 1832) states that Stillman was personally attacked simultaneously by six Indians, that his sword was torn from his side, that he fought them off and shot two of them (the implication being shot them dead) with his pistols, and that ". . . he leaped upon a spirited horse and escaped." Only those last eight words seem to have any semblance of truth. One final brief example of the need to create or embellish heroism occurs in regard to the death of Corporal Bird Ellis, who, while mortally wounded, managed to ride his horse just over two miles from the scene before falling from his horse in death. His was the last body recovered, and because it was so far from the others, the heroic story quickly appeared, as follows: Young Ellis, who was but a boy in years, was able to crawl two and a half miles south of the battlefield, where his body was found beside a strapping Indian, who had demanded his life, though it was then ebbing away. In this enfeebled condition he fought and killed his antagonist, sinking into death soon after. Ellis was found with his head partly cut off, embraced by the dead Indian. The young man had been tomahawked, and the Indian shot through the body. It is clear that the young man, after shooting the Indian, had no longer the means of defence, and that the Indian had strength enough left to tomahawk him, but in the act of cutting off his head, died, thus embracing his enemy in the last convulsive gasp of life. Ellis was buried on the spot, now the farm of Mr. A. C. Brown. Since there were only three Indian casualties and this was not one of them, the fancy of the story is exposed. The actual casualties for both sides in this skirmish were:

• Three Sac Indians killed, which were Sagano of the peace delegation and the two warriors (unidentified by name) downed from the party of five observers.
• Five militiamen wounded, including 1st Lieutenant Edward Shane and Private Adam Vancil, both of Captain Eads's company; Privates John Brumfield and John Perry, both of Captain Japhet Ball's company; and Private Jesse Dickey of Captain James Johnson's company.
• Eleven militiamen killed, including Privates Tyrus M. Childs and Joseph B. Farris and Corporal Bird W. Ellis, all of Captain David Barnes's company; Privates Isaac Perkins and David Kreeps, and Captain John G. Adams, all of Adams's company (see also Note no. 205); Private Joseph Draper of Captain Merritt Covell's company; Corporal James Milton of Captain James Johnson's company; Sergeant John Walters of Captain Asel Ball's company; and Private James Doty of Captain Abner Eads's company.
• One Government Scout killed: Gideon Munson.

203. Most accounts say the members of Stillman's detachment began arriving at Dixon's about 3:00 A.M., although Private A. H. Maxfield, first to arrive, always claimed he got there at 2:30 A.M. It took more than twenty-four hours before the last of those who were to return got in.

204. The Hennepin mentioned here by Governor Reynolds is the same as the present city of Hennepin, Putnam County seat, located on the left bank of the Illinois River seventy-five river miles downstream from present Joliet, Illinois, and forty-five river miles upstream from present Peoria, Illinois.

205. The two who had been beheaded and the skulls then skinned were Captain John G. Adams and Private Isaac Perkins of his company. (Captain Adams's wife, upon being informed of her husband's fate, lost her sanity and never recovered.)

206. Of the forty-one men still missing at this point, only one — Corporal Bird W. Ellis — had been killed by the Indians, and his remains were not discovered for several more days. The other forty represented those who, in their panic, fled directly south, skirting Dixon's and continuing without pause to the Illinois River towns with their grim news.

207. An example of how the Indian allies of the United States were provided for is given in the memorandum of George Boyd at Green Bay, agent of the Menominee Indians, to fellow agent Samuel C. Stambaugh:

Requisition for Military Stores and Subsistance [sic] *for the 200 Menominees called into the field under the orders and at the instance of General Atkinson — viz Green Bay, July 23d 1832 —*
110 Stands of Arms of all descriptions
250 lbs of Powder, 125 Rifle, 125 Common
600 lbs of Lead — 400 lbs furnished by the Garrison
200 lbs Buck-Shot furnished by the Garrison [Ft. Howard]
1000 flints
50 Fire Steels
150 Awls
100 Dressed Deer Skins
100 pieces of Deer's sinew
10 lbs of Candles
300 Needles
2 Tin Lanterns
300 Skeins of Coarse Thread
50 lbs of Soap
50 Scalping Knives — & 25 Tomhawks [sic]
150 lbs of Tobacco
20 lbs of Vermillion [sic]
25 yds of White muslin
25 yds of Red muslin
20 yds Blue ribbands [sic] for Chiefs medals
20 two gallon Tin-Kettles
3 Frying Pans
10 Knives & Forks
10 Tin Cups
10 Plates
2 Tea-kettles
2 Tea Pots
5 lbs of Tea
10 lbs good Sugar
50 lbs maple sugar
40 Bags of Coarse Linen
15 Wood Axes

Subsistence &c —
60 Bushels of white flint Corn — not in Store in Garrison
2 Barrels of Flour
1 Barrel of Hard Bread
1 Barrel of Fresh Bread
2 Barrels of Pork
1 Bushel of Salt

5000 lbs of fresh Beef, to be driven on the Hoof from the Grand Kakaulin 20 miles from the Bay, on the line of march of the expedition.

One Barge to transport Commissariat Stores, which I should be glad Capt: Clarke would furnish from his command together with the above list of Provisions.

. . . *To Colo. S. C. Stambaugh Comg the Menomonie [sic] Expedition Present.*

G. Boyd U.S. Ind Agent

208. Chaubenee's two sons and a nephew who aided him on their famous rides to warn the American settlers and peaceful Indians of the outbreak of hostilities were Pypegee, Shata, and Pypes. Chaubenee concentrated his efforts in the valley of Indian Creek and the north side of the Illinois River from Morris downstream to La Salle. His son Pypegee concentrated on the settlements and isolated cabins located in the Big Bureau Creek and Little Vermilion Creek valleys. His son Shata, who was chief of his own little village on the edge of the Big Wood [see Note no. 210], was responsible for the settlements and villages along the Des Plaines, Du Page, and Fox rivers west and southwest of Chicago to the Illinois River. Chaubenee's nephew, Pypes, covered the area from the mouth of the Kankakee River downstream on the south side of the Illinois River to Peru and then upstream (southeast) on the Vermilion River to the area of present Streator, all the way to the village of Potawatomi chief Rochelle, where he remained two days because he was enamored of the chief's daughter, Nunuquaya.

209. The lake in question is present Crystal Lake in McHenry County, Illinois.

210. The Big Wood was well known to the whites of the Chicago area as a place where travelers had sometimes disappeared, never to be seen again. The superstitious blamed evil spirits or other dimensions; the more logical blamed renegade whites, murderous Indians, fugitive criminals, ordinary bandits, or a combination of these. In any event, the Big Wood, which lay entirely within what is present Kane County, Illinois, some thirty-five miles just slightly north of due west of present downtown Chicago, was studiously avoided by most residents of the area. Ranging from two to five miles wide, it began at the present northern edge of the city of Elgin and followed the west side of the Fox River southward for about ten miles to near the site of the present town of St. Charles.

211. The location of this rest stop was on the site of present Janesville in Rock County, Wisconsin.

212. Yaharaseepe means River-of-the-Four-Lakes and is the present Yahara River. The names of the four lakes remain the same today, and it is on the land between the two upper lakes, Monona and Mendota, where the present capital of Wisconsin, Madison, was founded in 1837.

213. This island no longer exists, having been eroded away by floodwaters of the Rock and Bark rivers over the years. At that time, however, it was located a short distance downstream from the mouth of the Bark River, near the site of present Fort Atkinson in Jefferson County, Wisconsin.

214. The settlement established by the brothers John and Joseph Naper and others thirty-two miles west and a little south of Chicago was at the site of present Naperville in Du Page County, Illinois.

215. The youngest son of Chaubenee, Shata, pronounced SHAY-tuh, was born about 1805. His name, which has also variously been reported as Shatee, Shaytee, and Sha-atee, meant Wolf's Tail. His village was located at this time along the Fox River at the northeastern edge of present St. Charles, in Kane County, Illinois. Shata's older brother, Pypegee, was about five years his senior.

216. Present city of Riverside, in Cook County, Illinois. Both Laughton brothers died in 1834.

217. Hollenbeck's Grove had been on the site of the present town of Millbrook, Kendall County, Illinois.

218. Kaurayneta was pronounced Kaw-ray-NEE-tuh, which means Crow Feather.

219. The village of Spotted Arm was located in present Madison, Dane County, Wisconsin, adjacent to the present Shorewood Hills area, on the headland projecting into Lake Mendota, on the site where the University of Wisconsin campus is now located.

220. Juliette Kinzie, in her book, WAU-BUN [see Bibliography], which relates many of the occurrences at this time, was extremely fearful when her husband, John Kinzie, who had just learned of the war breaking out, announced he was leaving to council with the Winnebagoes. The "we" she uses below refers to herself and her brother, Arthur, who was visiting Fort

Winnebago from Kentucky. She wrote: "*In vain we pleaded and remonstrated against such an exposure. 'It was his duty to assemble and talk to them,' my husband said, 'and he must run the risk if there were any. He had perfect confidence in the Winnebagoes. The enemy, by all he could learn, were now far distant from the Four Lakes — probably at Kosh-ko-nong. He would set off early in the morning with Paquette, hold his council, and return to us the same evening.' It were useless to attempt to describe our feelings during that long and dreary day. When night arrived, the cry of a drunken Indian, or even the barking of a dog, would fill our hearts with terror. As we sat, at a late hour, at the open window, listening to every sound, with what joy did we at length distinguish the tramp of horses — we knew it to be Griffin and Jerry* [the horses were so named] *ascending the hill, and a cheerful shout soon announced that all was well. They had ridden seventy miles that day, besides holding a long 'talk' with the Indians.*"

221. Buffalo Grove was located at the site of present Polo in Ogle County, Illinois.

222. The organization of the 5th Regiment was as follows: Colonel, James Johnson; Lieutenant Colonel, Isaiah Stillman; Major, David Bailey; Adjutant, James W. Crain; Quartermaster, Hugh Woodrow; Paymaster, David C. Alexander; Surgeon, Samuel Pillsbury; Sergeant Major, Daniel McCall; Quartermaster Sergeant, Joshua C. Morgan.

223. William Selby Harney had entered the U.S. Army in 1818 and in 1825 had been appointed captain of the 1st Infantry. He later gained recognition for his valor during the Mexican War and in the wars against the Sioux in the Great Plains. He eventually became commander of the Western Department of the Army and retired as brevet major general in 1863. He finally died at eighty-nine in 1889. Jefferson Davis, born in Kentucky and taken to Mississippi as an infant, also served in the Mexican War. He became a member of the U.S. House of Representatives and later, United States senator from Mississippi. He was eventually chosen by the provisional congress as president of the Confederacy and inaugurated at Richmond, Virginia, on February 22, 1862. After the Civil War he was indicted for treason, imprisoned, and subsequently released on bond. Oddly enough, he died at the age of eighty-one the same year as Harney — 1889 — at his estate, Beauvoir, on the Gulf of Mexico near Biloxi, Mississippi. It is interesting to note that at this little frontier settlement of Dixon's Ferry at this time there were two future presidents of the United States — Captain Abraham Lincoln and Colonel Zachary Taylor — and the future president of the Confederacy — Lieutenant Jefferson Davis.

224. The principal forts being erected in the lead mining district of southwestern Wisconsin were as follows: Fort Union at Dodgeville; Mound Fort (or Blue Mounds Fort) at Blue Mounds; Fort Hamilton at William Hamilton's diggings (now Wiota); Fort Jackson at Mineral Point; Parish's Fort at Wingville; Fort Defiance on the farm of Daniel Parkinson, five miles southeast of Mineral Point; and forts officially unnamed at Gratiot's Grove, Cassville, White Oak Springs, Diamond Grove, Platteville, Shullsburg, New Diggings, the home of George Wallace Jones near Sinsinawa Mound; the farm of Justus De Seelhorst at Elk Grove, and the home of Benjamin Funk at Monticello.

225. There is now a monument at the site of the Indian Creek Massacre, honoring the fifteen victims who died at the hands of the Indians on May 20, 1832.

226. This unusual practice during the Black Hawk War of the Indians removing the genitals of their victims — an act rarely noticed before this time — seems to have had its impetus from a fable widely circulated and generally believed by the members of the British Band of the Sacs before and during the war. The origin of the practice was explained to William Clark by the Fox chief Taimah and the Sac chief Apenose after the Black Hawk War in this manner:

Father — we were told that the Americans were determined shortly to lay hands on all our males, both old and young, and deprive them of those parts which are said to be essential to courage; then a horde of Negro men were to be brought from the South, to whom our wives, sisters and daughters were to be given, for the purpose of raising a stock of slaves to supply the demand in this country, where Negroes are scarce. We assure you, Father, that this, and many other similar stories have had a great influence on the minds of all, or at least of most, of that unfortunate band which now seems abandoned from heaven and humanity. For the evidence of this fact, I refer you to the enthusiastic madness with which our women urged their husbands to this desperate resort; and, secondly, influenced by a belief of the above fables, they have uniformly treated the dead bodies of the unfortunate white men who have fallen into their hands with the same indignities which they themselves so much dreaded.

227. The only other Indian of this party positively identified was a Winnebago warrior named Wapanoset.

228. So far as can be ascertained, Aaron and Adam Payne were no kin to Christopher Payne of Naperville, who was a member of Captain Brown's Company, which arrived here at this time.

229. One of the multitude of embroidered stories of this period concerned the death of Adam Payne. Its account stated that after leaving Holderman's, ". . . he was awakened from a reverie by shots fired from a foe concealed in a clump of underbrush. One ball entered his shoulder and another inflicted a wound, which soon proved mortal, in the body of his beautiful mare. Realizing that no time was to be lost in garrulous appeals for sympathy and that the only possible chance for escape lay in the old-fashioned way of flight, he pricked his mare forward and for five miles maintained a safe distance ahead of his three pursuers on ponies. But the effect of the mare's wound was now apparent. She staggered and fell dead under her rider. The three pursuers quickly came upon him and leveled their guns, while he simply raised his hands to Heaven and appealed for mercy. The appeal was heeded by two of them, but, so we are told by one of the party, who subsequently moved west, the third pulled his trigger and fired and Mr. Payne dropped dead. If two of these fiends had been so humane in lowering their weapons it is remarkable that they should all have joined in severing the head from the body, as they did. A long black beard flowed from the victim's chin, and by this one of the party seized the head, threw it over his shoulder and together the three returned to camp." [The Black Hawk War, by Frank E. Stevens, pp. 167–158]

230. As nearly as can be determined, the first part of their ride, which ended near midnight, had taken the Hall girls northward along an Indian trail that probably came close to the present Illinois towns of Baker, Leland, Victor, and Waterman, just north of which the rest stop was made. The second part of the ride, from perhaps around 2:00 A.M. until 1:00–2:00 P.M., probably passed through or came close to the sites of the present towns of Elva, Malta, Esmond, and Fairdale, perhaps stopping about five miles north of there, just west of South Owens Creek in present northwestern De Kalb County.

231. This day's travel had carried the Hall girls generally north-northwestward, crossing the Kishwaukee River a mile or two east of present New Milford and meeting the Rock River at just about the center of present Rockford, Illinois. They continued upriver along the Indian path, approximately through present Loves Park, North Park, and Roscoe, and their stopping place was apparently somewhere close to the site of present South Beloit, Illinois, virtually on the Illinois-Wisconsin border and probably no more than a mile or so from the village of the Winnebago war chief White Crow — Kawraykawsawkaw — the Turtle Village, as it was called.

232. Benjamin Mills appears to have been cut from the same cloth as Strode. He had been living in mortal fear of the Indians eventually descending upon Galena and wiping it out, and he had no intention of being on hand when that happened. He volunteered with untoward eagerness to carry the dispatch from Strode to the secretary of war. This behavior did not go unnoticed, and when Mills became a candidate for Congress in 1834, many broadside attacks were launched against him for his precipitate haste to get away from Galena during the war. [See also Note no. 246.]

233. It is likely that such a letter to the president was never written. Certainly it was never received and no account is had of it, nor any identification as to who was supposed to have carried it.

234. Strode was evidently the only person ever to dignify Stillman's Defeat by calling it the Kishwaukee Battle.

235. No one has ever questioned why the men of this detail, when fired upon, chose to retreat fifty miles to Galena, rather than safely circling this area at a distance and reaching the army at Dixon's Ferry, only twelve miles distant.

236. Plum River Fort — a small, stockaded cabin — was located on the Mississippi at the mouth of Plum River, site of present Savanna, Carroll County, Illinois.

237. Toagra's full name was Toagranaukooraykaw — pronounced Toe-AH-grah-nau-KOO-ray-kaw, for which no translation has been found. Nausaunay's full name was Nausaunayhekaw — pronounced Naw-SAW-nay-HEE-kaw — and meant Sitting Chief.

238. The three men who escaped — Thomas Kenney, Aquilla Floyd, and Alexander Higginbotham — continued on their way toward Galena, but once again they were cut off by Indians and had to flee. They managed to escape and had just crossed Rush Creek at a place

approximately 3.5 miles northwest of present Elmo, Illinois, when again they saw more Indians. They backtracked, recrossed Rush Creek, and then headed south to Plum Creek. They spent the next two nights hiding in a thicket there, occasionally seeing Indians as they peered out. Finally, they made their dash for Galena and arrived there safely on May 27.

239. A monument was erected on the site of this attack at Kellogg's Grove. It is located in Kent Township, Stephenson County, Illinois, about a mile and a quarter northwest of the town of Kent, almost on the location where the Chicago & North Western Railroad enters Jo Daviess County.

240. Many accounts list this village site as being the village of White Crow. Some have called it Whirling Thunder's village, and a few have named it Little Priest's village. It was, in fact, the village of Spotted Arm. White Crow's village was the Turtle Village at the site of present Beloit, Wisconsin. Whirling Thunder's village was located across Lake Mendota from Spotted Arm's, at the head of the lake, close to where the Yahara River enters — an especially attractive village containing some six hundred lodges. Little Priest's village was located about two miles north of present Monticello, Wisconsin, close to the present community of Exeter.

241. John Marsh, a native of Massachusetts and Harvard graduate, was at this time thirty-three years old. He had an unusually colorful career. Employed at Fort Snelling (Minneapolis, Minnesota) as a tutor for the officers' children, he studied medicine under the fort surgeon. In 1824 he was given a temporary position at the St. Peters Indian Agency there, where he became an expert in the Dakotah Sioux tongue, compiling a dictionary of the Sioux language, and a skilled interpreter for the Sioux. The following year he was appointed by Michigan Territory governor Lewis Cass as subagent at Prairie du Chien, but earned the enmity of agent Joseph Street because in early April 1830 he provided information to the Sioux that a party of Fox Indians was expected in Prairie du Chien, which he had learned from Captain Wynkoop Warner. This resulted in the April 5 massacre of the Fox party by the Sioux, and though Warner took most of the public blame, there were those — Joseph Street among them — who contended that Marsh was responsible. Street had for some time been pressing for Marsh to be fired, in part because of his private trading ventures, his too-close attachment to the Sioux, and his liaison with a half-Sioux woman. Marsh was fired later that year. In 1832, to remove his family from a possible revenge slaying, he took his wife and six-year-old son, Charles, to live in New Salem, Illinois (where they became friends of Abraham Lincoln), while Marsh himself continued to live at Red Cedar with his Sioux half-breed. After the Black Hawk War, in which Marsh led his party of Sioux, he was charged with illegal sale of arms to the Indians, but fled before he could be arrested and became a trader in Independence, Missouri. About 1835 he moved to Santa Fe, New Mexico, and from there to California, where he practiced medicine and also became a successful cattle rancher. Shortly after a dramatic reunion with his son in 1856, he was finally murdered by three of his disgruntled employees.

242. The scalps that were found were not, as Whiteside presumed them to be, the scalps of the victims of the Indian Creek massacre. They were, in fact, old scalps taken during the period 1812–1829.

243. There was great outrage among the populace of Ottawa when Colonel Johnson, Lieutenant Colonel Stillman, Major Bailey, and their respective men elected to build the fort on the south side of the Illinois River opposite their town rather than adjacent to the town itself on the north side of the river. Imprecations of cowardice had little effect. The new fort, which Colonel Johnson named Fort Johnson after himself, was built on the south bank, and the inhabitants of Ottawa were told that if danger threatened and they wanted its protection, they could cross the river in boats and take shelter within, although there were not boats enough to move the population across in less than two or three days. Then, even while the fort was under construction, the majority of Johnson's regiment deserted and went home.

244. The blockhouse being erected on the south bank of the Illinois River at the foot of the Illinois Rapids was located at the mouth of the Vermilion River opposite present La Salle, Illinois. It was named Fort Deposit by Major Reddick Horn, who established it, but quickly became better known as Fort Wilbourn after Captain John S. Wilbourn of the Morgan County Militia.

245. The news Harriet Buckmaster wanted to pass on to her husband in person was that she was pregnant with their first child.

246. Benjamin Mills, a native of Massachusetts, moved to Bond County, Illinois, in 1819. Two years later he had been elected county judge and from 1823 to 1829 was registrar of the U.S.

Land Office at Vandalia, Illinois. Practicing law in Galena at the time of the Black Hawk War, he was elected in this year of 1832 to the Illinois House of Representatives, despite a considerable outcry against his seeming cowardice during that affair. He served as chairman of the House Impeachment Committee in the first Illinois impeachment trial in 1833, that of Supreme Court Justice Theophilus W. Smith. His political career ended in 1834, when he was defeated as candidate for the U.S. Congress. Not long after that he returned to Massachusetts, where he died in 1841.

247. The forty-two-year-old Joshua Pilcher, a native of Culpeper County, Virginia, had moved to Kentucky with his family when he was twenty years old, in 1810. He moved on by himself to St. Louis in 1815, at which time he entered the mercantile business and fur trade. Though he applied for a permanent Indian-agent position at the Rock Island Agency later in 1832, the appointment was not made. The following year he became an employee of the American Fur Company at Council Bluffs, where he soon became subagent to the Sioux. He became agent to the Sioux, Cheyenne, and Ponca tribes in 1837. On William Clark's death in 1838, he was appointed superintendent of Indian affairs until 1841. He died in 1843.

248. Some months after the Black Hawk War ended, Toquamee and Comee were arrested for the Indian Creek massacre. According to Frank E. Stevens in his book *The Black Hawk War* (Chicago, 1903), pp. 157–158: "*To-qua-mee and Co-mee, who were indicted for complicity in the murders, were brought to bar for the crime, but by reason of the uncertainty of the times and judges to try them, the first term of court passed with nothing done except to admit the culprits to bail on the bond of Shab-bo-na [Chaubenee], Shem-e-non, Snock-wine [Senachwine], Sha-a-toe, Mee-au-mese [Meau-eus] and Sash-au-quash, chiefs and head men of the Pottowatomie [sic] nation. Before the next term of court could be held the tribe had been removed west of the Mississippi, wither went the two defendants. When needed for trial they were sought by Sheriff George E. Walker, who alone journeyed into the Indian country. He gathered together the several chiefs, according to custom, who decided the two must return, which they did, with no effort or inclination to escape. This conduct, together with the lavish use of paint, rendered recognition almost impossible by the Hall girls, who were the chief witnesses for the State, and procured their acquittal by the jury.*

249. The Door Prairie was located four miles west of present La Porte, Indiana.

250. The Blue Mounds settlement was the closest of the lead mining camps of the whites to the villages of the Winnebagoes. It was located just a little over twenty miles west and slightly south of Spotted Arm's village — the site of present Madison, Wisconsin. One of the buildings there had been fortified over the past couple of months and was called Blue Mounds Fort (or, in some accounts, Fort Blue Mounds), and was situated a mile and a half south of the present community of East Blue Mounds. Eight miles west of the Blue Mounds Fort was Morrison's Grove, also known as Porter's Grove, located a mile north of present Ridgeway, in Iowa County, Wisconsin, adjacent to where the old Stagecoach Stop historical marker is located.

251. At this time the present Bark River was called by a variety of names, both Indian and English, including Meconi, Meekasipe, White River, Whitewater River, and Clearwater River. Reference in this account will be limited to Bark River, to avoid confusion.

252. Sylvia and Rachel Hall were unexpectedly reunited at Gratiot's Grove, where they were taken by Henry Gratiot, with two of their uncles who were in the militia, though the names of these two men were evidently not recorded. The girls were then taken to White Oak Springs, ten miles from Galena, where they had a more joyful reunion with their brother John W. Hall, who they thought had been killed in the massacre. He took them to Galena, where they stayed with family friends a few days. The three then went downstream by steamboat to St. Louis, where they remained for a week as guests in the mansion of Indian superintendent William Clark. They then took the steamboat to Beardstown on the Illinois River, where they remained with another uncle, Scott Horn. The two girls eventually married, Sylvia to William S. Horn and Rachel to William Munson. Both women lived very long lives.

253. This chief's principal name was Waucon Decorah, but he was most often called simply Decorah. His village, one of the largest among the Winnebago tribe, was located at what was then called Crosse Prairie, which is the site of present LaCrosse, Wisconsin. Decorah's name was probably derived from that of his grandfather, a French army officer named Sabrevoir DeCarrie, who married the daughter of a Winnebago chief. Decorah was known by a number of different names (see below) and often confused in historical works with his father, Old

Decorah (Chowpostkawkaw or Chahpostkawkaw), and his two brothers, Washington Decorah and Kowekosa — Snakeskin — who, because of a disfigurement was far better known as One-Eyed Decorah. He was the son of Chahpostkawkaw and a cousin of Chief Konoka, with whom he is also sometimes confused. Among other names Waucon Decorah was known by are Big Canoe, Big Boat, Grand Canoe, the One-Eye, Watshhatakaw, Watchhattykau, Watchkatoque, and Waudgkhatakan.

254. The first night's camp by Captain Iles's company was just a little south and east of the present town of Sublette in Lee County, Illinois.

255. The bodies were found just south of Kellogg's Grove. That of St. Vrain, identified by his brother-in-law, George W. Jones, had the head missing, and it was never found. Neither were the hands and feet, which had also been severed. Jones took charge of St. Vrain's papers that were found in a packet, and also his pocketbook. His coat, a bullet hole through its blood-stained collar, was found a considerable distance away, where it had evidently been dropped by one of the Indians. On January 6, 1834, the United States Congress passed a bill for the relief of the widow and heirs of Felix St. Vrain. The remains of Hale were identified by his son and son-in-law, who also recovered his blood-covered purse, in which there was thirty dollars cash that the Indians, in their haste to get away, had not taken. The body of Hawley was never found.

256. The community of Apple River, also called Apple River Fort during the Black Hawk War, was located at the site of the present town of Elizabeth, in Jo Daviess County, Illinois.

257. Actually, Atkinson had written five letters to the commanding general, Major General Alexander Macomb. These letters were written on May 10, 23, 25, and 30. The letter of May 10 had reached Washington in five days. The letter of May 23 was lost. The letters of May 25 and 30 were received on the same date, June 15, three days after John Robb's heated letter was written and mailed.

258. The river headwaters Keokuk mentioned — Nichnabatona, Nondowa, and Au Boyer — are, respectively, the present Nich Na Ba Tona River, the Nodaway River, and the Boyer River, all located in western Iowa.

259. Toogranau is pronounced TOOG-ray-naw. Koonay is pronounced KOO-nay.

260. Chaetar is pronounced CHAY-et-tar. Some accounts state that Black Hawk was being guided on this raid by Chaetar and One-Eyed Decorah, but the latter was definitely not one of the guides and was, in fact, a guide to Colonel Henry Dodge at this time.

261. The Spafford farm was located just about a mile and a half west of the site of present South Wayne in Lafayette County, Wisconsin.

262. The rifle called the U.S. Yaeger of 1832 was a variation of the German Yaeger, a hunting rifle. Though a flintlock rifle, the U.S. Yaeger was a forerunner of the 1841 Harper's Ferry rifle, which became commonly known as the Kentucky Rifle.

263. Hunkquat, pronounced HUNK-kwat, was a common shortening of his full name, which was Hunkquattshak Keereekaw — HUNK-kwat-chak KEE-ree-kaw. Wauzeeree, pronounced WAW-zeer-ee, was the common shortening of his full name, which was Wauzee-reekaykeeweekaw — WAW-zeer-ee-kay-KEE-wee-kaw.

264. Aubrey is believed to have suffered a fatal heart attack brought on by his wounds, exertions, and terror.

265. One of the many stories that sprang up around this incident was that while Blue Mounds Fort was being built, a Winnebago Indian known only as Thick Lips rode up to the Aubrey cabin, some distance from which William Griffith Aubrey — who was known as Griffith to his friends — was in the field planting corn. When Aubrey's wife came to the door, Thick Lips allegedly told her that soon she would have to do the corn planting, since the Indians were going to kill her husband. Mrs. Aubrey merely laughed and ridiculed him, according to the story, and Thick Lips went away very angry.

266. Colonel Dodge and Private Woodbridge, in their correspondence, reported that five men had been buried, but the number was actually four. They were including Francis Spencer, who was considered dead even though his body had not been found. Extensive searching for his body was undertaken during the following week, but it was not found, and the presumption of death was solidified. There was great amazement and joy when, nine days after the attack on the Spafford party, a weak and bedraggled Francis Spencer broke from hiding and rushed toward a group of scouts. Spencer's story, published as an article in *The Galenian* of June 27, told how,

when he split away from the Spafford group, which was under attack, he ran to a ravine, followed it up some distance, and then scrambled into hiding beneath some brush under the overhanging bank. One of the following Indians came very close to him but did not discover him, and as soon as the Indian was gone, he moved away to some more distant bushes and concealed himself there. Thoroughly frightened, he remained in that hiding place for three days. He finally emerged and made his way toward Ft. Hamilton, and when he got within view of it, he saw Indians around it. Actually, these were the Menominees that Colonel Hamilton had brought from Prairie du Chien to help fight the Sacs, but Spencer, not knowing this and believing them to be the enemy, went back into hiding, eating berries, roots, frogs, and crayfish to sustain himself for the next six days, until he spied the scouting party from a distance and ran to them.

267. The twenty-nine men who accompanied Colonel Dodge in pursuit of the Indians are identified as completely as possible as follows: Lt. Paschal Bequette, Pvt. Samuel Black, Lt. Charles Bracken, Pvt. Samuel Bunts, Pvt. William Carnes, Pvt. _____ Devies (or Devees), Pvt. Asa Duncan, Pvt. Matthew G. Fitch, Capt. James H. Gentry, Pvt. Alexander Higginbotham, Dr. Allen Hill, Pvt. John Hood, Pvt. Thomas Jenkins, Pvt. Richard H. Kirkpatrick, Pvt. Benjamin Lawhead, Pvt. Levin Leach, Pvt. Dominick McGraw, Pvt. John Messersmith, Jr., Pvt. F. Montaville Morris, Lt. Daniel M. Parkinson, Pvt. Peter Parkinson, Jr., Pvt. Samuel Patrick, Pvt. _____ Porter, Pvt. Thomas H. Price, Pvt. _____ Rankin, Pvt. H. S. Townsend, Pvt. Van Waggoner, Pvt. Samuel Wells, and Pvt. W. W. Woodbridge.

268. In some accounts it has been stated that the Sac war party was led by the Winnebago chief Little Priest, who was killed at the scene, but this is not true. Little Priest, in fact, was one of the signers of the treaty that was made between the Indians and whites shortly after the war ended. The site of the Battle of the Pecatonica (or Battle of Horseshoe Bend) was about one mile west by northwest of the present town of Woodford, Lafayette County, Wisconsin, on the site of present Black Hawk Memorial County Park.

269. Some accounts state there were thirteen Indians in the party, and some say seventeen. The correct number is eleven. The story of a French trapper the next winter finding three more Indian bodies beneath brushwood where they had allegedly crawled after being wounded is without foundation.

270. Private Samuel Black was taken into the care of his friend, Private Peter Parkinson, who transported the injured man to Fort Defiance, where the Parkinson family had forted up. For a few days after the battle they had hopes he would recover. Upon hearing that an eminent surgeon from Galena, Dr. Addison Philleo, was at Fort Hamilton, young Parkinson mounted his horse and went there. He brought Dr. Philleo back with him, but when the surgeon examined Black's wound, he shook his head and declared that there was no hope for him, that the skull bone had been so badly fractured by the lead ball that he would probably die in the next few days, possibly within the next twenty-four hours. The second night after that — ten days after the battle — Parkinson was watching at Black's side at about midnight when Black stirred, and Parkinson saw Black's lips take on a smile that spread until it became audible laughter. Parkinson leaned over and put his face close to Black's and said, "Why are you laughing, Sam?" Black opened his eyes and, still chuckling, replied, "Well, Peter, I was just laughing at the idea of Colonel Dodge saying he would charge them sword in hand and wanted everyone else to follow him in the same way, when there were only two swords in the whole crowd of us." These were his last words. He closed his eyes and died, the third fatality of the whites in the Battle of the Pecatonica.

271. The Hodges cabin was located about on the site of present Dover, in Bureau County, Illinois.

272. The area of the thicket where the party of Sacs took refuge was a short distance northeast of the large grove of timber known then as Waddam's Grove. A town of that name is presently at that site. The isolated thicket lay in the midst of an extensive prairie about three miles east of Waddam's Grove on the road leading to present McConnell, both in Stephenson County, Illinois.

273. In some accounts this private's name has been given as George Eames, but in later accounts the correction to Charles Eames was made by the dead man's relatives, N. B. Craig and Hiram B. Hunt.

274. On June 20, Colonel James Strode left Galena leading the companies of Captains Stephenson and Craig, went to the site where they located the bodies, and buried them along the trail

between present Waddam's Grove and McConnell. Fifty-four years later, in 1886, the bodies of the three Americans killed in this skirmish were disinterred, removed to the Kellogg's Grove Monument, and reburied there. In respect to Strode's party finding the remains of only one Indian, Stephenson, recuperating from his flesh wound, stated that the retreating Indians had undoubtedly carried their other dead away with them.

275. A copy of the adjutant general's Order No. 51, assigning various military units to General Winfield Scott for the purpose of putting a speedy end to the Black Hawk War was received by General Scott the day after he received his orders from the secretary of war. It read as follows:

Order, No. 51

I . . . *The commanding officer of Fort Monroe* [at Point Comfort, Va.] *will detach five companies from the Artillery School of Practice, prepared and equipped for active service as Infantry, with orders to proceed forthwith to Fort Dearborn, Chicago, via New York and the Lakes. The battalion will be commanded by Brevet Lieut. Colonel* [Ichabod Bennet] *Crane of the 4th Regiment of Artillery.*

II . . . *Brevet Major* [Matthew Mountjoy] *Payne, with his company, will proceed forthwith to Fort Columbus* [in New York City] *and, on being there joined by companies F. and H. of the 4th Artillery, now stationed in the harbor of New York, will, without loss of time, resume the line of march for Chicago.*

III . . . *The Garrisons of Forts Niagara* [at the mouth of the Niagara River on Lake Ontario] *and Gratiot* [at the foot of Lake Huron, one-half mile from the lake and on the west bank of the St. Clair River] *to be conducted by their respective commandants, Lieut. Colonel* [Alexander] *Cummings and Brevet Major* [Alexander Ramsay] *Thompson, of the 2nd Regiment of Infantry, will forthwith proceed to Chicago; and one company of the 5th Regiment from each of the Garrisons of Forts Brady* [at the Sault Ste. Marie rapids] *and Mackinac* [on Mackinac Island in the Mackinac Straits] *will be detached and be ordered by the respective commandants to proceed forthwith to the same point of Rendezvous.*

IV . . . *The commanding officer of Baton Rouge* [Colonel D. L. Clinch] *will order all the companies of the Garrison, except one, to proceed forthwith to the scene of Indian hostilities in Illinois, with orders to the commander of the battalion to report to the officer there in command of the troops. Should the commander of the troops from Baton Rouge, upon arriving at St. Louis, learn that Indian hostilities had ceased, he will, in such event, return to Baton Rouge with his command.*

V . . . *Lt. Col.* [David Emmanuel] *Twiggs, of the 4th Regiment of Infantry, will collect all the disposable recruits and assume command of the detachment, arm and equip such portion thereof as he may judge to be expedient, and forthwith proceed to Chicago.*

VI . . . *Surgeon* [Josiah] *Everett is assigned to duty with the battalion of Artillery ordered from Fort Monroe; and Assistant Surgeon* [Edward] *Macomb to the detachment from Fort McHenry* [at Baltimore, Maryland], *and the harbor of New York. Surgeon* [?] *Harney will accompany the troops ordered from Baton Rouge. Assistant Surgeons* [Henry] *Stevenson and* [Henry A.] *Stinnecke will accompany the commands from Forts Niagara and Gratiot. Assistant Surgeon* [Robert E.] *Kerr will forthwith proceed to join the command of Brevet Brigadier General Atkinson, via Chicago. And Assistant Surgeons* [Clement Alexander] *Finley and* [Edwin] *James, now on furlough, will forthwith repair to their respective stations, and report in person for duty.*

VII . . . *The Quartermaster General, Commissary General of Subsistence, Surgeon General, and Colonel of Ordnance, will take measures to furnish the means and supplies requisite for the prompt and efficient execution of the provisions and object of this order.*

VIII . . . *All absent Captains and subalterns attached to companies ordered to Chicago, or elsewhere on the northwestern frontier, will forthwith join their respective companies for active duty, unless exempted by special authority communicated through the Adjutant General's office. (NOTE: a follow-up order to Paragraph VIII was issued by the A.G.'s Office, to wit:*

1. In conformity with provisions of paragraph 8 of Order No. 51, the following named officers are hereby relieved from detached duty and will forthwith proceed to join their respective companies on the line of march for Chicago: —

1st Regt. of Artillery, 2d Lieut. E. S. Sibley.

3rd Regt. of Artillery, 1st Lieut. D. E. Vinton.

4th Regt. of Artillery, Brevet Captain James Monroe; 1st Lieuts. Pickell and Searle: 2d Lieuts. Cram, Drum, Norton, and Brevet 2nd Lieut. Ridgley.

2nd Infantry, 2nd Lieut. Izard.

2nd Lieut. Hanford, and Brevet 2nd Lieut. Ritner, of the 4th Regt. of Infantry will proceed forthwith to join their respective companies at St. Louis, or elsewhere, as circumstances may direct.

2. Brevet Colonel Eustis will detach one other company from Fort Monroe with instructions to the Captain to join, without delay, the battalion previously ordered to Chicago.

3. Colonel Eustis is assigned to the command of all the Artillery ordered up to the frontier, and will accordingly report for instructions to Brevet Major General Scott; and Brevet Lieut. Colonel Worth, Major of Ordnance, is assigned to duty in the Staff of that General, to whom he will report in person for orders.)

IX . . . Brevet Major [Benjamin Kendrick] Pierce, of the 4th Artillery, will forthwith proceed from New Castle to the harbor of New York with his entire command; and the companies A. and D. of that regiment will garrison Forts Columbus and Hamilton [both in New York City] in place of companies F. and H., which companies are not to await the arrival of the relief garrison from Delaware.

X . . . Brevet Major General Scott is charged with the execution of this order, and the prompt movement of the several detachments herein ordered from the seaboard and upper lakes.

General Scott will repair to Chicago, assume command of the forces, & direct the operations against the hostile Indians.

By order: R. Jones Adjutant General.

276. The force mentioned was the United States Battalion of Mounted Rangers, Henry Dodge, Major.

277. The death of Private William Brown just a short distance from Fort Payne — present Naperville in Du Page County, Illinois — was the closest known approach of Black Hawk's warriors to Chicago during the war.

278. The camp was established in what is now Evanston, Illinois, on the site presently occupied by Northwestern University.

279. The organization of the new army under the general command of Henry Atkinson at Fort Wilbourn was as follows:

FIRST BRIGADE

Commander: Brig. Gen. Alexander Posey

Aides: Alexander P. Hall and B. A. Clark

Brigade Inspector: John Raum

Brigade Paymaster: William M. Wallace

Asst. Qtmstrs.: John A. McClernand and Marshall Rawlings

1st Regiment

Cmdg. Offs.: Col. Willis Hargrave, Lt. Col. Jefferson Gatewood, Maj. James Huston

Co. Cmdrs.: Capts. John Bays, David B. Russell, Harrison Wilson (later Lieut. Gov.), Joel Holliday, Achilles Coffey

2nd Regiment

Cmdg. Offs.: Col. John Ewing, Lt. Col. _____ Storm, Maj. Johnson Wren

Co. Cmdrs.: Capts. George P. Bowyer, William J. Stephenson, Obediah West, Charles Dunn, Jonathan Durman, Armstead Holman

3rd Regiment

Cmdg. Offs.: Col. Samuel Leech, Lt. Col. _____ Campbell (soon succeeded by Lt. Col. William Adair), Maj. Joseph Shelton

Co. Cmdrs.: Capts. Ardin Biggerstaff, James Hall, John Onstott, James N. Clark, Berryman G. Wells

Spy Battalion

Cmdg. Offs.: Maj. John Dement, Adj. Stinson B. Anderson (later Lieut. Gov.), Paymaster

Zadock Casey (present Lieut. Gov.)
Co. Cmdrs.: Capts. William N. Dobbins, James Bowman

SECOND BRIGADE

Cmdg. Off.: Brig. Gen. Milton K. Alexander
Aide: William B. Archer
Brigade Inspector: Stephen B. Shelledy
Brigade Qtrmstr.: Henry G. Smith
   1st Regiment
Cmdg. Offs.: Col. James M. Blackburn, Lt. Col. William Wyatt, Maj. James S. Jones,
Surgeon J. J. Parrish
Co. Cmdrs.: Capts. Thomas B. Ross, Royal A. Nott, Samuel Brimberry, Isaac Sandford,
Robert Griffin, Jonathan Mayo
   2nd Regiment
Cmdg. Offs.: Col. Samuel Adams, Lt. Col. J. W. Barlow, Maj. George Bowers, Adj. Samuel
Dunlap
Co. Cmdrs.: Capts. John Barnes, Alexander M. Houston, William Highsmith, John Arnold,
Elias Jordan
   3rd Regiment
Cmdg. Offs.: Col. Hosea Pearce, Lt. Col. C. Jones, Maj. William Eubanks, Adj. Isaac
Parmenter, Surgeon Aaron Thrall
Co. Cmdrs.: Capts. Solomon Hunter, Champion S. Madding, John Haynes, William
Thomas, David Powell
   Spy Battalion
Cmdg. Offs.: Maj. William McHenry, Adj. Nineveh Shaw, Surgeon George Flanagan
Co. Cmdrs.: Capts. John F. Richardson, Abner Greer, John McCown

THIRD BRIGADE

Cmdg. Off.: Brig. Gen. James D. Henry
Aide: Alexander P. Field
Brigade Inspector: Murray McConnel
Brigade Paymaster: Cornelius Hook
Brigade Wagonmaster: Nathan Hussey
Asst. Brigade Qtrmstrs.: N. H. Johnston, Milton B. Roberts
   1st Regiment
Cmdg. Offs.: Col. Samuel T. Matthews, Lt. Col. James Gillham, Maj. James Evans, Adj.
William Weatherford, Surgeon E. K. Wood
Co. Cmdrs.: Capts. David Smith, William Gillham, William Gordon, George F. Bristow,
J. T. Arnett, Walter Butler
   2nd Regiment
Cmdg. Offs.: Col. Jacob Fry, Lt. Col. Jeremiah Smith, Maj. Benjamin James, Adj. John
O'Melvany, Surgeon William H. Terrel
Co. Cmdrs: Capts. Hiram Rountree, James Kincaid, Alexander Smith (replaced soon by
Gershom Patterson), Aaron Bannon, Thomas Stout
   3rd Regiment
Cmdg. Offs.: Col. Gabriel Jones, Lt. Col. Sidney Breese, Maj. John D. Wood, Adj. David
Baldridge
Co. Cmdrs.: Capts. Andrew Bankson, William Adair, Josiah S. Briggs, James Thompson,
Jacob Feaman (soon replaced by James Conner), James Burns
   4th Regiment
Cmdg. Offs.: Col. James Collins, Lt. Col. Powell H. Sharp, Maj. William Miller, Adj. Dr.
E. H. Merriman
Co. Cmdrs.: Capts. Bennett Nowlen, Ozias Hale, Jesse Claywell, Reuben Brown, Thomas
Moffett, Henry L. Webb
   Spy Battalion
Cmdg. Offs.: Maj. William L. D. Ewing, Surgeon John Allan Wakefield
Co. Cmdrs.: Capts. Allan F. Lindsay, Samuel Huston

280. The village of Chief Aptakisic (pronounced AP-tih-KISS-sick) was located on the site of the present community of Aptakisic, twenty-eight miles north-northwest of downtown Chicago. A mile and a quarter directly northeast is the present village of Half Day, located at the intersection of U.S. Route 45 and Illinois Route 22. The village is, of course, named after Potawatomi chief Half Day and not, as so many present Chicagoans seem to think, because it was a traveler's stop located a half-day's journey from Chicago on the road to Milwaukee, Wisconsin.

281. In the initial reports and letters, Welsh's name was given as Welch, but this was later corrected. Kirkpatrick's given name had variously been shown as David, Derek, or Donald, but most accounts have shown it as David.

282. The five men killed, all privates, were William Allen, James Black, Abner Bradford, James B. Bond, and Robert Meek.

283. Lieutenant Tramel Ewing managed to intercept General Posey on his way to the scene to investigate the Indian trail that had been found before dawn. Ewing told him of the attack presently being made against the Americans at Kellogg's Grove, and Posey thereupon ordered Ewing to continue to Dixon's and report to General Atkinson, who should have arrived by the time he got there. Posey then ordered his own force into double-speed march in order to reach and relieve the beleaguered units at Kellogg's Grove.

284. The Americans claimed, in various accounts, to having killed from nine to eighteen men. In his autobiography, Black Hawk states that his war party had nine men killed — seven warriors and two very important men in the band, the latter two being Chief Chekokalauko — Turtle Shell — who ranked as the sixth chief in status in the band, and the renowned brave named Patchetowart — the Liar — who ranked as fourth principal brave in the band. The only other Indian killed who was positively identified was the Sac warrior named Makesinnene (MOCK-kee-sih-NEE-nee). Although several Indians were thought to have been wounded, the only one of these positively identified was a warrior named Hardfish, who survived.

285. In various accounts the number of horses killed that belonged to the whites has been recorded from a minimum of twenty-six to a maximum of sixty-nine. The most common cited figure is "around thirty."

286. The five Americans who had been killed in the Battle of Kellogg's Grove were found and buried in various parts of the grove during the next few days. These graves were located and the bodies disinterred fifty-four years after the battle and reburied together on a knoll at the edge of the grove, along with the remains of five or six other whites who had been killed in other areas in what is present Stephenson County. A thirty-foot shaft of quarried stone was cut into an obelisk, and three of its sides inlaid with slabs of polished marble, upon which were inscribed the names of the dead. It was erected as a monument over the grave in a ceremony attended by twenty-five hundred people on September 30, 1886. As so often occurred, the whites hailed this battle as a great victory, mainly because the number of Sac dead outnumbered those of the whites. Yet, many of the men who participated in the battle considered it, at best, only a draw. Dement himself publicly stated that the Americans lost the battle. Black Hawk considered it neither a victory nor a defeat, only a good fight, but his praise for Dement, whom he referred to as the "young chief," was very high, as reflected in his comment: "This young chief deserves great praise for his courage and bravery, but fortunately for us, his army was not all composed of such brave men."

287. Little York eventually had its name changed to what it is today, Toronto, in Ontario, Canada.

288. Sinsinawa Mound, a lead mining community, was located on the site of present Sinsinawa in Grant County, Wisconsin.

289. At least one report states that one of the Winnebago Indians brought in was "shot and scalped for impertinence," but there seems to be no basis in fact for this account.

290. The camp was to be made just a half-mile east of present Cold Spring in Jefferson County, Wisconsin. The creek that Black Hawk's warriors were to follow upstream to this point is the present Galloway Creek, which passes through Cold Spring and empties into the Bark River a little over a mile north of the town.

291. Present Silver Creek, which empties into Rock River in the northern section of present Watertown, Wisconsin, at the county line for Jefferson and Dodge counties.

292. The Indian trail followed to Broken Tree actually led northeast to approximately the site of present Lebanon in Dodge County, Wisconsin, and from that point went almost due north to the Rapids of Rock River.

293. Present Sinissippi Lake on the north edge of the present town of Hutisford in Dodge County, Wisconsin.

294. In some historical accounts, written considerably after the fact, it is stated that White Crow was the guide for Dodge and Posey on their approach to Lake Koshkonong, but that is an error based on a simple error in one principal source. White Crow was, in fact, one of the Winnebagoes of a party under the interpreter Pierre Paquette, who joined the Dodge-Posey march at its onset. Aware that Black Hawk's ambush was calculated to attack Atkinson in his advance, White Crow realized that the combined army forces would be far too strong for only 350 warriors, even well hidden in ambush, to attempt to destroy. Therefore, White Crow left the whites temporarily, allegedly to make a scout to see if he could locate the precise position of Black Hawk, after which he would report back. In the interim, Whirling Thunder was acting as principal guide. A few days after this, White Crow returned. By that time the abandoned ambush site had been found, and White Crow was accused of treacherously trying to lead the Dodge-Posey party into that trap. And realizing at this point that Black Hawk's star was rapidly descending, White Crow from this time on became genuinely very helpful to the American army in its pursuit and attack of Black Hawk.

295. The names of the five Winnebago braves are pronounced as follows: Chikakemakaw is CHICK-uh-kee-MA-kaw; Hunkqua is HUNK-wha (a shortened form of his full name, which was Hunkquatshakeereekaw, pronounced HUNK-kwa-tcha-KEE-ree-kaw); Houkmenunkaw is HOWK-me-NUN-kaw; Waukeeaunskaw is WAW-kee-AWNs-kaw; Waukeeska is WAW-kee-skah, and Moychenunkaw is MOY-cheh-NUN-kaw.

296. Although this dead sentry was mentioned in many different accounts as being a private in the 1st Infantry company of Captain Thomas Floyd Smith, in no account the author has located has this soldier's name been mentioned.

297. Although General Scott did not know it at the time, the *Superior* moored itself to the wharf at Fort Gratiot with already over a quarter of the troops on board stricken with cholera. She had no sooner stopped than the men aboard who were still physically active enough to do so — whether afflicted or not — began jumping ship. Just behind, the *Henry Clay* came in. So many men of Colonel Twiggs's command were stricken that the ship's crew had reneged on their agreement to Scott's order to go to Bois Blanc Island and said they would not proceed beyond this point. In an effort to save at least some of the troops who were apparently still disease-free, Twiggs sent several hundred men ashore. Instead of assembling into the companies, discipline vanished, and the men scattered in all directions — into the town, into the woods, anywhere, just to avoid each other and possible further contact with infected individuals. With two-thirds of his command having deserted, Twiggs was now left with a sizable number of young officers with no troops to command. At once he ordered the *Henry Clay* to return to Detroit. They began passing the *William Penn*, still laboring up the St. Clair River, towing the schooner. Word of what had happened was shouted over, and immediately the skipper of the *William Penn* turned her around and followed the *Henry Clay* toward Detroit, where Colonel Twiggs hoped he would still be able to assemble the uninfected troops and start them by land on the march to Chicago. But on reaching Detroit they learned that the city was itself now severely stricken with cholera, and so they merely anchored and remained on board the ships. By the next morning, with the *William Penn* still not reporting a single case of cholera, aboard the *Henry Clay* all the new recruits had jumped ship during the night, and Colonel Twiggs was left with only six men of his command who had not contracted the disease. His order called over to the unaffected troops aboard the *William Penn* to disembark and march immediately to Chicago was rejected by the men, who were terror-stricken at the thought of entering the infected city, if only to pass through.

298. In later years, when he had become a political figure, Abraham Lincoln ridiculed efforts to portray men like himself and Lewis Cass and others as heroic figures of the Black Hawk War. As Lincoln put it at one point, "If General Cass went in advance of me in picking whortleberries, I guess I surpassed him in charges upon wild onions. If he saw any live fighting Indians, it was more than I did, but I had a good many bloody experiences with mosquitoes, and although I never fainted from loss of blood, I can truly say I was often very hungry."

299. Though first called Fort Koshkonong, the name of the little installation soon evolved into Fort Atkinson. It was located on the east side of what is presently the town of Fort Atkinson in

Jefferson County, Wisconsin. The little fort was garrisoned until the termination of the Black Hawk War, at which point it was abandoned and its garrison sent to Fort Winnebago.

300. The camp established by Major Whistler for his Fort Dearborn garrison was located on the grounds of present Lincoln Park in Chicago, slightly north of the present Chicago Academy of Sciences. Nevertheless, several men and officers of this body of troops contracted cholera and died.

301. Among the sailing ships that had fled into the lake and then returned later were several vessels belonging to Oliver Newberry of Detroit, who had been commissioned by the government to transport provisions and supplies to Chicago for the use of General Scott's troops.

302. The site of this burial place was approximately at the present northwest corner of East Lake Street and North Wabash Avenue.

303. As nearly as can be ascertained, the route Henry and Dodge followed under the guidance of White Pawnee was reasonably direct, considering the difficult nature of the terrain. Having begun at Fort Winnebago, located two miles east of the present city of Portage in Columbia County, Wisconsin, they traveled eastward to approximately present Pardeeville. Here the trail moved south to the North Branch of Duck Creek, which it followed upstream to about the area of present Cambria. From here it moved south on the high ground delineating the natural divide between streams running west to the Mississippi River and those running southeastward into the Crawfish River drainage. The high ground was followed generally southward until they entered an extensive marshy area near the headwaters of Beaver Creek. From here they slogged very slowly through often waist-deep water and muck covered by rank cattail and marsh weed growth until they reached present Calamus Creek at approximately the present village of South Beaver Dam. Following the east side of this creek downstream, they passed the site of present Leisig and continued their march downstream to where the confluence of Calamus Creek and Shaw Brook form the Beaverdam River. At about near the site of present Lowell, they turned generally eastward until they reached Man-eater's village some two miles northeast of present Clyman.

304. The lake referred to by the Winnebagoes in those days as "the Cranberry lake" is the long, narrow, marsh-surrounded body of water presently known as Horicon Lake. Some years ago the lake and its surrounding marshes were designated as the Horicon National Wildlife Refuge, due to the ideal natural habitat existing there for a wide variety of wildlife. It is located in present north-central Dodge County, Wisconsin, just north of the present town of Horicon.

305. The Winnebago Trail was a broad, well-beaten path that had been used for a century or more. It followed almost the exact route of the right-of-way of the Chicago & Northwestern Railroad running from present Milwaukee through the cities and towns of present Waukesha, Wales, Dousman, a mile north of Sullivan, crossing Rock River just over two miles north of Jefferson, past the south edge of Rock Lake, through London, Deerfield, Cottage Grove, and finally into Madison. The place where Black Hawk's band intercepted the trail was about three miles northwest of present Jefferson, just prior to where the trail crossed a fording place of the Crawfish River.

306. Caukeecamac is pronounced Caw-KEE-kuh-mack. He was believed to have been over ninety years old at this time.

307. The route walked by Abraham Lincoln and George Harrison from Havana to New Salem was essentially the route now followed by the right-of-way of the Chicago & Illinois Midland Railroad from Havana to Petersburg.

308. Dr. Philleo later sent this trophy and another like it to Galena. And later still, the *Cincinnati Chronicle* commented in an editorial:

We trust that The Galenian is the only paper in the Union that could boast of such a feat, and that its editor is the only one of the fraternity capable of perpetrating so disgusting and cruel an act.

309. The camp made by Black Hawk the night of July 19 was on the west side of present Door Creek, two miles west of the present village Cottage Grove in Dane County, Wisconsin, and about four miles east of the western shore of Lake Monona, about ten miles west of where General Henry's force had camped between the present towns of London and Deerfield.

310. The stream where Black Hawk's camp was made is present Pheasant Branch, which flows through the northern edge of present Middleton in Dane County, Wisconsin.

311. Black Hawk's ambush, as nearly as can be ascertained, was set up in the vicinity of the intersection of present Washington and Blair in Madison.

312. The location of this campsite was just east of where Madison's Williamson Street was later constructed to cross Catfish River — the Yahara.

313. The site of Black Hawk's camp on the south shore of the Wisconsin River was three miles due northwest of the present town of Mazomanie, where the county line of Dane and Iowa counties meets the Wisconsin River.

314. Pronunciation of the names of these chiefs: Meeneekau is MEE-nee-kaw; Machakeet is Muh-CHOCK-eet; Ninnamakee is NIN-nuh-MAH-kee; Weesheet is WEE-eh-sheet. The whites had one soldier killed and eight wounded, while statements regarding the casualties of the Indians ranged from a minimum of twenty killed and fifteen wounded to a maximum of sixty-five killed and "about that many more wounded." As nearly as can be ascertained from the official reports and body count on the field, thirty-five Indians were killed, and none of the bodies were taken away by the Indians, as was their custom, because they were too weak.

315. A great deal of controversy was generated by this letter written by Dodge, since he signed himself as colonel commanding the Michigan Volunteers. The title was accurate enough, in that he was, indeed, commander of the Michigan volunteer rangers, but he was attached to the militia command of General James D. Henry, who was with him and who was in chief command of this body of men.

316. Wabasha's village of Dakotah Sioux was located on the site of present Winona, seat of Winona County, Minnesota.

317. The abandoned mining community called Helena was on the site of present Helena in Sauk County, Wisconsin.

318. The encampment made by General Atkinson's army was located on the east bank of Pine River approximately four miles south-southeast of present Richland Center in Richland County, Wisconsin.

319. General Scott's party, upon his departure from Chicago for the front on July 29, included Captain Patrick Henry Galt, Captain Richard Bache, and Lieutenant William Maynadier, along with twelve enlisted men and two wagons.

320. The route taken by General Scott as he left Chicago for the front was a well-traveled path that eventually came to be called — and is still presently known as — Army Trail Road. From downtown Chicago it went westward over the route followed by present Lake Street through Oak Park and crossing the Des Plaines River at present River Forest, then through present Bellwood, Melrose Park, and Northlake to the present suburb of Addison, where it followed the route of Army Trail Road westward through present Bloomingdale to a fording place of the Fox River at an area presently called Fox River Estates, midway between the present cities of St. Charles and Elgin.

321. The point at which Black Hawk's band reached the Mississippi River was approximately two miles below the mouth of the present Bad Axe River, about one mile north of the present town of Victory in Vernon County, Wisconsin, and almost directly across the river from the present Iowa-Minnesota border. This was approximately forty river miles upstream from Prairie du Chien.

322. Kishkasshoi is pronounced KISH-cos-shoy.

323. Wabakawsawkaw is pronounced WAW-buh-kaw-SAW-kaw.

324. In Black Hawk's autobiography, the Sac leader states that after he left his people, he was stricken by remorse and turned back to them. In his words: "*Next morning, at daybreak, a young man overtook me, and said that all my party had determined to cross the Mississippi — that a number had already got over safe, and that he had heard the white army last night within a few miles of them. I now began to fear that the whites would come up with my people, and kill them before they could get across. I had determined to go and join the Chippewas; but reflecting that by this I could only save myself, I concluded to return, and die with my people, if the Great Spirit would not give us another victory!*" In view of subsequent events, including the interrogation of Sac survivors of the Battle of Bad Axe, Black Hawk had abandoned his people before the battle and had at no time returned, and was later captured in hiding in the area of the Wisconsin Dells. Thus, his statement above is apparently little more than a self-justification and in no matter based on fact.

325. Wakefield, in his subsequent book about the war (see Bibliography), wrote in regard to this: "*It*

was a horrid sight to witness little children, wounded and suffering the most excruciating pain. It was enough to make the heart of the most hardened being on earth to ache." Compare that to the comments later written about this aspect by Governor John Reynolds and Black Hawk, neither of whom were on the scene. Black Hawk wrote: *"Our braves, but few in number, finding that the enemy paid no regard to age or sex, and seeing that they were murdering helpless women and little children, determined to fight until they were killed."* Reynolds wrote: *"Some squaws were killed by mistake in the battle. They were mixed with the warriors and some of them dressed like males."*

326. The little Indian girl rescued by Lieutenant Anderson was found to have so severe a wound that her right arm had to be amputated. As Anderson wrote about it later, *". . . the operation was performed without drawing a tear or a shriek. The child was eating a piece of hard biscuit during the operation. It was brought to Prairie du Chien, and we learn that it has nearly recovered."*

327. The American fatalities, including those who died later of their wounds, were: 2nd Lts. Samuel Bowman and Samuel W. Miller, 1st Sgt. Russell Rose, and Pvts. Dexter Graves, Jonathan Smith, Pierce Hawley, William Rogers, Stephen Scott, William Smith, Rufus Brown, Andrew McCormick, Cornelius Van Horn, James Matthews, Elisha Fish, George McConnell, Russell E. Heacock, Jonathan Boardman, Alexander Hutchings, _____ Lawrence, _____ Hood, and _____ Lowry. The wounded were: Capt. Joseph Dickson, 2nd Lt. Daloss W. Brown, Sgt. George Willard, and Pvts. Aaron Payne, John White, _____ Skinner, _____ Young.

328. Aaron Payne, while safely brought to the hospital at Prairie du Chien, could not be operated on because the two balls were lodged too close to his spine, and he wound up carrying the lead balls in his body for the remainder of his life. While at the hospital, some days after the battle, he was visited by Major General Scott, who later wrote: *"While inspecting the hospital at Fort Crawford, I was struck with a remarkably fine head of a tall volunteer lying there on his side and seeking relief in a book. To my question, 'What have you there, my friend?', the wounded man pointed to the title page of 'Young's Night Thoughts.' I sat down on the edge of the bunk, already interested in the reader, to learn more of his history. The wounded volunteer said his brother, Rev. Adam Payne, fell an early victim to Black Hawk's band, and he (not in the spirit of revenge, but to protect the frontier settlements) volunteered as a private soldier. While riding into the battlefield of Bad Axe, he passed a small Indian boy, whom he might have killed, but thought him a harmless child. 'After passing, the boy fired, lodging two balls near my spine, when I fell from my horse.' The noble volunteer, although suffering great pain from his wound, said he preferred his condition to the remorse he should have felt if he had killed the boy, believing him to be harmless."*

329. Ironically, this Winnebago who was killed by one of the fleeing Sacs was White Pawnee, the son of White Crow.

330. Nasheweskaka is pronounced Nuh-SHE-wee-SKAH-kuh. His name, on the prisoner list, is shown as Achewayschuk. However, Lieutenant Robert Anderson, who was in direct charge of the prisoners being shipped downstream and who had made out the prisoner list, inserted a variation of the name in pencil, writing it as Nacheaskuck. Hodge showed the name as Nasheakusk, while George Catlin, who later painted his portrait, gave the name as Nahseuskuk. However, Black Hawk's great-granddaughter, Mary Mack, in 1940, gave the name as it is shown by the author.

331. Lieutenant Jefferson Davis, of course, later became president of the Confederate States when the South separated from the North. The twenty-seven prisoners he was guarding are shown on Lieutenant Robert Anderson's list as: Black Hawk (his Sac name shown incorrectly as both Muckcatamechecaca and Muccatamichacakig), Pashepahoe (Little Stabbing Chief, or the Stabber, whose name properly should have been spelled Chokepashepaho), Achewayschuk (Loud Thunder, son of Black Hawk), Waysahmesaw (also written as Ahtammasah and Ahtamasah), Asinneke (Little Rock), Kushkana (Bird), Mamewaneca (Bear), Methapay, Pashquayah, Sheekuck, Mahneeasqua (Deer), Wabashekah, Apatahane, Cheamuckquo (Little Bear), Pahmeahchaskuk, Mahnahquet, Mukquatahauquit, Kishcanah, Tahquame, Tucquo, Apahtistah, Takooschuck, Pasque, Tshokuk, Meekasanmeme, Wacheekeenequa, and Ahcomee. Oddly, although Wabokieshiek, the Prophet, was also on board as prisoner and taken to Jefferson Barracks, his name was not included on the list.

332. The saga of Black Hawk did not end with his death and burial. He was buried in the northeast corner of Davis County, Iowa, in Section 2, Township 70, Range 12; the site is approximately

fifteen river miles downstream from present Ottumwa (Wapello County) and about midway between the present villages of Eldon and Selma. Less than a year later his body was stolen from its grave by an Illinois physician. Complaint was made by Black Hawk's family to Governor Robert Lucas of the Territory of Iowa. Lucas, in turn, appealed to Illinois authorities, who began an investigation, but it was a year more before the skeleton of Black Hawk was returned to Burlington, then the capital of territorial Iowa. Later that same year the seat of government was transferred to Iowa City, and the box containing Black Hawk's bones was taken as well and placed in a law office there, supposedly for temporary storage, with the bones ultimately to be displayed in the museum of the Iowa Historical and Geological Institute. That storage in the same law office continued for thirteen years, until, on January 16, 1853, the building was consumed by fire, and Black Hawk's remains were forever lost.

SPECIFIC SOURCES

Note: The specific sources listed below, chapter by chapter, are keyed by the author or publication given here to the Bibliography of Principal Sources, which follows this section.

PROLOGUE

American State Papers, Indian Affairs, I, 711. Andreas, I, 34. Blair, II: 148, 187. Draper, 1–T–58, 9–T–6. Fenton, 246–247. Flexner, 269–271. Hadlock, 204–221. Hagan, 4–9. Hunt, George T., 96–110, 194. Jackson, 17, 22, 47. Jones, William, 82–83, 163–164. Lowie, 113. "Memorandum of Talks Between Edmund P. Gaines and the Sauk, June 4, 5, 7, 1831," Adjutant General's Office Files, War Records Branch, National Archives, Washington, D.C. Miller, W. B., 278. Mishkin, Bernard, 47–49. Newcomb, 317–330. Parkman, II: 168–169, 171. Prucha: 1–98. Schoolcraft, Henry Rowe, *Archives of Aboriginal Knowledge*, III, 562, 609. Skinner, *Observations* . . . Smith, Marian W., 348–365. Snyderman, 104. Stevens, 21. Tax, 243–244. Turney-High, 19–24. Wallace, 149. *Wisconsin Historical Collections*, IX, 301–302.

CHAPTER I

American State Papers: Indian Affairs, I, 575–578, 693, 695, 711; V, 663, 689–690. Andreas, I, 35, 410; II, 72–73. Barry, 28, 44, 47, 50, 58. Berton, 40–43. Berthrong: Zebulon Pike to Anthony Wayne, July 5, 1796. Blair, II, 148, 187, 203f76. Carter, XIII, 8–9, 31, 57–58, 76–80, 103–104. Clifton, 146, 149–150, 152–155. Cole, 30–31. Dawson, 36, 59. Draper, 6–T–85; 9–T–2–3, 9–T–54–59. Edmunds, 155–157, 160–165, 182. Esarey, I, 25–31, 41–46, 52–54, 56–57, 76–84, 101, 111–112, 114–115, 132–134. Flexner, *Revolution*, II, 329. Galland, I, No. 4, 53. Gibson, 53–55. *Glimpses*, 115–117. Great Lakes Indian Archives, Potawatomi File. Greene, 4. Hafen, 174–175. Hagan, 3, 5–6, 12–13, 16–22, 24–27, 92. Hatcher, 60. Howe, I, 34, 91, 529–530, 540, 747, 753–754, 814; II, 223–232. Hunt, 77–79. Jackson, *Black Hawk*, 53–53f9–10, 54–59, 59f21, 60–61, 61f24–26, 63f26, 64f, 93, 93f1, 180–186.; *Letters*, 162. Jones, William, 82–83, 163–164, 209–237, 235. *Journal of American Folklore*, XXIV, 1911: 209–237. Kappler, II, 54–66, 75. Kinnaird, 14–19. Kinzie, 491–493. Kroeber, 28–32. Laselle: Harrison to Secy/War, July 15, 1801; Secy/War to Harrison, March 3, 1803. Miller, W. B., 278. *Missouri*, "Glimpses of the Past," II, 89, 111. *Missouri Historical Review*, L: 10. Nasatir, II, 758–759. National Archives, M-15, Roll 1, 328–331; Roll 2, 4; Secy/War to Harrison, Feb. 21, 1803. Parkman, 257–258. Perkins, 546. Prucha, 6–7, 13–20, 22. Quaife, *Lake Michigan*, 113; *Life of Black Hawk*, 89. Royce, 189. Schoolcraft, III, 593. Sheehan, 171. Stevens, 21–32, 34–35. Swanton, 256–257. *Territorial Papers*, XIV: 438–441. Thwaites, . . . *Lewis and Clark* . . . , 9–21. Trager, 36363, 366–369. *Transactions*, Illinois, 1916: 57. *Treaties Between* . . . , 109. *United States Statutes*, VII: 84–87; *Indian Treaties*, 178. Webb,

143. Wentworth, 9–10. Wheat, II, 31–60. *Wisconsin Historical Collections*, XII: 218–219. *Writings of Thomas Jefferson*, IV, 472.

CHAPTER II

American State Papers: Indian Affairs, Vol. I, 805, John Johnson to Gov. Benjamin Howard, Jan. 7, 1812. *American Weekly Messenger*, I, 3, Nov. 6, 1813. Andreas, I, 35, 72–75, 80–83, 90, 98–99, 101, 123f, 166, 240, 264, 566, 640. Atwater, 176. Barry, 69–70, 72–73, 96, 405. Berton, 112–113. *Bulletin of the Chicago Historical Society*, 110–112. *Bulletin of the Missouri Historical Society*, V, 17–33. Carter, XIII: 138–139; XIV: 370–373, 652–654, "Council Held by Interpreter Maurice Blondeau (a Fox half-blood) with the Sacs, January 22, 1813," and Boilvin to Armstrong, March 20, 1813, both in Boilvin Letters, and Baron Vasques to Boilvin, February 27, 1813, 727–728; XVI, 193–194, Gov. Benj. Howard to Secy of War Eustis, March 3, 1812; 244–247, Gov. Edwards to Secy of War, July 21, 1812; 285–289, Gov. Edwards to Pres. Madison, Jan. 16, 1812; 261–265, 326, Thomas Forsyth to Gov. Ninian Edwards, Sep. 7, 1812; 534–535, John Johnson to Gov. Benj. Howard, March 9, 1812; 324–327. *Chicago Historical Society Collections*, 338–340. Clark Papers, Kansas; August 1825 Treaty at Prairie du Chien. Clark Papers, Missouri: Clark to J. B. Comegys (Kentucky Merchant), Nov. 20, 1813; Forsyth to Clark, March 31, 1814; Forsyth to Clark, May 5, 1814. Clifton 211–214, 218, 220, 225–226, 228, 231–232. *Collections and Researches Made by the Michigan Pioneer and Historical Society*, XV, 623–627. *Collections of the Illinois State Historical Society*, XXXVI, 4–5, 91f1; XXXVII, Part I: 7; Part II: 255–256, 1056–1057. Coues, 35–36, 239f, 303–304. Cruikshank, 143–147. Draper, 25–S–32–33; 26–S–126–127; 2–T–32, 4–T–190–195, 204–207, 265, 269–272; 6–T–85, 97–101, 104–105, 113–115, 7–T–89–93, 96–97; 8–T–54. Edmunds, 108, 179, 184, 199, 201, 216, 225, 229–230. Edwards, 288, 351–353. Forsyth Papers, Missouri; Forsyth to Clark, St. Louis, March 31, 1814. Fulton, *Annals of Iowa*, 3rd Series, (1897), 76, 97–110, 737; III, No. 2, 103; XII, 336; XXV, 263. Galloway, 152–161. Gibson, 64, 73–74, 80–81, 86–87, 99. Great Lakes Indian Archives, Potawatomi File, "A Report of the Horses, Hogs, Etc., Stolen and Killed within the Indian Agency for the State of Illinois" made by Robert Graham, June 1, 1821; "Minutes of a Council Between Clark and the Potawatomi Chief. Black Partridge, Jan. 2, 1814"; Edwards to Secy of War, XVI, 285–289; Governor Edwards to President Madison, Jan. 16, 1813; "Petition of the Citizens of Illinois, June 18, 1821; *Proceedings of the Treaty at Chicago, August*, 1821; Procter to Major General Roger Shaffe, XV, 215–216. Gregg, XXXIII, No. 8 (1939). Hagan, 39–42, 44–46, 50–53, 55–64, 67, 90, 94–96, 99–100, 102–104, 106–112, 115, 120, 144. Hodge, II, 475. *Illinois State Archives*, 91f1, 144–146; "Deposition by Samuel Mallory, May 17, 1828"; Tom McNeale to Gov. Edwards, May 18, 1828. Jackson, 33, 63–66, 66f, 68–69, 72–77, 82–83, 85–88, 97–101, 108–112. *Journal, Illinois State*, 142–150. Kappler, II: 198–201, 207–208, "Treaty Between the Indian Tribes, August 19, 1825" in 250–255; "Prairie du Chien Treaty, June 25, 1829," in 297–300. Kinzie, 138–141, 248, 255, 494–496. McAfee, 53–58, 321–322, 406, 438–440, 474–475, 477. McCall, 231. *Missouri Gazette*, July 30, 1814. National Archives, M–15, Roll 6, 7–8; M–21, Roll 1, 27; M–234, Roll 132, 28–33, Roll 419, 777–781, 789–792; Roll 748, 593–594; M–271, Roll 4, 41–42; M–494, Roll 2, 159–160; "Articles of a Treaty Made and Concluded at Prairie du Chien, 1829"; Letters Received, Secretary of War, Sep. 12, 1813, and June 5, 1814. Neill, 279. *Niles Weekly Register*, No. 4, 148; Governor Edwards to Governor Shelby, March 22, 1813 (originally in *Kentucky Argus*); No. 6, 113, April 16, 1814, 242; April 16, 1814, May 14, 1814, June 11, 1814. Pierce, I, 28–29, 35–36, 411. Prucha, 23, 25–32. Quaife, *Checagou*, 140; *Chicago and the Old Northwest*, 345–347; *Lake Michigan*, 108, 123, 126, 129–130, 316. Reynolds, 204. Schoolcraft, *Travels* . . . , 337, 347–348, 348f, 371, 387–388. Sibley Papers, Sibley to Clark, March 17, 1814, V, 200, 205–207. Stevens, 37–43, 43f, 44–46, 46f, 47–50, 67f, 68–73, 76, 79, 100–101, 109, 112–113, 124, 129, 132–133, 136–139, 176. Swanton, 251–253. Taliaferro Papers, Forsyth to Taliaferro, May 28, 1827. Thwaites, *Early Western Travels*, XXI, 175–176, Trager, 380, 383, 385, 390–391, 394, 397, 400, 402–404, 410. *Transactions, Illinois State Historical Society*, 1902: 170–171; 1904: 57, 65, 72–73, 96–97, 99–100, 146, 146f1, 147, 150–153, 156–161, 165; 1909: 161–162. Tucker, II, Plate XLIV. U.S. Congressional Record: 22nd Congress, 1st Session, *House Executive Document No. 38*, 5–6. U.S. Public Lands, IV, 852. *U.S. Statutes at Large*, VI: 192–207; VII: 218–221. Webb, 2. *Wisconsin State Historical Society Collections*; III: 239; VI: 191; IX: 148, 179–195, 262, 282–283, 286, 297–298, 301–302, 316–319; X: 71, 145, 147–152;

XII: 115, 133, 135–136, 138–139, 141–146, 152, 220–222, 228, 242; XV: 124–125; U. S. Miscellaneous Archives; Report of Jonathan Rigs, July 26, 1814; Report of Lt. John Campbell, July 24, 1814.

CHAPTER III

Andreas, I: 3, 111–112, 174, 198, 641. *Army Register, 1815–1837*, 212. Barry, 173. Carter, XIV: 644–645, 657–662; XVII: 3–5, 5–10. *Chicago Historical Society Collections*, Chicago Plat Map for 1830. *Clark Papers . . . Kentucky*, IV: 222–224; VI: 190–191, 259. Clifton, 234. *Collections of the Illinois State Historical Library*, XXXVI: vii; XXXVII, Part 1: 3–5, 5f, 11–13, 13f, 15, 17–26, 60–61, 138, 214, 290, 354; Part 2: 5–6, 11–13. Coues, 345. Davenport, IV: 165–166. *Davenport and Scott Country*, I: 48, 549. Draper, 6–T–125–131, 167–168; 9–T–54–59. Edmunds, 250. Foreman, 59. Gaston, 1. *Governor's Correspondence*, II: Reynolds to Clark, May 26, 1831. Hagan, 15, 97, 104, 118, 120–127, 136, 187. *Illinois Historical Collections*, IV: 166–168. *Iowa Journal*, XI: 543–545. Jackson, 93, 96, 118–124. *Journal . . . Illinois State*, XVII: 587; XXVII, 414; LXI: 37–39. Kappler, II: 122, 208, 250–251, 305–307. Kinzie, 114, 121, 124, 153, 153f, 159–160, 259, 401, 491, 496–497. *Lee County*, 56, 66, 150–158, 196, 237–260. McCall, 223–224, 249. McCoy, 400. McKenney, I: li, 231–234. *Michigan Historical Collections*, XV: 285; XVI: 192–196, 283–285, 325, 335–337, 339. *Minnesota Historial Collections*, II, 70–73. *Missouri Historical Society Bulletin*, II: 54–55. *Missouri Historical Society Collections*, III: 46f, 105f, 113–115, 198–199. Monroe & McIntosh, I: 202–203. *Ogle County*, I: 261, 266; II: 937. Pierce, I: 33. Prucha, *American . . .*, 32–36, 44, 224–249. Reynolds, 208. *Rock Island County*, 51, 134. *Sangamon County*, Vol. A: 46–47; Vol. B: 81. Satz, 81–86. Scanlan, Chapters VIII and IX. *Stephenson County*, 221. Stevens, 55–56, 82–91, 96, 99, 101, 107, 109–110, 129–130, 148–151, 169, 171, 176, 290–291, 295. Thwaites, *Early Western Travels*, XXI: 175–176. Trager, 414. *Transactions . . . Illinois*, 1902: 170–171. U.S. Congressional Record; 21st Congress, 1st Session, *Senate Document* 110, 2–3; 23rd Congress, 1st Session, *Senate Document* 512, II, 65. U.S. *Statutes at Large*, IV: 411. *Wisconsin State Historical Society Collections*, IX: 323–326; X: 80; XI: 269–270; XII: 224–226. Works Progress Administration, 441–443.

CHAPTER IV

Andreas, I: 267. Blair, II: 227. Carter, XIII: 165. *Clark Papers . . . Kentucky*, IV: 221–222; VI: 1–2, 124, 404, 425–426. *Collections . . . Illinois*, XXXVII, Part 1: 27–33, 35–37, 39–40, 47–52, 63–66, 73, 76–77, 84–88, 98–99, 169. Davidson and Steuve, 377. *Early Days . . . Rock Island*, 50. Edmunds, 235. Ford, 112–115. Fulton, *Annals of Iowa*, XXIII: 91–92; *Red Men of Iowa*, 194. Gibson, 87. *Glimpses of the Past*, IX: 73–84. Hagan, 127–134. Hobart, 74–75. *Illinois Advocate*, June 10, 1831; July 8, 1831. Jackson, 91, 125. Kappler, II: 74–77, 126–128, 250–255. *Lloyd Steamboat Directory*, 208. Kinzie, 576–577. McCall, 224–244. *Military and Naval . . .* , III, July, 1834: 245–252, 349–357. *Missouri . . . Collections*, III: 124, 127. Mitchell, 18. *Niles Weekly Register*, XL, July 2, 1831: 310. Pierce, I: 36. Prucha, 37–38, 42. Reynolds, 209, 214–215, 334. *Rock Island County*, 102, 105, 473. *Rock Island County Atlas*, 1894, 8, 16–17, 144; 1905, 27. *Schuyler County*, (1908), II: 679–680. Skinner, 129–130. Spencer, 49–50. Spencer and Burrows, 27, 46–48. Stevens, 86–90, 92–99, 121–123. *Transactions . . . Illinois*, XXVI: 132–133; XXVIII, 92–93, 99–106, 109; XXXVII: 224–225, 227–228. U.S. Congressional Record, *House Executive Documents*, 2, 195–197. Wallace, 13–24. *Warren County*, (1877), 119; (1903), 704–705. *Wisconsin State Historical Society Collections*, XI: 347–348; XII: 226.

CHAPTER V

Annals of Iowa, XIV: 436, 443, 457; XVI: 41–42, XXIII: 100. Andreas, I: 116, 120, 266–267, 297. Beggs, 97–101. Bowen, 13, 21. Carter, XXVII: 41–52. Cartwright, 333–335. *Clark Papers — Kansas*, IV: 7–8, 279–281, 295–296; VI: 248–249, 259–260, 302. *Clark Papers — Kentucky*, IV:

347; VI: 175, 435–438. Clark Papers — Missouri, II: 87 (April 16, 1832). *Collections . . . Illinois*, IV: 172–174, 178–179; XVII, No. 3, Oct. 1924: 390–391; XVIII: 303, 325; XXXV: 181–182; XXXVI: 365–366; XXXVII, Pt. 1: 89–90, 93–95, 104–105, 112, 114–121, 127–131, 143–147. Coues, I: 45f. Edmunds, 233, 235–237. Fulton, XVI; 25ff. *Galenian, The,* May 2, 1832. Gibson, 87. Hagan, 123, 134–149, 151, 165. *Illinois Advocate,* July 8, 15, 1831; April 20, May 8, June 12, 26, July 3, 1832. Indian Claims Commission, Wash., D.C., Docket 83, Exhibit 146, Affidavit of L. A. Dunlap, "Sale of Certain of the Lands in Royce's Cession 50, Between the Military Tract and the Indian Boundary Line Prior to June 1, 1832." *Illinois . . . Journal,* LXVI (Summer, 1973), 184–197. *Iowa Journal of History and Politics,* XIV: 483, 494. Jackson, 93, 98, 108–109, 112–114, 116, 130, 132–141, 146, 154f. James, 32–33. *Jo Daviess County,* 245–246, 285–292, 591, 758. *Journal of Felix St. Vrain,* April 15–May 9, 1832. Kappler, II: 207–208, 250–255, 300–301, 306. Keating, I: 181. Kinzie, 400–401. *Knox County,* 151. *Laws of Illinois,* Sec. 13, 47–56. Lokken, 267. Lyman, 22–25. Mahan, 14, 128–129, 136–137, 242, 275–277, 355–360. Matson, 11–14, 17–19, 118. *Mercer and Henderson Counties,* 119. *Minutes of a Council at Fort Armstrong, April 13, 1832. Missouri Historical Review,* IX: *Glimpses of the Past,* 1–39, 43–86; XXXVII: 150–161, 353. *Missouri Republican,* April 10, 19, 24, 1832. Monroe & McIntosh, I: 217–219. National Archives, Box 74: M–234, Roll 132, 180–182, M–567, Roll 66–67; Box 94: File A63, Roll 66, M–567; Box 194: M–21, Roll 7, 362; M–234, Roll 642, 31–33. Atkinson Order Book, 0–19, 0–20, SO–3; Atkinson Letter Book, 4–7–1832; 4–10–1832; 11–19–1832. Nicolay and Hay, I: Chapter II, Chapter III. Pierce, I: 36. *Pike County,* 320. Prucha, *American . . . ,* 112–114, 211–212, 266–267. Quaife, *Lake Michigan,* 140–141, 316. Reynolds, 227–228. *Rock Island County,* 42. *Rock River Valley,* I: 118. *Rock Spring Pioneer,* 152. *Sangamo Journal,* April 19, 26, May 17, June 28, 1832. Scanlan, 138, 145. Spencer, I: 48, 161–162. *Springfield Herald,* May 18, 1832. Stevens, 81, 99, 101–108, 110–113, 117, 119–120, 125–126, 148–149, 160–162, 166–167, 171, 238, 249, 278–279, 295. Swanton, 253. Trager, 417, 420. *Transactions . . . Illinois,* XXXVII: 222, 224–225, 228–230. United States Congressional Record, 22nd Congress, 1st Session, *House Executive Document No. 2,* 197–198; *Senate Executive Document No. 2,* Vol. I, Serial 216, 202–204; *No. 90. United States Register,* 101. Wallace, 29, 32–36, 38–39, 41–49, 133–134, 219–221, 223–225, 227–229, 232–233, 236–237, 240, 244–251, 255–256, 258–262, 264–270, 272–273, 275, 277–280, 282–283, 285, 287–290, 294–296, 299, 300–302, 327–328. *White Crow's Statement at Rock Island, September 11, 1832. Wisconsin Historical Collections,* II: 98–196, 170: V: 256; IX: 285; X: 152–156; XI: 331–332, 334, 348–349; XII: 226–234; XV: 122–123, 127, 283–284; XIX: 479f–480f; XXI: 232.

CHAPTER VI

Adams, 499. Andreas, I: 36, 91, 96, 109–110, 114–118, 122, 132–133, 192, 198, 240, 266–269, 517, 566, 641. *Annals of Iowa,* VII: 190–191. Basler, I: 10f. *Black Hawk War Papers,* I: 125–126, 129, 144–145, 171, 237f, 239, 239f–240f, 468, 570–571; Atkinson Order Book, Orders: 5–10, 12–14; Special Orders: 9–10. Bloom, XXVII: 1, 235. Brownell, 483. Browning, 1830: April 25–30, May 1–7, 10–12. Carter, XXVII: 105, 129. Clark Papers — Kentucky: IV: 363. Clifton, 233. *Collections . . . Illinois,* XVIII, 74–79; XXXV: 191; XXXVII, Pt.1: 324, 362, 513. Edmunds, 236–237. Elliott, XXIII: 23–37. Fergus, No. 16, 64. Furer, 1. *Galenian, The,* May 6, 9–10, 16, 1832. Gratiot, 1832: January. 1; April 19, 24, 26. Hagan, 148–162, 164–165, 168. Hodges, I: 151–152. Hoffman, April 5, 1879. *Illinois Advocate,* 1832: May 15, 22; 1833: February 9. *Illinois . . . Journal,* "Shabonee," by Alta P. Walters, XVII, No. 3, October, 1924. 391; "Shaw Family Papers." *Iowa Journal of History and Politics,* XVII: 322–323, 335. Jackson, 114, 116–125, 134, 136–141. *Jo Daviess and Carroll Counties,* 1889, 739. *Jo Daviess County,* 1878, 556. Johnston, 1832: April 25–26, May 4. Kappler, II: 250–255, 300–303, 305–310. Kinzie, 402. *McDonough County,* 1885, 204. *Madison County,* 1912, I: 141, 347, 501. Minutes of an Examination of Prisoners at Fort Crawford, Prairie du Chien, Michigan Territory, August 20, 1832. National Archives, RG–75, BIA, L, Vol. I, June 30, 1832; RG–94, Frames 215–217, 253–256, A–77, Roll 66, M–567; "Journal of the Council at Porter's Grove, June 3, 1832"; *Militia Commission Records, 1830–1848,* 9, 17. Nichols, 119–136. Pierce, I: 34–35. Reynolds, 226–227, 229–230, 235. Russell, Box 1, Folder 15. St. Vrain, 1832: April 27, May 4. *Sangamo Journal,* 1832: April 26, May 13, June 14, July 12. Skinner, 8. Smith, I: 266, 417. Stevens, 114–119, 119f, 120, 122–127, 127f, 128, 128f, 130–138, 148, 166, 176, 236–238, 254, 279, 281, 284, 292–294. Trager, 421. *Transactions . . .*

Illinois, 1902: 171–173, 176; IX: 329–330. *U.S. Register*, 1833, 89. Wakefield, 10–12, 14, 16. Wallace, 48–51, 302–310, 314–319, 321, 324–332, 334–340, 342–347, 349, 351–357, 359–360, 362–364, 366, 369–370. *Whiteside County*, 1877, 54. *Wisconsin Historical Collections*, II: 336, 488; V: 286; VIII: 270; X: 154–156, 235, 245, 253, 493; XI: 230; XII: 228–229, 232–236, 244–245; XIII: 451f–452f; XV: 344.

CHAPTER VII

Andreas, I: 107, 268–269. Armstrong, 386. *Atkinson Order Book*, Order No. 16, 17, 18, 19, 20. Bassman, 32–48. Bowen, 25–30. Brown, 363. *Bureau County Atlas*, 1875, 5. Clifton, 233. *Collections . . . Illinois*, IV: 202; XXXV: 183–184, 189–190, 193–194, 198, 219, 221, 531; XXXVI: 377–378. *Du Page County*, 1882. Edmunds, 236–238. Fergus, No. 7: 53. Ford, 172. *Galenian, The*, May 23, 1832. Hagan, 159–164. *Illinois Advocate*, May 22, 29, 1832. *Illinois Herald*, May 18, 1832. *Illinois . . . Journal*, "Shabonee," by Alta P. Walters, XVII, No. 3: 391–392; XVIII, 970–978. Jackson, 118–120, 122–124, 136, 139–148. *Jo Daviess County*, 1878, 282–284. Kappler, II: 404. Kilbourn, 52. Kinzie, 403–405. Kurtz, 28. Matson, 121–124. *Missouri Intelligencer*, May 26, 1832; July 10, 1832. *Missouri Republican*, June 19, 1832. National Archives, Letters Rec'd by Secy of War, Main Series, M–221, Roll–112, 9981; RG–94, Frames 450–452, File A–105, Roll–66, M–567. *Ogle County*, 1878, 266. *Ogle County Atlas*, 1912, 58–59. Quaife, *Lake Michigan*, 141. Reynolds, 230, 234, 238–239. *St. Louis Times*, May 26, 1832. *Sangamo Journal*, May 24, 31, 1832; June 4, 7, 10, 1832; July 19, 1832. Smith, II: 319–330. Stevens, 128, 130–137, 139–143, 145–158, 163–164, 166, 183, 238–239, 284, 292–293, 296. Strong, 176. *Transactions . . . Illinois*, 1902: 171, 173–179. Wakefield, 51–52, 54, 56–60. Wallace, 35, 42, 47, 50–51, 370–385, 388–393, 397–398, 425–429, 562–565, 856–858. *Wisconsin Historical Collections*, V, 285–286; X: 156–158, 209, 261; XII: 233–235, 237–240–242, 246. *Wisconsin Magazine of History*, III: 364–367; XXVIII: 67–68.

CHAPTER VIII

Andreas, I: 107, 118, 267–269. Armstrong, 386. *Atkinson Order Book*, Order No. 16, 17, 18, 19, 20. Bassman, 42–54. Bowen, 25–30. Brown, 363. Brownell, 483. *Bureau County Atlas*, 1875, 5–6. Clifton, 233. *Collections . . . Illinois*, V: 202; XXXV: 183–184, 189, 190, 193–194, 198, 219, 221, 531. *Du Page County*, 1882. Edmunds, 236–238. Fergus, No. 7: 53. Ford, 172. *Galenian, The*, May 16, 23, 30, 1832. Hagan, 138, 150, 157–164. Hodges, I: 151–152. *Illinois Advocate*, May 29, 1832. *Illinois Herald*, May 18, 1832. *Illinois . . . Journal*, "Shabonee," by Alta P. Walters, XVII: No. 3: 121–124, 391–392. Jackson, 117–120, 122–125, 138–147. *Jo Daviess County*, 1878, 280–285. Kappler, II: 404. Kilbourn, 142–146. Kinzie, 403–405. Kurtz, 28–30. *Missouri Intelligencer*, May 26, July 10, 1834. *Missouri Republican*, June 19, 1832. National Archives, AGOF, Stock Transcripts, Gratiot's Journal, Jan. 1, 1832; Stock Transcripts, Journal of the Council at Porter's Grove, June 3, 1832; "Black Hawk War Miscellaneous Papers"; Secretary of War, Letters Received, Reynolds to Cass, June 7, 1832; M–234, Roll 132, Frames 165–166; M–567, Roll 66, Frames 450–452. Nichols, 119–136, 160–161, 174–175. *Ogle County*, 1878, 263–267. *Ogle County Atlas*, 1912, 58–59. Peck, 321–322, 339. Quaife, *Lake Michigan*, 141. Reynolds, 230–235, 238–239. *St. Louis Times*, May 26, 1832. *Sangamo Journal*, May 18, 24, May 31, June 10, 14, July 19, 1832. Skinner, 8. Smith, II: 319–330. Smith, Henry, "Indian Campaign of 1832," 157. Spencer, 53–54. Stevens, 128, 130–158, 162–164, 166, 183, 238–239, 284, 292–293, 295–296. Strong, 176. Trager, 421. *Transactions . . . Illinois*, 1902: 171, 173–179. Wakefield, 11–12, 21, 55–60. Wallace, 35, 42, 47, 50–51, 371–373, 856–858. *Whiteside County*, 1877, 54. *Wisconsin Historical Collections*, V: 285; X: 156–158; XII: 235–242, 246. *Wisconsin Magazine of History*, III: 364–367; XXVIII: 67–68.

CHAPTER IX

Alton Spectator, May 30, 1832. Andreas, I: 27, 104, 118–119, 266, 268–270, 641. Armstrong, 489. *Atkinson Order Book*, Order No. 20–22, 24–25, 29, 31–33; Special Order No. 11–13, 15–17,

19–23. *Bannerman's Catalog*, January 1845, 27. Barge, 18. Barry, 210. Bateman & Selby Moses, I: 381f. *Beardstown Chronicle*, May 30, 1832. Beggs, 98–102. *Bond County*, 1915: 624. *Bond and Montgomery Counties*, 1882: 30. *Carroll County*, 1878: 249, 333. Clifton, 233–234. *Collections . . . Illinois*, XXXV: 183, 238–241, 497; XXXVI: 4, 146f1, 431–432, 505–506; XXXVII, Pt.1: 3–5, 5f, 130–131, 288, 447; XXXVIII: 100, 264. Custer, No. 7. *Du Page County*, 1857: 19–23. *Early History of Michigan . . .* , 131–132. Edmunds, 238–239. Elliott, 256. Fergus, No. 13: 38–40. Ford, 124. Fulton, XVI: 41–42. *Galenian, The*, May 30, June 7 (Extra), 13, 16, 20, 27, 1832. *Green County, Wisconsin*, 1881: 799. *Guide to Minnesota*, 263–264. Hagan, 160–169. Iles, 43. *Illinois Advocate*, June 12, 26, 1832. *Illinois Herald*, May 15, 1832. *Illinois . . . Journal*, IX: 503–504; XVII, No. 3: "Shabonee," by Alta P. Walters; Russell Family Papers, Box 1, Folder 15; Shaw Family Papers, Folder 2; Stevens Collection. *Illinois Patriot*, June 12, 1832. *Illustrated Histories of Iowa and Lafayette Counties*, 428–429. Hunt, 45. Jackson, 147, 154f107. *Jo Daviess County*, 1878: 287–288. *Kane County*, 1878: 276–277; 1904: 622. *Kane County Atlas*, 1872: 20, 23, 37, 39, 41. Kappler, II: 347. *Kendall County*, 1877: 56, 79–84, 91, 99, 101; 1914: 635–648, 670, 709–710, 890–891, 894. Kinzie, 153, 153f, 403–409, 497–499. *La Salle County Atlas*, 1876: 69. *Lafayette Free Press*, May 25, 1832. McKenney & Hall, II: 298, 308–315. *McLean County*, 1879: 483; 1908: 636. McMaster, 18. *Macoupin County*, 1911, I: 120. Matson, 20, 53, 81–82, 176, 206, 208–209, 220. *Michigan Historical Collections*, I: 121, 250; IV: 306–307; XXXI, 327, 379, 381, 384–385, 389–391, 394, 406, 427, 528; XXXVII, 32, 245. *Minnesota Geographical Names*, 555. *Missouri Historical Review*, VIII: 37. *Missouri Intelligencer*, n.d., 1832. *Missouri Republican*, May 23, 29, June 12, 1832. National Archives, AGOF, Stock Transcripts, Journal of the Council at Porter's Grove, June 3, 1832; "Black Hawk War Miscellaneous Papers"; Secretary of War, Letters Received, Atkinson to Macomb, July 13, 1832; Cass to Reynolds, May 5, 1832; Macomb to Atkinson, May 5, 1832; M–234, Roll 132, Frames 158–159; M–567, Roll 66, File A–55, A–82–83, A–94, A–105. *Niles Weekly Register*, No. 8, 1828. *Ogle County*, 1878, 264, 266. *Palmyra Courier*, June 2, 1832. Peck, 188–189. *Peoria County*, 1880: 592, Pierce, I:36. *Putnam and Marshall Counties*, 1880: 267, 269–270. Quaife, *Lake Michigan*, 141. *Randolph Free Press*, July 23, 1832. Reynolds, 252, 377. *St. Clair County*, 1907, II: 676, 690. *St. Louis Times*, June 9, 1832. Salter, 31. *Sangamo Journal*, May 24, 31, June 14, 21, 28, September 22, 1832; July 2, 1841. *Scioto Gazette*, July 10, 1832. Spencer, 61–62, 62f. Smith, *History of Wisconsin I*: 272, 416–417, 422–423; III: 209–214. Smith, Henry, "Indian Campaign of 1832." Smith, *Stream Flow . . .* , 660. *Springfield Week-by-Week*, December 31, 1832. "The Illinois Land Office" by H. W. Fay. Stevens, 140, 145–146, 151–154, 157, 159–164, 166–170, 171–183, 188–189, 192–193, 229–230, 255–257, 284–286. Sunder, 47. *Tazewell County*, 1873: 4. *Tazewell County Atlas*, 1873: 4. *Transactions . . . Illinois*, XI: 65–72; XXXI: 91–92; 1902: 178. *Vermilion County*, 1879: 671. Wallace, 395–397, 400–401, 403–404, 407, 409, 411. *Washington Constitution*, April 17, 1859. *Western Sun & General Advertiser*, June 9, 1832. *White County*, 1883: 227, 307, 623. *Will County*, 1878, Pt. 1: 347. *Wisconsin Historical Collections*, I: 275; II, 326–373, 383–384, "Bouchard's Narrative"; V: 297f, 306–309, 401–415; X: 76–77, 179–206, 209, 211–212, 245, 253, 495–496; XII: 241–246, 289–296; IX: 457; XIII: 451, 451f, 452–452f. *Wisconsin Magazine of History*, XII: 304–306.

CHAPTER X

Annals of Iowa, XVI: 3–22. Andreas, I: 84, 119–121, 163, 270, 458, 641. *Army Register 1815–1837*, 436, 451–452, 465–466. *Atkinson Order Book*, Order No. 34–43, 47–55; Special Order No. 24–34. Baldwin, 272, 436. *Bannerman's Catalog*, 27. Barge, 18–19. Barry, 235, 289. *Beardstown Chronicle*, June 5, 1832. Beggs, 104. *Bulletin of the Chicago Historical Society*, I, 1934–1935, "Chicago Indian Chiefs" by Juliette A. Kinzie, 112. Catlin, II: 49–50, 151. Clifton, 233. *Collections . . . Illinois*, IV: 203–207; V: 66, 79; VI: 322; XIII: 61–64; XVIII: 206, 225, 236; XXXV: 123, 288–289, 317, 474, 521, 528, 531, 572–573; XXXVI: 574–575; XXXVII, Pt. II, 770; XXXVIII: 253; Horatio Newhall Papers. *Congressional Globe*, 30 *Congr.*, 1st Sess., 1847–1848; Appendix, 1042. Cooke, 161–162. *Dane County, Wisconsin*, 414, 867. *De Kalb County*, 1907, I: 24. Edmunds, 238–239. Edwards, 367–372. Elliott, 262–263. *Fayette County*, 1878, 17. Fergus, No. 13: 72–76; Appendix L. *Galenian, The*, June 20, 27, July 4, 1832. *Grundy County*, 1882, 126–127, 140. Hafen, I, 249; IX: 157, 163–164. Hagan, 19, 163, 166–176, 193, 202, 210. Hatcher, 227–228. Hunt, 110, 143. Hurlbut, 443–450, 464. *Illinois Advocate*, June 21, July 1, 1832. *Illinois Blue Book*,

1931–32, 698, 739, 741. *Illinois Herald*, July 12, 1832. *Illinois . . . Journal*, V: 66–79; IX: 503–504; XVI: 69; XVII, No. 3: "Shabonee," by Alta P. Walters; L:377–384; Russell Family Papers, Box 1, Folder 15. *Illinois Patriot*, July 12, 1832. *Indiana Historical Collections*, XXIV: 735; XXV, 80, 104–105, 643; XXXV: 104; XXXVIII: 115, 117, 223f, 369–370. *Iowa Journal . . .* , 34. Jackson, 22, 26–27, 147–151, 154, 154f107, 155. *Jo Daviess County*, 1878, frontispiece map. Johnston, 36. *Kane County*, 1878: 276; 1904: 619–621; 1908, I: 42–44, 46. *Kansas Historical Quarterly*, XXXVIII: 132–143. Kappler, II: 298, 319–325, 347, 377–381. *Kendall County*, 1914, II: 634. Kinzie, 91, 189–191, 267–271, 275, 409–414. Kirkland, I: 53f. *Lee County*, 1893, 120, 123–124, 127. *McDonough County*, 1878, 116–119. McKenney & Hall, II: 194–200. McMaster, 10. *Macoupin County*, 1911, I: 120. Matson, 106–109. *Michigan Historical Collections*, XXXI: 317, 328, 356–360, 378, 386, 389–390, 402–403, 440, 442, 445–448, 463; XXXVI: 447f; XXXVII: 237f; *Glimpses of the Past*, IX, No. 3, 54, 54f, 55. *Michigan History Magazine*, XXXIII: 226–229. *Missouri Intelligencer*, June 30, 1832. *Missouri Republican*, June 19, 26, July 10, 1832. *Montgomery County*, 1918, II: 749–750. *Myers Journal*. National Archives, AGOF, Stock Transcripts, Journal of the Council at Porter's Grove, June 3, 1832; "Black Hawk War Miscellaneous Papers"; Secretary of War, Letters Received; M–234, Roll 132; M–567, Roll 66, File A–209. *Niles Weekly Register*, July 28, August 11, 1832. *Ogle County*, 1878, II: 741. Peck, 287. *Pennsylvania Magazine of History and Biography*, LXIV, 498–490. Pierce, I: 37. Prucha, *Guide . . .* , 59–60, 67, 76, 88, 95. Quaife, *Chicago and the Old Northwest*, 327–328; *Lake Michigan*, 141–145. *Randolph Free Press*, July 23, 1832. *Register of Debates in Congress*, 22nd Congr., 1st Sess., VIII:, Pt. 3, Appendix, xviii. Reynolds, 243, 245, 251–255. Salter, 42–43. *Sangamo Journal*, June 21; July 5, 12, August 11, 1832; September 7, October. 19, 1833. Smith, Henry, "Indian Campaign of 1832." Smith, William, III: 211–213, 219, 670. *Springfield Week-by-Week*, December 31, 1832, "The Illinois Land Office" by H. W. Fay. *Stephenson County*, 1910, I: 42. Stevens, 140, 154–155, 157–160, 169, 179, 183–187, 189, 190–215, 234–235, 242–247, 257–258, 286–288. Trager, 421. *Transactions . . . Illinois*, 1902: 131–132, 176–177; XXII: 116. *Vandalia Whig and Illinois Intelligencer*, July 11, 1832. Vogel, 13, 160–162, 164. Wakefield, 33. *Warren County*, 1877, 114. Washburne, 589–590. *Washington Globe*, June 9, 1832. *Weekly Free Press*, October 15, 1891; January 21, 1892. *Western Sun & General Advertiser*, July 21, 1832. Wilkie, 98–99. *Wisconsin Historical Collections*, II: 351–354, 404–405, 434–441; III: 284, 425; VII: 325; X: 159–161, 185, 190, 192, 209–210, 253, 314; XII: 241, 243–244, 244f, 246–250; XIII: 451–452; XV: 63. *Wisconsin Magazine of History*, XXXI: 429–440.

CHAPTER XI

Andreas, I; 119–121. *Atkinson Order Book*, Order No. 38, 39, 40, 41, 42, 50, 57, 59, 60, 61, 62, 63, 64, 65; Special Order No. 35. *Cincinnati Chronicle*, August 11, 1832. *Clark County*, 1907: 221, 633, 652. Clifton, 234. *Collections . . . Illinois*, IV: 207–209; XXXV: 378, 390–391, 397, 399, 401, 404, 407, 410, 449, 451–453, 509, 521, 563, 573; XXXVII, Part I: 574. Cullum, I: 421. Drake, 163–164. Edmunds, 239. Edwards, *Lawrence . . .* , 326. Fergus, No. 11. *Early Medical Chicago* by James N. Hyde, 18–19. Ford, 146–155. *Galenian, The*, June 13, July 11, 18, Aug. 1, 1832. Hagan, 19–20, 26–28, 174, 176–190, 194, Plate 3. Hunt, *Wisconsin . . .* , 26–27, 69, 159, Plate II. *Illinois Advocate*, July 31; Aug. 1832. *Illinois . . . Journal*, IX: 503–504; XVII, No. 3: "Shabonee," by Alta P. Walters. *Illinois Patriot*, Aug. 10, 1832. *Indiana Historical Collections*, XXIV: 161f; XXV: 653; XXXVIII: 105–108, 115, 120–122. *Iowa Journal of History . . .* , XIII: 154. Jackson, 2, 22–25, 130–133, 150–153, 154f107, 155–162. *Jackson County*, Murphreysboro, Ill., 1878. *Jo Daviess County*, 1878, 292, 294. Kinzie, 450. *Lee County*, I: 238, 249–251. *Marion and Clinton Counties*, 120, 173. *Missouri Republican*, August 14, 1832. National Archives, AGOF, Stock Transcripts, Journal of the Council at Porter's Grove, June 3, 1832; "Black Hawk War Miscellaneous Papers"; Secretary of War, Letters Received; M–234, Roll 132; M–567, Roll 66, File A–105, Frames 351–353, 356–360, 448–449, 479–486. Pierce, I: 37. Prucha, *Broadax . . .* , 152. Quaife, *Lake Michigan*, 142, 145–146. Reynolds, 262. *Sangamo Journal*, July 19, August 3, 11, 18, 25, 1832. Smith, Henry, "Indian Campaign of 1832" in *Wisconsin Historical Collections*, III: 163, 223. Smith, William, III: 228–232. *Springfield Week-by-Week*, December 31, 1832. "The Illinois Land Office" by H. W. Fay. Stevens, 159–160, 189–190, 211–212, 215–224, 226–227, 229, 234–235, 239, 247–248, 288. Trager, 420. Wakefield, 62–64, 66, 70, 72, 75–79, 83–86, 97–98,

123. *Wisconsin Historical Collections*, II: (*Pioneer Life in Wisconsin*, by Daniel M. Parkinson), 223, 334–341, 355–361, 390, 407–408; IV: 346; V: 261–264; VI: 407; VII: 350–351; IX: 293–296, 465–467; X: 77, 161–164, 166f, 207–208, 210; XI: 403; XII: 231, 242, 250–261, 265, 270–272, 431. *Wisconsin Magazine of History*, IV: 55–60.

EPILOGUE

American Quarterly Review, No. 35, 1834: 426. Andreas, I: 36, 36f, 108–109, 121–122, 124, 128, 240, 289, 641. Armstrong, 368. *Beloit Weekly Free Press*, October 15, 1891. *Burlington Gazette*, August 25, 1888. Catlin, II: 212. Drake 202, 204–206, 213–214, 663. Edmunds, 239. Fulton, *Annals of Iowa*, XX: 435–443; XXV: 58–60. Fulton, *Red Men of Iowa*, 212. *Galenian, The*, Sept. 4, 5, 1832. Green, 7–8, 16, 67. Hagan, 20, 190–192, 194–200, 208–210. Hatcher, 259. Hodge, I: 152; II: 32–33. *Illinois . . . Journal*, IX: 503–504; XVII: No. 3: "Shabonee," by Alta P. Walters, 383. *Indiana Magazine of History*, XLV, June, 1949: 152–157. Jackson, 1–4, 6f, 7, 7f–8f, 9, 9f15, 10–11, 11f15–f18, 12, 12f20, 13, 16–18, 33–34, 83f, 104, 162–163, 165, 167–171. Kappler, II: 353–355, 367–375. *Mississippi Valley Historical Review*, XLI: 457. *Missouri Republican*, Sept. 11, 1832. National Archives, AGOF, Stock Transcripts, Report of the Commissioners, Oct., 1832, T–924, Roll 2, 526–531; Deposition of J. H. Kintree, July 1, 1834, M–234, Roll 354, 874; Deposition by James Avaline, July 7, 1834, M–234, Roll 354, 66, 86; "Articles of a Treaty Made and Concluded . . . October 26, 1832"; "Black Hawk War Miscellaneous Papers"; Secretary of War, Letters Received; M–234, Roll 132; M–567, Roll 66, File A–102, Cass to Jennings, Davis & Crume, M–21, Roll, 9, 44–47; "Minutes of a Conference Between the U.S. and the Sac & Fox, Sept. 20, 1832, in Records of the Senate, 22nd Congress; Minutes of the 1st Conference Held Between U.S. Representatives and the Indians at Rock Island, Sept. 19, 1832; Indian Relations — Minutes Relating to the 1832 Treaty with the Sacs & Foxes. *National Intelligencer*, June 20, 1833. *Niles Weekly Register*, Sept. 8, 29, 1833. Pierce, I: 37. Quaife, *Lake Michigan*, 146. *Sangamo Journal*, Sept. 22, 1833. Stevens, 148, 224–225, 229–233, 239–241, 243, 247–248, 259–263, 267. Trager, 420. *Transactions . . . Illinois*, 1916: 57. *United States Statutes. . .* VII: 370–376. Wakefield, 91, 95–101. *Wisconsin Historical Collections*, V: 293–294; VIII: 316f; X: 164–166; XII: 261–263, 265.

BIBLIOGRAPHY OF PRINCIPAL SOURCES

Albach, James R. *Annals of the West*. Pittsburgh, 1857.
Aldrich, Charles. "Jefferson Davis and Black Hawk." *Midland Monthly*, vol. V (1896), 406–411.
Alton Spectator, Alton, Ill.
American State Papers. Indian Affairs, 2 vols., 1832–34; Military Affairs, 7 vols. Washington, D.C.,
      1832–61.
American Quarterly Review.
American Weekly Messenger.
Andreas, A. T. *History of Chicago, from the Earliest Periods to the Present Time*. 3 vols. Chicago,
      1884.
Armstrong, Perry A. *The Sauks and the Black Hawk War*. Springfield, Ill., 1887.
Army Register, 1815–1837. Library of Congress, Washington, D.C., 1985–.
Atkinson Letter Book. Ms. in Collection of Illinois Historical Library, Springfield, Ill.
Atkinson Order Book. Ms. in Collection of Illinois Historical Library, Springfield, Ill.
Atwater, Caleb. *Remarks Made on a Tour to Prairie du Chien*. Columbus, Ohio, 1831.
Baldwin, Henry. *La Salle County*. Ottawa, Ill., 1877.
Bannerman's Catalog, January 1845.
Barge, William D. *Early Lee County*. Dixon, Ill., 1891.
Barry, Louise. *The Beginning of the West: Annals of the Kansas Gateway to the American West,
      1540–1854*. Topeka, Kan., 1972.
Bassman, L. M., ed. *Riverside Then and Now*. Chicago, 1912.
Beggs, Stephen R. *Pages from the Early History of the West and North-west*. Cincinnati, Ohio, 1868.
Beloit Weekly Free Press, Beloit, Wis.
Berthrong, [Donald J.] Collection. Bizzell Memorial Library, University of Oklahoma, Norman.
Berton, Pierre. *The Invasion of Canada: 1812–1813*. Boston, 1980.
Black Hawk War Papers. Ms. in Collection of Illinois Historical Library, Springfield, Ill.
Blair, Emma Helen. *The Indian Tribes of the Upper Mississippi Valley and Region of the Great
      Lakes*. 2 vols. Cleveland, 1911.
Bond County, 1915. Greenville, Ill., 1915.
Bond and Montgomery Counties, 1882. Hillsboro, Ill., 1882.
Bowen, J. L. *Savanna*. Galena, Ill., 1882.
Brownell, Charles D. *The History of the Indian Races of North and South America*. Hartford, Conn.,
      1865.
Browning, Oliver H. *Journal — 1832*. Illinois Historical Library Collection, Springfield, Ill.
Burlington Gazette, Burlington, Iowa.
Carroll County, 1878. Mt. Carroll, Ill., 1878.

Carter, Clarence Edwin, ed. and comp. *The Territorial Papers of the United States.* 27 vols. Washington, D.C. 1934–. See especially *Territory of Michigan*, vol. XI, and *Wisconsin Territory*, vol. XXVII.

Cartwright, A. G. *Autobiography.* Philadelphia, 1881.

Catlin, George. *Letters and Notes on the Manners, Customs, and Condition of the North American Indians.* 9th ed., Philadelphia, 1850.

Chambers, John Sharpe. *The Conquest of Cholera, America's Greatest Scourge.* New York, 1902.

Chicago Historical Society Collections. Vol. III, Chicago, 1898.

Cincinnati Chronicle, Cincinnati.

Clark, William. The William Clark Papers Pertaining to the U.S. Superintendency of Indian Affairs at St. Louis. Ms. in Kansas State Historical Society, *Journal of the Proceedings of the Treaty of Prairie du Chien, August, 1825.* Topeka, Kan., 1923.

———. Clark Papers. Kentucky Historical Society, Frankfort, Ky.

———. Clark Papers. Missouri Historical Society, St. Louis, Mo.

Clifton, James A. *The Prairie People.* Lawrence, Kan., 1977.

Cole, Cyrenus. *I Am a Man: The Indian Black Hawk.* Iowa City, Iowa, 1938.

Collections and Researches Made by the Michigan Pioneer and Historical Society. 15 vols., Lansing, Mich., 1921–1927.

Collections of the Illinois Historical Library. 34 vols., Springfield, Ill., 1903–.

Congressional Globe, Washington, D.C.

Cooke, Philip St. George. *Scenes and Adventures in the Army.* Philadelphia, 1857.

Coues, Elliott, ed. *The Expeditions of Zebulon Montgomery Pike to the Headwaters of the Mississippi River, through Louisiana Territory, and in New Spain in the Years 1805–6–7.* 3 vols. Minneapolis, 1895.

Covington, James W. "The Liquor Trade at Peoria," *Journal of the Illinois State Historical Society*, vol. LXVI. Springfield, Ill., 1953.

Cruikshank, Ernest A. *Robert Dickson, the Indian Trader.* Wisconsin Historical Collections, Madison, Wis., vol. XII (1894), 1–13.

Custer, R. G. *A Few Family Records, No. 7.* Dubuque, Iowa, 1894.

Dane County, Wisconsin, 1880. Madison, Wis., 1880.

Davenport and Scott County, Iowa, 1910. Davenport, Iowa, 1910.

Davidson, Robert, and G. L. Stuve. *A Complete History of Illinois, from 1673 to 1884.* Springfield, Ill., 1884.

Dawson, Moses. *A Historical Narrative of the Civil and Military Service of Major General William Henry Harrison, and a Vindication of his Character and Conduct as a Statesman, a Citizen, and a Soldier.* Cincinnati, Ohio, 1834.

De Kalb County, 1907. Sycamore, Ill., 1907.

Drake, Benjamin. *The Great Indian Chief of the West, or The Life and Adventures of Black Hawk.* Cincinnati, Ohio, 1858.

Drake, Samuel G. *Indian Biography.* Boston, 1832.

Draper, Lyman C. The Lyman Copeland Draper Manuscript Collections (microfilm). Wisconsin State Historical Society, Madison, Wis.

Du Page County, 1882. Wheaton, Ill., 1882.

Early History of Michigan with Biographies of State Officers. Lansing, Mich., 1888.

Eckert, Allan W. *The Conquerors.* Boston, 1970.

———. *The Frontiersmen.* Boston, 1967.

———. *Gateway to Empire.* Boston, 1983.

———. *Wilderness Empire.* Boston, 1969.

———. *The Wilderness War.* Boston, 1978.

Edmunds, R. David. *The Potawatomies: Keepers of the Fire.* Norman, Okla., 1980.

Edwards, Josiah. *Lee County.* Dixon, Ill., 1914.

Edwards, Ninian W. *The History of Illinois: From 1778 to 1833.* Springfield, Ill., 1870.

———. *Life and Times of Ninian Edwards.* Springfield, Ill., 1872.

Elliott, Charles Winslow. *Winfield Scott: The Soldier and the Man.* New York, 1937.

Esarey, Logan, ed. *Governor's Messages and Letters: Messages and Letters of William Henry Harrison.* 2 vols. Indiana Historical Collections, Indianapolis, Ind., 1922.

Fayette County, 1878. Vandalia, Ill., 1878.

Fenton, William N. Review of *Primitive War*, by H. H. Turney-High, *American Anthropologist*, vol. LII (1950).

Fergus Historical Series. 35 numbered pamphlets, Chicago, 1916.

Flexner, James Thomas. *George Washington in the American Revolution, 1775–1783*. 2 vols. Boston, 1967–68.

———. *Mohawk Baronet: Sir William Johnson of New York*. New York, 1959.

Ford, Thomas. *A History of Illinois from its Commencement as a State in 1818 to 1847*. Chicago, 1854.

Foreman, Grant. *The Last Trek of the Indians*. Chicago, 1946.

Forsyth Papers. *Report to William Clark on the Illinois Country*. September 1826. Missouri Historical Society Collections, St. Louis, Mo.

Fulton, A. R. *Annals of Iowa*. 3rd series, 25 vols., Des Moines, Iowa, 1897.

———. *Red Men of Iowa*. Des Moines, Iowa, 1882.

Furer, Howard B. *Chicago: A Chronological and Documentary History: 1784–1970*. Chicago, 1974.

Galenian, The, Galena, Ill.

Galland, Isaac. *Chronicles of the North American Savage*. Publication of the Missouri Historical Society, St. Louis Mo., vol. II (May-September 1835).

Galloway, William Albert. *Old Chillicothe: Shawnee and Pioneer History; Conflicts and Romances in the Northwest Territory*. Xenia, Ohio, 1934.

Gaston, George H. "The History and Government of Chicago." *Educational Bimonthly*, vol. XVII no. 3 (June 1941), pp. 23–28, 49–51.

Gibson, A. M. *The Kickapoos: Lords of the Middle Border*. Norman, Okla., 1963.

Glimpses of the Past. Publication of the Missouri Historical Society, St. Louis, Mo., vol. II (May-September 1835).

Governor's Correspondence, 1809–1831. 2 vols. Illinois State Library, Archives Division, Springfield, Ill.

Governor's Letterbook. Illinois State Library, Archives Division, Springfield, Ill.

Grant County, Wisconsin, 1881. Lancaster, Wis., 1881.

Gratiot Journal, 1832–1833. Wisconsin Historical Society Archives, Madison, Wis.

Great Lakes–Ohio Valley Indian Archives Project. Potawatomi File, Glen A. Black Laboratory of Archaeology, Indiana University, Bloomington, Ind., n.d.

Green, Charles R. *Early Days in Kansas: In Keokuk's Time on the Kansas Reservation*. Topeka, Kan., 1956.

Green County, Wisconsin, 1881. Monroe, Wis., 1881.

Greene, Evarts Boutelle, and Clarence Walworth Alvord, eds. *The Governor's Letter-Books, 1818–1834*. Illinois Historical Collections (Springfield, Ill.), vol. IV, 1909.

Gregg, Kate L. "The War of 1812 on the Missouri Frontier." *Missouri Historical Review*, vol. XXXIII, no. 8 (1939).

Grundy County, 1882. Morris, Ill., 1882.

Hadlock, Wendell S. "War among the Northeastern Woodland Indians," *American Anthropologist*, vol. XLIX (1947), pp. 601–637.

Hafen, LeRoy R., with Carl Coke Rister. *The Mountain Men and the Fur Trade of the West*. 16 vols. New York, 1941.

———. *Western America: The Exploration, Settlement and Development of the Region Beyond the Mississippi*. 12 vols., New York, 1941.

Hagan, William T. *The Sac and Fox Indians*. Norman, Okla., 1958.

Hamilton, Holman. *Zachary Taylor: Soldier of the Republic*. Indianapolis, Ind., 1941.

Hatcher, Harlan. *Lake Erie*. New York, 1945.

Hobart, James. *Recollections*. Madison, Wis., 1872.

Hodge, Frederick Webb, ed. *Handbook of the American Indians North of Mexico*. 2 vols. Bulletin 30, Bureau of American Ethnology, Washington, D.C., 1910.

Hoffman, T. L. *Antique Dubuque*. Dubuque, Iowa, 1926.

Howe, Henry. *Historical Collections of Ohio*. 2 vols. Cincinnati, Ohio, 1888.

Hunt, George T. *The Wars of the Iroquois: A Study in Intertribal Trade Relations*. Madison, Wis., 1940.

———. *Wisconsin Gazetteer*. Madison, Wis., 1938.

Hurlbut, Henry. *Chicago Antiquities*. Chicago, 1890.

Iles, Elijah. *Early Life and Times*. Chicago, 1879.
Illinois Advocate, Edwardsville, Ill.
Illinois Herald, Springfield, Ill.
Illinois Patriot, Jacksonville, Ill.
Illinois State Archives: *Governor's Correspondence*. Springfield, Ill., 1938.
Indiana Historical Collections. Indianapolis, Ind.
Indiana Magazine of History. Indianapolis, Ind.
Iowa Journal of History and Politics. Des Moines, Iowa.
Jackson County. Murphysboro, Ill., 1878.
Jackson, Donald, ed. *Black Hawk: An Autobiography*. Urbana, Ill., 1955.
———. *Letters of the Lewis and Clark Expedition with Related Documents*. Urbana, Ill., 1962.
James, U. P. *James' River Guide* . . . Cincinnati, Ohio, 1856.
Jo Daviess County, 1878. Galena, Ill., 1878.
Johnston, A. S. *Journal* — 1832. Frankfort, Ky., 1848.
Johnston, William Preston. *The Life of General Albert Sidney Johnston*. New York, 1879.
Jones, William. *Ethnology of the Fox Indians*. Bulletin 125, Bureau of American Ethnology, Washington, D.C., 1929.
Journal of American Folklore, vol. XXIV (1911).
Journal of Felix St. Vrain. Ms. in Collection of the Iowa State Historical Society, Iowa City, Iowa.
Kane County. Geneva, Ill., 1878, 1904, 1908.
Kappler, Charles J., ed. *Indian Affairs: Laws and Treaties*, *1778–1883*. 2 vols. Washington, D.C., 1904.
Keating, William H. *Narrative of an Expedition to the Source of St. Peter's River*. 2 vols. Philadelphia, 1824.
Kendall County. Yorkville, Ill., 1877, 1914.
Kilbourn, Elijah. *Soldier's Cabinet*. Philadelphia, 1855.
Kinnard, Lawrence, ed. *Spain in the Mississippi Valley, 1765–1794: Translations of Materials from the Spanish Archives in the Bancroft Library*. 3 vols., Annual Report of the American Historical Society for . . . 1945, vols. II, III. Washington, D.C., 1946, 1949.
Kinzie, Juliette A. "Chicago Indian Chiefs," in *Bulletin of the Chicago Historical Society*, vol. I (1935–1936), pp. 107–110.
Kinzie, Juliette A. M. (Mrs. John M.). *Wau-Bun: The "Early-Day" in the North-West*. New York, 1856.
Kirkland, Joseph. *The Story of Chicago*. Chicago, 1893.
Knox County, Illinois, 1878. Galesburg, Ill., 1878.
Kroeber, A. L. *Cultural and Natural Areas of Native North America*. Berkeley, Calif., 1939.
Kurtz, Frank, *History of Dixon and Lee County*. Dixon, Ill., 1880.
La Salle County Atlas, 1876. Ottawa, Ill., 1876.
Lafayette Free Press, Lafayette, Ind.
Laselle Papers. Indiana State Library, Indianapolis, Ind.
Laws of Illinois, 1830–31. Springfield, Ill., 1878–.
Lee County, Illinois. Dixon, Ill., 1881, 1893.
Lloyd Steamboat Directory. St. Louis, Mo., 1856.
Lowie, Robert H. *The Crow Indians*. New York, 1935.
Lyman, George D., *John Marsh, Pioneer*. New York, 1930.
McAfee, Robert B. *History of the Late War in the Western Country*, ed. by Van Tassell. Bowling Green, Ky., 1919.
McCall, George A. *Letters from the Frontiers, Written During a Period of Thirty Years' Service in the Army of the United States*. Philadelphia, 1868.
McCoy, Isaac. *History of Baptist Indian Missions*. Washington, D.C., 1840.
McDonough County, 1878. Macomb, Ill., 1878.
McKenney, Thomas L., and James Hall. *A History of the Indian Tribes of North America, with Biographical Sketches and Anecdotes of the Principal Chiefs*. 3 vols. Philadelphia, 1838.
McLean County, 1879. Bloomington, Ill., 1879.
McMaster, John Bach. *Sixty Years on the Upper Mississippi*. St. Louis, Mo., 1899.
Macoupin County, 1911. Carlinville, Ill., 1911.
Madison County, 1912. East St. Louis, Ill., 1912.

Mahan, Bruce E. *Old Fort Crawford and the Frontier.* Iowa City, Iowa, 1926.
Marion and Clinton Counties. Salem, Ill., 1881.
Matson, Nehemiah. *Memories of Shau-be-na.* Chicago, 1880.
Memorandum of Talks Between Edmund P. Gaines and the Sauk, June 4, 5, 7, 1831. Adjutant General's Office Files, War Records Branch, National Archives, Washington, D.C., 1831.
Mercer and Henderson Counties, 1882. Oquawka, Ill., 1882.
Michigan Historical Collections, Lansing, Mich.
Michigan History Magazine.
Miller, W. B. "Two Concepts of Authority" *American Anthropologist,* vol. LVII (1955), pp. 211–236.
Military and Naval Magazine of the United States. Washington, D.C.
Minnesota Historical Collections. St. Paul, Minn.
Minutes of a Council at Fort Armstrong, April 13, 1832. In Black Hawk War Papers. Wisconsin State Historical Society Collection.
Mishkin, Bernard. *Rank and Warfare Among the Plains Indians.* Monographs of the American Ethnological Society, vol. III. New York, 1940.
Mississippi Valley Historical Review, Cedar Rapids, Iowa.
Missouri Gazette, Columbia, Mo.
Missouri Historical Review, vol. L, Columbia, Mo., 1912.
Missouri Historical Society Bulletin, Jefferson City, Mo.
Missouri Historical Society Collections, Jefferson City, Mo.
Missouri Historical Society Transactions, 1933–35, St. Louis, Mo.
Missouri Intelligencer, St. Louis, Mo.
Missouri Intelligencer and Boon's Lick Advertiser, Columbia, Mo.
Missouri Republican, St. Louis, Mo.
Mitchell, S. Augustus. *Illinois in 1837.* Philadelphia, 1837.
Montgomery County, 1918. Hillsboro, Ill., 1918.
Monroe, Day, and A. L. McIntosh, eds. *Jefferson Davis Papers.* New York, 1898.
Nasatir, A. P., ed. *Before Lewis and Clark: Documents Illustrating the History of Missouri, 1785–1804.* 2 vols. St. Louis, Mo., 1952.
National Archives, Washington, D.C., including:
  General Records of the U.S. Government (Record Group 11)
  Adjutant General's Office Files (AGOF)
  Ratified Indian Treaties (M-668) (microfilm), 1772–1848
  Secretary of War, Letters Received
  Records of the Bureau of Indian Affairs (Record Group 75)
  Documents Relating to the Negotiations of Treaties (T-494) (microfilm), 1801–1853
  Letters Received by the Office of Indian Affairs (M-234) (microfilm): from the Chicago Agency, 1824–1827; from the Forth Wayne Agency, 1824–1830; from the Green Bay Agency, 1824–1850; from the Indiana Agency, 1824–1850; from the Iowa Agency, 1825–1837; from the Iowa Superintendency, 1824–1851; from the Michigan Superintendency, 1824–1851; from the Ohio Agency, 1831–1843; from the Osage River Agency, 1824–1854; from the Potawatomi Agency, 1851–1852; from the St. Louis Superintendency, 1825–1851; from the Wisconsin Superintendency, 1836–1848
  Records of the Secretary of War Relating to Indian Affairs (microfilm): Letters Received (271), 1800–1823; Letters Sent (M-16), 1807–1823
  Atkinson Order Book
  Territorial Papers of the United States, Wisconsin, 1836–1848 (microfilm rolls 36–48 [M-236]).
Neill, E. D. *The History of Minnesota.* Philadelphia, 1858.
Newcomb, W. W., Jr. "A Re-examination of the Causes of Plains Warfare," *American Anthropologist,* vol. LII (1952), pp. 84–164.
Nicolay, John G and John Hay. *Abraham Lincoln: A History.* Chicago, 1966.
Nichols, Roger L. *General Henry Atkinson: A Western Military Career.* Norman, Okla., 1965.
Niles Weekly Register. 76 vols. Baltimore, Md., 1811–1849.
Ogle County, Illinois. Chicago, Ill., 1909.
Palmyra Courier, Palmyra, Mo.

Parkman, Francis. *The Conspiracy of Pontiac and the Indian War After the Conquest of Canada.* 2 vols. Boston, 1894.

Pease, T. C. *The Story of Illinois.* University of Chicago Press, 1975.

Peck, John Mason. *A Gazetteer of Illinois.* Jacksonville, Ill., 1834.

Pennsylvania Magazine of History and Biography, Harrisburg, Pa.

Perkins, H. E., and George Peck. *Annals of the West.* Cincinnati, Ohio, 1871.

Pierce, Bessie Louise. *A History of Chicago.* 3 vols. Chicago, 1975.

Pike County, 1880. Pittsfield, Ill., 1880.

Prucha, Francis Paul. *American Indian Policy in the Formative Years: The Indian Trade and Intercourse Acts, 1790–1834.* Lincoln, Neb., 1970.

————. *Broadax and Bayonet: The Role of the United States in the Development of the Northwest, 1815–1860.* Lincoln, Neb., 1967.

————. *Guide to Military Posts.* Lincoln, Neb., 1966.

Putnam and Marshall Counties, 1880. Hennepin, Ill., 1880.

Quaife, Milo Milton. *Checagou: From Indian Wigwam to Modern City, 1673–1835.* Chicago, 1933.

————. *Chicago and the Old Northwest, 1673–1835.* Chicago, 1913.

————. *Lake Michigan.* Indianapolis, Ind., 1944.

————, ed. *Life of Black Hawk: Ma-Ka-Tai-Me-She-Kia-Kiak.* Chicago, 1916.

Randolph Free Press, Kaskaskia, Ill.

Reynolds, John. *My Own Times: Embracing Also the History of My Life.* Chicago, 1879.

Rock Island County, 1908. Rock Island, Ill., 1908.

Rock Island County Atlas. Rock Island, Ill., 1905.

Rock Spring Pioneer, Rock Spring, Wis., 1832.

Royce, Charles C. *Indian Land Cessions in the Unites States.* 18th Annual Report of the Bureau of American Ethnology, Part 2. Washington, 1899–1900.

Russell Family Papers. Box 1, Folder 15, Ms. in Collection of Illinois Historical Society, Springfield, Ill.

St. Clair County, 1907. Belleville, Ill., 1907.

St. Louis Times, St. Louis, Mo.

St. Vrain, Felix. *Journal — 1832,* in Indian Papers of the Missouri Historical Society. St. Louis, Mo.

Salter, William. *The Life of Henry Dodge from 1782 to 1833.* Burlington, Iowa, 1890.

Sangamo Jounal, Springfield, Ill.

Sangamon County Commissioners' Court Records. vols. A, B. Springfield, Ill.

Satz, Ronald D. *American Indian Policy in the Jacksonian Era.* Lincoln, Neb., 1975.

Scanlan, Charles M. *Indian Creek Massacre and Captivity of Hall Girls.* Milwaukee, Wis., 1915.

Scanlan, Peter L. *Prairie du Chien, French, British, American.* Menasha, Wis., 1937.

Schoolcraft, Henry Rowe. *Archives of Aboriginal Knowledge.* Philadelphia, 1860.

————. *Travels in the Central Portions of the Mississippi Valley: Comprising Observations on its Mineral Geography, Internal Resources, and Aboriginal Population.* New York, 1825.

Schuyler County, 1908. Rushville, Ill., 1908.

Scioto Gazette, Chillicothe, Ohio.

Sheehan, Bernard. *Seeds of Extinction: Jeffersonian Philanthropy and the American Indian.* Chapel Hill, N.C., 1973.

Sibley Papers. Ms. in Missouri Historical Society Collections, St. Louis, Mo.

Skinner, Alanson. *Observations on the Ethnology of the Sauk Indians.* Bulletin of the Public Museum of the City of Milwaukee, vol. V, nos. 1–3 (1923–1926).

Smith, Henry. *Indian Campaign of 1832,* in Wisconsin Historical Collections, Madison, Wis.

Smith, Marian W. "American Indian Warfare," in *Transactions of the New York Academy of Sciences,* ser. 2, vol. XIII (1951).

Smith, William. *The History of Wisconsin in Three Parts, Historical, Documentary, and Descriptive.* 3 vols. Madison, Wis., 1854.

Snyderman, George. *Behind the Tree of Peace: A Sociological Analysis of Iroquois Warfare.* Ph.D. dissertation, University of Pennsylvania, Philadelphia, 1948.

Spencer, J. W. *Reminiscences of Pioneer Life in the Mississippi Valley*. Chicago, 1947.
———, and J. M. D. Burrows. *The Early Days of Rock Island and Davenport*, ed. by M. M. Quaife. Chicago, Ill., 1942.
Springfield Herald, Springfield, Ill., 1832.
Springfield Week-by-Week, Springfield, Ill., 1832.
Stephenson County, Illinois. Chicago, 1880, 1910.
Stevens, Frank E. *The Black Hawk War Including a Review of Black Hawk's Life*. Chicago, 1903.
Strong, M. N. *History of the Territory of Wisconsin from 1836–1848*. Madison, Wis., 1885.
———. *John A. Wakefield*. Madison, Wis., 1888.
Swanton, John R. *Indian Tribes of North America*. Smithsonian Institution Bureau of Ethnology Bulletin 145. U.S. Government Printing Office, Washington, D.C., 1953.
Tanner, John. *A Narrative of the Captivity and Adventures of John Tanner . . . During Thirty Years Residence Among the Indians of the Interior of North America*, prepared by Edwin James, M.D. New York, 1930.
Taliaferro Papers. Ms. in Collection of Minnesota Historical Society, St. Paul, Minn.
Tazewell County, 1873. Pekin, Ill., 1873.
Tazewell County Atlas, 1873. Pekin, Ill., 1873.
Tax, Sol. "The Social Organization of the Fox Indians," in *Social Anthropology of North American Indian Tribes*. ed. by Fred Eggan. Chicago, Ill., 1937, pp. 31–41.
Thwaites, Reuben Gold, ed. *Early Western Travels*, vol. XXI. 32 vols. Cleveland, Ohio, 1904–1907.
———. *Original Journals of Lewis and Clark Expedition, 1804–1806*. New York, 1904–05.
Trager, James. *The People's Chronology*. New York, 1979.
Transactions of the Illinois State Historical Society. Springfield, Ill.
Treaties Between the United States of America and the Several Indian Tribes. Washington, D.C., 1837.
Tucker, Sara Jones, comp. *Indian Villages of the Illinois Country*. 2 vols. Springfield, Ill., 1942.
Turney-High, Harry Holbert. *Primitive War: Its Practice and Concepts*. Columbia, S.C., 1949.
United States Congressional Record. 22nd Congress, Washington, D.C., 1832.
United States Public Lands. 5 vols. Washington, D.C., 1912.
United States Register, 1832–1833. Washington, D.C., 1889.
United States Statutes at Large: Indian Treaties, 1778–1842. Washington, D.C.,
Upham, William. *Minnesota Geographic Names*. Minneapolis, Minn., 1926.
Vandalia Whig and Illinois Intelligencer, Vandalia, Ill.
Vermilion County, 1879. Danville, Ill., 1879.
Vogel, Virgil. "Indian Place Names in Illinois," in *Journal of the Illinois State Historical Society*, vol. LI (1962), pp. 821–826.
Wakefield, John A. *History of the War Between the United States and the Sac and Fox Nation of Indians and Parts of Other Disaffected Tribes of Indians in the Years 1827–31–32*. Jacksonville, Ill., 1834.
Wallace, Anthony F. C. *Prelude to Disaster: The Course of Indian-White Relations which Led to the Black Hawk War of 1832*. Springfield, Ill., 1970.
———. *King of the Delawares: Teedyscung, 1700–1763*. Philadelphia, 1949.
———. "Political Organization and Land Tenure Among the Northeastern Indians, 1600–1830," *Southwestern Journal of Anthropology*, vol. XIII, (1957), pp. 1128–1199.
Warren County, 1877. Monmouth, Ill., 1877.
Washburne, E. B., ed. *The Edwards Papers*, in Chicago Historical Society Collections, vol. 5. Chicago, 1927–1928.
Washington Globe, Washington, D.C.
Washington Constitution, Washington, D.C.
Way, Royal B. *The Rock River Valley: Its History, Traditions, Legends and Charm*. 3 vols. Chicago, 1926.
Webb, George W. *Chronological List of Engagements Between the Regular Army of the United States and Various Tribes of Hostile Indians which Occurred During the Years 1790 to 1898 Inclusive*. N.p., n.d.

Webb, Walter Prescott. *The Great Plains*. Boston, 1936.
Weekly Free Press, Beloit, Wis.
Wendt, Lloyd. *Chicago Tribune: The Rise of a Great American Newspaper*. Chicago, 1979.
Wentworth, John. *Fort Dearborn*. Chicago, 1881.
Western Sun & General Advertiser, Vincennes, Ind.
White County, 1883. Carmi, Ill., 1883.
Whiteside County, 1877. Morrison, Ill., 1877.
Wisconsin Magazine of History, Madison, Wis.
Wisconsin State Historical Society Collections. Madison, Wis.
Works Progress Administration. *Guide to Minnesota*. Washington, D.C., 1934.
———. *Guide to Wisconsin*. Washington, D.C., 1934.

INDEX